Tuttle
Learner's
CHINESE-
ENGLISH
DICTIONARY

LI Dong 李冬

TUTTLE PUBLISHING
Boston • Rutland, Vermont • Tokyo

Published by Tuttle Publishing, an imprint of Periplus
Editions (HK) Ltd., with editorial offices at 153 Milk
Street, Boston, MA 02109 and 130 Joo Seng Road
#06-01/03 Singapore 368357.

Library of Congress Control Number: 2004115974
ISBN 0-8048-3552-7

First Edition 2005
Printed in Singapore

Distributed by:

North America, Latin America & Europe
Tuttle Publishing
Airport Business Park
364 Innovation Drive
North Clarendon, VT 05759-9436
Tel: (802) 773 8930
Fax: (802) 773 6993
Email: info@tuttlepublishing.com
www.tuttlepublishing.com

Japan
Tuttle Publishing
Yaekari Building, 3rd Floor
5-4-12 Osaki, Shinagawa-ku
Tokyo 141-0032
Tel: (03) 5437 0171
Fax: (03) 5437 0755
Email: tuttle-sales@gol.com

Asia Pacific
Berkeley Books Pte. Ltd.
130 Joo Seng Road #06-01/03
Singapore 368357
Tel: (65) 6280 1330
Fax: (65) 6280 6290
Email: inquiries@periplus.com.sg
www.periplus.com

09 08 07 06 05
6 5 4 3 2 1

Contents

A Guide for Learners of Chinese

1 PRONUNCIATION

1.1 The Pinyin Romanization System

The pronunciation of Chinese words is transcribed in this dictionary using the *pinyin* transliteration system, the official, internationally recognized Chinese romanization system. Every Chinese character in this dictionary is accompanied by its *pinyin* spelling so users will know how it is pronounced.

Pronouncing Chinese syllables normally involves three elements: vowels, consonants and tones. Modern standard Chinese, known as Putonghua, uses about 419 syllables without tones and 1,332 syllables with tones.

1.2 Vowels

1.2.1 Single Vowels

There are seven basic single vowels:

a	similar to *a* in *ah*
e	similar to *a* in *ago*
ê	similar to *e* in *ebb* (this sound never occurs alone and is transcribed as **e**, as in **ei, ie, ue**)
i	similar to *ee* in *cheese* (spelled **y** when not preceded by a consonant)
o	similar to *oe* in *toe*
u	similar to *oo* in *boot* (spelled **w** when not preceded by a consonant)
ü	similar to German *ü* in *über* or French *u* in *tu*; or you can also get *ü* by saying *i* and rounding your lips at the same time (spelled **u** after **j, q, x**; spelled **yu** when not preceded by a consonant)

1.2.2 Vowel Combinations

These single vowels enter into combinations with each other or the consonants of **n** or **ng** to form what are technically known as *diphthongs*. These combinations are pronounced as a single sound, with a little more emphasis on the first part of the sound.

You can learn these combinations in four groups:

Group 1:	diphthongs starting with a/e/ê	
	ai	similar to *y* in *my*
	ao	similar to *ow* in *how*
	an	
	ang	
	en	
	eng	
	ei	similar to *ay* in *may*

Group 2:   diphthongs starting with i
  ia
  ie   similar to *ye* in *yes*
  iao
  iou   similar to *you* (spelled **iu** when preceded by a consonant)
  ian
  ien   similar to *in* (spelled **in** when preceded by a consonant)
  ieng   similar to *En* in *English* (spelled **ing** when preceded by a consonant)
  iang   similar to *young*
  iong

Group 3:   diphthongs starting with u/o
  ua
  uo
  uai   similar to *why* in British English
  uei   similar to *way* (spelled **ui** when preceded by a consonant)
  uan
  uen   (spelled **un** when preceded by a consonant)
  ueng
  uang
  ong

Group 4:   diphthongs starting with ü
  üe   used only after **j, q, x**; spelled **ue**
  üen   used only after **j, q, x**; spelled **un**
  üan   used only after **j, q, x**; spelled **uan**

1.3   Consonants

Consonants may be grouped in the following ways.

Group 1:   These consonants are almost the same in Chinese and English.
Chinese   English
  m   *m*
  n   *n*
  f   *f*
  l   *l*
  s   *s*
  r   *r*
  b   pronounced as hard *p* (as in *speak*)
  p   *p* (as in *peak*)
  g   pronounced as hard *k* (as in *ski*)
  k   *k* (as in *key)*
  d   pronounced as hard *t* (as in *star*)
  t   *t* (as in *tar)*

Group 2: Some modification is needed to get these Chinese sounds from English.

Chinese	English
j	as *j* in *jeep* (but unvoiced, not round-lipped)
q	as *ch* in *cheese* (but not round-lipped)
x	as *sh* in *sheep* (but not round-lipped)
c	as *ts* as in *cats* (make it long)
z	as *ds* as in *beds* (but unvoiced, and make it long)

Group 3: No English counterparts

Chinese **zh**, **ch**, and **sh** have no English counterparts. You can learn to say **zh**, **ch** and **sh** starting from **z**, **c** and **s**. For example, say **s** (which is almost the same as the English *s* in *sesame*) and then roll up your tongue to touch the roof of your mouth. You get **sh**.

1.4 Tones

Chinese is a tonal language, i.e. a sound pronounced in different tones is understood as different words. So the tone is an indispensable component of the pronunciation of a word.

1.4.1 Basic Tones

There are four basic tones. The following five-level pitch graph shows the values of the four tones:

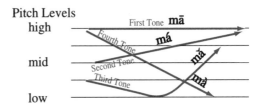

The **First Tone** is a high, level tone and is represented as ‾, e.g. 妈 **mā** (meaning *mother*, *mom*).

The **Second Tone** is a high, rising tone and is represented by the tone mark ´, e.g. 麻 **má** (*hemp* or *sesame*).

The **Third Tone** is a falling and rising tone. As you can see from the pitch graph it falls from below the middle of the voice range to nearly the bottom and then rises to a point near the top. It is represented by the tone mark ˇ, e.g. 马 **mǎ** (*horse*).

The **Fourth Tone** is a falling tone. It falls from high to low and is represented by the tone mark ` , e.g. 骂 **mà** (*curse*).

In Chinese speech, as in English speech, some sounds are unstressed, i.e. pronounced short and soft. They do not have any of the four tones. Such sounds are said to have **Neutral Tone**. Sounds with the neutral tone are not marked. For example in 爸爸 **bàba** (*daddy*) the first syllable is pronounced in the fourth tone and the second syllable in the neutral tone, i.e. unstressed.

1.4.2 Tone Changes

Tones may undergo changes in actual speech ("tone sandhi"). The third tone, when followed by a first, second, fourth or neutral tone sound, loses its final rise and stops at the low pitch. Followed by another third tone sound, it becomes the second tone. This is a general rule and the notation of third tone sounds remains unchanged.

For example, in 所以 **suǒyǐ** (*therefore, so*), notation remains the third tone for both syllables, but the word is actually pronounced like **suóyǐ**.

Two important words 不 **bù** (*no*) and 一 **yī** (*one*) also undergo tone changes. You will find the details of their tone changes under these entries.

1.5 Syllables

1.5.1 Chinese Syllables: Distinct Units

Normally a consonant and a vowel merge to form a syllable in Chinese. Every syllable is a distinct unit in speech. Learners should say each syllable clearly and give full value to most syllables in speech. The general impression of Chinese speech, described in musical terms, is staccato rather than legato (which could be used to describe English).

1.5.2 Syllable Division Mark

As Chinese syllables are distinct units and should not be liaised with preceding or following syllables, a syllable division mark (') is sometimes used to avoid confusion, e.g. **shí'èr, píng'ān, tiān'é**.

2   WRITING CHINESE CHARACTERS

2.1 Strokes

Each Chinese character is composed by strokes. The table below shows the basic strokes. Recognizing the strokes in a character is helpful for finding a character or radical in the Stroke Index, List of Radicals and Radical Index. Each of the following strokes is counted as one stroke.

Stroke	Writing the stroke	Examples
Héng	left to right ―	千 主 女
Shù	top to bottom ∣	千 山 北
Piě	top (right) to bottom (left) ノ	千 人 么

Stroke	Writing the stroke	Examples
Nà	top (left) to bottom (right)	人 木 又
Diǎn	top to bottom	主 心 习
Tí	Bottom (left) to top (right)	习 打 北
Stroke with hook	left to right, top to bottom	买 打 以 心
Stroke with turn(s)		山 马 女 么 又
Stroke with turn(s) and hook		北 习 认 马

2.2 Stroke Order

For the character to look correct, its strokes should be written in the correct order. Knowing the order will also help you remember characters. The general rules of stroke order are as follows.

Rule	Example	Stroke order
Top before bottom	三	一 二 三
Left before right	什	ノ 亻 仁 什
Horizontal before vertical/downward	天	一 二 于 天
"Enter the room, then close the door"	日	丨 冂 月 日
Vertical stroke before sides/bottom	小	亅 小 小

2.3   Simplified and Traditional Characters

The Chinese government simplified hundreds of Chinese characters in mid-1950 by reducing the numbers of their strokes. Such simplified characters are called 简体字 **jiǎntǐzì**. This dictionary uses *jiantizi*. Traditional versions (also known as complicated characters) are still used in Taiwan and Hong Kong, and they are shown after Trad where applicable, e.g.:

xué 学 Trad 學

2.4   How to Look Up a Word in a Chinese Dictionary

2.4.1 By *Pinyin* Romanization

To aid learners of Chinese, this dictionary arranges headwords alphabetically according to *pinyin*. So if you know how a word is pronounced, you can find it easily, just the way you will look up an English word in an English dictionary.

2.4.2 By Radical

Very often, however, you do not know the pronunciation of a word when you come across it in reading. In that case you can find it either by its radical or the number of its strokes.

Radicals (部首 **bùshǒu**) are certain component parts of characters that have been used in Chinese dictionary-making for nearly 2,000 years. Characters sharing a radical are grouped together under the heading of that radical. To find a character in a dictionary, follow these steps:

(i)   In the **List of Radicals**, look up the character's radical according to the number of strokes in the radical. This gives a Radical Index number.

(ii) Turn to the number in the **Radical Index**

(iii) Locate the character according to the number of remaining strokes needed to write the character (i.e. number of total strokes minus radical strokes = remaining strokes). You will find the pinyin by the character.

For example, to find 活:

(i)   The radical group of 活 is 氵, which has three strokes. In the **List of Radicals**, look up 氵 in the section marked "3 strokes":

       3 strokes
       氵   33

(ii) Turn to number 33 in the **Radical Index**.

(iii) As there are nine strokes in 活, and the radical has three strokes, six strokes remain to complete the character 活 (9 − 3 = 6). Look in the section "6 strokes" and locate 活:

       6 strokes
       活   **huó**

(iv) Turn to **huó** in the dictionary:

       huó 活 …

2.4.3 By Number of Strokes

Unfortunately, looking for a character by its radical is not an entirely satisfactory method as learners may not always know which part of the character is the radical. Therefore, this dictionary includes a **Stroke Index** to aid the learner further. Simply look for the character according to the number of its strokes, and then locate the character by its first stroke.

For example, to find 活:

(i)　There are nine strokes in 活. Go to the section of nine strokes.

9 strokes

(ii)　As the first stroke of 活 is " 丶 ", locate 活 under " 丶 ".

丶

…

活　huó

(iii) Turn to **huó** in the dictionary.

huó 活...

2.4.4 By English Meaning

To find out the Chinese equivalent or near-equivalent of an English word, use the English-Chinese Word Finder, which is practically a handy English-Chinese dictionary. Chinese equivalents or near-equivalents of over 4,100 English words are listed alphabetically in the Finder.

For example, to find out what *airport* is in Chinese, turn to "A" in the Finder and locate *airport* in the list of words beginning with "A":

airport **fēijī chǎng** 飞机场 63, **jīchǎng** 机场 100

The entry for 飞机场 **fēijī chǎng** is found on page 63 and the entry for 机场 **jīchǎng**, on page 100.

3　VOCABULARY

3.1　Words in this Dictionary

This dictionary gives detailed description of the 3,000-odd words prescribed for Level A and Level B of the Chinese government-sponsored, internationally-recognized Chinese Language Proficiency Test (汉语水平考试 **Hànyǔ Shuǐpíng Kǎoshì**, HSK). About a hundred words are added to reflect changing Chinese life, among which are:

手机 **shǒujī** (mobile phone), 短信 **duǎnxìn** (text message), 光碟 **guāngdié** (CD), 英特网 **yīngtèwǎng** (Internet), 网站 **wǎngzhàn** (Web site), 网吧 **wǎngbā** (Internet café), 信息 **xìnxī** (information), 资金 **zījīn** (fund), 财产 **cáicǎn** (property), 股票 **gǔpiào** (share, stock), 开发 **kāifā** (develop), 交税 **jiāoshuì** (pay taxes), 董事长 **dǒngshìzhǎng** (chairman of board of trustees)

A major feature of this dictionary is that it is self-contained, i.e. the words used to make the thousands of sample sentences are also found as headwords in the dictionary.

In other words, if you do not know a word used in the dictionary, you can always find it explained somewhere within the dictionary.

3.2 Word-formation

Like German, Chinese words are very transparent; that is, the way a word is formed tells you a lot about its meaning. Therefore it is very helpful to know the meanings of the components in a word and the way the word is formed, and it also makes understanding the word easier and more interesting.

This dictionary analyzes word-formation methods of headwords, whenever it is practical to do so. We recognize six methods of word-formation.

Compounding (shortened to "compound"): the components of a word are complementary to each other in meaning and are of the same status. For example:

> chóngfù 重复 [compound: 重 *once again* + 复 *repeat*] VERB = repeat

Modification ("modif"): one component modifies the other. For example:

> wàiguó 外国 [modif: 外 *outside* + 国 *country*] NOUN = foreign country

Verb+object ("v+obj"): the word has a verb-and-object relationship. For example:

> fāshāo 发烧 [v+obj: 发 *develop* + 烧 *burning, fever*] VERB = run a fever

Verb+complementation ("v+comp"): the word has a verb-and-complement relationship, that is, the first component is a verb and the second one modifies it. For example:

> tígāo 提高 [v+comp: 提 *raise* + 高 *high*] VERB = raise, advance

Suffixation ("suffix"): the word contains a suffix. For example:

> běnzi 本子 [suffix: 本 *a book* + 子 nominal suffix] NOUN = notebook

Idioms ("idiom"): the word is an idiomatic expression. For example:

> mǎshàng 马上 [idiom] ADVERB = at once, immediately

3.3 Definitions

In most cases English equivalents or near equivalents are given as definitions. For example:

> gāoxìng 高兴 ADJECTIVE = joyful, delighted, willing

For grammatical words that have no English equivalents, concise explanations are given in brackets. For example:

> **de** 的 PARTICLE = (attached to a word, phrase or clause to indicate that it is an attribute; 的 **de** is normally followed by a noun)

After the definition of a noun, the specific measure word used with the noun is shown, if it is one of headwords in the dictionary. For example:

> **shū** 书 Trad 書 NOUN = book (本 **běn**)

When the specific measure word is not within the scope of this dictionary and therefore is not shown, you can often use the default measure word 个 **ge**.

Antonyms are shown after the definition of most adjectives and some nouns, if they are headwords of this dictionary. For example:

> **duǎn** 短 ADJECTIVE = (of length, time) short (antonym 长 **cháng**)

When a headword has more than one meaning, the different meanings are indicated by **1, 2**, etc. For example:

> **yuè** 月 NOUN
> 1 = month
> …
> 2 = the moon
> …

Homonyms (words pronounced and written the same but with different, unrelated meanings) are treated as separate words, e.g.

> **dài** 代 1 VERB = take the place of, perform on behalf of
> …
> **dài** 代 2 NOUN
> 1 = generation
> …
> 2 = dynasty
> …

3.4   Collocations

Certain words are habitually juxtaposed with each other. Such juxtapositions are called *collocations*. This dictionary shows approximately 2,000 common collocations, with clear definitions and necessary example sentences. For example:

> **bāo** 包 NOUN = parcel, bag
> …
> qiánbāo 钱包 = wallet, purse
> shūbāo 书包 = schoolbag
> yóubāo 邮包 = mailbag, parcel for posting

The result is that this dictionary introduces you to many more words than the headwords, all learnt conveniently. In this way your word power will be significantly increased.

3.5 Sample Sentences

Words become really meaningful only when used in sentences. That is why this dictionary supplies a number of sample sentences for almost every headword. All the sentences are carefully constructed to be (1) idiomatic, (2) communicatively useful and (3) within the controlled vocabulary of this dictionary.

Studying the sentences carefully will help you learn how to use important Chinese words in everyday communication. Care was taken to include sentences that are good examples of how words behave in communication.

For example:

> **bàozhǐ 报纸** [modif: 报 *reporting* + 纸 *paper*]
> NOUN = newspaper (张 **zhāng**, 份 **fèn**)
> ■ 今天报纸上有什么重要消息? **Jīntiān bàozhǐ shang yǒu shénme zhòngyào xiāoxi?** = *What important news is there in today's paper?*
> ■ 我很少看报纸。**Wǒ hén shǎo kàn bàozhǐ.** = *I seldom read newspapers.*
> ■ 这份报纸广告比新闻多。**Zhè fèn bàozhǐ guǎnggào bǐ xīnwén duō.** = *There are more advertisements than news in this newspaper.*

Three sample sentences are given for the headword 报纸 **bàozhǐ**. In the first one

> ■ 今天报纸上有什么重要消息? **Jīntiān bàozhǐ shang yǒu shénme zhòngyào xiāoxi?** = *What important news is there in today's paper?*

the headword 报纸 **bàozhǐ** is used in the subject position and is collocated with the preposition 上 **shàng**.

In the second one

> ■ 我很少看报纸。**Wǒ hén shǎo kàn bàozhǐ.** = *I seldom read newspapers.*

报纸 **bàozhǐ** functions as an object after the common verb 看 **kàn**.

Another example is the entry of 办法 **bànfǎ**. As many as five sample sentences are provided, encompassing almost all situations in everyday communication. If you understand and learn the sentences, you will be able to use 办法 **bànfǎ** with ease and confidence. All sample sentences in this dictionary are accompanied by its *pinyin* and English translation to aid learning.

In some cases a second translation is provided in brackets to aid comprehension and idiomatic expression. -> indicates a freer, more idiomatic translation and <-, a more literal translation. For example:

ràng 让

…

你应该让那辆车先行。**Nǐ yīnggāi ràng nà liàng chē xiānxíng.** = *You should let that vehicle go first.* (→ *You should give way to that vehicle.*)

4 GRAMMAR

4.1 Main Features of Chinese Grammar

4.1.1 Topic+Comment Structure

The basic principle in making Chinese sentences is to follow the "topic+comment" structure. "Topic" means the subject matter you want to talk about, and "comment" is the information you give about the subject matter. To make a Chinese sentence, you simply first mention the subject matter you want to talk about, and then say what you have to say about it. For example, you can say 那本书 **nà běn shū** (*that book*) first as the "topic" and then add "comment":

- 那本书 很有意思。**Nà běn shū hěn yǒu yìshi.** = *That book is very interesting.*
- 那本书 卖完了。**Nà běn shū mài wán le.** = *That book has been sold.*
- 那本书 你有吗? **Nà běn shū nǐ yǒu mā?** = *Do you have that book?*
- 那本书 语言很优美。**Nà běn shū yǔyán hěn yōuměi.** = *The language of that book is beautiful.*

4.1.2 Ellipsis of Sentence Elements

Chinese speakers may leave out words that are supposed to be understood, and therefore need not be spoken. Subjects and conjunctions are often omitted. For example, you may translate the English sentence *If you like it, you may buy it, but if you don't like it, you don't have to.* into the Chinese sentence 喜欢就买，不喜欢就别买。**Xǐhuān jiù mǎi, bù xǐhuān jiù bié mǎi.** Compare the two sentences, and you will find that some English words, such as *if*, *you*, *it*, and *but* are not translated.

4.1.3 Word Classes: Flexibility, No Inflection

Chinese words do not have inflections, i.e. they do not change to indicate grammatical categories. For example, the verb 去 **qù** (*to go*) is invariably 去 **qù**; there is no past form or any other inflected form of this verb. Neither do Chinese words normally have formal markers of word class. Consequently it is rather easy for a word to be used in more than one word class. This relative flexibility in word classes, however, does not mean that Chinese does not have word classes (see Section 4.2).

4.1.4 Measure Words and Particles

Measure words (量词 **liàngcí**) and particles (助词 **zhùcí**) are two word classes found in Chinese but not in English and most other languages.

Measure words are usually required when a noun is modified by a numeral. For example, 两书 **liǎng shū** is unacceptable; you must use the measure word 本 **běn** between the numeral and the noun: 两本书 **liǎng běn shū** (*two books*). Furthermore, Chinese nouns require specific measure words to go with them. For example, the noun 书 **shū** (*book*) must be used with the measure word 本 **běn**.

In Chinese grammar, particles are words attached to other words or at the end of a sentence to indicate grammatical concepts or to express emotions. For example, the particles 了 **le**, 着 **zhe**, 过 **guo** are attached to verbs to indicate, respectively, whether the actions denoted are completed, in progress or past experiences.

4.2 Word Classes

Following are brief explanations of the basic terms in Chinese grammar used in this dictionary. (A word of warning: it is a rather complicated matter to define grammatical terms accurately. Here we will be content with some very general but useful ideas.)

ADJECTIVE	a describing word, a word that describes people, things or actions, typically used before a noun.
ADVERB	a word that modifies a verb, an adjective or another adverb.
CONJUNCTION	a word used to link two words, phrases or sentences, indicating certain relationships between them.
IDIOM	a set phrase, the meaning of which cannot be readily derived from its components.
INTERJECTION	a word that expresses strong emotions.
MEASURE WORD	a word that connects a numeral to a noun. Measure words are a special feature of Chinese; a list of measure words is included in the Appendices.
MODAL VERB	a word used before a verb to indicate necessity, possibility, willingness, etc.
NOUN	a naming word, a word that names people, animals, plants, things, ideas, etc.
NUMERAL	a word that represents a number, typically used with a noun.
ONOMATOPOEIA	a word that imitates the sounds of a thing or an action.
PARTICLE	a word used with another word, phrase, or sentence to indicate certain grammatical meanings or to express strong emotions.
PREPOSITION	a word used before a noun or pronoun to indicate time, place, direction, manner, reason of an action, etc.
PRONOUN	a word that is used in the place of a noun, a verb, an adjective, etc.
VERB	an action word, a word that indicates what somebody does or feels.

4.3 Other Grammar Terms

ATTRIBUTE	the element that modifies the subject or object of a sentence; or, in word-formation analysis, a word that modifies a noun.
ADVERBIAL	the element that is used before the predicate of a sentence

	and modifies it; or, in word-formation analysis, a word that precedes a verb or adjective to modify it.
COMPLEMENT	the element that is used after the predicate of a sentence and modifies it; or, in word-formation analysis, a word that follows a verb or adjective to modify it.
IMPERATIVE SENTENCE	a command or a request.
OBJECT	the element that follows a predicative verb, typically to indicate the target of an action.
PREDICATE	the comment or information about the subject, typically a verb or adjective.
PREFIX	an additional element that immediately precedes the word it is attached to.
SUBJECT	the topic of a sentence, what the speaker wants to talk about, typically a noun or pronoun.
SUFFIX	an additional element that closely follows the word it is attached to.

5   CULTURAL AND USAGE NOTES

Essential information on cultural context, pronunciation, grammar and usage is given to help you use the language in a socially acceptable and idiomatic way. For example:

Hànyǔ 汉语

...

> NOTE: In Chinese there are a number of words denoting "the Chinese language." 汉语 **Hànyǔ** literally means *the language of the Han Chinese people*, in contrast with the languages of the non-Han peoples in China. 汉语 **Hànyǔ** is therefore the accurate, scientific term for the language. However, the most popular term for *the Chinese language* is 中文 **Zhōngwén**. In Singapore and other Southeast Asian countries, the standard Chinese language is often referred to as 华语 **Huáyǔ** in contrast to the various Chinese dialects spoken there. Also see note on 普通话 **Pǔtōnghuà**.

hěn 很

...

> NOTE: When used as predicates, Chinese adjectives normally require an adverb. For example, 我高兴 **Wǒ gāoxìng** sounds unnatural, while 我很高兴 **Wǒ hěn gāoxìng** (*I'm [very] happy*), 我不高兴 **Wǒ bù gāoxìng** (*I'm not happy*) or 我非常高兴 **Wǒ fēicháng gāoxìng** (*I'm very happy*) are normal sentences. The adverb 很 **hěn** is often used as a default adverb before an adjective. In such cases the meaning of 很 **hěn** is very weak.

List of Radicals

1 stroke	卩 30	辶 60	牛 90	立 120	身 148
、 1	阝(on left) 31	彐 61	手 91	穴 121	角 149
一 2	阝(on right) 32	尸 62	毛 92	衤 122	言 150
乙 3		已 63	气 93	示 123	辛 151
丨 4	**3 strokes**	己 64	片 94	主 124	系 152
丿 5	氵 33	巳 65	斤 95	母 125	束 153
	忄 34	弓 66	爪 96	去 126	非 154
	小 35	女 67	月 97	疋 127	酉 155
2 strokes	宀 36	子 68	欠 98		豆 156
亠 6	丬 37	纟 69	天 99	**6 strokes**	
冫 7	广 38	马 70	风 100	老 128	**8 strokes**
讠 8	门 39		殳 101	耳 129	隹 157
二 9	辶 40	**4 strokes**	火 102	西 130	青 158
十 10	工 41	灬 71	礻 103	页 131	鱼 159
厂 11	干 42	文 72	戈 104	虫 132	雨 160
匚 12	土 43	方 73	水 105	缶 133	
匕 13	士 44	心 74	止 106	舌 134	**9 strokes**
卜 14	上 45	户 75		竹 135	革 161
刂 15	艹 46	斗 76	**5 strokes**	自 136	是 162
冖 16	廾 47	王, 玉 77	石 107	舟 137	食 163
冂 17	大 48	木 78	业 108	衣 138	音 164
勹 18	寸 49	犬 79	目 109	亦 139	
刀 19	扌 50	歹 80	田 110	羊 140	**11 strokes**
力 20	口 51	瓦 81	皿 111	米 141	麻 165
八 21	囗 52	车 82	钅 112	艮 142	
亻 22	巾 53	比 83	矢 113	羽 143	**12 strokes**
人 23	山 54	日 84	禾 114	糸 144	黑 166
儿 24	彳 55	曰 85	白 115		
几 25	彡 56	贝 86	用 116	**7 strokes**	
又 26	夕 57	见 87	母 117	走 145	
凵 27	夂 58	父 88	鸟 118	里 146	
厶 28	犭 59	攵 89	疒 119	足 147	
廴 29					

Radical Index

All characters are listed here under their radical plus the number of additional strokes needed to write them. For more information on looking up a character by its radical, see Section 2.4 of the Guide (page ix).

1 丶		再	zài	义	yì	离	lí
之	zhī	**6–9 strokes**		**3–4 strokes**		竞	jìng
为	wèi	丽	lì	升	shēng	**9–15 strokes**	
永	yǒng	更	gèng	乎	hū	竟	jìng
主	zhǔ	来	lái	长	cháng, zhǎng	商	shāng
举	jǔ	两	liǎng	乐	lè, yuè	童	tóng
2 一		求	qiú	生	shēng	就	jiù
一	yī, yí, yì	事	shì	失	shī	敲	qiāo
1–2 strokes		面	miàn	瓜	guā	赢	yíng
七	qī	哥	gē	**5–13 strokes**			
三	sān	夏	xià	丢	diū	**7 冫**	
于	yú	**3 乙**		年	nián	习	xí
下	xià	了	le, liǎo	向	xiàng	次	cì
才	cái	司	sī	复	fù	冰	bīng
与	yǔ	飞	fēi	重	chóng, zhòng	决	jué
丈	zhàng	也	yě	鬼	guǐ	况	kuàng
万	wàn	民	mín	够	gòu	冷	lěng
3 strokes		矛	máo	舞	wǔ	冻	dòng
无	wú	承	chéng			净	jìng
专	zhuān	**4 丨**		**6 亠**		凉	liáng
不	bú, bù	卜	bó	**2–4 strokes**		减	jiǎn
丰	fēng	书	shū	六	liù	准	zhǔn
互	hù	中	zhōng	市	shì		
牙	yá	且	qiě	交	jiāo	**8 讠**	
世	shì	师	shī	充	chōng	**2–3 strokes**	
五	wǔ	临	lín	齐	qí	订	dìng
尤	yóu	**5 丿**		弃	qì	计	jì
4–5 strokes		**1–2 strokes**		亩	mǔ	认	rèn
东	dōng	九	jiǔ	**6–8 strokes**		讯	xùn
册	cè	久	jiǔ	享	xiǎng	训	xùn
可	kě	么	me	京	jīng	议	yì
平	píng	千	qiān	亮	liàng	记	jì
正	zhèng			帝	dì	让	ràng
而	ér			弯	wān	讨	tǎo
				高	gāo		
4 strokes							
访	fǎng						
讲	jiǎng						
论	lùn						
设	shè						
许	xǔ						
5 strokes							
词	cí						
评	píng						
识	shí						
诉	sù						
译	yì						
诚	chéng						
证	zhèng						
6–8 strokes							
诗	shī						
详	xiáng						
该	gāi						
话	huà						
试	shì						
说	shuō						
误	wù						
语	yǔ						
诵	sòng						
谊	yì						
谅	liàng						
9–10 strokes							
调	diào, tiáo						
谓	wèi						
读	dú						
课	kè						
谅	liàng						
谁	shuí, shéi						
谈	tán						
请	qǐng						

谊 yì
谢 xiè

9 二

二 èr
元 yuán
云 yún
些 xiē

10 十

十 shí
午 wǔ
支 zhī
克 kè
卖 mài
直 zhí
南 nán
真 zhēn

11 厂

厂 chǎng
历 lì
厅 tīng
厉 lì
压 yā
厌 yàn
后 hòu
厕 cè
厚 hòu
厘 lí
咸 xián
原 yuán
厨 chú

12 匚

匹 pǐ
区 qū
医 yī

13 匕

北 běi
疑 yí

14 卜

卡 kǎ
占 zhàn

15 刂

4–5 strokes

刚 gāng
创 chuàng
列 liè
则 zé
利 lì
别 bié
判 pàn

6–8 strokes

到 dào
刮 guā
刻 kè
刷 shuā
制 zhì
刺 cì
剧 jù

9–10 strokes

副 fù
割 gē
剩 shèng

16 冖

写 xiě
军 jūn
农 nóng
冠 guàn

17 冂

内 nèi
肉 ròu
同 tóng
网 wǎng
周 zhōu

18 勹

勺 sháo
包 bāo
句 jù

19 刀

刀 dāo

2–4 strokes

切 qiè
召 zhào
争 zhēng
负 fù
色 sè
危 wéi

6–9 strokes

免 miǎn
兔 tù
剪 jiǎn

20 力

力 lì

2–4 strokes

办 bàn
加 jiā
劝 quàn
动 dòng
劳 láo

5–9 strokes

努 nǔ
助 zhù
励 lì
势 shì
劲 jìn
勇 yǒng
勉 miǎn

21 八

八 bā

2–4 strokes

分 fēn
公 gōng
兰 lán
半 bàn
共 gòng
关 guān
兴 xīng, xìng
并 bìng

5–6 strokes

兵 bīng
弟 dì
单 dān
典 diǎn
具 jù
其 qí

7–8 strokes

前 qián
首 shǒu
养 yǎng
益 yì

22 亻

1–2 strokes

亿 yì
化 huà
什 shén
仍 réng

3 strokes

传 chuán
代 dài
付 fù
们 men
他 tā
仪 yí

4 strokes

仿 fǎng
伙 huǒ
份 fèn
价 jià
件 jiàn
优 yōu
任 rèn
伟 wěi
似 sì

5 strokes

但 dàn
低 dī
何 hé
你 nǐ
伯 bó
体 tǐ
估 gū
位 wèi
住 zhù
作 zuò
伸 shēn
佛 fú

6 strokes

例 lì
使 shǐ
便 biàn, pián
俩 liǎ
供 gòng
修 xiū
依 yī
佩 pèi

7 strokes

侵 qīn
信 xìn
促 cù
保 bǎo
俱 jù

8 strokes

倍 bèi
倒 dǎo
值 zhí
候 hòu
健 jiàn
借 jiè

9–10 strokes

假 jiǎ, jià
偷 tōu
偏 piān
停 tíng

做	zuò	**26 又**		4–5 strokes		油	yóu	10–13 strokes	
傅	fù	又	yòu	阴	yīn	治	zhì	滚	gǔn
傲	ào	1–2 strokes		阳	yáng	注	zhù	源	yuán
11–12 strokes		叉	chā	阶	jiē	沿	yán	满	mǎn
催	cuī	反	fǎn	阵	zhèn	6 strokes		漂	piào
傻	shǎ	双	shuāng	陈	Chén	活	huó	演	yǎn
像	xiàng	友	yǒu	附	fù	测	cè	漏	lòu
		3–8 strokes		阿	ā	洞	dòng	澳	ào
23 人		对	duì	陆	lù	浪	làng	滴	dī
人	rén	发	fā	6–10 strokes		浓	nóng	激	jí
个	gè, ge	欢	huān	除	chú	洒	sǎ	澡	zǎo
2 strokes		艰	jiān	险	xiǎn	羊	yáng		
从	cóng	叔	shū	限	xiàn	洲	zhōu	**34 忄**	
介	jiè	难	nán	院	yuàn	济	jì	3–5 strokes	
今	jīn			陪	péi	洗	xǐ	忙	máng
以	yǐ	**27 凵**		隔	gé	派	pài	快	kuài
3–4 strokes		出	chū			浮	fú	怕	pà
令	lìng	画	huà	**32 阝 (on right)**		7–8 strokes		怪	guài
伞	sǎn			那	nà	海	hǎi	性	xìng
企	qǐ	**28 厶**		邮	yóu	浴	yù	怜	lián
合	hé	允	yǔn	部	bù	酒	jiǔ	6–8 strokes	
会	huì	台	tái	都	dōu	流	liú	恨	hèn
全	quán	县	xiàn			消	xiāo	悄	qiāo
5–10 strokes		参	cān	**33 氵**		港	gǎng	惭	cán
舍	shè	能	néng	2–4 strokes		清	qīng	惊	jīng
余	yú			汗	hàn	深	shēn	情	qíng
金	jīn	**29 廴**		污	wū	淡	dàn	9–13 strokes	
命	mìng	延	yán	沙	shā	渐	jiàn	愧	kuì
拿	ná	建	jiàn	汉	hàn	漠	mò	愤	fèn
盒	hé			江	jiāng	添	tiān	惯	guàn
舒	shū	**30 卩**		汤	tāng	涂	tú	愉	yú
		卫	wèi	没	méi	液	yè	慢	màn
24 儿		印	yìn	汽	qì	9 strokes		懂	dǒng
儿	ér	危	wéi	沉	chén	滑	huá	懒	lǎn
先	xiān	却	què	泛	fàn	湿	shī		
		卷	juǎn	5 strokes		温	wēn	**35 小**	
25 几				法	fǎ	湖	hú	小	xiǎo
几	jǐ	**31 阝 (on left)**		泼	pō	渴	kě	2–3 strokes	
凡	fán	2–3 strokes		河	hé	湾	wān	少	shǎo
		队	duì	浅	qiǎn	游	yóu	光	guāng
		防	fáng	泳	yǒng			当	dāng

4–9 strokes		38 广		还	hái, huán	巧	qiǎo	44 士	
尝	cháng	广	guǎng	迫	pò	功	gōng	声	shēng
省	shěng	3–4 strokes		进	jìn	左	zuǒ	志	zhì
党	dǎng	庆	qìng	近	jìn	式	shì	壶	hú
辉	huī	庄	zhuāng	连	lián	巩	gǒng	喜	xǐ
		床	chuáng	迎	yíng	攻	gōng		
36 宀		应	yīng	远	yuǎn	项	xiàng	45 上	
2–4 strokes		店	diàn	运	yùn			上	shàng
它	tā	府	fǔ	这	zhè, zhèi	42 干			
安	ān	5–8 strokes		5–6 strokes		干	gān, gàn	46 艹	
守	shǒu	底	dǐ	述	shù			1–4 strokes	
完	wán	庙	miào	迹	jí	43 土		艺	yì
字	zì	序	xù	迷	mí	土	tǔ	节	jié
灾	zāi	度	dù	选	xuǎn	3 strokes		花	huā
5–6 strokes		庭	tíng	追	zhuī	至	zhì	苍	cāng
宝	bǎo	席	xí	适	shì	场	chǎng	5–6 strokes	
定	dìng	座	zuò	送	sòng	地	de, dì	苦	kǔ
官	guān	康	kāng	逃	táo	在	zài	苹	píng
实	shí			退	tuì	4–6 strokes		英	yīng
宜	yì	39 门		7 strokes		址	zhǐ	范	fàn
客	kè	门	mén	造	zào	圾	jī	草	cǎo
室	shì	2–4 strokes		逐	zhú	坏	huài	茶	chá
宣	xuān	闪	shǎn	造	zào	坚	jiān	药	yào
7–9 strokes		问	wèn	递	dì	块	kuài	荣	róng
家	jiā	闲	xián	逗	dòu	坐	zuò	7–11 strokes	
室	shì	间	jiān	逛	guàng	坡	pō	获	huò
案	àn	5–7 strokes		速	sù	幸	xìng	菜	cài
害	hài	闹	nào	透	tòu	城	chéng	黄	huáng
宽	kuān	闻	wén	途	tú	7–12 strokes		葡	pú
容	róng	阅	yuè	通	tōng	埋	mái	萝	luó
宴	yàn			9–13 strokes		基	jī	营	yíng
密	mì	40 辶		遍	biàn	堆	duī	著	zhù
寄	jì	2–3 strokes		道	dào	堂	táng	萄	táo
宿	sù	边	biān	遇	yù	填	tián	蓝	lán
富	fù	过	guò	遗	yí	塔	tǎ	蕉	jiāo
寒	hán	达	dá	遭	zāo	塑	sù	薄	báo, bó
		迈	mài	遵	zūn	境	jìng		
37 丬		迅	xùn	避	bì	墙	qiáng	47 开	
状	zhuàng	4 strokes				增	zēng	开	kāi
将	jiāng	迟	chí	41 工		壁	bì		
				工	gōng				

48 大

大 dà, dài

1–3 strokes
夫 fū
太 tài
头 tóu
夺 duó
买 mǎi

5–7 strokes
奇 qí
奋 fèn
奖 jiǎng
套 tào

49 寸
封 fēng
耐 nài

50 扌

2–3 strokes
扔 rēng
扩 kuò
打 dǎ
扬 yáng

4 strokes
扫 sǎo
托 tuō
拒 jù
护 hù
扮 bàn
抄 chāo
抗 kàng
抢 qiǎng
扰 rǎo
投 tóu
折 zhé
抓 zhuā
把 bǎ
报 bào
技 jì
批 pī

找 zhǎo

5 strokes
抱 bào
拉 lā
拍 pāi
抬 tái
拆 chāi
抽 chōu
担 dàn
拣 jiǎn
拦 lán
披 pī
拖 tuō
拥 yōng
择 zé
招 zhāo

6 strokes
持 chí
挂 guà
挤 jǐ
拾 shí
挺 tǐng
指 zhǐ
按 àn
挥 huī
拼 pīn
挑 tiāo

7 strokes
换 huàn
挨 āi
据 jù
捞 lāo
损 sǔn
捉 zhuō

8 strokes
掉 diào
接 jiē
排 pái
推 tuī
措 cuò
描 miáo

捧 pěng
探 tàn

9 strokes
提 tí
握 wò
插 chā
搁 gē
援 yuán

10 strokes
摆 bǎi
搬 bān
搞 gǎo
摸 mō
摄 shè
摇 yáo
摊 tān

11–14 strokes
摘 zhāi
摔 shuāi
撞 zhuàng
播 bō
操 cāo
擦 cā

51 口

口 kǒu

2 strokes
叶 yè
兄 xiōng
史 shǐ
另 lìng
号 hào
叫 jiào

3 strokes
右 yòu
只 zhī, zhǐ
吃 chī
吗 ma
舌 shé
吸 xī
吓 xià

4 strokes
吧 ba
吹 chuī
告 gào
听 tīng
呀 yā, ya
员 yuán
吵 chǎo
吩 fēn
否 fǒu
吨 dūn
呆 dāi

5 strokes
咖 kā
呢 ne
哎 āi
咐 fù
呼 hū
味 wèi

6 strokes
哈 hā
咳 ké
哪 nǎ, na
虽 suī
响 xiǎng
咱 zán
品 pǐn
咽 yàn
咬 yǎo

7–9 strokes
啊 ā
哼 hēng
哲 zhé
唱 chàng
啡 fēi
唯 wéi
啦 la
啤 pí
喊 hǎn
喝 hē
喂 wèi

喷 pēn

10–13 strokes
嗯 ng
嘛 ma
嘿 hēi
噢 ō
嘱 zhǔ
嗽 sòu
器 qì
嘴 zuǐ
嚷 rǎng

52 囗

2–3 strokes
四 sì
回 huí
团 tuán
因 yīn

4–8 strokes
困 kùn
园 yuán
围 wéi
国 guó
固 gù
图 tú
圆 yuán
圈 quān

53 巾
巾 jīn
布 bù
希 xī
帮 bāng
带 dài
常 cháng
帽 mào
幅 fú

54 山
山 shān

岁	suì
岛	dǎo
岸	àn
崇	chóng

55 彳

行	háng, xíng
彻	chè
征	zhēng
往	wǎng
很	hěn
待	dāi, dài
律	lù
得	dé, de, děi
街	jiē
微	wēi
德	dé

56 彡

形	xíng
须	xū
彩	cǎi
影	yǐng

57 夕

外	wài
多	duō
名	míng
夜	yè

58 夂

处	chù
冬	dōng
务	wù
各	gè
备	bèi
梦	mèng

59 犭

犹	yóu
狗	gǒu

独	dú
狮	shī
狼	láng
猜	cāi
猫	māo
猪	zhū
猴	hóu

60 饣

饭	fàn
饱	bǎo
饺	jiǎo
饼	bǐng
饿	è
馆	guǎn
馒	mán

61 彐

录	lù
寻	xún

62 尸

尺	chǐ
尽	jǐn, jìn
层	céng
局	jú
尾	wěi
届	jiè
居	jū
屋	wū
展	zhǎn
属	shǔ

63 已

已	yǐ

64 己

己	jǐ

65 巳

导	dǎo

66 弓

引	yǐn
张	zhāng
弱	ruò
强	qiáng

67 女

女	nǚ

2–4 strokes

奶	nǎi
妇	fù
好	hǎo
妈	mā
如	rú
她	tā
妙	miào

5 strokes

姑	gū
姐	jiě
妹	mèi
妻	qī
始	shǐ
姓	xìng

6–11 strokes

姻	yīn
娘	niáng
婚	hūn
嫂	sǎo
嫩	nèn

68 子

子	zǐ, zi
孔	kǒng
存	cún
学	xué
孩	hái

69 纟

2–4 strokes

纠	jiū
红	hóng

丝	sī
纤	xiān
约	yuē
纺	fǎng
级	jí
纪	jì
纸	zhǐ

5 strokes

练	liàn
细	xì
终	zhōng
织	zhī
组	zǔ
线	xiàn

6 strokes

给	gěi
结	jié
经	jīng
统	tǒng
绝	jué
绕	rǎo

7–11 strokes

继	jì
紧	jǐn
绩	jì
绿	lù
续	xù
绳	shéng
维	wéi
编	biān
缝	féng
缩	suō

70 马

马	mǎ
驾	jià
骂	mà
骄	jiāo
骗	piàn
验	yàn
骑	qí

71 灬

5–6 strokes

烈	liè
点	diǎn
热	rè

8–12 strokes

然	rán
煮	zhǔ
照	zhào
熟	shú
熊	xióng

72 文

文	wén

73 方

方	fāng
放	fàng
施	shī
旅	lǚ
旁	páng
族	zú
旗	qí

74 心

1–4 strokes

心	xīn
必	bì
忘	wàng
忍	rěn
念	niàn
态	tài
忽	hū

5–6 strokes

急	jí
思	sī
怎	zěn
总	zǒng
息	xī
恳	kěn
恋	liàn

虑	lǜ	术	shù	桶	tǒng	暂	zàn	费	fèi
7–8 strokes		朴	pǔ	械	xiè	最	zuì	**6–12 strokes**	
您	nín	杀	shā	**8–11 strokes**		**85 日**		资	zī
悉	xī	林	lín	森	sēn			赔	péi
悠	yōu	朵	duǒ	棉	mián	日	rì	赚	zhuàn
悲	bēi	机	jī	概	gài	**1–4 strokes**		赛	sài
惹	rě	杂	zá	棵	kē	旧	jiù	赞	zàn
9–11 strokes		**3 strokes**		椅	yǐ	早	zǎo		
愁	chóu	村	cūn	**9–11 strokes**		时	shí	**87 见**	
感	gǎn	材	cái	楼	lóu	明	míng	见	jiàn
想	xiǎng	杆	gǎn	榜	bǎng	易	yì	观	guān
意	yì	极	jí	橘	jú	者	zhě	规	guī
愿	yuàn	李	Lǐ			**5–6 strokes**		觉	jué
慰	wèi	条	tiáo	**79 犬**		映	yìng	览	lǎn
		4 strokes		哭	kū	春	chūn		
75 户		松	sōng	献	xiàn	是	shì	**88 父**	
户	hù	枪	qiāng			星	xīng	父	fù
启	qǐ	构	gòu	**80 歹**		昨	zuó	爷	yé
房	fáng	板	bǎn	死	sǐ	晓	xiǎo	爸	bà
扁	biǎn	杯	bēi	殊	shū	**7–9 strokes**			
扇	shàn	果	guǒ			晨	chén	**89 攵**	
		5 strokes		**81 瓦**		曾	céng	**2–5 strokes**	
76 斗		柿	shì	瓶	píng	景	jǐng	收	shōu
斗	dòu	染	rǎn			普	pǔ	改	gǎi
斜	xié	某	mǒu	**82 车**		暑	shǔ	故	gù
		查	chá	车	chē	晴	qíng	政	zhèng
77 王, 玉		树	shù	转	zhuǎn	晚	wǎn	**6–9 strokes**	
王	Wáng	相	xiāng	轮	lún	暖	nuǎn	致	zhì
玉	yù	**6 strokes**		轻	qīng	暗	àn	敌	dí
环	huán	柴	chái	辅	fú			效	xiào
玩	wán	格	gé	辆	liàng	**86 贝**		教	jiāo, jiào
现	xiàn	根	gēn	输	shū	**3–4 strokes**		救	jiù
玻	bō	桥	qiáo			财	cái	敢	gǎn
班	bān	校	xiào	**83 比**		败	bài	散	sàn
理	lǐ	样	yàng	比	bǐ	质	zhì	数	shǔ, shù
球	qiú	桌	zhuō	毕	bì	货	huò		
		7 strokes				**5 strokes**		**90 牛**	
78 木		检	jiǎn	**84 日**		贯	guàn	牛	niú
木	mù	梨	lí	显	xiǎn	贴	tiē	物	wù
1–2 strokes		梁	liáng	量	liáng, liàng	贸	mào	牲	shēng
本	běn	梯	tī	替	tì	贵	guì	牺	xī

特　　　　tè

91 手
手　　　　shǒu
掌　　　　zhǎng

92 毛
毛　　　　máo
毫　　　　háo
毯　　　　tǎn

93 气
气　　　　qì

94 片
片　　　　piàn
版　　　　bǎn
牌　　　　pái

95 斤
斤　　　　jīn
所　　　　suǒ
新　　　　xīn
断　　　　duàn

96 爪
爬　　　　pá
采　　　　cǎi
爱　　　　ài

97 月
月　　　　yuè

2–3 strokes

有　　　　yǒu
肚　　　　dù
肝　　　　gān

4 strokes

肥　　　　féi
股　　　　gǔ
肩　　　　jiān
服　　　　fú

朋　　　　péng
育　　　　yù

5 strokes

胃　　　　wèi
脉　　　　mài
胡　　　　hú
胆　　　　dǎn
背　　　　bèi
肺　　　　fèi
骨　　　　gǔ
胖　　　　pàng
胜　　　　shèng

6 strokes

脆　　　　cuì
胳　　　　gē
胸　　　　xiōng
朗　　　　lǎng
脑　　　　nǎo
脏　　　　zāng

7–8 strokes

脚　　　　jiǎo
脖　　　　bó
脸　　　　liǎn
脱　　　　tuō
望　　　　wàng
脾　　　　pí
朝　　　　cháo
期　　　　qī

9–10 strokes

腿　　　　tuǐ
腰　　　　yāo
膊　　　　bó
膀　　　　bǎng

98 欠
欠　　　　qiàn
欧　　　　ōu
软　　　　ruǎn
款　　　　kuǎn
歇　　　　xiē
歌　　　　gē

99 天
天　　　　tiān

100 风
风　　　　fēng
飘　　　　piāo

101 殳
段　　　　duàn

102 火
火　　　　huǒ

2–5 strokes

灭　　　　miè
灰　　　　huī
灯　　　　dēng
灵　　　　líng
炼　　　　liàn
炮　　　　pào

6–12 strokes

烦　　　　fán
烂　　　　làn
烫　　　　tàng
煤　　　　méi
燃　　　　rán

103 礻
礼　　　　lǐ
社　　　　shè
视　　　　shì
祝　　　　zhù
神　　　　shén
祖　　　　zǔ
福　　　　fú

104 戈
成　　　　chéng
划　　　　huà
戏　　　　xì
我　　　　wǒ
或　　　　huò

武　　　　wǔ
战　　　　zhàn
戴　　　　dài

105 水
水　　　　shuǐ

106 止
止　　　　zhǐ
步　　　　bù
些　　　　xiē
肯　　　　kěn
龄　　　　líng

107 石
石　　　　shí

3–5 strokes

矿　　　　kuàng
码　　　　mǎ
础　　　　chǔ
破　　　　pò

6–9 strokes

研　　　　yán
确　　　　què
硬　　　　yìng
碎　　　　suì
碟　　　　dié
碰　　　　pèng
碍　　　　ài
碗　　　　wǎn
磁　　　　cí

108 业
业　　　　yè

109 目
目　　　　mù

2–4 strokes

盯　　　　dīng
看　　　　kàn
冒　　　　mào

盾　　　　dùn
盼　　　　pàn

5–12 strokes

眼　　　　yǎn
睁　　　　zhēng
睛　　　　jīng
睡　　　　shuì
瞒　　　　mán
瞧　　　　qiáo

110 田
田　　　　tián
由　　　　yóu
电　　　　diàn
男　　　　nán
界　　　　jiè
留　　　　liú
累　　　　lèi
野　　　　yě

111 皿
盆　　　　pén
盘　　　　pán

112 钅

2–4 strokes

针　　　　zhēn
钓　　　　diào
钥　　　　yào
钢　　　　gāng
钟　　　　zhōng

5–6 strokes

钻　　　　zuān
铃　　　　líng
铁　　　　tiě
铅　　　　qiān
钱　　　　qián
铜　　　　tóng

7–11 strokes

锅　　　　guō
锐　　　　ruì

铺 pù
银 yín
错 cuò
键 jiàn
锻 duàn
镜 jìng

113 矢

知 zhī
短 duǎn
矮 ǎi

114 禾

2–4 strokes

私 sī
秀 xiù
和 hé
秒 miǎo
科 kē
秋 qiū
香 xiāng
种 zhǒng, zhòng

5–9 strokes

租 zū
称 chēng
乘 chéng
积 jī
秩 zhì
移 yí
税 shuì
稳 wěn

115 白

白 bái
百 bǎi
皂 zào
的 de
皇 huáng

116 用

用 yòng

117 母

母 mǔ

118 鸟

鸟 niǎo
鸡 jī
鹅 é

119 疒

病 bìng
疼 téng
疲 pí
痛 tòng
瘦 shòu

120 立

立 lì
产 chǎn
亲 qīn
站 zhàn
章 zhāng
端 duān

121 穴

究 jiū
穷 qióng
空 kōng, kòng
穿 chuān
突 tū
窗 chuāng

122 衤

2–3 strokes

补 bǔ
初 chū
衬 chèn
衫 shān

4–7 strokes

袖 xiù
被 bèi
袜 wà
裤 kù
裙 qún

123 示

示 shì

124 主

责 zé

125 母

母 mǔ
每 měi

126 去

去 qù

127 疋

楚 chǔ

128 老

考 kǎo
老 lǎo

129 耳

耳 ěr
取 qǔ
耽 dān
聊 liáo
职 zhí
联 lián
聪 cōng

130 西

西 xī
要 yāo, yào
票 piào

131 页

页 yè
顺 shùn
顿 dùn
顾 gù
预 yù
领 lǐng
颜 yán

132 虫

虫 chóng
蚊 wén
蛇 shé
蛋 dàn
蛙 wā
蝇 yíng
蜜 mì

133 缶

缺 quē
罐 guàn

134 舌

乱 luàn

135 竹

竹 zhú

3–5 strokes

笔 bǐ
笑 xiào
第 dì
笨 bèn
符 fú

6–7 strokes

答 dā, dá
筑 zhù
等 děng
简 jiǎn
签 qiān
筷 kuài

8–9 strokes

算 suàn
管 guǎn
箭 jiàn
篇 piān

136 自

自 zì
臭 chòu
鼻 bí

137 舟

般 bān
航 háng
船 chuán

138 衣

衣 yī
表 biǎo
袋 dài
装 zhuāng

139 亦

变 biàn

140 羊

羊 yáng
美 měi
差 chà
着 zháo, zhe
善 shàn
羡 xiàn
群 qún

141 米

米 mǐ

3–5 strokes

类 lèi
料 liào
粉 fěn
粒 lì
粗 cū

7–11strokes

粮 liáng
精 jīng

糊	hú
糕	gāo
糟	zāo
糖	táng

142 艮

良	liáng
既	jì

143 羽

羽	yǔ
翅	chì
翻	fān

144 糸

索	suǒ
素	sù
紫	zǐ
繁	fán

145 走

走	zǒu
赶	gǎn
起	qǐ
超	chāo
越	yuè

趁	chèn
趟	tàng

146 里

里	lǐ

147 足

足	zú

3–5 strokes

跃	yuè
距	jù
跌	diē
践	jiàn
跨	kuà
踩	cǎi
跑	pǎo

6–7 strokes

跟	gēn
路	lù
跳	tiào
踢	tī

148 身

身	shēn
躺	tǎng
躲	duǒ

149 角

角	jiǎo
解	jiě
触	chù

150 言

言	yán
警	jǐng

151 辛

辛	xīn
辟	pì

152 系

系	xì

153 束

束	shù
整	zhěng

154 非

非	fēi
靠	kào

155 酉

配	pèi

酱	jiàng
酸	suān
醉	zuì
醋	cù

156 豆

豆	dòu
登	dēng

157 隹

集	jí
雄	xióng
雌	cí

158 青

青	qīng
静	jìng

159 鱼

鱼	yú
鲜	xiān

160 雨

雨	yǔ
雪	xuě
零	líng

雾	wù
需	xū
露	lù

161 革

鞋	xié

162 是

匙	shì
题	tí

163 食

食	shí
餐	cān

164 音

音	yīn

165 麻

麻	má

166 黑

黑	hēi
墨	mò
默	mò

Stroke Index

This index lists all characters in this dictionary according to the number of strokes used to write them. Characters with the same number of strokes are grouped together according to the first stroke used. These groups are listed in the following order:

1. 一 (including ㇔ ㇀)
2. 丨 (including 丿 ㇚)
3. 丿 (including 丿 一 丿)
4. 丶 (including 丶 ㇏)
5. 乛 (including 乛 乛 ㇗ 乙 乙 乚)
6. ㄑ (including 乚 ㄥ ㄑ ㄣ ㄅ)

Within each group, characters are arranged alphabetically according to *pinyin*.

1–2 strokes							
一		万	wàn	习	xí	元	yuán	什	shén

1–2 strokes

一

一 yī, yí, yì
厂 chǎng
二 èr
七 qī
十 shí

丨

卜 bó

丿

儿 ér
几 jī, jǐ
人 rén
入 rù

乛

刀 dāo
力 lì
了 le, liǎo
又 yòu

3 strokes

一

才 cái
寸 cùn
大 dà, dài
工 gōng
三 sān
士 shì
土 tǔ
万 wàn
下 xià
于 yú
丈 zhàng

丨

口 kǒu
山 shān
上 shàng
小 xiǎo

丿

凡 fán
干 gān, gàn
个 gè
久 jiǔ
么 me
千 qiān
勺 sháo
义 yì
亿 yì

丶

广 guǎng
门 mén
之 zhī

乛

叉 chā
飞 fēi
己 jǐ
马 mǎ
卫 wèi

习 xí
也 yě
已 yǐ
子 zǐ, zi

ㄑ

女 nǚ
与 yǔ

4 strokes

一

不 bú, bù
车 chē
夫 fū
互 hù
开 kāi
木 mù
匹 pǐ
区 qū
世 shì
太 tài
天 tiān
厅 tīng
王 Wáng
无 wú
五 wǔ
牙 yá
艺 yì
尤 yóu
友 yǒu

元 yuán
云 yún
支 zhī
专 zhuān

丨

见 jiàn
内 nèi
日 rì
少 shǎo
水 shuǐ
中 zhōng

丿

长 cháng, zhǎng
从 cóng
反 fǎn
分 fēn
丰 fēng
风 fēng
父 fù
公 gōng
化 huà
介 jiè
斤 jīn
今 jīn
毛 máo
牛 niú
片 piàn
气 qì
欠 qiàn

什 shén
升 shēng
手 shǒu
午 wǔ
月 yuè

丶

订 dìng
斗 dòu
方 fāng
户 hù
火 huǒ
计 jì
六 liù
认 rèn
为 wèi
文 wén
心 xīn

乛

办 bàn
尺 chǐ
队 duì
孔 kǒng
劝 quàn
书 shū
双 shuāng
卫 wèi
引 yǐn

ㄑ

比 bǐ

以 yǐ
允 yǔn

5 strokes
一
本 běn
布 bù
东 dōng
功 gōng
节 jié
可 kě
厉 lì
龙 lóng
灭 miè
平 píng
巧 qiǎo
切 qiè
去 qù
扔 rēng
仍 rěng
石 shí
示 shì
术 shù
未 wèi
右 yòu
玉 yù
正 zhèng
左 zuǒ
丨
北 běi
出 chū
电 diàn
号 hào
叫 jiào
旧 jiù
卡 kǎ
另 lìng
目 mù
且 qiě
史 shǐ

四 sì
田 tián
兄 xiōng
叶 yè
业 yè
由 yóu
占 zhàn
只 zhī, zhǐ
丿
白 bái
包 bāo
册 cè
处 chǔ, chù
传 chuán
代 dài
冬 dōng
付 fù
瓜 guā
乎 hū
化 huà
句 jù
乐 lè
令 lìng
们 men
鸟 niǎo
生 shēng
失 shī
他 tā
外 wài
务 wù
休 xiū
仪 yí
印 yìn
用 yòng
乐 yuè
、
半 bàn
必 bì
汉 hàn
记 jì

兰 lán
礼 lǐ
立 lì
让 ràng
闪 shǎn
市 shì
它 tā
讨 tǎo
头 tóu
写 xiě
讯 xùn
议 yì
永 yǒng
主 zhǔ
乛
边 biān
对 duì
加 jiā
矛 máo
民 mín
加 jiā
司 sī
召 zhào
乚
发 fā
纠 jiū
母 mǔ
奶 nǎi
台 tái

6 strokes
一
百 bǎi
场 chǎng
存 cún
达 dá
打 dǎ
地 de, dì
动 dòng
夺 duó

而 ér
耳 ěr
巩 gǒng
共 gòng
过 guò
划 huà
灰 huī
机 jī
圾 jī
考 kǎo
扩 kuò
老 lǎo
列 liè
迈 mài
朴 pǔ
扫 sǎo
式 shì
死 sǐ
吐 tù
压 yā
亚 yà
厌 yàn
有 yǒu
西 xī
扬 yáng
页 yè
在 zài
至 zhì
丨
吃 chī
虫 chóng
此 cǐ
当 dāng
刚 gāng
光 guāng
回 huí
吗 ma
肉 ròu
师 shī
岁 suì

同 tóng
团 tuán
网 wǎng
吸 xī
迅 xùn
吓 xià
因 yīn
早 zǎo
则 zé
丿
成 chéng
创 chuàng
丢 diū
多 duō
朵 duǒ
份 fèn
负 fù
各 gè
行 háng
合 hé
后 hòu
会 huì
伙 huǒ
价 jià
件 jiàn
军 jūn
名 míng
年 nián
企 qǐ
全 quán
任 rèn
伞 sǎn
色 sè
杀 shā
伤 shāng
舌 shé
似 sì
危 wēi
伟 wěi
先 xiān

向	xiàng	训	xùn	材	cái	运	yùn	饭	fàn
血	xiě	羊	yáng	苍	cāng	找	zhǎo	佛	fú
行	xíng	衣	yī	抄	chāo	折	zhé	告	gào
血	xuě	澡	zǎo	村	cūn	址	zhǐ	估	gū
延	yán	庄	zhuāng	豆	dòu	志	zhì	何	hé
爷	yé	字	zì	否	fǒu	走	zǒu	鸡	jī
优	yōu			杆	gān			角	jiǎo
杂	zá	导	dǎo	更	gèng	吧	ba	近	jìn
争	zhēng	防	fáng	攻	gōng	别	bié	利	lì
竹	zhú	观	guān	护	hù	步	bù	邻	lín
自	zì	欢	huān	还	hái, huán	财	cái	乱	luàn
		阶	jiē	花	huā	吵	chǎo	每	měi
安	ān	尽	jín, jǐn	坏	huài	吹	chuī	你	nǐ
冰	bīng	那	nà	极	jí	呆	dāi	身	shēn
并	bìng	戏	xì	技	jì	盯	dīng	体	tǐ
产	chǎn	寻	xún	进	jìn	吨	dūn	条	tiáo
充	chōng	阳	yáng	拒	jù	坚	jiān	位	wèi
次	cì	阴	yīn	抗	kàng	困	kùn	我	wǒ
灯	dēng	羽	yǔ	克	kè	里	lǐ	希	xī
访	fǎng	阵	zhèn	块	kuài	男	nán	系	xì
关	guān			来	lái	时	shí	秀	xiù
汗	hàn	毕	bì	劳	láo	听	tīng	犹	yóu
江	jiāng	妇	fù	丽	lì	围	wéi	余	yú
讲	jiǎng	好	hǎo	励	lì	县	xiàn	迎	yíng
交	jiāo	红	hóng	连	lián	些	xiē	皂	zào
决	jué	级	jí	弄	lòng	呀	yā, ya	住	zhù
论	lùn	纪	jì	两	liǎng	邮	yóu	作	zuò
忙	máng	妈	mā	批	pī	员	yuán	坐	zuò
米	mǐ	纤	xiān	抢	qiǎng	园	yuán		
农	nóng	如	rú	求	qiú	助	zhù	补	bǔ
齐	qí	收	shōu	却	què	足	zú	沉	chén
庆	qìng	丝	sī	扰	rǎo			初	chū
设	shè	她	tā	忍	rěn	兵	bīng	床	chuáng
守	shǒu	约	yuē	声	shēng	伯	bó	词	cí
汤	tāng			束	shù	彻	chè	弟	dì
完	wán	**7 strokes**		投	tóu	但	dàn	冻	dòng
问	wèn			形	xíng	岛	dǎo	泛	fàn
污	wū	把	bǎ	严	yán	的	de	间	jiān
闲	xián	扮	bàn	医	yī	低	dī	究	jiū
兴	xīng, xìng	报	bào	远	yuǎn	肚	dù	快	kuài
许	xǔ								

况	kuàng			其	qí	明	míng	征	zhēng
冷	lěng	努	nǔ	奇	qí	呢	ne	知	zhī
良	liáng	纺	fǎng	青	qīng	叔	shū	制	zhì
亩	mǔ	妙	miào	枪	qiāng	图	tú	质	zhì
没	méi	纸	zhǐ	取	qǔ	味	wèi	周	zhōu
判	pàn			软	ruǎn	些	xiē		
评	píng	**8 strokes**		事	shì	易	yì	宝	bǎo
启	qǐ			势	shì			怖	bù
弃	qì	板	bǎn	松	sōng	爸	bà	变	biàn
汽	qì	抱	bào	抬	tái	版	bǎn	衬	chèn
穷	qióng	杯	bēi	态	tài	饱	bǎo	诚	chéng
沙	shā	表	biǎo	拖	tuō	备	bèi	单	dān
社	shè	厕	cè	玩	wán	采	cǎi	底	dǐ
识	shí	拆	chāi	武	wǔ	钓	diào	店	diàn
诉	sù	抽	chōu	现	xiàn	肥	féi	定	dìng
忘	wàng	刺	cì	幸	xìng	服	fú	法	fǎ
辛	xīn	担	dān	英	yīng	肝	gān	房	fáng
序	xù	到	dào	拥	yōng	供	gòng	放	fàng
言	yán	范	fàn	雨	yǔ	狗	gǒu	府	fǔ
译	yì	奋	fèn	责	zé	股	gǔ	该	gāi
应	yīng	构	gòu	择	zé	刮	guā	怪	guài
灾	zāi	规	guī	招	zhāo	和	hé	官	guān
这	zhè, zhèi	画	huà	者	zhě	货	huò	河	hé
证	zhèng	环	huán	直	zhí	金	jīn	话	huà
状	zhuàng	或	huò	转	zhuǎn	命	mìng	京	jīng
		拣	jiǎn			例	lì	净	jìng
阿	ā	苦	kǔ	哎	āi	念	niàn	刻	kè
层	céng	矿	kuàng	岸	àn	爬	pá	空	kōng, kòng
陈	Chén	拉	lā	败	bài	佩	pèi	肩	jiān
承	chéng	拦	lán	典	diǎn	朋	péng	卷	juǎn
迟	chí	林	lín	非	fēi	迫	pò	怜	lián
附	fù	轮	lún	咐	fù	侵	qīn	庙	miào
改	gǎi	码	mǎ	固	gù	舍	shè	闹	nào
际	jì	卖	mài	国	guó	使	shǐ	怕	pà
局	jú	欧	ōu	果	guǒ	所	suǒ	泼	pō
灵	líng	拍	pāi	呼	hū	往	wǎng	浅	qiǎn
陆	lù	披	pī	虎	hǔ	委	wěi	衫	shān
买	mǎi	苹	píng	具	jù	物	wù	诗	shī
尾	wěi	坡	pō	咖	kā	依	yī	实	shí
张	zhāng	妻	qī	肯	kěn	鱼	yú	试	shì

视	shì	帮	bāng	要	yāo, yào	胆	dǎn	种	zhǒng, zhòng
享	xiǎng	标	biāo	政	zhèng	独	dú	重	chóng, zhòng
性	xìng	玻	bō	指	zhǐ	段	duàn	追	zhuī
学	xué	草	cǎo			盾	dùn		
夜	yè	茶	chá	背	bēi, bèi	肺	fèi	扁	biǎn
宜	yì	查	chá	尝	cháng	复	fù	测	cè
泳	yǒng	城	chéng	点	diǎn	钢	gāng	穿	chuān
油	yóu	持	chí	骨	gǔ	逛	guàng	帝	dì
育	yù	春	chūn	贵	guì	鬼	guǐ	洞	dòng
治	zhì	带	dài	哈	hā	很	hěn	度	dù
注	zhù	挡	dǎng	界	jiè	候	hòu	冠	guàn
		费	fèi	咳	ké	皇	huáng	恨	hèn
驾	jià	封	fēng	览	lǎn	急	jí	活	huó
艰	jiān	革	gé	临	lín	饺	jiǎo	迹	jī
建	jiàn	故	gù	骂	mà	看	kàn	济	jì
降	jiàng	挂	guà	冒	mào	科	kē	将	jiāng
届	jiè	厚	hòu	哪	nǎ, na	俩	liǎ	奖	jiǎng
居	jū	胡	hú	盼	pàn	律	lù	举	jǔ
录	lù	挥	huī	省	shěng	脉	mài	觉	jué
刷	shuā	厘	lǐ	是	shì	贸	mào	客	kè
肃	sù	挤	jǐ	思	sī	免	miǎn	烂	làn
限	xiàn	面	miàn	虽	suī	秒	miǎo	浪	làng
		某	mǒu	胃	wèi	胖	pàng	类	lèi
参	cān	南	nán	显	xiǎn	盆	pén	炼	liàn
姑	gū	耐	nài	响	xiǎng	秋	qiū	亮	liàng
姐	jiě	配	pèi	星	xīng	牲	shēng	迷	mí
练	liàn	拼	pīn	咽	yàn	胜	shèng	美	měi
妹	mèi	品	pǐn	咬	yǎo	狮	shī	浓	nóng
始	shǐ	轻	qīng	映	yìng	食	shí	派	pài
细	xì	荣	róng	咱	zán	适	shì	炮	pào
线	xiàn	拾	shí	战	zhàn	顺	shùn	前	qián
详	xiáng	柿	shì	昨	zuó	逃	táo	亲	qīn
姓	xìng	树	shù			香	xiāng	染	rǎn
沿	yán	挑	tiāo	保	bǎo	信	xìn	洒	sǎ
织	zhī	挺	tǐng	版	bǎn	修	xiū	神	shén
组	zǔ	歪	wāi	饼	bǐng	须	xū	施	shī
		咸	xián	便	biàn, pián	选	xuǎn	室	shì
9 strokes		项	xiàng	臭	chòu	钥	yào	首	shǒu
		相	xiāng	促	cù	怎	zěn	说	shuō
按	àn	药	yào	待	dāi, dài	钟	zhōng	送	sòng

诵	sòng	班	bān	虑	lù	途	tú	旅	lǚ
庭	tíng	翅	chì	紧	jǐn	息	xī	旁	páng
突	tū	础	chǔ	哭	kū	牺	xī	疲	pí
弯	wān	耽	dān	哦	ō	笑	xiào	悄	qiāo
闻	wén	都	dōu	贴	tiē	胸	xiōng	瓶	píng
误	wù	逗	dòu	蚊	wén	脏	zāng	请	qǐng
席	xí	顿	dùn	晓	xiǎo	造	zào	容	róng
洗	xǐ	赶	gǎn	圆	yuán	值	zhí	扇	shàn
宣	xuān	哥	gē	桌	zhuō	秩	zhì	谁	shuí, shéi
洋	yáng	根	gēn			逐	zhú	烫	tàng
养	yǎng	顾	gù	爱	ài	租	zū	谈	tán
音	yīn	壶	hú	般	bān	钻	zuān	疼	téng
语	yǔ	换	huàn	倍	bèi			袜	wà
洲	zhōu	获	huò	笔	bǐ	案	àn	消	xiāo
祝	zhù	教	jiāo, jiào	称	chēng	被	bèi	效	xiào
总	zǒng	捞	lāo	乘	chéng	病	bìng	袖	xiù
祖	zǔ	烈	liè	脆	cuì	部	bù	宴	yàn
		埋	mái	倒	dǎo	差	chà	谊	yì
除	chú	破	pò	敌	dí	递	dì	益	yì
孩	hái	起	qǐ	饿	è	调	diào, tiáo	浴	yù
既	jì	桥	qiáo	胳	gē	读	dú	阅	yuè
骄	jiāo	殊	shū	航	háng	烦	fán	站	zhàn
退	tuì	素	sù	候	hòu	粉	fěn	准	zhǔn
屋	wū	速	sù	积	jī	浮	fú	资	zī
险	xiǎn	损	sǔn	健	jiàn	高	gāo	座	zuò
勇	yǒng	索	suǒ	脚	jiǎo	海	hǎi		
院	yuàn	热	rè	借	jiè	害	hài	悬	kěn
		套	tào	俱	jù	家	jiā	剧	jù
给	gěi	夏	xià	狼	láng	竞	jìng	难	nán
贯	guàn	校	xiào	留	liú	酒	jiǔ	陪	péi
结	jié	样	yàng	秘	mì	课	kè	弱	ruò
经	jīng	原	yuán	拿	ná	宽	kuān	通	tōng
绝	jué	哲	zhé	脑	nǎo	朗	lǎng	验	yàn
绕	rǎo	真	zhēn	铅	qiān	离	lí	预	yù
统	tǒng	致	zhì	钱	qián	恋	liàn	展	zhǎn
姻	yīn	捉	zhuō	缺	quē	凉	liáng		
				特	tè	谅	liàng	继	jì
10 strokes		啊	ā	铁	tiě	铃	líng	能	néng
		柴	chái	透	tòu	流	liú	娘	niáng
挨	āi	党	dǎng						

11 strokes

一

菜	cài
措	cuò
掉	diào
堵	dǔ
堆	duī
辅	fú
副	fù
黄	huáng
基	jī
检	jiǎn
接	jiē
救	jiù
据	jū
理	lǐ
历	lì
粒	lì
辆	liàng
聊	liáo
萝	luó
梦	mèng
描	miáo
排	pái
捧	pěng
票	piào
球	qiú
探	tàn
萄	táo
梯	tī
桶	tǒng
推	tuī
雪	xuě
研	yán
营	yíng
械	xiè
职	zhí
著	zhù

丨

常	cháng

唱	chàng
晨	chén
崇	chóng
哼	hēng
辉	huī
距	jù
啦	la
累	lèi
啤	pí
圈	quān
蛇	shé
匙	shì
堂	táng
唯	wéi
虚	xū
眼	yǎn
野	yě
跃	yuè

丿

笨	bèn
脖	bó
猜	cāi
彩	cǎi
船	chuán
袋	dài
得	dé, de, děi
第	dì
符	fú
够	gòu
馆	guǎn
盒	hé
忽	hū
假	jiǎ, jià
梨	lí
利	lì
脸	liǎn
领	lǐng
猫	māo
勉	miǎn
您	nín

牌	pái
盘	pán
偏	piān
售	shòu
停	tíng
铜	tóng
偷	tōu
脱	tuō
悉	xī
斜	xié
移	yí
银	yín
悠	yōu
猪	zhū
做	zuò

丶

惭	cán
粗	cū
淡	dàn
断	duàn
港	gǎng
惯	guàn
毫	háo
混	hùn
寄	jì
剪	jiǎn
减	jiǎn
渐	jiàn
惊	jīng
竟	jìng
康	kāng
粒	lì
梁	liáng
麻	má
密	mì
清	qīng
情	qíng
商	shāng
深	shēn
宿	sù

添	tiān
望	wàng
谓	wèi
液	yè
章	zhāng
着	zháo, zhe
族	zú

乛

蛋	dàn
敢	gǎn
骑	qí

㇄

婚	hūn
绩	jì
绿	lù
绳	shéng
维	wéi
续	xù

12 strokes

一

悲	bēi
插	chā
超	chāo
朝	cháo
趁	chèn
厨	chú
概	gài
棵	kē
款	kuǎn
联	lián
棉	mián
期	qī
确	què
散	sàn
森	sēn
提	tí
替	tì
填	tián
握	wò

喜	xǐ
雄	xióng
椅	yǐ
硬	yìng
越	yuè
暂	zàn
煮	zhǔ

丨

跌	diē
幅	fú
喊	hǎn
喝	hē
践	jiàn
量	liáng, liàng
帽	mào
跑	pǎo
晴	qíng
贴	tiē
蛙	wā
晚	wǎn
喂	wèi
遗	yí
遇	yù
最	zuì

丿

傲	ào
傍	bàng
答	dā, dá
等	děng
短	duǎn
鹅	é
傅	fù
猴	hóu
集	jí
街	jiē
脾	pí
然	rán
锐	ruì
剩	shèng
释	shì

税 shuì
舒 shū
毯 tǎn
筑 zhù

遍 biàn
曾 céng
窗 chuāng
道 dào
愤 fèn
富 fù
割 gē
寒 hán
湖 hú
滑 huá
就 jiù
渴 kě
裤 kù
普 pǔ
裙 qún
痛 tòng
湾 wān
湿 shī
童 tóng
温 wēn
羡 xiàn
谢 xiè
游 yóu
愉 yú
掌 zhǎng
装 zhuāng
尊 zūn

登 dēng
隔 gé
骗 piàn
强 qiáng
属 shǔ

编 biān

嫂 sǎo

13 strokes

碍 ài
摆 bǎi
搬 bān
楚 chǔ
碟 dié
感 gǎn
搞 gǎo
搁 gé
鼓 gǔ
蓝 lán
零 líng
楼 lóu
摸 mō
碰 pèng
葡 pú
摄 shè
碎 suì
输 shū
摊 tān
雾 wù
碗 wǎn
献 xiàn
想 xiǎng
摇 yáo

暗 àn
跟 gēn
睛 jīng
景 jǐng
跨 kuà
龄 líng
路 lù
嗯 ng
暖 nuǎn
喷 pēn

暑 shǔ
睡 shuì
跳 tiào
歇 xiē
照 zhào
置 zhì

矮 ǎi
愁 chóu
触 chù
催 cuī
错 cuò
躲 duǒ
锅 guō
简 jiǎn
键 jiàn
解 jiě
筷 kuài
铺 pù
签 qiān
傻 shǎ
腿 tuǐ
微 wéi
箱 xiāng
像 xiàng
腰 yāo

福 fú
滚 gǔn
粮 liáng
酱 jiàng
满 mǎn
煤 méi
漠 mò
善 shàn
数 shǔ, shù
塑 sù
新 xīn
意 yì
源 yuán

辟 pì
群 qún

缝 féng

14 strokes

磁 cí
榜 bǎng
歌 gē
蕉 jiāo
静 jìng
墙 qiáng
摔 shuāi
酸 suān
需 xū
愿 yuàn
摘 zhāi

雌 cí
黑 hēi
嘛 ma
嗽 sòu
遭 zāo
赚 zhuàn

膀 bǎng
鼻 bí
膊 bó
锻 duàn
馒 mán
貌 mào
算 suàn
躺 tǎng
稳 wěn
舞 wǔ
鲜 xiān

察 chá

滴 dī
端 duān
腐 fǔ
精 jīng
漏 lòu
慢 màn
蜜 mì
漂 piào
旗 qí
敲 qiāo
赛 sài
瘦 shòu
演 yǎn

嫩 nèn
缩 suō
疑 yí

15 strokes

播 bō
聪 cōng
醋 cù
飘 piāo
趟 tàng
鞋 xié
增 zēng
撞 zhuàng
醉 zuì

踩 cǎi
嘿 hēi
瞒 mán
墨 mò
噢 ō
踢 tī
题 tí
影 yǐng
嘱 zhǔ

丿

德 dé
管 guǎn
箭 jiàn
靠 kào
篇 piān
躺 tǎng

丶

澳 ào
懂 dǒng
糊 hú
熟 shú

颜 yán
遵 zūn

𠃌

慰 wèi
豫 yù

16 strokes

一

薄 báo, bó
操 cāo
橘 jú
整 zhěng

丨

餐 cān
默 mò
器 qì
嘴 zuǐ

丿

镜 jìng
邀 yāo
赞 zàn

丶

糕 gāo
激 jí

懒 lǎn
糖 táng

𠃌

壁 bì
避 bì

17-23 strokes

一

擦 cā
戴 dài
警 jǐng

露 lù

丨

瞧 qiáo
嚷 rǎng

丿

翻 fān
繁 fán
罐 guàn

丶

燃 rán
赢 yíng

A

ā 阿 PREFIX = (used to address certain relatives or friends to convey sentiment of intimacy)
ā bà 阿爸 = daddy
ā pó 阿婆 = (maternal) granny

Ālābówén 阿拉伯文 NOUN = the Arabic language (especially the writing)
■ 阿拉伯文是从右向左写。**Ālābówén shì cóng yòu xiàng zuǒ xiě.** = *Arabic is written from right to left.*

Ālābóyǔ 阿拉伯语 NOUN = the Arabic language
■ 阿拉伯语是一种古老而优美的语言。**Ālābóyǔ shì yì zhǒng gǔlǎo ér yōuměi de yǔyán.** = *Arabic is an ancient and beautiful language.*

āyí 阿姨 NOUN = mother's sister
■ 我妈妈有一个姐姐，一个妹妹，所以我有两个阿姨。**Wǒ māma yǒu yí ge jiějie, yí ge mèimei, suǒyǐ wǒ yǒu liǎng ge āyí.** = *My mother has an elder sister and a younger sister, so I have two aunts.*

NOTES: (1) 阿姨 **āyí** is a form of address used by a child for a woman about his/her mother's age. It is also common to put a family name before 阿姨 **āyí**, e.g. 张阿姨 **Zhāng āyí**. (2) 阿姨 **āyí** is also used by adults and children for domestic helpers and female nursery staff.

ā 啊
1 INTERJECTION = (used to express strong emotions such as surprise, admiration, regret etc.) oh, ah
■ 啊，海风多么凉爽！**Ā, hǎifēng duōme liángshuǎng!** = *How refreshing the sea breeze is!*
2 PARTICLE = (attached to a sentence to express strong emotions such as surprise, admiration, regret etc.)
■ 海风真凉爽啊！**Hǎifēng zhēn liángshuǎng a!** = *How refreshing the sea breeze is!*
■ 北京的冬天真冷啊！**Běijīng de dōngtiān zhēn lěng a!** = *How cold the winter in Beijing is!*

āi 哎 INTERJECTION = (used to attract attention or express surprise)
■ 哎，你还在玩电子游戏？**Āi, nǐ hái zài wán diànzǐ yóuxì?** = *Oh, you're still playing computer games?*

āiyā 哎呀 INTERJECTION = (used to express surprise or annoyance)
■ 哎呀，我说了半天，你怎么还不明白？**Āiyā, wǒ shuō le bàntiān, nǐ zěnme hái bù míngbai?** = *Goodness, I've been explaining for ages, how come you still don't see the point?*

ái 挨 VERB = undergo (some painful or unpleasant experience)
■ 那个小偷挨了一顿打。**Nàge xiǎotōu ái le yí dùn dǎ.** = *That thief was beaten up.*

ǎi 矮 ADJECTIVE = (of a person or plant) of short stature; short (antonym 高 **gāo**)
■ 他虽然长得矮，但是篮球打得挺好。**Tā suīrán zhǎng de ǎi, dànshì lánqiú dǎ de tǐng hǎo.** = *Although he's short, he's a good basketball player.*
■ 妹妹比我矮一点儿。**Mèimei bǐ wǒ ǎi yìdiǎnr.** = *My younger sister is a bit shorter than me.*

ài 爱 Trad 愛 VERB
1 = love
■ 我爱爸爸妈妈，爸爸妈妈也爱我。**Wǒ ài bàba māma, bàba māma yě ài wǒ.** = *I love my mom and dad, and they love me too.*
2 = like, be fond of
■ 她爱表现自己。**Tā ài biǎoxiàn zìjǐ.** = *She likes to show off.*

àihào 爱好 [compound: 爱 *love* + 好 *like, be fond of*]
1 VERB = like, be interested in, have as a hobby
■ 我爱好旅行，爱好了解世界各地人民的风俗习惯。**Wǒ àihào lǚxíng, àihào liǎojiě shìjiè gèdì rénmín de fēngsú xíguàn.** = *I like travelling; I like getting to know the social customs and practices of peoples everywhere.*
2 NOUN = hobby, interest
■ "你有什么爱好？""我的爱好比较广泛，不过我最大的爱好是玩电子游戏。" **"Nǐyǒu shénme àihào?" "Wǒde àihào bǐjiào guǎngfàn, búguò wǒ zuìdà de àihào shì wán diànzǐ yóuxì."** = *"What's your hobby?" I have many*

A

hobbies, but my favorite one is playing computer games."

àihù 爱护 [compound: 爱 *love* + 护 *protect*]
VERB = care for and protect, cherish
■ 父母都爱护自己的孩子。**Fùmǔ dōu àihù zìjǐ de háizi.** = *All parents care for and protect their children.*
■ 我们应该爱护我们之间的友谊。**Wǒmen yīnggāi àihù wǒmen zhī jiān de yǒuyì.** = *We should cherish our friendship.*

àiqíng 爱情 [compound: 爱 *love* + 情 *feeling, affection*] NOUN = romantic love
■ 年轻人都希望获得爱情。**Niánqīngrén dōu xīwàng huòdé àiqíng.** = *Young people all yearn for love.*
■ 婚姻一定要建立在爱情的基础上。**Hūnyīn yídìng yào jiànlì zài àiqíng de jīchǔ shang.** = *Marriage must be based on love.*

àirén 爱人 [modif: 爱 *love* + 人 *person*] NOUN = husband or wife
■ 我和爱人结婚十年了。**Wǒ hé àirén jiéhūn shí nián le.** = *My husband (or wife) and I have been married for ten years.*

NOTE: 爱人 **àirén** as *husband* or *wife* is only used in Mainland China as a colloquialism. On formal occasions 丈夫 **zhàngfu** (*husband*) and 妻子 **qīzi** (*wife*) are used instead. Now there is a decreasing tendency to use 爱人 **àirén** in China. In its place 先生 **xiānsheng** and 太太 **tàitai** are used to refer to *husband* and *wife*, a long established practice in Taiwan, Hong Kong and overseas Chinese communities. For example:
■ 你先生近来忙吗？ **Nǐ xiānsheng jìnlái máng ma?** = *Is your husband busy these days?*
■ 我太太要我下班回家的路上买些菜。**Wǒ tàitai yào wǒ xiàbān huíjiā de lù shang mǎi xiē cài.** = *My wife wants me to buy some vegetables on my way home.*

ài 碍 Trad 礙 VERB = hinder (See 妨碍 **fáng'ài.**)

ān 安 ADJECTIVE = peaceful, safe

ānjìng 安静 [compound: 安 *peace* + 静 *quiet*] ADJECTIVE = quiet, peaceful, serene

■ 这里很少有车开过，环境很安静。**Zhèlǐ hěn shǎo yǒu chē kāiguò, huánjìng hěn ānjìng.** = *There is very little traffic here. The environment is very peaceful.*
■ 请大家安静！**Qǐng dàjiā ānjìng!** = *Please be quiet, everyone!*
■ 这位老人只想过安静的生活。**Zhè wèi lǎorén zhǐ xiǎng guò ānjìng de shēnghuó.** = *This old man only wants to live a quiet life.*

ānpái 安排 [compound: 安 *to settle, to arrange* + 排 *to arrange, to put in order*] VERB = arrange, make arrangement; plan
■ 大学生一般都很忙，因此必须安排好时间。**Dàxuéshēng yìbān dōu hěn máng, yīncǐ bìxū ānpái hǎo shíjiān.** = *University students are generally busy people, so they must plan their time well.*
■ 董事长下个月去中国旅行，请你安排一下。**Dǒngshìzhǎng xià ge yuè qù Zhōngguó lǚxíng, qǐng nǐ ānpái yíxià.** = *The chairman of the board is going to China for a trip next month. Please make the arrangements.*

ānquán 安全 [compound: 安 *peace* + 全 *complete, all-around*]
1 NOUN = security, safety
■ 开车安全第一。**Kāichē ānquán dì yī.** = *When you are driving, safety is the most important thing.*
2 ADJECTIVE = safe, secure
■ 在这里夜里一个人在街上走，安全吗？**Zài zhèlǐ yèlǐ yí ge rén zài jiē shang zǒu, ānquán ma?** = *Is it safe to walk alone in the streets here at night?*

ānwèi 安慰 [compound: 安 *make peace* + 慰 *comfort*] VERB = comfort, console
■ 他们失去了心爱的女儿，心情悲痛，朋友们都来安慰他们。**Tāmen shīqùle xīn'ài de nǚ'ér, xīnqíng bēitòng, péngyoumen dōu lái ānwèi tāmen.** = *They are in deep sorrow as they have lost their beloved daughter. Their friends have all come to comfort them.*

ānxīn 安心 [v+obj: 安 *make peace* + 心 *the heart*] ADJECTIVE = be relaxed and content
■ 她不安心在小学教书，她想当电影演员。**Tā bù ānxīn zài xiǎoxué jiāoshū, tā xiǎng dāng diànyǐng yǎnyuán.** = *She is not content to be a*

primary school teacher; she wants to be a movie star.

àn 岸 NOUN = bank or shore (of a river, lake, or sea)

■ 河的两岸是一个个小村子。**Hé de liǎng àn shì yí gège xiǎo cūnzi.** = *The river is flanked by small villages.*

hǎi àn 海岸 = coast
shàng àn 上岸 = go ashore

àn 按 PREPOSITION = according to, in accordance with

■ 按计划，这座工厂将在明年四月建成。**Àn jìhuà, zhè zuò gōngchǎng jiāng zài míngnián Sìyuè jiànchéng.** = *According to our plan, the factory will be built by April next year.*
■ 我一定按你说的做。**Wǒ yídìng àn nǐ shuō de zuò.** = *I will definitely do as you say.*

ànshí 按时 [v+obj: 按 *according to* + 时 *time*] ADVERB = according to a fixed time, on time

■ 学生要按时完成作业。**Xuésheng yào ànshí wánchéng zuòyè.** = *Students must finish their assignments on time.*
■ 你得按时吃药，病才会好。**Nǐ děi ànshí chī yào, bìng cái huì hǎo.** = *You've got to take the medicine on time, or you won't get well.*

ànzhào 按照 PREPOSITION = according to, in accordance with (same as 按 **àn**)

àn 案 NOUN = case, plan (See 答案 **dá'àn**, 方案 **fāng'àn**.)

àn 暗 ADJECTIVE = dark, dim

■ 房间里太暗了，你要看书得开灯。**Fángjiān li tài àn le, nǐ yào kàn shū děi kāi dēng.** = *The room is dim. You've got to turn on the light if you want to read.*

ànshì 暗室 = darkroom

ào 傲 ADJECTIVE = arrogant (See 骄傲 **jiāo'ào**.)

ào 澳 NOUN = deep waters

Àodàlìyà 澳大利亚 NOUN = Australia

B

bā 八 NUMERAL = eight

■ 八八六十四 **Bā bā liùshísì.** = *Eight times eight is sixty-four.*

bā 巴 NOUN = cheek (See 尾巴 **wěiba**.)

bǎ 把

1 MEASURE WORD = (for objects with handles)
■ 一把刀 **yì bǎ dāo** = a knife
2 MEASURE WORD = a handful of
■ 一把米 **yì bǎ mǐ** = a handful of rice
3 PREPOSITION = (used before a noun or pronoun to indicate it is the object of the sentence)
■ 哥哥把自行车修好了。**Gēge bǎ zìxíngchē xiūhǎo le.** = *My elder brother has fixed the bike.*
■ 请你把这封信交给李先生。**Qǐng nǐ bǎ zhè fēng xìn jiāogěi Lǐ xiānsheng.** = *Please deliver this letter to Mr Li.*
■ 我可以把车停在这里吗？**Wǒ kěyǐ bǎ chē tíng zài zhèli ma?** = *May I park my car here?*

bà 爸 NOUN = dad, daddy, papa

bàba 爸爸 NOUN = daddy, papa

■ 我爸爸工作很努力。**Wǒ bàba gōngzuò hěn nǔlì.** = *My father works hard.*
■ 爸爸，这个星期五晚上我想用一下你的车，行不行？**Bàba, zhègè Xīngqīwǔ wǎnshang wǒ xiǎng yòng yíxià nǐ de chē, xíng bu xíng?** = *Daddy, I'd like to use your car this Friday evening. Is it all right?*

ba 吧 PARTICLE

1 = (used to make a suggestion)
■ 我们一块儿去吃中饭吧。**Wǒmen yíkuàir qù chī zhōngfàn ba.** = *Let's go and have lunch together.*
■ 今天太冷了，别去游泳吧！**Jīntiān tài lěng le, bié qù yóuyǒng ba!** = *It's too cold today. Don't go swimming, OK?*
2 = (used to indicate supposition)
■ 你是新加坡来的张先生吧？**Nǐ shì Xīnjiāpō lái de Zhōng xiānsheng ba?** = *Aren't you Mr Zhang from Singapore?*
■ 你对这个地方很熟悉吧？**Nǐ duì zhège dìfāng hěn shúxi ba?** = *You're familiar with this place, aren't you?*

bái 白

1 ADJECTIVE = white
- 下雪以后，路上一片白。 **Xiàxuě yǐhòu, lù shang yí piàn bái.** = *The road was all white after the snow.*
- 她穿白衣服特别好看。 **Tā chuān bái yīfu tèbié hǎokàn.** = *She looks especially beautiful in white.*

báikāishuǐ 白开水 = plain boiled water
- 感冒了要喝白开水。 **Gǎnmào le yào hē báikāisuǐ.** = *You should drink a lot of boiled water when you've got a cold.*

báirén 白人 = Caucasian person, Caucasian people

NOTE: In Chinese tradition, white symbolizes death and is the color for funerals.

2 ADVERB = in vain, without any result
- 他根本不思改进，你说了也白说。 **Tā gēnběn bù sī gǎijìn, nǐ shuōle yě bái shuō.** = *He does not want to improve his work at all. You said all that in vain.*
- 我忘了在电脑里保存文件，一个晚上的工作白做了。 **Wǒ wàngle zài diànnǎo lǐ bǎocún wénjiàn, yí ge wǎnshang de gōngzuò dōu bái zuò le.** = *I forgot to save my document in the computer. An evening's work all came to nothing.*

3 ADVERB = for free
- 世界上没有白吃的午餐。 **Shìjiè shang méiyǒu bái chī de wǔcān.** = *There is no free lunch in the world. (→ There's no such thing as a free lunch.)*

báicài 白菜 [modif: 白 white + 菜 vegetable]

NOUN = cabbage (棵 **kē**)
- 在中国北方，白菜是冬天最便宜、最普通的蔬菜。 **Zài Zhōngguó běifāng, báicài shì dōngtiān zuì piányi, zuì pǔtōng de shūcài.** = *In North China, cabbage is the cheapest, most ordinary vegetable in winter.*

báitiān 白天 [modif: 白 white + 天 day] NOUN

= daytime
- 春天来了，白天越来越长了。 **Chūntiān lái le, báitiān yuèlaiyuè cháng le.** = *Spring has come. Days become longer and longer.*
- 他家白天一般没有人，你还是晚上去吧。 **Tā jiā báitiān yìbān méiyǒu rén, nǐ háishi wǎnshang qù ba.** = *There is usually nobody at his home during the day. You should go there in the evening.*

bǎi 百 NUMERAL = hundred
- 三百元 **sān bǎi yuán** = *three hundred yuan/ dollars*

bǎirìké 百日咳 = whooping cough
bǎixìng 百姓 = common people
lǎobǎixìng 老百姓 = common people

NOTE: 百 **bǎi** may have the abstract sense of *a great deal of* and *a multitude of*. This sense can be found in many expressions, e.g. 百闻不如一见 **Bǎi wén bùrú yí jiàn**, which literally means *A hundred sounds are not as good as one sight* and may be translated as *Seeing is believing.* Another example is 百忙 **bǎi máng**, meaning *very busy.* For example:
- 你百忙中还来看我，太好了。 **Nǐ bǎi máng zhōng hái lái kàn wǒ, tài hǎo le.** = *It's very kind of you to come to see me when you're so busy.*

bǎi 摆 Trad 擺 VERB = put, place, arrange
- 桌子上摆着一只大花瓶。 **Zhuōzi shang bǎizhe yì zhī dà huāpíng.** = *On the table is placed a big vase.*
- 吃饭了，你把碗筷摆好吧！ **Chīfàn le, nǐ bǎ wǎnkuài bǎihǎo ba!** = *It's mealtime, will you please set the table?*

bài 败 Trad 敗 VERB = be defeated (antonym 胜 shèng)
- 我们球队又败了，得研究一下原因。 **Wǒmen qiúduì yòu bài le, děi yánjiū yíxià yuányīn.** = *Our (ball) team was defeated again. We've got to look into the reason.*

bài 拜 VERB = visit (See 礼拜天 Lǐbàitiān.)

bān 班 NOUN

1 = class (in school)
- 我们班有十二个男生，十四个女生。 **Wǒmen bān yǒu shí'èr ge nánshēng, shísì ge nǔshēng.** = *Our class has twelve male students and fourteen female students.*

2 = shift (in a workplace)
- 这位护士上个星期上白天班，这个星期上夜班。 **Zhè wèi hùshi shàng ge xīngqī shàng báitiān bān, zhège xīnqī shàng yèbān.** = *This nurse was on day shift last week, and is on night shift this week.*

jiābān 加班 = work overtime
shàngbān 上班 = go to work
xiàbān 下班 = leave work
■ 我妈妈每天九点上班，五点下班。**Wǒ māma měi tiān jiǔ diǎn shàngbān, wú diǎn xiàbān.** = *My mother goes to work at nine o'clock and leaves work at five o'clock.*

bānzhǎng 班长 [modif: 班 *class, squad* + 长 *leader*] NOUN = leader (of a class in school, a squad in the army, etc.)
■ 你打算选谁当班长？**Nǐ dǎsuàn xuǎn shéi dāng bānzhǎng?** = *Whom are you going to elect as class monitor?*

bān 般 NOUN = kind, sort (See 一般 yìbān.)

bān 搬 VERB = move (heavy objects)
■ 我们把这张桌子搬到房间外面去吧。**Wǒmen bǎ zhè zhāng zhuōzi bān dào fángjiān wàimiàn qù ba.** = *Let's move this table out of the room.*
bān bu dòng 搬不动 = cannot move/cannot be moved
bān de dòng 搬得动 = can move/can be moved
bānjiā 搬家 = move (house)
■ 我们这个周末搬家，有几位朋友来帮忙。**Wǒmen zhège zhōumò bānjiā, yǒu jǐ wèi péngyou lái bāngmáng.** = *We're moving house this weekend. Some friends will come to help.*

bǎn 板 NOUN = board (See 黑板 hēibǎn.)

bǎn 版 NOUN = printing plate (See 出版 chūbǎn.)

bàn 办 Trad 辦 VERB = handle, manage
■ 这件事不容易办。**Zhè jiàn shì bù róngyì bàn.** = *This matter is not easy to handle.*
■ 你办事我很放心。**Nǐ bànshì wǒ hěn fàngxīn.** = *I feel reassured when you're handling a matter.* (→ *I have confidence in you when you're in charge.*)
■ 这件事我来办。**Zhè jiàn shì wǒ lai bàn.** = *Let me handle this matter.*

bànfǎ 办法 [modif: 办 *handle, manage* + 法 *method*] NOUN = way of doing things, method
■ 这些老办法都不行。**Zhèxie lǎo bànfǎ dōu bùxíng.** = *All these old methods won't work.*
■ 你试试我的办法。**Nǐ shìshi wǒ de bànfǎ.** = *Do try my method.*

xiǎng bànfǎ 想办法 = think up a plan/find a way of doing things
■ 我们正在想办法解决这个问题。**Wǒmen zhèngzài xiǎng bànfǎ jiějué zhège wèntí.** = *We're trying to find a way to solve this problem.*
yǒu bànfǎ 有办法 = have a way with ..., be resourceful
■ 他对小孩很有办法。**Tā duì xiǎohái hěn yǒu bànfǎ.** = *He has a way with children.*
méiyǒu bànfǎ 没有办法 = there's nothing we can do
■ 飞机票全卖完了，我们明天不能走，没有办法。**Fēijī piào quán màiwán le, wǒmen míngtiān bù néng zǒu, méiyǒu bànfǎ.** = *All the air tickets are sold out. We won't be able to leave tomorrow. There's nothing we can do.*

bàngōng 办公 [compound: 办 *handle* + 公 *public, public office*] VERB = work (as a white-collar worker, usually in an office)
■ 王经理在办公，你有事可以给他留个话。**Wáng jīnglǐ zài bàngōng, nǐ yǒushì kěyǐ gěi tā liú ge huà.** = *Mr Wang, the manager, is working in his office. You can leave him a message, if you've any business.*
bàngōng shíjiān 办公时间 = office hours, working hours
bàngōng dàlóu 办公大楼 = office building

bàngōngshì 办公室 NOUN = office (间 jiān) [compound: 办 *handle* + 公 *public, public office* + 室 *room*]
■ 大华公司的办公室在十四楼。**Dàhuá gōngsī de bàngōngshì zài shísì lóu.** = *The Dahua Company office is on the fourteenth floor.*
■ 请你到我办公室来一下。**Qǐng nǐ dào wǒ bàngōngshì lái yíxià.** = *Please come to my office.*

bàn 半 MEASURE WORD = half
■ 我等她等了一个半小时。**Wǒ děng tā děngle yí ge bàn xiǎoshí.** = *I waited for her for one and a half hours.*

bàntiān 半天 [modif: 半 *half* + 天 *day*] NOUN
1 = half a day
2 = a period of time felt to be very long, a very long time

■我等你等了半天了。**Wǒ děng nǐ děng le bàntiān le.** = *I've been waiting for you for a long time.*
■那本书我找了半天，还没找到。**Nà běn shū wǒ zhǎo le bàntiān, hái méi zhǎodào.** = *I've been looking for the book for a long time but I still haven't found it.*

bànyè 半夜 [modif: 半 *half* + 夜 *night*] NOUN = midnight, at midnight
■他经常工作到半夜才睡。**Tā jīngcháng gōngzuò dào bànyè cái shuì.** = *He often works till midnight before going to bed.*

bàn 扮 VERB = disguise as (See 打扮 **dǎbàn**.)

bāng 帮 VERB = help, assist
■上个周末，很多朋友来帮他搬家。**Shàng ge zhōumò, hěn duō péngyou lái bāng tā bānjiā.** = *Last weekend, many friends came to help him move house.*
■你能帮我找一下这本书吗？ **Nǐ néng bāng wǒ zhǎo yíxià zhè běn shū ma?** = *Can you help me find this book?*

NOTES: 帮 **bāng**, 帮忙 **bāngmáng** and 帮助 **bāngzhù** are synonyms. Their differences are: (1) 帮忙 **bāngmáng** is a verb that takes no object, while 帮 **bāng** and 帮助 **bāngzhù** are usually followed by an object. (2) As verbs, 帮 **bāng** and 帮助 **bāngzhù** are interchangeable, but 帮 **bāng** is more colloquial than 帮助 **bāngzhù**. (3) 帮助 **bāngzhù** can also be used as a noun.

bāngmáng 帮忙 VERB = help
■上个周末，他搬家，很多朋友来帮忙。**Shàng ge zhōumò tā bānjiā, hěnduō péngyou lái bāngmáng.** = *Last weekend, he moved house. Many friends came to help.*

NOTE: See note on 帮 **bāng**.

bāngzhù 帮助 [compound: 帮 *help* + 助 *assist*]
1 VERB = help, assist
■富国应该帮助穷国。**Fùguó yīnggāi bāngzhù qióngguó.** = *Rich countries should help poor countries.*
■李先生帮助我们解决了很多困难。**Lǐ xiānsheng bāngzhù wǒmen jiějuéle hěn duō**

kùnnán. = *Mr Li helped us overcome many difficulties.*
2 NOUN = help, assistance
■非常感谢你的帮助。**Fēicháng gǎnxiè nǐ de bāngzhù.** = *Thank you very much for your help.*
■没有你的帮助，我们不可能及时完成任务。**Méiyǒu nǐ de bāngzhù, wǒmen bù kěnéng jíshí wánchéng rènwù.** = *Without your help we couldn't have accomplished the task in time.*

NOTE: See note on 帮 **bāng**.

bǎng 榜 NOUN = list of names, honor roll

bǎngyàng 榜样 NOUN = (positive) example, role model
■我们的老师是美国人，说一口标准中文，真是我们的好榜样！ **Wǒmen de lǎoshī shì Měiguórén, shuō yì kǒu biāozhǔn Zhōngwén, zhēn shì wǒmen de hǎo bǎngyàng!** = *Our teacher is an American and speaks standard Chinese. He really is a good role model for us.*

bǎng 膀 NOUN = upper arm (See 翅膀 **chìbǎng**.)

bàng 傍 VERB = be close to

bàngwǎn 傍晚 [modif: 傍 *towards, close to* + 晚 *evening*] NOUN = dusk, at dusk
■他们傍晚的时候才走出树林，不一会天就黑了。**Tāmen bàngwǎn de shíhòu cái zǒuchū shùlín, bú yìhuǐ tiān jiù hēi le.** = *They came out of the woods at dusk, and soon it was dark.*

bāo 包
1 NOUN = parcel, bag
■他在路边拣到一个包，马上交给警察。**Tā zài lùbiān jiǎn dào yíge bāo, mǎshàng jiāo gei jǐngchá.** = *He picked up a parcel by the roadside and immediately handed it over to the police.*
2 VERB = wrap up
■顾客："请你把这只花瓶好好包起来。" **Gùkè: "Qǐng nǐ bǎ zhè zhī huāpíng hǎohǎo bāo qǐlai."** = *Customer: "Could you please wrap up this vase carefully?"*
qiánbāo 钱包 = wallet, purse
shūbāo 书包 = schoolbag
yóubāo 邮包 = mailbag, parcel for posting

bāokuò 包括 [compound: 包 *embrace* + 括 *include*] VERB = include, embrace
■ 旅行团包括一名翻译一共十五人。 **Lǚxíngtuán bāokuò yì míng fānyì yígòng shíwǔ rén.** = *There are fifteen people in the tour group, including an interpreter.*

bāozi 包子 [suffix: 包 *bun* + 子 nominal suffix] NOUN = steamed bun with filling
■ 我早饭吃了两个包子。 **Wǒ zǎofàn chīle liǎng ge bāozi.** = *I had two steamed buns for breakfast.*

báo 薄 ADJECTIVE = thin, flimsy (antonym 厚 hòu)
■ 天冷了，这条被子太薄，要换一条厚一点儿的。 **Tiān lěng le, zhè tiáo bèizi tài báo, yào huàn yì tiáo hòu yìdiǎnr de.** = *It's getting cold. This blanket is too thin. You need a thicker one.*

NOTE: See note on 薄 **bó**.

bǎo 宝 Trad 寶 NOUN = treasure

bǎoguì 宝贵 [compound: 宝 *precious* + 贵 *valuable*] ADJECTIVE = valuable, precious
■ 世界上什么最宝贵？ **Shìjiè shang shénme zuì bǎoguì?** = *What is the most valuable thing in the world?*
■ 我不想浪费你们的宝贵时间，就直话直说了。 **Wǒ bù xiǎng làngfèi nǐmen de bǎoguì shíjiān, jiù zhí huà zhí shuō le.** = *I don't want to waste your precious time, and will say what I have to say without mincing words.*

bǎo 保 VERB = conserve, protect
■ 这房子用了新材料，特别保暖。 **Zhè fángzi yòngle xīn cáiliào, tèbié bǎo nuǎn.** = *This house uses a new material that is particularly good at keeping the house warm.*
bǎo'ān 保安 = security guard

bǎochí 保持 [compound: 保 *conserve* + 持 *maintain*] VERB = keep, maintain
■ 他去年在学校运动会上得了长跑冠军，今年能保持吗？ **Tā qùnián zài xuéxiào yùndònghuì shang déle chángpǎo guànjūn, jīnnián néng bǎochí ma?** = *He was the champion in long-distance running at the school sports meet last year. Can he maintain it this year?* (→ *Can he defend his position this year?*)

bǎocún 保存 [compound: 保 *conserve* + 存 *keep*] VERB = keep, save
■ 这个文件很重要，你打好以后，千万别忘了保存。 **Zhège wénjiàn hěn zhòngyào, nǐ dǎhǎo yǐhòu, qiānwàn bié wàngle bǎocún.** = *This is an important document. After you've done (← typed) it, do remember to save it.*

bǎohù 保护 [compound: 保 *conserve* + 护 *protect*] VERB = protect, safeguard, conserve
■ 这片大森林一定要保护好，不能开发为旅游区。 **Zhè piàn dà sēnlín yídìng yào bǎohù hǎo, bù néng kāifā wéi lǚyóuqū.** = *This vast forest must be conserved and mustn't be developed into a tourist area.*

bǎoliú 保留 [compound: 保 *conserve* + 留 *retain*] VERB = retain, reserve
■ 这张飞机票我们给你保留三天。 **Zhè zhāng fēijī piào wǒmen gěi nǐ bǎoliú sān tiān.** = *We'll reserve this air ticket for you for three days.*
■ 你可以保留自己的意见，但是大家的决定不能违反。 **Nǐ kěyǐ bǎoliú zìjǐ de yìjiàn, dànshì dàjiā de juédìng bù néng wéifǎn.** = *You can have your reservations, but the collective decision must not be opposed.*

bǎowèi 保卫 [compound: 保 *protect* + 卫 *defend*] VERB = defend
■ 当外敌入侵时，每个人都应该保卫自己的国家。 **Dāng wài dí rùqīn shí, měi ge rén dōu yīnggāi bǎowèi zìjǐ de guójiā.** = *When an enemy invades our country, everybody should defend it.*

bǎozhèng 保证 [compound: 保 *protect* + 证 *evidence*]
1 VERB = guarantee, pledge
■ 我保证以后不犯这样的错误。 **Wǒ bǎozhèng yǐhòu bú fàn zhèyàng de cuòwù.** = *I guarantee that I won't repeat this mistake.*
■ 本公司保证产品质量。 **Běn gōngsī bǎozhèng chǎnpǐn zhìliàng.** = *This company guarantees the quality of its products.*
2 NOUN = guarantee
■ 你们能为产品提供保证吗？ **Nǐmen néng wèi chǎnpǐn tígōng bǎozhèng ma?** = *Can you provide a guarantee for your products?*
chǎnpǐn bǎozhèng shū 产品保证书 = (product) quality guarantee

B

bǎo 饱 Trad 飽 ADJECTIVE = having eaten one's fill, full (antonym 饿 **è**)

■ 谢谢，我饱了。 **Xièxie, wǒ bǎo le.** = *Thank you. I'm full.*

■ 您吃饱了吗? **Nín chī bǎo le ma?** = *Have you had (←eaten) enough?*

chī de bǎo 吃得饱 = have enough to eat

chī bu bǎo 吃不饱 = not have enough to eat (→not have enough food)

> NOTE: It is customary for a Chinese host to ask a guest who seems to have finished the meal 您吃饱了吗? **Nín chī bǎo le ma?** = *Have you had (←eaten) enough?* The guest is expected to reply 吃饱了。多谢。您慢慢吃。 **Chī bǎo le. Duō xiè. Nín mànman chī.** = *Yes, I have. Thank you. Please take your time to eat.*

bào 报 Trad 報 NOUN = newspaper (same as 报纸 **bàozhǐ**)

bàodào 报到 VERB = report for duty, register

■ 学校九月一日开学，学生从八月二十五日起报到。 **Xuéxiào Jiǔyuè yīrì kāixué, xuésheng cóng Bāyuè èrshíwǔ rì qǐ bàodào.** = *The academic year begins on September 1, and students start registration on August 25.*

bàodào 报道

1 VERB = report (news), cover

■ 今天城里各家报纸都报道了昨天的交通事故。 **Jīntiān chéng li gè jiā bàozhǐ dōu bàodàole zuótiān de jiāotōng shìgù.** = *Today all the newspapers in the city covered yesterday's road accident.*

2 NOUN = news story

■ 你看了关于昨天交通事故的报道没有? **Nǐ kànle guānyú zuótiān jiāotōng shìgù de bàodào méiyǒu?** = *Have you read the news story about yesterday's road accident?*

bàogào 报告

1 VERB = report, make known

■ 播音员：现在报告新闻。 **Bōyīnyuán: "Xiànzài bàogào xīnwén."** = *Newscaster: "Now the news."*

■ 医院发现生这种病的病人，没有立即向卫生局报告。 **Yīyuàn fāxiàn shēng zhè zhǒng bìng de bìngrén, méiyǒu lìjì xiàng wèishēngjú bàogào.** = *The hospital failed to report to the*

Bureau of Health immediately after finding a case of this disease.

2 NOUN = report, talk (at a large-scale meeting)

■ 董事会收到了一份重要报告。 = **Dǒngshìhuì shōudàole yí fèn zhòngyào bàogào.** *The Board of Directors received an important report.*

zuò bàogào 作报告 = give a talk at a large-scale meeting

bàomíng 报名 VERB = enter one's name, sign up, apply for (a place in school)

■ 我已经向一所大学报名。 **Wǒ yǐjīng xiàng yì suǒ dàxué bàomíng.** = *I have applied for a place in a university.*

■ 有六百多人报名参加星期天的长跑。 **Yǒu liùbǎi duō rén bàomíng cānjiā Xīngqītiān de chángpǎo.** = *Over 600 people have signed up for Sunday's long-distance run.*

bàozhǐ 报纸 [modif: 报 *reporting* + 纸 *paper*] NOUN = newspaper (张 **zhāng**, 份 **fèn**)

■ 今天报纸上有什么重要消息? **Jīntiān bàozhǐ shang yǒu shénme zhòngyào xiāoxi?** = *What important news is there in today's paper?*

■ 我很少看报纸。 **Wǒ hěn shǎo kàn bàozhǐ.** = *I seldom read newspapers.*

■ 这份报纸广告比新闻多。 **Zhè fèn bàozhǐ guǎnggào bǐ xīnwén duō.** = *There are more advertisements than news in this newspaper.*

> NOTE: In colloquial Chinese, 报 **bào** is often used instead of 报纸 **bàozhǐ**, e.g.:
> ■ 你看得懂中文报吗? **Nǐ kàndedǒng Zhōngwén bào ma?** = *Can you understand Chinese newspapers?*

bào 抱 VERB = hold...in arms, embrace, hug

■ 妈妈抱着孩子。 **Māma bàozhe háizi.** = *The mother is holding her baby in her arms.*

■ 让我抱抱你。 **Ràng wǒ bàobao nǐ.** = *Let me hug you.*

bàoqiàn 抱歉 ADJECTIVE = apologetic, sorry, regretful

■ 很抱歉，今天我不能加班。 **Hěn bàoqiàn, jīntiān wǒ bù néng jiābān.** = *I'm sorry, but I won't be able to work overtime today.*

■ 我忘了昨天的会议，实在抱歉! **Wǒ wàngle zuótiān de huìyì, shízài bàoqiàn!** = *I'm awfully sorry that I forgot the meeting yesterday.*

bēi 杯 NOUN = cup, mug, glass (只 **zhī**)
  bēizi 杯子 = cup, mug, glass
  ■ 这些杯子要洗一下。**Zhèxiē bēizi yào xǐ yíxià.** = *These cups/mugs/glasses need washing.*
  chábēi 茶杯 = teacup
  jiǔbēi 酒杯 = wine glass
  yì bēi chá/jiǔ 一杯茶／酒 = a cup of tea/a glass of wine

> NOTE: 杯 **bēi** may denote either *cup*, *mug*, or *glass*. 杯 **bēi** is seldom used alone. It is usually suffixed with 子 **zi**: 杯子 **bēizi**, or combined with 茶 **chá** or 酒 **jiǔ**: 茶杯 **chábēi**, 酒杯 **jiǔbēi**.

bēi 背 VERB = carry...on the back
  ■ 孩子每天高高兴兴背着书包上学校。**Háizi měi tiān gāo-gāo-xìng-xìng bēizhe shūbāo shàng xuéxiào.** = *Every day the child goes to school happily, his schoolbag on his back.*

bēi 悲 NOUN = grieved

bēiguān 悲观 [compound: 悲 *grieved, sad* + 观 *view*] ADJECTIVE = pessimistic (antonym 乐观 **lèguān**)
  ■ 你太悲观了，情况不会这么坏吧。**Nǐ tài bēiguān le, qíngkuàng bú huì zhème huài ba.** = *You're too pessimistic. Things can't be that bad.*

bēitòng 悲痛 [compound: 悲 *grieved, sad* + 痛 *agony*] ADJECTIVE = deeply grieved, agonized, with deep sorrow
  ■ 他在交通事故中失去了妻子、女儿，悲痛极了。**Tā zài jiāotōng shìgù zhōng shīqùle qīzi, nǚ'ér, bēitòng jíle.** = *He lost his wife and daughter in a road accident and is deeply grieved.*

běi 北 NOUN = north, northern
  ■ 在北半球，刮北风，天就冷。**Zài běi bànqiú, guā běifēng, tiān jiù lěng.** = *In the north hemisphere, the weather becomes cold when a north wind blows.*
  běijí 北极 = the North Pole (← the north extreme)
  běijíxīng 北极星 = the North Star, Polaris

běibian 北边 [modif: 北 *north* + 边 *side*] NOUN = north side, to the north, in the north

  ■ 山的北边是一大片草原。**Shān de běibian shì yí dà piàn cǎoyuán.** = *North of the mountains is a vast pasture.*
  ■ 加拿大在美国的北边。**Jiānádà zài Měiguó de běibian.** = *Canada is to the north of USA.*

běifāng 北方 [modif: 北 *north* + 方 *region*] NOUN = northern region
  ■ 中国南方和北方以长江为界。**Zhōngguó nánfāng hé běifāng yǐ Chángjiāng wéi jiè.** = *South China and North China are demarcated by the Yangtze River.*

Běijīng 北京 NOUN = Beijing (Peking) (the capital of the People's Republic of China)

běimiàn 北面 NOUN = same as 北边 **běibian**

bèi 备 Trad 備 VERB = prepare (See 具备 **jùbèi**, 设备 **shèbèi**, 预备 **yùbèi**, 准备 **zhǔnbèi**.)

bèi 背 VERB = learn by heart

bèisòng 背诵 [compound: 背 *learn by heart* + 诵 *recite*] VERB = repeat from memory
  ■ 他们六岁的孩子能背诵好几首唐诗。**Tāmen liù suì de háizi néng bèisòng hǎojǐ shǒu Táng shī.** = *Their six-year-old child can recite quite a few Tang poems.*

bèi 被 PREPOSITION = by (introducing the doer of an action)
  ■ 花瓶被小明打破了。**Huāpíng bèi Xiǎo Míng dǎ pò le.** = *The vase was broken by Xiao Ming.*
  ■ 他被人欺负了。**Tā bèi rén qīfu le.** = *He was bullied by somebody.*

bèizi 被子 NOUN = quilt, blanket (条 **tiáo**)
  ■ 冬天出太阳的时候，很多中国人喜欢晒被子。**Dōngtiān chū tàiyang de shíhou, hěn duó Zhōngguórén xǐhuan shài bèizi.** = *Many Chinese like to sun quilts when it's sunny in winter. (→ On sunny winter days, many Chinese like to air their quilts.)*

bèi 倍 MEASURE WORD = fold, time
  ■ 这个学校的学生人数比我们学校多一倍。(= 这个学校的学生人数是我们学校的两倍。) **Zhège xuéxiào de xuésheng rénshù bǐ wǒmen xuéxiào duō yí bèi. (= Zhège xuéxiào de xuésheng rénshù shì wǒmen xuéxiào de liǎng**

B

bèi.) = *The student number of this school is twice as big as that of our school.* (→ *The student population of this school is twice of ours.*)

běn 本

1 NOUN = principal, capital
péi běn 赔本 = lose one's capital in investments or other business dealings
■ 他做生意赔了本，没法还银行的钱。**Tā zuò shēngyì péile běn, méifǎ huán yínháng de qián.** = *He lost his capital in business and was unable to repay the bank loan.*
běnqián 本钱 = the money with which one makes investments or conducts other business dealings, capital
2 ADVERB = same as **本来 běnlái** ADVERB
3 MEASURE WORD = (for books, magazines, etc.)
■ 一本书 **yì běn shū** = *a book*
4 ADJECTIVE = this one, one's own
■ 本店春节照常营业。**Běn diàn chūnjié zhàocháng yíngyè.** = *This store will do business as usual during the Spring Festival.* (→ *We'll be open during the Chinese New Year.*)

NOTE: 本 **běn** in the sense of *this one* is only used on formal occasions.

běndì 本地 [modif: 本 *this* + 地 *place*] NOUN = this locality
■ 我向你介绍一个本地的名菜。**Wǒ xiàng nǐ jièshao yí ge běndì de míngcài.** = *I'll recommend you a famous dish of this town.*

běnlái 本来 ADVERB = originally, at first
■ 这个旅馆本来是一个富商的家。= **Zhège lǚguǎn běnlái shì yí ge fù shāng de jiā.** *This hotel was originally a rich merchant's residence.*
■ 我本来不想去看电影，他一定要我去，我就去了。**Wǒ běnlái bù xiǎng qù kàn diànyǐng, tā yídìng yào wǒ qù, wǒ jiù qù le.** = *At first I did not want to go to the movie, but he insisted I should go, so I went with him.*

běnlǐng 本领 NOUN = skill, ability, capability
■ 他已经二十多岁了，还没有本领独立生活。**Tā yǐjīng èrshí duō suì le, hái méiyǒu běnlǐng dúlì shēnghuó.** = *He is over twenty, but still lacks the skills to live independently.*

běnshì 本事 NOUN = ability, capability
■ 他自以为本事很大，其实什么都做不好。

Tā zì yǐwéi běnshì hěn dà, qíshí shénme dōu zuò bu hǎo. = *He thinks himself very capable; actually he can't get anything done properly.*

NOTE: 本领 **běnlǐng** and 本事 **běnshì** are synonyms, but 本领 **běnlǐng** emphasizes skills while 本事 **běnshì** has a more general sense of "the ability to get things done" and may be used with negative connotations.

běnzhì 本质 [compound: 本 *origin* + 质 *nature*] NOUN = innate character, true nature
■ 研究问题我们要透过表面现象看到本质。**Yánjiū wèntí, wǒmen yào tòuguo biǎomiàn xiànxiàng kàndào běnzhì.** = *When studying a problem we should see beyond appearances and get to its essence.*

běnzi 本子 [suffix: 本 *a book* + 子 nominal suffix] NOUN = notebook (本 **běn**)
■ 他丢了一个很重要的本子。**Tā diūle yí ge hěn zhòngyào de běnzi.** *He's lost an important notebook.*
■ 这本本子记了朋友的电话号码，传真号码和电子邮件地址。**Zhè běn běnzi jì le péngyou de diànhuà hàomǎ, chuánzhēn hàomǎ hé diànzǐ yóujiàn dìzhǐ.** *In this notebook are recorded his friends' telephone numbers, fax numbers and e-mail addresses.*

bèn 笨 ADJECTIVE = dumb, stupid
■ 他不善于言词，其实一点都不笨。**Tā bú shànyú yáncí, qíshí yìdiǎn dōu bú bèn.** = *He is not good at expressing himself, but he is by no means stupid.*
■ 千万不能对孩子说 "你真笨！" 这样的话。**Qiānwàn bù néng duì háizi shuō "Nǐ zhēn bèn!" zhèyàng de huà.** = *Never, ever say to a child such things as "How stupid you are!"*

bí 鼻 NOUN = same as 鼻子 **bízi**

bízi 鼻子 NOUN = the nose
■ 有些中国人叫西方人 "大鼻子"，这是不礼貌的。**Yǒuxiē Zhōngguórén jiào Xīfāngrén "dà bízi", zhe shì bù lǐmào de.** = *Some Chinese call Westerners "Big Noses"; this is impolite.*

bǐ 比

1 PREPOSITION = (introducing the object that is compared with the subject of a sentence), than

■ 你比他高一点。**Nǐ bǐ tā gāo yìdiǎn.** = *You're a bit taller than he is.*
■ 今天比昨天冷得多。**Jīntiān bǐ zuótiān lěng de duō.** = *Today is much colder than yesterday.*
■ 我跑得比你快。**Wǒ pǎo de bǐ nǐ kuài.** = *I run faster than you.*
■ 你写汉字没有我写得快，但是写得比我好看。**Nǐ xiě hànzì méiyǒu wǒ xiě de kuài, dànshì xiě de bǐ wǒ hǎokàn.** = *You write Chinese characters more slowly, but more beautifully than I do.*
2 VERB = compete, compare, contrast
■ 你们俩谁跑得快? 比一比! **Nǐmen liǎ shuí pǎo de kuài? Bǐ yì bǐ!** = *Of you two, who runs faster? Let's see!*

bǐjiào 比较

1 VERB = compare
■ 这两种方法哪个好，我们要比较一下。**Zhè liǎng zhǒng fāngfǎ nǎge hǎo, wǒmen yào bǐjiào yíxià.** = *Which of the two approaches is the better one? We need to compare them.*
hé ... bǐjiào 和 … 比较 = compare...with
■ 和农村比较，城市的生活方便得多。**Hé nóngcūn bǐjiào, chéngshì de shēnghuó fāngbiàn de duō.** = *Compared to living on a farm, city life is much more convenient.*
2 ADVERB = relatively, quite, to some degree
■ 这两天天气比较好。**Zhè liǎng tiān tiānqì bǐjiào hǎo.** = *The weather these days is not bad.*
■ 李先生在海外生活多年了，但还是比较喜欢吃中国菜。**Lǐ xiānsheng zài hǎiwài shēnghuó duō nián le, dàn háishi bǐjiào xǐhuan chī Zhōngguó cài.** = *Mr Li has been living overseas for quite a few years, but he still prefers Chinese food.*

bǐlì 比例 NOUN = percentage
■ 这个学校海外留学生在学生人数中占多少比例? **Zhège xuéxiào hǎiwài liúxuéshēng zài xuésheng rénshù zhōng zhàn duōshǎo bǐlì?** = *What percentage of this school's enrolment are overseas students?*

bǐrú 比如 CONJUNCTION = for example
■ 今年我们都取得了很大进步，比如约翰，现在已经会用中文写电子邮件了。**Jīnnián wǒmen dōu qǔdéle hěn dà jìnbù, bǐrú Yuēhàn, xiànzài yǐjīng huì yòng Zhōngwén xiě diànzǐ yóujiàn le.** = *We have all made good progress this year. Take John for example, now he can write e-mail in Chinese.*

NOTE: In spoken Chinese you can also use 比如说 **bǐrúshuō.**

bǐsài 比赛 [compound: 比 *compare* + 赛 *compete*]

1 VERB = compete, have a match
■ 我们比赛一下，看谁打字打得又快又好。**Wǒmen bǐsài yíxià, kàn shéi dǎizì dǎ de yòu kuài yòu hǎo.** = *Let's have a contest to see who types quickly and accurately. (→ Let's compete and see who types better.)*
■ 今天晚上我们和他们比赛篮球。**Jīntiān wǎnshang wǒmen hé tāmen bǐsài lánqiú.** = *This evening we'll have a basketball match with them.*
2 NOUN = competition, match, game
■ 昨天晚上的篮球比赛精彩级了! **Zuótiān wǎnshang de lánqiú bǐsài jīngcǎi jíle!** = *The basketball match yesterday evening was wonderful!*
■ 下个月北京举行中国武术比赛。**Xià ge yuè Běijīng jǔxíng Zhōngguó wǔshù bǐsài.** = *There will be a Chinese martial arts contest in Beijing next month.*
bǐsài xiàngmù 比赛项目 = event (of a sports meet)
cānjiā bǐsài 参加比赛 = participate in a game (or sports event)
hégēn...bǐsài 和 / 跟...比赛 = have a match/race with
kàn bǐsài 看比赛 = watch a game (or sports event)

bǐ 笔 Trad 筆 NOUN = writing instrument, pen, pencil (支 zhī)
■ 这支笔很好写。**Zhè zhī bǐ hěn hǎoxiě.** = *This pen writes well.*
■ 我可以借用你的笔吗? **Wǒ kěyǐ jièyòng nǐ de bǐ ma?** = *May I borrow your pen?*
huàbǐ 画笔 = paintbrush (for art)
máobǐ 毛笔 = Chinese writing brush

bǐjì 笔记 NOUN = notes (taken in class or while reading)
jì bǐjì 记笔记 = take notes (in class, at a lecture, etc.)
■ 老师要求学生上课记笔记。**Lǎoshī yāoqiú xuésheng shàngkè jì bǐjì.** = *The teacher requires that students take notes in class.*
■ 她有边读书边做笔记的好习惯。**Tā yǒu biān dúshū biān zuò bǐjì de hǎo xíguàn.** = *She*

has formed the good habit of making notes while reading.

zuò bǐjì 做笔记 = make notes (while reading)
■ 我昨天没来上课，你的笔记能借我看一下吗？ **Wǒ zuótiān méi lái shàngkè, nǐ de bǐjì néng jiè wǒ kàn yíxià ma?** = *I was absent from class yesterday. Could you let me have a look at your notes?*

bǐjì běn 笔记本 = notebook

bì 币 Trad 幣 NOUN = currency (See 人民币 **Rénmíngbì**.)

bì 必 ADVERB = inevitably

bìrán 必然 ADJECTIVE = inevitable, be bound to
■ 他因为骄傲而失败，这是必然的。**Tā yīnwèi jiāo'ào ér shībài, zhè shì bìrán de.** = *He failed because he was conceited. This was inevitable.*

bìxū 必须 [compound: 必 *must* + 须 *need, have to*] MODAL VERB = must
■ 每个公民都必须遵守法律。**Měi ge gōngmín dōu bìxū zūnshǒu fǎlǜ.** = *Every citizen must abide by the law.*
■ 你要在那个大学学习，必须在半年前报名。**Nǐ yào zài nàge dàxué xuéxí, bìxū zài bànnián qián bàomíng.** = *You must apply for enrolment half a year earlier if you want to study in this university.*

bìyào 必要 [compound: 必 *must* + 要 *require*] ADJECTIVE = necessary
■ 你不必要送这么贵的礼物。**Nǐ bú bìyào sòng zhème guì de lǐwù.** = *You don't have to give such an expensive present.*
■ 你外出旅行两天，带这么多衣服，必要吗？ **Nǐ wàichū lǚxíng liǎngtiān, dài zhème duō yīfu, bìyào ma?** = *Is it necessary to take so many clothes with you for a trip of two days?*

bì 毕 Trad 畢 VERB = finish

bìyè 毕业 [v+obj: 毕 *finish* + 业 *course of study*] VERB = graduate from school
■ 你哪一年毕业？ **Nǐ nǎ yì nián bìyè?** = *When will you graduate?*
■ 我父亲二十多年前从一所著名大学毕业。**Wǒ fùqin èrshí duō nián qián cóng yì suǒ zhùmíng dàxué bìyè.** = *My father graduated*

from a famous university over twenty years ago.

bì 闭 Trad 閉 VERB = close, shut up
■ 老人看报看累了，闭上眼睛休息一会。**Lǎorén kàn bào kàn lèi le, bìshang yǎnjing xiūxi yíhuìr.** = *The old man was tired from reading the newspapers. He closed his eyes to rest.*
■ 她愤怒地喊："闭嘴！" **Tā fènnù de hǎn: "Bì zuǐ!"** = *She shouted angrily, "Shut up!"*

NOTE: 闭嘴! **Bìzuǐ!** = *Shut your mouth!* is a very impolite expression to tell people to stop talking. You can also say 闭上你的嘴! **Bì shang nǐ de zuǐ!** = *Shut your mouth!*

bì 避 VERB = evade, avoid
■ 很多人在商场里避雨。**Hěn duō rén zài shāngchǎng li bì yǔ.** = *Many people are in the shopping mall to shelter from the rain.*

bìmiǎn 避免 [compound: 避 *evade* + 免 *be free from*] VERB = avoid, avert
■ 她避免和以前的男朋友见面。**Tā bìmiǎn hé yǐqián de nán péngyou jiànmiàn.** = *She avoids meeting her former boyfriend.*
■ 自然灾害是无法避免的。**Zìrán zāihài shì wúfǎ bìmiǎn de.** = *Natural disasters cannot be avoided.*

bì 壁 NOUN = wall (See 隔壁 **gébì**.)

biān 边 Trad 邊 NOUN = side, border
■ 山的这一边有很多树，那一边没有树。**Shān de zhè yì biān yǒu hěn duō shù, nà yì biān méiyǒu shù.** = *On this side of the hill there are lots of trees, and there are no trees on the other side.*

NOTE: The most frequent use of 边 **biān** is to form "compound location nouns": 东边 **dōngbian** = *east side*, 南边 **nánbian** = *south side*, 西边 **xībian** = *west side*, 北边 **běibian** = *north side*, 里边 **lǐbian** = *inside*, 外边 **wàibian** = *outside*. 边 **biān** in such cases is often pronounced in the neutral tone.

biān ... biān 边...边 CONJUNCTION = (used with verbs to indicate simultaneous actions)
■ 他们边走边谈，不一会儿就到市中心了。

Tāmen biān zǒu biān tán, bùyíhuìr jiù dào shì zhōngxīn le. = *They chatted while walking, and soon reached the city centre.*

biān 编 Trad 編 VERB = compile, compose
■ 那本词典是一位有丰富教学经验的老教授编的。**Nà běn cídiǎn shì yí wèi yǒu fēngfù jiàoxué jīngyàn de lǎo jiàoshòu biān de.** = *That dictionary was compiled by an old professor with rich teaching experience.*

biǎn 扁 ADJECTIVE = flat
■ 面包放在这么多菜的下面，都压扁了。**Miànbāo fàng zài zhème duō cài de xiàmiàn, dōu yà biǎn le.** = *Placed under so many groceries, the bread was crushed flat.*

biàn 变 Trad 變 VERB = transform, change
■ 世界上任何事情都在变。**Shìjiè shang rènhé shìqing dōu zài biàn.** = *Everything in the world is changing.*

biànchéng 变成 [v+comp: 变 *change* + 成 *into*] VERB = change into
■ 几年不见，小女孩变成了大姑娘。**Jǐnián bújiàn, xiǎo nǚhái biànchéngle yí ge dà gūniang.** = *I hadn't seen her for several years and the little girl had changed into a young lady.*

biànhuà 变化 [compound: 变 *change* + 化 *transform*]
1 VERB = transform, change
■ 情况变化了，不能仍然用老办法。**Qíngkuàng biànhuà le, bùnéng réngrán yòng lǎo bànfǎ.** = *Things have changed. We cannot use old ways of doing things as before. (→ We cannot continue doing things the old way.)*
2 NOUN = transfomation, change
■ 几年没来，我觉得这里变化很明显。**Jǐnián méi lái, wǒ juéde zhèli biànhuà hěn míngxiǎn.** = *After a few years absence, I find obvious changes in this place.*
■ 这些年来这个城市没有多大变化。**Zhèxiē nián lái zhège chéngshì méiyǒu duō dà biànhuà.** = *This city has not had much change over these years.*

NOTE: As a verb 变化 **biànhuà** is interchangeable with 变 **biàn**, 变化 **biànhuà** being a little more formal than 变 **biàn**.

biàn 便 ADVERB = same as 就 **jiù** 3 ADVERB. Used only in written Chinese.

biàntiáo 便条 [modif: 便 *handy* + 条 *note*]
NOUN = informal written message, note
liú biàntiáo 留便条 = leave a note
■ 老王给我留了一张便条，说他明天下午三点半来看我。**Lǎo Wáng gěi wǒ liúle yì zhāng biàntiáo, shuō tā míngtiān xiàwǔ sān diǎn bàn lái kàn wǒ.** = *Lao Wang left a note for me, saying that he would come to see me at 3:30 tomorrow afternoon.*

biàn 遍 MEASURE WORD = (used to indicate the frequency of an action done in its complete duration from the beginning to the end)
■ 这本书我看了三遍。**Zhè běn shū wǒ kànle sān biàn.** = *I've read this book three times.*
■ 上个月我看了三个电影，其中一个看了两遍。**Shàng ge yuè wǒ kànle sān ge diànyǐng, qízhōng yí ge kànle liǎng biàn.** = *I saw three movies last month, one of which I saw twice.*

biāo 标 Trad 標 VERB = mark

biāodiǎn 标点 [compound: 标 *mark* + 点 *point*] NOUN = punctuation mark
■ 你这个标点用得不对。**Nǐ zhège biāodiǎn yòng de bú duì.** = *The punctuation mark you used is not correct. (→ You used a wrong punctuation mark.)*
■ 我这里应该用什么标点？**Wǒ zhèli yīnggāi yòng shénme biāodiǎn?** = *Which punctuation mark should I use here?*

biāozhǔn 标准 [compound: 标 *standard* + 准 *accuracy*]
1 NOUN = standard, criterion
fúhé biāozhǔn 符合标准 = conform to the standard
■ 这些产品不符合标准，不能出厂。**Zhèxiē chǎnpǐn bù fúhé biāozhǔn, bù néng chūchǎng.** = *These products do not conform to the standard and cannot leave the factory. (→ These products do not meet the standard and cannot be shipped.)*
dádào biāozhǔn 达到标准 = reach the standard
■ 你们的汉语水平达到什么标准？**Nǐmen de Hànyǔ shuǐpíng dádào shénme biāozhǔn?** = *What level has your Chinese proficiency reached?*

B

B

2 ADJECTIVE = standard, perfect
■ 外国人说汉语发音不太标准，问题不大；在中国，又有多少人说标准的普通话呢？
Wàiguórén shuō Hànyǔ fāyīn bú tài biāozhǔn, wèntí bú dà; zài Zhōngguó, yòu yǒu duōshǎo rén shuō biāozhǔn de Pǔtōnghuà ne? = *It doesn't matter if a foreigner doesn't speak Chinese with perfect pronunciation. After all, how many Chinese speak perfect Putonghua?*

biǎo 表 NOUN
1 Trad 錶 = watch (块 **kuài**, 只 **zhi**)
■ 我的表慢了一点。**Wǒ de biǎo màn le yìdiǎn.** = *My watch is a bit slow.*
■ 我的表停了，你的表几点? **Wǒ de biǎo tíng le, nǐ de biǎo jǐ diǎn?** = *My watch has stopped. What time is it by your watch?*
dài biǎo 戴表 = wear a watch
■ 他戴了一块新表。**Tā dàile yí kuài xīn biǎo.** = *He wears a new watch.*
nán biǎo 男表 = men's watch
nǚ biǎo 女表 = ladies' watch
2 = form (张 **zhāng**, 份 **fèn**)
■ 这张表我不会填，你能帮帮我吗? **Zhè zhāng biǎo wǒ bú huì tián, nǐ néng bāngbang wǒ ma?** = *I don't know how to fill in this form. Could you help me?*

biǎodá 表达 [compound: 表 *express* + 达 *reach*] VERB = express (thoughts or emotions)
■ 你能不能用简单的中文把意思表达清楚? **Nǐ néng bu néng yòng jiǎndān de Zhōngwén bǎ yìsi biǎodá qīngchu?** = *Can you express the meaning clearly in simple Chinese?*
■ 我当时的心情很复杂，很难表达清楚。**Wǒ dāngshí de xīnqíng hěn fùzá, hěn nán biǎodá qīngchu.** = *I had mixed feelings at that moment, it was difficult to express them clearly.*

biǎomiàn 表面 [modif: 表 *surface* + 面 *face*] NOUN = surface
■ 他表面上很友好，其实完全不是这样。**Tā biǎomiàn shang hěn yǒuhǎo, qíshí wánquán búshì zhèyàng.** = *He appears to be very friendly; actually he is not friendly at all.*

biǎomíng 表明 [v+comp: 表 *express* + 明 *clear*] VERB = make clear, demonstrate
■ 她一直不说话，表明她其实不赞成。**Tā yìzhí bù shuōhuà, biǎomíng tā qíshí bú**

zànchéng. = *She was silent all the way, showing that actually she disapproved.*
■ 我向他清楚地表明，我们公司完全保证产品质量。**Wǒ xiàng tā qīngchu de biǎomíng, wǒmen gōngsī wánquán bǎozhèng chǎnpǐn zhìliàng.** = *I made it very clear to him that our company completely guarantees the quality of our products.*

biǎoshì 表示 [compound: 表 *show, express* + 示 *indicate*] VERB = express, show
■ 一般点头表示同意，摇头表示不同意。**Yìbān diǎntóu biǎoshì tóngyì, yáotóu biǎoshì bù tóngyì.** = *Generally, nodding indicates agreement and shaking one's head indicates disagreement.*
■ 他一句话也没说，表示不高兴。**Tā yí jù huà yě méi shuō, biǎoshì bù gāoxìng.** = *He did not say a word, showing his displeasure.*

biǎoxiàn 表现 [compound: 表 *show, express* + 现 *display*] VERB = display, show
1 = display, show
■ 他表现得很热情。**Tā biǎoxiàn dé hěn rèqíng.** = *He showed great enthusiasm.*
2 = perform
■ 新工人表现很好，老板决定增加他的工资。**Xīn gōngrén biǎoxiàn hěn hǎo, lǎobǎn juédìng zēngjiā tā de gōngzī.** = *The new worker performed well, and the boss decided to raise his wages.*

biǎoyǎn 表演 [compound: 表 *show* + 演 *act*]
1 VERB = put on (a show), perform, demonstrate
■ 他们星期六在这里表演歌舞。**Tāmen Xīngqīliù zài zhèlǐ biǎoyǎn gēwǔ.** = *They perform singing and dancing here on Saturday.*
2 NOUN = performance, show
■ 他们的表演很精彩。**Tāmen de biǎoyǎn hěn jīngcǎi.** = *Their performance was wonderful.*
kàn biǎoyǎn 看表演 = watch a performance/ demonstration
■ 今天晚上你去看表演吗? **Jīntiān wǎnshang nǐ qù kàn biǎoyǎn ma?** = *Are you going to see the performance tonight?*
cānjiā biǎoyǎn 参加表演 = participate in a performance/demonstration

biǎoyáng 表扬 [compound: 表 *display* + 扬 *raise, make known*] VERB = praise, commend (antonym 批评 **pīpíng**)

■ 他学习进步很大，老师在班上表扬了他。**Tā xuéxí jìnbù hěn dà, lǎoshī zài bān shang biǎoyángle tā.** = *He made great progress in his studies and the teacher praised him in class.*

bié 别 ADVERB = don't
■ 别说话了，电影开始了。**Bié shuōhuà le, diànyǐng kāishǐ le.** = *Don't talk. (→ Stop talking.) The movie has started.*
■ 你不愿意去，就别去了。**Nǐ bú yuànyì qù, jiù bié qù le.** = *If you don't want to go, then don't go.*

NOTE: 别 **bié** is a contraction of 不要 **búyào** in an imperative sentence. It is used colloquially only.

biéde 别的 PRONOUN = other
■ 他大学毕业以后一直在教书，没有做过别的工作。**Tā dàxué bìyè yǐhòu yìzhí zài jiāoshū, méiyǒu zuòguo biéde gōngzuò.** = *He has been teaching since graduating from university and has not held any other job (← done any other work).*

biérén 别人 [modif: 别 *other* + 人 *person, people*] PRONOUN = other people, others
■ 别人怎么说我不管，只要你喜欢就行。**Biérén zěnme shuō wǒ bù guǎn, zhǐyào nǐ xǐhuan jiù xíng.** = *I don't mind what others may say. It's OK as long as you like it.*

bīn 宾 Trad 賓 NOUN = guest

bīnguǎn 宾馆 [modif: 宾 *guest* + 馆 *house*] NOUN = guesthouse
■ 这是政府宾馆，不对外开放。**Zhè shì zhèngfǔ bīnguǎn, bú duì wài kāifàng.** = *This is a government guesthouse. It is not open to the public.*

bīng 冰 NOUN = ice
■ 水到零度就结成冰。**Shuǐ dào líng dù jiù jiéchéng bīng.** = *Water freezes to ice at zero degrees Celsius.*

bīngxiāng 冰箱 [modif: 冰 *ice* + 箱 *box*] NOUN = refrigerator
■ 冰箱里没有什么东西，看来得出去吃晚饭了。**Bīngxiāng li méiyǒu shénme dōngxi, kànlái děi chūqu chī wǎnfàn le.** = *There isn't*

much in the fridge. Looks like we'll have to eat dinner out.*
diàn bīngxiāng 电冰箱 = refrigerator

bīng 兵 NOUN = soldier
dāng bīng 当兵 = be a soldier, serve in the armed forces
■ 她哥哥在部队当兵。**Tā gēge zài bùduì dāng bīng.** = *Her brother is serving in the armed forces.*

bǐng 饼 Trad 餅 NOUN = cake

bǐnggān 饼干 [modif: 饼 *cake* + 干 *dried food*] NOUN = cookie(s), biscuit(s) (片 **piàn**, 包 **bāo**)
■ 他肚子饿了，就吃饼干。**Tā dùzi è le, jiù chī bǐnggān.** = *He ate some biscuits when he was hungry.*

bìng 并 Trad 並
1 ADVERB = (used before a negative word for emphasis)
■ 事情并不象你想象的那样简单。**Shìqing bìng bú xiàng nǐ xiǎngxiàng de nàyàng jiǎndān.** = *Things are not at all as simple as you imagine.*
■ 他并不是没有试过，但是不成功。**Tā bìng bú shì méiyǒu shìguo, dànshi bù chénggōng.** = *It was not the case that he never tried, but that he was not successful.*
2 CONJUNCTION = same as 并且 **bìngqiě**. Used only in written Chinese.

NOTE: 并 **bìng** is used to emphasize the negation. It is not grammatically essential; without 并 **bìng** the sentences still stand. The following is perfectly acceptable:
■ 事情不象你想象的那样简单。**Shìqing bú xiàng nǐ xiǎngxiàng de nàyàng jiǎndān.** = *Things are not as simple as you imagine.*

bìngqiě 并且 CONJUNCTION = moreover, what's more, and
■ 技术员发现并且解决了问题。**Jìshùyuán fāxiàn bìngqiě jiějuéle wèntí.** = *The technician discovered the problem and solved it. (←The technician discovered the problem; what's more, he solved it.)*
■ 他去机场接朋友，并且带他游览市区。**Tā qù jīchǎng jiē péngyou, bìngqiě dài tā yóulǎn**

B

shìqū. = *He met the friend at the airport and took him on a sightseeing trip of the city.*

bìng 病

1 VERB = fall ill, be ill
■ 我爸爸病了，在家休息。**Wǒ bàba bìng le, zài jiā xiūxi.** = *My father's ill and is taking a rest at home.*

2 NOUN = illness, disease
■ 他的病很严重，得住院。**Tā bìng de hěn zhòng, děi zhùyuàn.** = *He is seriously ill and needs to be hospitalized.*
■ 张先生什么病? **Zhāng xiānsheng shénme bìng?** = *What is Mr Zhang ill with? (→ What's wrong with Mr Zhang?)*
■ 这一点儿小病，没关系。**Zhè yìdiǎnr xiǎo bìng, méi guānxi.** = *This is a mild case (of illness); it doesn't matter.*

bìng jià 病假 = sick leave
qǐng bìngjià 请病假 = ask for/apply for sick leave
■ 她请了三天病假。**Tā qǐngle sāntiān bìngjià.** = *She asked for three days' sick leave.*
shēng bìng 生病 = to fall ill

bìngfáng 病房 [modif: 病 sickness + 房 room]

NOUN = (hospital) ward
■ 医生每天上午十点查病房。**Yīshēng měi tiān shàngwǔ shí diǎn chá bìngfáng.** = *The doctors make their rounds of the wards at ten o'clock every morning.*
zhòng bìngfáng 重病房 = intensive care ward

bìngrén 病人 [modif: 病 sick + 人 person]

NOUN = patient
■ 病人要听医生的嘱咐。**Bìngrén yào tīng yīshēng de zhǔfu.** = *Patients should take their doctors' advice.*
zhùyuàn bìngrén 住院病人 = inpatient

bō 玻 NOUN = glass (See 玻璃 bōli.)

bōli 玻璃 NOUN = glass

■ 大楼的正面全部是玻璃。**Dàlóu de zhèngmiàn quánbù shì bōli.** = *The front of the big building is all covered by glass.*
bōli bēi 玻璃杯 = glass
bōli chuāng 玻璃窗 = glass window, window

bō 播 VERB = sow (See 传播 chuánbō, 广播 guǎngbō.)

bó 伯 NOUN = same as 伯父 bófù

bófù 伯父 NOUN = father's elder brother

■ 伯父只比爸爸大两岁，但是看来比爸爸老得多。**Bófù zhǐ bǐ bàba dà liǎng suì, dànshì kànlái bǐ bàba lǎo de duō.** = *My father's elder brother is only two years older than he is, but looks much older.*

NOTE: 伯父 **bófù** is also a form of address for men older than your father but not old enough to be your grandfather. The colloquialism for 伯父 **bófù** is 伯伯 **bóbo**.

bómǔ 伯母 NOUN = father's elder brother's wife

■ 我的伯父伯母住在香港。**Wǒ de bófù bómǔ zhù zài Xiānggǎng.** = *My uncle (← father's elder brother) and aunt (his wife) live in Hong Kong.*

NOTE: 伯母 **bómǔ** is also a form of address for women older than your father but not old enough to be your grandmother. It is generally used by well-educated urban Chinese.

bó 脖 NOUN = neck

bózi 脖子 [suffix: 脖 neck + 子 nominal suffix]

NOUN = neck
■ 我的脖子扭伤了。**Wǒ de bózi niǔ shāng le.** = *My neck was sprained.*

bó 膊 NOUN = arm (See 胳膊 gēbo.)

bó 薄 ADJECTIVE = meager, small (antonym 厚 hòu)

■ 请收下这份薄礼。**Qǐng shōu xia zhè fèng bó lǐ.** = *Please accept this insignificant gift.*

NOTE: The character 薄 has two pronunciations: **báo** and **bó**. While 薄 **báo** is used to describe material "thin-ness," 薄 **bó** is used in a figurative sense. See 薄 **báo** for examples.

bo 卜 Trad 蔔 See 萝卜 luóbo.

búbì 不必 [modif: 不 not + 必 necessary]

ADVERB = need not, not have to, unnecessarily
■ 你不必送这么贵重的礼物。**Nǐ búbì sòng zhème guìzhòng de lǐwù.** = *You don't have to give such an expensive gift.*

■ 孩子会很快恢复健康的，你完全不必担心。**Háizi huì hěn kuài huīfù jiànkāng de, nǐ wánquán búbì dānxīn.** = *The child will recover very soon. You really don't have to worry.*

búcuò 不错 [modif: 不 *not* + 错 *wrong*]
ADJECTIVE
1 = not wrong
■ 你告诉我的电话号码不错。**Nǐ gàosu wǒ de diànhuà hàomǎ bú cuò.** = *The telephone number you gave (← told) me is correct.*
2 = quite right; not bad, quite good
■ 这个电影不错。**Zhè ge diànyǐng búcuò.** = *This movie is rather good.*
■ 这孩子画得真不错。**Zhè háizi huà de zhēn búcuò.** = *This child really doesn't draw badly.* (→ *This child draws quite well.*)

NOTE: ...得不错 **...de búcuò** is ambiguous. It may mean either ... *correctly* or ... *rather well.* For example, the sentence 你说得不错。**Nǐ shuō de búcuò.** may mean either *You spoke correctly.* (→ *You're right.*) or *You spoke quite well.* (→ *Well said.*)

búdà 不大 ADVERB = not very, not much
■ 今天不大热。**Jīntiān búdà rè.** = *Today is not very hot.*
■ 我不大喜欢吃日本菜。**Wǒ búdà xǐhuan chī Rìběn cài.** = *I'm not very fond of Japanese food.*

búdàn 不但 CONJUNCTION = not only ... (but also)
■ 这家饭店的菜不但好吃，而且好看。**Zhè jiā fàndiàn de cài búdàn hǎochī, érqiě hǎokàn.** = *The dishes in this restaurant are not only delicious but also beautiful.*
■ 她不但唱歌唱得好听，而且跳舞跳得好看。**Tā búdàn chànggē chàng de hǎotīng, érqiě tiàowǔ tiào de hǎokàn.** = *She not only sings beautifully, but also dances gracefully.*

búduàn 不断 [modif: 不 *not* + 断 *interrupt*]
ADVERB = without interruption, continuously, incessantly
■ 只有不断努力，才能永远进步。**Zhǐyǒu búduàn nǔlì, cái néng yǒngyuǎn jìnbù.** = *Only by continuous efforts can one make progress forever.*

búguò 不过 CONJUNCTION = same as 但是 **dànshì**. Used colloquially.

búlùn 不论 CONJUNCTION = same as 不管 **bùguǎn**. Used more in writing.

búxìng 不幸 [modif: 不 *not* + 幸 *fortunate*]
ADJECTIVE = unfortunate
■ 这次交通事故死了一人，伤了三人，真是一件不幸的事。**Zhè cì jiāotōng shìgù sǐle yì rén, shāngle sān rén, zhēn shì yí jiàn búxìng de shì.** = *One person died and three were injured in this road accident, which is indeed an unfortunate event.*

NOTE: 不幸 **búxìng** is used to describe serious events or matters, often involving death. Do not use 不幸 **búxìng** for trivial matters. For example, even though in English it is acceptable to say, "Unfortunately, I haven't seen the film," in Chinese it would be wrong to say 我不幸没有看过那个电影。**Wǒ búxìng méiyǒu kànguo nàge diànyǐng.**

búyào 不要 ADVERB = (used in an imperative sentence or as advice) do not
■ 你们不要说话了，电影开始了。**Nǐmen búyào shuōhuà le, diànyǐng kāishǐ le.** = *Please don't talk any more. The movie has started.*
■ 你不要着急，你孩子的病很快会好的。**Nǐ búyào zháojí, nǐ háizi de bìng hěnkuài huì hǎo de.** = *Don't you be worried, your child will recover soon.*

NOTE: See note on 别 **bié**.

búyòng 不用 ADVERB = no need, there's no need, don't have to
■ 如果你明天不舒服，就不用来了。**Rúguǒ nǐ míngtiān bù shūfu, jiù búyòng lái le.** = *If you're not well tomorrow, you don't have to come.*
■ 不用麻烦了，我们一会儿就走。**Búyòng máfan le, wǒmen yíhuǐr jiù zǒu.** = *Don't bother. We'll be leaving soon.*

bǔ 补 Trad 補 VERB = mend, patch
■ 衣服破了，补一下还能穿。**Yīfu pò le, bǔ yíxià hái néng chuān.** = *The coat is torn, but mend it and it can still be worn.*
bǔkè 补课 = make up for missed lessons
■ 上星期一王老师开会，没有上课，今天下午补课。**Shàng Xīngqīyī Wáng lǎoshī kāihuì,**

méiyǒu shàngkè, jīntiān xiàwǔ bǔkè. = *Last Monday Teacher Wang had a meeting and missed a class. He will make up for it this afternoon.*

bǔxí 补习 = take or give supplementary lessons
■ 他英文不行，妈妈给他请家庭教师补习。**Tā Yīngwén bù xíng, māma gěi tā qǐng jiātíng jiàoshī bǔxí.** = *He is poor at English, and his mother hired a home tutor to give him extra lessons.*

bǔchōng 补充 [compound: 补 *supplement* + 充 *fill up*] VERB = make up, supplement
■ 刚才小李谈了这个问题，我想补充几句。**Gāngcái Xiǎo Lǐ tánle zhège wèntí, wǒ xiǎng bǔchōng jǐ jù.** = *Just now Xiao Li spoke of this problem. I'd like to add a few points.*

bù 不 ADVERB = no, not
■ 今天不冷。**Jīntiān bù lěng.** = *It's not cold today.*
■ 你说得不对。**Nǐ shuō de búduì.** = *You're not correct.*
■ "你是美国人吗？""不，我是加拿大人。" = **"Nǐ shì Měiguórén ma?" "Bù, wǒ shì Jiānádàrén."** = *"Are you an American?" "No, I'm a Canadian."*

NOTE: When followed by a syllable in the fourth (falling) tone, 不 undergoes tone change (tone sandhi) from the normal fourth tone to the second (rising) tone, e.g. 不对 **búduì**, 不是 **búshì**.

bùdébù 不得不 ADVERB = have to, having no choice but
■ 我做错了题目，不得不重做。**Wǒ zuòcuòle tímù, bùdébù chóng zuò.** = *I did the wrong question [for a school assignment] and had to do it all over agian.*
■ 这个星期去上海的飞机票全部卖完了，我们不得不改到下星期去。**Zhège xīngqī qù Shànghǎi de fēijī piào quánbù màiwán le, wǒmen bùdébù gǎi dào xià xīngqī qù.** = *This week's air tickets to Shanghai are sold out, so we have no choice but change our departure date to next week.*

bùdéliǎo 不得了 ADJECTIVE
1 = horrible, extremely serious
■ 不得了了，对面房子着火了！**Bùdéliǎo le, duìmiàn fángzi zháohuǒ le!** = *How terrible, the*

house opposite is on fire!
■ 你没有什么不得了的事，就别麻烦朋友了。**Nǐ méiyǒu shénme bùdéliǎo de shì, jiù bié máfan péngyou le.** = *If it isn't anything really serious, don't bother your friends.*
2 = extremely (used after an adjective and introduced by 得 de)
■ 昨天热得不得了。**Zuótiān rè de bùdéliǎo.** = *It was extremely hot yesterday.*
■ 爬那座雪山危险得不得了，你们非充分准备不可。**Pá nà zuò xuěshān wēixiǎn de bùdéliǎo, nǐmen fēi chōngfèn zhǔnbèi bùkě.** = *It is extremely dangerous to climb that snowy mountain. You must be well prepared.*

bùgǎndāng 不敢当 IDIOM = Thank you, I don't dare to accept (a polite/modest reply to a compliment)
■ "您中文说得很标准。""不敢当，还要不断练习。" **"Nín Zhōngwén shuō de hěn biāozhǔn." "Bùgǎndāng, háiyào búduàn liànxí."** = *"You speak standard Chinese. (→ Your Chinese is perfect.)" "Thank you very much. I still need constant practice."*
■ "您对这个问题分析得极其深刻。""不敢当，您对这个问题有什么看法？" **"Nín duì zhège wèntí fēnxī de jíqí shēnkè." "Bùgǎndāng, nín duì zhège wèntí yǒu shénme kànfǎ?"** *"You've made a penetrating analysis of this problem." "I don't deserve [such praise]. What's your view on this matter?"*

bùguǎn 不管 CONJUNCTION = no matter (what, who, how, etc.)
■ 不管你在那里看到他，他都带着他的小狗。**Bùguǎn nǐ zài nǎlǐ kàndào tā, tā dōu dàizhe tā de xiǎo gǒu.** = *No matter where you see him, he is with his puppy.*
■ 不管你明天来不来，都给我一个电话。**Bùguǎn nǐ míngtiān lái bu lái, dōu gěi wǒ yí ge diànhuà.** = *Whether you come or not tomorrow, give me a call.*
■ 不管他多么忙，他总是每天给妈妈发一份电子邮件。**Bùguǎn tā duōme máng, tā zǒngshì měi tiān gěi māma fā yí fèn diànzǐ yóujiàn.** = *No matter how busy he is, he always sends his mother a daily e-mail.*

NOTE: 不管 **bùguǎn** may be replaced by 不论 **búlùn** or 无论 **wúlùn**, but 不管 **bùguǎn** is more colloquial.

bù hǎoyìsi 不好意思 IDIOM = I'm embarrassed (polite phrase used when you are offering an apology, giving a gift, or receiving a gift or other acts of kindness)
- 不好意思，我又迟到了。**Bù hǎoyìsi, wǒ yòu chídào le.** = *I'm sorry I'm late agian.*
- 又让你送我礼物，真不好意思。**Yòu ràng nǐ sòng wǒ lǐwù, zhēn bù hǎoyìsi.** = *Oh, you gave me a gift again, it's embarrassing.*
- 这点小礼物，请您收下，不好意思。**Zhè diǎn xiǎo lǐwù, qǐng nín shōuxià, bù hǎoyìsi.** *Please accept this little present.*

NOTE: 不好意思 **bù hǎoyìsi** literally means "I'm embarrassed." It is easy to understand why you say it when you are apologising or receiving a gift. When you are giving a gift, however, you also say it to imply that the gift is so insignificant that you feel embarrassed about it.

bùjǐn 不仅 CONJUNCTION = same as 不但 **búdàn**. Tends to be used in writing.

bùjiǔ 不久 NOUN = not long afterwards, near future, soon
- 他们不久就要回国了。**Tāmen bùjiǔ jiù yào huíguó le.** = *They're returning to their country soon.*

bùrán 不然 CONJUNCTION = otherwise, or
- 你别说了，不然我真要生气了。**Nǐ bié shuō le, bùrán wǒ zhēn yào shēngqì le.** = *Don't say any more, or I'll really be angry.*
- 他一定遇到了非常麻烦的事，不然情绪不会这么坏。**Tā yídìng yùdàole fēicháng máfan de shì, bùrán qíngxù bú huì zhème huài.** = *He must have gotten into big trouble, otherwise he wouldn't be in such a bad mood.*

NOTE: To be more emphatic, you can use 不然的话 **bùrán de huà** instead of 不然 **bùrán**.

bùrú 不如 VERB = be not as good as, not as...as
- 走路不如骑车快。**Zǒulù bùrú qíchē kuài.** = *Walking is not as fast as riding a bicycle.*
- 我体育不如你，但是你功课不如我。**Wǒ tǐyù bùrú nǐ, dànshì nǐ gōngkè bùrú wǒ.** = *I'm not as good as you are in sports, but you're not as good as me in academic work.*

bùshǎo 不少 [modif: 不 not + 少 few, little] ADJECTIVE = quite a few
- 我在这个城市有不少好朋友。**Wǒ zài zhège chéngshì yǒu bùshǎo hǎo péngyou.** = *I have quite a few good friends in this city.*
- 我做了不少解释，她还是不原谅我。**Wǒ zuòle bùshǎo jiěshì, tā háishì bù yuánliàng wǒ.** = *I have given many explanations, but she still won't forgive me.*

bùtíng 不停 [modif: 不 not + 停 stop] ADVERB = without letup, incessantly
- 雨不停地下了两天。**Yǔ bùtíng de xiàle liǎng tiān.** = *It rained for two days without letup.*

bùtóng 不同 ADJECTIVE = not the same, different
- 人和人不同，不能比较。**Rén hé rén bùtóng, bù néng bǐjiào.** = *People are different and cannot be compared.*
- 这两个字发音相同，写法不同，意思也不同。**Zhè liǎng ge zì fāyīn xiāngtóng, xiěfǎ bùtóng, yìsi yě bùtóng.** = *These two characters have the same pronunciation but they are different in writing and meaning.*
...hé/gēn...bùtóng …和／跟…不同 = … is/are different from ...
- 我的意见跟他的意见不同。**Wǒ de yìjiàn gēn tā de yìjiàn bùtóng.** = *My opinion is different from his.*

bùxíng 不行 ADJECTIVE
1 = will not do, not allowed
- "妈妈，这个周末我带十几个同学来家里玩，行不行？""不行。" **"Māma, zhège zhōumò wǒ dài shí jǐ ge tóngxué lái jiāli wán, xíng bu xíng?" "Bù xíng."** = *"Mom, may I bring a dozen classmates home for a party this weekend?" "No, you may not."*
2 = not [be] good [at …]
- 我的中文不行，请你多多帮助。**Wǒ de Zhōngwén bù xíng, qǐng nǐ duōduō bāngzhù.** = *My Chinese is not good. Please help me.*
- 他体育很好，但是功课不行。**Tā tǐyù hěn hǎo, dànshì gōngkè bùxíng.** = *He is good at sports, but poor at schoolwork.*

bùxǔ 不许 VERB = not permitted, not allowed
- 不许逃学。**Bùxǔ táo xué.** = *Truancy is not allowed.*
- 爸爸不许她和那个男孩出去玩。**Bàba bùxǔ**

tā hé nèi ge nán hái chūqu wán. = *Father does not allow her to go out with that boy.*

bù 布 NOUN = cotton or linen cloth (块 **kuài**, 片 **piàn**)

■ 这块布很好看，做裙子正合适。**Zhè kuài bù hěn hǎokàn, zuò qúnzi zhèng héshì.** = *This piece of cotton cloth looks good, just right for a skirt.*

bù 布 Trad 佈 VERB = arrange, deploy

bùzhì 布置 VERB = decorate

■ 他们马上要结婚了，这几天正在布置新房。**Tāmen mǎshàng yào jiēhūn le, zhè jǐ tiān zhèngzài bùzhì xīnfáng.** = *They're getting married soon and are decorating their new home these days.*

bù 步 NOUN = step

■ 走几步就到了，不用开车。**Zǒu jǐ bù jiù dào le, bú yòng kāi chē.** = *It's just a few steps away. There's no need to drive.*

bù 怖 VERB = fear (See 恐怖 **kǒngbu**.)

bù 部 NOUN = part, unit

bùduì 部队 NOUN = troops, the army

■ 部队是锻炼年轻人的好地方。**Bùduì shì duànliàn niánqīngrén de hǎo dìfang.** = *The army is a good place to toughen up young people.*

bùfen 部分 [compound: 部 *part* + 分 *division*] NOUN = portion, part

■ 中国的中学分初中和高中两部分。**Zhōngguó de zhōngxué fēn chūzhōng hé gāozhōng liǎng bùfen.** = *Chinese high schools have two parts—junior high and senior high.*

dà bùfen 大部分 = most of ..., the majority of ....

bùmén 部门 [compound: 部 *department* + 门 *gate, door*] NOUN = department

■ 他们虽然都在市政府工作，但是在不同的部门，相互不熟悉。**Tāmen suīrán dōu zài shì zhèngfǔ gōngzuò, dànshì zài bùtóng de bùmén, xiānghù bù shúxi.** = *Although they both work in the city government, they work at different departments and do not know each other well.*

bùzhǎng 部长 [modif: 部 *ministry* + 长 *chief, the person in charge*] NOUN = (government) minister

■ 教育部长对中小学的外语教学很关心。**Jiàoyù Bùzhǎng duì zhōng-xiǎoxué de wàiyǔ jiàoxué hěn guānxīn.** = *The Minister of Education is very concerned for foreign language teaching at schools.*

C

cā 擦 VERB = clean or erase by wiping or rubbing

■ 窗户脏了，要擦一下。**Chuānghu zāng le, yào cā yíxià.** = *The window is dirty and needs cleaning.*

■ 每个星期一他去公司上班前，总要把皮鞋擦得很亮。**Měi ge Xīngqīyī tā qù gōngsī shàngbān qián, zǒngyào ba píxié cā de hěn liàng.** = *Every Monday before going to work in his company, he will polish his shoes.*

■ 我的自行车太脏了，我要把它擦干净。**Wǒ de zìxíngchē tài zāng le, wǒ yào ba tā cā gānjing.** = *My bike is dirty. I'll wipe it clean.*

cāi 猜 VERB = guess

■ "谁来了？你猜猜看。""我猜不着。告诉我吧。" = "**Shéi lái le? Nǐ cāicai kàn." "Wǒ cāi bu zháo. Gàosu wǒ ba."** = *"Guess who's come!" "I can't. Just tell me."*

cái 才 ADVERB

1 = (before a verb) a short time ago, just

■ 我才来，不知道这件事。**Wǒ cái lái, bù zhīdào zhè jiàn shì.** = *I've just arrived and don't know anything about this matter.*

■ 我才认识他，对他还不了解。**Wǒ cái rènshi tā, duì tā hái bù liǎojiě.** = *I came to know him not long ago, and I don't know him very well.*

2 = (used before a word of time or quantity to indicate that the speaker feels the time is too early, too short or the quantity is too little), only, as early as, as few/little as

■ 我学中文才一年，说得不好。**Wǒ xué Zhōngwén cái yì nián, shuō de bù hǎo.** = *I've learned Chinese for only one year, and can't speak it very well.*

■ 这本书才十块钱，太便宜了。**Zhè ben shū cái shí kuài qián, tài piányì le.** = *This book is only ten dollars. It's really cheap.*

3 = (used after a word of time to indicate that the speaker feels the time is too late or there is too much delay), as late as

■ 这个小孩三岁才会走。**Zhège xiǎo hái sānsuì cái huì zǒu.** = *This child learned to walk as late as three years old.*

■ 妈妈等到孩子都回来了才睡觉。**Māma děngdào háizi dōu huílai le, cái shuìjiào.** = *Mother did not go to bed until all her children came home.*

cái 财 Trad 財 NOUN = wealth, property

cáichǎn 财产 [compound: 财 *property, fortune* + 产 *property*] NOUN = property, belongings

■ 国家保护合法的个人财产。**Guójiā bǎohù héfǎ de gèrén cáichǎn.** = *The state protects legitimate private property.*

■ 这是我的个人财产，你们不能动。**Zhè shì wǒ de gèrén cáichǎn, nǐmen bù néng dòng.** = *These are my personal belongings. You can't touch them.*

cái 材 NOUN = material

cáiliào 材料 NOUN

1 = materials, e.g. steel, timber, plastic

■ 建筑材料越来越贵，房子的造价也就越来越贵。**Jiànzhú cáiliào yuèlaiyuè guì, fángzi de zàojià yě jiù yuèlaiyuè guì.** = *As building materials become more and more expensive, building houses also becomes more and more expensive.*

2 = data (for a thesis, a report, etc.)

■ 报上提供的材料对我写文章很有帮助。**Bào shang tígòng de cáiliào duì wǒ xiě wénzhāng hěn yǒu bāngzhù .** = *The data provided in the newspapers are very helpful to my writing.*

cǎi 采 Trad 採

VERB = pick, pluck

■ 公园里的花，是给大家看的，任何人不能采。**Gōngyuán li de huā shì gěi dàjiā kàn de, rènhé rén bù néng cǎi.** = *The flowers in the park are for everyone to admire. Nobody is allowed to pick them.*

cǎiqǔ 采取 [compound: 采 *pick* + 取 *take*]

VERB = adopt (a policy, a measure, an attitude, etc.)

■ 对这个重大的经济问题，政府准备采取什么措施？ **Duì zhège zhòngdà de jīngjì wèntí, zhèngfǔ zhǔnbèi cǎiqǔ shénme cuòshī?** = *What measures is the government ready to adopt to deal with this major ecomonic problem?*

cǎiyòng 采用 [compound: 采 *pick* + 用 *use*]

VERB = use, employ

■ 采用新技术以后，产品质量有了明显提高。**Cǎiyòng xīn jìshù yǐhòu, chǎnpǐn zhìliàng yǒule míngxiǎn tígāo.** = *After adopting the new technique, product quality has improved remarkably.*

cǎi 彩 ADJECTIVE = colorful

cǎisè 彩色 [modif: 彩 *multi-colored* + 色 *color*] ADJECTIVE = multi-colored

■ 现在大部分人家都有彩色电视机，谁还看黑白电视机？ **Xiànzài dà bùfen rénjiā dōu yǒu cǎisè diànshìjī, shéi hái kàn háibái diànshìjī?** = *Now that most families have color TV sets, who wants to watch black and white TV?*

cǎi 踩 VERB = step on, tread on

■ 你们在花园里玩球，可别踩了花。**Nǐmen zài huāyuán li wán qiú, kě bié cǎile huā.** = *When you play ball in the garden, don't step on the flowers.*

cài 菜 NOUN

1 = vegetables

■ 一个人既要吃肉，又要吃菜，才能健康。**Yí ge rén jì yào chī ròu, yòu yào chī cài, cái néng jiànkāng.** = *One should eat both meat and vegetables in order to be in good health.*

zhòng cài 种菜 = grow vegetables

■ 这菜是我们自己种的，你尝尝。**Zhè cài shì wǒmen zìjǐ zhòng de. Nǐ chángchang.** = *We grew this vegetable ourselves. Do try some.*

2 = any non-staple food such as vegetables, meat, fish, eggs etc.

mǎi cài 买菜 = buy non-staple food, do grocery shopping

■ 妈妈每个星期五都要买很多菜，有鱼、有肉、还有蔬菜。**Māma měi ge Xīngqíwǔ dōu yào mǎi hěn dōu cài, yǒu yú, yǒu ròu, háiyǒu shūcài.** = *Every Friday, mother buys lots of food: fish, meat and vegetables.*

C

3 = cooked dish

■ 这个菜又好吃又好看，是谁做的？ **Zhège cài yòu hǎokàn yòu hǎochī, shì shuí zuò de?** = *This dish is both beautiful and delicious. Who cooked it?*

■ 请别客气，多吃点菜！ **Qǐng bié kèqi, duō chī diǎn cài!** = *Please don't be too polite. Eat more food!*

diǎn cài 点菜 = **order a dish (in a restaurant)**

■ 我们每个人点一个菜，好吗？ **Wǒmen měi ge rén diǎn yí ge cài, hǎo ma?** = *Shall we each order a dish?*

Zhōngguó cài 中国菜 = **Chinese dishes, Chinese food**

■ 你会做中国菜吗？ **Nǐ huì zuò Zhōngguó cài ma?** = *Can you cook Chinese dishes?*

cān 参 Trad 參 VERB = call, enter

cānguān 参观 [compound: 参 call + 观 watch, see] VERB = visit (a place)

■ 这个古迹十分有名，每天有很多人来参观。 **Zhège gǔjì shífēn yǒumíng, měi tiān yǒu hěn duō rén lái cānguān.** = *This historical site is well known. Many people come to visit it every day.*

■ 我在中国的时候，参观了很多学校。 **Wǒ zài Zhōngguó de shíhou, cānguānle hěn duō xuéxiào.** = *I visited many schools when I was in China.*

cānjiā 参加 [v+comp: 参 enter + 加 add] VERB
1 = join

■ 我可以参加中文班吗？ **Wǒ kěyǐ cānjiā Zhōngwén bān ma?** = *May I join the Chinese class?*

■ 欢迎你参加我们的俱乐部。 **Huānyíng nǐ cānjiā wǒmen de jùlèbù.** = *You're welcome to join our club.*

2 = participate, attend

■ 我们出版社有兴趣参加这个书展。 **Wǒmen chūbǎnshè yǒu xìngqù cānjiā zhège shūzhǎn.** = *Our publishing house is interested in participating in this book fair.*

■ 欢迎您来参加我们的晚会。 **Huānyíng nín lái cānjiā wǒmen de wǎnhuì.** = *You're welcome to our evening party.*

cān 餐 NOUN = meal

cāntīng 餐厅 [modif: 餐 meal + 厅 hall] NOUN = restaurant

■ 旅馆的餐厅在十二楼。 **Lǚguǎn de cāntīng zài shí'èr lóu.** = *The restaurant in the hotel is on the twelfth floor.*

cán 惭 Trad 慚 NOUN = shame

cánkuì 惭愧 [compound: 惭 shame + 愧 sense of guilt] ADJECTIVE = be ashamed

■ 由于我的错误，给你带来了不便，我深感惭愧。 **Yóuyú wǒ de cuòwù, gěi nǐ dàiláile búbiàn, wǒ shēn gǎn cánkuì.** = *My error has caused you inconvenience. I feel deeply ashamed.*

cāng 苍 Trad 蒼 NOUN = dark green

cāngying 苍蝇 NOUN = housefly

■ 那里有一只苍蝇，拍死它！ **Nàli yǒu yì zhī cāngying, pāi sǐ tā!** = *There's a fly, kill it!*

cáng 藏 VERB = hide, conceal

■ 他把玩具藏在床下，不让妈妈看见。 **Tā bǎ wánjù cáng zài chuáng xia, bú ràng māma kànjiàn.** = *He hid the toy under the bed so mother wouldn't see.*

cāo 操 NOUN = drill, exercise

cāochǎng 操场 [modif: 操 drill, exercise + 场 ground] NOUN = sports ground, playground

■ 我们学校的操场很大。 **Wǒmen xuéxiaò de cānchǎng hěn dà.** = *Our school sports ground is very big.*

(zài) cāochǎng shang (在) 操场上 = on the sports ground

■ 很多学生在操场上玩。 **Hěn duō xuésheng zài cāochǎng shang wán.** = *Many students are playing on the sports ground.*

cǎo 草 NOUN = grass, weed (棵 kē)

■ 你们每天给马喂几次草？ **Nǐmen měi tiān gěi mǎ wèi jǐ cì cǎo?** = How many times *a day do you feed the horses?* (← *How many times a day do you feed the horses grass?*)

cǎodì 草地 [modif: 草 grass + 地 land] NOUN = lawn

■ 我家房前有一片草地。 **Wǒ jiā fáng qián yǒu yí piàn cǎodì.** = *There is a lawn in front of our house.*

cǎoyuán 草原 [modif: 草 *grass* + 原 *flat land*]
NOUN = grassland, steppe, pasture
■ "你见过真正的草原吗？""没有，我一直住在大城市里。" **"Nǐ jiànguo zhēnzhèng de cǎoyuán ma?" "Méiyǒu, wǒ yìzhí zhù zài dà chéngshì li."** = *"Have you ever seen real grasslands?" "No, I've been living in a big city all along."*

cè 册 MEASURE WORD = (used for books) volume
■ 两千册图书 **liǎngqiān cè túshū** = *two thousand [volumes of] books*

cè 厕 Trade 厠 NOUN = toilet

cèsuǒ 厕所 NOUN = toilet
■ 请问，男厕所在哪里？ **Qǐngwèn, nán cèsuǒ zài nǎli?** = *Excuse me, where is the men's toilet?*
gōnggòng cèsuǒ 公共厕所 = public toilet
nán cèsuǒ 男厕所 = men's toilet
nǚ cèsuǒ 女厕所 = women's toilet

NOTE: See note on 洗手间 **xǐshǒujiān** (in 洗 **xǐ**).

cè 测 Trad 測 VERB = measure, gauge

cèyàn 测验 [compound: 测 *measure* + 验 *test*]
1 VERB = test (in a school)
■ 明天数学测验，请同学们好好准备。 **Míngtiān shùxué cèyàn, qǐng tóngxuémen hǎohǎo zhǔnbèi.** = *There will be a mathematics test tomorrow. Be well prepared, everyone.*
2 NOUN = test, examination
■ 这个学期一共有四次测验。 **Zhège xuéqī yígòng yǒu sì cì cèyàn.** = *There will be four tests this semester.*

cè 策 NOUN = plan (See 政策 **zhèngcè**.)

céng 层 Trad 層 MEASURE WORD = story (storey), level, floor
■ 这座大楼一共有二十层。 **Zhè zuò dàlóu yígòng yǒu èrshí céng.** = *This building has twenty levels.*
■ "你住在第几层？""我住在第三层。" **"Nǐ zhù zài dì jǐ céng?" "Wǒ zhù zài dì sān céng."** = *"Which floor do you live on?" "I live on the third floor."*

NOTE: See note on 楼 **lóu**.

céng 曾 ADVERB = same as 曾经 **céngjīng**. Used more in writing.

céngjīng 曾经 ADVERB = once, formerly
■ 我曾经在那个城市里住过两年。 **Wǒ céngjīng zài nàge chéngshì li zhùguo liǎng nián.** = *I lived in that city for two years.*
■ 这位老人曾经是一位著名的科学家。 **Zhè wèi lǎorén céngjīng shì yí wèi zhùmíng de kēxuéjiā.** = *That old gentleman was once a famous scientist.*

NOTE: 曾经 **céngjīng** is used to emphasize that an action or situation took place in the past.

chā 叉 NOUN = fork

chāzi 叉子 NOUN = fork (把 **bǎ**)
■ 这把叉子掉在地上，脏了，请再给我一把。 **Zhè bǎ chāzi diào zai dìshang, zāng le, qǐng zài gěi wǒ yì bǎ.** = *This fork dropped on the floor and got dirty. Please give me another one.*

chā 插 VERB = insert, stick in
■ 花瓶里要插一些花才好。 **Huāpíng li yào chā yìxiē huā cái hǎo.** = *It would be good to have some flowers in the vase.*

chá 茶 NOUN = tea
■ 茶凉了，快喝吧。 **Chá liáng le, kuài hē ba.** = *The tea is no longer hot. Please drink it.*
hóngchá 红茶 = black tea
lǜchá 绿茶 = green tea
■ 您喝红茶还是绿茶？ **Nín hē hóngchá háishì lǜchá?** = *Do you drink black tea or green tea?*
hē chá 喝茶 = drink tea
■ 经常喝茶，特别是绿茶，对身体很有好处。 **Jīngcháng hē chá, tèbié shì lǜchá, duì shēntǐ hěn yǒu hǎochù.** = *Drinking tea regularly, especially green tea, is very beneficial to health.*
chábēi 茶杯 = teacup
chá hú 茶壶 = teapot

chá 查 VERB = check, look up
■ 我可以用一下你的词典吗？ 我要查一个字。 **Wǒ kěyǐ yòng yíxià nǐ de cídiǎn ma? Wǒ**

yào chá yí ge zì. = *May I use your dictionary? I want to look up a word.*

■ 请你查查，你们学校有没有这个学生。**Qǐng nǐ chácha, nǐmen xuéxiào yǒu méiyǒu zhège xuésheng.** = *Please find out if your school has this student.*

chá cídiǎn 查词典 = look up words in a dictionary

■ 你会查中文词典吗？ **Nǐ huì chá Zhōngwén cídiǎn ma?** = *Do you know how to look up words in a Chinese dictionary?*

chá 察 VERB = examine, look over closely (See 观察 **guānchá**, 警察 **jǐngchá**.)

chà 差

1 VERB = be short of, lack in

■ 我还差二十块钱，你可以借给我吗？ **Wǒ hái chà èrshí kuài qián, nǐ kěyǐ jiè gěi wǒ ma?** = *I'm still short of twenty dollars. Can you give me a loan?*

■ 现在是十一点差五分。**Xiànzài shì shíyī diǎn chà wǔ fēn.** = *It's five to eleven now.*

2 ADJECTIVE = poor, not up to standard

■ 这种电冰箱不但价格贵，而且质量差。**Zhè zhǒng diànbīngxiāng búdàn jiàgé guì, érqiě zhìliàng chà.** = *This refrigerator is not only expensive but also of poor quality.*

■ 他身体很差，经常生病。**Tā shēntǐ hěn chà, jīngcháng shēngbìng.** = *He is in poor health and often falls ill.*

chàbuduō 差不多 ADJECTIVE

1 = more or less the same

■ 他们俩年龄差不多，经历也差不多，很快成了好朋友。**Tāmen liǎ niánlíng chàbuduō, jīnglì yě chàbuduō, hěnkuài chéngle hǎo péngyou.** = *They were more or less the same age and had more or less the same experiences, and soon became good friends.*

2 = almost

■ "你报告写完了吗？" "差不多了。" **"Nǐ bàogào xiěwánle ma?" "Chàbuduō le."** = *"Have you finished writing the report?" "Almost."*

■ 我们晚饭吃得差不多了，弟弟才回来。**Wǒmen wǎnfàn chī de chàbuduō le, dìdi cái huílai.** = *We had almost finished dinner when my younger brother came home.*

■ 差不多十二点了，她怎么还不来上班？ **Chàbuduō shí'èr diǎn le, tā zěnme hái bù lái**

shàngbān? = *It's almost twelve o'clock. Why hasn't she turned up for work?*

chàdiǎnr 差点儿 ADVERB = almost, nearly

■ 今天是妻子的生日，陈先生差点儿忘了。**Jīntiān shì qīzi de shēngrì, Chén xiānsheng chàdiǎnr wàngle.** = *Today is his wife's birthday. Mr Chen almost forgot it. (→ Mr Chen nearly forgot it was his wife's birthday today.)*

■ 去年他几次犯错误，差点儿丢了饭碗。**Qùnián tā jǐ cì fàn cuòwù, chàdiǎnr diūle fànwǎn.** = *Last year he made several mistakes and nearly lost his job.*

chāi 拆 VERB = take apart, demolish

■ 小孩把玩具拆开了，可是不知道怎样再装起来。**Xiǎohái bǎ wánjù chāikāi le, kěshì bù zhīdào zěnyàng zài zhuāng qǐlai.** = *The child took the toy apart, but did not know how to re-assemble it.*

chái 柴 NOUN = firewood (See 火柴 **huǒchái**.)

chǎn 产 Trad 產 VERB = produce

chǎnliàng 产量 [modif: 产 product + 量 quantity] NOUN = (production) output, yield

■ 仅仅增加产量是没有意义的。**Jǐnjǐn zēngjiā chǎnliàng shì méiyǒu yìyì de.** = *Increasing output alone is meaningless.*

■ 你们工厂去年的产量是多少？ **Nǐmen gōngchǎng qùnián de chǎnliàng shì duōshǎo?** = *What was the output of your factory last year?*

chǎnpǐn 产品 [modif: 产 production + 品 goods] NOUN = product

■ 我们必须不断研究和开发新产品。**Wǒmen bìxū búduàn yánjiū hé kāifā xīn chǎnpǐn.** = *We must continually research and develop new products.*

■ 产品质量是企业的生命。**Chǎnpǐn zhìliàng shì qǐyè de shēngmìng.** = *The quality of its products is the lifeblood of an enterprise.*

chǎnshēng 产生 [compound: 产 produce + 生 grow] VERB = produce, give rise to, lead to

■ 新科技的应用产生了一些新的社会现象。**Xīn kējì de yìngyòng chǎnshēngle yìxiē xīn de shèhuì xiànxiàng.** = *The use of new technology has given rise to some new social phenomena.*

cháng 长 Trad 長 ADJECTIVE = long (antonym 短 **duǎn**)
- 中国的历史很长。**Zhōngguó de lìshǐ hěn cháng.** = *China has a long history.*
- 你还年轻，生活道路还长着呢。**Nǐ hái niánqīng, shēnghuó dàolù hái chángzhe ne.** = *You're still young, and have a long way to go in life.*

chángpǎo 长跑 = **long distance running**
- 他是一名长跑运动员。**Tā shì yì míng chángpǎo yùndòngyuán.** = *He is a long-distance athlete.*

chángchéng 长城 = the Great Wall (a historic landmark in Northern China)

Cháng Jiāng 长江 = the Yangtze River (China's longest river)

chángqī 长期 [modif: 长 *long* + 期 *period*] NOUN = a long period of time
- 他长期研究汉语语法，发表过很多文章。**Tā chángqī yánjiū Hànyǔ yǔfǎ, fābiǎoguo hěn duō wénzhāng.** = *He has studied Chinese grammar for a long time, and has published many essays.*
- 农民问题长期没有受到重视。**Nóngmín wèntí chángqī méiyǒu shòudào zhòngshì.** = *For a long time the peasants' problem has not been paid attention to.*

chángtú 长途 [modif: 长 *long* + 途 *way*] NOUN = long distance

chángtú diànhuà 长途电话 = long-distance telephone call

guójì chángtú diànhuà 国际长途电话 = international telephone call
- 我要打一个国际长途电话到纽约。**Wǒ yào dǎ yí ge guójì chángtú diànhuà dào Niǔyuē.** = *I want to make an international call to New York.*

chángtú qìchē 长途汽车 = long-distance bus, coach

cháng 肠 Trad 腸 NOUN = intestine (See 香肠 **xiāngcháng**.)

cháng 尝 Trad 嘗 VERB = taste
- 这种水果我没有吃过，想尝尝。**Zhè zhǒng shuǐguǒ wǒ méiyǒu chīguo, xiǎng chángchang.** = *I've never eaten this fruit. I'd like to taste it.*

cháng 常 ADVERB = often
- 我常去市图书馆借书。**Wǒ cháng qù shì túshūguǎn jiè shū.** = *I often go to the city library to borrow books.*

chángcháng 常常 = often
- 我常常去市图书馆借书。**Wǒ chángcháng qù shì túshūguǎn jiè shū.** = *I often go to the city library to borrow books.*

bù cháng 不常 = not often, seldom
- 他住在乡下，不常进城。**Tā zhù zài xiāngxia, bù cháng jìn chéng.** = *He lives in a village and seldom goes to town.*

NOTE: Colloquially, 常常 **chángcháng** is often used instead of 常 **cháng**.

chǎng 厂 Trad 廠 NOUN = factory (See 工厂 **gōngchǎng**.)

chǎng 场 Trad 場
1 NOUN = ground, field
cāochǎng 操场 = sports ground, playground
tǐyùchǎng 体育场 = stadium
fēijīchǎng 飞机场 = airport
shìchǎng 市场 = market
2 MEASURE WORD = (for movies, sport events, etc.)
- 一场电影 **yì chǎng diànyǐng** = *a show of film*
- 这个电影院一天放六场电影。**Zhège diànyǐngyuàn yìtiān fàng liù chǎng diànyǐng.** = *This cinema has six film shows a day.*
- 一场球赛 **yì chǎng qiúsài** = *a ball game, a ball match*
- 昨天我看了一场精彩的球赛。**Zuótiān wǒ kànle yì chǎng jīngcǎi de qiúsài.** = *I watched a wonderful ball game yesterday.*

chàng 倡 VERB = initiate (See 提倡 **tíchàng**.)

chàng 唱 VERB = sing
- 你会唱中文歌吗？**Nǐ huì chàng Zhōngwén gē ma?** = *Can you sing Chinese songs?*

chànggē 唱歌 = sing songs, sing
- 你唱歌唱得真好听！**Nǐ chànggē chàng de zhēn hǎotīng!** = *You really sing well!*

chāo 抄 VERB = copy by hand
- 这些数字很重要，我要抄下来。**Zhèxiē shùzì hěn zhòngyào, wǒ yào chāo xiàlai.** = *These are important numbers. I'll write them down.*

chāoxiě 抄写 VERB = same as 抄 **chāo**

chāo 超 VERB = go beyond, exceed

chāoguò 超过 VERB
1 = overtake
■ 我前面的车开得太慢，我要超过它。**Wǒ qiánmiàn de chē kāi de tài màn, wǒ yào chāoguò tā.** = The car in front of me is moving too slowly. I want to overtake it.
2 = exceed
■ 去年到这个国家的旅游者超过了三百万。**Qùnián dào zhège guójiā de lǚyóuzhě chāoguòle sān bǎiwàn.** = The number of tourists visiting this country last year exceeded three million.

chāojí 超级 [modif: 超 exceed + 级 grade]
ADJECTIVE = super
chāojí shìchǎng 超级市场 = supermarket
■ 你经常去哪一家超级市场？ **Nǐ jīngcháng qù nǐ yì jiā chāojí shìchǎng?** = Which supermarket do you often go to?
chāojí dàguó 超级大国 = **superpower**
■ 现在世界上只有一个超级大国。**Xiànzài shìjiè shang zhǐ yǒu yí ge chāojí dàguó.** = There is only one superpower in the world today.
chāojí gōnglù 超级公路 = super-highway, motorway

cháo 朝
1 VERB = face
■ 中国人的房子大多朝南。**Zhōngguórén de fángzi dàduō cháo nán.** = Chinese people's houses mostly face the south. (→ Most Chinese houses face south.)
2 PREPOSITION = towards, to
■ 你一直朝前走十分钟左右，就到公园了。**Nǐ yìzhí cháo qián zǒu shí fēnzhōng zuǒyòu, jiù dào gōngyuán le.** = Walk straight ahead for about ten minutes and you'll reach the park.

chǎo 吵 VERB
1 = quarrel
■ 他们夫妻俩又吵了。**Tāmen fūqī liǎ yòu chǎo le.** = The couple quarreled again.
2 = make a big noise, be noisy
■ 这间房面对大街，太吵了。**Zhè jiān fáng miànduì dàjiē, tài chǎo le.** = This room faces a main street. It's too noisy.

NOTE: For quarrel, 吵架 **chǎojià** is more commonly used than 吵 **chǎo**, for example:
■ 他们夫妻俩又吵架了。**Tāmen fūqī liǎ yòu chǎojià le.** = The couple quarreled again.

chē 车 Trad 車 NOUN = vehicle, traffic (辆 **liàng**)
■ 我的车坏了。**Wǒ de chē huài le.** = My car (or bicycle) has broken down.
■ 路上车很多。**Lùshang chē hěn duō.** = There is lots of traffic on the road.
■ 我可以借用你的车吗？ **Wǒ kěyǐ jièyòng nǐ de chē ma?** = May I borrow your car (or bicycle)?
chē pái 车牌 = (vehicle) license plate
chē pái hào 车牌号 = (vehicle) license plate number
kāi chē 开车 = drive an automobile
qí chē 骑车 = ride a bicycle
tíngchēchǎng 停车场 = car park
xué chē 学车 = learn to drive (or to ride a bicycle)
xiū chē 修车 = repair a car/bicycle
xiū chē háng 修车行 = motor vehicle repair and servicing shop

chējiān 车间 NOUN = workshop (in a factory)
■ 这个车间有多少工人？ **Zhège chējiān yǒu duōshǎo gōngrén?** = How many workers work in this workshop?

chēzhàn 车站 [modif: 车 vehicle + 站 station]
NOUN = bus stop, coach station, railway station
■ "车站离这里远不远？" "不远，开车只要十分钟。" **"Chēzhàn lí zhèli yuǎn bu yuǎn?" "Bù yuǎn, kāi chē zhǐyào shí fēnzhōng."** = "Is the railway (or bus) station far from here?" "No, it's only ten minutes' drive."
■ 王先生去车站接朋友了。**Wáng xiānsheng qù chēzhàn jiē péngyou le.** = Mr Wang's gone to the railway (or coach) station to meet a friend.
chángtú qìchē zhàn 长途汽车站 = coach station
chūzū qìchē zhàn 出租汽车站 = taxi stand
huǒchē zhàn 火车站 = railway station

chè 彻 Trad 徹 ADJECTIVE = thorough

chèdǐ 彻底 [compound: 彻 thorough + 底 end, bottom] ADJECTIVE = thorough, complete
■ 经过彻底调查，确定这个地区没有这种病。**Jīngguò chèdǐ diàochá, quèdìng zhège dìqū**

méiyǒu zhè zhǒng bìng. = *After a thorough investigation it is confirmed that this region is free from this disease.*

chén 沉 VERB = sink
■ 一公斤铁在水里会沉，一公斤棉花沉吗？ **Yì gōngjīn tiě zài shuǐ li bú huì chén, yì gōngjīn miánhuā huì chén ma?** = *While a kilogram of iron will sink in water, will a kilogram of cotton?*

chénmò 沉默 [compound: 沉 *deep* + 默 *silent*] ADJECTIVE = silent, reticent
■ 他总是很沉默，没人知道他到底在想什么。 **Tā zǒngshì hěn chénmò, méi rén zhīdào tā dàodǐ zài xiǎng shénme.** = *He is always reticent, and nobody knows what he is thinking.*

Chén 陈 Trad 陳 NOUN = a common family name

chén 晨 NOUN = early morning (See 早晨 zǎochén.)

chèn 衬 Trad 襯 NOUN = lining, underwear

chènshān 衬衫 NOUN = shirt (件 jiàn)
■ 你去公司上班，当然要每天换衬衫。 **Nǐ qù gōngsī shàngbān, dāngrán yào měitiān huàn chènshān.** = *If you work in a company, of course you should change shirts every day.*

chènyī 衬衣 NOUN = shirt or similar underwear (件 jiàn)
■ 他拿着干净的衬衣短裤，进浴室去洗澡。 **Tā názhe gānjìng de chènyī duǎnkù, jìn yùshì qù xǐzǎo.** = *Carrying clean underwear, he went into the bathroom to take a bath.*

chèn 趁 PREPOSITION = taking advange of, while, when
■ 我想趁这个机会，向大家说几句话。 **Wǒ xiǎng chèn zhège jīhuì, xiàng dàjiā shuō jǐ jù huà.** = *I'd like to take this opportunity to say a few words to you.*
■ 趁王董事长也在这里，我想报告一下最近的营业情况。 **Chèn Wáng dǒngshìzhǎng yě zài zhèli, wǒ xiǎng bàogào yíxià zuìjìn de yíngyè qíngkuàng.** = *Now that Chairman Wang is here, I'd like to report our recent business situation.*

chēng 称 Trad 稱 VERB
1 = call, be known as, address … as
■ 电脑又称计算机。 **Diànnǎo yòu chēng jìsuànjī.** = *"Diannao" is also known as "jisuanji."*
■ 他比我们都大一点，我们都称他"李大哥"。 **Tā bǐ wǒmen dōu dà yìdiǎn, wǒmen dōu chēng tā "Lǐ dàgē".** = *As he is older than we are, we all call him "Elder Brother Li."*
2 = weigh
■ 他上飞机场之前，称了一下行李，看看有没有超重。 **Tā shàng fēijīchǎng zhī qián, chēngle yíxià xíngli, kànkan yǒu méi yǒu chāozhòng.** = *He weighed his luggage before leaving for the airport to make sure it was not overweight.*

chēngzàn 称赞 [compound: 称 *praise* + 赞 *praise*] VERB = compliment, praise
■ 老板称赞他工作努力，成绩优秀。 **Lǎobǎn chēngzàn tā gōngzuò nǔlì, chéngjì yōuxiù.** = *The boss praised him as a hardworking high achiever.*

chéng 成 VERB = become, turn into
■ 几年没见，她成了一个漂亮的大姑娘了。 **Jǐnián méi jiàn, tā chéngle yí ge piàoliang de dàgūniang le.** = *After several years' absence, she had become a pretty young lady.*
■ 他是我小学时的同学，没想到成了一位大人物。 **Tā shì wǒ xiǎoxué shí de tóngxué, méi xiǎngdào chéngle yí wèi dàrénwù.** = *He was my primary school classmate and, unexpectedly, has become a big shot.*
chéng míng 成名 = become famous
■ 她写了那本小说，几乎一夜成名。 **Tā xiěle nà běn xiǎoshuō, jīhū yí yè chéng míng.** = *She wrote that novel and became famous almost overnight.*

chéngfèn 成分 [compound: 成 *percentage* + 分 *element*] NOUN = component part, ingredient (种 zhǒng)
■ 这种中药有哪些成分？ **Zhè zhǒng Zhōngyào yǒu nǎxiē chéngfèn?** = *What are the ingredients in this Chinese medicine?*

chénggōng 成功 [v+obj: 成 *accomplish* + 功 merits, feat]
1 VERB = succeed
■ 经过无数次的试验，科学家们终于成功

了。**Jīngguò wúshù cì de shìyàn, kēxuéjiāmen zhōngyú chénggōng le.** = *After numerous experiments, the scientists finally succeeded.*
■ 祝你成功！**Zhù nǐ chénggōng!** = *I wish you success!*
2 ADJECTIVE = successful
■ 在一个成功的男人背后，总有一位好妻子。**Zài yí ge chénggōng de nánrén bèihou, zǒng yǒu yí wèi hǎo qīzi.** = *Behind a successful man, there stands a good wife.*
■ 这次会谈十分成功。**Zhè cì huìtán shífēn chénggōng.** = *This formal talk was a success.*

chéngguǒ 成果 [compound: 成 *achievement* + 果 *fruit, good result*] NOUN = positive result, achievement (项 **xiàng**)
■ 我们中文学习进步这么大，都是老师辛苦工作的成果。**Wǒmen Zhōngwén xuéxí jìnbù zhème dà, dōu shì lǎoshī xīnkǔ gōngzuò de chéngguǒ.** = *The rapid progress we have made in our Chinese studies is the result of our teachers' hard work.*

chéngjì 成绩 [compound: 成 *accomplish* + 绩 *result*] NOUN = achievement, examination result
kǎoshì chéngjì 考试成绩 = examination result
■ 他去年的考试成绩非常好。**Tā qùnián de kǎoshì chéngjì fēicháng hǎo.** = *His examination results last year were very good.*
■ 你的工作成绩不理想，必须努力改进。**Nǐ de gōngzuò chéngjì bù lǐxiǎng, bìxū nǔlì gǎijìn.** = *Your work results are not good enough. You must work harder to improve them.*
qǔdé chéngjì 取得成绩 = make achievement, get (positive, good) results.

chéngjiù 成就 [compound: 成 *achievment* + 就 *achievement*] NOUN = great achievement (项 **xiàng**)
■ 我们在经济发展方面取得了很大成就。**Wǒmen zài jīngjì fāzhǎn fāngmiàn qǔdéle hěn dà chéngjiù.** = *We have won great achievements in economic development.*

chénglì 成立 [compound: 成 *accomplish* + 立 *establish*] VERB = establish, set up
■ 你们公司是哪一年成立的？**Nǐmen gōngsī shì nǎ yì nián chénglì de?** = *When was your company set up?*

chéngshú 成熟 [compound: 成 *accomplish* + 熟 *mature*]
1 VERB = mature
■ 秋天是很多水果成熟的季节。**Qiūtiān shì hěn duō shuǐguǒ chéngshú de jìjié.** = *Autumn is the season when many fruits ripen.*
2 ADJECTIVE = ripe, mature
■ 他虽然二十多岁了，但是还不够成熟。**Tā suīrán èrshí duō suì le, dànshì hái bú gòu chéngshú.** = *Although he is over twenty, he is not mature enough.*

chéngwéi 成为 [compound: 成 *become* + 为 *be*] VERB = become
■ 这个小城已经成为著名的大学城。**Zhège xiǎo chéng yǐjīng chéngwéi zhùmíng de dàxué chéng.** = *This town has become a well-known university town.*
■ 她想成为一名电影演员。**Tā xiǎng chéngwéi yì míng diànyǐng yǎnyuán.** = *She wants to become a film star.*

chéngzhǎng 成长 [compound: 成 *become* + 长 *grow*] VERB = grow up
■ 他已经成长为一名优秀青年。**Tā yǐjīng chéngzhǎng wéi yìmíng yōuxiù qīngnián.** = *He has grown into a fine young man.*

chéng 承 VERB = bear, undertake

chéngrèn 承认 VERB
1 = acknowledge, recognize
■ 大家都承认他是一位有成就的科学家。**Dàjiā dōu chéngrèn tā shì yí wèi yǒu chéngjiù de kēxuéjiā.** = *Everyone acknowledges that he is a scientist who has made great achievements.*
2 = admit (mistake, error, etc.)
■ 他错了，还不承认。**Tā cuò le, hái bù chéngrèn.** = *He is wrong, but he still doesn't admit it.*
■ 我承认自己不了解情况，批评错了。**Wǒ chéngrèn zìjǐ bù liǎojiě qíngkuàng, pīpíng cuò le.** = *I admit that I did not know the situation well and made a wrong criticism.*

chéng 城 NOUN = city, town (座 **zuò**)
chénglǐ 城里 = in town, downtown
chéngwài 城外 = out of town, suburban area
jìn chéng 进城 = go to town, go to the city center

■ 我今天下午进城, 有什么事要我办吗? **Wǒ jīntiān xiàwǔ jìn chéng, yǒu shénme shì yào wǒ bàn ma?** = I'm going to town this afternoon. Is there anything you want me to do for you?

chéngshì 城市 [compound: 城 city wall, city + 市 market] NOUN = city, urban area (as opposed to rural area) (座 **zuò**)
■ 城市的中心是商业区, 东面是工业区。**Chéngshì de zhōngxīn shì shāngyè qū, dōngmiàn shì gōngyè qū.** = The city centre is a business district and the east part is an industrial area.
■ 这个城市不大, 但是很漂亮。**Zhège chéngshì bú dà, dànshì hěn piàoliang.** = This city is not big, but it's quite beautiful.
■ 我喜欢住在大城市里。**Wǒ xǐhuan zhù zài dà chéngshì li.** = I like to live in big cities.
chéngshì shēnghuó 城市生活 = city life

chéng 乘 VERB = use (a means of transport), travel (by car, train, plane, etc.)
■ 爸爸每天乘公共汽车上班。**Bàba měi tiān chéng gōnggòng qìchē shàngbān.** = Father goes to work by bus every day.
■ 你打算乘火车, 还是乘飞机到北京去? **Nǐ dǎsuàn chéng huǒchē, háishì chéng fēijī qù Běijīng?** = Do you plan to go to Beijing by train or by plane?

chéng 程 NOUN = regulation, procedure

chéngdù 程度 NOUN = level, degree
■ 汽车坏到这种程度, 已经修不好了。**Qìchē huài dao zhè zhǒng chéngdù, yǐjīng xiū bù hǎo le.** = The car is damaged to such a degree that it cannot be repaired.

chéng 诚 Trad 誠 ADJECTIVE = sincere

chéngkěn 诚恳 [compound: 诚 sincere + 恳 sincere] ADJECTIVE = sincere
■ 我们诚恳地希望你提出批评建议。**Wǒmen chéngkěn de xīwàng nǐ tíchū pīpíng jiànyì.** = We sincerely hope you will give us your criticism and suggestions.

chéngshí 诚实 [compound: 诚 sincere + 实 true] ADJECTIVE = honest, simple
■ 爸爸从小教育我做人要诚实。**Bàba cóng xiǎo jiàoyù wǒ zuòrén yào chéngshí.** = Since

my childhood, father has taught me to be an honest person.

chī 吃 VERB = eat
■ "你吃过早饭没有?" "吃过了。" **"Nǐ chī guo zǎofàn méiyǒu?" "Chī guo le."** = "Have you had breakfast?" "Yes, I have."

chījīng 吃惊 VERB = be shocked, be startled, be alarmed
■ 股票跌得这么快, 王先生很吃惊。**Gǔpiào diē de zhènme kuài, Wáng xiānsheng hěn chījīng.** = Mr Wang was shocked that the share prices fell so quickly.
dà chī yì jīng 大吃一惊 = greatly shocked, have the fright of one's life
■ 他回家时, 发现家门大开, 大吃一惊。**Tā huíjiā shí, fāxiàn jiā mén dà kāi, dà chī yì jīng.** = When he got home, he had the fright of his life when he saw the door wide open.

chí 迟 Trad 遲 ADJECTIVE = late

chídào 迟到 [modif: 迟 late + 到 arrive] VERB = come late, be late (for work, school, etc.)
■ 对不起, 我迟到了。**Duìbuqǐ, wǒ chídào le.** = I'm sorry I'm late.
■ 我今天早上差点儿迟到。**Wǒ jīntiān zǎoshang chàdiǎnr chídào.** = I was almost late this morning.
■ "你今天迟到了二十分钟, 明天不要再迟到了。" "请您原谅, 我明天一定不迟到。" **"Nǐ jīntiān chídàole èrshí fēnzhōng, míngtiān bú yào zài chídào le." "Qǐng nín yuánliàng. Wǒ míngtiān yídìng bù chídào."** = "You were late twenty minutes today. Don't be late tomorrow." "My apologies. I'll definitely not be late tomorrow."

chí 持 VERB = persevere (See 保持 **bǎochí**, 坚持 **jiānchí**, 支持 **zhīchí**.)

chǐ 尺
1 NOUN = ruler (把 **bǎ**)
■ 要划直线, 就要有一把尺。**Yào huà zhí xiàn, jiù yào yǒu yì bǎ chǐ.** = You need a ruler if you want to draw a straight line.
chǐcùn 尺寸 = size, measurements
■ 你做衣服以前, 要量一下尺寸。**Nǐ zuò yīfu yǐqián, yào liáng yíxià chǐcùn.** = Before a garment is made for you, measurements should be taken.

chǐmǎ 尺码 = size (of shoes, shirts, ready-made clothing, etc.)
- 我们有各种尺码的裙子，保证您满意。**Wǒmen yǒu gè zhǒng chǐmǎ de qúnzi, bǎozhèng nín mǎnyì.** = We have skirts of various sizes. Your satisfaction is guaranteed.

2 MEASURE WORD = a traditional Chinese unit of length (equal to ⅓ meter)
- 三尺等於一公尺，也就是说一尺等於三分之一公尺。**Sān chǐ děngyú yì gōngchǐ, yé jiù shì shuō yì chǐ děngyú sān fēnzhī yì gōngchǐ.** = Three chi make a meter; that is to say, one chi is a third of a meter.

gōngchǐ 公尺 = meter
yīngchǐ 英尺 = foot (as a measurement of length)

chì 翅 NOUN = wing

chìbǎng 翅膀 NOUN = wing (of a bird)
- 这只鸟翅膀受伤了，不能飞了。**Zhè zhī niǎo chìbǎng shòu shāng le, bù néng fēi le.** = This bird's wing is injured, it can't fly.

chōng 充 ADJECTIVE = sufficient, full

chōngfèn 充分 ADJECTIVE = abundant, ample, adequate
- 对明天的会谈双方都作了充分的准备。**Duì míngtiān de huìtán shuāngfāng dōu zuòle chōngfèn de zhǔnbèi.** = Both parties made ample preparations for the talk tomorrow.

chōngmǎn 充满 [compound: 充 filled + 满 full] ADJECTIVE = full of, be filled with
- 他充满了信心，一定能完成公司的任务。**Tā chōngmǎnle xìnxìn, yídìng néng wánchéng gōngsī de rènwù.** = He is full of confidence that he will complete the task set by the company.

chōngzú 充足 [compound: 充 filled + 足 enough] ADJECTIVE = sufficient, adequate, enough
- 我有充足的理由相信，这次试验能成功。**Wǒ yǒu chōngzú de lǐyóu xiāngxìn, zhè cì shìyàn néng chénggōng.** = I have enough reason to believe that the experiment will succeed this time.
- 他们有充足的资金研究和开发这项新技术。**Tāmen yǒu chōngzú de zījīn yánjiū hé kāifā zhè xiàng xīn jìshù.** = They have sufficient funds to research and develop this new technology.

chóng 虫 Trad 蟲 NOUN = insect, worm

chóngzi 虫子 [suffix: 虫 insect + 子 nominal suffix] NOUN = insect, worm (只 zhī)
- 有一只虫子在你背上爬。**Yǒu yì zhī chóngzi zài nǐ bèi shang pá.** = There's an insect crawling on your back.

chóng 重 ADVERB = again, once again
- 我在电脑上做的文件没有保存，只好重做。**Wǒ zài diànnǎo shang zuò de wénjiàn méiyǒu bǎocún, zhǐ hǎo chóng zuò.** = I failed to save the file in the computer, and had to redo [the work].

chóngfù 重复 [compound: 重 once again + 复 repeat] VERB = repeat
- 我离家前，妈妈又把话重复了一遍。**Wǒ lí jiā qián, māma yòu bǎ huà chóngfùle yí biàn.** = Before I left home, mother repeated what she had said.

chóngxīn 重新 [compound: 重 once again + 新 renew] ADVERB = same as 重 **chóng**

chóng 崇 ADJECTIVE = high, lofty

chónggāo 崇高 [compound: 崇 high, lofty + 高 high] ADJECTIVE = lofty, sublime
- 不少人不相信世界上有什么崇高的东西。**Bùshǎo rén bù xiāngxìn shìjiè shang yǒu shénem chónggāo de dōngxi.** = Quite a few people do not believe there is anything lofty in the world.

chōu 抽 VERB = take out (from in between)

chōuxiàng 抽象 ADJECTIVE = abstract
- 这么抽象的道理，有多少人听得懂？**Zhème chōuxiàng de dàolǐ, yǒu duōshǎo rén tīng de dǒng?** = How many people understand such abstract concepts?

chóu 绸 Trad 綢 NOUN = silk (See 丝绸 sīchóu.)

chóu 愁 VERB = worry
- 你别愁，大伙儿会帮助你的。**Nǐ bié chóu,**

dàhuǒr huì bāngzhù nǐ de. = *Don't worry. We'll all help you.*

chòu 臭 ADJECTIVE = smelly, stinking (antonym 香 **xiāng**)
■ 他的脚爱出汗，一脱鞋就闻到臭味。 **Tā de jiǎo ài chūhàn, yì tuō xié jiù wéndào chòu wèi.** = *He has sweaty feet. The moment he takes off his shoes, one scents the foul smell.*
■ 臭豆腐，闻闻臭，吃起来香。 **Chòu dòufu, wénwen chòu, chī qǐlai xiāng.** = *The preserved beancurd smells bad but tastes delicious.*

chū 出 VERB = emerge from, get out of
chūlai 出来 = **come out**
■ 请你出来一下。 **Qǐng nǐ chūlai yíxià.** = *Would you please step out for a while?*
chūqu 出去 = go out
■ 请你出去一下。 **Qǐng nǐ chūqu yíxià.** = *Please go out for a while. (→ Please leave us for a while.)*
chūguó 出国 = go abroad, go overseas
■ 我爸爸每年都要出国开会。 **Wǒ bàba měi nián dōu yào chūguó kāihuì.** = *My father goes abroad for conferences every year.*

chūbǎn 出版 VERB = publish
■ 这本词典由一家国际出版公司出版。 **Zhè běn cídiǎn yóu yì jiā guójì chūbǎn gōngsī chūbǎn.** = *This dictionary is published by an international publishing house.*
■ 老教授又出版了一本书。 **Lǎo jiàoshòu yòu chūbǎnle yì běn shū.** = *The old professor has published another book.*

chūfā 出发 [compound: 出 *depart* + 发 *discharge*] VERB = set off (on a journey), start (a journey)
■ 他们天不亮就出发了。 **Tāmen tiān bú liàng jiù chūfā le.** = *They set off before dawn.*
■ "我们明天什么时候出发？" "早上八点。" **"Wǒmen míngtiān shénme shíhou chūfā?" "Zǎoshang bā diǎn."** = *"When do we set off tomorrow?" "Eight o'clock in the morning."*

chūkǒu 出口 [v+obj: 出 *leave* + 口 *mouth, port*]
1 VERB = export (antonym 进口 **jìnkǒu**)
■ 这个国家出口大量工业品到世界各地。 **Zhège guójiā chūkǒu dàliàng gōngyèpǐn dào shìjiè gè dì.** = *This country exports large*

amounts of industrial products to various places in the world.
2 NOUN = exit
■ 这是停车场的出口，不能从这里进。 **Zhè shì tíngchēchǎng de chūkǒu, bù néng cóng zhèlǐ jìn.** = *This is the car park exit. You can't enter here.*
chūkǒu gōngsī 出口公司 = export company
chūkǒu màoyì 出口贸易 = export business in foreign trade

chūshēng 出生 [compound: 出 *come out* + 生 *be born*] VERB = be born
■ 他出生在1980年。 **Tā chūshēng zài yī-jiǔ-bā-líng nián.** = *He was born in 1980.*
■ 他于1980年出生在中国。 **Tā yú yī-jiǔ-bā-líng nián chūshēng zài Zhōngguó.** = *He was born in China in the year 1980.*
chūshēng dì 出生地 = place of birth
chūshēng rìqī 出生日期 = date of birth
chūshēng zhèng 出生证 = birth certificate

chūxí 出席 VERB = attend (a meeting, a court trial, etc.)
■ 你出席明天的会议吗？ **Nǐ chūxí míngtiān de huìyì ma?** = *Are you going to attend the meeting tomorrow?*

chūxiàn 出现 [compound: 出 *emerge* + 现 *appear*] VERB = come into view, appear, emerge
■ 开车两小时，一座漂亮的小山城出现在我们面前。 **Kāichē liǎng xiǎoshí, yí zuò piàoliang de xiǎo shānchéng chūxiàn zài wǒmen miànqián.** = *After two hours' drive, a beautiful small mountain town appeared before us.*
■ 最近社会上出现了一些奇怪的现象。 **Zuìjìn shèhuì shang chūxiànle yìxiē qíguài de xiànxiàng.** = *Unusual phenomena have emerged in society recently.*

chūyuàn 出院 VERB = be discharged from hospital
■ 医生，我什么时候可以出院？ **Yīshēng, wǒ shénme shíhou kěyǐ chūyuán?** = *When can I be discharged, doctor?*

chūzū 出租 [compound: 出 *out* + 租 *rent*] verb = have ... for hire, rent
■ 这家商店出租电视机。 **Zhè jiā shāngdiàn chūzū diànshìjī.** = *This store has TV sets for hire.*

chūzū qìchē 出租汽车 = taxi
- 我要一辆出租汽车去飞机场。**Wǒ yào yí liàng chūzū qìchē qù fēijīchǎng.** = *I want a taxi to go to the airport.*

NOTE: The slang expression 打的 **dǎdī**, which means *to call a taxi* or *to travel by taxi*, is very popular in everyday Chinese.

chū 初

1 NOUN = beginning
yuèchū 月初 = at the beginning of a month
niánchū 年初 = at the beginning of a year

2 ADJECTIVE = at the beginning, for the first time
- 我初来贵国，情况还不熟悉。**Wǒ chū lái guì guó, qíngkuàng hái bù shúxi.** = *I have just arrived in your country, and do not know much about it.*

3 PREFIX = (used for the first ten days of a lunar month), the first
- 初一 **chū yī** = *the first day (of a lunar month)*
- 五月初八 **Wǔyuè chū bā** = *the eighth day of the fifth lunar month*
- 年初一 / 大年初一 **nián chū yī / dà nián chū yī** = *the first day of the first lunar month (Chinese New Year's Day)*

chūbù 初步 [modif: 初 *initial* + 步 *step*]

ADJECTIVE = initial, tentative
- 这仅仅是我们的初步打算。**Zhè jǐnjǐn shì wǒmen de chūbù dǎsuàn.** = *This is but our tentative plan.*

chūjí 初级 [modif: 初 *initial* + 级 *grade*]

ADJECTIVE = elementary, initial
chūjí xiǎoxué 初级小学 / chūxiǎo 初小
= elementary school (from Grade 1 to Grade 4 of a primary school)
chūjí zhōngxué 初级中学 / chūzhōng 初中
= junior high school

chú 除 VERB = get rid of

chú cǎo 除草 = to weed
chú chóng 除虫 = to kill insects, insecticide

chúle ... (yǐwài) 除了 ... (以外) PREPOSI-

TION = except, besides
- 这个动物园除了圣诞节每天开放。**Zhège dòngwùyuán chúle shèngdànjié měi tiān kāifàng.** = *This zoo is open to the public all year round except on Christmas Day.*

- 我除了英文以外，还会说一点儿中文。**Wǒ chúle Yīngwén yǐwài, hái huì shuō yìdiǎnr Zhōngwén.** = *Besides English I speak a little Chinese.*

NOTES: (1) While *except* and *besides* are two distinct words in English, 除了 ... 以外 **chúle ... yǐwài** may mean either *except* or *besides*, as is shown in the examples. (2) 以外 **yǐwài** may be omitted, i.e. 除了 ... **chúle ... (yǐwài)** and 除了 ... **chúle** are the same.

chú 厨 NOUN = kitchen

chúfáng 厨房 [modif: 厨 *kitchen* + 房 *room*]

NOUN = kitchen
- 厨房又乱又脏，要收拾一下。**Chúfáng yòu luàn yòu zāng, yào shōushi yíxia.** = *The kitchen is dirty and messy. It needs tidying up.*
- 她在厨房里忙了好久了。**Tā zài chúfáng mángle hǎojiǔ le.** = *She has been busy working in the kitchen for a long time.*

chǔ 处 Trad 處 VERB = handle, deal with

chǔfèn 处分

1 VERB = take disciplinary action
- 处分这名学生 是为了教育全校所有的学生。**Chǔfèn zhè míng xuésheng shì wèile jiàoyù quán xiào suǒyǒu de xuésheng.** = *The purpose of taking disciplinary action against this student is to educate all the students of the school.*

2 NOUN = disciplinary action
- 十名官员因接受贵重礼物受到处分。**Shí míng guānyuán yīn jiēshòu guìzhòng lǐwù shòudào chǔfèn.** = *Disciplinary action was taken against ten officials who had accepted expensive gifts.*

chǔlǐ 处理 VERB = handle, deal with

- 对於顾客提出的意见，我们都会认真处理。**Duìyú gùkè tíchū de yìjiàn, wǒmen dōu huì rènzhēn chǔlǐ.** = *We deal with customers' complaints seriously.*
- 这种关系很难处理。**Zhè zhǒng guānxi hěn nán chǔlǐ.** = *This kind of relationship is difficult to handle.*

chǔ 础 Trad 礎 NOUN = plinth (See 基础 jīchǔ.)

chǔ 楚 ADJECTIVE = clear, neat (See 清楚 qīngchu.)

chù 处 Trad 處 NOUN = place, location
■ 你知道他现在的住处吗？ **Nǐ zhīdào tā xiànzài de zhùchù ma?** = *Do you know where he lives now?*

chù 触 Trad 觸 VERB = touch (See 接触 jiēchù.)

chuān 穿 VERB
1 = wear (clothes or shoes), be dressed in
■ 你穿黑衣服去参加中国人的婚礼，不合适。 **Nǐ chuān hēi yīfu qù cānjiā Zhōngguórén de hūnlǐ, bù héshì.** = *It is not appropriate for you go to a Chinese wedding in black.*
2 = put on (clothes or shoes)
■ 这个小孩会穿衣服了，可是还不会穿鞋子。 **Zhège xiǎohái huì chuān yīfu le, kěshì hái bú huì chuān xiézi.** = *This child can put on clothes, but still can't put on shoes.*
chuānzhe 穿着 = be dressed in
■ 那个穿着红衣服的女孩子是我哥哥的女朋友。 **Nàge chuānzhe hóng yīfu de nǚháizi shì wǒ gēge de nǚ péngyou.** = *The girl in red is my elder brother's girlfriend.*

chuán 船 NOUN = boat, ship
zuòchuán 坐船 = travel by boat/ship
■ 从香港坐船到上海去，只要两天。 **Cóng Xiānggǎng zuòchuán dào Shànghǎi qù, zhǐ yào liǎng tiān.** *It only takes two days to travel from Hong Kong to Shanghai by sea.*
huáchuán 划船 = row a boat

chuán 传 Trad 傳 VERB
1 = pass (something) on
■ 你看完这份文件后，请按照名单传给下一个人。 **Nǐ kàn wán zhè fèn wénjiàn hòu, qǐng ànzào míngdān chuán gěi xià yí ge rén.** = *After reading this document, please pass it on to the next person on the list.*
2 = spread (news, rumor)
■ 好事不出门，坏事传千里。 **Hǎo shì bù chūmén, huài shì chuán qiān lǐ.** = *Good news stays at home, but bad news travels far and wide.*

chuánbō 传播 [compound: 传 *spread* + 播 *sow*] VERB = propagate, disseminate
■ 学校不仅仅是传播知识的地方。 **Xuéxiào**

bù jǐnjǐn shì chuánbō zhīshi de dìfang. = *A school is more than a place to disseminate knowledge.*
■ 这种病传播得很快。 **Zhè zhǒng bìng chuánbō de hěn kuài.** = *This disease spreads fast.*

chuántǒng 传统 NOUN = tradition
■ 每个民族都有自己的传统。 **Měi ge mínzú dōu yǒu zìjǐ de chuántǒng.** = *Every ethnic group has its own traditions.*
■ 中医、武术、国画都是中国人的传统文化。 **Zhōngyī, wǔshù, guóhuà dōu shì Zhōngguórén de chuántǒng wénhuà.** = *Chinese medicine, martial arts and Chinese painting are all part of traditional Chinese culture.*

chuánzhēn 传真 [v+obj: 传 *transmit* + 真 *true*] NOUN = fax
■ 我的传真号码和电话号码是一样的。 **Wǒ de chuánzhēn hàomǎ hé diànhuà hàomǎ shì yíyàng de.** = *My fax number is the same as my telephone number.*
■ 我发了一份传真给他。 **Wǒ fāle yí fèn chuánzhēn gěi tā.** = *I sent him a fax.*

chuāng 窗 NOUN = window

chuānghu 窗户 [compound: 窗 *window* + 户 *door*] NOUN = window
■ 我房间的窗户朝东。 **Wǒ fángjiān de chuānghu cháo dōng.** = *The window in my room faces east.*
■ 马上要下雨了，把窗户关上吧。 **Mǎshang yào xià yǔ le, bǎ chuānghu guānshang ba.** = *It's going to rain soon. Let's close the window.*
dǎkāi chuānghu 打开窗户 = open a window
guānshang chuānghu 关上窗户 = close a window

chuáng 床 NOUN = bed (张 zhāng)
■ 这张床很舒服。 **Zhè zhāng chuáng hěn shūfu.** = *This bed is very comfortable.*
■ 这个房间很小，放了一张大床，就剩下不多地方了。 **Zhè ge fángjiān hěn xiǎo, fàngle yì zhāng dà chuáng, jiù shèngxia bù duō dìfang le.** = *This room is small. With a big bed in it, there is not much space left.*
dānrén chuáng 单人床 = single bed
shuāngrén chuáng 双人床 = double bed

chuàng 创 Trad 創 VERB = create

chuàngzào 创造 [compound: 创 *create* + 造 *build, make*] VERB = create
- 有人说神创造了天地。**Yǒurén shuō shén chuàngzàole tiān-dì.** = *Some people say God created the universe.*

chuàngzàoxìng 创造性 NOUN = creativity
- 创造性是艺术作品的生命。**Chuàngzàoxìng shì yìshù zuòpǐn de shēngmìng.** = *Creativity is the life of a work of art.*

chuàngzuò 创作 [compound: 创 *create* + 作 *make*]
1 VERB = create (works of art and literature)
- 这位作家创作了反映农民生活的小说。**Zhè wèi zuòjiā chuàngzuòle fǎnyìng nóngmín shēnghuó de xiǎoshuō.** = *This author wrote novels about peasant life.*
2 NOUN = work of art or literature
- 这位作家的新创作是中国文学的伟大成就。**Zhè wèi zuòjiā de xīn chuàngzuò shì Zhōngguó wénxué de wěidà chéngjiù.** = *This author's new work is a great achievement in Chinese literature.*

chuī 吹 VERB = blow, puff
- 风吹草动。**Fēng chuī cǎo dòng.** = *Winds blow and the grass stirs. (→ There are signs of disturbance/trouble.)*
chuīniú 吹牛 = brag, boast
- 你别相信他，他在吹牛。**Nǐ bié xiāngxìn tā, tā zài chuīniú.** = *Don't believe him. He's bragging.*

chūn 春 NOUN = spring

chūnjié 春节 [modif: 春 *spring* + 节 *festival*] NOUN = Spring Festival (the Chinese New Year)
- 春节是中国人最重要的节日。**Chūnjié shì Zhōngguórén zuì zhòngyào de jiérì.** = *The Spring Festival is the most important festival for the Chinese.*
- 小明的哥哥，姐姐都要回家过春节。**Xiǎo Míng de gēge, jiějie dōu yào huí jiā guò chūnjié.** = *Xiao Ming's elder brothers and sisters will be coming home for the Spring Festival.*

chūntiān 春天 [modif: 春 *spring* + 天 *days*] NOUN = spring
- 春天来了，花园里的花都开了。**Chūntiān lái le, huāyuán lǐ de huā dōu kāi le.** = *Spring has come. The flowers in the garden are in full bloom.*
- 我最喜欢春天，不太热，也不太冷。**Wǒ zuì xǐhuan chūntiān, bú tài lěng, yě bú tài rè.** = *I like spring the best; it's neither too hot nor too cold.*

cí 雌 ADJECTIVE = (of animals) female (antonym 雄 xióng)
- 我不知道家里的狗是雌的还是雄的。**Wǒ bù zhīdào jiāli de gǒu shì cí de háishì xióng de.** = *I don't know whether our family dog is female or male.*

cí 词 Trad 詞 NOUN = word
- 现代汉语的词一般是由两个字组成。**Xiàndài Hànyǔ de cí yìbān shì yǒu liǎng ge zì zǔchéng.** = *Modern Chinese words are generally comprised of two characters.*
- 我没有听说过这个词。**Wǒ méiyǒu tīngshuōguo zhè ge cí.** = *I haven't heard of this word.*

cídiǎn 词典 NOUN = dictionary (本 běn)
- 这本词典对我们很有帮助。**Zhè ben cídiǎn duì wǒmen hěn yǒu bāngzhù.** = *This dictionary is very helpful to us.*
- 你看，我买了一本新词典。**Nǐ kàn, wǒ mǎile yì běn xīn cídiǎn.** = *Look, I've bought a new dictionary.*
chá cídiǎn 查词典 See 查 chá.

cí 磁 NOUN = magnetism

cídài 磁带 [modif: 磁 *magnetic* + 带 *tape*] NOUN = magnetic tape, audio tape
- 这一盘磁带是我最喜欢的，几乎每天都听。**Zhè yì pán cídài shì wǒ zuì xǐhuan de, jīhu měi tiān dōu tīng.** = *This is my favourite tape. I listen to it almost every day.*

cǐ 此 PRONOUN
1 = this
- 此路不通。**Cǐ lù bù tōng.** = *This road is blocked. (→ No through road.)*
cǐshícǐdì 此时此地 = here and now
2 = here
- 会议到此结束。**Huìyì dào cǐ jiéshù.** = *The meeting ends here/at this point. (→ This is the end of the meeting.)*

cǐwài 此外 CONJUNCTION = besides, apart from (that), as well
■ 他买了一台新电脑，此外，还买了一些软件。**Tā mǎile yì tái xīn diànnǎo, cǐwài, hái mǎile yìxiē ruǎnjiàn.** = *He bought a new computer and some software as well.*

cì 次 MEASURE WORD = time (expressing frequency of an act)
■ 我去过他家两次。**Wǒ qùguo tā jiā liǎng cì.** = *I've been to his home twice.*
■ 这是我第一次出国旅行。**Zhè shì wǒ dì-yī cì chūguó lǚxíng.** = *This is my first trip abroad.*

cì 刺 VERB = prick
■ 花儿很美，但是会刺人。**Huār hěn měi, dànshì huì cì rén.** = *The flower is beautiful, but it may prick you.*

cōng 聪 Trad 聰 ADJECTIVE = acute hearing

cōngmíng 聪明 [compound: 聪 *acute hearing* + 明 *keen eyesight*] ADJECTIVE = clever, bright, intelligent
■ 他不但聪明，而且用功，所以考试总是第一名。**Tā búdàn cōngmíng, érqiě yònggōng, suǒyǐ kǎoshì zǒngshi dì-yī míng.** = *He is not only clever, but also hardworking, so he always comes out first in the exams.*

cóng 从 Trad 從 PREPOSITION = following, from
■ "你从哪里来？" "我从很远的地方来。" **"Nǐ cóng nǎlǐ lái?" "Wǒ cóng hěn yuǎn de dìfang lái."** = *"Where do you come from?" "I come from a faraway place."*
cóng...chūfā 从...出发 = set out from ...

cóngbù 从不 ADVERB = never
■ 我从不吸烟。**Wǒ cóngbù xīyān.** = *I never smoke.*

cóngcǐ 从此 CONJUNCTION = since then, from then on
■ 我上次跟他开玩笑，他竟生气了，从此我不跟他开玩笑了。**Wǒ shàng ci gēn tā kāi wánxiào, tā jìng shěngqì le, cóngcǐ wǒ bù gēn tā kāi wánxiào le.** = *He got angry when I joked with him the last time. Since then I have never joked with him.*

cóng ... dào... 从...到... PREPOSITION = from ... to ..., from ... till ...
■ 我从上午九点到下午三点都要上课。**Wǒ cóng shàngwǔ jiǔ diǎn dào xiàwǔ sān diǎn dōu yào shàngkè.** = *I've classes from nine o'clock in the morning till three o'clock in the afternoon.*
■ 从中国到英国要经过许多国家。**Cóng Zhōngguó dào Yīngguó yào jīngguò xǔduō guójiā.** = *Travelling from China to England, one has to pass through many countries.*
cóng-zǎo-dào-wǎn 从早到晚 = from morning till night, long hours in a day
■ 夏天他从早到晚都在农场工作。**Xiàtiān tā cóng-zǎo-dào-wǎn dōu zài nóngchǎng gōngzuò.** = *In summer he works on the farm from morning till night.*
cóng-gǔ-dào-jīn 从古到今 = from remote past till now in history
■ 从古到今，出现过多少英雄人物！**Cóng-gǔ-dào-jīn, chūxiàngguo duōshǎo yīngxióng rénwù!** = *From the remote past till now, history has produced so many heroes!*

cóng'ér 从而 CONJUNCTION = thus, thereby
■ 我要认真学好中文，从而了解中华文化。**Wǒ yào rènzhēn xué hǎo Zhōngwén, cóng'ér liǎojiě Zhōnghuá wénhuà.** = *I will study the Chinese language earnestly, thereby gaining an understanding of Chinese culture.*

cónglái 从来 ADVERB = always, ever
■ 有钱的越来越有钱，没钱的越来越没钱，从来如此。**Yǒuqiánde yuèláiyuè yǒu qián, méiqiánde yuèláiyuè méi qián, cónglái rúcǐ.** = *The rich get richer and the poor get poorer—it has always been this way.*
cónglái bù 从来不 = never
■ 我从来不喝酒。**Wǒ cónglái bù hē jiǔ.** = *I never drink wine.*

cóng ... qǐ 从 ... 起 PREPOSITION = starting from ...
■ 我决定从明年一月一日起每天早上跑步。**Wǒ juédìng cóng míngnián Yīyuè yīrì qǐ měi tiān zǎoshang pǎobù.** = *I've decided to jog every morning starting from January 1 next year.*

cóngqián 从前 NOUN
1 = past time, past, in the past
■ 我从前不知道学中文多么有意思。**Wǒ cóngqián bù zhīdào xué Zhōngwén duōme yǒu**

yìsi. = *I did not know how interesting it is to learn Chinese.*

2 = once upon a time (used in story-telling)

■ 从前有个农民，他… **Cóngqián, yǒu ge nóngmín, tā...** = *Once upon a time there was a farmer, who...*

cū 粗 ADJECTIVE = thick (antonym 细 **xì**)

■ 这根绳子太细了，要粗点儿的。**Zhè gēn shéngzi tài xì le, yào cū diǎnr de.** = *This rope is too thin. We need a thicker one.*

cù 促 VERB = urge

cùjìn 促进 [v+obj: 促 *promote* + 进 *progress*] VERB = promote, advance

■ 工会的目的是促进工人的利益。**Gōnghuì de mùdì shì cùjìn gōngrén de lìyì.** = *The purpose of the trade union is to advance workers' interests.*

■ 让我们为促进友谊努力。**Ràng wǒmen wèi cùjìn yǒuyí nǔlì.** = *Let's work hard to promote our friendship.*

cù 醋 NOUN = vinegar

■ 他喜欢吃酸的，什么东西都放醋。**Tā xǐhuan chī suān de, shénme dōngxi dōu fàng cù.** = *He is fond of sour flavours, and adds vinegar to whatever he eats.*

cuī 催 VERB = urge, hurry

■ 他催我还钱。**Tā cuī wǒ huán qián.** = *He urged me to pay him back.*

■ 别催她，时间还早。**Bié cuī tā, shíjiān hái zǎo.** = *Don't hurry her. There's enough time.*

cuì 脆 ADJECTIVE = crisp (See 干脆 **gāncuì**.)

cūn 村 NOUN = village

cūnzi 村子 [suffix: 村 *village* + 子 *nominal suffix*] NOUN = village (座 **zuò**)

■ 你们村子有多少户人家？**Nǐmen cūnzi yǒu duōshǎo hù rénjiā?** = *How many households are there in your village?*

cún 存 VERB = store, keep

■ 她一有钱就存在银行里。**Tā yì yǒu qián jiù cún zài yínháng lǐ.** = *As soon as she gets some money, she deposits it in the bank.*

■ 他出国前把一些东西存在姐姐家。**Tā chū guó qián bǎ yìxiē dōngxi cún zài jiějie jiā.** = *Before going abroad he stored some stuff at his sister's home.*

cúnzài 存在 VERB = exist

■ 这家公司存在严重问题。**Zhè jiā gōngsī cúnzài yánzhòng wèntí.** = *There are serious problems with this company.*

cùn 寸 MEASURE WORD = a traditional Chinese unit of length (equal to ⅓₀ meter)

yīngcùn 英寸 = inch

cuò 错 Trad 錯 ADJECTIVE = wrong (antonym 对 **duì**)

■ 我错了，我不应该那么做。**Wǒ cuò le, wǒ bù yīnggāi nàme zuò.** = *I was wrong. I shouldn't have done that.*

■ 你这个字写错了。**Nǐ zhège zì xiě cuò le.** = *You've written this character wrong.*

cuòzì 错字 = a wrong character

cuòwù 错误 [compound: 错 *wrong* + 误 *miss*]

1 NOUN = mistake, error

■ 你这次作业有很多错误。**Nǐ zhè cì zuòyè yǒu hěn duō cuòwù.** = *You've made many mistakes in this assignment.*

fàn cuòwù 犯错误 = make a mistake

■ 人人都会犯错误。**Rénrén dōu huì fàn cuòwù.** = *Everybody makes mistakes.*

jiūzhèng cuòwù 纠正错误 = correct a mistake

2 ADJECTIVE = wrong, erroneous

■ 这是一个错误的决定。**Zhè shì yí ge cuòwù de juédìng.** = *This is a wrong decision.*

cuò 措 VERB = arrange, handle

cuòshī 措施 NOUN = measure, step

■ 我们必须迅速采取有效措施。**Wǒmen bìxū xùnsù cǎiqǔ yǒuxiào cuòshī.** = *We must take immediate and effective measures.*

■ 由於措施不当，问题更加严重了。**Yóuyú cuòshī bú dàng, wèntí gèngjiā yánzhòng le.** = *Owing to inappropriate measures, the problem became even more serious.*

D

dā 答 VERB = answer

dāying 答应 [compound: 答 *reply* + 应
respond] VERB
1 = answer, reply
■ 我按了半天门铃，也没人答应。**Wǒ ànle
bàntiān ménlíng, yě méi rén dāying.** = *I pressed
the doorbell for a long time, but nobody
answered.*
2 = promise
■ 爸爸答应给他买一台笔记本电脑。**Bàba
dāying gěi tā mǎi yì tái bǐjìběn diànnǎo.** = *Father has promised to buy him a notebook
computer.*

dá 达 Trad 達 VERB = reach, attain

dádào 达到 [compound: 达 *reach* + 到 *reach*]
VERB = reach, achieve
■ 需要学几年才能达到一级汉语水平？
**Xūyào xué jǐ nián cái néng dádào yī jí Hànyǔ
shuǐpíng?** = *How many years do I have to study
to reach Level A of the Chinese proficiency
standard?*
■ 他的要求太高，很难达到。**Tā de yāoqiú tài
gāo, hěn nán dádào.** = *His demands are too
high. It is difficult to meet them.*
■ 不能为了达到目的，而不择手段。**Bù néng
wèile dádào mùdì, ér bù zé shǒuduàn.** = *One
shouldn't stop at nothing in order to achieve
one's aim. (→ The end doesn't always justify
the means.)*

dá 答 VERB = answer, reply
■ 这个问题我不会答。**Zhège wèntí wǒ bú huì
dá.** = *I can't answer this question.*

dá'àn 答案 [modif: 答 *anwer* + 案 *file*] NOUN =
answer (to a list of questions)
■ 测验以后，老师发给学生标准答案。**Cèyàn
yǐhòu, lǎoshī fā gei xuésheng biāozhǔn dá'àn.**
= *After the test, the teacher distributed stan-
dardized answers among students.*
■ 关于这个问题，还是没有答案。**Guānyú
zhège wèntí, háishì méiyǒu dá'àn.** = *There is
still no answer to this question.*

dǎ 打 VERB = strike, hit; play (certain games)
■ 不能打人。**Bù néng dǎ rén.** = *You can't hit
people*
dǎ qiú 打球 = play basketball/volleyball/netball
dǎ diànhuà 打电话 = make a telephone call

dǎbàn 打扮 VERB = dress up, make up
■ 新娘打扮得很漂亮。**Xīnniáng dǎbàn de hěn
piàoliang.** = *The bride was beautifully dressed*
■ 她每天要花很多时间打扮。**Tā měi tiān yào
huā hěn duō shíjiān dǎbàn.** = *Every day she
spends lots of time putting on makeup.*

dǎrǎo 打扰 VERB = disturb, interrupt
■ 爸爸在写一份重要的报告，你别去打扰
他。**Bàba zài xiě yí fèn zhòngyào de bàogào,
nǐ bié qù dǎrǎo tā.** = *Daddy is working on an
important report. Don't disturb him.*

NOTE: You can use 打搅 **dǎjiǎo** instead of 打
扰 **dǎrǎo**, with exactly same meaning. When
you call on someone, especially at their home,
you can say 打扰你们了 **Dǎrǎo nǐmen le** as a
polite expression.

dǎsǎo 打扫 VERB = clean up
■ 中国人在过春节前，要打扫屋子。
**Zhōngguórén zài guò chūnjié qián, yào dǎsǎo
wūzi.** = *Before the Spring Festival, Chinese
people clean up their houses.*

dǎsuàn 打算 [compound: 打 *act* + 算
calculate] VERB = plan, contemplate
■ 你打算毕业以后做什么？ **Nǐ dǎsuàn bìyè
yǐhòu zuò shénme?** = *What do you plan to do
after graduation?*
■ 我不打算买什么。**Wǒ bù dǎsuàn mǎi
shénme.** = *I don't intend to buy anything.*

dǎtīng 打听 VERB = inquire, ask
■ 您从北京大学来，我想跟您打听一位教
授。**Nín cóng Běijīng Dàxué lái. Wǒ xiǎng gēn
nín dǎtīng yí wèi jiàoshòu.** = *As you're from
Beijing University, I'd like to ask you about a
professor.*
■ 你到了那里打听一下就知道了。**Nǐ dàole
nàli dǎtīng yíxià jiù zhīdào le.** = *When you're
there, just make some inquiries and you'll find
out.*

dǎzhēn 打针 VERB = give (or get) an injection
- 病人每天要打针吃药。**Bìngrén měi tiān yào dǎzhēn chīyào.** = *The patient must get injections and take medicine every day.*

dǎzì 打字 VERB = type
- 他打字打得又快又好。**Tā dǎzì dǎ de yòu kuài yòu hǎo.** = *He types fast and well. (→ He has excellent keyboard skills.)*

dà 大 ADJECTIVE = big, large (antonym 小 **xiǎo**)
- 中国实在很大。**Zhōngguó shízài hěn dà.** = *China is indeed big.*
- 我爷爷种的树都长大了。**Wǒ yéye zhòng de shù dōu zhǎngdà le.** = *The trees that my grandfather planted have all matured.*

dà hòutiān 大后天 = three days from now
dà rénwù 大人物 = great personage, big shot, very important person (VIP)
dàshì 大事 = matter of importance

dàdǎn 大胆 [modif: 大 *big* + 胆 *gallbladder*]
ADJECTIVE = bold, courageous
- 你可以大胆地试验，失败了不要紧。**Nǐ kěyǐ dàdǎn de shìyàn, shībàile búyàojǐn.** = *You can experiment boldly. It doesn't matter if you fail.*

NOTE: The ancient Chinese believed that the gallbladder was the organ of courage—if one had a big gallbladder it meant that the person was endowed with courage and daring, and if one was timid it was because he had a small gallbladder. Therefore, 他胆子很大 **Tā dǎnzi hěn dà** and 他很大胆 **Tā hěn dàdǎn** means *He is bold*; 他胆子很小 **Tā dǎnzi hěn xiǎo** and 他很胆小 **Tā hěn dǎnxiǎo** means *He is timid.*

dàduō 大多 [modif: 大 *big* + 多 *many*] ADVEB = mostly
- 这个国家的人大多会说一点儿英文。**Zhège guójiā de rén dàduō huì shuō yìdiǎnr Yīngwén.** = *Most people in this country can speak a little English.*
- 商场里卖的衣服大多是中国制造的。**Shāngcháng li mài de yīfu dàduō shì Zhōngguó zhìzào de.** = *Most of the garments sold in shopping malls are made in China.*

dàduōshù 大多数 [modif: 大 *big* + 多数 *majority*] NOUN = great majority, overwhelming majority
- 大多数人支持新政府。**Dàduōshù rén zhīchí xīn zhèngfǔ.** = *Most of the people support the new government.*
- 大多数时间这位科学家都在实验室工作。**Dàduōshù shíjiān zhè wèi kēxuéjiā dōu zài shíyànshì gōngzuò.** = *Most of the time this scientist works in the lab.*

dàgài 大概
1 ADJECTIVE = general, more or less
- 他的话我没听清楚，但是大概的意思还是懂的。**Tā de huà wǒ méi tīng qīngchu, dànshì dàgài de yìsi háishì dǒng de.** = *I did not catch his words clearly, but I understood the general idea.*
2 ADVERB = probably
- 商店大概已经关门了，你明天去吧。**Shāngdiàn dàgài yǐjīng guānmén le, nǐ míngtiān qù ba.** = *The shop is probably closed. You should go tomorrow.*

dàhuì 大会 [modif: 大 *big* + 会 *meeting*] NOUN = assembly, congress, rally
- 全国人民代表大会每年三月在北京举行会议。**Quánguó Rénmín Dàibiǎo Dàhuì měi nián Sānyuè zài Běijīng jǔxíng huìyì.** = *The National People's Congress [of China] holds meetings in Beijing in March every year.*

dàhuǒr 大伙儿 PRONOUN = everybody, all the people
- 大伙儿都说他是个好小伙子。**Dàhuór dōu shuō tā shì ge hǎo xiǎohuǒzi.** = *Everybody says he is a good lad.*
- 我们大伙儿一条心，一定能把事办好。**Wǒmen dàhuǒr yìtiáoxīn, yídìng néng bǎ shì bàn hǎo.** = *All of us are united and we're sure to do a good job.*

NOTE: 大伙儿 **dàhuǒr** is a very colloquial word. For general use, 大家 **dàjiā** is preferred.

dàjiā 大家 PRONOUN = all, everybody
- 既然大家都赞成这个计划，那么就执行吧。**Jìrán dàjiā dōu zànchéng zhège jìhua, nàme jiù zhíxíng ba.** = *As everybody is for this plan, let's carry it out.*
- 请大家安静一下，我有一件重要的事跟大家说。**Qǐng dàjiā ānjìng yíxià, wǒ yǒu yí jiàn zhòngyào de shì gen dàjiā shuō.** = *Please be quiet, everybody. I've something important to say to you all.*

wǒmen dàjiā 我们大家 = all of us
nǐmen dàjiā 你们大家 = all of you
tāmen dàjiā 他们大家 = all of them
■ 我们大家都想去参观那个展览会。**Wǒmen dàjiā dōu xiǎng qù cānguān nàge zhǎnlǎnhuì.** = *We all want to visit that exhibition.*

dàjiē 大街 [modif: 大 *big* + 街 *street*] NOUN = main street
■ 大街两旁是大大小小的商店。**Dàjiē liǎng páng shì dà-dà-xiǎo-xiǎo de shāngdiàn.** = *On both sides of the street are stores big and small.*
guàng dàjiē 逛大街 = take a stroll in the streets, do window-shopping

dàliàng 大量 ADJECTIVE = a large amount of, a large number of
■ 每年夏季大量大学毕业生进入人才市场。**Měi nián xiàjì dàliàng dàxué bìyèshēng jìnrù réncái shìchǎng.** = *In summer every year, large numbers of graduates enter the labor market.*
■ 人们可以从英特网获取大量信息。**Rénmen kěyǐ cóng yīngtèwǎng huòqǔ dàliàng xìnxī.** = *People can obtain a great deal of information from the Internet.*

dàlù 大陆 [modif: 大 *big* + 陆 *land*] NOUN = continent, mainland
■ 亚洲大陆是世界上人口最多的地方。**Yàzhōu dàlù shì shìjiè shang rénkǒu zuì duō de dìfang.** = *The Asian continent is the most populated place in the world.*
Zhōngguó dàlù 中国大陆 = mainland China

dàmǐ 大米 [modif: 大 *big* + 米 *rice*] NOUN = rice
■ 日本每年消费大量大米。**Rìběn měi nián xiāofèi dàliàng dàmǐ.** = *Japan consumes a large quantity of rice every year.*

dàpī 大批 [modif: 大 *big* + 批 *batch*] ADJECTIVE = a large quantity of, lots of
■ 大批农民离开农村，到城市找工作。**Dàpī nóngmín líkāi nóngcūn, dào chéngshì zhǎo gōngzuò.** = *Large numbers of peasants leave their villages to seek jobs in cities.*

dàren 大人 [modif: 大 *big* + 人 *person*] NOUN = adult, grown-up (antonym 小孩儿 xiǎoháir)
■ 小孩儿都希望很快变成大人。**Xiǎoháir dōu xiǎng hěn kuài biànchéng dàren.** = *Children all hope to become adults very soon. (→All children hope to grow up quickly.)*
■ 你已经是大人了，怎么还和孩子一样？**Nǐ yǐjīng shì dàren le, zěnme hái hé háizi yíyàng?** = *You're a grown-up. How can you behave like a child?*
NOTE: 大人 **dàren** is a colloquialism. The general word for *adult* is 成年人 **chéngnián rén**.

dàshēng 大声 [modif: 大 *big* + 声 *sound, voice*] ADJECTIVE = in a loud voice
■ 请你大声点，我听不清。**Qǐng nǐ dàshēng diǎn, wǒ tīng bu qīng.** = *Speak up, please. I can hardly hear you.*

dàshǐguǎn 大使馆 [modif: 大 *big* + 使 *envoy* + 馆 *house*] NOUN = embassy
■ 你有英国大使馆的电话号码吗？**Nǐ yǒu Yīngguó dàshǐguǎn de diànhuà hàomǎ ma?** = *Do you have the telephone number of the British embassy?*
NOTE: 大使 **dàshǐ** means *ambassador*.

dàxiǎo 大小 [compound: 大 *big* + 小 *small*] NOUN = size
■ 你知道那间房间的大小吗？**Nǐ zhīdào nà jiān fángjiān de dàxiǎo ma?** = *Do you know the size of the room?*
NOTE: 大 **dà** and 小 **xiǎo** are opposites. Put together, 大小 **dàxiǎo** means *size*. There are other Chinese nouns made up of antonyms e.g. 高矮 **gāo'ǎi** = *height*, 长短 **chángduǎn** = *length*, 好坏 **hǎohuài** = *quality*.

dàxíng 大型 [modif: 大 *big* + 型 *model*] ADJECTIVE = large-scale, large-sized
■ 今年十月这个城市要举行一个大型汽车展览会。**Jīnnián Shíyuè zhège chéngshì yào jǔxíng yí ge dàxíng qìchē zhǎnlǎnhuì.** = *In October this year a large-scale auto show will be held in this city.*

dàxué 大学 [modif: 大 *big* + 学 *school*] NOUN = university (座 **zuò**, 所 **suǒ**)
■ 这座大学很有名。**Zhè zuò dàxué hěn**

D

yǒumíng. = *This university is well known.*
■ 你们国家有多少所大学？ **Nǐmen guójiā yǒu duōshǎo suǒ dàxué?** = *How many universities are there in your country?*
kǎo dàxué 考大学 = sit for the university entrance examination
■ 他在准备考大学。**Tā zài zhǔnbèi kǎo dàxué.** = *He's preparing for the university entrance examination.*
kǎo shàng dàxué 考上大学 = pass the university entrance examination
■ 我今年一定要考上大学。**Wǒ jīnnián yídìng yào kǎo shàng dàxué.** = *I'm determined to pass the university entrance examination this year.*
shàng dàxué 上大学 = go to university, study in a university

Dàyángzhōu 大洋洲 [modif: 大 *big* + 洋 *ocean* + 洲 *continent*] NOUN = Oceania
■ 新西兰在大洋洲。**Xīnxīlán zài Dàyángzhōu.** = *New Zealand is in Oceania.*

dàyī 大衣 [modif: 大 *big* + 衣 *clothes, coat*] NOUN = overcoat
■ 今天很冷，外出要穿大衣，戴帽子。**Jīntiān hěn lěng, wàichū yào chuān dàyī, dài màozi.** = *It's cold today. You need to wear an overcoat and a hat when going out.*

dàyuē 大约 ADVERB = approximate, approximately, about, nearly
■ 昨天下午大约四点钟有人给你打电话。**Zuótiān xiàwǔ dàyuē sì diǎnzhōng yǒu rén gěi nǐ dǎ diànhuà.** = *Someone telephoned you at about four o'clock yesterday afternoon.*

dāi 呆
1 ADJECTIVE = foolish, stupid
■ 她很呆，竟会相信这个广告。**Tā hěn dāi, jìng huì xiāngxìn zhège guǎnggào.** = *It is foolish of her to believe the commercial.*
2 VERB = same as 待 **dāi**

dāi 待 VERB = stay
■ 我这次来只待两三天。**Wǒ zhè cì lái zhǐ dāi liǎng-sān tiān.** = *For this visit I'll stay only a couple of days.*

NOTE: 待 **dāi** in the sense of *stay* may be replaced by 呆 **dāi**.

dàifu 大夫 NOUN = doctor (位 **wèi**) same as 医生 **yīshēng**, used more as a colloquialism.

dài 代 1 VERB = take the place of, perform on behalf of
■ 这件事你得亲自做，别人不能代你做。**Zhè jiàn shì nǐ děi qīnzì zuò, biérén bù néng dài nǐ zuò.** = *You must do it by yourself; nobody can do it on your behalf.*
dàikè lǎoshī 代课老师 = relief teacher
dài xiàozhǎng / dài bùzhǎng 代校长 / 代部长 = acting principal / acting minister

dài 代 2 NOUN
1 = generation
■ 李家在这个村子里住了好几代了。**Lǐ jiā zài zhège cūnzi li zhùle hǎo jǐ dài le.** = *The Lis have been living in this village for generations.*
2 = dynasty
■ 唐代中国是当时世界上最强大的国家。**Táng dài Zhōngguó shì dāngshí shìjiè shang zuì qiángdà de guójiā.** = *China in Tang Dynasty was the most powerful country in the world at that time.*

NOTE: The major Chinese dynasties are 秦 **Qín**, 汉 **Hàn**, 唐 **Táng**, 宋 **Sòng**, 元 **Yuán**, 明 **Míng**, 清 **Qīng**.

dàibiǎo 代表 [compound: 代 *substitute* + 表 *manifest*]
1 NOUN = representative
■ 工会代表拒绝了公司的方案。**Gōnghuì dàibiǎo jùjué le gōngsī de fāng'àn.** = *The trade union representative has rejected the company's proposal.*
■ 谁是你们的代表？ **Shuí shì nǐmen de dàibiǎo?** = *Who is your representative?*
2 VERB = represent, indicate
■ 这只是他个人的意见，不代表公司的立场。**Zhè zhǐ shì tā gèrén de yìjiàn, bú dàibiǎo gōngsī de lìchǎng.** = *This is only his personal opinion, which does not represent the view of the company.*

dàitì 代替 VERB = substitute for, replace, instead of
■ 这次家长会你爸爸妈妈一定要出席，不能请人代替。**Zhè cì jiāzhǎnghuì nǐ bàba māma yídìng yào chūxí, bù néng qǐng rén dàitì.** = *Your parents must attend this parents' meeting and nobody can go on their behalf.*

dài 带 Trad 帶 VERB = bring, take
- 出去旅游，别忘了带照相机。**Chūqù lǚyóu, bié wàngle dài zhàoxiàngjī.** = *Don't forget to bring along your camera when you go out sightseeing.*
- 明天上课的时候，把词典带来。**Míngtiān shàngkè de shíhou, bǎ cídiǎn dàilai.** = *Please bring your dictionary with you when you come to class tomorrow.*

dàilai/dài ... lái 带来 / 带 ... 来 = bring ...
dàiqu/dài ... qù 带去 / 带 ... 去 = take
- ...你不知道图书馆在哪儿？我带你去。**Nǐ bù zhīdào túshūguǎn zài nǎr? Wǒ dài nǐ qù.** = *You don't know where the library is? I'll take you there.*

dài 待 VERB = treat, deal with
- 他待朋友很热心。**Tā dài péngyou hěn rèxīn.** = *He is warmhearted in dealing with friends.*
- 人家怎么待我，我就怎么待人家。**Rénjiā zěnme dài wǒ, wǒ jiù zěnme dài rénjiā.** = *I treat people the way they treat me.*

dài 袋 NOUN = sack, bag
- 他带了一个大袋子来装书。**Tā dàile yí ge dà dàizi lái zhuāng shū.** = *He brought a big bag for books.*

kǒudài 口袋 = pocket

NOTE: 袋 **dài** is seldom used alone. It is either used with the nominal suffix 子 **zi** to form 袋子 **dài zi**, or with another noun to form a compound word, e.g. 口袋 **kǒudài** (*pocket*).

dài 戴 VERB = wear, put on
- 外面很冷，戴上帽子吧！**Wàimiàn hěn lěng, dàishang màozi ba!** = *It's cold outside. Do put on your cap.*

dài shǒutàor 戴手套儿 = wear gloves
dài yǎnjìng 戴眼镜 = wear spectacles

dān 单 Trad 單 ADJECTIVE = single, separate
- 他不习惯和别人合住，一定要单住一个房间。**Tā bù xíguàn hé biérén hé zhù, yídìng yào dān zhù yī ge fángjiān.** = *He is not used to sharing a room with another person and insists on having a room to himself.*

dānrén chuáng 单人床 = single bed
dānrén fángjiān 单人房间 = (hotel) room for a single person
dānshù 单数 = odd number

dāncí 单词 [modif: 单 *single* + 词 *word*] NOUN = word
- 光学单词用处不大，一定要把单词放在句子中学。= **Guāng xué dāncí yòngchu bú dà, yídìng yào bǎ dāncí fàng zài jùzi zhōng xué.** = *Learning words in insolation is not very useful. You must learn words in sentences.*

dānwèi 单位 NOUN = work unit, e.g. a factory, a school, a government department
- 你是哪个单位的？ **Nǐ shì nǎge dānwèi de?** = *Which work unit do you belong to?*

dān 担 Trad 擔 VERB = shoulder

dānrèn 担任 [compound: 担 *shoulder* + 任 *act as*] verb = assume the office of, act in the capacity of
- 今年谁担任我们的中文老师？ **Jīnián shuí dānrèn wǒmen de Zhōngwén lǎoshī?** = *Who'll be our Chinese teacher this year?*
- 政府邀请这位大学校长担任教育部长。**Zhèngfǔ yāoqǐng zhè wèi dàxué xiàozhǎng dānrèn jiàoyù bùzhǎng.** = *The government has invited this university president to be Minister of Education.*

dānxīn 担心 VERB = worry
- 他担心考试不及格。**Tā dānxīn kǎoshì bù jígé.** = *He is worried that he may fail the exam.*
- 我为爸爸的身体担心。**Wǒ wèi bàba de shēntǐ dānxīn.** = *I'm worried about daddy's health.*

dān 耽 VERB = delay

dānwù 耽误 [compound: 耽 *delay* + 误 *miss*] VERB = delay
- 你们没有按时交货，耽误了我们的生产。**Nǐmen méiyǒu ànshí jiāohuò, dānwùle wǒmen de shēngchǎn.** = *Your failure to deliver the goods on time has delayed our production.*
- 有病得马上看，不要耽误。**Yǒubìng děi mǎshàng kàn, búyào dānwù.** = *If you are sick you should go to see a doctor immediately. Don't delay.*

dǎn 胆 NOUN = gallbladder (See 大胆 **dàdǎn**.)

dàn 但 CONJUNCTION = same as 但是 **dànshì**. Used in writing.

dànshì 但是 CONJUNCTION = but, yet
- 这种产品价格很低，但是质量不好。**Zhè zhǒng chǎnpǐn jiàgé hěn dī, dànshì zhìliàng bù hǎo.** = *This product is cheap but is of low quality.*
- 虽然他星期天不上班，但是好象比哪一天都忙。**Suīrán tā Xīngqītiān bù shàngbān, dànshì hǎoxiàng bǐ nǎ yì tiān dōu máng.** = *He does not go to work on Sundays, but seems to be busier than any other day.*
- 这个女孩子长得很漂亮，但是大家都不喜欢她。**Zhège nǚ háizi zhǎng de hěn piàoliang, dànshì dàjiā dōu bù xǐhuan tā.** = *This girl is quite pretty, but nobody likes her.*

dàn 淡 ADJECTIVE
1 = not salty, tasteless, bland
- 汤太淡了，得放些盐。**Tāng tài dàn le, děi fàng xie yán.** = *The soup is tasteless. Put some salt in it.*
2 = weak (of tea, coffee) (antonym 浓 **nóng**)
- 茶淡一点儿好，我喝浓茶睡不着。**Chá dàn yìdiǎnr hǎo, wǒ hē nóngchá shuì bu zháo.** = *I prefer weak tea. I can't fall asleep after drinking strong tea.*

dàn 蛋 NOUN = egg (especially chicken egg)
- 他每天早上吃一个蛋。**Tā měi tiān zǎoshàng chī yí ge dàn.** = *He eats an egg every morning.*
- 鸡蛋营养丰富。**Jīdàn yíngyíng fēngfù.** = *Eggs are very nutritious.*

dàngāo 蛋糕 [modif: 蛋 *egg* + 糕 *cake*] NOUN = (western-style) cake
- 你饿吗？先吃点蛋糕当点心吧。**Nǐ è ma? Xiān chī diǎn dàngāo dàng diǎnxīn ba.** = *Are you hungry? Have some cake for a snack.*

dāng 当 Trad 當
1 PREPOSITION = at the time of, when
- 当他赶到火车站，火车已经开走了。**Dāng tā gǎndào huǒchēzhàn, huǒchē yǐjīng kāizǒu le.** = *When he hurried to the railway station, the train had already left.*
2 VERB = work as, serve as
- "你长大了想当什么？""我想当医生。" **"Nǐ zhǎngdàle xiǎng dāng shénme?" "Wǒ xiǎng dāng yīshēng."** = *"What do you want to be when you grow up?" "I'd like to be a doctor."*

dāng ... de shíhou 当 ... 的时候 CONJUNCTION = when ...
- 当我在工作的时候，不希望别人来打扰我。**Dāng wǒ zài gōngzuò de shíhou, bù xīwàng biérén lái dǎrǎo wǒ.** = *When I am working, I don't want to be disturbed.*
- 当我认识她的时候，她正在一家医院当护士。**Dāng wǒ rènshi tā de shíhou, tā zhèngzài yì jiā yīyuàn dāng hùshi.** = *When I came to know her, she was working as a nurse in a hospital.*

NOTE: 当 **dāng** may be omitted, especially colloquially, e.g. 我在工作的时候，不希望别人来打扰我。**Wǒ zài gōngzuò de shíhou, bù xīwàng biérén lái dá rǎo wǒ.**

dāngdì 当地 NOUN = at the place in question, local
- 他来自一个小城市，当地没有大学。**Tā láizi yí ge xiǎo chéngshì, dāngdì méiyǒu dàxué.** = *He came from a small city, where there was no university.*
dāngdì rén 当地人 = a local
dāngdì shíjiān 当地时间 = local time

dāngnián 当年 NOUN = in those years, then
- 想当年，亲戚朋友之间主要靠写信联系。哪有什么电子邮件？ **Xiǎng dāngnián, qīnqi péngyou zhī jiān zhǔyào kào xiě xìn liánxì. Nǎyǒu shénme diànzǐ yóujiàn?** = *In those years, relatives and friends relied on letter-writing to keep in touch with each other. How could there be e-mail? (→ There was no such thing as e-mail.)*

dāngqián 当前 NOUN = at present, now
- 王经理向我们介绍了当前市场情况。**Wáng jīnglǐ xiàng wǒmen jièshàole dāngqián shìchǎng qíngkuàng.** = *Mr Wang, the manager, briefed us on the current marketing situation.*

dāngrán 当然 ADJECTIVE = of course
- 他们受到这么热情的招待，当然很高兴。**Tāmen shòudào zhème rèqíng de zhāodài, dāngrán hěn gāoxìng.** = *They were of course delighted to be received so warmly.*
- "你到了北京别忘了给我发一份电子邮件。""那当然，忘不了。" **"Nǐ dàole Běijīng bié wàngle gěi wǒ fā yí fèn diànzǐ yóujiàn." "Nà dāngrán, wàng bu liǎo."** = *"Don't forget to*

*send me an e-mail when you arrive in Beijing."
"Of course, I won't forget."*

dāngshí 当时 NOUN = at that time, then
■ 当时我没有想到这一点。**Dāngshí wǒ
méiyǒu xiǎngdào zhè yìdiǎn.** = *At that time I
missed this point.*

dǎng 党 Trad 黨 NOUN = political party
■ 他不参加任何党。**Tā bù cānjiā rènhé dǎng.** =
He does not join any party.

NOTE: As China is under one-party rule, when
people mention 党 **dǎng** in China, it usually
refers to 中国共产党 **Zhōngguó Gòngchǎn
Dǎng** = *the Chinese Communist Party.*

dǎngyuán 党员 [modif: 党 *party* + 员
member] NOUN = party member
■ 在中国重要官员几乎都是中国共产党党
员。**Zài Zhōngguó zhòngyào guānyuán jīhū
dōu shì Zhōngguó Gòngchǎn Dǎng dǎngyuán.**
= *In China almost all important officials are
members of the Chinese Communist Party.*

dǎng 挡 VERB = block, keep off
■ 记者被挡在门外。**Jìzhě bèi dǎng zài
ménwài.** = *The reporters were barred from the
house.*

dàng 当 Trad 當 VERB
1 = treat as, regard as
■ 他非常节省，一块钱当两块钱用。**Tā
fēicháng jiéshěng, yí kuài qián dàng liǎng kuài
qián yòng.** = *He is very thrifty and wishes he
could make one dollar go twice as far.*
2 = think
■ 你中文说得这么好，我还当你是中国人
呢！**Nǐ Zhōngwén shuōde zhème hǎo, wǒ hái
dàng nǐ shì Zhōngguórén ne!** = *You speak Chinese so well that I thought you were a Chinese!*

dàngzuò 当做 VERB = treat as, regard as
■ 我一直把他当做好朋友。**Wǒ yìzhí bǎ tā
dàngzuò hǎo péngyou.** = *I always regard him
as a good friend.*

dāo 刀 NOUN = knife (把 **bǎ**)
■ "我可以借用一下你的刀吗？" "可以。"
"Wǒ kěyǐ jièyòng yíxià nǐ de dāo ma?" "Kěyǐ."
= *"May I use your knife?" "Yes."*

qiānbǐ dāo 铅笔刀 = pencil sharpener
shuǐguǒ dāo 水果刀 = penknife

dāozi 刀子 [suffix: 刀 *knife* + 子 nominal
suffix] NOUN = same as 刀 **dāo**

dǎo 导 Trad 導 VERB = lead, guide (See 辅导
fǔdǎo, 领导 **lǐngdǎo**, 指导 **zhǐdǎo**.)

dǎo 岛 Trad 島 NOUN = island
■ 新西兰有两个大岛：南岛和北岛。**Xīnxīlán
yǒu liǎng ge dà dǎo: nán dǎo hé běi dǎo.** = *New
Zealand has two big islands: South Island and
North Island.*

dǎo 倒 VERB = fall, topple
■ 风大极了，把很多树都刮倒了。**Fēng dà
jíle, bǎ hěn duō shù dōu guā dǎo le.** = *The
winds were so strong that many trees were
blown down.*

dào 到 VERB = arrive, come to; up to
■ 北京来的飞机什么时候到？**Běijīng lái de
fēijī shénme shíhou dào?** = *When will the flight
from Beijing arrive?*
■ 陈经理下个月要到香港去。**Chén jīnglǐ xià
ge yuè yào dào Xiānggǎng qù.** = *Mr Chen, the
manager, will go to Hong Kong next month.*
■ 我们已经学到第十八课了。**Wǒmen yǐjīng
xué dào dì-shíbā kè le.** = *We've studied up to
Lesson 18.*

dàochù 到处 ADVERB = everywhere
■ 坏人到处都有，好人也到处都有。**Huàirén
dàochù dōu yǒu, hǎorén yě dàochù dōu yǒu.**
= *There are villains everywhere but there are
good people everywhere, too.*
■ 王老师家里到处都是书。**Wáng lǎoshī jiā li
dàochù dōu shì shū.** = *There are books everywhere in Teacher Wang's home.*
■ 他到处游览名胜古迹。**Tā dàochù yóulǎn
míngshèng gǔjì.** = *He visits well-known scenic
spots and historical sites everywhere.*

NOTE: 到处 **dàochù** is always placed before a
verb phrase, and is often followed by 都 **dōu**.

dàodá 到达 [compound: 到 *get to* + 达 *reach*]
VERB = arrive, reach
■ 张部长乘坐的飞机将在晚上六点三刻到达
北京机场。**Zhāng bùzhǎng chéngzuò de fēijī**

jiāng zài wǎnshang liù diǎn sān kè dàodá Běijīng jīchǎng. = *The airplane Minister Zhang is travelling in will arrive at Beijing Airport at a 6:45.*

dàodǐ 到底 [v+obj: 到 *get to* + 底 *bottom*]
ADVERB
1 = in the end, finally
■ 她到底还是找到了理想的丈夫。**Tā dàodǐ háishì zhǎodàole lǐxiǎng de zhàngfu.** = *Finally she found her ideal husband.*
2 = after all (used in a question)
■ 你到底去不去啊？ **Nǐ dàodǐ qù bu qù a?** = *Are you going or not?*
■ 他到底想要什么？ **Tā dàodǐ xiǎng yào shénme?** = *What does he want after all?*

dào 倒
1 VERB = put upside down
■ 他把画挂倒了。**Tā bǎ huà guà dào le.** = *He hung the picture upside down.*
2 VERB = pour (water), make (tea)
■ 她给客人倒了一杯水。**Tā gěi kèrén dàole yì bēi shuǐ.** = *She gave the visitor a glass of water.*
3 ADVERB = contrary to what may be expected (used before a verb or adjective to indicate an unexpected action or state)
■ 弟弟倒比哥哥高。**Dìdi dào bǐ gēge gāo.** = *The younger brother is unexpectedly taller than his elder brother.*
■ 用了电脑人们倒好象更忙了。**Yòngle diànnǎo rénmen dào hǎoxiàng gèng máng le.** = *With the use of computer people seem to be busier.*

dào 盗 NOUN = robber, bandit (See 强盗 **qiángdào.**)

dào 道 1 VERB = same as 说 **shuō**, used only in old-fashioned writing

dào 道 2 MEASURE WORD
1 = (for things in the shape of a line)
■ 一道光线 **yí dào guāngxiàn** = *a ray of sunshine*
2 = (for questions in a school exercises, examinations, etc.)
■ 两道难题 **liǎng dào nántí** = *two difficult questions*

dàodé 道德 [modif: 道 *the way* + 德 *virtue*]
NOUN = moral, ethics
■ 赚钱也要讲道德。**Zhuànqián yě yào jiǎng dàodé.** = *When making money you should also pay attention to ethics.*
bú dàodé 不道德 = immoral
■ 这样做是不道德的。**Zhèyàng zuò shì bú dàodé de.** = *Such conduct is immoral.*

dàolǐ 道理 [compound: 道 *way, principle* + 理 *pattern, reason*] NOUN = principle, reason, hows and whys
■ 这个道理人人都懂。**Zhège dàolǐ rénrén dōu dǒng.** = *Everybody understands this principle.* (→ *Everybody understands why this is true/correct.*)
jiǎng dàolǐ 讲道理 = (of a person) reasonable
■ 他这个人很不讲道理。**Tā zhège rén hěn bù jiǎng dàolǐ.** = *This man is very unreasonable.*
yǒu dàolǐ 有道理 = reasonable, true
■ 你说的话很有道理。**Nǐ shuō de huà hěn yǒu dàolǐ.** = *What you said is reasonable/true.*
■ 他说得很好听，其实没有什么道理。**Tā shuō de hěn hǎotīng, qíshí méiyǒu shénme dàolǐ.** = *He mouthed fine words but was not quite right.*

NOTE: 道 **dào** and 理 **lǐ** are two important concepts in Chinese thought. The original meaning of 道 **dào** is *path, way*. By extension it denotes "the fundamental principle of the universe." 理 **lǐ** originally meant *the grain of a piece of jade* and came to mean "the underlying logic of things."

dàolù 道路 [compound: 道 *way* + 路 *road*]
NOUN = road, path
■ 盖房子以前，先要修道路。**Gài fángzi yǐqián, xiān yào xiū dàolù.** = *Before putting up houses, roads must be built.*
■ 车辆把前面的道路堵住了。**Chēliàng bǎ qiánmiàn de dàolù dǔzhù le.** = *Traffic has blocked the road ahead.*

dàoqiàn 道歉 [v+obj: 道 *say* + 歉 *apology*]
NOUN = apologize, say sorry
■ 你应该向他们道歉。**Nǐ yīnggāi xiàng tāmen dàoqiàn.** = *You should apologize to them.*

dào 稻 NOUN = rice, paddy (See 水稻 **shuǐdào.**)

dé 得 VERB = get, obtain
■ 她去年英文考试得了A。 **Tā qùnián Yīngwén kǎoshì déle A.** = She got A for the English examination last year.

dédào 得到 = succeed in getting/obtaining
■ 他得到一个去中国学汉语的机会。 **Tā dédào yí ge qù Zhōngguó xué Hànyǔ de jīhuì.** = He got a chance to go to China to study Chinese.
■ 我得到他们很大帮助。 **Wǒ dédào tāmen hěn dà bāngzhù.** = I was greatly helped by them.

NOTE: The verb 得 **dé** is seldom used alone. It is often followed by 到 **dào**, grammatically a complement, to mean get or obtain.

dé 德 Trad 德 NOUN = virtue

Déguó 德国 NOUN = Germany

Déwén 德文 NOUN = the German language (especially the writing)

Déyǔ 德语 NOUN = the German language

de 地 PARTICLE = (attached to a word or phrase to indicate that it is an adverbial. 地 **de** is normally followed by a verb or an adjective.)
■ 慢慢地说 **mànman de shuō** = speak slowly
■ 愉快地旅行 **yúkuài de lǚxíng** = travel pleasantly

NOTE: See note on 的 **de**.

de 得 PARTICLE = (introducing a word, phrase or clause to indicate that it is a complement. 得 **de** is normally preceded by a verb or an adjective.)
■ 来得很早 **lái de hěn zǎo** = come early
■ 说得大家都笑了起来 **shuò de dàjiā dōu xiàole qǐlái** = talk in such a way that everybody starts laughing
■ 贵得很 **guì de hěn** = very expensive

NOTE: See note on 的 **de**.

de 的 PARTICLE = (attached to a word or phrase to indicate that it is an attribute. 的 **de** is normally followed by a noun.)
■ 我的电脑 **Wǒ de diànnǎo** = my computer
■ 最新型的电脑 **zuì xīnxíng de diànnǎo** = the latest model computer
■ 学校刚买来的电脑 **xuéxiào gāng mǎilai de diànnǎo** = the computer that the school just bought

NOTE: 的, 得, 地 have different functions and are three distinct words. However, as they are pronounced the same (**de**) in everyday speech, some Chinese speakers do not distinguish them.

... de huà ... 的话 CONJUNCTION = if
■ 明天下雨的话，就改期举行。 **Míngtiān xià yǔ de huà, jiù gǎiqī jǔxíng.** = If it rains tomorrow, we'll change the date for the meeting.

NOTE: See note on 要是 **yàoshì**.

děi 得 MODAL VERB = have to, has to
■ 时间不早了，我们得走了。 **Shíjiān bù zǎo le, wǒmen děi zǒu le.** = It's quite late. We've got to go.
■ 这件事怎么办，我们还得想个办法。 **Zhè jiàn shì zěnme bàn, wǒmen děi xiǎng ge bànfǎ.** = We've got to find a way of dealing with this matter.

dēng 灯 Trad 燈 NOUN = lamp, lighting
■ 这个房间的灯坏了。 **Zhège fángjiān de dēng huài le.** = The light in this room is out of order.
■ 最后一个离开办公室的人，别忘了关灯。 **Zuìhòu yī ge líkāi bàngōngshì de rén, bié wàngle guān dēng.** = The last one to leave the office, please turn off the light.
diàndēng 电灯 = light, electric light
guān dēng 关灯 = turn off the light
kāi dēng 开灯 = turn on the light
rìguāngdēng 日光灯 = fluorescent lamp
táidēng 台灯 = desk lamp

dēng 登 VERB = publish (in a newspaper, a journal, etc.)
■ 今天各大报纸都登了这条新闻。 **Jīntiān gè dà bàozhǐ dōu dēngle zhè tiáo xīnwén.** = This news is published in all the major newspapers today.

dēngjì 登记 VERB = register, check in
■ 在旅馆里住，都要登记。 **Zài lǚguǎn li zhù, dōu yào dēngjì.** = To stay in a hotel, one has to register.

děng 等 1 VERB = wait, wait for
- 她在等一个重要的电话。**Tā zài děng yí ge zhòngyào de diànhuà.** = *She is waiting for an important telephone call.*
- 我昨天等你等了半小时。**Wǒ zuótiān děng nǐ děngle bàn xiǎoshí.** = *I waited for you for half an hour yesterday.*

děng yíxià 等一下 = wait a minute
- 等一下，我马上就来。**Děng yíxià, wǒ mǎshang jiù lái.** = *Wait a minute, I'll come soon.*

děng 等 2 NOUN = grade, rank, class
- 我们商店只卖一等品。**Wǒmen shāngdiàn zhǐ mài yī-děng pǐn.** = *Our store sells first class goods only. (→ We sell only the best here.)*

děng 等 3 PARTICLE
1 = and so on and so forth, et cetera
- 我们在中国参观了北京、上海、西安等地。**Wǒmen zài Zhōngguó cānguānle Běijīng, Shànghǎi, Xī'ān děng dì.** = *In China we visited Beijing, Shanghai, Xi'an and other places.*
2 = (used at the end of an enumeration)
- 我们在中国游览了北京、上海、西安等三个大城市。**Wǒmen zài Zhōngguó yóulǎn le Běijīng, Shànghǎi, Xī'ān déng sānge dà chéngshì.** = *We toured the three major cities of Beijing, Shanghai and Xi'an.*

děngdài 等待 [compound: 等 wait + 待 await, anticipate] VERB = wait (usually used in writing)
- 你不能总是等待机会，要主动寻找机会。**Nǐ bù néng zǒngshì děngdài jīhuì, yào zhǔdòng xúnzhǎo jīhuì.** = *You mustn't always wait for an opportunity; you should proactively search for it.*

děngyú 等于 VERB = be equal to, equal
- 一加二等于三。**Yī jiā èr děngyú sān.** = *One plus two equals three.*

dī 低
1 ADJECTIVE = low (antonym 高 **gāo**)
- 这把椅子太低了，坐着不舒服。**Zhè ba yǐzi tài dī le, zuòzhe bù shūfu.** = *This chair is too low, it's uncomfortable to sit in.*
- 她说话声音很低，你得仔细听才行。**Tā shuōhuà shēngyīn hěn dī, nǐ děi zǐxì tīng cái xíng.** = *She speaks in a low voice. You've got to listen attentively.*

2 VERB = lower
- 他低着头，离开校长办公室。**Tā dīzhe tóu, líkāi xiàozhǎng bàngōngshì.** = *He left the principle's office with his head hung low.*

dī 滴 MEASURE WORD = drop (used with liquids)
- 节约每一滴水。**Jiéyuē měi yì dī shuǐ.** = *Save every drop of water.*

díquè 的确 ADVERB = really, truly
- 这个名胜的确美丽。**Zhège míngshèng díquè měilì.** = *This well-known scenic spot is truly beautiful.*

dí 敌 Trad 敵 NOUN = enemy

dírén 敌人 [modif: 敌 enemy + 人 person, people] NOUN = enemy
- 我想我在公司里没有敌人。**Wǒ xiǎng wǒ zài gōngsī li méiyǒu dírén.** = *I don't think I have any enemies in the company.*
- 吸烟是健康的敌人。**Xīyān shì jiànkāng de dírén.** = *Smoking is an enemy of health.*

dǐ 底 NOUN = base, bottom

dǐxia 底下 [compound: 底 bottom + 下 under] NOUN = underneath, under
- 床底下有一双拖鞋。**Zhuáng dǐxia yǒu yì shuāng tuōxié.** = *There's a pair of slippers under the bed.*
- 孩子躲在桌子底下。**Háizi duǒ zài zhuōzi dǐxia.** = *The child hid under the table.*

dì 地 NOUN = earth, ground

dìdiǎn 地点 [compound: 地 place + 点 point] NOUN = the place of an event or activity, venue
- 会议的地点还没有定。**Huìyì de dìdiǎn hái méiyǒu dìng.** = *The venue of the meeting has not been decided on.*
- 展览会的时间和地点决定以后，我会立即通知你。**Zhǎnlǎnhuì de shíjiān hé dìdiǎn juédìng yǐhòu, wǒ huì lìjì tōngzhī nǐ.** = *After the time and venue of the exhibition are decided on, I will inform you immediately.*

dìfang 地方 [compound: 地 earth + 方 place] NOUN
1 = place, location, area (个 ge)
- 你住在什么地方？**Nǐ zhù zài shénme**

dìfang? = *Where do you live?*
- 他们正在找开会的地方。**Tāmen zhèngzài zhǎo kāihuì de dìfang.** = *They're looking for a venue for their conference.*

2 = part of, aspect
- 这本书我有些地方不大明白。**Zhè ben shū wǒ yǒuxie dìfang búdà míngbai.** = *I'm not quite clear about parts of the book.*

NOTE: 地方 **dìfang** is a word of wide application. It has both concrete, specific senses and abstract, general senses, as in the following examples:
- 医生: 你什么地方不舒服? **Yīshēng: Nǐ shénme dìfang bù shūfu?** = *Doctor: What spot ails you? (→ What's wrong with you?)*
- 照顾不到的地方，请多多原谅。**Zhàogù búdào de dìfang, qǐng duōduō yuánliàng.** = *If there's anything not well attended to, please accept my sincere apology.*

dìmiàn 地面 NOUN = the earth's surface
- 这里的地面比海平面高出二百公尺。**Zhèli de dìmiàn bǐ hǎipíngmiàn gāochū èrbǎi gōngchǐ.** = *The ground here is 200 meters above sea level.*

dìqiú 地球 [modif: 地 *ground* + 球 *ball*] NOUN = the earth
- 人类只有一个家园－地球。**Rénlèi zhǐ yǒu yí ge jiāyuán – dìqiú.** = *Mankind has only one home—the earth.*

dìqū 地区 [modif: 地 *place* + 区 *region*] NOUN = region, area
- 这个国家东部地区比西部地区发达。**Zhège guójiā dōngbù dìqū bǐ xībù dìqū fādá.** = *In this country, the eastern regions are more developed than the western regions.*

dìtú 地图 NOUN = map (张 **zhāng**)
- 这张地图太旧了，没多大用处。**Zhè zhāng dìtú tài jiù le, méi duō dà yòngchu.** = *This map is too old and is not of much use.*
dìtú cè 地图册 = atlas

dìwèi 地位 [compound: 地 *place* + 位 *seat*] NOUN = status, position
- 他在公司里有很高的地位。**Tā zài gōngsī li yǒu hěn gāo de dìwèi.** = *He holds a high position in the company.*

dìxià 地下 [modif: 地 *ground* + 下 *under*] NOUN = underground
dìxià shāngchǎng 地下商场 = underground shopping center
dìxià tiělù (dìtiě) 地下铁路 (地铁) = underground railway, subway
dìxià tíngchēchǎng 地下停车场 = underground car park

dìzhǐ 地址 NOUN = address
- 这是我的地址和电话号码，请你记一下。**Zhè shi wǒ de dìzhǐ he diànhuà hàomǎ, qǐng nǐ jì yíxia.** = *Here are my address and telephone number. Please write them down.*

dì 弟 NOUN = younger brother

dìdi 弟弟 NOUN = younger brother
- 我弟弟比我小两岁。**Wǒ dìdi bǐ wǒ xiǎo liǎng suì.** = *My younger brother is two years younger than me.*
- "你有没有弟弟?""没有，我只有一个哥哥。" **"Nǐ yǒu méiyǒu dìdi?" "Méiyǒu, wǒ zhǐ yǒu yī ge gēge."** = *"Do you have a younger brother?" "No, I only have an older brother."*
- 她弟弟还在念小学。**Tā dìdi hái zài niàn xiǎoxué.** = *Her younger brother is still studying in a primary school.*

dì 帝 NOUN = the Supreme Being (See 皇帝 **huángdì**.)

dì 递 Trad 遞 VERB = hand over, pass on
- 请你把那本词典递给我。**Qǐng nǐ bǎ nà běn cídiǎn dì gei wǒ.** = *Please pass me that dictionary.*

dì 第 PREFIX = (used before a number to form an ordinal numeral)
- 第一 **dì-yī** = *the first*
- 第一天 **dì-yī tiān** = *the first day*
- 第十 **dì-shí** = *the tenth*
- 第十课 **dì-shí kè** = *the tenth lesson, Lesson 10*

diǎn 点 Trad 點
1 NOUN = drop, point, dot
- 雨点打在窗户上。**Yǔdiǎn dǎ zài chuānghu shang.** = *Raindrops beat on the windowpane.*
- "点" 字下面有四点。**"Diǎn" zì xiàmian yǒu sì diǎn.** = *There're four dots at the bottom of the character 点.*

D

mò diǎn 墨点 = ink stain
shuǐ diǎn 水点 = water stain
2 NOUN = (indicating decimal)
■ 三点四 **sān diǎn sì** = 3.4 (three point four)
■ 十二点三五 **shí'èr diǎn sān wǔ** = 12.35 (twelve point three five)
3 VERB = drip, put a dot, touch
■ 你给我点眼药水，行吗？ **Nǐ gěi wǒ diǎn yǎnyàoshuǐ, xíng ma?** = Could you please put my eye drops in for me?
4 MEASURE WORD = a little, a bit
■ 他喜欢在睡觉前喝一点儿酒。 **Tā yǐhuan zài shuìjiào qián hē yìdiǎnr jiǔ.** = He likes to drink a little wine before going to bed.
■ 我去商店买一点儿东西，很快就回来。 **Wǒ qù shāngdiàn mǎi yìdiǎnr dōngxi, hěn kuài jiù huílai.** = I'll go to the store to do a little shopping and will be back soon.
5 MEASURE WORD = o'clock
■ "现在几点？""三点正。" **"Xiànzài jídiǎn?" "Sān diǎn zhèng."** = "What time is it?" "Three o'clock sharp."
■ 现在才八点一刻，还早呢。 **Xiànzài cái bā diǎn yí kè, hái zǎo ne.** = It's only a quarter past eight. It's still early.
yǒu (yì) diǎnr… 有(一)点儿… = a bit…, a little… (used before noun and adjective)
■ 我有一点儿累，想休息一会儿。 **Wǒ yǒu yìdiǎnr lèi, xiǎng xiūxi yíhuìr.** = I'm a bit tired. I want to take a little break.

diǎnxīn 点心 NOUN = snack, light refreshments
■ 有点儿饿了吧？ 吃一点儿点心吧。 **Yǒu diǎnr è le ba? Chī yìdiǎnr diǎnxīn ba.** = Aren't you a bit hungry? Have a snack!

NOTE: The Cantonese pronunciation of 点心 is "dim sum." Many Chinese restaurants overseas sell Cantonese-style refreshments or snack known as "dim sum." To have such refreshments for a meal is "yum cha," Cantonese pronunciation of 饮茶 **yìnchá**, which literally means drink tea.

diǎnzhōng 点钟 NOUN = o'clock
■ "现在几点钟？""三点钟。" **"Xiànzài jí diǎnzhōng?" "Sān diǎnzhōng."** = "What time is it?" "Three o'clock."
■ 我每天十点钟睡觉，七点钟起床。 **Wǒ měi tiān shí diǎnzhōng shuìjiào, qī diǎnzhōng qǐchuáng.** = Every day, I go to bed at ten o'clock and get up at seven o'clock.

NOTE: In colloquial Chinese 点钟 **diǎnzhōng** can be shortened to 点 **diǎn**, e.g.:
■ "现在几点？""三点。" **"Xiànzài jí diǎnzhōng?" "Sān diǎnzhōng."** = "What time is it?" "Three o'clock."

diǎn 典 NOUN = standard, law (See 词典 **cídiǎn**.)

diàn 电 Trad 電 NOUN = electricity, power; electronics
■ 我们这里电比较便宜。 **Wǒmen zhèli diàn bǐjiào piányi.** = Power is rather cheap here.
■ 今天停电。 **Jīntiān tíng diàn.** = No power today. (→ There's a blackout/power failure today.)
■ 整个地区停电。 **Zhěng ge dìqū tíng diàn.** = There is a blackout in the entire region.

diànbào 电报 [modif: 电 electric + 报 report] NOUN = telegram, cable (份 **fèn**)
■ 现在还有人打电报吗？ **Xiànzài háiyǒu rén dǎ diànbào ma?** = Do people still send telegrams?

diànchē 电车 [modif: 电 electricity + 车 vehicle] NOUN = trolley bus, streetcar (辆 **liàng**)
■ 这辆电车去哪儿？ **Zhè liàng diànchē qù nǎr?** = Where does this trolley bus go?
■ 他每天坐电车上班。 **Tā měi tiān zuò diànchē shàngbān.** = He goes to work by trolley bus every day.

diàndēng 电灯 [modif: 电 electricity + 灯 lamp] NOUN = electric light (个 **ge**)
■ 这个房间的电灯坏了。 **Zhège fángjiān de diàndēng huài le.** = The lights in this room are out of order.
■ 你会装电灯吗？ **Nǐ huì zhuāng diàndēng ma?** = Do you know how to install an electric light?
kāi diàndēng 开电灯 = turn on the light
guān diàndēng 关电灯 = turn off the light

diànhuà 电话 [modif: 电 electricity + 话 speech] NOUN = telephone, telephone call (个 **ge**)
■ "电话在哪里？""在桌子上。" **"Diànhuà zài nǎli?" "Zài zhuōzi shang."** = "Where's the telephone?" "It's on the table."
■ "我可以用一下你的电话吗？""当然可以。" **"Wǒ kěyǐ yòng yíxia nǐ de diànhuà ma?"**

"Dāngrán kěyǐ." = *"May I use your telephone?" "Sure."*

dǎ diànhuà 打电话 = use the telephone, be on the phone

■ 王先生在打电话。**Wáng xiānsheng zài dǎ diànhuà.** = *Mr Wang is on the phone.*

gěi ... dǎ diànhuà 给 ... 打电话 = call ... on the telephone, ring ...

■ "你常常给你妈妈打电话吗?""常常打。" **"Nǐ chángcháng gěi nǐ māma dǎ diànhuà ma?" "Chángcháng dǎ."** = *"Do you often ring your mother?" "Yes."*

tīng diànhuà 听电话 = answer a telephone call

■ 李小姐，请你听电话。**Lǐ xiǎojiǎ, qǐng nǐ tīng diànhuà.** = *Miss Li, you're wanted on the phone.*

diànnǎo 电脑 [modif: 电 *electricity* + 脑 *brain*] NOUN = computer (台 **tái**)

■ 我会用电脑写汉字。**Wǒ huì yòng diànnǎo xiě Hànzì.** = *I can write Chinese characters on a computer.*

■ 这个机器是由电脑控制的。**Zhège jīqì shì yóu diànnǎo kòngzhì de.** = *This machine is controlled by a computer.*

diànshàn 电扇 [modif: 电 *electricity* + 扇 *fan*] NOUN = electric fan

■ 夜里热极了，我得开着电扇睡觉。**Yèli rè jíle, wǒ děi kāizhe diànshàn shuìjiào.** = *It's so hot at night that I have to sleep with the electric fan on.*

diànshì 电视 [modif: 电 *electricity* + 视 *view*] NOUN = television

■ "今天晚上的电视有没有好节目?""没有。" **"Jīntiān wǎnshang de diànshì yǒu méiyǒu hǎo jiémù?" "Méiyǒu."** = *"Are there any good programs on TV tonight?" "No."*

kàn diànshì 看电视 = watch TV

■ 我很少看电视。**Wǒ hěn shǎo kàn diànshì.** = *I seldom watch TV.*

diànshì jī 电视机 = TV set

diànshì tái 电视台 = TV station

diàntái 电台 [modif: 电 *electricity* + 台 *station*] NOUN = radio station

■ 我常常听这个电台。**Wǒ chángcháng tīng zhège diàntái.** = *I often listen to this radio station.*

diàntī 电梯 [modif: 电 *electricity* + 梯 *stairs*] NOUN = elevator, lift

■ 大楼着火的时候，千万不能用电梯。**Dàlóu zháohuǒ de shíhou, qiānwàn bù néng yòng diàntī.** = *Do not use the elevator when there is a fire in the building.*

chéng diàntī 乘电梯 = go up/down by elevator

diànyǐng 电影 [modif: 电 *electricity* + 影 *shadow*] NOUN = film, movie (场 **chǎng**, 个 **ge**)

■ 我昨天看的电影很有意思。**Wǒ zuótiān kàn de diànyǐng hěn yǒu yìsi.** = *The film I saw yesterday was very interesting.*

kàn diànyǐng 看电影 = see a film, go to the movies

■ 他常常和女朋友一起看电影。**Tā chángcháng hé nǚpéngyou yìqǐ kàn diànyàng.** = *He often goes to the movies with his girlfriend.*

diànyǐng piào 电影票 = film ticket

diànyǐngyuàn 电影院 [modif: 电影 *film, movie* + 院 *place* (for certain activities)] NOUN = cinema, cinema complex, movie theater (座 **zuò**)

■ 这座新建的电影院有五个电影场。**Zhè zuo xīn jiàn de diànyǐngyuàn yǒu wǔ ge diànyǐngchǎng.** *This newly-built cinema complex has five cinemas.*

diànzǐ 电子 [suffix: 电 *electricity, electron* + 子 *nominal suffix*] NOUN = electron

diànzǐ gōngyè 电子工业 = electronics industry

diànzǐ hèkǎ 电子贺卡 = e-card

diànzǐ yóujiàn 电子邮件 = e-mail

■ 我今天收到两个电子邮件，发了三个电子邮件。**Wǒ jīntiān shōudào liǎng ge diànzǐ yóujiàn, fāle sān ge diànzǐ yóujiàn.** = *I received two e-mail messages and sent three today.*

diànzǐ yóuxì 电子游戏 = electronic game

diàn 店 NOUN = same as 商店 **shāngdiàn**

diào 掉 VERB = fall, drop

■ 杯子从桌子上掉到地上。**Bēizi cóng zhuōzi shang diàodao dì shang.** = *The cup fell from the table to the floor.*

NOTE: 掉 **diào** is often used after a verb, as a complement to mean "finish [doing ...]," e.g.

chīdiao 吃掉 = eat up
■ 水果都吃掉了。 **Shuǐguǒ dōu chīdiao le.** = *The fruit is all eaten up.*
màidiao 卖掉 = sell out
■ 那些书还没有卖掉。 **Nà xiē shū hái méiyǒu màidiao.** = *Those books aren't sold out yet.*
rēngdiao 扔掉 = throw away, discard
■ 这件衣服太小了，不能穿了，你扔掉吧！ **Zhè jiàn yīfu tài xiǎo le, bù néng chuān le, nǐ rēngdiao ba!** = *This dress is too small for you. You'd better throw it away.*
wàngdiao 忘掉 = forget
■ 这件事我怎么也忘不掉。 **Zhè jiàn shì wǒ zěnme yě wàng bu diao.** = *I can't forget this incident, no matter how hard I try.*
yòngdiao 用掉 = use up
■ 我上个月用掉了一千块钱。 **Wǒ shàng ge yuè yòngdiaole yìqiān kuài qián.** = *I used up one thousand dollars last month. (→ I spent a thousand dollars last month.)*

diào 钓 Trad 釣 VERB = angle
■ 你钓到几条鱼？ **Nǐ diàodao jǐ tiáo yú?** = *How many fish have you caught [with hook and line]?*

diào 调 Trad 調 VERB
1 = exchange, swap
■ 你想和我调一下座位吗？ **Nǐ xiǎng hé wǒ diào yíxià zuòwèi ma?** = *Would you like to swap seats with me?*
2 = transfer
■ 他调到总公司去工作了。 **Tā diàodào zǒnggōngsī qù gōngzuò le.** = *He has been transferred to the company headquarters.*

diàochá 调查
1 VERB = investigate
■ 政府有关部门正在调查这家公司的商业活动。 **Zhèngfǔ yǒuguān bùmén zhèngzài diàochá zhè jiā gōngsī de shāngyè huódòng.** = *The relevant government departments are investigating this company's commercial activities.*
2 NOUN = investigation
■ 经过半年调查，发现这家公司违反了法律。 **Jīnguò bàn nián diàochá, fāxiàn zhè jiā gōngsī wéifǎnle fǎlǜ.** = *After six months' investigation the company was found to have violated the law.*
■ 关于这个事件，警察正在进行调查。

Guānyú zhège shìjiàn, jǐngchá zhèngzài jìnxíng diàochá. = *The police are conducting an investigation of this incident.*

diē 跌 VERB
1 = fall, tumble
■ 老人跌了一交，摔断了左腿。 **Lǎorén diē le yì jiāo, shuāiduànle zuǒ tuǐ.** = *The old man (or woman) fell down and broke his (or her) left leg.*
2 = (prices) fall, drop
■ 昨天股票跌了，还是升了？ **Zuótián gǔpiào diē le, háishì shēng le?** = *Did the shares fall or rise yesterday?*

dié 碟 NOUN = disk (See 光碟 guāngdié.)

dīng 盯 VERB = gaze, stare
■ 你别老盯着人家看，多不礼貌！ **Nǐ bié lǎo dīngzhe rénjiā kàn, duō bù lǐmào!** = *You shouldn't stare at people. How rude!*

dǐng 顶 Trad 頂
1 NOUN = top (of the head), peak, summit
shāndǐng 山顶 = peak
■ 今天我们能爬到山顶吗？ **Jīntiān wǒmen néng pádào shāndǐng ma?** = *Can we climb to the mountain top today?*
tóudǐng 头顶 = crown of the head
wūdǐng 屋顶 = roof
2 VERB = carry on the head, hit with the head
■ 九号队员顶球入门。 **Jiǔhào duìyuán dǐng qiú rù mén.** = *Number Nine headed the ball into the goal.*

dìng 定 VERB = fix, set, decide
■ 你去北京的日期定了吗？ **Nǐ qù Běijīng de rìqí dìng le ma?** = *Have you decided on the date to leave for Beijing?*

dìng 订 Trad 訂 VERB = book
dìng fángjiān 订房间 = reserve a hotel/motel room, book a table/a seat
■ 我想订一个双人房间。 **Wǒ xiǎng dìng yí ge shuāngrén fángjiān.** = *I'd like to book a double room.*
dìng piào 订票 = book a ticket
■ 我现在订机票，万一有事能退吗？ W6 **xiànzài dìng jī piào, wànyī yǒushì néng tuì ma?** = *If I book an air ticket now, can I cancel it in case of emergency?*

dìng zuò 订座 = book a table (at a restaurant), book a seat (in a theatre)

diū 丢 VERB = lose, throw away
- 我的表丢了。**Wǒ de biǎo diū le.** = *I've lost my watch.*

diūliǎn 丢脸 = lose face, be disgraced
- 他考试门门不及格，真丢脸! **Tā kǎoshì ménmen bù jígé, zhēn diūliǎn!** = *It was disgraceful for him to fail every subject in the exam.*

diū-sān-là-sì 丢三落四 = be forgetful, be scatter-brained
- 年纪大了，容易丢三落四的。**Niánjì dà le, róngyì diū-sān-là-sì de.** = *When one gets old, one tends to be more forgetful.*

diūshī 丢失 = lose

dōng 东 Trad 東 NOUN = east, eastern
- 我在体育馆东门等你.。**Wǒ zài tǐyùguǎn dōng mén děng nǐ.** = *I'll be waiting for you at the east gate of the gymnasium.*
- 一直向东走，就是我们的学校。**Yìzhí wàng dōng zǒu, jiùshì wǒmen de xuéxiào.** = *Walk straight towards the east and you'll come to our school.*

dōngběi 东北 [compound: 东 *east* + 北 *north*] NOUN = northeast, the Northeast
- 中国东北天气非常冷。**Zhōngguó Dōngběi tiānqì fēicháng lěng.** = *It's very cold in Northeast China.*

NOTE: 东北 **dōngběi** as a specific geographical term refers to the northeastern part of China, which used to be known in the West as Manchuria.

dōngbian 东边 NOUN = the east side, to the east, in the east
- 我们学校的东边是一座公园。**Wǒmen xuéxiào de dōngbian shì yí zuò gōngyuán.** = *To the east of our school is a park.*
- 日本在中国的东边。**Rìběn zài Zhōngguó de dōngbian.** = *Japan lies to the east of China.*

dōngfāng 东方 [modif: 东 *east* + 方 *direction, part*] NOUN = the East, the Orient
- 东方文化和西方文化有很大的不同。**Dōngfāng wénhuà hé xīfāng wénhuà yǒu hěn dà de bùtóng.** = *There are major differences between the cultures of East and West.*

dōngmiàn 东面 NOUN = same as 东边 **dōngbian**

dōngnán 东南 [compound: 东 *east* + 南 *south*] NOUN = southeast
- 中国东南地区经济发达，人口很多。**Zhōngguó dōngnán dìqū jīngjì fādá, rénkǒu hěn duō.** = *The southeastern regions in China are economically well-developed and densely populated.*

dōngxi 东西 NOUN
1 = thing, things (个 **ge**, 件 **jiàn**, 种 **zhǒng**)
- 这些东西都是小明的。**Zhèxiē dōngxi dōu shì Xiǎo Míng de.** = *All these things are Xiao Ming's.*
- 我没有看到过这种东西。**Wǒ méiyǒu kàndànguo zhè zhǒng dōngxi.** = *I've never seen such a thing.*
2 = a person or animal (used affectionately or disapprovingly in colloquial Chinese)
- 这小东西真可爱。**Zhè xiǎo dōngxi zhēn kě'ài.** = *What a cute little thing.* (Referring to a baby or kitten)
- 你这个坏东西又在骗人了。**Nǐ zhè ge huài dōngxi yòu zài piànrén le.** = *You rascal! You're trying to deceive me again.*

NOTE: 东西 **dōngxi**, which literally means *east and west*, is an extremely common "all-purpose" noun that can denote any object or objects in Chinese. More examples:
- 妈妈出去买东西了。**Māma chūqu mǎi dōngxi le.** = *Mother's gone shopping.*
- 图书馆里不能吃东西。**Túshūguǎn lǐ bù néng chī dōngxi.** = *No food in the library.*
- 我想喝点儿东西。**Wǒ xiǎng hē diǎnr dōngxi.** = *I'd like to have a drink.*

dōng 冬 NOUN = winter

dōngtiān 冬天 [modif: 冬 *winter* + 天 *days*] NOUN = winter
- 今年的冬天比去年冷。**Jīnnián de dōngtiān bǐ qùnián lěng.** = *This year's winter is colder than last year's.*
- 这一对老人喜欢在暖和的地方过冬天。**Zhè yí duì lǎorén xǐhuan zài nuǎnhuo de dìfang guò dōngtiān.** = *This old couple likes to spend winter in a warm region.*
- 我妈妈冬天常常生病。**Wǒ māma dōngtiān chángcháng shēngbìng.** = *My mother is often sick in winter.*

D

dǒng 懂 VERB = comprehend, understand
■ 我不懂你的意思。**Wǒ bù dǒng nǐ de yìsi.** = I don't understand what you mean.
■ 我听得懂一些简单的中文。**Wǒ tīng de dǒng yìxiē jiǎndān de Zhōngwén.** = I can understand a little simple spoken Chinese.
■ 这首歌的意思你懂不懂? **Zhè shǒu gē de yìsi nǐ dǒng bu dǒng?** = Do you understand the meaning of this song?
dúdǒng 读懂 = read and understand
■ 这本书我读了两遍才读懂。**Zhè běn shū wǒ dúle liǎng biàn cái dúdǒng.** = I understood this book only after reading it twice.
kàndǒng 看懂 = see (or read) and understand
■ 这个电影我没有看懂。**Zhège diànyǐng wǒ méiyǒu kàndǒng.** = I didn't understand that movie.
tīngdǒng 听懂 = listen and understand

dǒngshìzhǎng 董事长 [modif: 董事 in charge + 长 chief] NOUN = chairman of the board of directors
■ 大华公司王董事长在记者招待会上宣布了重大消息。**Dàhuá Gōngsī Wáng dǒngshìzhǎng zài jìzhě zhāodàihuì shang xuānbùle zhòngdà xiāoxi.** = Mr Wang, chairman of the board of Da Hua Company, announced important news at the press conference.

dòng 动 Trad 動 VERB = move
■ 别动, 我给你照张像。**Bié dòng, wǒ gěi nǐ zhào zhāng xiàng.** = Stay put, I'll take your picture.
dònggōng 动工 = begin construction

dòngrén 动人 [modif: 动 moving + 人 people] ADJECTIVE = moving, touching
■ 这个电影的故事十分动人。**Zhège diànyǐng de gùshi shífēn dòngrén.** = This film has a moving story line.

dòngshēn 动身 [v+obj: 动 act + 身 the body] VERB = start (a journey), set off (on a journey)
■ 你如果要在天黑前到达, 就得早上动身。**Nǐ rúguǒ yào zài tiān hēi qián dàodá, jiù děi zǎoshang dòngshēn.** = If you want to arrive before dark, you've got to set off early in the morning.

dòngshǒu 动手 [v+obj: 动 act + 手 hand] VERB = start work
■ 我们现在动手, 一定能在七点前完成任务。**Wǒmen xiànzài dòngshǒu, yídìng néng zài qī diǎn qián wánchéng rènwù.** = If we start work now we're sure to be able to finish the job before seven o'clock.

dòngwù 动物 [modif: 动 moving + 物 object] NOUN = animal (只 zhī)
■ 这些小动物真可爱! **Zhèxiē xiǎo dòngwù zhēn kě'ài!** = These little animals are really lovable!
■ 小孩子特别喜欢动物。**Xiǎo háizi tèbié xǐhuan dòngwù.** = Children are particularly fond of animals.
dòngwùxué 动物学 = zoology

dòngwùyuán 动物园 NOUN = zoo
■ 下星期五我们班参观动物园。**Xià Xīngqīwǔ wǒmen bān cānguān dòngwùyuán.** = Our class will visit the zoo next Friday afternoon.

dòngzuò 动作 [compound: 动 act + 作 do] NOUN = movement (of the body)
■ 你跳舞的动作真优美! **Nǐ tiàowǔ de dòngzuò zhēn yōuměi!** = The movements of your dance are really beautiful! (→ You're a graceful dancer!)

dòng 冻 Trad 凍 VERB = freeze
■ 天这么冷, 我真冻坏了。**Tiān zhème lěng, wǒ zhēn dòng huài le.** = It's so cold. I'm frozen to death.
dòngròu 冻肉 = frozen meat
ròudòng 肉冻 = jellied meat
shuǐguǒ dòng 水果冻 = fruit jelly

dòng 洞 NOUN = hole, cave, cavity
■ 你敢进这个山洞吗? **Nǐ gǎn jìn zhège shāndòng ma?** = Do you dare to enter this mountain cave?

dōu 都 ADVERB = all, both, without exception
■ 学生们都喜欢上中文课。**Xuéshengmen dōu xǐhuan shàng Zhōngwén kè.** = All the students like having Chinese classes.
■ 我每天都跑步。**Wǒ měi tiān dōu pǎobù.** = I jog every day.
■ 我所有的朋友都来了。**Wǒ suǒyǒu de péngyou dōu lái le.** = All my friends have come.

NOTE: When words like 每天 **měi tiān** (*every day*), 每个 **měi ge** (*every one*), 大家 **dàjiā** (*everybody*) or 所有的 **suǒyǒu de** (*all*) are used, they usually occur with the adverb 都 **dōu**.

dòu 斗 Trad 鬥 VERB = fight

dòuzhēng 斗争 [compound: 斗 *fight* + 争 *strive*]

1 VERB = struggle, fight
- 为世界和平而斗争！ **Wèi shìjiè hépíng ér dòuzhēng!** = *Struggle for world peace!*

2 NOUN = struggle, fight
- 你们的斗争一定会胜利。 **Nǐmen de dòuzhēng yídìng huì shènglì.** = *Your struggle will definitely be victorious.*

dòu 豆 NOUN = bean, pea

dòufu 豆腐 [modif: 豆 *soybean* + 腐 *curd*]
NOUN = bean curd, tofu
- 豆腐价格便宜，营养丰富。 **Dòufu jiàgé piányì, yíngyíng fēngfù.** = *Bean curd is cheap and nutritious.*

dòu 逗 VERB = play with, tease
- 他下班以后，最爱逗孩子玩。 **Tā xiàbān yǐhòu, zuì ài dòu háizi wán.** = *After work, the thing he likes to do best is play with the baby.*

dú 独 Trad 獨 ADJECTIVE = solitary, alone

dúlì 独立 [modif: 独 *solitary* + 立 *stand*] VERB
= be independent
- 孩子大了都想独立，父母不用太担心。 **Háizi dàle dōu xiǎng dúlì, fùmǔ búyòng tài dānxīn.** = *When children grow up, they all want to be independent. Parents should not be too worried.*

dú 读 Trad 讀 VERB

1 = read, read aloud
- 他正在读一份重要文件。 **Tā zhèng zài dú yí fèn zhòngyào wénjiàn.** = *He is reading an important document.*

2 = attend (a school), study (in a school)
- 他们的大儿子在读中学，小女儿在读小学。 **Tāmen de dà érzi zài dú zhōngxué, xiǎo nǚ'er**

zài dú xiǎoxué. = *Their elder son is studying in a high school and their young daughter is studying in a primary school.*

dú xiǎoxué/zhōngxué/dàxué 读小学 / 中学 / 大学 = attend a primary school/high school/university.

NOTES: (1) In colloquial Chinese, 读 **dú** may be replaced by 看 **kàn** when used in the sense of "read," e.g. 看书 **kàn shū**, 看报 **kàn bào**. (2) When used in the sense of "attend (school)" or "study (in a school)" 读 **dú** may be replaced by 念 **niàn** to become 念小学 / 中学 / 大学 **niàn xiǎoxué/zhōngxué/dàxué**, which is more colloquial.

dúshū 读书 [v+obj: 读 *read* + 书 *book*] VERB
1 = read
- 这孩子喜欢读书，他爸爸妈妈看了真高兴。 **Zhè háizi xǐhuan dúshū, tā bàba māma kànle zhēn gāoxìng.** = *The child likes reading, much to the delight of his parents.*
2 = be a student, study (in a school)
- 我姐姐工作了，可是我妹妹还在读书。 **Wǒ jiějie gōngzuò le, kěshì wó mèimei háizài dúshū.** = *My elder sister is working but my younger sister is still a student.*

dúzhě 读者 [suffix: 读 *read* + 者 nominal suffix] NOUN = reader
- 今天报上登了很多读者来信，对这个问题发表意见。 **Jīntiān bào shang dēng le hěn duō dúzhě láixìn, duì zhège wèntí fābiǎo yìjian.** = *Today's newspaper publishes many readers' letters airing views on this issue.*

dǔ 堵 VERB = block
- 什么东西堵住了下水道。 **Shénme dōngxi dǔzhùle xiàshuǐdào.** = *Something is blocking the sewer.*

dù 肚 NOUN = stomach

dùzi 肚子 [suffix: 肚 *stomach* + 子 nominal suffix] NOUN = abdomen, stomach, belly
- 我肚子痛。 **Wǒ dùzi tóng.** = *I have a stomachache. (← My stomach hurts.)*

dù 度
1 NOUN = limit, extent
nándù 难度 = degree of difficulty

■ 这篇课文难度太高。**Zhè piān kèwén nándù tài gāo.** = *This text is too difficult.*

2 MEASURE WORD = degree (of temperature, longitude, latitude, etc.)

■ 今天最高气温是二十五度。**Jīntiān zuì gāo qìwēn shì èrshíwǔ dù.** = *The highest temperature today is 25 degrees.*

dùguò 度过 VERB = spend (a period of time)

■ 孩子们在爷爷奶奶家度过了愉快的暑假。**Háizimen zài yéye nǎinai jiā dùguòle yí ge yúkuài de shǔjià.** = *The children spent a pleasant summer vacation with their grandpa and grandma.*

D

dù 渡 VERB = cross (a body of water, e.g. a river, a strait, etc.)

■ 我们怎么渡江呢？ **Wǒmen zěnme dù jiāng ne?** = *How are we going to cross the river?*

dùlún 渡轮 = ferry boat

duān 端 VERB = carry ... level with one or both hands

■ 她端了一大盘水果走了进来。**Tā duānle yí dà pán shuǐguǒ zǒule jìnlai.** = *She came in, carrying a big plate of fruit.*

duǎn 短 ADJECTIVE = (of length, time) short (antonym 长 **cháng**)

■ 这条街很短，只有十几座房子。**Zhè tián jiē hěn duǎn, zhǐ yǒu shíjǐ zuò fángzi.** = *This is a short street, with only a dozen houses.*

■ 我在上海的时间很短，没有好好玩。**Wǒ zài Shànghǎi de shíjiān hěn duǎn, méiyǒu hǎohǎo wán.** = *I only stayed in Shanghai for a short time and did not have much time for fun* (e.g. sightseeing, window-shopping, dining in restaurants).

duǎnqī 短期 [modif: 短 *short* + 期 *period*] NOUN = short-term

■ 她要去北京参加一个短期汉语口语训练班。**Tā yào qù Běijīng cānjiā yí ge duǎnqī Hànyǔ kǒuyǔ xùnliàn bān.** = *She is going to Beijing to attend a short course in spoken Chinese.*

■ 这个目标不可能在短期内达到。**Zhège mùbiāo bù kěnéng zài duǎnqī nèi dádào.** = *This goal cannot be reached in a short time.*

duǎnxìn 短信 [modif: 短 *short* + 信 *letter*] NOUN = text message (by cell phone), text

■ 我昨天收到他发来的两份短信。**Wǒ zuótiān shōudao tā fālai de liǎng fèn duǎnxìn.** = *I received two text messages from him yesterday.*

duàn 段 MEASURE WORD = section (of something long)

■ 一段路 **yí duàn lù** = *a section of a road/ street, part of a journey*

■ 这段路不平，开车要特别小心。**Zhè duàn lù bù píng, kāi chē yào tèbié xiǎoxīn.** = *This section of the road is quite rough. One should be particularly careful when driving.*

■ 一段时间 **yi duàn shíjiān** = *a period of time*

■ 一段经历 **yi duàn jīnglì** = *an experience [in life]*

duàn 断 Trad 斷 VERB

1 = break, snap

■ 把电线剪断。**Bǎ diànxiàn jiǎn duàn.** = *Cut the electric wire.*

■ 我和她的联系断了，我不知道她在哪里。**Wǒ hé tā de liánxì duàn le, wǒ bù zhīdào tā zài nǎlǐ.** *I have lost contact with her. I do not know where she is.*

2 = break off, cut off

duàn diàn 断电 = cut off electricity

■ 一场大雪使这个地区断电三天。**Yì chǎng dà xuě shǐ zhège dìqù duàn diàn sān tiān.** = *A heavy snow cut off electricity supply to this region for three days.*

duàn shuǐ 断水 = cut off water supply

duàn nǎi 断奶 = wean (a child)

duàn 锻 Trad 鍛 VERB = forge, shape metal

duànliàn 锻炼 [comp: 锻 *shape metal* + 炼 *smelt*] VERB = undergo physical training, do physical exercises

■ 你要成为一名好运动员，就得天天锻炼。**Nǐ yào chéngwéi yì míng hǎo yùndòngyuán, jiù děi tiāntiān duànliàn.** = *If you want to become a good athlete, you have to train every day.*

duī 堆 VERB = heap up, pile up

■ 你要扔的东西都堆在墙角，明天打扫出去。**Nǐ yào rēng de dōngxi dōu duī zài qiángjiǎo, míngtiān dǎsǎo chūqu.** = *Pile up whatever you want to dump in the corner. Tomorrow we'll get rid of it.*

duì 对 Trad 對 1

1 VERB = treat, deal with
- 她对我很好。**Tā duì wǒ hěn hǎo.** = *She treats me well.* (→ *She is nice to me.*)
- 我的批评是对事不对人。**Wǒ de pīpíng shì duì shì bú duì rén.** = *My criticism concerns the issue, not the person.*

2 VERB = same as 对于 **duìyú**

duì 对 Trad 對 2 ADJECTIVE = correct, true
(antonym 错 **cuò**)
- 你的话很对。**Nǐ de huà hěn duì.** = *Your words are correct.* (→ *You're right.*)
- 你说得很对。**Nǐ shuō de hěn duì.** = *You spoke correctly.* (→ *You're right.*)

NOTE: 对不对 **duì bu duì** is used at the end of a sentence to form a question, e.g.
- 他回答得对不对？ **Tā huídá de duì bu duì?** = *Did he answer correctly?*
- 你是英国人，对不对？ **Nǐ shì Yīngguórén, duì bu duì?** = *You're from the UK, aren't you?*
- 中华文明是世界上最古老的文明，对不对？ **Zhōnghuá wénmíng shì shìjiè shang zuì gǔlǎo de wénmíng, duì bu duì?** = *Chinese civilization is the oldest in the world, isn't it?*

duì 对 Trad 對 3 MEASURE WORD = pair, two
(matching people or things)
- 一对花瓶 **yí duì huāpíng** = *two matching vases*
- 他们结婚的时候，我送了一对花瓶。**Tāmen jiéhūn de shíhuo, wǒ sòngle yí duì huāpíng.** = *I gave them two matching vases when they married.*
- 一对夫妻 **yí duì fūqī** = *a couple (husband and wife)*

duìbǐ 对比 [compound: 对 check + 比 compare, contrast] VERB = compare and contrast
- 你对比一下中文和英文，就会发现很多有趣的问题。**Nǐ duìbǐ yíxià Zhōngwén hé Yīngwén, jiù huì fāxiàn hěn duō yǒuqù de wèntí.** = *If you compare and contrast Chinese and English, you will find many interesting issues.*

duìbuqǐ 对不起 IDIOM = I'm sorry, I beg your pardon
- 对不起，打错电话了。**Duìbuqǐ, dǎ cuò diànhuà le.** = *Sorry, I've dialed a wrong number.*

- 对不起，我迟到了。**Duìbuqǐ, wǒ chídào le.** = *Sorry, I'm late.*
- 对不起，我没听清楚，请你再说一遍。**Duìbuqǐ, wǒ méi tīng qīngchu, qǐng nǐ zài shuō yíbiàn.** = *I'm sorry, I didn't catch it. Could you please say it again?*

NOTE: 对不起 **duìbuqǐ** is a very useful idiomatic expression in colloquial Chinese. It is used when you've done something wrong or caused some inconvenience to others. For more formal occasions, use 请原谅 **qǐng yuánliàng** = *please forgive me.*

duìfāng 对方 [modif: 对 the opposite side + 方 side] NOUN = the other side, the other party
- 你必须清楚地了解对方的企图。**Nǐ bìxū qīngchu de liáojiě duìfāng de qǐtú.** = *You must have a clear idea of the other party's intention.*

duìfu 对付 VERB = cope with, deal with
- 这种不讲道理的人，实在难对付。**Zhè zhǒng bù jiǎng dàolǐ de rén, shízài nán duìfu.** = *It is indeed difficult to deal with such unreasonable people.*
- 我不知道怎么样对付这种情况。**Wǒ bù zhīdào zěnmeyàng duìfu zhè zhǒng qíngkuàng.** = *I don't know how to cope with such a situation.*

duìhuà 对话

1 VERB = have a dialogue
- 他能够流利地用中文对话。**Tā nénggòu liúlì de yòng Zhōngwén duìhuà.** = *He is able to have a dialogue in fluent Chinese.*

2 NOUN = dialogue
- 工人已经和老板进行了两次对话。**Gōngrén yǐjīng he lǎobǎn jìnxíng le liǎng cì duìhuà.** = *Workers have conducted two talks with the boss.*

duìmiàn 对面 NOUN = opposite, the opposite side
- 学校的对面是一座公园。**Xuéxiào de duìmiàn shì yí zuò gōngyuán.** = *Opposite the school is a park.*

duìxiàng 对象 NOUN

1 = person or thing to which action or feeling is directed, object
- 她研究的对象是学前儿童。**Tā yánjiū de**

duìxiàng shì xué-qián értóng. = *Preschool children are the object of her study.*

2 = marriage partner, fiancé(e)

■ 他已经三十多岁了，还没有对象。**Tā yǐjīng sānshí duō suì le, hái méiyǒu duìxiàng.** = *He is over thirty, but still has no fiancée.*

zhǎo duìxiàng 找对象 = look for a marriage partner

duìyú 对于 PREPOSITION

1 = (introducing the object of an action), regarding

■ 我对于这个理论还没有完全理解。**Wǒ duìyú zhège lǐlùn hái méiyǒu wánquán lǐjiě.** = *I still haven't understood this question completely.*

■ 对于产品质量，工厂十分重视。**Duìyú chǎnpǐn zhìliàng gōngchǎng shífēn zhòngshì.** = *The factory attaches great importance to the quality of its products.*

2 = (indicating a certain relationship), to, towards

■ 学习中文对于了解中国人和中国文化很有帮助。**Xuéxí Zhōngwén duìyú liǎojiě Zhōngguórén he Zhōngguó wénhuà hěn yǒu bāngzhù.** = *Learning Chinese is very helpful to understanding the Chinese people and Chinese culture.*

duì 队 Trad 隊 NOUN = team

duìyuán 队员 = member of a team

lánqiú duì 篮球队 = basketball team

zúqiú duì 足球队 = soccer team

duìwu 队伍 NOUN = troops

■ 队伍天黑后进了村。**Duìwu tiānhēi hòu jìnle cūn.** = *The troops entered the village after dark.*

duìzhǎng 队长 [modif: 队 team + 长 chief] NOUN = team leader

■ 队员都服从队长。**Duìyuán dōu fúcóng duìzhǎng.** = *All the team members submit to the team leader.*

dūn 吨 Trad 噸 MEASURE WORD = ton

■ 一吨等於一千公斤。**Yí dūn děngyú yìqiān gōngjīn.** = *One ton equals 1,000 kilograms.*

dùn 盾 NOUN = shield (See 矛盾 **máodùn.**)

dùn 顿 Trad 頓 MEASURE WORD = (for meals)

■ 我们一天吃三顿饭：早饭、午饭、晚饭。**Wǒmen yì tiān chī sān dùn fàn: zǎofàn, wǔfàn, wǎnfàn.** = *We have three meals a day: breakfast, lunch and supper* (or *dinner*).

■ 她好好地吃了一顿晚饭。**Tā hǎohǎo de chīle yí dùn wǎnfàn.** = *She had a good meal for supper.* (→ *She had a good supper.*)

duō 多

1 ADJECTIVE = many, much (antonym 少 **shǎo**)

■ 今天的作业不多。**Jīntiān de zuòyè bù duō.** = *There isn't much homework today.*

■ 他有很多中国朋友。**Tā yǒu hěn duō Zhōngguó péngyou.** = *He has many Chinese friends.*

■ 他昨天酒喝得太多，今天头疼。**Tā zuótiān jiǔ hē de tài duō, jīntiān tóu téng.** = *He drank too much last night. Today he has a headache.*

bǐ ... de duō 比 ... 得多 = much more ... than

■ 今天比昨天热得多。**Jīntiān bǐ zuótiān rè de duō.** = *Today is much hotter than yesterday.*

2 NUMERAL = more, over

■ 我们学了五百多个汉字。**Wǒmen xuéle wǔbǎi duō ge Hànzì.** = *We've learned more than five hundred Chinese characters.*

■ 他在台湾住了八个多月。**Tā zài Táiwān zhùle bā ge duō yuè.** = *He lived in Taiwan for over eight months.*

3 ADVERB = how ...!

■ 要是我能去北京学中文，多好啊！**Yàoshì wǒ néng qù Běijīng xué Zhōngwén, duō hǎo a!** = *How nice it would be if I could go to Beijing to study Chinese!*

4 ADVERB = how ...?

■ 老先生，您多大了？**Lǎo xiānsheng, nín duō dà le?** = *How old are you, sir?* (to an elderly man)

duōme 多么 ADVERB = same as 多 3 ADVERB. Used in colloquial Chinese.

duōshǎo 多少 [compound: 多 many, much + 少 few, little] PRONOUN = how many, how much

■ 你们班多少人学中文？**Nǐmen bān duōshǎo rén xué Zhōngwén?** = *How many in your class are studying Chinese?*

...duōshǎo qián ...多少钱 = How much is ...?

■ 这本书多少钱？**Zhè běn shū duōshǎo qián?** = *How much is this book?*

méiyǒu duōshǎo 没有多少 = not many, not much

■ 他没有多少钱，可是要装出很有钱的样子。**Tā méiyǒu duōshǎo qián, kěshì yào zhuāngchū hěn yǒuqián de yàngzi.** = He hasn't got much money, but he pretends to be rich.

NOTE: See note on 几 **jǐ**.

duōshù 多数 [modif: 多 *many* + 数 *number*]
NOUN = majority
■ 世界上多数国家都实行民主制度。**Shìjiè shang duōshù guójiā dōu shíxíng mínzhǔ zhìdù.** = *The majority of countries in the world practice democracy.*

duó 夺 Trad 奪 VERB = take by force, win
■ 我们队夺得了冠军。**Wǒmen duì duódéle guànjūn.** = *Our team has won the championship.*

duǒ 朵 MEASURE WORD = (for flowers)
■ 送给你一朵花。**Sòng gei nǐ yì duō huā.** = *I'll give you a flower.*

duǒ 躲 VERB = hide (oneself)
■ 他躲在门背后。**Tā duǒ zài mén bèihòu.** = *He hid behind the door.*

E

é 俄 NOUN = (a shortened form of *Russia* or *Russian*)

Éguó 俄国 NOUN = Russia

Éyǔ 俄语 [compound: 俄 *Russia* + 语 *speech*]
NOUN = the Russian language
■ 俄语的语法很复杂。**Éyǔ de yǔfǎ hěn fùzá.** = *Russian grammar is complicated.*

Éwén 俄文 [compound: 俄 *Russian* + 文 *writing*] NOUN = the Russian language (especially the writing)

é 鹅 Trad 鵝 NOUN = goose (只 **zhī**)
tiān'é 天鹅 = swan

è 饿 Trad 餓 ADJECTIVE = hungry (antonym 饱 **bǎo**)
■ 我饿了，我们去吃饭吧！**Wǒ è le, wǒmen**

qù chī fàn ba!** = *I'm hungry. Let's go and eat.*
■ 看到这么多好吃的东西，我感到饿了。**Kàndào zhème duō hǎochī de dōngxi, wǒ gǎndào è le.** = *At the sight of so much delicious food, I feel hungry.*

ér 儿 Trad 兒 NOUN = child, son

értóng 儿童 [compound: 儿 *child* + 童 *child*]
NOUN = child, children
■ 这种电影不适合儿童看。**Zhè zhǒng diànyǐng bù shìhé értóng kàn.** = *This kind of film is not suitable for children.*
értóng shídài 儿童时代 = childhood

érzi 儿子 [suffix: 儿 *son* + 子 nominal suffix]
NOUN = son (个 **ge**)
■ 他们有两个儿子，大儿子工作了，小儿子还在念大学。**Tāmen yǒu liǎng ge érzi, dà érzi gōngzuò le, xiǎo érzi háizài niàn dàxué.** = *They have two sons. While the elder son has started working, the younger son is still studying in a university.*
■ 他希望妻子生一个儿子。**Tā xīwàng qīzi shēng yí ge érzi.** = *He hopes that his wife will give birth to a son.*

ér 而 CONJUNCTION = (indicating a contrast) but, yet, on the other hand
■ 学而不用，等于没学。**Xué ér bú yòng, děngyú méi xué.** = *If you learn skills but do not use them, it is tantamount to not having learnt them at all.*
■ 他姐姐功课很好，而他呢，去年考试三门不及格。**Tā jiějie gōngkè hěn hǎo, ér tā ne, qùnián kǎoshì sān mén bù jígé.** = *His sister's schoolwork is excellent, but he failed in three subjects last year.*

érqiě 而且 CONJUNCTION = moreover, what's more
■ 这件衣服大了一点儿，而且比较贵，还是不买吧。**Zhè jiàn yīfu dàle yìdiǎnr, érqiě bǐjiào guì, háishì bù mǎi ba.** = *This dress is a bit too big and also expensive. You shouldn't buy it.*
búdàn ..., érqiě ... 不但 ..., 而且 ... = not only ..., but also ...
■ 我爸爸不但会开车，而且会修车。**Wǒ bàba búdàn huì kāi chē, érqiě huì xiū chē.** = *My daddy can not only drive but also fix cars.*
■ 这个电脑游戏不但小孩爱玩，而且大人也

E

爱玩。**Zhège diànnǎo yǒuxì búdàn xiǎohái ài wán, érqiě dàren yě ài wán.** = *Not only children but also grownups like to play this electronic game.*

ěr 耳 NOUN = ear

ěrduō 耳朵 NOUN = the ear (只 **zhī**)
■ 人有两只耳朵，就说明应该听不同的声音。**Rén yǒu liǎng zhī ěrduō, jiù shuōmíng yīnggāi tīng bùtóng de shēngyīn.** = *A man has two ears, which means he should listen to different voices.* (→ *A man has two ears, which means he should hear out different opinions.*)

èr 二 NUMERAL = second, two
■ 二千二百二十二 **èrqiān èrbǎi èrshí'èr** = *two thousand and two hundred and twenty-two*
■ 我二哥去年结婚了。**Wǒ èrgē qùnián jiéhūn le.** = *My second elder brother got married last year.*

NOTE: See note on 两 **liǎng**.

F

fā 发 Trad 發 VERB
1 = send out, release
■ 我上个星期给他发了一封信，今天上午又发了一个传真。**Wǒ shàng ge xīngqī gěi tā fāle yì fēng xìn, jīntiān shàngwǔ yòu fāle yí ge chuánzhēn.** = *I sent him a letter last week and sent him a fax this morning.*
2 = develop (into a state)
fācái 发财 = make a fortune, become prosperous
fā chuánzhēn 发传真 = send a fax
fā diànzǐ yóujiàn 发电子邮件 = send an e-mail message
fā (shǒujī) duǎnxìn 发（手机）短信 = send a text message (by cell phone)
fāhuǒ 发火 = lose one's temper, flare up

fābiǎo 发表 [compound: 发 *release* + 表 *express*] VERB = publicize, make known, publish
■ 请您发表对目前经济形势的看法。**Qǐng nín fābiǎo duì mùqián jīngjì xíngshì de kànfǎ.** = *Please express your views on the current economic situation.*

fāchū 发出 [compound: 发 *release* + 出 *out*] VERB
1 = produce, emit, give off
■ 水果成熟会发出特殊的香味。**Shuǐguǒ chéngshóu huì fāchū tèshū de xiāngwèi.** = *Ripe fruit gives off a special fragrance.*
2 = send out
■ 学校已经向新生发出通知。**Xuéxiào yǐjīng xiàng xīnshēng fāchū tōngzhī.** = *The school has sent out notifications to the new students.*

fādá 发达 ADJECTIVE = developed, well-developed
■ 这个国家制造业很发达。**Zhège guójiā zhìzàoyè hěn fādá.** = *This country has a well-developed manufacturing industry.*

fādòng 发动 VERB = launch (a massive campaign)
■ 毛泽东发动的文化大革命给中国人民带来巨大灾难。**Máo Zédōng fādòng de Wénhuà Dà Gémìng gěi Zhōngguó rénmín dàilái jùdà zāinàn.** = *The Cultural Revolution launched by Mao Zedong brought terrible disaster to the Chinese people.*

fādǒu 发抖 VERB = tremble
■ 她冷得发抖。**Tā lěng de fādǒu.** = *She trembled with cold.*

fāhuī 发挥 VERB = allow display, give free rein to
■ 这项工作能够充分发挥他在这方面的能力。**Zhè xiàng gōngzuò nénggòu chōngfèn fāhuī tā zài zhè fāngmiàn de nénglì.** = *This job allows him to display his ability in this area fully.*

fāmíng 发明
1 VERB = invent
■ 飞机是谁发明的？**Fēijī shì shuí fāmíng de?** = *Who invented the airplane?*
2 NOUN = invention (项 **xiàng**)
■ 这项新发明会给公司带来巨大的利益。**Zhè xiàng xīn fāmíng huì gěi gōngsī dàilái jùdà de lìyì.** = *This new invention will bring tremendous benefit to the company.*

fāshāo 发烧 [v+obj: 发 *develop* + 烧 *burning, fever*] VERB = run a fever
■ 她昨天着凉了，夜里就发烧了。**Tā zuótiān zháoliáng le, yèlǐ jiù fāshāo le.** = *She caught a*

cold yesterday and began to run a fever at night.

fāshēng 发生 [compound: 发 develop + 生 grow] VERB = take place, happen
■ 这里发生了什么事？ **Zhèli fāshēngle shénme shì?** = What happened here?
■ 前面发生了交通事故，车辆必须绕道。 **Qiánmiàn fāshēngle jiāotōng shìgù, chēliàng bìxū ràodào.** = A road accident happened up ahead. Traffic must detour.

fāxiàn 发现 [compound: 发 develop + 现 show] VERB = discover, find, find out
■ 谁先发现新西兰的？ **Shuí xiān fāxiàn Xīnxīlán de?** = Who first discovered New Zealand?
■ 我发现他爱打扮了，是不是有了女朋友？ **Wǒ fāxiàn tā ài dǎbàn le, shì bu shì yǒule nǚpéngyou?** = I notice that he is paying more attention to his grooming. Has he gotten a girlfriend?

fāyán 发言 [v+obj: 发 release + 言 words]
1 VERB = speak (at a meeting), make a speech
■ 代表们在会上纷纷发言。 **Dàibiǎomen zài huìshang fēnfēn fāyán.** = The delegates spoke at the meeting, one after another.
2 NOUN = speech
■ 他在会上的发言引起了代表们的争论。 **Tā zài huìshang de fāyán yǐnqǐle dàibiǎomen de zhēnglùn.** = His speech at the meeting gave rise to a debate among the delegates.

fāyáng 发扬 [compound: 发 develop + 扬 unfold] VERB = develop, carry forward
■ 希望你发扬优点，克服缺点。 **Xīwàng nǐ fāyáng yōudiǎn, kèfú quēdiǎn.** = I hope you will develop your strong points and overcome your shortcomings.

fāyīn 发音 [v+obj: 发 send out + 音 sound] NOUN = pronunciation
■ 我这个字发音对不对？ **Wǒ zhège zì fāyīn duì bu duì?** = Did I pronounce this character correctly?
■ 他中文说得很流利，虽然发音不太好。 **Tā Zhōngwén shuō de hěn liúlì, suīrán fāyīn bú tài hǎo.** = He speaks Chinese fluently, though his pronunciation is not too good.

fāzhǎn 发展 [compound: 发 develop + 展 unfold] VERB = develop
■ 经济要发展，政治要民主。 **Jīngjì yào fāzhǎn, zhèngzhì yào mínzhǔ.** = The economy should be developed, and politics should be democratized.
■ 公司决定发展在这个地区的业务。 **Gōngsī juédìng fāzhǎn zài zhè ge dìqū de yèwù.** = The company has decided to develop its business in this region.
fāzhǎnzhōng guójiā 发展中国家 = developing country
■ 中国是世界上最大的发展中国家。 **Zhōngguó shì shìjiè shang zuìdà de fāzhǎnzhōng guójiā.** = China is the largest developing country in the world.

fá 乏 VERB = lack (See 缺乏 quēfá.)

fǎ 法 NOUN = method, law

Fǎguó 法国 [modif: 法 France + 国 state, country] NOUN = France
■ 法国是一个重要的国家。 **Fǎguó shì yí ge zhòngyào de guójiā.** = France is an important country.

fǎlǜ 法律 [compound: 法 law + 律 rule] NOUN = law
■ 他哥哥在读法律，他想当律师。 **Tā gēge zài dú fǎlǜ, tā xiǎng dāng lǜshī.** = His brother is studying law; he wants to be a lawyer.
■ 每一个公民都必须遵守法律。 **Měi yí ge gōngmín dōu bìxū zūnshǒu fǎlǜ.** = Every citizen must obey the law.
lǜshī 律师 = lawyer
wéifǎn fǎlǜ 违反法律 = violate the law
xiūgǎi fǎlǜ 修改法律 = amend a law

Fǎwén 法文 [compound: 法 France + 文 writing] NOUN = the French language (especially the writing)

Fǎyǔ 法语 [compound: 法 France + 语 speech] NOUN = the French language
■ 她法语说得很漂亮。 **Tā Fǎyǔ shuō de hěn piàoliang.** = She speaks French beautifully.

fān 翻 VERB = turn, turn over
■ 请把书翻到二十页。 **Qǐng bǎ shū fāndào èrshí yè.** = Please turn your books to page twenty.

fānyì 翻译

1 VERB = translate, interpret
bǎ ... fānyì chéng … 把 ... 翻译成... = translate ... into ...
- 你能不能把这封信翻译成中文? **Nǐ néng bu néng bǎ zhè fēng xìn fānyì chéng Zhōngwén?** = *Can you translate this letter into Chinese?*
- 这本小说已经被翻译成八种语言。**Zhè běn xiǎoshuō yǐjīng bèi fānyì chéng bā zhǒng yǔyán.** = *This novel has been translated into eight languages.*
2 NOUN = translator, interpreter
- 这位翻译中文英文都好极了。**Zhè wèi fānyì Zhōngwén Yīngwén dōu hǎo jíle.** = *This translator* (or *interpreter*) *has very good command of both Chinese and English.*
dāng fānyì 当翻译 = to work as a translator (or interpreter)
- 明天有中国朋友来参观我们工厂，请你当翻译。**Míngtiān yǒu Zhōngguó péngyou lái cānguān wǒmen gōngchǎng, qǐng nǐ dāng fānyì.** = *Tomorrow some Chinese friends will come to visit our factory. I'll ask you to act as interpreter.*

fán 凡 ADVERB = every

fánshì 凡是 ADVERB = every, all
- 凡是我姐姐的朋友，我都认识。**Fánshì wǒ jiějie de péngyou, wǒ dōu rènshi.** = *I know every one of my sister's friends.*
- 凡是违反法律的事，都不能做。**Fánshì wéifǎn fǎlǜ de shì, dōu bù néng zuò.** = *You must not do anything that violates the law.*

NOTE: 凡是 **fánshì** is used before a noun phrase to emphasize that what is referred to is all-embracing, without a single exception. The phrase introduced by 凡是 **fánshì** usually occurs at the beginning of a sentence, and 都 **dōu** is used in the second half of the sentence.

fán 烦 Trad 煩 ADJECTIVE = annoyed (See 麻烦 máfan, 耐烦 nàifán.)

fán 繁 ADJECTIVE = numerous, abundant

fánróng 繁荣 [compound: 繁 abundant + 荣 flourishing] ADJECTIVE = prosperous, thriving
- 由于经济繁荣，人民的生活水平不断提

高。**Yóuyú jīngjì fánróng, rénmín de shēnghuó shuǐpíng búduàn tígāo.** = *With a prosperous economy, the people's standard of living keeps rising.*

fǎn 反 ADJECTIVE = reverse, opposite (antonym 正 zhèng)
- 请看反面。**Qǐng kàn fǎnmiàn.** = *Please read the reverse side.*

fǎndòng 反动 [modif: 反 reverse + 动 action] ADJECTIVE = reactionary
- 反对民主就是反动。**Fǎnduì mínzhǔ jiù shì fǎndòng.** = *Opposing democracy is reactionary.*

fǎnduì 反对 [modif: 反 opposing + 对 deal with] VERB = oppose, object (antonym 同意 tóngyì)
- 我不反对你的计划，但是我觉得很难做到。**Wǒ bù fǎnduì nǐ de jìhuà, dànshì wǒ juéde hěn nán zuòdào.** = *I don't object to your plan, but I think it'll be difficult to implement.*
fǎnduì yìjiàn 反对意见 = opposing opinion
fǎnduì dǎng 反对党 = the Opposition [party]

fǎnfù 反复 [compound: 反 reverse + 复 duplicate] ADVERB = repeatedly, over and over again
- 董事长反复强调市场调查的重要性。**Dǒngshìzhǎng fǎnfù qiángdiào shìchǎng diàochá de zhòngyàoxìng.** = *The chairman of the board emphasized over and over again the importance of market surveys.*

fǎnkàng 反抗 [compound: 反 oppose + 抗 resist] VERB = resist, fight back, rebel
- 当父母的如果管得太多，孩子会反抗。**Dāng fùmǔ de rúguǒ guǎn de tài duō, háizi huì fǎnkàng.** = *If a parent is too bossy, the child will rebel.*

fǎnyìng 反应 [compound: 反 opposite + 应 reply, respond] NOUN = response, reaction
- 病人还在昏迷中，医生问他话，没有反应。**Bìngrén háizài hūnmí zhōng, yīshēng wèn tā huà, méiyǒu fǎnyìng.** = *The patient is still in coma and gives no response to the doctor's questions.*
- 对于这个新产品，市场反应非常好。**Duìyú zhège xīn chǎnpǐn, shìchǎng fǎnyìng fēicháng**

hǎo. = *There is excellent market response to this new product.*

fǎnyìng 反映 VERB

1 = reflect, mirror

■ 这篇小说反映了当代大学生的生活。**Zhè piān xiǎoshuō fǎnyìng le dāndài dàxuéshēng de shēnghuó.** = *This novel reflects the life of contemporary university students.*

2 = report, make known, convey

■ 我要把你们的意见反映给领导。**Wǒ yào bǎ nǐmen de yìjiàn fǎnyìng gei lǐngdǎo.** = *I will convey your views to the leadership.*

fàn 犯 VERB = violate, offend

■ 他犯了一个严重错误，心里很难过。**Tā fànle yí ge yánzhòng cuòwù, xīnli hěn nánguò.** = *He is very sad that he made a serious mistake.*

fàn cuòwù 犯错误 = make a mistake, commit an offence

fàn fǎ 犯法 = violate the law

fàn guī 犯规 = foul (in sports), break a rule

fàn 饭 Trad 飯 NOUN

1 = cooked rice

■ 小王每顿吃两碗饭。**Xiǎo Wáng měi dùn chī liǎng wǎn fàn.** = *Xiao Wang eats two bowls of rice every meal.*

■ 他是南方人，爱吃米饭，不爱吃馒头和面条儿。**Tā shì nánfāngrén, ài chī mǐfàn, bú ài chī mántou hé miàntiáor.** = *He is a Southerner. He loves rice and doesn't like steamed buns or noodles.*

2 = meal (顿 **dùn**)

■ 他们常常在外面吃饭。**Tāmen chángcháng zài wàimiàn chīfàn.** = *They often have their meals outside. (→ They often dine out.)*

■ 我请你吃饭。**Wǒ qǐng nǐ chīfàn.** = *I'll treat you to a meal.*

fànwǎn 饭碗 = rice bowl; way of making a living, job

fàndiàn 饭店 [modif: 饭 meal + 店 shop, store] NOUN

1 = restaurant (家 **jiā**)

■ 这家饭店饭菜好吃，价钱也便宜。**Zhè jiā fàndiàn fàncài hǎochī, jiàqián yě piányi.** = *The dishes in this restaurant are delicious and affordable.*

■ 市中心新开了一家饭店，都说不错。

Shìzhōngxīn xīn kāile yì jiā fàndiàn, dōu shuō búcuò. = *A new restaurant opened downtown recently, and everyone says it's good.*

2 = hotel (家 **jiā**)

■ 他住在一家五星饭店里。**Tā zhù zài yì jiā wǔxīng fàndiàn lǐ.** = *He lives in a five-star hotel.*

NOTE: The original meaning of 饭店 **fàndiàn** is *restaurant*, but it is also used to denote a hotel. For example, 北京饭店 **Běijīng fàndiàn** may mean *Beijing Restaurant* or *Beijing Hotel.*

fàn 范 Trad 範 NOUN = border; model

fànwéi 范围 [compound: 范 border + 围 boundary] NOUN = scope, range, limits

■ 这不属于我的工作范围。**Zhè bù shǔyú wǒ de gōngzuò fànwéi.** = *This is outside my job description.*

■ 这家公司的营业范围很广。**Zhè jiā gōngsī de yíngyè fànwéi hěn guǎng.** = *The business range of this company is very wide.*

fàn 泛 ADJECTIVE = general, extensive (See 广泛 guǎngfàn.)

fāng 方 ADJECTIVE = square

■ 中国人传统在方桌或者圆桌上吃饭，不用长桌吃饭。**Zhōngguórén chuántǒng zài fāngzhuō huòzhě yuánzhuō shang chīfán, bú yòng chángzhuō chīfán.** = *Traditionally, the Chinese dine at a square or round table, not at an oblong one.*

zhèngfāng 正方 = square

chángfāng 长方 = oblong, rectangular

fāng'àn 方案 [compound: 方 method + 案 file] NOUN = plan, program (for a major project)

■ 经过反复讨论，委员会通过了这个方案。**Jīngguò fǎnfù tǎolùn, wěiyuánhuì tōngguòle zhège fāng'àn.** = *After repeated discussions the committee approved the program.*

fāngbiàn 方便 ADJECTIVE = convenient, handy (antonym 麻烦 máfan)

■ 住在城里买东西很方便。**Zhù zài chéngli mǎi dōngxi hěn fāngbiàn.** = *With city living, shopping is convenient.*

■ 你方便的话，请帮我找一下这本书。**Nǐ**

F

fāngbiàn de huà, qǐng bāng wǒ zhǎo yíxià zhè běn shū. = *If it's not too much trouble, please help me locate this book.*
fāngbiàn miàn 方便面 = instant noodles

NOTE: A euphemism for "going to the toilet" is 方便一下 **fāngbiàn yíxià**, e.g.
■ 我要方便一下。**Wǒ yào fāngbiàn yíxià.** = *I'm going to use the restroom.*

fāngfǎ 方法 [compound: 方 *method, way of doing things* + 法 *method*] NOUN = method
■ 这个方法不行，要另想办法。**Zhège fāngfǎ bùxíng, yào lìng xiǎng bànfǎ.** = *This method won't do. We'll have to find another way.*
■ 学中文有没有什么好方法。**Xué Zhōngwén yǒu méiyǒu shénme hǎo fāngfǎ.** = *Are there any good methods of learning Chinese?*

fāngmiàn 方面 [compound: 方 *side* + 面 *face, surface*] NOUN = side, aspect
■ 政府应该考虑社会各方面的意见。**Zhèngfǔ yīnggāi kǎolǜ shèhuì gè fāngmiàn de yìjiàn.** = *The government should consider viewpoints from various aspects of society.*
■ 大量生产这种产品，在技术方面还有些问题。**Dàliàng shēngchǎn zhèzhǒng chǎnpǐn, zài jìshù fāngmiàn hái yǒu xiē wèntí.** = *There are still some technological problems if this new product is to be mass-produced.*

fāngshì 方式 [compound: 方 *method* + 式 *manner*] NOUN = manner, way
■ 说话的内容很重要，说话的方式同样重要。**Shuōhuà de nèiróng hěn zhòngyào, shuōhuà de fāngshì tóngyàng zhòngyào.** = *What you say is important, and how you say it is equally important.*
shénghuó fāngshì 生活方式 = way of life, lifestyle

fāngxiàng 方向 NOUN = direction, orientation
■ 你的方向错了。**Nǐ de fāngxiàng cuò le.** = *You're in the wrong direction.*
■ 汽车朝飞机场方向开去。**Qìchē cháo fēijīchǎng fāngxiàng kāiqu.** = *The car headed in the direction of the airport.*

fāngzhēn 方针 NOUN = guiding principle, policy
■ 你们国家的教育方针是什么？**Nǐmen guójiā de jiàoyù fāngzhēn shì shénme?** = *What*

are the guiding principles of education in your country?

fáng 防 VERB = prevent, guard against
■ 防火比救火重要，防病比治病重要。**Fánghuǒ bǐ jiùhuǒ zhòngyào, fángbìng bǐ zhìbìng zhòngyào.** = *Preventing fires is more important than fire fighting; preventing disease is more important than curing disease.*
fánghuǒ 防火 = fire prevention
fángbìng 防病 = disease prevention
fángdào 防盗 = anti-burglary measures

fángzhǐ 防止 [compound: 防 *prevent* + 止 *stop*] VERB = prevent, guard against
■ 政府将采取措施防止人才外流。**Zhèngfǔ jiāng cǎiqǔ cuòshī fángzhǐ réncái wàiliú.** = *The government will adopt measures to prevent brain drain.*
■ 我们取得了优秀成绩，要防止骄傲情绪。**Wǒmen qǔdéle yōuxiù chéngjì, yào fángzhǐ jiāo'ào qíngxù.** = *After achieving excellent results we should guard against conceit.*

fáng'ài 妨碍 [compound: 妨 *prevent* + 碍 *hinder*] VERB = hinder, hamper, disturb
■ 你们把车停在这里，会妨碍交通。**Nǐmen bǎ chē tíng zài zhèli, huì fáng'ài jiāotōng.** = *If you park your car here, it will block traffic.*

fáng 房 NOUN
1 = house
■ 他们现在租房住，打算明年买房。**Tāmen xiànzài zū fáng zhù, dǎsuàn míngnián mǎi fáng.** = *They now live in a rented house and are planning to buy a house next year.*
cǎofáng 草房 = thatched cottage
lóufáng 楼房 = house of two or more levels
píngfáng 平房 = single-story house, bungalow
2 = room (间 **jiān**)
■ 楼上有三间房。**Lóu shang yǒu sān jiān fáng.** = *There are three bedrooms upstairs.*
bìngfáng 病房 = sick room, ward
kèfáng 客房 = guest room

fángjiān 房间 [compound: 房 *room, home* + 间 *space*] NOUN = room (间 **jiān**)
■ 这间房间不大，但是挺舒服。**Zhè jiān fángjiān bú dà, dànshì tǐng shūfu.** = *This room is not big, but it's very comfortable.*

fángzi 房子 [suffix: 房 *house* + 子 *nominal suffix*] NOUN = house, housing
■ 他们有了钱就买房子。**Tāmen yǒule qián jiù mǎi fángzi.** = *They will buy a house once they have the money.*

fǎng 仿 VERB = imitate

fǎngfú 仿佛 VERB = be like, be alike
■ 他们俩年龄相仿佛，经历也差不多。**Tāmen liǎ niánlíng xiāng fǎngfú, jīnglì yě chàbuduō.** = *The two of them are of similar age and share similar life experiences.*

fǎng 纺 Trad 紡 VERB = spin (into thread/yarn)

fǎngzhī 纺织 [compound: 纺 *spin* + 织 *weave*] VERB = spin and weave
■ 在这个山村里，还有老人会纺织土布。**Zài zhège shāncūn lǐ háiyǒu lǎorén huì fǎngzhī tǔbù.** = *In this mountain village there are old people who still make homespun cloth.*
fǎngzhī gōngyè 纺织工业 = textile industry
fǎngzhīpǐn 纺织品 = textile goods

fǎng 访 Trad 訪 VERB = visit

fǎngwèn 访问 [compound: 访 *visit* + 问 *ask, ask after*] VERB = visit, interview
■ 这位老人很有名，经常有人来访问他。**Zhè wéi lǎorén hěn yǒumíng, jīngcháng yǒu rén lái fǎngwèn tā.** = *This old man is famous. People often come to visit him.*
■ 已经有一百多万人访问过这个网站。**Yǐjīng yǒu yìbǎi duō wàn rén fǎngwènguo zhège wǎngzhàn.** = *Over a million people have visited this web site.*

fàng 放 VERB = put, put in
■ 请你不要把你的书放在我的桌子上。**Qǐng nǐ bú yào bǎ nǐ de shū fàng zài wǒ de zhuōzi shang.** = *Please don't put your books on my desk.*
■ 你的咖啡里要不要放糖？ **Nǐ de kāfēi li yào bú yào fàng táng?** = *Shall I put sugar in your coffee?*

fàngdà 放大 [compound: 放 *expand* + 大 *large*] VERB = enlarge
■ 这张照片请放大。**Zhè zhāng zhàopiàn qǐng fàngdà.** = *Please enlarge this photo.*
fàngdàjìng 放大镜 = magnifying glass

fàngjià 放假 [v+obj: 放 *release* + 假 *holiday*] VERB = be on holiday, have the day off
■ 我们学校从十二月十五日到一月二十日放假。**Wǒmen xuéxiào cóng Shí'èr yuè shíwǔ rì dào Yīyuè èrshí rì fàngjià.** = *We have school holidays from December 15 to January 20.*
■ 明日停电，学校放假一天。**Míngrì tíngdiàn, xuéxiào fàngjià yìtiān.** = *School's closed tomorrow due to a power cut.*

fàngqì 放弃 [compound: 放 *release* + 弃 *abandon*] VERB = abandon, give up
■ 这个机会十分难得，你不要放弃。**Zhège jīhuì shífēn nándé, nǐ bú yào fàngqì.** = *This is a very rare opportunity. Don't pass it up.*
■ 我们已经放弃了原来的计划。**Wǒmen yǐjīng fàngqìle yuánlái de jìhuà.** = *We have abandoned our original plan.*

fàngxīn 放心 [v+obj: 放 *set in place* + 心 *the heart*] VERB = set one's mind at ease, be at ease (antonym 担心 **dānxīn**)
■ 你办事，我放心。**Nǐ bànshì, wǒ fàngxīn.** = *With you in charge, my mind's at ease.*
■ 才十几岁的孩子出国留学，父母怎么会放心呢？ **Cái shí jǐ suì de háizi chūguó liúxué, fùmǔ zénme huì fàngxīn ne?** = *How can parents not worry when their teenage children go overseas to study?*

fēi 飞 Trad 飛 VERB = fly
■ 小鸟飞走了。**Xiǎo niǎo fēi zǒu le.** = *The little bird flew away.*

fēijī 飞机 [modif: 飞 *flying* + 机 *machine*] NOUN = airplane
■ 从北京来的飞机什么时候到？ **Cóng Běijīng lái de fēijī shénme shíhou dào?** = *When does the plane from Beijing arrive?*
zuò/chéng fēijī 坐／乘飞机 = travel by plane
■ 我们全家明天坐飞机去上海。**Wǒmen quán jiā míngtiān zuò fēijī qù Shànghǎi.** = *My family will go to Shanghai tomorrow by air.*
fēijī piào 飞机票 = air ticket
fēijī chǎng 飞机场 = airport
kāi fēijī 开飞机 = pilot a plane

fēi 非 ADVERB = not, do not

fēi … bùkě 非 … 不可 ADVERB = have no choice but to …, simply must …

■我今天非写完这个报告不可。**Wǒ jīntiān fēi xiěwán zhège bàogào bùkě.** = *I simply must finish writing this report today.*

NOTE: 非...不可 **fēi ... bùkě** is used to emphasize the verb after 非 **fēi**. 不可 **bùkě** may be omitted, e.g. 我今天非写完这个报告。**Wǒ jīntiān fēi xiěwán zhège bàogào.** = *I simply must finish writing this report today.*

fēicháng 非常 [modif: 非 *not* + 常 *usual*]
ADVERB = unusually, very
■中国非常大。**Zhōngguó fēicháng dà.** = *China is very big.*
■我非常想去新加坡旅行。**Wǒ fēicháng xiǎng qù Xīnjiāpō lǚxíng.** = *I very much want to take a trip to Singapore.*

Fēizhōu 非洲 [modif: 非 *Africa* + 洲 *continent*] NOUN = Africa

féi 肥 ADJECTIVE = fat, fattened
■这头猪真肥! **Zhè tóu zhū zhēn féi!** = *What a fat pig!*

NOTE: 肥 **féi** is normally used to describe animals. It is insulting to use it to describe humans.

fèi 肺 NOUN = the lungs
■吸烟伤害肺。**Xīyān shānghài fèi.** = *Smoking harms the lungs.*

fèi 费 Trad 費
1 NOUN = fee, charge
■我一个月要花很多钱交各种各样的费。**Wǒ yí ge yuè yào huā hěnduō qián jiāo gè-zhǒng-gè-yàng de fèi.** = *I spend a lot of money on various fees every month.*
guǎnlǐ fèi 管理费 = administration charge
jīchǎng fèi 机场费 = airport tax
jiāo fèi 交费 = pay fees, a charge, etc.
shuǐdiàn fèi 水电费 = water and electricity bill
xué fèi 学费 = tuition fee
2 VERB = cost, spend
■他费了很多钱才把车修好。**Tā fèi le hěn duō qián cái bǎ chē xiūhǎo.** = *Only after spending a small fortune did he get his car repaired.*
fèi le jiǔ-niú-èr-hǔ zhī lì 费了九牛二虎之力 = spend the strength of nine bulls and two tigers, make tremendous efforts

■我费了九牛二虎之力才完成这个任务。**Wǒ fèi le jiǔ-niú-èr-hǔ zhī lì cái wánchéng zhège rènwù.** = *It was with tremendous effort that I accomplished the task.*

fèiyòng 费用 NOUN = expense, cost
■在这个国家念大学，一年的费用是多少? **Zài zhège guójiā niàn dàxué, yìnián de fèi yòng shì duōshǎo?** = *How much is the annual cost of studying in a university in this country?*
shēnghuó fèiyòng 生活费用 = living expenses, cost of living
bàngōng fèiyòng 办公费用 = administration cost, overheads

fēn 分
1 VERB = divide
■今天是你的生日，你来分生日蛋糕。**Jīntiān shì nǐ de shēngrì, nǐ lái fēn shēngrì dàngāo.** = *Today's your birthday, come and cut your birthday cake.*
fēnxiǎng 分享 = share (joy, benefits, etc.)
2 NOUN = point, mark
■你去年中文考试得了多少分? **Nǐ qùnián Zhōngwén kǎoshì dé le duōshǎo fēn?** = *What marks did you get for the Chinese examination last year?*
3 NOUN = minute
■现在是十点二十分。**Xiànzài shì shí diǎn èrshí fēn.** = *It's ten twenty now.*
4 MEASURE WORD = (Chinese currency; 1 分 fēn = 0.1 角 **jiǎo** = 0.01 元 **yuán**), cent

... fēnzhī ... ... 分之 ... NUMERAL = (indicating fraction)
■三分之二 **sān fēnzhī èr** = *two thirds*
■八分之一 **bā fēnzhī yī** = *one eighth*
bǎi fēnzhī ... 百分之 ... = ... percent
■百分之七十 **bǎi fēnzhī qīshí** = *seventy percent*
■百分之四十五 **bǎi fēnzhī sìshíwǔ** = *forty-five percent*

fēnbié 分别 VERB
1 = part with, be separated from
■我和姐姐分别三年了，今天见面，多高兴啊! **Wǒ hé jiějie fēnbié sānnián le, jīntiān jiànmiàn, duō gāoxìng a!** = *I'm meeting my older sister today after three years' separation. How happy I am!*
2 = distinguish

■ 对于犯错误的人，我们要分别情况，不同对待。**Duìyú fàn cuòwù de rén, wǒmen yào fēnbié qíngkuàng, bùtóng duìdài.** = *Regarding those who have made mistakes, we should distinguish between circumstances and deal with them accordingly.*

fēnpèi 分配 [compound: 分 *divide* + 配 *ration*] NOUN = distribute, allocate
■ 根据各人的能力，分配不同的工作。**Gēnjù gèrén de nénglì, fēnpèi bùtóng de gōngzuò.** = *Different jobs are allocated according to people's abilities.*

fēnxī 分析 [compound: 分 *divide* + 析 *analyze*]
1 VERB = analyze
■ 我们要仔细分析这两件事之间的关系。**Wǒmen yào zǐxì fēnxī zhè liǎng jiàn shì zhī jiān de guānxi.** = *We should analyze the relationship between these two events carefully.*
2 NOUN = analysis
■ 经过分析他们知道了这个药的化学成分。**Jīngguò fēnxī tāmen zhīdào le zhège yào de huàxué chéngfèn.** = *After an analysis, they learned the drug's chemical components.*

fēnzhōng 分钟 NOUN = minute (of an hour)
■ 五分钟不是一段很长的时间。**Wǔ fēnzhōng bú shì yí duàn hěn cháng de shíjiān.** = *Five minutes is not a long time.*
■ 我等你等了四十多分钟。**Wǒ děng nǐ děngle sìshí duō fēnzhōng.** = *I waited for you for over forty minutes.*
■ 打长途电话，以每分钟计费。**Dǎ chángtú diànhuà, yǐ měi fēnzhōng jìfèi.** = *The cost of long-distance telephone calls is calculated by the minute.*

fēn 吩 VERB = instruct

fēnfù 吩咐 VERB = instruct, tell (what to do)
■ 她吩咐旅馆服务员把晚饭送到房间来。**Tā fēnfù lǚguǎn fúwùyuán bǎ wǎnfàn sòngdào fángjiān lái.** = *She instructed the hotel attendant to deliver the dinner to her room.*

fēn 纷 Trad 紛 ADJECTIVE = numerous, varied

fēnfēn 纷纷 ADJECTIVE = numerous and disorderly
■ 对于这个处分，大家议论纷纷，有人说太

重，有人说太轻。**Duìyú zhège chǔfèn, dàjiā yìlùn fēnfēn, yǒurén shuō tài zhòng, yǒurén shuō tài qīng.** = *There is great controversy over this disciplinary action; some say it is too severe, others say it is too light.*

fěn 粉 NOUN = powder

fěnbǐ 粉笔 [modif: 粉 *powder* + 笔 *pen*] NOUN = chalk (支 zhī)
■ 约翰，请你到办公室去给我拿几支粉笔来。**Yuēhàn, qǐng nǐ dào bàngōngshì qu gěi wǒ ná jǐ zhī fěnbǐ lái.** = *John, please go to the office and get me a few pieces of chalk.*

fènliàng 分量 NOUN = weight
■ 你们这批货物分量不足。**Nǐmen zhè pī huòwù fènliàng bù zú.** = *This batch of your goods is short weight.*
■ 他在公司里工作了二十多年了，说话很有分量。**Tā zài gōngsī li gōngzuòle èrshí duō nián le, shuōhuà hěn yǒu fènliàng.** = *He has been working in the company for over twenty years and what he says carries a lot of weight.*

fèn 份 MEASURE WORD = (for a set of things or newspapers, documents, etc.)
■ 一份礼物 **yí fèn lǐwù** = *a present*
■ 一份晚报 **yí fèn wǎnbào** = *a copy of the evening papers*
■ 一份报告 **yí fèn bàogào** = *a report*

fèn 奋 Trad 奮 VERB = exert oneself

fèndòu 奋斗 [modif: 奋 *exert oneself* + 斗 *fight*] VERB = fight, struggle, strive
■ 要成功就要奋斗。**Yào chénggōng jiù yào fèndòu.** = *If you want to succeed, you must fight for it.*

fèn 愤 Trad 憤 NOUN = anger

fènnù 愤怒 [compound: 愤 *angry* + 怒 *enraged*] ADJECTIVE = enraged, angry
■ 她发现又受了欺骗，十分愤怒。**Tā fāxiàn yòu shòule qīpiàn, shífēn fènnù.** = *She was enraged to discover that she had been cheated again.*

fēng 丰 Trad 豐 ADJECTIVE = abundant

F

fēngfù 丰富 [compound: 丰 *abundance* + 富 *wealth*] ADJECTIVE = abundant, rich, plenty
- 我们的生活很丰富。**Wǒmen de shēnghuó hěn fēngfù.** = *Our life is very rich.* (→ *We live a full life.*)
- 这位老师有丰富的经验。**Zhè wèi lǎoshī yǒu fēngfù de jīngyàn.** = *This teacher has rich experience.*
- 这本书的内容非常丰富，值得反复阅读。**Zhè běn shū de nèiróng fēicháng fēngfù, zhídé fǎnfù yuèdú.** = *This book has very rich content and is worth repeated reading.*

fēng 风 Trad 風 NOUN = wind
- 今天风很大。**Jīntiān fēng hěn dà.** = *It's very windy today.*
- 冬天中国常常刮西北风。**Dōngtiān Zhōngguó chángcháng guā xīběi fēng.** = *In winter a northwestern wind prevails in China.*
fēngxiàng 风向 = wind direction

fēngjǐng 风景 NOUN = landscape, scenery
- 山顶上的风景特别优美。**Shāndǐng shang de fēngjǐng tèbié yōuměi.** = *The scenery on top of the mountain is particularly beautiful.*

fēnglì 风力 [modif: 风 *wind* + 力 *force*] NOUN = wind force, wind power
- 今天风力很大，不能划船。**Jīntiān fēnglì hěn dà, bù néng huáchuán.** = *Today the wind is too strong for us to go boating.*

fēngsú 风俗 NOUN = custom, social customs
- 他每到一个地方就了解当地的风俗。**Tā měi dào yí ge dìfang jiù liáojiě dāngdì de fēngsú.** = *Wherever he goes he will learn the local customs.*
- 有些旧风俗正在渐渐消失。**Yǒuxiē jiù fēngsú zhèngzài jiànjiàn xiāoshī.** = *Some old customs are gradually disappearing.*

fēng 封 MEASURE WORD = (for letters)
- 王先生，有你一封信。**Wáng xiānsheng, yǒu nǐ yì fēng xìn.** = *Mr Wang, here's a letter for you.*

fēng 蜂 NOUN = wasp (See 蜜蜂 **mìfēng**.)

féng 逢 VERB = come upon, meet
- 每逢结婚纪念日，他们夫妻总要庆祝一下。**Měi féng jiéhūn jìniànrì, tāmen fūqī zǒngyào qìngzhù yíxià.** = *Every time their wedding anniversary comes around, that couple will celebrate it.*
féng-nián-guò-jié 逢年过节 = on festival days and the New Year's Day, on festive occasions

féng 缝 Trad 縫 NOUN = sew
- 现在很少人自己缝衣服了。**Xiànzài hěn shǎo rén zìjǐ féng yīfu le.** = *Very few people make their own clothes nowadays.*

fǒu 否 VERB = negate

fǒudìng 否定 VERB = negate, deny (肯定 **kěndìng**)
- 我不想否定你们的成绩。**Wǒ bù xiǎng fǒudìng nǐmen de chéngjì.** = *I don't want to deny your achievements.*

fǒuzé 否则 CONJUNCTION = otherwise, or
- 这个问题必须尽快解决，否则会危害整个工程。**Zhège wèntí bìxū jìnkuài jiějué, fǒuzé huì wēihài zhěngge gōngchéng.** = *This problem must be solved as soon as possible, otherwise it will jeopardize the entire project.*
- 你们一定要在十天内付清电费，否则要断电。**Nǐmen yídìng yào zài shí tiān nèi fùqīng diànfèi, fǒuzé yào duàndiàn.** = *You must pay the electricity bill in ten days or face an electricity cutoff.*

fū 夫 NOUN = man

fūrén 夫人 NOUN = (formal term for another person's) wife
- 王董事长和夫人将出席宴会。**Wáng dǒngshìzhǎng hé fūrén jiāng chūxí yànhuì.** = *Chairman Wang and his wife will attend the dinner party.*

fū 肤 Trad 膚 NOUN = skin (See 皮肤 **pífū**.)

fú 佛 See 仿佛 **fǎngfú**.

fú 服 VERB = obey

fúcóng 服从 [compound: 服 *obey* + 从 *follow*] VERB = obey, submit to
- 少数服从多数。**Shǎoshù fúcóng duōshù.** = *The minority submits to the majority.*
- 我服从总公司的决定。**Wǒ fúcóng**

zǒnggōngsī de juédìng. = *I will defer to the decision of the company headquarters.*

fúwù 服务 [compound: 服 *obey* + 务 *work*]
VERB = serve, work for

wèi ... fúwù 为 ... 服务 = serve ..., work for ...
■ 我能为大家服务，感到很高兴。**Wǒ néng wèi dàjiā fúwù, gǎndào hěn gāoxìng.** = *I'm happy to be able to serve you all.*

fúwù yè 服务业 = service industry

fúwùyuán 服务员 [suffix: 服务 *serve* + 员 *person*] NOUN = attendant, waiter/waitress
■ 这位服务员态度不大好。**Zhè wèi fúwùyuán tàidu bú dà hǎo.** = *This attendant's work attitude is not very good.*
■ 请你叫一下服务员。**Qǐng nǐ jiào yíxià fúwùyuán.** = *Please call the attendant.*
■ 要付服务员小费吗？**Yào fù fúwùyuán xiǎofèi ma?** = *Do we tip the attendants?*

NOTE: Though 服务员 **fúwùyuán** is the word to refer to or address an attendant, a waiter or waitress, in everyday usage 小姐 **xiǎojiě** is more common (if the attendant is a woman).

fú 浮 VERB = float
■ 你说说铁做的大轮船为什么会浮在水上？**Nǐ shuōshuo tiě zuò de dà lúnchuán wèishénme huì fú zài shuǐ shang?** = *Can you tell me why a big ship made of iron floats on water?*

fú 幅 MEASURE WORD = (for pictures, posters, maps, etc.)
■ 一幅中国画 **yì fú Zhōngguó huà** = *a Chinese painting*

fú 福 NOUN = blessing (See 幸福 **xìngfú**.)

fú 府 NOUN = government office (See 政府 **zhèngfǔ**.)

fú 符 VERB = be in accord

fúhé 符合 [compound: 符 *conform to* + 合 *accord with*] VERB = conform to, accord with
■ 这种产品的质量不符合要求。**Zhè zhǒng chǎnpǐn de zhìliàng bù fúhé yāoqiú.** = *The quality of this product does not meet the requirements.*
■ 政府的政策必须符合多数人的利益。

Zhèngfǔ de zhèngcè bìxū fúhé duōshùrén de lìyì. = *Government policies must conform to the interest of the majority of people.*

fú 辅 Trad 輔 NOUN = assistance, supplement

fǔdǎo 辅导 VERB = coach, tutor
■ 王小姐辅导我们学中文。**Wáng xiǎojiě fǔdǎo wǒmen xué Zhōngwén.** = *Miss Wang tutors us in Chinese.*
■ 王老师，您的辅导对我们很有帮助。**Wáng lǎoshī, nín de fǔdǎo duì wǒmen hěn yǒu bāngzhù.** = *Teacher Wang, your tutorial is helpful to us.*

fǔdǎo kè 辅导课 = tutorial class, tutorial
fǔdǎo lǎoshī 辅导老师 = tutor, teaching assistant

fǔ 腐 ADJECTIVE = rotten (See 豆腐 **dòufu**.)

fù 父 NOUN = father

fùqin 父亲 [modif: 父 *father* + 亲 *parent*] NOUN = father
■ 您父亲作什么工作？**Nín fùqin zuò shénme gōngzuò?** = *What does your father do?*
■ 我爱我父亲。**Wǒ ài wǒ fùqin.** = *I love my father.*
■ 父亲的话，有的有道理，有的没有什么道理。**Fùqin de huà, yǒude yǒudàolǐ, yǒude méiyǒu shénme dàolǐ.** = *Some of my father's words are reasonable, others are not so reasonable.*

NOTE: 爸爸 **bàba** and 父亲 **fùqin** denote the same person. While 爸爸 **bàba** is colloquial, like "daddy," 父亲 **fùqin** is formal, equivalent to "father." When referring to another person's father, 父亲 **fùqin** is preferred. As a form of address to your own father, only 爸爸 **bàba** is normally used.

fù 付 VERB = pay
■ 提供服务后请立即付费。**Tígòng fúwù hòu qǐng lìjí fù fèi.** = *You are expected to pay as soon as a service is provided. (→ Pay promptly for services rendered.)*
■ 我已经付给眼镜店百分之二十的定金。**Wǒ yǐjīng fù gei yǎnjìngdiàn bǎifēn zhī èrshí de dìngjīn.** = *I have paid the optician a deposit of twenty percent.*

F

fù 负 Trad 負 VERB = carry on the back

fùzé 负责 [v+obj: 负 *carry on back* + 责 *responsibility*] VERB = be responsible, be in charge
- 这件事我负责。**Zhè jiàn shì wǒ fùzé.** = *I'm responsible for this matter.* (or *I'm in charge of this matter.*)
- 他做事非常负责。**Tā zuòshì fēicháng fùzé.** = *He has a strong sense of responsibility.*
- 你现在负责哪一方面的工作? **Nǐ xiànzài fùzé nǎ yì fāngmiàn de gōngzuò?** = *Which part of the job are you responsible for?*
fùzérén 负责人 = the person in charge
- 我很不满意,我要见你们的负责人。**Wǒ hěn bù mǎnyì, wǒ yào jiàn nǐmen de fùzérén.** = *I'm very dissatisfied* (or *disappointed*). *I want to see the person in charge here.*

fù 妇 Trad 婦 NOUN = woman

fùnǚ 妇女 [compound: 妇 *woman* + 女 *woman*] NOUN = woman, womankind
- 妇女的地位有了很大提高。**Fùnǚ de dìwèi yòule hěn dà tígāo.** = *The social status of women has risen remarkably.*

fù 附 VERB = be close to

fùjìn 附近 [compound: 附 *close to* + 近 *close by*] NOUN = the area nearby
- 附近有没有邮局? **Fùjìn yǒu méiyǒu yóujú?** = *Is there a post office nearby?*
- 李先生就住在附近。**Lǐ xiānsheng jiù zhù zài fùjìn.** = *Mr Li lives near here.*
- 附近的学校都很好。**Fùjìn de xuéxiào dōu hěn hǎo.** = *The schools nearby* (or *in this area*) *are all very good.*

fù 咐 VERB = instruct (See 吩咐 fēnfù, 嘱咐 zhǔfù.)

fù 复 Trad 復 VERB = repeat, compound

fùshù 复述 [modif: 复 *repeat* + 述 *narrate*] VERB = retell, repeat
- 请你把她的话一个一个字地复述一下。**Qǐng nǐ bǎ tā de huà yí ge yí ge zì de fùshù yíxia.** = *Please repeat what she says verbatim.*

fùxí 复习 [modif: 复 *repeat* + 习 *study*] VERB = review (one's lesson)
- 下星期要考试,这几天我在复习。**Xià xīngqī yào kǎoshì, zhè jǐ tiān wǒ zài fùxí.** = *I'll be having an examination next week. I'm reviewing my lesson these days.*

fùzá 复杂 [compound: 复 *multiple* + 杂 *miscellaneous*] ADJECTIVE = complicated, complex (antonym 简单 jiǎndān)
- 这件是很复杂,我说不清楚。**Zhè jiàn shì hěn fùzá, wǒ shuō bu qīngchu.** = *This is a complicated matter. I can't explain it clearly.*
- 这么复杂的中文句子,我不会说。**Zhème fùzá de Zhōngwén jùzi, wǒ bú huì shuō.** = *I can't say such a complicated sentence in Chinese.*
- 他把这件事搞得很复杂。**Tā bǎ zhè jiàn shì gǎo de hěn fùzá.** = *He has complicated the matter.*

fù 副
1 MEASURE WORD = (for objects in pairs or sets) pair, set
- 一副手套 **yí fù shǒutàor** = *a pair of gloves*
- 一副眼镜 **yí fù yǎnjìng** = *a pair of spectacles*
2 ADJECTIVE = deputy, vice-…
- 这几天校长生病,有事可以找副校长。**Zhè jǐtiān xiàozhǎng shēngbìng, yǒu shì kěyǐ zhǎo fù xiàozhǎng.** = *The principal is ill these days. You can go and talk to the deputy principal if there are any problems.*

fù 富 ADJECTIVE = rich, wealthy (antonym 穷 qióng)
- 这个地区很富,房子都很漂亮。**Zhège dìqū hěn fù, fángzi dōu hěn piàoliang.** = *This is a wealthy area with beautiful houses.*
fùrén 富人 = rich person, rich people

> NOTE: In everyday Chinese, 富 **fù** is not used as much as 有钱 **yǒuqián** to mean *rich*.

fù 傅 NOUN = teacher, advisor (See 师傅 shīfu.)

G

gāi 该 Trad 該 1 MODAL VERB
1 = should, ought to
- 你不该常常迟到。**Nǐ bù gāi chángcháng chídào.** = *You shouldn't be late so often.*

■ 他不该答应了你，又不去办。**Tā bù gāi dāyìngle nǐ, yòu bú qù bàn.** = *He shouldn't have made you a promise and then done nothing.*

2 VERB = be somebody's turn to do something
■ 今天该你洗碗。**Jīntiān gāi nǐ xǐ wǎn.** = *It's your turn to wash dishes today.*

gāi 该 Trad 該 2 PRONOUN = that, the said, the abovementioned
■ 该校学生人数在五年内增加一倍。**Gāi xiào xuésheng rénshù zài wǔ nián nèi zēngjiā yí bèi.** = *The student population of that school has doubled in five years.*

NOTE: 该 **gāi** in this sense is used only in formal writing.

gǎi 改 VERB = alter, change, correct
■ 你这个字写错了，要改一下。**Nǐ zhège zì xiě cuò le, yào gǎi yíxià.** = *You've written a wrong character. You should correct it.*
■ 你这个坏习惯一定要改。**Nǐ zhège huài xíguàn yídìng yào gǎi.** = *You must break this bad habit.*
gǎiqī 改期 = change a scheduled time, change the date (of an event)

gǎibiàn 改变 [compound: 改 *alter* + 变 *change*]
1 VERB = transform, change
■ 我想改变一下我们的旅行路线。**Wǒ xiǎng gǎibiàn yíxià wǒmende lǚxíng lùxiàn.** = *I'd like to change our itinerary.*
■ 青年人要改变世界，老年人知道得改变自己。**Qīngniánrén yào gǎibiàn shìjiè, lǎoniánrén zhīdào děi gǎibiàn zìjǐ.** = *Young people want to change the world, and old people know they have to change themselves.*
2 NOUN = change, transformation
■ 你明年的计划有没有什么改变？**Nǐ míngnián de jìhuà yǒu méiyǒu shénme gǎibiàn?** = *Are there any changes in your plan for the next year?*
gǎiháng 改行 = change one's profession (or trade)

gǎigé 改革 [compound: 改 *change* + 革 *remove*]
1 VERB = reform
■ 大学考试制度应该改革。**Dàxué kǎoshì**

zhìdù yīnggāi gǎigé. = *The university entrance examination system should be reformed.*
■ 只有不断改革，才能跟上时代。**Zhíyǒu búduàn gǎigé, cáinéng gēnshàng shídài.** = *Only by constant reform can we keep abreast with the times.*
2 NOUN = reform
■ 改革开放是中国八十年代以来的两项重大政策。**Gǎigé, kāifàng shì Zhōngguó bāshí niándài yǐlái de liǎng xiàng zhòngdà zhèngcè.** = *Reform and opening-up have been two major policies in China since the 80s.*

gǎijìn 改进 [v+comp: 改 *change* + 进 *progress*]
1 VERB = improve, make ... more advanced/sophisticated
■ 这个方法有一些问题，需要改进。**Zhège fāngfǎ yǒu yìxiē wèntí, xūyào gǎijìn.** = *There are some problems with this method. It needs improving.*
■ 怎么样改进我们的服务？请您多提意见。**Zěnmeyàng gǎijìn wǒmen de fúwù? Qǐng nín duō tí yìjiàn.** = *What should we do to improve our service? Please feel free to make suggestions.*
2 NOUN = improvement (项 **xiàng**)
■ 这项技术改进使产量大大增加。**Zhè xiàng jìshù gǎijìn shǐ chǎnliàng dàdà zēngjiā.** = *This technological improvement greatly increased production.*

gǎishàn 改善 [v+comp: 改 *change* + 善 *good*]
1 VERB = ameliorate, make ... better/more favorable
■ 人人都想改善生活条件。**Rénrén dōu xiǎng gǎishàn shēnghuó tiáojiàn.** = *Everybody wants to improve their living conditions.*
■ 我们要改善和邻居的关系。**Wǒmen yào gǎishàn hé línjū de guānxi.** = *We should improve our relationship with our neighbors.*
2 NOUN = improvement, amelioration
■ 人们的居住条件得到了改善。**Rénmen de jūzhù tiáojiàn dédàole gǎishàn.** = *People's housing conditions have been improved.*

gǎizào 改造 [compound: 改 *change* + 造 *build up*]
1 VERB = remold, rebuild, reform
■ 这个城区要全面改造。**Zhège chéngqū yào quánmiàn gǎizào.** = *This urban district will undergo comprehensive rebuilding.*

2 NOUN = remolding, rebuilding
- 这个城区的改造需要大量资金。**Zhège chéngqū de gǎizào xūyào dàliàng zījīn.** = *The rebuilding of this urban district needs a large amount of funding.*

găizhèng 改正 [v+comp: 改 *change* + 正 *correct*] VERB = put ... right, rectify
- 改正下面句子中的错误。**Gǎizhèng xiàmiàn jùzi zhōng de cuòwù.** = *Correct the errors in the following sentences.*

gài 概 ADVERB = totally

gàikuò 概括 [compound: 概 *total* + 括 *include*] VERB = summarize
- 你能不能把这份报告概括成五百个字左右的短文。**Nǐ néng bu néng bǎ zhè fèn bàogào gàikuò chéng wǔbǎi ge zì zuǒyòu de duǎn wén.** = *Can you summarize this report in about 500 Chinese characters?*

gàiniàn 概念 [modif: 概 *total* + 念 *idea*] NOUN = concept, notion
- 你用老概念解释不了新现象。**Nǐ yòng lǎo gàiniàn jiěshì bù liǎo xīn xiànxiàng.** = *You cannot explain fresh phenomena with outdated concepts.*

gān 干 Trad 乾 ADJECTIVE = dry
- 衣服干了，收进来吧。**Yīfu gān le, shōu jìnlái ba.** = *The clothes are dry. Let's take them in.*

gānbēi 干杯 [v+obj: 干 *to dry* + 杯 *cup*] VERB = drink a toast, "Bottoms up!"
- 为我们的友谊，干杯！**Wèi wǒmen de yǒuyì, gānbēi!** = *To our friendship!*

gāncuì 干脆 [compound: 干 *dry* + 脆 *crisp*]
1 ADJECTIVE = decisive, not hesitant, straight to the point
- 做事要干脆，别犹犹豫豫。**Zuò shì yào gāncuì, bié yóu-yóu-yù-yù.** = *Be decisive in action, don't be hesitant.*
- 行就行，不行就不行，就干脆地说吧！**Xíng jiù xíng, bù xíng jiù bù xíng, jiù gāncuì de shuō ba!** = *Whether it's OK or not, just say it directly without mincing words.*
2 ADVERB = just, simply
- 你既然这么讨厌男朋友，干脆不要他了！

Nǐ jìrán zhème tǎoyàn nánpéngyou, gāncuì bú yào tā le! = *Since you dislike your boyfriend so much, just dump him!*

gānjing 干净 [compound: 干 *dry* + 净 *clean*] ADJECTIVE = clean (antonym 脏 zāng)
- 这些衣服很干净，不用洗。**Zhèxiē yīfu hěn gānjing, bú yòng xǐ.** = *These clothes are clean. They don't need washing.*
- 这些是干净的衣服。**Zhèxiē shì gānjing de yīfu.** = *These are clean clothes.*
- 这件衣服洗不干净了。**Zhè jiàn yīfu xǐ bu gānjing le.** = *This dress cannot be washed clean.*

gānzào 干燥 [compound: 干 *dry* + 燥 *arid*] ADJECTIVE = dry, arid
- 沙漠上天气干燥。**Shāmò shang tiānqì gānzào.** = *In the desert, the weather is dry.*

gān 杆 NOUN = pole
diànxiàn gān 电线杆 = electric pole, telephone/utility pole

gān 肝 NOUN = the liver
- 他有肝病，不能喝酒。**Tā yǒu gān bìng, bù néng hē jiǔ.** = *He has liver trouble and cannot drink alcohol.*

gǎn 赶 Trad 趕 VERB
1 = catch up with
- 他跑得这么快，我怎么赶得上？**Tā pǎo de zhème kuài, wǒ zénme gǎn de shàng?** = *How can I catch up with him when he is running so fast?*
2 = hurry up, rush for, try to catch
- 我得马上走，去赶最后一辆公共汽车。**Wǒ děi mǎshàng zǒu, qù gǎn zuì hòu yìbān gōnggòng qìchē.** = *I've got to go right now to catch the last bus.*
gǎn de shàng 赶得上 = can catch up
gǎn bu shàng 赶不上 = cannot catch up
gǎn shàng 赶上 = succeed in catching up
méi gǎn shàng 没赶上 = fail to catch up

gǎnjǐn 赶紧 ADVERB = hasten (to do something)
- 他母亲生重病住院了，他得赶紧回家。**Tā mǔqin shēng zhòngbìng zhùyuàn le, tā děi gǎnjǐn huíjiā.** = *His mother is hospitalized owing to severe illness and he has to rush back home.*

gǎnkuài 赶快 ADVERB = same as 赶紧 **gǎnjǐn**

gǎn 敢 MODAL VERB = dare
- 这么多人，我不敢讲话。**Zhè me duō rén, wǒ bù gǎn jiǎnghuà.** = There're so many people here, I don't dare to speak.

gǎn 感 VERB = feel

gǎndào 感到 [v+comp: 感 feel + 到 arrive (as a complement)] VERB = feel
- 我有机会访问你们的国家，感到很高兴。**Wǒ yǒu jīhuì fǎngwèn nǐmen de guójiā, gǎndào hěn gāoxìng.** = I feel very happy to have the opportunity to visit your country.
- 听了他的不幸经历，我感到很难过。= **Tīngle tā de búxìng jīnglì, wǒ gǎndào hěn nánguò.** = After hearing his tragic experience, I felt very sad.

gǎndòng 感动 [compound: 感 feel + 动 move] VERB = move, touch emotionally
- 这个电影很感动人，不少观众感动得哭了。**Zhège diànyǐng hěn gǎndòng rén, bùshǎo guānzhòng gǎndòng de kū le.** = This film was so moving that many in the audience wept.

gǎnjī 感激 [compound: 感 feel + 激 excite] VERB = feel deeply grateful
- 你在我最困难的时候帮助我，我十分感激。**Nǐ zài wǒ zuì kùnnán de shíhou bāngzhù wǒ, wǒ shífēn gǎnjī.** = I'm very grateful to you as you helped me in my most difficult times.

gǎnjué 感觉 [compound: 感 feel + 觉 be conscious of]
1 VERB = feel
- 我感觉他对我们不大友好。**Wǒ gǎnjué tā duì wǒmen bú dà yǒuhǎo.** = I feel that he is not very friendly to us.
2 NOUN = feeling, impression
- 她相信自己的感觉，常常跟着感觉走。**Tā xiāngxìn zìjǐ de gǎnjué, chángcháng gēnzhe gǎnjué zǒu.** = She believes her instinct and often follows it.

gǎnmào 感冒 VERB = catch a cold
- 突然变冷，很多人感冒了。**Tūrán biàn lěng, hěn duō rén gǎnmào le.** = It suddenly became cold, so quite a few people caught colds.
- 穿上衣服吧，当心感冒！**Chuān shang yīfu ba, dāngxīn gǎnmào!** = Put on your clothes. Take care not to catch a cold.

gǎnqíng 感情 [compound: 感 feeling + 情 emotion, affection] NOUN
1 = feelings, emotion
- 你要理解她的感情。**Nǐ yào lǐjiě tā de gǎnqíng.** = You should understand her feelings.
2 = affection, love
- 他们在一起工作多年，渐渐产生了感情。**Tāmen zài yìqǐ gōngzuò duō nián, jiànjiàn chǎnshēng le gǎnqíng.** = Having worked together for quite a few years, they have gradually become fond of each other.

gǎnxiǎng 感想 [compound: 感 feeling + 想 thoughts] NOUN = impressions, reflections
- 请问，您参观了这个学校，有什么感想？**Qǐngwèn, nín cānguānle zhège xuéxiào, yǒu shénme gǎnxiǎng?** = Could you please tell us your impressions of the school you've just visited?

gǎnxiè 感谢 [v+obj: 感 feel + 谢 grateful] VERB = be grateful, thank
- 我感谢你对我的帮助。**Wǒ gǎnxiè nǐ duì wǒ de bāngzhù.** = I'm grateful for your help.
- 我真不知道怎么样感谢你才好。**Wǒ zhēn bù zhīdào zénmeyàng gǎnxiè nǐ cái hǎo.** = I really don't know how to thank you enough.

gǎn xìngqù 感兴趣 VERB = be interested (in)
- 我对小说不感兴趣。**Wǒ duì xiǎoshuō bù gǎn xìngqù.** = I'm not interested in fiction.

gàn 干 Trad 幹 VERB = do, work
- 你干了一下午了，该休息休息了。**Nǐ gànle yíxiàwǔ le, gāi xiūxi xiūxi le.** = You've been working for the entire afternoon. You should take a break.
- 这活儿我干不了。**Zhè huór wǒ gàn bu liǎo.** = I can't do this job.

gànbù 干部 NOUN = cadre, official (位 **wèi**)

NOTE: 干部 **gànbù** is a communist party term, denoting party (or government) officials. It is not commonly used today. In its stead, 官员 **guānyuán** is the word for government officials.

gāng 刚 Trad 剛 ADVERB = just, barely
- 他去年考试刚及格。**Tā qùnián kǎoshì gāng jígé.** = *He barely passed the exam last year.*

gāngcái 刚才 [compound: 刚 *just* + 才 *only*]
NOUN = a short while ago, just
- 刚才王先生来电话，说明天的会见要改期。**Gāngcái Wáng xiānsheng lái diànhuà, shuō míngtiān de huìjiàn yào gǎiqī.** = *Mr Wang called just now, saying that tomorrow's meeting would be rescheduled.*
- 我刚才看见小明到图书馆去，你去那儿一定能找到他。**Wǒ gāngcái kànjiàn Xiǎo Míng dào túshūguǎn qù, nǐ qù nàr yídìng néng zhǎodào tā.** = *I saw Xiao Ming going to the library a short while ago. You're sure to find him there.*

gānggāng 刚刚 ADVERB = same as 刚 **gāng**, but more emphatic.

gāng 钢 Trad 鋼 NOUN = steel

gāngbǐ 钢笔 [modif: 钢 *steel* + 笔 *pen*] NOUN = fountain pen (支 **zhī**)
- 你的钢笔我用一下，行吗？**Nǐ de gāngbǐ wǒ yòng yíxià, xíng ma?** = *I'll use your fountain pen for a while, is it OK? (→ May I use your fountain pen for a while?)*
- 现在有各种各样的笔，很少人用钢笔。**Xiànzài yǒu gè-zhǒng-gè-yàng de bǐ, hěn shǎo rén yòng gāngbǐ.** = *Now there are many varieties of pens. Very few people use fountain pens.*

gāngtiě 钢铁 [compound: 钢 *steel* + 铁 *iron*] NOUN = iron and steel, steel
- 钢铁制造是基础工业。**Gāngtiě zhìzào shì jīchǔ gōngyè.** = *Steel and iron manufacturing is a basic (or primary) industry.*

gǎng 岗 Trad 崗 NOUN = sentry post (See 下岗 **xiàgǎng.**)

gǎng 港 NOUN = port, harbor
hǎigǎng 海港 = seaport
- 上海港是中国最重要的海港之一。**Shànghǎi gǎng shì Zhōngguó zuì zhòngyào de hǎigǎng zhī yī.** = *The Port of Shanghai is one of the most important seaports in China.*
gǎngkǒu 港口 = port, harbor

gāo 高 ADJECTIVE = tall, high (antonym 矮 **ǎi**, 低 **dī**)
- 我哥哥比我高。**Wǒ gēge bǐ wǒ gāo.** = *My elder brother is taller than I am.*
- 那座高高的楼房是一座新医院。**Nà zuò gāogāo de lóufáng shì yí zuò xīn yīyuàn.** = *That tall building is a new hospital.*
- 一年不见，那孩子长高了不少。**Yì nián bú jiàn, nà háizi zhǎng gāole bùshǎo.** = *I haven't seen the child for a year. He's grown much taller.*

gāodà 高大 ADJECTIVE = tall and big (antonym 矮小 **ǎixiǎo**)
- 他们有三个儿子，都长得很高大。**Tāmen yǒu sān ge érzi, dōu zhǎng de hěn gāodà.** = *They have three sons who are all tall and big.*

gāodù 高度 [compound: 高 *high* + 度 *degree*]
1 NOUN = altitude, height
- 从三十公尺的高度往下跳，当然很危险。**Cóng sānshí gōngchǐ de gāodù wàng xià tiào, dāngrán hěn wēixiǎn.** = *Jumping from a height of thirty meters is certainly very risky.*
2 ADJECTIVE = a high degree
- 日本的汽车制造工业高度发达。**Rìběn de qìchē zhìzào gōngyè gāodù fādá.** = *Japan has a highly developed car manufacturing industry.*

gāojí 高级 [modif: 高 *advanced, senior* + 级 *grade*] ADJECTIVE = advanced, high-level
gāojí xiǎoxué (gāoxiǎo) 高级小学 (高小)
= higher primary school (Grades 5 and 6)
gāoji zhōngxué (gāozhōng) 高级小学 (高中)
= senior high school

gāoxìng 高兴 [compound: 高 *high* + 兴 *excited*] ADJECTIVE = joyful, delighted, willing
- 见到你，我很高兴。**Jiàndào nǐ, wǒ hěn gāoxìng.** = *I'm delighted to see you.*
- 我可不高兴给他送什么生日贺卡。**Wǒ kě bù gāoxìng gěi tā sòng shénme shēngrì hèkǎ.** = *I'm unwilling to send him any kind of birthday card.*

gāoyuán 高原 [modif: 高 *high* + 原 *plain*]
NOUN = highland, plateau
- 高原的阳光特别强烈。**Gāoyuán de yángguāng tèbié qiángliè.** = *Sunshine is particularly intense on a plateau.*

gāo 膏 NOUN = paste, ointment (See 牙膏 yágāo.)

gāo 糕 NOUN = cake (See 蛋糕 dàngāo, 糟糕 zāogāo.)

gǎo 搞 VERB = do, be engaged in (a trade, profession, etc.)
■ "你父亲搞什么工作?" "他搞软件设计。" **"Nǐ fùqin gǎo shénme gōngzuò?" "Tā gǎo ruǎnjiàn shèjì."** = *"What does your father do?" "He's engaged in software design."*
■ 搞了半天, 你原来不是我要找的人。 **Gǎole bàntiān, nǐ yuánlái bú shì wǒ yào zhǎo de rén.** = *After so much ado, you turn out not to be the person I'm looking for.*

gào 告 VERB
1 = tell, inform
■ 我告你一件事, 你别对别人说。 **Wǒ gào nǐ yí jiàn shì, nǐ bié duì biérén shuō.** = *I'll tell you something. Don't tell others.*
2 = sue, bring a legal action against
■ 有人告他偷东西。 **Yǒurén gào tā tōu dōngxi.** = *He was charged with theft.*

gàobié 告别 VERB = bid farewell to, part with
■ 我告别父母到中国来学汉语, 已经八个月了。 **Wǒ gàobié fùmǔ dào Zhōngguó lái xué Hànyǔ, yǐjīng bā ge yuè le.** = *It is eight months since I bade my parents farewell and came to China to study Chinese.*

gàosu 告诉 [compound: 告 tell + 诉 inform] VERB = tell, inform
■ 他告诉我一个重要消息。 **Tā gàosu wǒ yī ge zhòngyào xiāoxi.** = *He told me an important piece of news.*
■ 这件事千万别告诉他。 **Zhè jiàn shì qiānwàn bié gàosu tā.** = *You mustn't tell him about this matter.*

gē 哥 NOUN = elder brother

gēge 哥哥 NOUN = elder brother
■ 我哥哥踢足球踢得很好。 **Wǒ gēge tī zúqiú tī de hěn hǎo.** = *My elder brother plays soccer very well.*
■ 她把哥哥介绍给自己最好的朋友。 **Tā bǎ gēge jièshào gěi zìjǐ zuìhǎo de péngyou.** = *She introduced her elder brother to her best friend.*

gē 胳 NOUN = arm

gēbo 胳膊 NOUN = the arm (只 zhī)
■ 这位举重运动员胳膊特别粗。 **Zhè wèi jǔzhòng yùndòngyuán gēbo tèbié cū.** = *This weightlifter has unusually thick arms.*

gē 割 VERB = cut
■ 夏天割草, 冬天可以喂牛羊。 **Xiàtiān gē cǎo, dōngtiān kěyǐ wèi niúyáng.** = *Grass is cut in summer to feed cattle and sheep in winter.*

gē 歌 NOUN = song
■ 这个歌很好听, 我想再听一遍。 **Zhè ge gē hěn hǎotīng, wǒ xiǎng zài tīng yí biàn.** = *This song is beautiful. I want to hear it once more.*
■ 你会唱中文歌吗? **Nǐ huì chàng Zhōngwén gē ma?** = *Can you sing Chinese songs?*
chànggē 唱歌 = sing a song
gēcí 歌词 = words of a song
gēshǒu 歌手 = professional singer

gē 搁 Trad 擱 VERB = put, place
■ 你先把脏衣服搁在洗衣机里。 **Nǐ xiān bǎ zāng yīfu gē zài xǐyījī li.** = *You put the dirty clothes in the washing machine first.*

gé 革 VERB = expel

géming 革命 NOUN = revolution (场 chǎng)
■ 在那场革命中牺牲了很多人。 **Zài nà chǎng géming zhōng xīshēngle hěn duō rén.** = *Many people died in that revolution.*

gé 格 NOUN = pattern, standard (See 及格 jígé, 价格 jiàgé, 性格 xìnggé, 严格 yángé.)

gé 隔 VERB = separate, partition
■ 隔一条江就是另一个国家。 **Gé yì tiáo jiāng jiù shì lìng yí ge guójiā.** = *Beyond the river is another country.*
gélí 隔离 = isolate (a patient, a criminal), quarantine
gélí bìngfáng 隔离病房 = isolation ward

gébì 隔壁 NOUN = next door
■ 我们家隔壁住着一对老夫妻。 **Wǒmen jiā gébì zhùzhe yí duì lǎo fūqī.** = *Next door to our home lives an old couple.*

gè 个 Trad 個 MEASURE WORD = (the most commonly used measure word, used in default of any other measure word; normally pronounced in the neutral tone)
- 一个人 **yí ge rén** = *a person*
- 两个苹果 **liǎng ge píngguǒ** = *two apples*
- 三个工厂 **sān ge gōngchǎng** = *three factories*

gèbié 个别 ADJECTIVE
1 = very few, exceptional
- 这是个别现象。**Zhè shì gèbié xiànxiàng.** = *This is an isolated case.*
2 = individual, one-to-one
- 对学习特别困难的学生，老师个别辅导。**Duì xuéxí tèbié kùnnán de xuésheng, lǎoshī gèbié fúdǎo.** = *The teacher gives individual tutoring to students with special difficulties.*

gèrén 个人 [modif: 个 *individual* + 人 *person*]
NOUN = individual (antonym 集体 **jítǐ**)
- 个人利益和集体利益产生矛盾时，怎么处理？**Gèrén lìyì hé jítǐ lìyì chǎnshēng máodùn shí, zénme chǔlǐ?** = *How should we handle cases where there is a conflict between an individual's interest and the collective interest?*
- 这是我个人的意见，不代表公司。**Zhè shì wǒ gèrén de yìjiàn, bù dàibiǎo gōngsī.** = *This is my personal opinion and it does not represent that of the company.*

gèzi 个子 NOUN = height and size (of a person), build
- 他因为营养不良，个子很小。**Tā yīnwèi yíngyǎng bùliáng, gèzi hěn xiǎo.** = *Due to malnutrition, he is of small build.*

gè 各 PRONOUN = each, every
- 各人的事，各人自己负责。**Gè rén de shì, gè rén zìjǐ fùzé.** = *Everyone should be responsible for his own affairs.*
- 爸爸妈妈各有主张，他不知道该听谁的。**Bàba māma gè yǒu zhǔzhāng, tā bù zhīdào gāi tīng shuí de.** = *Dad and mom each have their own views. He doesn't know whom to listen to.*
gè zhǒng 各种 = all kinds of
- 我各种水果都喜欢吃。**Wǒ gè zhǒng shuídōu dòu xǐhuan chī.** = *I like to eat all kinds of fruit.*

gěi 给 Trad 給
1 VERB = give, provide
- 妈妈每两个星期给小明五十块钱。**Māma měi liǎng ge xīngqī gěi Xiǎo Míng wǔshí kuài qián.** = *Mom gives Xiao Ming fifty dollars every fortnight.*
- 在我写论文的过程中，王老师给了我很多指导。**Zài wǒ xiě lùnwén de guòchéng zhōng, Wáng lǎoshī gěile wǒ hěn duō zhídǎo.** = *In the course of writing this thesis, Teacher Wang gave me a great deal of guidance.*
2 PREPOSITION = for, to
- 她给我们做了一顿很好吃的中国饭。**Tā gěi wǒmen zuòle yí dùn hěn hǎochī de Zhōngguó fàn.** = *She cooked us a delicious Chinese meal.*
- 今天晚上你们去看电影吧，我给你们照顾孩子。**Jīntiān wǎnshang nǐmen qù kàn diànyǐng ba, wǒ gěi nǐmen zhàogù háizi.** = *You go and watch the film tonight. I'll take care of your child for you (→ I'll baby-sit your child).*

gēn 根
1 NOUN = root
- 这棵树非常大，根一定很深。**Zhè kē shù fēicháng dà, gēn yídìng hěn shēn.** = *This tree is very big. Its roots must be deep.*
2 MEASURE WORD = (for long, thin things)
- 一根筷子 **yì gēn kuàizi** = *a chopstick*

gēnběn 根本 [compound: 根 *root* + 本 *root*]
1 NOUN = essence, what is fundamental
- 问题的根本在于产品的质量不合格。**Wèntí de gēnběn zàiyú chǎnpǐn de zhìliàng bù hégé.** = *The essence of the problem is that product quality is not up to standard.*
2 ADJECTIVE = essential, fundamental, basic
- 我们不能头痛医头，脚痛医脚，而必须找到一个根本的解决方法。**Wǒmen bù néng tóutòng yī tóu, jiǎotòng yī jiǎo, ér bìxū zhǎodào yí ge gēnběn de jiějué fāngfǎ.** = *We cannot just take temporary and cosmetic measures, but must find a fundamental solution.*

gēnjù 根据
1 VERB = do according to, on the basis of
- 我们根据最新情况，对计划作了修改。**Wǒmen gēnjù zuìxīn qíngkuàng, duì jìhuà zuòle xiūgǎi.** = *We have amended our plan according to the latest situation.*
2 NOUN = grounds, basis
- 你对我的批评没有根据。**Nǐ duì wǒ de**

pīpíng méiyǒu gēnjù. = *Your criticism of me is groundless.*

gēn 跟

1 VERB = follow

■ 我在前面走，我的小狗在后面跟。**Wǒ zài qiánmiàn zǒu, wǒ de xiǎogǒu zài hòumiàn gēn.** = *I walked in front and my puppy followed behind.*

2 PREPOSITION = with

■ 老师：“请大家跟我念。”**Lǎoshī: "Qǐng dàjiā gēn wǒ niàn."** = *Teacher: "Read after me, please."*

gēnshàng 跟上 = catch up with, keep abreast with

gēn ... yìqǐ 跟 ... 一起 = together with ...

■ 我常常跟爸爸一起去看足球赛。**Wǒ chángcháng gēn bàba yìqǐ qù kàn zúqiú sài.** = *I often go to watch soccer games with my father.*

gèng 更 ADVERB = still more, even more

■ 美国很大，加拿大更大。**Měiguó hěn dà, Jiānádà gèng dà.** = *America is big and Canada is even bigger.*

■ 我爱我的老师，但我更爱真理。**Wǒ ài wǒ de lǎoshī, dàn wǒ gèng ài zhēnlǐ.** = *I love my teacher, but I love truth more.*

gèngjiā 更加 ADVERB = same as 更 gèng

gōng 工 NOUN = work

gōngchǎng 工厂 [modif: 工 work + 厂 factory] NOUN = factory, works (座 zuò, 家 jiā)

■ 这座工厂生产什么？**Zhè zuò gōngchǎng shēngchǎn shénme?** = *What does this factory make?*

■ 他在中国参观了三家工厂。**Tā zài Zhōngguó cānguānle sān jiā gōngchǎng.** = *He visited three factories in China.*

bàn gōngchǎng 办工厂 = run a factory

jiàn gōngchǎng 建工厂 = build a factory

kāi gōngchǎng 开工厂 = set up a factory

gōngchéng 工程 [modif: 工 work + 程 course] NOUN = project, construction work, engineering

■ 这个工程从设计，施工到完成一共花了三年半时间。**Zhège gōngchéng cóng shèjì, shīgōng dào wánchéng yígòng huāle sānnián bàn shíjiān.** = *From design, construction till*

completion, this project took three and a half years.

tǔmù gōngchéng 土木工程 = civil engineering

shuǐlì gōngchéng 水利工程 = water conservancy project

gōngchéngshī 工程师 [modif: 工程 engineering + 师 master] NOUN = engineer (位 wèi)

■ 这座著名的大学培养了大批工程师。**Zhè zuò zhùmíng dàxué péiyǎngle dàpī gōngchéngshī.** = *This well-known university has trained a large number of engineers.*

zǒnggōngchéngshī 总工程师 = chief engineer

gōngfu 工夫 NOUN

1 = time

■ 他用了一个晚上的工夫把报告修改了一遍。**Tā yòngle yí ge wǎnshang de gōngfu bǎ bàogào xiūgǎile yí biàn.** = *He spent an entire evening revising this report.*

2 = efforts

■ 王老师每天花很大工夫备课。**Wáng lǎoshī měi tiān huā hěn dà gōngfu bèikè.** = *Teacher Wang makes great efforts to prepare his lessons every day.*

gōnghuì 工会 [modif: 工 workers + 会 association] NOUN = trade union

■ 工会代表工人要求增加工资，改善工作条件。**Gōnghuì dàibiǎo gōngrén yāoqiú zèngjiā gōngzī, gǎishàn gōngzuò tiáojiàn.** = *On behalf of the workers, the trade union demanded a wage increase and improvement in working conditions.*

gōngjù 工具 [modif: 工 work + 具 implement] NOUN = tool

■ 没有合适的工具，这活儿没法干。**Méiyǒu héshì de gōngjù, zhè huór méifǎ gàn.** = *This job can't be done without the proper tools.*

gōngrén 工人 [modif: 工 work + 人 person] NOUN = workman, worker

■ 工人在建一座新学校。**Gōngrén zài jiàn yí zuò xīn xuéxiào.** = *Workers are building a new school.*

■ 大批农民离开农村，到城市当工人。**Dàpī nóngmín líkāi nóngcūn, dào chéngshì dāng gōngrén.** = *Large numbers of peasants leave rural areas to be workers in cities.*

■ 这道门坏了，要请工人来修一下。**Zhè dào**

G

mén huài le, yào qǐng gōngrén lái xiū yíxià. = *Something is wrong with this door. We should ask a worker to fix it.*

gōngyè 工业 [modif: 工 *work* + 业 *industry*] NOUN = (manufacturing) industry
■ 工业发展了，国家才能富。**Gōngyè fāzhǎn le, guójiā cái néng fù.** = *Only when industry is developed, can a country be rich.*
■ 这个国家没有汽车工业。**Zhège guójiā méiyǒu qìchē gōngyè.** = *This country does not have an automobile industry.*

gōngyìpǐn 工艺品 [modif: 工艺 *craft* + 品 *article*] NOUN = handicraft
■ 约翰打算买一些中国工艺品带回国送人。**Yuēhàn dǎsuàn mǎi yìxiē Zhōngguó gōngyìpǐn dàihuí guó sòng rén.** = *John planned to buy some Chinese handicrafts and bring them home as gifts.*

gōngzī 工资 [modif: 工 *work* + 资 *fund*] NOUN = wages, salary
■ 你们是每月发工资，还是每两个星期发工资？**Nǐmen shì měi yuè fā gōngzī, háishì měi liǎng ge xīngqī fā gōngzī?** = *Do you pay wages every month or every fortnight?*

gōngzuò 工作 [compound: 工 *work* + 作 *do*]
1 VERB = work
■ 我们一星期工作五天。**Wǒmen yì xīngqī gōngzuò wǔ tiān.** = *We work five days in a week.*
■ 她在一家跨国公司工作。**Tā zài yì jiā kuàguó gōngsī gōngzuò.** = *She works in a multinational company.*
2 NOUN = work, job (件 jiàn)
■ 这件工作不太难。**Zhè jiàn gōngzuò bú tài nán.** = *This job is not too difficult.*
■ 他找工作找了两个月了。**Tā zhǎo gōngzuò zhǎole liǎng ge yuè le.** = *He's been looking for a job for two months.*

gōng 公 ADJECTIVE = male (of certain animals) (antonym 母 mǔ)
■ 公牛脾气很大，你千万别惹它。**Gōngniú píqì hěn dà. Nǐ qiānwàn bié rě tā.** = *Bulls have a fierce temper. Never provoke one.*

gōng'ān 公安 [modif: 公 *public* + 安 *security*] NOUN = public security

gōng'ān jú 公安局 = public security bureau (police bureau)
gōng'ān rényuán 公安人员 = public security personnel, policeman

NOTE: See note on 警察 **jǐngchá**.

gōngchǐ 公尺 [modif: 公 *metric* + 尺 a traditional Chinese measurement of length] MEASURE WORD = meter
■ 这个游泳池长二十五公尺，宽十公尺。**Zhège yóuyǒngchí cháng èrshíwǔ gōngchǐ, kuān shí gōngchǐ.** = *This swimming pool is 25 by 10 meters.*

gōnggòng 公共 [compound: 公 *public* + 共 *shared*] ADJECTIVE = public
■ 这是一座公共图书馆，任何人都可以进去看书。**Zhè shì yí zuò gōnggòng túshūguǎn, rènhé rén dōu kěyǐ jìnqù kàn shū.** = *This is a public library. Anybody can go in and read.*
gōnggòng qìchē 公共汽车 = bus
■ 我的车卖了，我现在坐公共汽车上班。**Wǒ de chē mài le, wǒ xiànzài zuò gōnggòng qìchē shàngbān.** = *I've sold my car. Now I go to work by bus.*

NOTE: The word for *bus* in Taiwan is 公车 **gōngchē**. In Hong Kong, *bus* is 巴士 **bāshì**, obviously a transliteration of the English word *bus*.

gōngjīn 公斤 [modif: 公 *metric* + 斤 a traditional Chinese measurement of weight] MEASURE WORD = kilogram
■ 这里有五公斤苹果，我送给你。**Zhèli yǒu wǔ gōngjīn píngguǒ, wǒ sòng gei nǐ.** = *Here are five kilograms of apples, my gift to you.*

gōngkāi 公开 [compound: 公 *public* + 开 *open*]
1 ADJECTIVE = open, public (antonym 秘密 mìmì)
■ 他发表公开谈话，反对政府的计划。**Tā fābiǎo gōngkāi tánhuà, fǎnduì zhèngfǔ de jìhuà.** = *He gave a public talk opposing the government plan.*
2 VERB = make public, reveal
■ 希望你能公开自己的观点。**Xīwàng nǐ néng gōngkāi zìjǐ de guāndiǎn.** = *I hope you will make your views known.*

gōnglǐ 公里 [modif: 公 *metric* + 里 *a traditional Chinese measurement of distance*] NOUN = kilometer
- 从城里到飞机场大概有十公里。**Cóng chéngli dào fēijīchǎng dàgài yǒu shí gōnglǐ.** = *It's about ten kilometers from town to the airport.*

gōnglù 公路 [modif: 公 *public* + 路 *road*] NOUN = public road, highway (条 tiáo)
- 全国公路四通八达。**Quán guó gōnglù sì-tōng-bā-dá.** = *Public roads reach every corner of the country.*
gāosù gōnglù 高速公路 = motorway, expressway

gōngmín 公民 [modif: 公 *public* + 民 *people, person*] NOUN = citizen
- 你拿哪个国家的护照，你就是哪个国家的公民。**Nǐ ná nǎige guójiā de hùzhào, nǐ jiù shì nǎge guójiā de gōngmín.** = *You are a citizen of the country whose passport you hold.*

gōngsī 公司 NOUN = commercial firm, company, corporation
- 我们公司的营业范围很广泛。**Wǒmen gōngsī de yíngyè fànwéi hěn guǎngfàn.** = *Our company has an extensive range of business activities.*
- 贵公司是哪一年成立的？ **Guì gōngsī shì nǎ yì nián chénglì de?** = *In which year was your company founded?*
zǒng gōngsī 总公司 = company headquarters
fēn gōngsī 分公司 = branch of a company

gōngyòng diànhuà 公用电话 [modif: 公用 *public use* + 电话 *telephone*] NOUN = public telephone, payphone
- 现在很多人都有手机，公用电话不象从前那样重要了。**Xiànzài hěn duō rén dōu yǒu shǒujī, gōngyòng diànhuà búxiàng yǐqián nàyàng zhòngyào le.** = *Nowadays many people have cell phones, so public telephones are not as important as before.*

gōngyuán 公元 NOUN = of the Christian/common era, AD (*anno Domini*)
- 他生于公元前二十五年，死于公元三十一年。**Tā shēng yú gōngyuán qián èrshíwǔ nián, sǐ yú gōngyuán sānshíyī nián.** = *He was born in 25 BC and died in AD 31.*

gōngyuán qián 公元前 公元前 = BC (before Christ), BCE (before the Christian/common era)

gōngyuán 公园 [modif: 公 *public* + 园 *garden*] NOUN = public garden, park (座 zuò)
- 这个公园春天特别美。**Zhège gōngyuán chūntiān tèbié měi.** = *This park is especially beautiful in spring.*
- 早上很多人在公园里跑步。**Zǎoshang hěn duō rén zài gōngyuán li pǎobù.** = *Many people jog in the park early in the morning.*

gōng 功 NOUN = skill

gōngfu 功夫 NOUN
1 = same as 工夫 gōngfu
2 = martial arts
liàn gōngfu 练功夫 = practice martial arts
- 每天一大早他就起来练功夫。**Měitiān yí dà zǎo tā jiù qǐlai liàn gōngfu.** = *Every day he gets up in the early morning and practices the martial arts.*
gōngfu piàn 功夫片 = martial arts film

gōngkè 功课 NOUN = schoolwork, homework
- 他功课不错，考试成绩总是很好。**Tā gōngkè búcuò, kǎoshì chéngjì zǒngshì hěn hǎo.** = *His schoolwork is quite good, and his examination results are always very good.*

gōng 攻 VERB = attack (See 进攻 jìngōng.)

gōng 供 VERB = supply
- 大风期间，城市供水供电正常。**Dàfēng qījiān, chéngshì gōngshuǐ gōngdiàn zhèngcháng.** = *During the storm, the city's water and electricity supply was maintained.*
- 供大于求。**Gōng dà yú qiú.** = *Supply exceeds demand.*
- 供不应求。**Gōng bù yìng qiú.** = *Supply falls short of demand.*

gōngjǐ 供给 [compound: 供 *supply* + 给 *provide*] VERB = supply, provide
- 对于经济特别困难的学生，政府供给生活费。**Duìyú jīngjì tèbié kùnnan de xuésheng, zhèngfǔ gōngjǐ shēnghuófèi.** = *The government provided a living stipend to students with special financial difficulties.*

gǒng 巩 Trad 鞏 VERB = consolidate

G

gǒnggù 巩固 [compound: 巩 *consolidate* + 固 *reinforce*]
1 VERB = consolidate, strengthen
■ 我们这次会谈是为了巩固和发展我们之间的合作关系。**Wǒmen zhè cì huìtán shì wèile gǒnggù hé fāzhǎn wǒmen zhījiān de hézuò guānxi.** = *The purpose of our talks is to strengthen and develop cooperation.*
2 ADJECTIVE = solid, firm
■ 他们夫妻之间关系很巩固。**Tāmen fūqī zhī jiān guānxi hěn gǒnggù.** = *Their marital relationship has a solid foundation.*

gòng 共 ADVERB
1 = altogether, in total
■ 那座大学共有学生一万三千五百四十名。**Nà zuò dàxué gòng yǒu xuésheng yíwàn sānqiān wǔbǎi sìshí míng.** = *That university has a total student population of 13,540.*
2 = jointly, together (used only in writing)
■ 两家公司的董事长将共进午餐。**Liǎng jiā gōngsī de dǒngshìzhǎng jiāng gòngjìn wǔcān.** = *The chairmen of the two companies will have luncheon together.*

gònghéguó 共和国 NOUN = republic
■ 中国的全称是中华人民共和国. **Zhōngguó de quánchēng shì Zhōnghuá Rénmín Gònghéguó.** = *China's full name is the People's Republic of China.*
■ 什么样的国家才是真正的共和国? **Shénmeyàng de guójiā cái shì zhēnzhèng de gònghéguó?** = *What kind of country is a genuine republic?*

gòngchǎndǎng 共产党 [modif: 共 *to share* + 产 *property* + 党 *party*] NOUN = communist party
■ 你是中国共产党党员吗? **Nǐ shì Zhōngguó Gòngchǎndǎng dǎngyuán ma?** = *Are you a member of the Chinese Communist Party?*

gòngtóng 共同 [compound: 共 *together* + 同 *shared*] ADJECTIVE = common, shared
■ 我们共同努力，保护我们共同的家园 – 地球。**Wǒmen gòngtóng nǔlì, bǎohù wǒmen gòngtóng de jiāyuán – dìqiú.** = *Let's work together to protect our common homeland—the Earth.*
■ 我们之间缺乏共同语言，就不必多谈了。**Wǒmen zhī jiān quēfá gòngtóng yǔyán, jiù bú bì duō tán le.** = *As we do not have a common language, there is no need for further conversation.*

gòngxiàn 贡献 [compound: 贡 *tribute* + 献 *offer*] VERB = contribute, dedicate
■ 这位科学家为环境保护贡献了自己的一生。**Zhè wèi kēxuéjiā wèi huánjìng bǎohù gòngxiàn le zìjǐ de yìshēng.** = *This scientist dedicated his life to environment protection.*
■ 在过去的一年中全体职工为公司的繁荣作出了贡献。**Zài guòqù de yì nián zhōng quántǐ zhígōng wèi gōngsī de fánróng zuòchu le gòngxiàn.** = *In the past year, all the staff have contributed to the prosperity of the company.*
wèi ... zuòchu gòngxiàn 为 ... 作出贡献 = make a contribution to ...

gǒu 狗 NOUN = dog (只 zhī, 条 tiáo)
■ 我喜欢狗，但是不会象有些人那样让狗睡在我的床上。**Wǒ xǐhuan gǒu, dànshì bú huì xiàng yǒuxiē rén nàyàng ràng gǒu shuì zai wǒ de chuáng shang.** = *I like dogs but, unlike some people, I won't let a dog sleep on my bed.*
mǔ gǒu 母狗 = bitch
xiǎo gǒu 小狗 = puppy

gòu 构 Trad 構 VERB = construct, form

gòuchéng 构成 VERB = make up, form
■ 远山近水构成了美丽的风景。**Yuǎn-shān-jìn-shuǐ gòuchéngle měilì de fēngjǐng.** = *Hills in the background and a lake in the foreground make up a beautiful landscape.*

gòuzào 构造 NOUN = structure
■ 小小的手机构造极其复杂。**Xiǎoxiǎo de shǒujī gòuzào jíqí fùzá.** = *The cell phone, small as it is, has an extremely complex structure.*

gòu 够 ADJECTIVE = enough, sufficient
■ 够了，够了，谢谢你! **Gòu le, gòu le, xièxie nǐ!** = *That's enough. Thank you!*
■ 我们的汽油不够了，得加满才能开到目的地。**Wǒmen de qìyóu bú gòu le, děi jiā mǎn cái néng kāi dào mùdìdì.** = *Our petrol is not enough. We've got to fill up to reach our destination.*

gū 估 VERB = estimate

gūjì 估计 [compound: 估 *estimate* + 计 *calculate*]

1 VERB = estimate, reckon, size up
■ 我估计整个工程要花三百万元。**Wǒ gūjì zhénggè gōngchéng yào huā sānbǎiwàn yuán.** = *I estimate the entire project will cost three million yuan.*
■ 你估计他什么时候到？ **Nǐ gūjì tā shénme shíhou dào?** = *When do you reckon he will arrive?*

2 NOUN = estimate, approximate calculation, appraisal
■ 根据专家估计，今年经济增长可达百分之五。**Gēnjù zhuānjiā gūjì, jīnnián jīngjì zēngzhǎng kě dá bǎifēn zhī wǔ.** = *According to expert estimates, economic growth will reach five percent this year.*

gū 姑 NOUN = aunt, woman

gūgu 姑姑 NOUN = father's sister, aunt
■ 我姑姑一直没有结婚，把我当做自己的孩子。**Wǒ gūgu yìzhí méiyǒu jiéhūn, bǎ wǒ dāngzuo zìjǐ de háizi.** = *My father's sister never married and treats me as her own child.*

gūniang 姑娘 NOUN = unmarried young woman, girl, lass
■ 那个姑娘是谁家的孩子？ **Nàge gūniang shì shuí jiā de háizi?** = *Whose child is that girl?*
xiǎo gūniang 小姑娘 = little girl
■ 小姑娘一般比小男孩懂事。**Xiǎo gūniang yìbān bǐ xiǎo nánhái dǒngshì.** = *Little girls are generally more sensible than little boys.*
dàgūniang 大姑娘 = young woman (usually unmarried), lass

NOTE: 姑娘 **gūniang** is a colloquial word. When used to mean *unmarried young lady*, 姑娘 **gūniàng** is used together with the word 小伙子 **xiǎohuǒzi** (*young man*), e.g.
■ 姑娘小伙子都爱热闹。**Gūniang xiǎohuǒzi dōu ài rènao.** = *Young people all like having fun.*

gǔ 古 ADJECTIVE = ancient
■ 中国是一个文明古国，有很多古建筑。**Zhōngguó shì yí ge wénmíng gǔguó, yǒu hěnduō gǔ jiànzhù.** = *China is a country of ancient civilization and boasts a large number of ancient buildings.*

gǔdài 古代 [modif: 古 *ancient* + 代 *generation, time*] NOUN = ancient times
■ 古代中国创造了伟大的文明。**Gǔdài Zhōngguó chuàngzàole wěidà de wénmíng.** = *Ancient China created a great civilization.*

gǔjì 古迹 [modif: 古 *ancient* + 迹 *footprints*] NOUN = historic site, place of historic interest
■ 这个古迹每年吸引几万人参观。**Zhège gǔjì měi nián xīyǐn jǐ wàn rén cānguān.** = *This historic site attracts tens of thousands of visitors every year.*
■ 有些古迹没有得到有效保护，多么可惜！ **Yǒuxiē gǔjì méiyǒu dédào yǒuxiào bǎohù, duōme kěxī!** = *What a shame it is that some places of historic interest have not been protected effectively.*

gǔlǎo 古老 [compound: 古 *ancient* + 老 *old*] ADJECTIVE = ancient, time-honored
■ 中国的苏州有两千五百多年的历史，真是一座古老的城市。**Zhōngguó de Sūzhōu yǒu liǎngqiān wǔbǎi duō nián de lìshǐ, zhēn shì yí zuò gǔlǎo de chéngshì.** = *The city of Suzhou in China has a history of over 2,500 years. It is indeed an ancient city.*

gǔ 骨 NOUN = bone

gǔtou 骨头 NOUN = bone (根 gēn)
■ 他扔给小狗一根骨头。**Tā rēng gěi xiǎogǒu yì gēn gǔtou.** = *He threw the puppy a bone.*

gǔ 股 NOUN = share

gǔpiào 股票 [modif: 股 *share* + 票 *ticket*] NOUN = share
■ 他上个月买了这家公司十万股票。**Tā shàngge yuè mǎile zhè jiā gōngsī shíwàn gǔpiào.** = *He bought 10,000 shares of the company last month.*

gǔ 鼓 NOUN = drum

gǔlì 鼓励 VERB = encourage
■ 新加坡政府鼓励华人说华语。**Xīnjiāpō zhèngfǔ gǔlì Huárén shuō Huáyǔ.** = *The Singapore government encourages ethnic Chinese people to speak Mandarin.*
wùzhì gǔlì 物质鼓励 = material incentive

G

jīngshén gǔlì 精神鼓励 = moral incentive, moral encouragement

gǔwǔ 鼓舞 [compound: 鼓 *drum up* + 舞 *dance*] VERB = inspire, fire ... with enthusiasm, hearten
■ 这个消息真是鼓舞人心! **Zhège xiāoxi zhēn shì gǔwǔ rénxīn.** = *This news is really inspiring!*

gǔzhǎng 鼓掌 [v+obj: 鼓 *drum* + 掌 *palm*] VERB = applaud
■ 小明要给大家唱一首中国歌曲，让我们鼓掌欢迎。**Xiǎo Míng yào gěi dàjiā chàng yì shǒu Zhōngguó gēqǔ, ràng wǒmen gǔzhǎng huányíng.** = *Xiao Ming is going to sing us a Chinese song. Let's give him a big hand.*

gù 固 VERB = strengthen (See 巩固 **gǒnggù**.)

gù 故 ADJECTIVE = old, former

gùshi 故事 [modif: 故 *old, past* + 事 *happening, event*] NOUN = story, tale
■ 这是一个真实的故事。**Zhè shì yí ge zhēnshí de gùshi.** = *This is a true story.*
■ 他每天晚上都给孩子讲一个故事。**Tā měi tiān wǎnshang dōu gěi háizi jiǎng yí ge gùshi.** = *He tells his child a story every evening.*
jiǎng gùshi 讲故事 = tell a story
tīng gùshi 听故事 = listen to a story

gùxiāng 故乡 [modif: 故 *former years* + 乡 *village, homeland*] NOUN = native place, hometown, home village
■ 他退休以后，要回故乡定居。**Tā tuìxiū yǐhòu yào huí gùxiāng dìngjū.** = *After retirement he will return to his hometown to live.*

gùyì 故意 [modif: 故 *on purpose* + 意 *intention*] ADJECTIVE = deliberate, intentional, on purpose (antonym 无意 **wúyì**)
■ 他犯的错误是无意的，不是故意的。**Tā fàn de cuòwù shì wúyì de, búshì gùyì de.** = *He did not commit this mistake deliberately, but by accident.*

gù 顾 Trad 顧 VERB = attend to, care for
■ 你不能只顾自己，不管别人。**Nǐ bù néng zhǐ gù zìjǐ, bù guǎn biérén.** = *You shouldn't care for only yourself and nobody else.*

■ 他忙得顾不上吃饭。**Tā máng de gù bu shàng chīfàn.** = *He was so busy that he did not have time for meals.*

gùkè 顾客 NOUN = customer, client (位 **wèi**)
■ 我们尽量满足顾客的要求。**Wǒmen jìnliàng mǎnzú gùkè de yāoqiú.** = *We try our best to meet customers' demands.*

guā 瓜 NOUN = melon, gourd (See 黄瓜 **huángguā**, 西瓜 **xīguā**.)

guā 刮 VERB = (of a wind) blow
■ 这儿冬天经常刮西北风。**Zhèr dōngtiān jīngcháng guā xīběi fēng.** = *A northwestern wind often blows here in winter.*

guà 挂 Trad 掛 VERB = hang up
■ 墙上挂着一幅世界地图。**Qiáng shang guàzhe yì fú shìjiè dìtú.** = *A map of the world hung on the wall.*

guàhào 挂号 VERB = register (at a hospital)
■ 在中国看病的第一件事就是挂号。**Zài Zhōngguó kànbìng de dì-yī jiàn shì jiù shì guàhào.** = *In China, when you go to a doctor the first thing to do is to register.*
guàhào fèi 挂号费 = registration fee, doctor's consultation fee
guàhào chù 挂号处 = registration office

NOTE: In China if you are sick you go to a hospital where doctors work in their specialist departments, e.g. internal medicine, gynecology and dermatology. 挂号 **guàhào** means to tell a receptionist which department you want to go to and pay the consultation fee. Dentistry is usually one of the departments and a dentist is generally considered just another doctor.

guǎi 拐 VERB = turn, make a turn
■ 往前走，再向左拐，就是火车站。**Wàng qián zǒu, zài xiàng zuǒ guǎi, jiù shì huǒchēzhàn.** = *Walk straight on, then turn left, and you will find the railway station.*

guài 怪
1 ADJECGIVE = strange, odd, queer
■ 我刚才放在这儿的书怎么一会儿就不见了，真怪! **Wǒ gāngcái fàng zài zhèr de shū**

zénme yíhuìr jiù bú jiàn le, zhēn guài! = *I left a book here just now and it's vanished. How odd!*
■ 昨天我碰到了怪事。**Zuótiān wǒ pèngdàole guài shì.** = *Something strange happened to me yesterday.*

2 VERB = blame
■ 都怪我，没讲清楚。**Dōu guài wǒ, méi jiǎng qīngchu.** = *It was all my fault. I did not make it clear.*
■ 你们别怪来怪去的，看看该怎么办吧。**Nǐmen bié guài-lái-guài-qù de, kànkan gāi zénme bàn ba.** = *Don't blame each other. Try to find out what should be done.*

guān 关 Trad 關 VERB = close; turn off
■ 你离开的时候，请把灯关掉，把门关上。**Nǐ líkāi de shíhou, qǐng bǎ dēng guāndiào, bǎ mén guānshàng.** = *When you leave, please turn off the lights and close the door.*
■ 学校晚上十一点半关大门。**Xuéxiào wǎnshang shíyī diǎn bàn guān dàmén.** = *The school gate is closed at 11:30 p.m.*
bǎ diàndēng / diànshì jī / lùyīng jī / jīqì guāndiào 把 电灯 / 电视机 / 录音机 / 机器关掉 = turn off the lights/TV/recorder/machine
bǎ mén/chuāng guānshang 把门 / 窗关上 = close the door/window

guānjiàn 关键 [compound: 关 *pass* + 键 *key*]
NOUN = what is crucial or critical
■ 一家公司的成功，关键在于人力资源。**Yì jiā gōngsì de chénggōng, guānjiàn zàiyú rénlì zīyuán.** = *The success of a company lies in its human resources.*
■ 他踢进了关键的一球。**Tā tījìnle guānjiàn de yì qiú.** = *He scored the crucial goal.*

guānxi 关系 [compound: 关 *related* + 系 *connected*]
1 NOUN = connection, relation
这两件事有没有关系？ **Zhè liǎng jiàn shì yǒu méiyǒu guānxi?** = *Is there any connection between these two matters? (→Are these two matters related?)*
■ 我和他只是一般朋友关系。我希望保持这种关系。**Wǒ hé tā zhǐ shì yìbān péngyou guānxi. Wǒ xīwàng bǎochí zhè zhǒng guānxi.** = *He and I are merely ordinary friends, and I intend to keep it that way.*
2 VERB = affect, have bearing on

■ 睡得好不好，关系到你的健康。**Shuì de hǎo bù hào, guānxi dào nǐ de jiànkāng.** = *Whether you sleep well or not affects your health.*
■ 能不能考上大学，关系到青年人的前途。**Néng bù néng kǎoshàng dàxué, guānxi dào qīngniánrén de qiántú.** = *Whether a young man passes the university entrance examination or not has bearing on his future.*
hé ... yǒu guānxi 和 ... 有关系 = have something to do with
■ 这件事和大家都有关系。**Zhè jiàn shì hé dàjiā dōu yǒu guānxi.** = *This matter concerns everybody.*
méi(yǒu)guānxi 没(有)关系 = it doesn't matter, it's OK
■ "对不起。" "没关系。" **"Duìbuqǐ." "Méiguānxi."** = [when you have unintentionally hurt somebody] *"I'm sorry." "It's OK."*

guānxīn 关心 [v + obj: 关 *connected* + 心 *the heart*] VERB = be concerned about, care for
■ 妈妈总是关心孩子的健康。**Māma zǒngshì guānxīn háizi de jiànkāng.** = *Mothers are always concerned about their children's health.*
■ 对公司的业务情况，每个职工都很关心。**Duì gōngsī de yèwù qíngkuàng, měi ge zhígōng dōu hěn guānxīn.** = *Every employee is deeply concerned about the business of the company.*

guānyú 关于 PREPOSITION = about, on
■ 我很久没有听到关于他的消息了。**Wǒ hěn jiǔ méiyǒu tīngdào guānyú tā de xiāoxi le.** = *I haven't heard about him for a long time.*
■ 关于这个月的营业情况，你得问王经理。**Guānyú zhège yuè de yíngyè qíngkuàng, nǐ děi wèn Wáng jīnglǐ.** = *You should ask Mr Wang, the manager, about business this month.*

guānzhào 关照 [compound: 关 *concerned* + 照 *look after*] VERB
1 = look after, take care of
■ 这里的工作请你关照一下。**Zhèli de gōngzuò qǐng nǐ guānzhào yíxia.** = *Please keep an eye on the work here.*
2 = notify, inform
■ 我已经关照服务员叫出租汽车了。**Wǒ yǐjīng guānzhào fúwùyuán jiào chūzū qìchē le.** = *I've asked the attendant to call a taxi.*

NOTE: 请你多关照。**Qǐng nǐ duō guānzhào.** is often said by someone who has just arrived or started working in a place, to someone who has been working there longer. It is a polite expression meaning something to the effect of "I'd appreciate your guidance."

guān 观 Trad 觀 VERB = look at, observe

guānchá 观察 [compound: 观 *see* + 察 *examine*] VERB = observe, watch
■ 这个人是否可靠，还需进一步观察。**Zhège rén shìfǒu kěkào, hái xū jìnyíbù guānchá.** = *Further observation is needed to determine whether this man is reliable or not.*
■ 对于市场情况，他观察得很仔细。**Duìyú shìchǎng qíngkuàng, tā guānchá de hěn zǐxì.** = *He watches the market very carefully.*
guāncháyuán 观察员 = observer (at a conference, especially an international conference)

guāndiǎn 观点 [modif: 观 *observe* + 点 *point*] NOUN = viewpoint, view
■ 对问题有不同的观点，是很正常的。**Duì wèntí yǒu bù tóng de guāndiǎn, shì hěn zhèngcháng de.** = *It is normal to have different views on an issue.*

guānzhòng 观众 [modif: 观 *watch* + 众 *crowd*] NOUN = audience (in a theatre, of TV, etc.), spectator
■ 观众对这个戏反映很好。**Guānzhòng duì zhège xì fǎnyìng hěn hǎo.** = *The audience responded very well to this play.*
■ 很多观众起立鼓掌。**Hěn duō guānzhòng qǐlì gǔzhǎng.** = *Many people in the audience stood up to applaud.*

guān 官 NOUN = (government) official
■ 很多中国人想当官。**Hěn duō Zhōngguórén xiǎng dāng guān.** = *Many Chinese want to be officials.*

NOTE: 官 **guān** is a colloquial word. For more formal occasions, use 官员 **guānyuán**.

guānyuán 官员 [suffix: 官 *official* + 员 nominal suffix] NOUN = official (位 **wèi**)
■ 这位官员很负责。**Zhè wèi guānyuán hěn fùzérèn.** = *This official has a strong sense of responsibility.*

■ 我想见一下这里的负责官员。**Wǒ xiǎng jiàn yíxià zhèli de fùzé guānyuán.** = *I want to see the official in charge here.*

NOTE: See note on 干部 **gànbù**.

guǎn 管 VERB = be in charge, take care (of)
■ 王老师管一年级的教学。**Wáng lǎoshī guǎn yī-niánjí de jiàoxué.** = *Teacher Wang is in charge of the first-year courses.*
■ 你们公司谁管人力资源？**Nǐmen gōngsī shéi guǎn rénlì zīyuán?** = *Who is in charge of human resources in your company?*
■ 别管我！**Bié guǎn wǒ!** = *Leave me alone!*

guǎnlǐ 管理 [compound: 管 *be in charge* + 理 *put in order*] VERB = manage, administer
■ 他管理工厂很有办法。**Tā guǎnlǐ gōngchǎng hěn yǒu bànfǎ.** = *He is resourceful and efficient in managing the factory.*
■ 这些图书资料管理得很好。**Zhèxiē túshū zīliào guǎnlǐ de hěn hǎo.** = *These books and files are well taken care of.*
shāngyè guǎnlǐ 商业管理 = business administration

guǎn 馆 Trad 館 NOUN = building (for a specific purpose)
fànguǎn 饭馆 = restaurant
guǎnzi 馆子 = restaurant (colloquial)
tǐyùguǎn 体育馆 = gymnasium
túshūguǎn 图书馆 = library

guàn 贯 Trad 貫 VERB = pass through

guànchè 贯彻 VERB = implement, carry out
■ 贯彻这项新政策，大约要半年时间。**Guànchè zhè xiàng xīn zhèngcè, dàyuē yào bànnián shíjiān.** = *Implementing the new policy will take about half a year.*

guàn 冠 NOUN = the best

guànjūn 冠军 NOUN = champion, championship
■ 我们学校获得了全市中学生篮球邀请赛冠军。**Wǒmen xuéxiào huòdéle quán shì zhōngxuéshēng lánqiú yāoqǐngsài guànjūn.** = *Our school has won the city high school basketball invitational tournament championship.*

guàn 惯 Trad 慣 ADJECTIVE = accustomed to
(See 习惯 **xíguàn**.)

guàn 罐 NOUN = tin, jar

guàntou 罐头 [suffix: 罐 *tin, can* + 头 *nominal suffix*] NOUN = can, tin
■ 这个罐头里面是什么呀? **Zhège guàntou lǐmiàn shì shénme ya?** = *What's in this can?*
guàntou shípǐn 罐头食品 = canned food

guāng 光
1 NOUN = light
■ 发光的不一定是金子。**Fā guāng de bù yídìng shì jīnzi.** = *All that glitters is not gold.*
dēngguāng 灯光 = lamplight
yángguāng 阳光 = sunlight
yuèguāng 月光 = moonlight
2 ADVERB = only, sole
■ 光有钱就能幸福吗? **Guāng yǒu qián jiù néng xìngfú ma?** = *Can money alone make you happy?*
■ 她光练口语, 不写汉字, 可不行。**Tā guāng liàn kǒuyǔ, bù xiě Hànzì, kě bù xíng.** = *She only practices oral Chinese and does not write characters. This won't do.*

guāngdié 光碟 [modif: 光 *light, laser* + 碟 *disk*] NOUN = compact disk (CD) (盘 **pán**)

guānghuī 光辉 [compound: 光 *light* + 辉 *splendor*]
1 NOUN = brilliance, radiance
■ 云挡不住太阳的光辉。**Yún dǎng bu zhù tàiyang de guānghuī.** = *The clouds cannot shut out the brilliance of the sunshine.*
2 ADJECTIVE = brilliant, splendid
■ 他在医学研究上取得了光辉的成绩。**Tā zài yīxué yánjiū shang qǔdé le guānghuī de chéngjì.** = *He achieved brilliant results in medical research.*

guāngmíng 光明 [compound: 光 *light* + 明 *bright*] ADJECTIVE = bright, promising
■ 只要努力就会有光明的前途。**Zhǐyào nǔlì jiùhuì yǒu guāngmíng de qiántú.** = *If only you work hard, you will have a bright future.*

guāngróng 光荣 [compound: 光 *light* + 荣 *glory*] ADJECTIVE = glorious, honorable
■ 他代表全校参加这次比赛, 是很光荣的。

Tā dàibiǎo quánxiào cānjiā zhè cì bǐsài, shì hěn guāngróng de. = *He represented the school in the competition, which was a great honor.*

guāngxiàn 光线 [compound: 光 *light* + 线 *string*] NOUN = light, ray (道 **dào**)
■ 这个房间光线太暗。**Zhège fángjiān guāngxiàn tài àn.** = *This room is not bright enough.*

guǎng 广 Trad 廣 ADJECTIVE = extensive, wide

guǎngbō 广播 [modif: 广 *extensive, wide* + 播 *sow, spread*]
1 VERB = broadcast
■ 今天早上广播了一条重要新闻。**Jīntiān zǎoshang guǎngbōle yì tiáo zhòngyào xīnwén.** = *A piece of important news was broadcast early this morning.*
2 NOUN = broadcasting
■ 这位老人每天都听新闻广播。**Zhè wèi lǎorén měi tiān dōu tīng xīnwén guǎngbō.** = *This old man listens to the news broadcast every day.*
guǎngbō diàntái 广播电台 = radio station
guǎngbō gōngsī 广播公司 = broadcasting company
guǎngbōyuán 广播员 = newsreader
Yīngguó Guǎngbō Gōngsī 英国广播公司 = the British Broadcasting Company (BBC)

guǎngchǎng 广场 [modif: 广 *broad* + 场 *ground*] NOUN = square
■ 中国最著名的广场是天安门广场。
Zhōngguó zuì zhùmíng de guǎngchǎng shì Tiān'ānmén Guǎngchǎng. = *The best-known square in China is Tiananmen Square.*

guǎngdà 广大 [compound: 广 *broad* + 大 *big*] ADJECTIVE = vast, extensive
■ 中国西北广大地区还没有充分开发。
Zhōngguó xīběi guǎngdà dìqū hái méiyǒu chōngfèn kāifā. = *The vast area of China's Northwest is yet to be fully developed.*

guǎngfàn 广泛 [compound: 广 *broad* + 泛 *extensive*] ADJECTIVE = widespread, wide-ranging, extensive
■ 他们对市场进行了广泛的调查。**Tāmen duì shìchǎng jìnxíngle guǎngfàn de diàochá.**

G

= *They conducted an extensive market investigation.*

guǎnggào 广告 [modif: 广 *broad* + 告 *inform*] NOUN = advertisement
■ 一般电视观众都讨厌电视广告。**Yìbān diànshì guānzhòng dōu tǎoyàn diànshì guǎnggào.** = *TV viewers generally hate commercials.*
■ 开店以前，他们先在报上登了大广告。**Kāidiàn yǐqián, tāmen xiān zài bào shang dēngle dà guǎnggào.** = *Before the store opened, they ran a huge advertisement in the newspaper.*

guǎngkuò 广阔 [compound: 广 *broad* + 阔 *wide*] ADJECTIVE = vast, wide
■ 中国东北有一片广阔的平原。**Zhōngguó dōngběi yǒu yípiàn guǎngkuò de píngyuán.** = *China's Northeast boasts a vast plain.*

guàng 逛 VERB = stroll, take a random walk
■ 我这么忙，哪有时间陪你逛街？**Wǒ zhème máng, nǎ yǒu shíjiān péi nǐ guàng jiē?** = *I'm so busy. How can I find time to go window-shopping with you?*
guàng gōngyuán 逛公园 = stroll in the park
guàng jiē 逛街 = stroll around the streets, do window shopping

guī 规 Trad 規 NOUN = regulation, rule

guīdìng 规定 [compound: 规 *stipulate* + 定 *decide*]
1 VERB = stipulate
■ 政府规定，珍贵文物不能带出国。**Zhèngfǔ guīdìng, zhēnguì wénwù bù néng dàichū guó.** = *The government stipulates that precious cultural relics may not be taken out of the country.*
2 NOUN = regulation
■ 必须遵守海关的规定。**Bìxū zūnshǒu hǎiguān de guīdìng.** = *Customs regulations must be obeyed.*

guīlǜ 规律 [compound: 规 *regulation* + 律 *law*] NOUN = law, regular pattern
■ 经济活动十分复杂，但是还是有规律的。**Jīngjì huódòng shífēn fùzá, dànshì háishì yǒu guīlǜ de.** = *Economic activities are very complicated, but they also follow regular patterns.*

guīmó 规模 NOUN = scale
■ 这次航空展览会规模很大。**Zhè cì hángkōng zhǎnlǎnhuì guīmó hěn dà.** = *This is a large-scale air show.*

guǐ 鬼 NOUN = ghost
■ "你怕鬼吗？" "不怕，我根本不相信有鬼。" **"Nǐ pà guǐ ma?" "Bú pà, wǒ gēnběn bù xiāngxìn yǒu guǐ."** = *"Are you afraid of ghosts?" "No, I don't believe in ghosts at all."*
guǐ gùshi 鬼故事 = ghost story
guǐ wū 鬼屋 = haunted house

guì 贵 Trad 貴 ADJECTIVE = expensive, of great value (antonym 便宜 **piányì**)
■ 这家商店的东西很贵。**Zhè jiā shāngdiàn de dōngxi hěn guì.** = *The goods in this shop are all very expensive.*
■ 什么？要一千块钱？太贵了！**Shénme? Yào yìqiān kuài qián? Tài guì le.** = *What? One thousand dollars? It's too expensive.*

guìxìng 贵姓 [modif: 贵 *valuable* + 姓 *family name*] IDIOM = your family name
■ "请问，您贵姓？" "我姓王。" **"Qǐngwèn, nín guìxìng?" "Wǒ xìng Wáng."** = *"What's your family name?" "Wang."*
■ "您大名是…？" "我叫宝华。" **"Nín dàmíng shì…?" "Wǒ jiào Bǎohuá."** = *"And your given name is…?" "It's Baohua."*
■ "您是王宝华先生？" "是，是。" **"Nín shì Wáng Bǎohuá xiānsheng?" "Shì, shì."** = *"Oh, you're Mr Wang Baohua?" "That's right."*

NOTES: (1) While 贵姓 **guìxìng** is the polite form when asking about somebody's family name, the polite way to ask somebody's given name is 请问，您大名是…? **Qǐngwèn, nín dàmíng shì…?** 大名 literally means *big name*. The answer to this question is 我叫XX。**Wǒ jiào XX.** (2) The word 贵 **guì** in the sense of *valuable* is added to certain nouns to mean *your…*, e.g. 贵姓 **guìxìng** = *your family name*, 贵国 **guìguó** = *your country*, 贵校 **guìxiào** = *your school.* They are only used in formal and polite contexts.

gǔn 滚 VERB = roll
■ 球滚到沙发下面去了。**Qiú gǔn dào shāfā xiàmiàn qu le.** = *The ball rolled under the armchair.*

NOTE: 滚 **gǔn** is used to tell somebody "get out of here" or "beat it," e.g.
- 滚! 滚出去! **Gǔn! Gǔn chūqu!** = *Get lost! Get out of here!*
- 滚开! **Gǔn kāi!** = *Beat it!*

These are highly offensive.

guō 锅 Trad 鍋 NOUN = pot, pan, wok
- 做好菜，要把锅洗干净。**Zuòhao cài, yào bǎ guō xǐ gānjìng.** = *After cooking, you should wash the pot clean.*

guó 国 Trad 國 NOUN = country
- 国与国之间应该是平等的。**Guó yú guó zhī jiān yīnggāi shì píngděng de.** = *There should be equality among nations.*

Déguó 德国 = Germany
Fǎguó 法国 = France
Měiguó 美国 = the United States of America
Yīngguó 英国 = England, the United Kingdom
Zhōngguó 中国 = China

guójì 国际 NOUN = international
- 反对恐怖活动已经成为一个国际问题。**Fǎnduì kǒngbù huódòng yǐjīng chéngwéi yí ge guójì wèntí.** = *Anti-terrorism has become an international issue.*
- 打国际长途电话越来越便宜了。**Dǎ guójì chángtú diànhuà yuèlaiyuè piányì le.** = *International long-distance calls have become less and less expensive.*

guójì fǎ 国际法 = international law
guójì huìyì 国际会议 = international conference

guójiā 国家 [compound: 国 *country* + 家 *family*] NOUN = country, state
- 这个国家历史很长。**Zhège guójiā lìshǐ hěn cháng.** = *This country has a long history.*
- 他代表国家参加运动会。**Tā dàibiǎo guójiā cānjiā yùndònghuì.** = *He represented his country in the sports meet.*
- "你去过几个国家?" **"Nǐ qùguo jǐ ge guójiā?"** = *"How many countries have you been to?"*

NOTE: It is significant that the Chinese word meaning *country*— 国家 **guójiā**—is composed of the word 国 **guó** (*country*) and the word 家 **jiā** (*family*). In traditional Chinese thought, China was one big family and the country was ruled as such, with the emperor as the patriarch.

Guómǐndǎng 国民党 NOUN = the Kuomintang (KMT, the political party which ruled China before 1949 and is now a major party in Taiwan.)

guǒ 果 NOUN = fruit (See 成果 **chéngguǒ**, 结果 **jiéguǒ**, 苹果 **píngguǒ**, 水果 **shuǐguǒ**, 效果 **xiàoguǒ**.)

guò 过 Trad 過 VERB
1 = pass, cross
- 过马路，一定要小心。**Guò mǎlù, yídìng yào xiǎoxīn.** = *You must be very careful when crossing the street.*
2 = spend (time), live (a life), observe (a festival)
- 他在国外过了这么多年，生活习惯有些改变了。**Tā zài guówài guòle zhème duō nián, shēnghuó xíguàn yǒu xiē gǎibiàn le.** = *He has spent so many years overseas that some of his habits have changed.*
- 从此以后，他们俩过得很幸福。**Cóngcǐ yǐhòu, tāmen liǎ guò de hěn xìngfú.** = *They lived happily ever after.*

guòlai 过来 = come over, come across (towards the speaker)
- 他正从马路那边过来。**Tā zhèng cóng mǎlù nàbiān guòlai.** = *He's coming over from the other side of the street.*
- 公共汽车开过来了。**Gōnggòng qìchē kāi guòlai le.** = *A bus is coming over.*

guòqu 过去 = go over, go across (away from the speaker)
- 街上车太多，很难过去。**Jiē shang chē tài duō, hěn nán guòqu.** = *Traffic in the street is too heavy. It's very difficult to go across.*
- 河水很急，我游不过去。**Héshuǐ hěn jí, wǒ yóu bù guòqu.** = *The river runs swiftly. I can't swim across it.*

guò rìzi 过日子 = live a life
guò nián 过年 = observe New Year's Day
guò jié 过节 = observe a festival

guòchéng 过程 NOUN = process, course
- 从葡萄变成酒，是一个又长又复杂的过程。**Cóng pútao biànchéng jiǔ, shì yí ge yòu cháng yòu fùzá de guòchéng.** = *The process by which grapes become wine is a long and complicated one.*

guònián 过年 VERB = observe the (Chinese) New Year's Day

G

■ 小孩子最喜欢过年。**Xiǎoháizi zuì xǐhuan guònián.** = *Children are most enthusiastic about celebrating New Year's Day.*

guòqù 过去 [compound: 过 *pass* + 去 *gone*]
NOUN = (something) in the past
■ 过去的事，不要多想了。**Guòqù de shì, bú yào duō xiǎng le.** = *Don't keep thinking about what's past. (→ Let bygones be bygones.)*
■ 他过去常常生病，现在身体好多了。**Tā guòqù chángcháng shēngbìng, xiànzài shēntǐ hǎo duō le.** = *He was often sick in the past. Now he is in much better health.*

guo 过 Trad 過 PARTICLE = (used after a verb or adjective to emphasize a past experience)
■ "你去过中国没有？""去过，我去过中国很多地方。" **"Nǐ qùguo Zhōngguó méiyǒu?" "Qùguo, wǒ qùguo Zhōngguó hěn duō dìfang."** = *"Have you been to China?" "Yes, I've been to many parts of China."*

H

hā 哈 ONOMATOPOEIA = (sound of loud laughter)

hāhā 哈哈 ONOMATOPOEIA = (representing loud laughter)
■ 听了孩子天真的话，老人哈哈大笑起来。**Tīngle háizi tiānzhēn de huà, lǎorén hāhā dàxiào qǐlai.** = *Hearing the child's naïve words, the old man burst into laughter.*

hái 还 Trad 還 ADVERB = still, as before
■ 时间还早，我还想看一会儿书再睡。**Shíjiān hái zǎo, wǒ xiǎng kàn yíhuìr shū zài shuì.** = *It's still early. I want to do a little reading before going to bed.*
■ 已经上午十点钟了，我还没有吃早饭呢。**Yǐjīng shàngwǔ shí diǎnzhōng le, wǒ hái méiyǒu chī zǎofàn ne.** = *It's already ten o'clock, and I still haven't had my breakfast.*

háishì 还是 1 ADVERB = still, as before
■ 老师说了两遍，我还是不大懂。**Lǎoshī shuō le liǎng biàn, wǒ háishì bú dà dǒng.** = *The teacher has explained twice, but I still don't quite understand.*

háishì 还是 2 CONJUNCTION = or
■ 你喝茶还是喝咖啡？**Nǐ hē chá háishì hē kāfēi?** = *Would you like tea or coffee?*
■ 我们今天去看电影还是明天去？**Wǒmen jīntiān qù kàn diànyǐng háishì míngtiān qù?** = *Shall we go and see the movie today or tomorrow?*

hái 孩 NOUN = child

háizi 孩子 [suffix: 孩 *child* + 子 nominal suffix] NOUN = child, children
■ 这个孩子真聪明！**Zhège háizi zhēn cōngmíng!** = *This child is really smart! (→ What a bright child!)*
■ 他们有一个男孩子，两个女孩子。**Tāmen yǒu yí ge nán háizi, liǎng ge nǚ háizi.** = *They have a son and two daughters.*

hǎi 海 NOUN = sea
■ 没有风，海很平静。**Méiyǒu fēng, hǎi hěn píngjìng.** = *There's no wind. The sea is calm.*
■ 这个国家任何地方都离海很近。**Zhège guójiā rènhe dìfang dōu lí hǎi hěn jìn.** = *Anywhere in this country is close to the sea.*
■ 海水冷吗？可以游泳吗？**Hǎi shuǐ lěng ma? Kěyǐ yóuyǒng ma?** = *Is the seawater cold? Can we swim?*

hǎiguān 海关 [modif: 海 *sea* + 关 *pass*] NOUN = customs, customs house
■ 通过海关的时候，要检查护照。**Tōngguò hǎiguān de shíhou, yào jiǎnchá hùzhào.** = *Your passport will be examined when you pass through customs.*
hǎiguān jiǎnchá 海关检查 = customs inspection, customs examination
hǎiguān shǒuxù 海关手续 = customs formalities
hǎiguān rényuán 海关人员 = customs officer

hǎiyáng 海洋 [compound: 海 *sea* + 洋 *ocean*] NOUN = sea, ocean
■ 地球表面十分之七是海洋。**Dìqiú biǎomiàn shí fēnzhī qī shì hǎiyáng.** = *Seven-tenths of the Earth's surface is covered by seas and oceans.*
hǎiyáng shēngwù 海洋生物 = sea life

hài 害 VERB = harm, cause harm to
■ 吸烟不但害自己，而且害别人。**Xīyān búdàn hài zìjǐ, érqiě hài biérén.** = *Smoking not only harms the smoker, it harms others too.*

yǒuhài 有害 = harmful
- 吸烟有害健康。**Xīyān yǒuhài jiànkāng.** = *Smoking is harmful to health.*

hàichóng 害虫 = pest (insect)

hàichu 害处 [modif: 害 *harmful* + 处 *place*] NOUN = harm (antonym 好处 **hǎochu**)
- 大家都知道吸烟的害处。**Dàjiā dōu zhīdào xīyān de hàichu.** = *Everybody knows the harm that smoking causes.*
- 对孩子严格一点，只有好处，没有害处。**Duì háizi yángé yìdiǎn, zhǐyǒu hǎochu, méiyǒu hàichu.** = *To be strict with children has only benefits, and will cause no harm.*

hàipà 害怕 VERB = fear, be fearful
- 她夜里一个人走回家，心里有点害怕。**Tā yèli yí ge rén zǒu huí jiā, xīnli yǒudiǎn hàipà.** = *She was fearful walking home alone at night.*

hán 含 VERB = hold in the mouth, contain, have … as ingredient
- 孩子嘴里含着一块糖，说不清话。**Háizi zuǐ li hánzhe yí kuài táng, shuō bu qīng huà.** = *The child had a piece of candy in his (or her) mouth and couldn't speak clearly.*

hán 寒 ADJECTIVE = cold

hánjià 寒假 [modif: 寒 *cold* + 假 *holiday*] NOUN = winter vacation
- 中国的学校一般在一月开始放寒假。**Zhōngguó de xuéxiào yìbān zài Yīyuè kāishǐ fàng hánjià.** = *In China, schools generally begin their winter holidays in January.*

hánlěng 寒冷 [compound: 寒 *freezing* + 冷 *cold*] ADJECTIVE = freezing cold
- 世界上最寒冷的地方在南极。**Shìjiè shang zuì hánlěng de dìfang zài Nánjí.** = *The coldest place on earth is in the Antarctic.*
- 加拿大北部天气寒冷，一年中有半年多下雪。**Jiānádà běibù tiānqì hánlěng, yì nián zhōng yǒu bànnián duō xià xuě.** = *North Canada is very cold; it snows over six months in a year.*

hǎn 喊 VERB = shout
- 有人在外面喊你。**Yǒu rén zài wàimiàn hǎn nǐ.** = *Someone is calling for you outside.*

hàn 汗 NOUN = sweat, perspiration

chūhàn 出汗 = to sweat, to perspire
- 这个房间热得我出汗。**Zhège fángjiān rè de wǒ chūhàn.** = *The room was so hot that I perspired.*

Hàn 汉 Trad 漢 NOUN = the Han people

Hànyǔ 汉语 [modif: 汉 *the Han people* + 语 *speech*] NOUN = the language of the Han people, the Chinese language
- 你学了几年汉语了？**Nǐ xuéle jǐ nián Hànyǔ le?** = *How many years have you been learning Chinese?*
- 我会说一点汉语。**Wǒ huì shuō yìdiǎn Hànyǔ.** = *I speak a little Chinese.*

NOTE: In Chinese there are a number of words denoting "the Chinese language." 汉语 **Hànyǔ** literally means *the language of the Han Chinese people*, in contrast with the languages of the non-Han peoples in China. 汉语 **Hànyǔ** is therefore the accurate, scientific term for the language. However, the most popular term for *the Chinese language* is 中文 **Zhōngwén**. In Singapore and other Southeast Asian countries, the standard Chinese language is often referred to as 华语 **Huáyǔ** in contrast to the various Chinese dialects spoken there. Also see note on 普通话 **Pǔtōnghuà**.

Hànzì 汉字 [modif: 汉 *the Han people* + 字 *word, character*] NOUN = Chinese character
- 这个汉字我不认识。**Zhège Hànzì wǒ bú rènshi.** = *I don't know this Chinese character.*
- 你会写多少汉字？**Nǐ huì xiě duōshǎo Hànzì?** = *How many Chinese characters can you write?*

hàn 憾 NOUN = regret (See 遗憾 **yíhàn**.)

háng 行 MEASURE WORD = line, row, queue (used with nouns that are formed in lines)
- 第四页第二行 **dì-sì yè dì-èr háng** = *line two on page four*

shísì háng shī 十四行诗 = sonnet

háng 航 VERB = navigate

hángkōng 航空 NOUN = aviation
hángkōng gōngsī 航空公司 = aviation company, airline

H

hángkōng xuéxiào 航空学校 = aviation school

háo 毫 NOUN = fine long hair

háo bù 毫不 ADVERB = not in the least, not at all
■ 他读书不用功，考试成绩不好毫不奇怪。**Tā dúshū bú yònggōng, kǎoshì chéngjì bù hǎo háo bù qíguài.** = *He didn't study hard, so it's no wonder he got very poor grades at the exams.*

> NOTE: 毫不 **háo bù** is an adverb used before an adjective of two or more syllables. For example, you can say 毫不奇怪 **háo bù qíguài** = *not at all strange*, but you cannot say 毫不怪 **háo bú guài**.

háo wú 毫无 VERB = have no ... at all, be in total absence of
■ 他心很硬，对不幸的人毫无同情心。**Tā xīn hěn yìng, duì búxìng de rén háo wú tóngqíngxīn.** = *He is hardhearted, and has no sympathy at all for less fortunate people.*

> NOTE: The object 毫无 **háo wú** usually takes a word of two or more syllables. The object usually refers to something abstract, like 同情心 **tóngqíngxīn** = *sympathy.*

hǎo 好 1 ADJECTIVE = good, all right (antonym 坏 **huài**, 差 **chà**)
■ 他总是愿意帮助学生，他是个好老师。**Tā zǒngshì yuànyì bāngzhù xuésheng, tā shì ge hǎo lǎoshī.** = *He is always ready to help his students. He is a good teacher.*
■ 我爸爸身体很好。**Wǒ bàba shēntǐ hěn hǎo.** = *My father is in good health.*
■ 你中文说得很好。**Nǐ Zhōngwén shuō de hěn hǎo.** = *You speak Chinese very well.*
hǎoxīn 好心 = kindhearted
■ 她是个好心人。**Tā shì ge hǎoxīn rén.** = *She is a kindhearted person.*

hǎo 好 2 ADVERB
1 = very, very much
■ 我生日那天，好多朋友都送给我贺卡和礼物。**Wǒ shēngrì nà tiān, hǎo duō péngyou dōu gěi wǒ sòng hèkǎ hé lǐwù.** = *Many friends gave me greeting cards and gifts on my birthday.*
2 = How...!
■ 你这件新衣服好漂亮！**Nǐ zhè jiàn xīn yīfu hǎo piàoliang!** = *How pretty your new dress is!*
hǎo duō 好多 = a good many, many, much

hǎochī 好吃 ADJECTIVE = delicious
■ 这种水果我没有尝过，好吃不好吃？**Zhè zhǒng shuǐguǒ wǒ méiyǒu chīguo, hǎochī bu hǎochī?** = *I've never tried this fruit before, is it good?*
■ 王太太做的这个菜，好吃极了！**Wáng tàitai zuò de zhège cài, hǎochī jíle!** = *This dish cooked by Mrs Wang is really delicious!*

hǎochu 好处 NOUN = benefit, being beneficial (antonyms 坏处 **huàichu**, 害处 **hàichu**)
■ 你惹爸爸生气，有什么好处呢？**Nǐ rě bàba shēngqì, yǒu shénme hǎochu ne?** = *What is the good of offending daddy?*
duì ... yǒu hǎochu 对...有好处 = be beneficial to
■ 经常锻炼对身体有很多好处。**Jīngcháng duànliàn duì shēntǐ yǒu hěnduō hǎochu.** = *Regular physical exercise is very beneficial to health.*

hǎohǎor 好好儿 ADJECTIVE = normal, nothing wrong
■ 她昨天还好好儿的，今天怎么病了呢？**Tā zuótiān hái hǎohǎor de, jīntiān zěnme bìng le ne?** = *She was quite well yesterday. How come she should fall ill today?*

hǎojiǔ 好久 ADVERB = a long time
■ 我好久没玩得这么痛快了。**Wǒ hǎojiǔ méi wán de zhème tòngkuai le.** = *I haven't had such fun for a long time.*
■ 他等了她好久，她才来。**Tā děngle tā hǎojiǔ, tā cái lái.** = *He waited for her for a long time before she came.*

hǎokàn 好看 ADJECTIVE
1 = pleasant to the eye, good-looking, pretty (antonym 难看 **nánkàn**)
■ 她妈妈年轻的时候很好看。**Tā māma niánqīng de shíhou hěn hǎokàn.** = *Her mother was beautiful when young.*
2 = interesting, absorbing
■ 这本小说好看不好看？**Zhè běn xiǎoshuō hǎokàn bu hǎokàn?** = *Is this novel interesting?*

hǎo róngyì 好容易 ADVERB = with great difficulty
■ 我好容易找到他家，他偏不在。**Wǒ hǎo róngyì zhǎodào tā jiā, tā piān bú zài.** = *I found his home with great difficulty, and he had to be out.*

NOTE: 好容易 **hǎo róngyì** is an idiomatic expression. You can also say 好不容易 **hǎo bù róngyì**, with exactly the same meaning, e.g. ■我好不容易找到他家，他偏不在。 **Wǒ hǎo bù róngyì zhǎodào tā jiā, tā piān bú zài.** = *I found his home with great difficulty, and he must be out.*

hǎotīng 好听 ADJECTIVE = pleasant to the ear, melodious (antonym 难听 **nántīng**)
■这首歌真好听，我越听越想听。 **Zhè shǒu gē zhēn hǎotīng, wǒ yuè tīng yuè xiǎng tīng.** = *This song is beautiful. The more I listen, the more I want to hear it.*
■他说话的声音很好听。 **Tā shuōhuà de shēngyīn hěn hǎotīng.** = *The voice he speaks in is pleasant. (→ He has a pleasant voice.)*

hǎowánr 好玩儿 ADJECTIVE = great fun
■这个游戏很好玩儿。 **Zhège yóuxì hěn hǎowánr.** = *This game is great fun.*

hǎoxiàng 好像 VERB = be like, similar to
■天边的白云好像一座雪山。 **Tiānbiān de bái yún hǎoxiàng yí zuò xuěshān.** = *The white cloud on the horizon looks like a snow mountain.*
■他今天好像不大高兴，你知道为什么吗？ **Tā jīntiān hǎoxiàng bú dà gāoxìng, nǐ zhīdào wèishénme ma?** = *He looks unhappy today. Do you know why?*
■你好像对这个地方很熟悉。 **Nǐ hǎoxiàng duì zhège dìfang hěn shúxī.** = *You seem to be familiar with this place.*

hǎoxiē 好些 ADJECTIVE = a good many, a large number of, lots of
■我有好些日子没见到他了。 **Wǒ yǒu hǎoxiē rìzi méi jiàndao tā le.** = *I haven't seen him for a long time.*

NOTE: 好些 **hǎoxiē** is a colloquial word, only used in casual, familiar styles.

hào 好 VERB = be fond of
■这个学生虚心好学，进步很快。 **Zhège xuésheng xūxīn hào xué, jìnbù hěn kuài.** = *This student is modest and fond of learning. He is making rapid progress.*
hào chī 好吃 = fond of eating, gluttonous
hào dòng 好动 = hyperactive
hào sè 好色 = oversexed, lewd

hào xué 好学 = fond of learning, thirsty for knowledge

hào 号 Trad 號 NOUN
1 = order of sequence
■小王住在三号楼五号房间。 **Xiǎo Wáng zhù zài sān hào lóu, wǔ hào fángjiān.** = *Xiao Wang lives in Building 3, Room 5.*
2 = date of month
■"今天几号？""今天二十号，九月二十号。" **"Jīntiān jǐ hào?" "Jīntiān èrshí hào, Jiǔyuè èrshí hào."** = *"What is the date today?" "It's the 20th, September 20th."*

NOTE: See note on 日 **rì**.

hàomǎ 号码 [compound: 号 order of sequence + 码 size] NOUN = serial number; size
■你知道张先生的电话号码吗？ **Nǐ zhīdào Zhāng xiānsheng de diànhuà hàomǎ ma?** = *Do you know Mr Zhang's telephone number?*
■"你穿多大号码的衬衫？""我穿四十码。" **"Nǐ chuān duō dà hàomǎ de chènshān?" "Wǒ chuān sìshí mǎ."** = *"What size shirt do you wear?" "Size 40."*
■这双鞋小了一点，有没有大一号码的？ **Zhè shuāng xié tài xiǎo le yìdiǎn, yǒu méiyǒu dà yī hàomǎ de?** = *This pair of shoes is a bit too small. Do you have a bigger size?*

hàozhào 号召 VERB = call upon, appeal
■中国政府号召一对夫妻只生一个孩子。 **Zhōngguó zhèngfǔ hàozhào yí duì fūqī zhǐ shēng yí ge háizi.** = *The Chinese government appeals to each couple to have only one child.*

hē 喝 VERB = drink
■我口渴，我想喝点水。 **Wǒ kǒu kě, wǒ xiǎng hē diǎn shuǐ.** = *I'm thirsty. I'd like to drink some water.*
■中国人一般先吃饭后喝汤，或者边吃饭边喝汤。 **Zhōngguórén yìbān xiān chī fàn zài hē tāng, huòzhě biān chī fàn biān hē tāng.** = *The Chinese usually have the main course before soup, or have the main course and soup at the same time.*

NOTE: 喝 **hē** (*drink*) and 渴 **kě** (*thirsty*) look similar. Be careful not to confuse the two characters.

hé 合 VERB = close
- 他太累了，一合上眼就睡着了。**Tā tài lèi le, yì hé shang yǎn jiù shuìzháo le.** = *He was so tired that he fell asleep the moment he closed his eyes.*

hélǐ 合理 [v+obj: 合 *conform* + 理 *reason*]
ADJECTIVE = conforming to reason, reasonable, logical
- 你这个建议十分合理。**Nǐ zhège jiànyì shífēn hélǐ.** = *Your proposal is very reasonable.*
- 对于你们的合理要求，我们会尽力满足。**Duìyú nǐmen de hélǐ yāoqiú, wǒmen huì jìnlì mǎnzú.** = *We will do our best to meet your reasonable demands.*

héshì 合适 [compound: 合 *harmony* + 适 *fit*]
ADJECTIVE = suitable, appropriate
- 他做这个工作非常合适。**Tā zuò zhège gōngzuò fēicháng héshì.** = *He is very suitable to do this job.*
- 他比你年纪大，你叫他小张不合适。**Tā bǐ nǐ niánjì dà, nǐ jiào tā Xiǎo Zhāng bù héshì.** = *He is older than you. It's inappropriate for you to call him "Little Zhang."*
- 这个工作对他不合适。**Zhège gōngzuò duì tā bù héshì.** = *This job is not right for him.*

hétóng 合同 NOUN = contract, agreement (份 fèn)
- 我们公司已经和市政府签订合同，在新区建一座小学。**Wǒmen gōngsī yǐjīng hé shì zhèngfǔ qiāndìng hétóng, zài xīn qū jiàn yí zuò xiǎoxué.** = *Our company has signed a contract with the city government to build a primary school in the new district.*

hézuò 合作 [modif: 合 *jointly* + 作 *operate*]
1 VERB = cooperate
- 我们非常高兴和你们合作。**Wǒmen fēicháng gāoxìng hé nǐmen hézuò.** *We're very happy to cooperate with you.*
- 两国正在合作研究开发新能源。**Liǎng guó zhèngzài hézuò yánjiū kāifā xīn néngyuán.** = *The two countries are cooperating in the development of new energy sources.*
2 NOUN = cooperation
- 我们应该加强合作。**Wǒmen yīnggāi jiāqiáng hézuò.** = *We should strengthen our cooperation.*
- 王董事长对我们两家公司之间的合作十分满意。**Wáng dǒngshìzhǎng duì wǒmen liǎng jiā gōngsī zhī jiān de hézuò shífēn mǎnyì.** = *Chairman Wang is very pleased with the cooperation between our two companies.*

hé 何 PRONOUN = which, what (See 任何 rènhé.)

hé 河 NOUN = river
- 这条河太宽，我游不过去。**Zhè tiáo hé tài kuān, wǒ yóu bu guòqu.** = *This river is too broad. I can't swim across it.*

NOTE: In modern Chinese, 江 **jiāng** and 河 **hé** both mean *river*. Usually (not always) rivers in the south are known as 江 **jiāng** and rivers in the north are 河 **hé**.

hé 和
1 CONJUNCTION = and
- 我和你都在学中文。**Wǒ hé nǐ dōu zài xué Zhōngwén.** = *You and I are both learning Chinese.*
2 PREPOSITION = with
- 我想和你谈谈。**Wǒ xiǎng hé nǐ tántan.** = *I'd like to have a word with you.*
hé … yìqǐ 和...一起 = together with…
- 昨天我和朋友一起吃中饭。**Zuótiān wǒ hé péngyou yìqǐ chī zhōngfàn.** = *Yesterday I had lunch with a friend of mine.*

hé 盒 NOUN = box

hézi 盒子 [suffix: 盒 *box* + 子 nominal suffix]
NOUN = box (只 zhī)
- 她的铅笔盒子里有四支铅笔。**Tāde qiānbǐ hé li yǒu sì zhī qiānbǐ.** = *There are four pencils in her pencil box.*

hè 贺 Trad 賀 VERB = congratulate

hèkǎ 贺卡 [modif: 贺 *greeting* + 卡 *card*] NOUN = greeting card (张 zhāng)
- 去年圣诞节你收到多少贺卡？**Qùnián shèngdànjié nǐ shōudao duōshǎo hèkǎ?** = *How many cards did you get last Christmas?*
- 明天是小王生日，我们送他一张生日贺卡吧。**Míngtiān shì Xiǎo Wáng shēngrì, wǒmen sòng tā yì zhāng hèkǎ ba.** = *Tomorrow is Xiao Wang's birthday. Let's give him a card.*
diànzǐ hèkǎ 电子贺卡 = e-card
shèngdàn hèkǎ 圣诞贺卡 = Christmas card

shēngrì hèkǎ 生日贺卡 = birthday card
xīnnián hèkǎ 新年贺卡 = New Year's Day card

hēi 黑 ADJECTIVE = black, dark
■ 我不喜欢穿黑颜色的衣服。**Wǒ bù xǐhuan chuān hēi yánsè de yīfu.** = *I don't like to wear black.*
■ 天快黑了，他们还在踢球。**Tiān kuài hēi le, tāmen hái zài tīqiú.** = *It's almost dark, but they're still playing soccer.*

hēibǎn 黑板 NOUN = blackboard
■ 我们现在不用黑板，用白板。**Wǒmen xiànzài bú yòng hēibǎn, yòng báibǎn.** = *Now we don't use the blackboard; we use the whiteboard.*

hēi'àn 黑暗 [compound: 黑 *black, dark* + 暗 *dim*]
ADJECTIVE = dark (antonym 光明 **guāngmíng**)
■ 他很天真，不知道社会的黑暗面。**Tā hěn tiānzhēn, bù zhīdào shèhuì de hēi'àn miàn.** = *He is naive, unaware of the seamy side of society.*

hēi 嘿 INTERJECTION
1 = (used to attract someone's attention in a casual or impolite manner)
■ 嘿，这里不准吸烟。**Hēi, zhèlǐ bùzhǔn xīyān.** = *Hey! You can't smoke here.*
2 = (used to indicate admiration)
■ 嘿，昨天的球赛咱们队打得真棒！**Hēi, zuótiān de qiúsài zánmen duì dǎ de zhēn bàng!** = *Hey, our team played marvelously in yesterday's match!*

hěn 很 ADVERB = very
■ 见到你，我很高兴。**Jiàndào nǐ, wǒ hěn gāoxìng.** = *I'm glad to meet you.*
■ 我很讨厌下雨天。**Wǒ hěn tǎoyàn xià yǔ tiān.** = *I hate rainy days.*

NOTE: When used as predicates, Chinese adjectives normally require an adverb. For example, 我高兴 **Wǒ gāoxìng** sounds unnatural, while 我很高兴 **Wǒ hěn gāoxìng** (*I'm [very] happy*), 我不高兴 **Wǒ bù gāoxìng** (*I'm not happy*) or 我非常高兴 **Wǒ fēicháng gāoxìng** (*I'm very happy*) are normal sentences. The adverb 很 **hěn** is often used as a default adverb before an adjective. In such cases the meaning of 很 **hěn** is very weak.

hèn 恨 VERB
1 = hate, be angry with (antonym 爱 **ài**)
■ 她恨男朋友欺骗了她。**Tā hèn nán péngyou qīpiàn le tā.** = *She hates her boyfriend for cheating on her.*
2 = regret deeply
■ 他恨自己念书不用功，但是太晚了。**Tā hèn zìjǐ niànshū bú yònggōng, dànshì tài wǎn le.** = *He deeply regrets not having studied hard, but it's too late.*

hēng 哼 VERB
1 = snort
■ 他哼了一声，翻过身去，又睡了。**Tā hēngle yìshēng, fānguo shēn qù, yòu shuì le.** = *He gave a snort, turned over and fell asleep again.*
2 = hum
■ 她一边做饭，一边哼着歌。**Tā yìbiān zuòfàn, yìbiān hēngzhe gē.** = *While she cooked, she hummed a song.*

hóng 红 Trad 紅 ADJECTIVE = red
■ 中国人传统上喜欢红颜色。**Zhōngguórén chuántǒng shang xǐhuan hóng yánsè.** = *Traditionally the Chinese love the color red.*
■ 红花绿树，你的花园真好看。**Hóng huā, lù shù, nǐ de huāyuán zhēn hǎokàn.** = *With red flowers and green trees, your garden is really beautiful.*

hóngbāo 红包 = a red envelope (containing money), bribe
■ 在那里办事，要送红包。**Zài nàli bànshì, yào sòng hóngbāo.** = *To get things done there, bribes must be given.*

hónglùdēng 红绿灯 = traffic lights, stoplights

hóngchá 红茶 [modif: 红 *red* + 茶 *tea*] NOUN = black tea
■ 中国人喝红茶，不放糖和牛奶。**Zhōngguórén hē hóngchá, bú fàng táng hé niúnǎi.** = *The Chinese don't put sugar or milk in their black tea.*

hóu 猴 NOUN = monkey

hóuzi 猴子 [suffix: 猴 *monkey* + 子 suffix]
NOUN = monkey
■ 动物园里的猴子每天吸引很多小朋友。**Dòngwùyuán li de hóuzi měi tiān xīyǐn hěn duō**

H

xiǎo péngyou. = *The monkeys in the zoo attract many children every day.*

hòu 后 Trad 後 NOUN = back, rear (antonyms 前 qián, 先 xiān)
- 请用后门。**Qǐng yòng hòumén.** = *Please use the back door.*

hòubian 后边 [modif: 后 back, rear + 边 side] NOUN = back, rear, (antonym 前边 qiánbian)
- 我家的后边有一条小河。**Wǒ jiā de hòubian yǒu yì tiáo xiǎo hé.** = *There is a stream behind our house.*
- 听课的时候我喜欢坐在前边，不喜欢坐在后边。**Tīng kè de shíhou, wǒ xǐhuān zuò zài qiánbiān, bù xǐhuān zuò zài hòubian.** = *When attending lectures, I like to sit in the front row, not the back row.*

hòuhuǐ 后悔 [modif: 后 afterwards + 悔 regret, repent] VERB = regret, feel sorry (for having done something)
- 我真后悔，没听爸爸的话。**Wǒ zhēn hòuhuǐ, méi tīng bàba de huà.** = *I really regret not taking father's advice.*
- 你放弃这么好的机会，以后会后悔的。**Nǐ fàngqì zhème hǎo de jīhuì, yǐhòu huì hòuhuǐ de.** = *You'll regret giving up such a good opportunity.*

hòulái 后来 [modif: 后 late + 来 come] NOUN = afterwards, later on
- 他刚到北京的时候，不爱吃中国菜，后来就慢慢习惯了。**Tā gāng dào Běijīng de shíhou, bú ài chī Zhōngguó cài, hòulái mànman xíguàn le.** = *When he first came to Beijing he did not like Chinese food, but later on he gradually got used to it.*

hòumiàn 后面 NOUN = same as 后边 hòubian

hòunián 后年 [modif: 后 late + 年 year] NOUN = the year after next
- 我今年十九岁，后年就二十一岁了。**Wǒ jīnnián shíjiǔ suì, hòunián jiù èrshíyī suì le.** = *I'm nineteen this year, and I'll be twenty-one the year after next.*

hòutiān 后天 [modif: 后 late + 天 day] NOUN = the day after tomorrow
- 今天刚星期三，后天才星期五呢。**Jīntiān gāng Xīngqīsān, hòutiān cái Xīngqīwǔ ne.** = *It's only Wednesday today. Friday will be the day after tomorrow.*

hòu 厚 ADJECTIVE = thick (antonym 薄 baó)
- 这么厚的小说，她两天就看完了。**Zhème hòu de xiǎoshuō, tā liǎng tiān jiù kànwán le.** = *It took her only two days to finish reading such a thick novel.*

hou 候 VERB = wait (See 气候 qìhou, 时候 shíhou, 问候 wènhou, 有时候 yǒushíhou.)

hū 乎 PARTICLE = (added to another word to express strong emotions) (See 几乎 jīhū, 似乎 sìhū.)

hū 呼 VERB = exhale

hūxī 呼吸 [compound: 呼 exhale + 吸 inhale] VERB = breathe
- 我刚才不大舒服，在花园里呼吸了新鲜空气，感到好多了。**Wǒ gāngcái búdà shūfu, zài huāyuán li hūxīle xīnxiān kōngqì, gǎndào hǎo duō le.** = *I didn't feel well just now. I'm feeling much better now that I've had some fresh air in the garden.*

hū 忽 ADVERB = suddenly

hūrán 忽然 ADVERB = suddenly
- 刚才天气还好好儿的，忽然下起大雨来了。**Gāngcái tiānqì hái hǎohǎor de, hūrán xià qǐ dà yǔ lái le.** = *Just now the weather was still fine. Suddenly it's raining hard.*

hú 胡 Trad 鬍 NOUN = beard, moustach

húzi 胡子 [suffix: 胡 beard, whiskers + 子 nominal suffix] NOUN = beard, whiskers
- 你的胡子长了，要刮一下。**Nǐ de húzi cháng le, yào guā yíxià.** = *You've grown quite a beard. You need a shave.*
- guā húzi 刮胡子 = shave (beard, whiskers)

hú 壶 Trad 壺 NOUN = kettle (把 bǎ)
- 壶里还有水吗？**Hú li hái yǒu shuǐ ma?** = *Is there any water left in the kettle?*
- shuǐhú 水壶 = kettle

hú 糊 VERB = paste

hútu 糊涂 [compound: 糊 *muddled* + 涂 *mire*]
ADJECTIVE = muddle-headed, muddled, confused
■ 你真糊涂，怎么又忘了把钥匙放在哪儿
了？ **Nǐ zhēn hútu, zěnme yòu wàngle bǎ
yàoshi fàng zài nǎli le?** = *You're really muddle-
headed. How is it that you've forgotten where
you've left the keys again?*
■ 你越解释，我越糊涂，还是让我自己再看
一遍书吧。 **Nǐ yuè jiěshì, wǒ yuè hútu, háishì
ràng wǒ zìjǐ zài kàn yí biàn shū ba.** = *The more
you explain, the more confused I am. I'd better
read the book once more by myself.*
hútu chóng 糊涂虫 = muddle-headed person,
bungler

hú 湖 NOUN = lake
■ 中国最大的湖是青海省的青海湖。
**Zhōngguó zuì dà de hú shì Qīnghǎi Shěng de
Qīnghǎi Hú.** = *China's biggest lake is Qinghai
Lake in Qinghai Province.*
húbiān 湖边 = lakeside
■ 湖边的房子越来越贵。 **Húbiān de fángzi
yuèláiyuè guì.** = *Lakeside houses are becoming
more and more expensive.*

hǔ 虎 NOUN = tiger (See 老虎 lǎohǔ, 马虎
mǎhu.)

hù 户 MEASURE WORD = (used with nouns
denoting households and families)
■ 这条街上有三十几户人家。 **Zhè tiáo jiē
shang yǒu sānshí jǐ hù rénjiā.** = *There are over
thirty households [living] along this street.*

hù 互 ADJECTIVE = reciprocal

hùliánwǎng 互联网 [modif: 互 *each other* +
联 *linked* + 网 *net*] NOUN = the Internet, the
World Wide Web
■ 有了互联网，信息交流方便多了。 **Yǒule
hùliánwǎng, xìnxi jiāoliú fāngbiàn duōle.** =
*With the Internet, information exchange is so
much more convenient.*
■ 我每天都上互联网，看新闻，找资料。 **Wǒ
měitiān dōu shàng hùliánwǎng, kàn xīnwén,
zhǎo zīliào.** = *I get on the Internet every day to
read news or search for data.*

hùxiāng 互相 ADVERB = each other, one
another
■ 我们是好朋友，应当互相关心，互相帮

助。 **Wǒmen shì hǎo péngyou, yīngdāng
hùxiāng guānxīn, hùxiāng bāngzhù.** = *We're
good friends, so we should care for each other
and help each other.*

hù 护 Trad 護 VERB = protect

hùshi 护士 NOUN = nurse
■ 护士按照医生的嘱咐给病人吃药。 **Hùshi
ànzhào yīshēng de zhǔfu gěi bìngrén chī yào.**
= *Nurses administer medicine to patients according to doctors' instructions.*

NOTE: In China nurses are almost exclusively
women. To address a nurse politely, use 护士
小姐 **hùshì xiǎojiě**, e.g.
■ 护士小姐，我还需要吃这个药吗？ **Hùshì
xiǎojiě, wǒ hái xūyào chī zhè ge yào ma?** =
Nurse, do I still need to take this medicine?
or you can put her family name before 护士
hùshì, e.g. 张护士 **Zhāng hùshì**, 李护士 **Lǐ
hùshì**.

hùzhào 护照 NOUN = passport
■ 约翰在北京旅行的时候，发现护照丢了，
就马上和大使馆联系。 **Yuēhàn zài Běijīng
lǚxíng de shíhou, fāxiàn hùzhào diū le, jiù
mǎshang hé dàshǐguǎn liánxì.** = *While traveling
in Beijing, John found that he had lost his passport and immediately contacted the embassy.*

huā 花 1 NOUN = flower (朵 duǒ)
■ 花瓶里插了几朵美丽的花。 **Huāpíng li chāle
jǐ duǒ měilì de huā.** = *Some beautiful flowers
were placed in the vase.*
■ 去医院看病人，可以带一些花。 **Qù yīyuàn
kàn bìngrén, kěyǐ dài yìxiēhuā.** = *You can take
some flowers with you when you visit a patient
in the hospital.*
huā píng 花瓶 = vase
zhòng huā 种花 = plant flowers, do gardening

NOTE: In colloquial Chinese 花儿 **huār** may be
used instead of 花 **huā**, e.g.
■ 去医院看病人，可以带一些花儿 **Qù yīyuàn
kàn bìngrén, kěyǐ dài yìxiēhuār.** = *You can take
some flowers with you when you visit a patient
in the hospital.*

huā 花 2 VERB
1 = spend
■ 去年我花了两百元买书。 **Qùnián wǒ huāle**

liángbái yuán mǎi shū. = *Last year I spent 200 yuan on books.*
■ 你每天花多少时间做作业？ **Nǐ měitiān huā duōshǎo shíjiān zuò zuóyè?** = *How much time do you spend on assignments every day?*

2 = cost (money)
■ 这次旅行花了我三千块钱。**Zhè cì lǚxíng huāle wó sānqiān kuái qián.** = *This trip cost me 3,000 yuan.*
■ 在英国留学一年要花多少钱？ **Zài Yīngguó liúxué yì nián yào huā duōshǎo qián?** = *How much would it cost to study in the UK for a year?*

3 = take (time)
■ 写这篇文章花了我整整两天。**Xiě zhè piān wénzhāng huāle wó zhěngzhěng liǎng tiān.** = *It took me two full days to write this essay.*

NOTE: In writing, the character 化 **huā** can be used instead of 花 **huā** as a verb meaning *spend*, *cost*, etc.

huār 花儿 ADJECTIVE = full of colours, mottled, loud
■ 这条裙子太花儿了，你穿不合适。**Zhè tiáo qúnzi tài huǎr le, nǐ chuān bù héshì.** = *This skirt is too flashy. It's unsuitable for you to wear.*

huāyuán 花园 [modif: 花 *flower* + 园 *garden*] NOUN = garden (座 **zuò**)
■ 这里几乎每座房子都有一个小花园。**Zhèli jīhū měi zuò fángzi dōu yǒu yí ge xiǎo huāyuán.** = *Almost every house here has a small garden.*

huá 划 Trad 劃 VERB = scratch or scrape with a sharp object
■ 我的手划破了，不能在花园里干活了。**Wǒ de shǒu huá pò le, bù néng zài huāyuán li gànhuó le.** = *I've scratched my hand. I can't work in the garden any more.*

huá 滑 ADJECTIVE = slippery
■ 下雪以后，路上很滑。**Xià xuě yǐhòu, lù shang hěn huá.** = *After a snowfall, roads are slippery.*
huábīng 滑冰 = skate (on ice), ice-skating
huáxuě 滑雪 = ski, skiing

huà 化 VERB = melt
■ 太阳出来，雪很快化了。**Tàiyang chūlai,**

xuě hěn kuài huà le. = *When the sun came out, the snow melted very quickly.*

huàxué 化学 [modif: 化 *change, transform* + 学 *study*] NOUN = chemistry
■ 他对化学感兴趣，以后想当化学工程师。**Tā duì huàxué gǎn xìngqu, yǐhòu xiǎng dāng huàxué gōngchéngshī.** = *He is interested in chemistry, and hopes to become a chemical engineer.*
huàxué gōngyè 化学工业 = chemical industry
huàgōng 化工 = shortened form of 化学工业 **huàxué gōngyè** (chemical industry)
huàgōngchǎng 化工厂 = chemical plant

huàyàn 化验 [modif: 化 *chemical* + 验 *test*] NOUN = chemical test, laboratory test
■ 你必须化验一下血。**Nǐ bìxū huàyàn yíxià xuě.** = *You must have your blood tested.*
huàyàn bàogào 化验报告 = laboratory test report
huàyàn dān 化验单 = laboratory test application (a form signed by a doctor for the patient to have a test done in a laboratory)
huàyàn shì 化验室 = laboratory
huàyàn yuán 化验员 = laboratory assistant, laboratory technician

huà 划 Trad 劃 VERB = plan (See 计划 **jìhuà**.)

huà 画 Trad 畫 VERB = draw, paint
■ 这个小孩喜欢画各种动物，而且画得挺好。**Zhège xiǎohái xǐhuān huà gè zhǒng dòngwù, érqiě huà de tǐng hǎo.** = *This child likes to draw animals, and is very good at it.*
qiānbǐ huà 铅笔画 = pencil drawing
shuǐcǎi huà 水彩画 = watercolor (painting)
yóuhuà 油画 = oil painting

huàr 画儿 NOUN = picture, drawing (张 **zhāng**, 幅 **fú**)
■ 这张画儿画得真好！**Zhè zhāng huàr huà de zhēn hǎo!** = *This picture is so well done!*

NOTE: You can use 画 **huà** instead of 画儿 **huàr**, e.g.
■ 这张画画得真好！**Zhè zhāng huà huà de zhēn hǎo!** = *This picture is so well done!*

huàbào 画报 [modif: 画 *picture* + 报 *paper*] NOUN = illustrated magazine, pictorial (份 **fèn**, 本 **běn**)

■ 星期天的报纸大多有一份画报。**Xīngqītiān de bàozhǐ dàduō yǒu yí fèn huàbào.** = *Most Sunday newspapers carry a pictorial* (or *color*) *supplement.*

huàjiā 画家 [suffix: 画 *paint* + 家 nominal suffix denoting an expert] NOUN = painter, artist (位 **wèi**)
■ 这位画家风景画画得特别好。**Zhè wèi huàjiā huà fēngjǐng tèbié hǎo.** = *This artist is particular good at landscapes.*

huà 话 Trad 話 NOUN = speech, what is said, words (句 **jù**)
■ 你这句话很有道理。**Nǐ zhè jù huà hěn yǒu dàolǐ.** = *Your words are very reasonable.* (→ *You're quite right there.*)
■ 他说的话没有一句是真的。**Tā shuō de huà méiyǒu yí jù shì zhēn de.** = *Nothing that he said is true.*
■ 别忘了我的话。**Bié wàngle wǒ de huà.** = *Don't forget what I said.*

huài 坏 Trad 壞
1 ADJECTIVE = bad (antonym 好 **hǎo**)
■ 小孩子看电影，总爱问谁是好人，谁是坏人。**Xiǎoháizi kàn diànyǐng, zǒng ài wèn shéi shì hǎorén, shéi shì huàirén.** = *When children watch movies, they like to ask who is the good guy and who is the bad guy.*
2 VERB = break down, be out of order
■ 这台电脑已经用坏了，得买台新的。**Zhè tái diànnǎo yǐjīng yòng huài le, děi mǎi yì tái xīn de.** = *This computer has already broken down, you need to buy a new one.*
■ 电视机坏了，今天没法看电视新闻了。**Diànshìjī huài le, jīntiān méi fǎ kàn diànshì xīnwén le.** = *The TV set has broken down. There's no way we can watch the TV news today.*
■ 他们的车半路上坏了。**Tāmen de chē bànlù shang huài le.** = *Their car broke down halfway.*

huàichu 坏处 [modif: 坏 *bad* + 处 *place*] NOUN = negative effect, disadvantage (antonym 好处 **hǎochu**)
■ 这样做好处很多，但是也有不少坏处。**Zhèyàng zuò hǎochu hěn duō, dànshì yě yǒu bù shǎo huàichu.** = *This way of doing things has many advantages, but it also has quite a few disadvantages.*

NOTE: 坏处 **huàichu** and 害处 **hàichu** both refer to the undesirable effects of an action or actions. 坏处 **huàichu** connotes general negativity while 害处 **hàichu** emphasizes the harm that results.

huān 欢 Trad 歡 ADJECTIVE = joyful

huānsòng 欢送 [modif: 欢 *joyfully* + 送 *send off*] VERB = send off
■ 我们明天到机场去欢送中国公司的代表。**Wǒmen míngtiān dào jīchǎng qù huānsòng Zhōngguó gōngsī de dàibiǎo.** = *We're going to the airport tomorrow to send off the representative from the Chinese company.*
huānsònghuì 欢送会 = a send-off party (e.g. a farewell tea party)

huānyíng 欢迎 [modif: 欢 *joyfully* + 迎 *meet*] VERB = welcome
■ 热烈欢迎您！**Rèliè huānyíng nín!** = *A warm welcome to you!*
■ 怎样改进我们的服务？欢迎顾客们提建议。**Zěnyàng gǎijìn wǒmen de fúwù? Huānyíng gùkèmen tí jiànyì.** = *What can we do to improve our service? Customers are welcome to give us their suggestions.*

huán 还 Trad 還 VERB = return, pay back
■ 他向银行借了十万元，要在五年内还清。**Tā xiàng yínháng jièle shíwàn yuán, yào zài wǔ nián nèi huán qīng.** = *He borrowed 100,000 yuan from a bank and must repay the loan within five years.*
■ 这本书在这个星期一定要还给图书馆。**Zhè běn shū zài zhège xīngqī yídìng yào huán gei túshūguǎn.** = *This book must be returned to the library within this week.*
■ 有借有还，再借不难。**Yǒu jiè yǒu huán, zài jiè bù nán.** = *Return what you borrowed, and it won't be difficult to borrow again.*

huán 环 Trad 環 NOUN = circle

huánjìng 环境 [compound: 环 *surroundings* + 境 *boundary, area*] NOUN = environment
■ 这座大学在城外，三面环山，环境安静美丽。**Zhè zuò dàxué zài chéngwài, sān miàn huán shān, huánjìng ānjìng měilì.** = *This university is outside the city, surrounded by hills*

H

on three sides. *The environment is peaceful, quiet, and beautiful.*
■ 这家造纸厂污染环境，引起当地居民的强烈不满。**Zhè jiā zàozhǐ chǎng wūrǎn huánjìng, yínqǐ dāngdì jūmín de qiángliè bùmǎn.** = *This paper mill pollutes the environment, arousing the local people's great displeasure.*

huàn 换 Trad 換 VERB = change, replace
■ 她的地址换了，我不知道她的新地址。**Tā de dìzhǐ huàn le, wǒ bù zhīdào tā de xīn dìzhǐ.** = *She has changed her address. I don't know her new one.*
■ 这双鞋太小了，我想换大一号的。**Zhè shuāng xié tài xiǎo le, wǒ xiǎng huàn dà yí hào de.** = *This pair of shoes is too small. I'd like to replace it with a bigger size.*

huāng 慌 VERB = be flustered, panic
■ 他考试要迟到了，慌得坐错了车。**Tā kǎoshì yào chídào le, huāng de zuòcuòle chē.** = *As he was about to be late for the examination, he was so flustered that he took the wrong bus.*
huāngle shǒu jiǎo 慌了手脚 = be so flustered as to not know what to do

huáng 皇 NOUN = emperor

huángdì 皇帝 NOUN = emperor
■ 中国历史上第一个皇帝是秦始皇帝。**Zhōngguó lìshǐ shang dì yī ge huángdì shì Qín Shǐ Huángdì.** = *The first emperor in Chinese history was Qin Shi Huangdi.*

huáng 黄 ADJECTIVE = yellow
■ 香蕉和桔子都是黄的。**Xiāngjiāo hé júzi dōu shì huáng de.** = *Bananas and tangerines are yellow.*
huángsè diànyǐng 黄色电影 = pornographic movie
huángsè zázhì 黄色杂志 = pornographic magazine

huángguā 黄瓜 NOUN = cucumber (根 gēn)
■ 我夏天爱吃新鲜黄瓜。**Wǒ xiàtiān ài chī xīnxiān huángguā.** = *I love to eat fresh cucumber in summer.*

huángyóu 黄油 NOUN = butter
■ 在新鲜面包上涂一层黄油，可好吃了！**Zài xīnxiān miànbāo shang tú yì céng**

huángyóu, kě hǎo chī le! = *If you spread a thin layer of butter on freshly baked bread, how delicious it is!*

huī 灰 ADJECTIVE = gray
■ 这个城市污染很严重，天空总是灰灰的。**Zhège chéngshì wūrǎn hěn yánzhòng, tiānkōng zǒng shì huīhuī de.** = *This city has a serious pollution problem. Its sky is always gray.*

huī 恢

huīfù 恢复 VERB = recover, restore
■ 祝你早日恢复健康！**Zhù nǐ zǎorì huīfù jiànkāng!** = *I wish you a speedy recovery of health!*
■ 经过十几天的圣诞和新年假期，城市生活又恢复正常了。**Jīngguò shí jǐ tiān de shèngdàn hé xīnnián jiàqī, chéngshì shēnghuó yòu huīfù zhèngcháng le.** = *After a dozen days of Christmas and New Year holidays, city life returned to normal.*

huī 挥 Trad 揮 VERB = wave (See 发挥 fāhuī.)

huī 辉 Trad 謹 NOUN = splendor (See 光辉 guānghuī.)

huí 回
1 VERB = return (to a place), go back
■ 时间不早了，我们回家吧。**Shíjiān bù zǎo le, wǒmen huí jiā ba.** = *It's quite late. Let's go back home.*
■ 小陈在英国大学毕业以后，就回中国找工作。**Xiǎo Chén zài Yīngguó dàxué bìyè yǐhòu, jiù huí Zhōngguó zhǎo gōngzuò.** = *After graduating from university in the UK, Xiao Chen returned to China to look for a job.*
huílai 回来 = return to a place (coming towards the speaker)
■ 哥哥要从国外回来过圣诞节。**Gēge yào cóng guówài huílai guò shèngdànjié.** = *My elder brother is coming home from abroad for Christmas.*
■ 妈，我回来了！**Mā, wǒ huílai le!** = *Mom, I'm home!*
huíqu 回去 = return to a place (away from the speaker)
■ 你回去以后，要常常给我们发电子邮件，保持联系。**Nǐ huíqu yǐhòu, yào chángcháng gěi wǒmen fā diànzǐ yóujiàn, bǎochí liánxì.**

= *After you've returned home, you should send us e-mail often to keep in touch.*

huíguó 回国 = return to one's home country

■ 每年在美国的留学生大学毕业后，有多少人回国？ **Měi nián zài Měiguó de liúxuéshēng dàxué bìyé hòu, yǒu duōshǎo rén huí guó?** = *How many foreign students in the USA return to their home countries after graduation every year?*

2 MEASURE WORD = number of times (of doing something)

■ 我去看了他们两回了，他们一次都没有来过。**Wǒ qù kànle tāmen liǎng huí le, tāmen yí cì dōu méiyǒu láiguo.** = *I've visited them twice, but they haven't come to see me even once.*

huídá 回答 [compound: 回 *reply* + 答 *answer*]
VERB = reply, answer

■ 警察说："我问你几个问题，你要老实回答。" **Jǐngchá shuō: "Wǒ wèn nǐ jǐ ge wèntí, nǐ yào lǎoshí huídá."** = *The policeman said, "I'm going to ask you some questions. You must answer truthfully."*

■ 他上个周末向女朋友求婚，女朋友说要考虑考虑再回答。**Tā shàng ge zhōumò xiàng nǚpéngyǒu qiúhūn, nǚpéngyǒu shuō yào kǎolǜ kǎolǜ zài huídá.** = *Last weekend he asked his girlfriend to marry him, but she said she needed to think it over before replying.*

huítóu 回头 ADVERB = later

■ 回头见！**Huítóu jiàn!** = *See you later!*
■ 回头再说。**Huítóu zài shuō.** = *I'll talk to you later.*

NOTE: 回头 **huítóu** is a colloquialism, used only in very informal styles.

huíxìn 回信 [modif: 回 *reply* + 信 *message*]
NOUN = reply (either spoken or written)

■ 我们上个月送去了报价，还没有收到他们回信。**Wǒmen shàng ge yuè sòngqule bàojià, hái méiyǒu shōudào tāmen huíxìn.** = *We sent them quotations last month, and still haven't gotten a reply from them.*

huíyì 回忆

1 VERB = recall, recollect

■ 你回忆一下，最后一次是在哪里用那把钥匙的。**Nǐ huíyì yíxià, zuìhòu yí cì shì zài nálì yòng nà bǎ yàoshi de.** = *Try to remember where you used that key for the last time.*

2 NOUN = recollection, memory

■ 根据被害人的回忆，事故发生在夜里十一点钟左右。**Gēnjù bèihàirén de huíyì, shìgù fāshēng zài yèlǐ shíyī diǎnzhōng zuǒyòu.** = *According to the victim's recollection, the accident took place around eleven o'clock at night.*

huǐ 悔 VERB = regret (See 后悔 **hòuhuǐ**.)

huì 会 Trad 會 1 MODAL VERB

1 = know how to, can

■ 我会游泳，但是今天不能去游泳，因为我感冒了。**Wǒ huì yóuyǒng, dànshì jīntiān bù néng qù yóuyǒng, yīnwèi wǒ gǎnmào le.** = *I can swim, but I'm not able to today because I've got a cold.*

= probably, will

■ 我看夜里会下雨。**Wǒ kàn yèlǐ huì xiàyǔ.** = *I think it will rain tonight.*

■ 只要努力工作，就会取得满意的成绩。**Zhǐyào nǔlì gōngzuò, jiù huì qǔdé mǎnyì de chéngjì.** = *Provided you work hard, you will achieve satisfactory results.*

2 VERB = have the ability or knowledge

■ 你会日文吗？**Nǐ huì Rìwén ma?** = *Do you speak (or write) Japanese?*

■ 这道题目我不会。**Zhè dào tímù wǒ bú huì.** = *I don't know how to do this question.*

NOTE: 会 **huì** as a full verb meaning *have the ability or knowledge* is used with a limited range of nouns, such as nouns denoting languages. Using 会 **huì** in this way is colloquial.

huì 会 Trad 會 2 NOUN = meeting, conference

■ 我去开会了，这里请你照顾一下。**Wǒ qù kāi huìle, zhèlǐ qǐng nǐ zhàogù yíxià.** = *I'm going to a meeting. Please keep an eye on things here.*

■ 明天的会非常重要，请您一定参加。**Míngtiān de huì fēicháng zhòngyào, qǐng nín yídìng cānjiā.** = *The meeting tomorrow is very important. Please be sure to attend it.*

dàhuì 大会 = an assembly, a rally
kāi huì 开会 = have a meeting

huìchǎng 会场 [modif: 会 *meeting, conference* + 场 *venue*] NOUN = venue for a meeting, conference, assembly or rally

H

■大会会场布置得很庄严。**Dàhuì huìchǎng bùzhì de hěn zhuāngyán.** = *The assembly hall was solemnly decorated.*

huìhuà 会话

1 VERB = talk, hold a conversation
■我和她一天用中文会话，一天用英文话。**Wǒ hé tā yìtiān yòng Zhōngwén huìhuà, yìtiān yòng Yīngwén huìhuà.** = *She and I talk in Chinese one day, and in English the next day.*
2 NOUN = conversation
■中文会话不太难，难的是写汉字。**Zhōngwén huìhuà bú tài nán, nán de shì xiě hànzì.** = *Chinese conversation is not too difficult. What is difficult is writing Chinese characters.*

huìjiàn 会见 [compound: 会 *meet* + 见 *see*]

VERB = (formal) meet
■明天上午商业部长会见我们公司的王董事长。**Míngtiān shàngwǔ Shāngyè Bùzhǎng huìjiàn wǒmen gōngsī de Wáng dǒngshìzhǎng.** = *The Minister of Commerce will meet Chairman Wang from our company tomorrow morning.*

huìkè 会客 [v+obj: 会 *meet* + 客 *guest*] VERB = receive visitors

■今天市长有重要会议，不能会客。**Jīntiān shìzhǎng yǒu zhòngyào huìyì, bù néng huì kè.** = *Today the mayor is at an important conference and is not able to receive visitors.*

huìtán 会谈 [compound: 会 *meet* + 谈 *talk*]

VERB = (formal) talk
■两个大学的校长将举行会谈，讨论怎样加强合作。**Liǎng ge dàxué de xiàozhǎng jiāng jǔxíng huìtán, tǎolùn zěnyàng jiāqiáng hézuò.** *The presidents of the two universities will hold a talk to discuss how to strengthen cooperation.*

huìyì 会议 [compound: 会 *meet* + 议 *discuss*]

NOUN = meeting, conference
■这次会议讨论什么问题？**Zhè cì huìyì tǎolùn shénme wèntí?** = *What questions will be discussed at the conference? (→ What is on the conference agenda?)*
cānjiā huìyì 参加会议 = participate in a meeting or conference
■参加会议的还有全国各地的中学校代表。**Cānjiā huìyì de háiyǒu quán guó gè dì de zhōngxué xiàozhǎng dàibiǎo.** = *Representatives of high school principals from various parts of the country also attended the conference.*
chūxí huìyì 出席会议 = attend a meeting or conference
■教育部长和几位重要人物出席了会议。**Jiàoyù bùzhǎng hé jǐ wèi zhòngyào rénwù chūxíle huìyì.** = *The Minister of Education and several other VIPs attended this conference.*
jǔxíng huìyì 举行会议 = hold a meeting or conference
■下个月这个城市要举行一个国际会议。**Xià ge yuè zhège chéngshì yào jǔxíng yī ge guójì huìyì.** = *An international conference will be held in this city next month.*
qǔxiāo huìyì 取消会议 = cancel a meeting or conference
■你知道为什么取消这次会议吗？**Nǐ zhīdào wèishénme qǔxiāo zhè cì huìyì ma?** = *Do you know why this meeting was canceled?*
zhāokāi huìyì 召开会议 = convene a meeting or conference
■校长召开全体教师会议，讨论学生纪律问题。**Xiàozhǎng zhāokāi quántǐ jiàoshī huìyì, tǎolùn xuésheng jìlǜ wèntí.** = *The principal convened a teachers' meeting to discuss the issue of student discipline.*

hūn 昏 VERB = faint

hūnmí 昏迷 [compound: 昏 *faint* + 迷 *coma*]

VERB = fall into a coma
■他在交通事故中受伤，昏迷了一天一夜才醒来。**Tā zài jiāotōng shìgù zhōng shòule shāng, hūnmíle yì-tiān-yí-yè cái xǐnglai.** = *He was injured in an traffic accident and was unconscious for twenty-four hours.*

hūn 婚 VERB = marry

hūnyīn 婚姻 [compound: 婚 *marriage* + 姻 *marriage*] NOUN = marriage

■婚姻是人生大事。**Hūnyīn shì rénshēng dà shì.** = *Marriage is an important event in one's life.*

hùn 混 VERB = mix up

■这两个词发音相同，意思不同，你别把它们混起来。**Zhè liǎng ge cí fāyīn xiāngtóng, yìsi bù tóng, nǐ bié bǎ tāmen hùn qǐlai.** = *These* *two words have the same pronunciation, but different meanings. Do not mix them up.*

hùn wéi yì tán 混为一谈 = lump different things together, fail to make distinction between different things

huó 活 VERB = be alive
■ 很多中国人只吃活鱼，不吃死鱼。**Hěn duō Zhōngguórén zhǐ chī huó yú, bù chī sǐ yú.** = *Many Chinese only eat live (→ freshly caught) fish, not dead ones.*

huór 活儿 NOUN = work, job
■ 这活儿不容易，你干得了吗? **Zhè huór bù róngyì, nǐ gàn de liǎo ma?** = *This job is not easy. Can you manage it?*
■ 没有适当的工具，这活儿没法干。**Méiyǒu shìdàng de gōngjù, zhè huór méi fǎ gàn.** = *This job can't be done without the proper tools.*

gàn huór 干活儿 = work, do a job

NOTE: 活儿 **huór** and 干活儿 **gàn huór** are very colloquial, and usually refer to manual work.

huódòng 活动 [compound: 活 alive + 动 move]
1 VERB = do physical exercise
■ 他每天起床后，先在花园里活动活动，再吃早饭。**Tā měi tiān qǐchuáng hòu, xiān zài huāyuán li huódòng huódòng, zài chī zǎofàn.** = *Every day after getting up he does a bit of exercise in the garden before having breakfast.*
2 NOUN = activity
■ 您退休以后，最好参加一些活动，别老待在家里。**Nín tuìxiū yǐhòu, zuìhǎo cānjiā yìxiē huódòng, bié lǎo dāi zài jiā li.** = *After retirement it's best that you participate in some activities. Don't stay at home all the time.*

cānjiā huódòng 参加活动 = participate in an activity

huópo 活泼 ADJECTIVE = lively, vivacious
■ 她性格活泼，爱交朋友，到处受欢迎。**Tā xìnggé huópo, ài jiāo péngyou, dàochù shòu huānyíng.** = *She is vivacious by nature and likes to make friends, so she is popular wherever she goes.*

huóyuè 活跃 [compound: 活 alive + 跃 leap, jump] ADJECTIVE = active, brisk
■ 这两天股票市场十分活跃。**Zhè liǎng tiān gǔpiào shìchǎng shífēn huóyuè.** = *The share market is very brisk these days.*

huǒ 火 NOUN = fire
■ 生了火，房间里就暖和了。**Shēngle huǒ, fángjiān li jiù nuǎnhuo le.** = *After a fire was lit, the room became warm.*

zháo huǒ 着火 = catch fire, be caught on fire
■ 着火了! 着火了! **Zháo huǒ le! Zháo huǒ le!** = *Fire! Fire!*

huǒchái 火柴 [modif: 火 fire + 柴 wood] NOUN = match (根 gēn, 盒 hé)
■ "你有火柴吗?" "没有，我有打火机。" **"Nǐ yǒu huǒchái ma?" "Méiyǒu, wǒ yǒu dǎhuǒjī."** = *"Have you got a match?" "No, but I've got a cigarette lighter."*

huá huǒchái 划火柴 = strike a match
huǒchái hé 火柴盒 = a matchbox

huǒchē 火车 [modif: 火 fire + 车 vehicle] NOUN = train (辆 liàng, 列 liè)
■ 我们坐火车到北京去。**Wǒmen zuò huǒchē dào Běijīng qù.** = *We'll go to Beijing by train.*
■ 上海来的火车晚上八点二十五分到达。**Shànghǎi lái de huǒchē wǎnshang bā diǎn èrshíwǔ fēn dàodá.** = *The train from Shanghai arrives at 8:25 in the evening.*

huǒchē zhàn 火车站 = railway station
huǒchē piào 火车票 = train ticket
huǒchē shíkè biǎo 火车时刻表 = railway timetable

huǒ 伙 Trad 夥 NOUN = partner

huǒshí 伙食 NOUN = meals (provided by a school, a factory, etc.)
■ 部队里的伙食很好。**Bùduì li de huǒshí hěn hǎo.** = *The army canteens provide good meals.*

huò 或 CONJUNCTION = same as 或者 huòzhě. Used more in writing.

huòzhě 或者 CONJUNCTION = or
■ 你明天一定要给我回信，可以打电话，或者发电子邮件。**Nǐ míngtiān yídìng yào gěi wǒ huíxìn, kěyǐ dǎ diànhuà, huòzhě fā diànzǐ yóujiàn.** = *You must give me a reply tomorrow, either by phone or by email.*

H

huò 货 Trad 貨 NOUN = goods
■ 暂时没有货，过两天再来问吧。**Zànshí méiyǒu huò, guò liǎng tiān zài lái wèn ba.** = *It's out of stock for the time being. Do come and inquire after a couple of days.*

huò 获 Trad 獲 VERB = gain, win

huòdé 获得 [compound: 获 *gain, win* + 得 *get*] VERB = win, obtain, get
■ 他工作努力，获得了优秀成绩。**Tā gōngzuò nǔlì, huòdéle yōuxiù chéngjì.** = *He works hard and has won excellent achievements.*

J

jī 几 ADVERB = nearly

jīhū 几乎 ADVERB = almost, nearly
■ 这个国家的人几乎都会说一点英语。**Zhège guójiā de rén jīhū dōu huì shuō yìdiǎn Yīngyǔ.** = *Almost everyone in this country speaks some English.*
■ 她的工资几乎全用来买新衣服。**Tā de gōngzī jīhū quán yònglai mǎi xīn yīfu.** = *She spends nearly all her salary on new clothes.*

jī 机 Trad 機 NOUN = machine

jīchǎng 机场 [modif: 机 *airplane* + 场 *ground, field*] NOUN = airport
■ "机场离这里远不远？" "不远，大概十公里。" **"Jīchǎng lí zhèlǐ yuǎn bu yuǎn?" "Bù yuǎn, dàgài shí gōnglǐ."** = *"Is the airport far from here?" "Not very far. About ten kilometers."*
■ 下午我要去机场接一个朋友。**Xiàwǔ wǒ yào qù jīchǎng jiē yí ge péngyou.** = *I'm going to the airport this afternoon to meet a friend.*
jīchǎng ānquán jiǎnchá 机场安全检查 = airport security check
jīchǎng fèi 机场费 = airport tax

jīchuáng 机床 NOUN = machine tool (台 **tái**)
■ 这一台机床是从国外进口的。**Zhè yì tái jīchuáng shì cóng guówài jìnkǒu de.** = *This machine tool was imported from overseas.*

jīguān 机关 NOUN = government office, state organ
■ 这一地区有很多重要的政府机关。**Zhè yí dìqū yǒu hěn duō zhòngyào de zhèngfǔ jīguān.** = *There are many important government offices in this district.*

jīhuì 机会 [compound: 机 *situation, opportunity* + 会 *by chance*] NOUN = opportunity, chance
■ 这个机会很难得，不要错过。**Zhège jīhuì hěn nándé, bú yào cuòguò.** = *This is a rare opportunity. Don't miss it.*
■ 你有没有机会去北京学中文？**Nǐ yǒu méiyǒu jīhuì qù Běijīng xué Zhōngwén?** = *Do you have any chance of going to Beijing to learn Chinese?*
fàngqì jīhuì 放弃机会 = give up an opportunity
zhuāzhù jīhuì 抓住机会 = grasp an opportunity

jīqì 机器 [compound: 机 *device, machine* + 器 *utensil*] NOUN = machine (台 **tái**)
■ 这种机器很有用。**Zhè zhǒng jīqì hěn yǒuyòng.** = *This kind of machine is very useful.*
■ 你会不会使用这台机器？**Nǐ huì bu huì shǐyòng zhè tái jīqì?** = *Do you know how to use this machine?*
jīqì rén 机器人 = robot
shǐyòng jīqì 使用机器 = operate a machine
xiūlǐ jīqì 修理机器 = repair a machine

jīxiè 机械 [compound: 机 *machinery* + 械 *tool*] NOUN = machine, machinery
■ 建筑机械已经进入工地，马上要开工了。**Jiànzhù jīxiè yǐjīng jìnrù gōngdì, mǎshàng yào kāigōng le.** = *Construction machinery has entered the construction site. (→ Construction machinery is on the site now.) Work will begin soon.*

jī 鸡 Trad 雞 NOUN = chicken, hen, rooster (只 **zhī**)
■ 我们晚饭吃鸡，好吗？**Wǒmen wǎnfàn chī jī, hǎo ma?** = *We'll have chicken tonight, OK?*
■ 我最爱喝鸡汤。**Wǒ zuì ài hē jītāng.** = *Chicken soup is my favorite food.*
gōngjī 公鸡 = rooster
mǔjī 母鸡 = hen
xiǎojī 小鸡 = chick
Kěn dé jī kǎojī 肯德基烤鸡 = Kentucky Fried Chicken (KFC)

NOTE: 鸡 **jī** may denote either a hen, a rooster or chick, though they may be specified by 公鸡 **gōngjī** = *cock*, 母鸡 **mǔjī** = *hen* and 小鸡 **xiǎojī** = *chicken*. As food, it is always 鸡 **jī**.

jīdàn 鸡蛋 [modif: 鸡 *hen* + 蛋 *egg*] NOUN = hen's egg (只 **zhī**, 个 **ge**)
- 妈妈每星期买两斤鸡蛋。**Māma měi xīngqī mǎi liǎng gōngjīn jīdàn.** = *Mom buys two kilograms of eggs every week.*
- 新鲜鸡蛋营养丰富。**Xīnxiān jīdàn yíngyǎng fēngfù.** = *Fresh eggs are very nutritious.*

jī 圾 NOUN = garbage (See 垃圾 **lājī**.)

jī 积 Trad 積 VERB = accumulate

jījí 积极 ADJECTIVE
1 = enthusiastic, active
- 王老师积极推广普通话。**Wáng lǎoshī jījí tuīguǎng Pǔtōnghuà.** = *Teacher Wang is very enthusiastic about popularizing Putonghua.*
- 我对这件事不积极；我觉得没多大意思。**Wǒ duì zhè jiàn shì bù jījí; wǒ juéde méi duōdà yìsi.** = *I'm not enthusiastic about this matter; I don't think it makes much sense.*
2 = positive
- 对于困难，我们应该争采取积极的态度。**Duìyú kùnán, wǒmen yīnggāi cǎiqǔ jījí de tàidu.** = *We should adopt a positive attitude towards difficulties.*

jījíxìng 积极性 NOUN = initiative, enthusiasm, zeal
- 要使我们的公司成功，每一名职工必须发挥积极性。**Yào shǐ wǒmen de gōngsī chénggōng, měi yì míng zhígōng bìxū fāhuī jījíxìng.** = *To make our company a success, every staff member must exercise initiative.*

jīlěi 积累 [compound: 积 *accumulate* + 累 *pile up*] VERB = accumulate, build up
- 他在三十年工作中积累了丰富的经验。**Tā zài sānshí nián gōngzuò zhōng jīlěile fēngfù de jīngyàn.** = *He accumulated rich experience in the course of his career of over thirty years.*

jī 基 NOUN = (earthen) foundation

jīběn 基本 [compound: 基 *(earthen) foundation* + 本 *root*] ADJECTIVE = fundamental, basic
- 这件事的基本情况我已经知道了。**Zhè jiàn shì de jīběn qíngkuàng wǒ yǐjīng zhīdào le.** = *I've learned the basic facts of this matter* (or *event*).

jīběn shang 基本上 = basically, on the whole
- 我基本上同意你的计划。**Wǒ jīběn shang tóngyì nǐ de jìhuà.** = *I basically approve of your plan.*

jīchǔ 基础 [compound: 基 *foundation* + 础 *plinth, base*] NOUN = foundation, base
- 你想建高楼，就要先打好基础。**Nǐ xiǎng jiàn gāolóu, jiù yào xiān dǎhao jīchǔ.** = *If you want to erect a high building, you must first of all lay a good foundation.*
- 学中文，第一年是打基础。**Xué Zhōngwén, dì-yī nián shì dǎ jīchǔ.** = *The first year of your Chinese studies lays the foundation.*

jī 激 VERB = arouse, excite

jīdòng 激动 [compound: 激 *arouse emotion* + 动 *move*] ADJECTIVE
1 = exciting
- 比赛结束前两分钟，他踢进一球，真是激动人心！**Bǐsài jiéshù qián liǎng fēnzhōng, tā tījìn yì qiú, zhēnshì jīdòng rénxīn!** = *Two minutes before the end of the match he scored a goal. How exciting!*
2 = excited, very emotional
- 我妹妹听了这个消息激动得一夜没睡。**Wǒ mèimei tīngle zhège xiāoxi jīdòng de yíyè méi shuì.** = *After hearing the news my sister was so excited that she didn't sleep the entire night.*

jīliè 激烈 [compound: 激 *exciting* + 烈 *fierce*] ADJECTIVE = fierce, intense
- 运动会上运动员之间的竞赛十分激烈。**Yùndònghuì shang yùndòngyuán zhī jiān de jìngsài shífēn jīliè.** = *At the sports meet competition between athletes was very fierce.*

jí 及 CONJUNCTION = and, with
- 他父亲、伯父、及祖父都是商人。**Tā fùqin, bófù, jí zǔfù dōu shì shāngrén.** = *His father, uncle and grandfather were all businessmen.*

J

jígé 及格 [compound: 及 *reach* + 格 *grade*]
VERB = pass (a test, an examination etc.)
- "王老师，我这次测验及格吗？" "你不但及格，而且取得优秀成绩。" **"Wáng lǎoshī, wǒ zhè cì cèyàn jígé ma?" "Nǐ búdàn jígé, érqiě qǔdé yōuxiù chéngjī."** = *"Teacher Wang, did I pass the test?" "Yes, you did, and you also got an excellent grade."*

jíshí 及时 [v+obj: 及 *reach* + 时 *time*] ADJECTIVE
1 = timely, at the proper time
- 这场雨下得真及时，农民高兴极了。 **Zhè cháng yǔ xià de zhēn jíshí, nóngmín gāoxìng jíle.** = *This rain came at the right time. Farmers are delighted.*
2 = immediately, promptly, without delay
- 感谢您及时回复我们的信。 **Gǎnxiè nín jíshí huífù wǒmen de xìn.** = *Thank you for replying promptly to our letter.*

jí 级 Trad 級 NOUN = grade, rank
- 他是一级教师。 **Tā shì yī-jí jiàoshī.** = *He is a first-class teacher.*
... niánjí ...年级 = grade ... (in a school)
yī-niánjí 一年级 = Grade One, first year of study
yī-niánjí xuésheng 一年级学生 = grade one student, first-year student

jí 极 Trad 極 ADVERB = extremely, highly
- 今天天气极好。 **Jīntiān tiānqì jí hǎo.** = *The weather is extremely good today.*

jíle 极了 ADJECTIVE = extremely, very
- 这两天我忙极了。 **Zhè liǎng tiān wǒ máng jíle.** = *I'm extremely busy these days.*

NOTE: 极了 **jíle** is used after adjectives or some verbs to mean *extremely* ... or *very* ... For example:
- 忙极了 **máng jíle.** = *extremely busy*
- 高兴极了 **gāoxìng jíle** = *very happy, delighted*

jíqí 极其 ADVERB = extremely, highly
- 我们极其重视产品质量。 **Wǒmen jíqí zhòngshì chǎnpǐn zhìliàng.** = *We attach great importance to the quality of our products.*
- 顾客对这样的服务态度极其不满。 **Gùkè duì zhèyàng de fúwù tàidu jíqí bùmǎn.** = *Customers are extremely unhappy with such service.*

jí 急 ADJECTIVE
1 = anxious
- 他心里很急。 **Tā xīnlǐ hěn jí.** = *He's very anxious.*
2 = urgent
- 这件事很急。 **Zhè jiàn shì hěn jí.** = *This is an urgent matter.*
- 他家里有急事，今天没来上班。 **Tā jiāli yǒu jíshì, jīntiān méi lái shàngbān.** = *He has an urgent family matter [to attend to] and did not come to work today.*
jíxìngzi 急性子 = an impatient or impetuous person
- 我妈妈是个急性子，爸爸是个慢性子，但是他们俩好象很合得来。 **Wǒ māma shì ge jíxìngzi, bàba shì ge mànxìngzi, dànshì tāmen liǎ hǎoxiàng hěn hé de lái.** = *My mother is an impatient person while my father moves slowly. However, they seem to get along quite well.*

jímáng 急忙 [compound: 急 *hurried* + 忙 *hastened*] ADJECTIVE = hurried, hasty
- 听说孩子病了，她急忙赶回家。 **Tīngshuō háizi bìng le, tā jímáng gǎn huíjiā.** = *Hearing that her child was sick, she rushed back home.*

jí 集 VERB = gather

jíhé 集合 [compound: 集 *assemble* + 合 *combine*] VERB = gather together, assemble
- 我们明天上午十点钟在火车站集合。 **Wǒmen míngtiān shàngwǔ shí diǎnzhōng zài huǒchēzhàn jíhé.** = *We'll assemble at the railway station at ten o'clock tomorrow morning.*

jítǐ 集体 [modif: 集 *collective* + 体 *body*] NOUN = collective (antonym 个人 **gèrén**)
- 这是董事会集体的决定。 **Zhè shì dǒngshìhuì jítǐ de juédìng.** = *This is the collective decision of the board of directors.*

jízhōng 集中
1 VERB = concentrate, focus
- 这个国家的重工业集中在一个很小的地区。 **Zhège guójiā de zhònggōngyè jízhōng zài yí ge hěn xiǎo de dìqū.** = *The heavy industry of this country is concentrated in a small region.*
- 我要集中精力，学好中文。 **Wǒ yào jízhōng jīnglì, xuéhao Zhōngwén.** = *I will concentrate my energy on gaining a good command of the Chinese language.*

2 ADJECTIVE = concentrated, focused
■ 这个学生上课时注意力不集中。**Zhège xuésheng shàngkè shí zhùyìlì bù jízhōng.** = This student's attention is not focused in class. (→ This student doesn't pay attention in class.)

jǐ 几 Trad 幾 PRONOUN
1 = several, some
■ 我上星期买了几本书。**Wǒ shàng xīngqī mǎi le jǐ běn shū.** = I bought several books last week.
2 = how many
■ 你上星期买了几本书? **Nǐ shàng xīngqī mǎi le jǐ běn shū?** = How many books did you buy last week?

NOTE: When 几 **jǐ** is used in a question to mean *how many*, it is presumed that the answer will be a number less than ten. Otherwise 多少 **duōshǎo** should be used instead. Compare:
■ 你有几个哥哥? **Nǐ yǒu jǐ ge gēge?** = How many elder brothers do you have?
■ 你们学校有多少学生? **Nǐmen xuéxiào yǒu duōshǎo xuésheng?** = How many students are there in your school?

jǐ 己 PRONOUN = self (See 自己 zìjǐ.)

jǐ 挤 Trad 擠
1 VERB = squeeze, crowd
■ 你会挤牛奶吗? **Nǐ huì jǐ niúnǎi ma?** = Do you know how to milk cows?
■ 他再忙也要挤出时间和孩子玩玩。**Tā zài máng yě yào jǐchu shíjiān hé háizi wánwan.** = No matter how busy he is, he always finds time to play with his children.
■ 这间房间挤不下这么多人。**Zhè jiān fángjiān jǐ bú xià zhème duō rén.** It is impossible to pack so many people in this room.
2 ADJECTIVE = crowded
■ 圣诞节前几天商店很挤。**Shèngdànjié qián jǐ tiān shāngdiàn hěn jǐ.** = Stores are crowded days before Christmas.

jǐ 给 See 供给 gōngjǐ.

jì 计 Trad 計 VERB = plan

jìhuà 计划 [compound: 计 plan + 划 plan]
1 NOUN = plan

■ 这个计划不可行。**Zhè ge jìhuà bù kéxíng.** = This plan is not feasible.
■ 他们还在制定明年的计划。**Tāmen hái zài zhìdìng míngnián de jìhuà.** = They are working on their plan for next year.
■ 你明年有什么计划? **Nǐ míngnián yǒu shénme jìhuà?** = What's your plan for next year?
zhìdìng jìhuà 制定计划 = draw up a plan
zhíxíng jìhuà 执行计划 = implement a plan
2 VERB = plan
■ 我计划明年去美国旅游。**Wǒ jìhuà míngnián qù Měiguó lǚyóu.** = I plan to tour the States next year.

jìsuàn 计算 [compound: 计 calculate + 算 calculate] VERB = calculate
■ 请你计算一下这个班去年考试的平均成绩。**Qǐng nǐ jìsuàn yíxià zhège bān qùnián kǎoshì de píngjūn chéngjì.** = Please calculate the average marks of this class for last year's examination.
jìsuànjī 计算机 = same as 电脑 diànnǎo. Used as a more formal term.

jì 记 Trad 記 VERB
1 = remember, recall
■ 那条街叫什么,我记不清了。**Nà tiáo jiē jiào shénme, wǒ jì bu qīng le.** = I don't remember clearly the name of that street. (→ I can't quite recall the name of that street.)
■ 我们第一次是在什么地方见面的,你还记得吗? **Wǒmen dì-yī cì shì zài shénme dìfang jiànmiàn de, nǐ hái jìdé ma?** = Do you still remember where we first met?
2 = record (usually by writing down), bear in mind
■ 你说得慢一点儿,我把它记下来。**Nǐ shuō de màn yìdiǎnr, wǒ bǎ tā jì xiàlai.** = Speak slowly. I'll write it down.
■ 你要记住我的话,别忘了! **Nǐ yào jìzhù wǒ de huà, bié wàng le!** = You should bear in mind what I said. Don't forget it.
■ 我把他要我买的东西都记下来了。**Wǒ bǎ tā yào wǒ mǎi de dōngxi dōu jì xiàlai le.** = I've written down the things she wants me to buy.
jìdé 记得 = can remember, can recall
jì bu dé 记不得 = cannot remember, cannot recall
jìzhù 记住 = learn by heart, bear in mind
jì bǐjì 记笔记 = take notes

jìlù 记录 [compound: 记 *record* + 录 *record*]

1 VERB = record

■ 护士把病人的体温记录下来。**Hùshi bǎ bìngrén de tǐwēn jìlù xiàlai.** = *The nurse recorded the patient's temperatures.*

2 NOUN = record

■ 这位运动员打破了世界记录。**Zhè wèi yùndòngyuán dǎpòle shìjiè jìlù.** = *This athlete broke the world record.*

huìyì jìlù 会议记录 = minutes (of a meeting)

jìyì 记忆 [compound: 记 *remember* + 忆 *recall*]

1 VERB = remember, memorize

■ 童年的经历老人还记忆犹新。**Tóngnián de jīnglì lǎorén hái jìyì yóuxīn.** = *The old man still vividly remembers his childhood experiences.*

2 NOUN = memory

■ 他们俩在海边共度的夏天，成了他难忘的记忆。**Tāmen liǎ zài hǎibiān gòngdù de xiàtiān, chéngle tā nánwàng de jìyì.** = *The summer they spent together by the seaside has become an indelible memory for him.*

jìzhě 记者 [suffix: 记 *record* + 者 nominal suffix] NOUN = correspondent

■ 记者及时报导了那次交通事故。**Jìzhě jíshí bàodǎole nà cì jiāotōng shìgù.** = *Journalists reported the road accident promptly.*

jìzhě zhāodàihuì 记者招待会 = press conference, news conference

xīnwén jìzhě 新闻记者 = news reporter, journalist

jì 纪 Trad 紀 NOUN = discipline

jìlǜ 纪律 [compound: 纪 *discipline* + 律 *rule*] NOUN = discipline (条 tiáo)

■ 军队的纪律很严格。**Jūnduì de jìlǜ hěn yángé.** = *Discipline in the army is very strict.*

■ 他违反学校纪律，受到了批评。**Tā wéifǎn xuéxiào jìlǜ, shòudàole pīpíng.** = *He violated school discipline and was reprimanded.*

jìniàn 纪念 [compound: 纪 *record* + 念 *remember*] VERB = commemorate

■ 这个节日纪念一位伟大的爱国诗人。**Zhège jiérì jìniàn yí wèi wěidà de àiguó shīrén.** = *This festival commemorates a great patriotic poet.*

jì 技 NOUN = skill

jìshù 技术 [compound: 技 *skill* + 术 *craft*] NOUN = technique, technology, skill

■ 由于新技术的应用，产品质量有了很大提高。**Yóuyú xīn jìshù de yìngyòng, chǎnpǐn zhìliàng yǒule hěn dà tígāo.** = *Thanks to the application of the new technology, the product quality has been greatly improved.*

■ 你得学点技术，走到哪儿都有用。**Nǐ děi xué diǎn jìshù, zǒu dào nǎr dōu yǒuyòng.** = *You've got to learn some skills, which will be useful wherever you go.*

jìshù gōngrén 技术工人 = skilled worker

jìshùyuán 技术员 [modif: 技术 *technique, technology* + 员 *person*] NOUN = technician (位 wèi)

■ 车床出问题了，要请技术员来看一下。**Chēchuáng chū wèntí le, yào qǐng jìshùyuán lái kàn yíxià.** = *Something has gone wrong with the machine tool. Please send for the technician.*

jì 际 Trad 際 NOUN = boundary, border (See 国际 guójì, 实际 shíjì.)

jì 季 NOUN = season

jìjié 季节 [compound: 季 *season* + 节 *solar term*] NOUN = season

■ 春夏秋冬，你最喜欢哪个季节？**Chūn-xià-qiū-dōng, nǐ zuì xǐhuan nǎge jìjié?** = *Spring, summer, autumn and winter—which season do you like the best?*

jì 济 Trad 濟 VERB = aid (See 经济 jīngjì.)

jì 迹 NOUN = remains, trace (See 古迹 gǔjì.)

jì 既 CONJUNCTION

1 = same as 既然 jìrán. Used more in writing.

2 = both … and …

jì … yòu … 既 … 又 … = both … and …

jì … yě … 既 … 也 … = both … and …

■ 她既要上班，又要管孩子。**Tā jì yào shàngbān, yòu yào guǎn háizi.** = *She has to both work and care for the children.*

■ 你既要看到一个人的优点，也要看到一个人的缺点。**Nǐ jì yào kàndao yí ge rén de yōudiǎn, yěyào kàndao yí ge rén de quēdiǎn.** = *You should see both the merits and shortcomings of a person.*

jìrán 既然 CONJUNCTION = now that, since, as
■ 他既然已经决定，你就不必多说了。**Nǐ jìrán yǐjīng juédìng, wǒ jiù búbì duō shuō le.** = *Now that he's made up his mind, you needn't say anything more.*
■ 既然你不喜欢他，为什么还要和他一起出去玩呢? **Jìrán nǐ bù xǐhuan tā, wèishénme háiyào hé tā yìqǐ chūqu wán ne?** = *Since you don't like him, why do you still go out with him?*

jì 绩 Trad 績 NOUN = accomplishment (See 成绩 **chéngjì**.)

jì 继 Trad 繼 VERB = continue

jìxù 继续 [compound: 继 *continue* + 续 *keep on*] VERB = continue
■ 我们吃午饭吧，下午继续开会。**Wǒmen chī wǔfàn ba, xiàwǔ jìxù kāihuì.** = *Let's have lunch. The meeting will continue in the afternoon.*
■ 这种情况不能再继续下去了。**Zhè zhǒng qíngkuàng bùnéng zài jìxù xiàqu le.** = *This situation must not be allowed to go on.*

jì 寄 VERB = send by mail, post
■ 请你马上把这些书寄给王先生。**Qǐng nǐ mǎshàng bǎ zhèxiē shū jìgei Wáng xiānsheng.** = *Please post these books to Mr Wang immediately.*
■ 我要寄这封信去香港。**Wǒ yào jì zhè fēng xìn qù Xiānggǎng.** = *I want to post this letter to Hong Kong.*
jì kuàijiàn 寄快件 = post by express mail

jiā 加 VERB = add, plus
■ 一加二等于三。**Yì jiā èr děngyú sān.** = *One plus two equals three.*

jiāgōng 加工 [v+obj: 加 *add* + 工 *work*] VERB = process (unfinished products)
■ 这个工厂主要做来料加工。**Zhège gōngchǎng zhǔyào zuò láiliào jiāgōng.** = *This factory mainly processes supplied materials.*
láiliào jiāgōng 来料加工 = processing of supplied materials
shípǐn jiāgōng 食品加工 = food processing

Jiānádà 加拿大 NOUN = Canada

jiāqiáng 加强 [compound: 加 *add* + 强 *strong*] VERB = strengthen, reinforce
■ 我们要加强研究开发工作。**Wǒmen yào jiāqiáng yánjiū kāifā gōngzuò.** = *We should strengthen research and development work.*

jiāyǐ 加以
1 VERB = (used before a verb to indicate what should be done)
■ 这个问题应及时加以解决。**Zhège wèntí yīng jíshí jiāyǐ jiějué.** = *This problem should be solved promptly.*
■ 对违反纪律的学生必须加以严肃处理。**Duì wéifàn jìlǜ de xuésheng bìxū jiāyǐ yánsù chǔlǐ.** = *Students who have violated disciplines must be dealt with seriously.*
2 CONJUNCTION = in addition, moreover
■ 他身体很差，加以工作太辛苦，终于病倒在床上。**Tā shēntǐ hěn chà, jiāyǐ gōngzuò tài xīnkǔ, zhōngyú bìngdǎo zài chuáng shang.** = *He was in poor health; moreover, he worked too hard and was finally bedridden with illness.*

NOTE: 加以 **jiāyǐ** as a verb smacks of officialese and is chiefly used in writing. The sentence still stands when 加以 **jiāyǐ** is omitted, e.g.
■ 这个问题应及时解决。**Zhège wèntí yīng jíshí jiějué.** = *This problem should be solved promptly.*

jiā 夹 VERB = pinch, squeeze, wedge between, sandwich
■ 你会不会用筷子夹一个蛋? **Nǐ huì bu huì yòng kuàizi jiā yì ge dàn?** = *Can you use chopsticks to pick up an egg?*

jiā 家
1 NOUN = family, household
■ 我家有四口人：父亲，母亲，姐姐和我。**Wǒ jiā yǒu sì kǒu rén: fùqin, mǔqin, jiějie hé wǒ.** = *There're four people in my family: my father, my mother, my sister and I.*
2 NOUN = home
■ 下课以后我就回家。**Xià kè yǐhòu wǒ jiù huíjiā.** = *I go home as soon as school is over.*
3 MEASURE WORD = (for families or businesses)
■ 四家人家 **sì jiā rénjiā** = *four families*
■ 一家商店 **yì jiā shāngdiàn** = *a store*

J

■ 两家工厂 **liǎng jiā gōngchǎng** = *two factories*
4 SUFFIX = (denoting an accomplished expert)
huàjiā 画家 = painter, artist
jiàoyùjiā 教育家 = educator
kéxuéjiā 科学家 = scientist

jiājù 家具 [modif: 家 *home* + 具 *implements*]
NOUN = furniture (套 **tào**, 件 **jiàn**)
　■ 他们结婚时买了一套漂亮而实用的家具，
后来又添了几件小家具。**Tāmen jiéhūn shí
mǎile yí tào piàoliang ér shíyòng de jiājù,
hóulái yòu tiānle jǐ jiàn xiǎo jiājù.** = *When they
got married, they bought a beautiful and practical set of household furniture, and later on
added several pieces of occasional furniture.*

jiātíng 家庭 [compound: 家 *home, family* + 庭
courtyard] NOUN = family (个 **gè**)
　■ 他的家庭很幸福。**Tā de jiātíng hěn xìngfú.**
= *He has a happy family.*
　■ 她在这里没有家庭，也没有朋友。**Tā zài
zhèli méiyǒu jiātíng, yě méiyou péngyou.**
= *She has neither family nor friends here.*
　■ 中国人比较重视家庭。**Zhōngguórén bǐjiào
zhòngshì jiātíng.** = *The Chinese attach much
importance to the family.*

> NOTE: 家 **jiā** has more meanings than 家庭
> **jiātíng**. While 家庭 **jiātíng** means only *family*,
> 家 **jiā** may mean *family*, *household* or *home*.

jiāwù 家务 [modif: 家 *family, home* + 务 *work,
duty*] NOUN = household chores, housework (件
jiàn)
　■ 你帮太太做家务吗? **Nǐ bāng tàitai zuò
jiāwù ma?** = *Do you help your wife with household chores?*

jiāxiāng 家乡 [modif: 家 *home* + 乡 *village*]
NOUN = hometown, home village
　■ 这几年家乡发生了巨大变化。**Zhè jǐ nián,
jiāxiāng fāshēngle jùdà biànhuà.** = *In the past
few years great changes have taken place in my
hometown.*

jiā 稼 See 庄稼 **zhuāngjiā**.

jiǎ 假 ADJECTIVE = false, untrue
　■ 他说的这些话都是假的。**Tā shuō de zhèxiē
huà dōu shì jiǎ de.** = *All he said was untrue.*
jiǎhuà 假话 = lie

jiǎhuò 假货 = fake (goods)
jiǎtuǐ 假腿 = artificial leg
jiǎyá 假牙 = dentures

jià 价 Trad 價 NOUN = price

jiàgé 价格 NOUN = price
　■ 新汽车价格合理，卖得很快。**Xīn qìchē
jiàgé hélǐ, màide hěn kuài.** = *The new car is
reasonably priced and sells quickly.*

jiàqián 价钱 [compound: 价 *price* + 钱 *money*]
NOUN = price
　■ 价钱太贵，还是不要买吧。**Jiàqián tài guì,
háishì bú yào mǎi ba.** = *The price is too high.
Don't buy it.*
　■ 他只是问一下价钱，没打算买。**Tā zhǐshì
wèn yíxià jiàqián, méi dǎsuàn mǎi.** = *He only
asked the price and didn't intend to buy it.*

jiàzhí 价值 [compound: 价 *price* + 值 *worth*]
NOUN = value
　■ 这些书太旧了，没有多大价值。**Zhèxiē shū
tài jiù le, méiyǒu duō dà jiàzhí.** = *These books
are too old and do not have much value.*
jiàzhíguān 价值观 = values
　■ 对不起，我的价值观和你不一样。**Duìbuqǐ,
wǒ de jiàzhíguān hé nǐ bù yíyàng.** = *Sorry, my
values are different from yours.*

jià 驾 Trad 駕 VERB = drive, pilot (See 劳驾
láojià.)

jià 架 MEASURE WORD = (used for machines,
aircraft etc.)
　■ 一架客机 **yí jià kèjī** = *a passenger plane*

jià 嫁 VERB = (of a woman) marry
　■ 他们的女儿嫁给了一个美国人。**Tāmen de
nǚ'ér jiàgeile yí ge Měiguórén.** = *Their daughter married an American.*
　■ 嫁鸡随鸡，嫁狗随狗。**Jià jī suí jī, jià gǒu
suí gǒu.** = *Marry a rooster and you follow a
rooster; marry a dog and you follow a dog.*
(An old saying meaning that a woman com-
plies with whoever she marries.)

jià 假 NOUN = holiday, leave

jiàqī 假期 [modif: 假 *holiday* + 期 *period*]
NOUN = holiday period, leave

■ 假期你打算做什么？ **Jiàqī nǐ dǎsuàn zuò shénme?** = *What do you plan to do during the holidays?*
■ 假期的时候，火车飞机都很挤。 **Jiàqī de shíhou, huǒchē fēijī dōu hěn jǐ.** = *During the holiday period, trains and planes are all crowded.*

jiàtiáo 假条 [compound: 假 *leave* + 条 *slip*]
NOUN = an application for leave, a leave form
■ 明天家里有重要的事不能来上课，这是假条。 **Míngtiān jiāli yǒu zhòngyào de shì, bù néng lái shàngkè, zhè shì jiàtiáo.** = *I can't come to class tomorrow as there's important family business to attend to. Here's my leave application.*
bìngjiàtiáo 病假条 = an application for sick leave, a doctor's certificate of illness, a medical certificate
■ 医生给他开了病假条。 **Yīshēng gěi tā kāile bìngjiàtiáo.** = *The doctor gave him a medical certificate.*

jiān 尖 ADJECTIVE = sharp, pointed
■ 这孩子耳朵尖，我们这么小声说话她都听见了。 **Zhè háizi ěrduo jiān, wǒmen zhème xiǎoshēng shuōhuà tā dōu tīngjiànle.** = *This child has sharp ears. We talked in such low voices but she heard us.*

jiānruì 尖锐 [compound: 尖 *pointed* + 锐 *sharp*] ADJECTIVE
1 = very sharp, penetrating
■ 多家报纸对政府提出尖锐批评。 **Duō jiā bàozhǐ duì zhèngfǔ tíchū jiānruì pīpíng.** = *Several newspapers made biting criticism of the government.*
2 = fierce, uncompromising
■ 他们之间的矛盾很尖锐。 **Tāmen zhī jiān de máodùn hěn jiānruì.** = *There is bitter conflict between them.*

jiān 坚 Trad 堅 ADJECTIVE = hard, firm

jiānchí 坚持 [modif: 坚 *firm, firmly* + 持 *hold*]
VERB = uphold, persist (in)
■ 不管刮风下雨，他坚持每天跑步。 **Bùguǎn guāfēng xià yǔ, tā jiānchí měi tiān pǎobù.** = *He persists in jogging every day no matter how wet or windy it is.*
■ 尽管大家不同意，他仍然坚持自己的观

点。 **Jǐnguǎn dàjiā dōu bù tóngyì, tā réngrán jiānchí zìjǐ de guāndiǎn.** = *Despite everyone's disagreement, he still holds on to his views.*

jiāndìng 坚定 [compound: 坚 *solid* + 定 *fixed*]
ADJECTIVE = firm
■ 我坚定地相信公司的决定是正确的。 **Wǒ jiāndìng de xiāngxìn gōngsī de juédìng shì zhèngquè de.** = *I'm firmly convinced that the company's decision is correct.*

jiānjué 坚决 [compound: 坚 *solid* + 决 *determined*] ADJECTIVE = resolute, determined
■ 我坚决执行公司的决定。 **Wǒ jiānjué zhíxíng gōngsī de juédìng.** = *I will resolutely carry out the company's decision.*

jiānyìng 坚硬 [compound: 坚 *solid* + 硬 *hard*]
ADJECTIVE = solid and hard
■ 大门是用坚硬的木头做的。 **Dàmén shì yòng jiānyìng de mùtou zuò de.** = *The gate is made from very hard timber.*

jiān 间 Trad 間
1 MEASURE WORD = (for rooms)
■ 一间教室 **yì jiān jiàoshì** = *a classroom*
■ 两间办公室 **liǎng jiān bàngōngshì** = *two offices*
2 NOUN = room (for a special purpose)
■ 洗澡间 **xǐzǎo jiān** = *bathroom*
■ 手术间 **shǒushù jiān** = *operating theatre, surgical room*

jiān 肩 NOUN = the shoulder
■ 我左肩疼。 **Wǒ zuǒ jiān téng.** = *My left shoulder hurts.*

jiān 艰 Trad 艱 ADJECTIVE =difficult

jiānjù 艰巨 [compound: 艰 *difficult* + 巨 *gigantic*] ADJECTIVE = (of a big and important task) very difficult, strenuous
■ 他们要到外国去开辟市场，这是一项艰巨的任务。 **Tāmen yào dào wàiguó qù kāipì shìchǎng, zhè shì yí xiàng jiānjù de rènwù.** = *They are going overseas to open up new market, which is a difficult and immense undertaking.*

jiānkǔ 艰苦 [compound: 艰 *difficult* + 苦 *bitter, harsh*] ADJECTIVE = difficult, hard, tough

J

■城里人往往不了解很多农民的艰苦生活。**Chénglǐrén wǎngwǎng bù liáojiě hěnduō nóngmín de jiānkǔ shēnghuó.** = *People in the city usually do not know the hard life many peasants live.*

jiǎn 拣 Trad 揀 VERB = choose, select
■这么多漂亮衣服，她不知道拣哪一件好。**Zhème duō piàoliang yīfu, tā bù zhīdào jiǎn nǎ yí jiàn hǎo.** = *There were so many pretty dresses, she did not know which to choose.*

jiǎn 剪 VERB = cut (with scissors), shear
■剪羊毛是很辛苦的，不过工资挺高。**Jiǎn yángmáo shì hěn xīnkǔ de, búguò gōngzī tǐng gāo.** = *Sheep shearing is a hard job, but it is well paid.*

jiǎn 减 VERB = subtract, deduct
■三百六十七减二百八十六是多少？**Sānbǎi liùshíqī jiǎn èrbǎi bāshíliù shì duōshǎo?** = *How much is 367 minus 268?*
jiǎnshù 减数 = subtrahend (e.g. 268 in the example)
bèi jiǎnshù 被减数 = minuend (e.g. 367 in the example)

jiǎnqīng 减轻 [v+comp: 减 *subtract* + 轻 *light*] VERB = lighten, alleviate
■使用电脑以后，人们的工作量并没有减轻。**Shǐyòng diànnǎo yǐhòu, rénmen de gōngzuò liàng bìng méiyǒu jiǎnqīng.** = *After the use of the computer, people's workload has not in fact been lightened.*

jiǎnshǎo 减少 [v+comp: 减 *subtract* + 少 *few, little*] VERB = make fewer, make less, reduce
■在过去三年中，这个学校的学生人数减少了百分之二十。**Zài guòqù sān nián zhōng, zhège xuéxiào de xuésheng rénshù jiǎnshǎo le bǎifēn zhī èrshí.** = *In the past three years, the student population of this school has been reduced by twenty percent.*

jiǎn 检 Trad 檢 VERB = examine

jiǎnchá 检查 [compound: 检 *examine* + 查 *inspect, check*] VERB = examine, inspect, check
■先生，我要检查一下你的行李。**Xiānsheng, wǒ yào jiǎnchá yíxià nǐ de xínglǐ.** = *I need to inspect your luggage, sir.*

■他每年检查一次身体。**Tā měi nián jiǎnchá yí cì shēntǐ.** = *He has a physical examination (or medical checkup) once a year.*
■下个月总公司要派人来检查我们的工作。**Xià ge yuè zǒnggōngsī yào pài rén lái jiǎnchá wǒmen de gōngzuò.** = *Next month the head office will dispatch people to inspect our work.*

jiǎn 简 Trad 簡 ADJECTIVE = simple

jiǎndān 简单 [compound: 简 *simple* + 单 *single*] ADJECTIVE = simple (antonym 复杂 **fùzá**)
■这个问题不简单，要好好想一想。**Zhège wèntí bù jiǎndān, yào hǎohǎo xiǎng yi xiǎng.** = *This question is not a simple one. It needs careful consideration.*
■中饭吃得简单些，不要搞这么多菜。**Zhōngfàn chī de jiǎndān xie, búyào gǎo zhème duō cài.** = *Let's just have a simple lunch and not have so many dishes.*

jiàn 件 MEASURE WORD = (for things, affairs, clothes or furniture)
■一件东西 **yí jiàn dōngxi** = *a thing, something*
■我有一件东西忘在机场了。**Wǒ yǒu yí jiàn dōngxi wàng zài jīchǎng le.** = *I've [inadvertently] left something in the airport.*
■一件事情 **yí jiàn shìqing** = *a matter*
■我有几件事情要跟你说。**Wǒ yǒu jǐ jiàn shìqing yào gēn nǐ shuō.** = *I've something to discuss with you.*
■一件衣服 **yí jiàn yīfu** = *a piece of clothing (e.g. a jacket, dress)*
■他上星期买了三件衣服。**Tā shàng xīngqī mǎile sān jiàn yīfu.** = *He bought three pieces of clothing last week.*

jiàn 见 Trad 見 VERB = see, perceive
■我能不能见一下王先生？**Wǒ néng bu néng jiàn yíxià Wáng xiānsheng?** = *May I see Mr Wang?*
■经理，有一位小姐要见你。**Jīnglǐ, yǒu yí wèi xiǎojiě yào jiàn nǐ.** = *There's a young lady here who wants to see you, sir (← manager).*

jiànmiàn 见面 [v + obj: 见 *see* + 面 *face*] VERB = meet, see (a person)
■"我们以前见过面吗？""见过一次。" **"Wǒmen yǐqián jiànguo miàn ma?" "Jiànguo yí cì."** = *"Have we met before?" "Yes, once."*
■这个周末她要带男朋友回家和父母见面。

Zhège zhōumò tā yào dài nánpéngyou huíjiā hé fùmǔ jiànmiàn. = *This weekend she will bring her boyfriend home to meet her parents.*

jiàn 建 VERB

1 = build, construct
■ 在新区里要建两座学校。**Zài xīnqū li yào jiàn liǎng zuò xuéxiào.** = *Two schools will be built in the new district.*

2 = found, set up
■ 这座大学建于1950年。**Zhè zuò dàxué jiàn yu yījiǔwǔlíng nián.** = *This university was founded in 1950.*

jiànlì 建立 [compound: 建 *found* + 立 *establish*] VERB

1 = establish, set up
■ 我们希望和你们建立友好合作关系。**Wǒmen xīwàng hé nǐmen jiànlì yǒuhǎo hézuò guānxi.** = *We hope to establish a relationship of friendly cooperation with you.*

2 = same as 建 **jiàn**

jiànshè 建设 [compound: 建 *build* + 设 *install*] VERB = build, construct
■ 我们努力工作，建设自己的国家。**Wǒmen nǔlì gōngzuò, jiànshè zìjǐ de guójiā.** = *We work hard to build our country.*
■ 真难想象，在一片沙漠上建设起这样一座城市。**Zhēn nán xiǎngxiàng, zài yí piàn shāmò shang jiànshèqi zhèyàng yí zuò chéngshì.** = *It's hard to imagine that such a city could have been built in the desert.*
■ 国家的建设靠全体人民的长期努力。**Guójiā de jiànshè kào quántǐ rénmín de chángqī nǔlì.** = *Building a country depends on the long term hard work of all the people.*

jiànyì 建议 VERB = suggest, propose
■ 他建议用电脑系统控制生产过程。**Tā jiànyì yòng diànnǎo xìtǒng kòngzhì shēngchǎn guòchéng.** = *He suggests that the production process be controlled by a computer system.*
■ 他的建议没有被采用，甚至没有被考虑。**Tā de jiànyì méiyǒu bèi cǎiyòng, shènzhì méiyǒu bèi kǎolǜ.** = *His suggestion was not adopted; it was not even considered.*

jiànzhù 建筑 [compound: 建 *build* + 筑 *build*]

1 NOUN = building, edifice (座 **zuò**)
■ 这座古代建筑具有很高的艺术价值。**Zhè**

zuò gǔdài jiànzhù jùyǒu hěn gāo de yìshù jiàzhí. = *This ancient building has high artistic value.*

2 NOUN = architecture
■ 他写过一本关于当代美国建筑的书。**Tā xiěguo yì běn guānyú dāngdài Měiguó jiànzhù de shū.** = *He has written a book on contemporary American architecture.*

3 VERB = build
■ 他们想建筑世界上最高的大楼。**Tāmen xiǎng jiànzhù shìjiè shang zuì gāo de dàlóu.** = *They want to build the tallest building in the world.*

jiànzhùxué 建筑学 = (the discipline of) architecture
jiànzhùshī 建筑师 = architect

jiàn 荐 Trad 薦 VERB = recommend (See 推荐 **tuījiàn.**)

jiàn 健 ADJECTIVE = strong

jiànkāng 健康 [compound: 健 *energetic* + 康 *good health*]

1 NOUN = health
■ 母亲很关心孩子的健康。**Mǔqin hěn guānxīn háizi de jiànkāng.** = *Mothers are very concerned for their children's health.*
■ 生了病才知道健康多么宝贵。**Shēngle bìng cái zhīdào jiànkāng duōme bǎoguì.** = *You don't know how precious good health is until you are ill.*

2 ADJECTIVE = healthy, in good health
■ 这位老人身体很健康。**Zhè wèi làorén shēntǐ hěn jiànkāng.** = *This old person is in good health.*
■ 祝您健康！／祝您身体健康！**Zhù nín jiànkāng! / Zhù nín shēntǐ jiànkāng!** = *I wish you good health.*

jiàn 渐 Trad 漸 ADVERB = same as 渐渐 **jiànjiàn**

jiànjiàn 渐渐 ADVERB = gradually, by and by
■ 他渐渐习惯了那里的生活。**Tā jiànjiàn xíguànle nàli de shēnghuó.** = *He gradually grew accustomed to the life there.*

jiàn 践 Trad 踐 VERB = carry out, perform (See 实践 **shíjiàn.**)

J

jiàn 箭 NOUN = arrow
- 你会射箭吗？ **Nǐ huì shè jiàn ma?** = *Do you know how to shoot an arrow?*

jiàn 键 Trad 鍵 NOUN = key (See 关键 **guānjiàn**.)

jiāng 江 NOUN = river (条 **tiáo**)
- 这条江从西向东流。**Zhè tiáo jiāng cóng xī xiàng dōng liú.** = *This river flows from west to east.*
- 你能游过江吗？ **Nǐ néng yòuguo jiāng ma?** = *Can you swim across the river?*

NOTE: The most famous 江 **jiāng** in China is 长江 **Cháng jiāng**, the longest river in China. 长江 **Cháng jiāng**, which literally means *long river*, is also known as the Yangtze River. See note on 河 **hé**.

jiāng 将 Trad 將 1 PREPOSITION = same as 把 **bǎ**, but only used in writing.

jiāng 将 Trad 將 2 ADVERB = will, shall, be going to, be about to
- 张部长将在下周二出席会议，并发表重要讲话。**Zhāng bùzhǎng jiāng zài xià zhōuèr chūxí huìyì, bìng fābiǎo zhòngyào jiǎnghuà.** = *Minister Zhang will attend the conference next Tuesday and deliver an important speech.*

jiānglái 将来 [modif: 将 *shall, will* + 来 *come*] NOUN = future
- 我现在看不懂中文报纸，将来一定看得懂。**Wǒ xiànzài kàn bu dǒng Zhōngwén bàozhǐ, jiānglái yídìng kàn de dǒng.** = *I can't read Chinese newspapers now, but I'll certainly be able to in the future.*
- 将来的世界会怎么样？谁也不知道。**Jiānglái de shìjiè huì zěnmeyàng? Shéi yě bù zhīdào.** = *What will the world be like in the future? Nobody knows.*

jiāngyào 将要 ADVERB = same as 将 **jiāng** 2 ADVERB

jiǎng 讲 Trad 講 VERB = talk
- 别讲了，这些事我知道。**Bié jiǎng le, zhè xiē shì wǒ zhīdào.** = *Say no more. I know all about these matters.*
- 他讲得多，做得少。**Tā jiǎng de duō, zuò de shǎo.** = *He talks a lot but does little.*

jiǎng dàolǐ 讲道理 = See 道理 **dàolǐ**.
jiǎng gùshi 讲故事 = See 故事 **gùshi**.

jiǎnghuà 讲话 [compound: 讲 *speak* + 话 *speak*] NOUN = speech, talk
- 我的讲话只是代表个人的意见，不代表公司立场。**Wǒ de jiǎnghuà zhǐshì dàibiǎo wǒ gèrén de yìjiàn, bú dàibiǎo gōngsī lìchǎng.** = *My talk expresses only my personal opinion, and does not reflect the stand of the company.*

jiǎngzuò 讲座 NOUN = lecture, course of lectures
- 李教授在下学期要做当代中国经济讲座，共分十二讲。**Lǐ jiàoshòu zài xià xuéqī yào zuò dāngdài Zhōngguó jīngjì jiǎngzuò, gòng fēn shí'èr jiǎng.** = *Next semester, Professor Li will offer a course in Contemporary Chinese Economy, which will be given in twelve lectures.*

jiǎng 奖 Trad 獎
1 NOUN = prize, award
- 这个电影得过奖，不过一点也不好看。**Zhège diànyǐng déguo jiǎng, búguó yìdiǎn yě bù hǎokàn.** = *This film has won an award, but isn't at all interesting.*
2 VERB = award
- 这首诗怎么翻译成中文？谁翻得好，就奖给谁一本词典。**Zhè shǒu shī zěnme fānyì chéng Zhōngwén? Shéi fānde hǎo, jiù jiǎnggei shéi yì běn cídiǎn.** = *How may this poem be translated into Chinese? Whoever gives the best translation will be awarded a dictionary.*
jiǎngbēi 奖杯 = trophy, cup (given as a prize)
jiǎngjīn 奖金 = prize money, bonus, award

jiǎngxuéjīn 奖学金 [modif: 奖 *award* + 学 *study* + 金 *gold, money*] NOUN = scholarship
- 他获得了教育部奖学金，去英国进修一年。**Tā huòdéle jiàoyùbù jiǎngxuéjīn, qù Yīngguó jìnxiū yì nián.** = *He was granted a Ministry of Education scholarship for a year of advanced studies in the UK.*

jiàng 降 VERB = fall, lower (antonym 升 **shēng**)
- 一天中气温降了十度。**Yì tiān zhōng qìwēn jiàngle shí dù.** = *The temperature fell by ten degrees within a day.*

J

jiàngdī 降低 [compound: 降 *fall* + 低 *lower*] (antonym 升高 **shēnggāo**) VERB = lower, cut, reduce
- 顾客很少，他们只能降低价格。**Gùkè hěn shǎo, tāmen zhǐnéng jiàngdī jiàgé.** = *As there were few customers, they had to reduce prices.*
- 很多老年人觉得社会道德水平降低了。**Hěn duō lǎoniánrén juéde shèhuì dàodé shuǐpíng jiàngdī le.** = *Quite a few elderly people feel that the level of morality in society has declined.*

jiàng 酱 Trad 醬 NOUN = soy paste

jiàngyóu 酱油 [compound: 酱 *soybean* + 油 *oil, sauce*] NOUN = soy sauce
- 做中国菜怎么少得了酱油呢？**Zuò Zhōngguó cài zěnme shǎodeliǎo jiàngyóu ne?** = *How can one cook Chinese dishes without soy sauce?*

jiāo 交 VERB = hand over, pay (bills, fees)
- 这件事交给我办吧。**Zhè jiàn shì jiāogei wǒ bàn ba.** = *Hand this matter over for me to deal with.*
- 这个月的电费你交了吗？**Zhè ge yuè de diànfèi nǐ jiāole ma?** = *Have you paid this month's electricity bill?*

jiāohuàn 交换 [compound: 交 *transfer* + 换 *exchange*] VERB = exchange
- 主客交换了礼物。**Zhǔ-kè jiāohuànle lǐwù.** = *The host and the guest exchanged gifts.*
- 这两个大学每年交换五名学生。**Zhè liǎng ge dàxué měi nián jiāohuàn wǔmíng xuésheng.** = *The two universities exchange five students every year.*

jiāojì 交际
1 NOUN = social contact, social intercourse, communication
- 她和外人没有什么交际。**Tā hé wàirén méiyǒu shénme jiāojì.** = *She doesn't have many social contacts.*
2 VERB = make social contacts
- 他善於交际，朋友很多。**Tā shànyú jiāojì, péngyou hěn duō.** = *He is good at making social contacts and has numerous friends.*
- 和不同的人交际要用不同的方法。**Hé bùtóng de rén jiāojì yào yòng bùtóng de fāngfǎ.** = *You should use different ways to maintain social contact with different people.*

jiāojìwǔ 交际舞 = ballroom dancing
jiāojìfèi 交际费 = entertainment expense
jiāojìhuā 交际花 = social butterfly

jiāoliú 交流 [compound: 交 *associate with* + 流 *flow*] VERB = exchange, communicate
- 老师们常常在一起交流教学经验。**Lǎoshīmen chángcháng zài yìqǐ jiāoliú jiàoxué jīngyàn.** = *Teachers often get together to exchange teaching experiences.*

jiāotōng 交通 [compound: 交 *transfer* + 通 *open, through*] NOUN = transport, transportation, traffic
- 火车仍然是中国最主要的交通工具。**Huǒchē réngrán shì Zhōngguó zuì zhǔyào de jiāotōng gōngjù.** = *The railway remains China's chief means of transport.*
- 住在市中心，交通很方便。**Zhù zài shìzhōngxīn, jiāotōng hěn fāngbiàn.** = *Transportation is convenient for those living in the city center.*
jiāotōng shìgù 交通事故 = traffic accident, road accident
jiāotōng jǐngchá 交通警察 = traffic policeman, traffic police

jiāoqū 郊区 NOUN = suburbs, outskirts (of a city)
- 在西方人们一般都喜欢居住在郊区。**Zài Xīfāng rénmen yìbān dōu xǐhuan jūzhù zài jiāoqū.** = *In the West, people generally prefer to live in the suburbs.*

jiāo 教 VERB = teach
- 张小姐教我们中文。**Zhāng xiǎojiě jiāo wǒmen Zhōngwén.** = *Miss Zhang teaches us Chinese.*
- 请你教教我怎么使用这台新电脑。**Qǐng nǐ jiāojiao wǒ zěnme shǐyòng zhè tái xīn diànnǎo.** = *Please teach me how to use this new computer.*

jiāo 骄 Trad 驕 ADJECTIVE = conceited

jiāo'ào 骄傲 [compound: 骄 *conceited, proud* + 傲 *arrogant*] ADJECTIVE = proud, conceited, arrogant

J

■ 他为自己的孩子感到骄傲。**Tā wèi zìjǐ de háizi gǎndào jiāo'ào.** = *He is proud of his children.*
■ 你能力很强，但也不能骄傲啊！**Nǐ nénglì hěn qiáng, dàn yě bù néng jiāo'ào a!** = *You're very capable, but you mustn't be conceited.*

jiāo 蕉 NOUN = banana (See 香蕉 **xiāngjiāo**.)

jiǎo 角 1 NOUN = corner
■ 不少人常常在公园的一角练习英语口语，那地点就成"英语角"。**Bùshǎo rén chángcháng zài gōngyuán de yì jiǎo liànxí Yīngyǔ kǒuyǔ, nà dìdiǎn jiù chéngle "Yīngyǔ Jiǎo".** = *Many people often practice oral English in a corner of the park, and that spot becomes the "English Corner."*

jiǎo 角 2 MEASURE WORD = (Chinese currency: 1 角 **jiǎo** = 0.1 元 **yuán** = 10 分 **fēn**) ten cents, a dime
■ 两角钱 **liǎng jiǎo qián** = *two jiao; twenty cents*
■ 八块九角五分 **bā kuài jiǔ jiǎo wǔ fēn** = *eight yuan nine jiao and five fen; eight dollars and ninety-five cents*

NOTE: In colloquial Chinese 毛 **máo** is often used instead of 角 **jiǎo**, e.g. 两毛钱 **liǎng máo qián** = *two mao; twenty cents*

jiāo 饺 Trad 餃 NOUN = same as 饺子 **jiǎozi**

jiǎozi 饺子 [suffix: 饺 *dumpling* + 子 *nominal suffix*] NOUN = stuffed dumpling, *jiaozi*
■ 你晚饭吃了多少个饺子？**Nǐ wǎnfàn chīle duōshǎo ge jiǎozi?** = *How many dumplings did you eat for supper?*
bāo jiǎozi 包饺子 = wrap jiaozi, make jiaozi

jiǎo 脚 NOUN = foot (只 **zhī**)
■ 我的脚很大，穿不下这双鞋。**Wǒ de jiǎo hěn dà, chuān bú xià zhè shuāng xié.** = *My feet are big. This pair of shoes doesn't fit.*
■ 他的左脚受伤了。**Tā de zuǒ jiǎo shòushāng le.** = *His left foot is injured.*

jiào 叫 1 VERB = call, address, shout, cry out
■ 大家都叫他小王。**Dàjiā dōu jiào tā Xiǎo Wáng.** = *Everybody calls him Xiao Wang.*

■ 我见了你的父母，应该叫什么？**Wǒ jiànle nǐ de fùmǔ, yīnggāi jiào shénme?** = *How should I address your parents when I meet them?*

jiào 叫 2 PREPOSITION = same as 被 **bèi**. Used more in colloquialisms.

jiàozuò 叫做 VERB = be called, be known as, be referred to as
■ 这种病叫做百日咳。**Zhè zhǒng bìng jiàozuò bǎirìké.** = *This illness is called the "hundred-day cough (or whooping cough)."*

jiào 教 NOUN = teaching

jiàocái 教材 [modif: 教 *teaching* + 材 *material*] NOUN = teaching material, textbook, coursebook (份 **fèn**, 本 **běn**)
■ "你们上中文课用什么教材？""用我们老师自己编的教材。"**"Nǐmen shàng Zhōngwén kè yòng shénme jiàocái?" "Yòng wǒmen lǎoshī zìjǐ biān de jiàocái."** = *"What textbook do you use for Chinese?" "The one written by our teacher."*

jiàoshī 教师 [modif: 教 *teaching* + 师 *teacher, master*] NOUN = teacher (位 **wèi**, 名 **míng**)
■ 在中国人的传统中，严格的教师才是好教师。**Zài Zhōngguórén de chuántǒng zhōng, yángé de jiàoshī cái shì hǎo jiàoshī.** = *In the Chinese tradition, only a strict teacher was a good teacher.*

jiàoshì 教室 [modif: 教 *teaching* + 室 *room*] NOUN = classroom (间 **jiān**)
■ "你们的教室在哪里？""在二楼，二二三房间。"**"Nǐmen de jiàoshì zài nǎli?" "Zài èrlóu, èr-èr-sān fángjiān."** = *"Where is your classroom?" "It's on the second floor, Room 223."*
■ 我们在那间教室上数学课。**Wǒmen zài nà jiān jiàoshì shàng shùxué kè.** = *We have our mathematics class in that classroom.*
jiàoshì dàlóu 教室大楼 = classroom building

jiàoshòu 教授 [compound: 教 *teach* + 授 *teach*] NOUN = university professor
■ 李教授既要教学，又要研究。**Lǐ jiàoshòu jìyào jiāoxué, yòu yào yánjiū.** = *Professor Li is engaged in both teaching and research.*

J

jiàoxué 教学 NOUN = teaching
■ 老师们每月开会，讨论教学中出现的问题。**Lǎoshīmen měi yuè kāihuì, tǎolùn jiàoxué zhong chūxiàn de wèntí.** = *The teachers have a monthly meeting to discuss problems emerging in teaching.*

jiàoxùn 教训 [compound: 教 *teach* + 训 *lecture*]
1 VERB = lecture, talk down to
■ 你可以不同意别人的意见，可别老是教训别人。**Nǐ kěyǐ bù tóngyì biérén de yìjiàn, kě bié lǎoshì jiàoxùn biérén.** = *You may hold different opinions from others, but you shouldn't always talk down to people.*
2 NOUN = lesson (learnt from mistakes or experience)
■ 犯错误不要紧，重要的是接受教训。**Fàn cuòwù bú yàojǐn, zhòngyào de shì jiēshòu jiàoxùn.** = *Making mistakes doesn't matter, what's important is to learn your lesson.*

jiàoyù 教育 [modif: 教 *teach* + 育 *nurture*]
1 VERB = educate, teach
■ 父母应该教育自己的孩子。**Fùmǔ yīnggāi jiàoyù zìjǐ de háizi.** = *Parents should educate their children.*
2 NOUN = education
■ 教育关系到国家的将来。**Jiàoyù guānxi dào guójiā de jiānglái.** = *Education has an important bearing on the future of a country.*
■ 我姐姐在大学念教育。**Wǒ jiějie zài dàxué niàn jiàoyù.** = *My elder sister studies education at the university.*

jiàoyuán 教员 [modif: 教 *teaching* + 员 *staff*]
NOUN = teacher (in a particular school)
■ 这个学校有二十四名教员。**Zhège xuéxiào yǒu èrshísì míng jiàoyuán.** = *This school has twenty-four teachers.*

jiào 较 Trad 較
1 PREPOSITION = same as 比 **bǐ** 1 PREPOSITION. Used only in writing.
2 ADVERB = same as 比较 **bǐjiào** 2 ADVERB. Used only in writing.

jiē 阶 Trad 階 NOUN = steps, grade

jiēduàn 阶段 [compound: 阶 *steps, stair* + 段 *section*) NOUN = period, stage
■ 这项工程正处在开始阶段。**Zhè xiàng gōngchéng zhèng chù zài kāishǐ jiēduàn.** = *This project is just at an initial stage.*

jiējí 阶级 [compound: 阶 *steps, stair* + 级 *grade*] NOUN = social class
■ 今天的中国社会有哪些阶级？**Jīntiān de Zhōngguó shèhuì yǒu nǎxiē jiējí?** = *What classes does today's Chinese society have?*

jiē 结 Trad 結 VERB = bear (fruit)

jiēshi 结实 ADJECTIVE = sturdy, strong, robust
■ 他们做的家具都很结实。**Tāmen zuò de jiājù dōu hěn jiēshi.** = *The furniture they make is very sturdy.*
■ 他身体很结实。**Tā shēntǐ hěn jiēshi.** = *He has a robust body.*

jiē 接 VERB
1 = receive (a letter, a telephone call)
我昨天接到一封信，两个传真和八个电子邮件。**Wǒ zuótiān jiēdao yì fēng xìn, liǎng ge chuánzhēn hé bā ge diànzǐ yóujiàn.** = *Yesterday I received a letter, two faxes and eight e-mail messages.*
■ 我要休息一会儿，谁的电话都不接。**Wǒ yào xiūxi yíhuìr, shuí de diànhuà dōu bù jiē.** = *I'll have a rest and take no calls.*
2 = meet and greet (a visitor)
■ 王先生是第一次到这里来，你应该去机场接他。**Wáng xiānsheng shì dī-yī cì dào zhèli lái, nǐ yīnggāi qù jīchǎng jiē tā.** = *This is the first time that Mr Wang's coming here. You should go and meet him at the airport.*

jiēchù 接触 [compound: 接 *join* + 触 *touch*] VERB = get in touch (with)
■ 我先和他们初步接触一下，了解他们的想法。**Wǒ xiān hé tāmen chūbù jiēchù yíxià, liǎojiě tāmen de xiǎngfǎ.** = *I'll first get in touch with them tentatively to find out their thoughts.*

jiēdài 接待 [compound: 接 *receive* + 待 *entertain*] VERB = receive (a visitor)
■ 今天市长不接待。**Jīntiān shìzhǎng bù jiēdài.** = *The mayor does not receive visitors today.*

jiēdao 接到 [v+comp: 接 *receive* + 到 *arrive*] VERB = have received

J

■ 我还没有接到会议邀请信。**Wǒ hái méiyǒu jiēdao huìyì yāoqǐngxìn.** = *I have not yet received a letter of invitation to the conference.*

jiējiàn 接见 [compound: 接 *receive* + 见 *see*]

VERB = receive (somebody), meet (somebody), give an audience

■ 教育部长昨天接见了中学教师代表。**Jiàoyù bùzhǎng zuótiān jiējiànle zhōngxué jiàoshī dàibiǎo.** = *The Minister of Education received representatives of secondary school teachers yesterday.*

NOTE: 接见 **jiējiàn** meaning *receive* or *meet* is only used for formal or official occasions. It implies that the receiving party is superior in status to the one being received.

jiējìn 接近 VERB = be close to, be near

■ 她接近董事会，很了解内情。**Tā jiējìn dǒngshìhuì, hěn liǎojiě nèiqíng.** = *She is close to the board of directors and knows the inside information.*

■ 已经接近下班时间了，工作只作了一半。**Yǐjīng jiējìn xiàbān shíjiān le, gōngzuò zhǐ zuòle yí bàn.** = *It is close to the time to get off work, but the job is only half done.*

jiēshòu 接受 [compound: 接 *receive* + 受 *accept*] VERB = accept

■ 我们不接受礼物。**Wǒmen bù jiēshòu lǐwù.** = *We do not accept gifts.*

jiēzhe 接着 CONJUNCTION = and immediately, then, at the heels of (a previous action or event)

■ 我先听到有人叫我，接着小王跑了进来。**Wǒ xiān tīngdao yǒu rén jiào wǒ, jiēzhe Xiǎo Wáng pǎole jìnlai.** = *I first heard someone calling me, and then Xiao Wang ran into the room.*

jiē 街 NOUN = street (条 tiáo)

■ 我家前边的那条街总是很安静。**Wǒ jiā qiánbian de nà tiáo jiē zǒngshì hén ānjìng.** = *The street in front of my home is always quiet.*
jiē shang 街上 = on the street
■ 街上人很多。**Jiē shang rén hěn duō.** = *There are many people in the street.*
bùxíng jiē 步行街 = pedestrian street
guàng dàjiē 逛大街 = stroll the streets, do window shopping

jiēdào 街道 [compound: 街 *street* + 道 *way*]

NOUN = street (条 tiáo)

■ 这里的街道很安静。**Zhèli de jiēdào hěn ānjìng.** = *The streets in this area are quiet.*

jié 节 Trad 節 1 NOUN = festival

■ 这个节我过得很愉快。**Zhège jié wǒ guò de hěn yúkuài.** = *I had a very happy festival.*
■ 这个地方一年有好几个节。**Zhège dìfang yì nián yǒu hǎo jí ge jié.** = *There're quite a number of festivals in this area.*
chūnjié 春节 = Spring Festival (Chinese New Year)
féngnián guòjié 逢年过节 = on New Year's Day and other festivals
guò jié 过节 = observe a festival, celebrate a festival
shèngdànjié 圣诞节 = Christmas
zhōngqiūjié 中秋节 = Mid-Autumn Festival (the Moon Festival, on the eighth day of the eighth lunar month)

jié 节 Trad 節 2 MEASURE WORD = a period of time

■ 一节课 **yì jié kè** = *a period of class*

jiémù 节目 [compound: 节 *section* + 目 *item*]

NOUN = program

■ 昨天的电视节目很精彩。**Zuótiān de diànshì jiémù hěn jīngcǎi.** = *The TV program yesterday was wonderful!*
■ 这个节目是谁编的？谁演的？**Zhège jiémù shì shuí biǎn de? Shuí yǎn de?** = *Who wrote this program? Who acted it?*
értóng jiémù 儿童节目 = children's program
tǐyù jiémù 体育节目 = sports program
wényì jiémù 文艺节目 = theatrical program
xīnwén jiémù 新闻节目 = news program (on TV or radio)

jiérì 节日 [modif: 节 *festival* + 日 *day*] NOUN = festival day

■ 中国人最重要的节日是春节，也就是中国人的新年。**Zhōngguórén zuì zhòngyào de jiérì shì chūnjié, yě jiùshì Zhōngguórén de xīnnián.** = *The most important festival for the Chinese is the Spring Festival, which is the Chinese New Year.*

jiéshěng 节省 VERB = save, be frugal with (antonym 浪费 làngfèi)

■ 你平时节省一点钱，几年下来就可能有一大笔钱。**Nǐ píngshí jiéshěng yìdiǎn qián, jǐ nián xiàlai jiù kěnéng yǒu yídà bǐ qián.** = *If you save a little money routinely, after several years you may have a substantial sum of money.*

jiéyuē 节约 VERB = economize, save, practice thrift (antonym 浪费 **làngfèi**)
■ 我们应当节约用电，节约用水。**Wǒmen yīngdāng jiéyuē yòngdiàn, jiéyuē yòngshuǐ.** = *We should cut down electricity and water consumption.*

jié 结 Trad 結 VERB = tie, bear (fruit)

jiégòu 结构 NOUN = structure, construction
■ 这座古代建筑是木结构的。**Zhèzuò gǔdài jiànzhù shì mù jiégòu de.** = *This ancient building is a timber structure.*

jiéguǒ 结果 [v+obj: 结 *bear* + 果 *fruit*]
1 NOUN = result, consequence
■ 这次试验的结果很鼓舞人心。**Zhè cì shìyàn de jiéguǒ hěn gǔwǔ rénxīn.** = *The result of this test is heartening.*
2 CONJUNCTION = as a result, consequently, finally
■ 我们找了他半天，结果在图书馆找到了他。**Wǒmen zhǎole tā bàntiān, jiéguǒ zài túshūguǎn zhǎodàole tā.** = *We looked for him for a long time and finally found him in the library.*
■ 他们讨论了半天，结果取得了一致意见。**Tāmen tǎolùnle bàntiān, jiéguǒ qǔdéle yízhì yìjiàn.** = *They discussed it for a long time, and finally reached a unanimous agreement.*
■ 技术员连续工作二十小时，结果解决了问题。**Jìshùyuán liánxù gōngzuó èrshí xiǎoshí, jiéguǒ jiějuéle wèntí.** = *Technicians worked for twenty hours continuously, and finally solved the problem.*

jiéhé 结合 [compound: 结 *tie* + 合 *merge*] VERB = combine, integrate
■ 热情的态度要和冷静的头脑相结合。**Rèqíng de tàidu yào hé lěngjìng de tóunǎo xiāng jiéhé.** = *Enthusiasm should be combined with a cool head.*
■ 他们俩终于结合为一对幸福的夫妻。**Tāmen liǎ zhōngyú jiéhéwéi yí duì xìngfú de fūqī.** = *They were finally joined as happy husband and wife.*

jiéhūn 结婚 [v+obj: 结 *tie* + 婚 *marriage*] VERB = marry (antonym 离婚 **líhūn**)
■ 他和中学时的女朋友结婚。**Tā hé zhōngxué shí de nǚpéngyou jiéhūn.** = *He married his high school sweetheart.*
■ 他结过两次婚，下个月又要结婚了。**Tā jiéguo liǎng cì hūn, xià ge yuè yòu yào jiéhūn le.** = *He has been married twice and will marry again next month.*

jiélùn 结论 [modif: 结 *end* + 论 *view, treatise*] NOUN = verdict, conclusion
■ 经过调查，我们的结论如下。**Jīngguò diàochá, wǒmen de jiélùn rú xià.** = *As a result of the investigation, our conclusions are as follows.*
■ 我不同意你的结论。**Wǒ bù tóngyì nǐ de jiélùn.** = *I don't agree with your conclusion.*

jiéshù 结束 [compound: 结 *tie* + 束 *knot*] VERB = end, terminate (antonym 开始 **kāishǐ**)
■ 电影什么时候结束？**Diànyǐng shénme shíhou jiéshù?** = *When does the movie end?*
■ 第二次世界大战是哪一年开始，哪一年结束的？**Dì-èr ci shìjiè dàzhàn shì nǎ yì nián kāishǐ, nà yì nián jiéshù de?** = *In which year did the Second World War begin, and in which year did it end?*

jiě 姐 NOUN = same as 姐姐 **jiějie**

jiějie 姐姐 NOUN = elder sister
■ 我姐姐对我很好。**Wǒ jiějie duì wǒ hěn hǎo.** = *My elder sister is very nice to me.*
■ 你有没有姐姐？**Nǐ yǒu méiyǒu jiějie?** = *Do you have an elder sister?*

jiě 解 VERB = untie, undo
■ 医生：请你把上衣解开，我要听听你的心肺。**Yīshēng: Qǐng nǐ bǎ shàngyī jiě kāi, wǒ yào tīngting nǐ de xīnfèi.** = *Doctor: Please undo your jacket. I want to listen to your heart and lungs.*

jiědá 解答 [compound: 解 *untie* + 答 *reply*] VERB = provide an answer, give an explanation
■ 这个问题谁会解答？**Zhè ge wèntí shuí huì jiědá?** = *Who can answer this question?*

jiěfàng 解放 [compound: 解 *untie* + 放 *release*]

J

1 VERB = set free, liberate, emancipate
■ 美国南北战争解放了南方的黑人。**Měiguó nánběi zhànzhēng jiěfàngle nánfāng de hēirén.** = *The American South-North War (→ the American Civil War) emancipated Black people in the South.*
2 NOUN = liberation, emancipation
■ 民族解放需要伟大的民族领袖。**Mínzú de jiěfàng xūyào wěidà de mínzú lǐngxiù.** = *The emancipation of a nation calls for great national leaders.*

jiějué 解决 [compound: 解 *dissect* + 决 *finalize*]
VERB = solve (a problem), settle (an issue)
■ 这个问题还没有解决。**Zhè ge wèntí hái méiyǒu jiějué.** = *This problem has not been resolved.*
■ 要解决目前的困难，必须和各方面合作。**Yào jiějué mùqián de kùnnán, bìxū hé gè fāngmiàn hézuò.** = *We must cooperate with all parties if the present difficulties are to be overcome.*

jiěshì 解释 [compound: 解 *untie* + 释 *clarify*]
1 VERB = explain, account for
■ 请你解释一下这个句子。**Qǐng nǐ jiěshì yíxià zhè ge jùzi.** = *Please explain this sentence to me.*
■ 科学家无法解释这种现象。**Kēxuéjiā wú fǎ jiěshì zhè zhǒng xiànxiàng.** = *Scientists cannot account for this phenomenon.*
2 NOUN = explanation, interpretation
■ 对这种现象，我有一个解释。**Duì zhè zhǒng xiànxiàng, wǒ yǒu yí ge jiěshì.** = *I have an explanation for this phenomenon.*

jiè 介 VERB = intervene

jièshào 介绍 [compound: 介 *intervene* + 绍 *connect*] VERB = introduce
■ 我来介绍一下，这位是李先生，这位是王小姐。**Wǒ lái jièshào yíxià, zhè wèi shì Lǐ xiānsheng, zhè wèi shì Wáng xiǎojiě.** = *Let me introduce [the people here]. This is Mr. Li. This is Miss Wang.*
■ 你刚从中国回来，请你介绍一下中国的情况。**Nǐ gāng cóng Zhōngguó huílai, qǐng nǐ jièshao yíxià Zhōngguó de qíngkuàng.** = *As you've just come back from China, please tell us something about the current situation in China.*

jièsháo rén 介绍人 = matchmaker, sponsor (for membership in a club, a political party, an association etc.)

jiè 届 MEASURE WORD = (used for a conference or congress held at regular intervals, for graduating classes)
■ 我是那个中学九九届的毕业生。**Wǒ shì nà ge zhōngxué jiǔjiǔ jiè de bìyèshéng.** = *I was a graduate of the class of '99 of that high school.*
■ 第十届国际生物学大会将于十二月在新加坡举行。**Dì-shí jiè guójì shēngwùxué dàhuì jiāng yú Shí'èr yuè zài Xīnjiāpō jǔxíng.** = *The 10th International Conference on Biology will be held in Singapore in December.*

jiè 界 NOUN = realm (See 世界 **shìjiè**.)

jiè 借 VERB = borrow, lend
■ 他借给我一百元。**Tā jiègei wǒ yìbǎi yuán.** = *He lent me one hundred dollars.*
■ 我向他借了一百元。**Wǒ xiàng tā jièle yìbǎi yuán.** = *I borrowed one hundred dollars from him.*
■ 借东西要还。**Jiè dōngxi yào huán.** = *If you borrow something, you must return it.*

NOTE: This verb may mean either *borrow* or *lend*, depending on the patterns in which it occurs:
A jiègei B ... A 借给 B ... = A lends B ...
A xiàng B jiè... A 向 B 借... = A borrows ... from B

jīn 巾 NOUN = towel (See 毛巾 **máojīn**.)

jīn 今 NOUN = now, the present

jīnhòu 今后 NOUN = from today, from now on
■ 我保证今后不迟到，不早退。**Wǒ bǎozhèng jīnhòu bù chídào, bù zǎotuì.** = *I assure you that from now on I will not be late for work or leave work earlier than is allowed.*

jīnnián 今年 [modif: 今 *now* + 年 *year*] NOUN
= this year
■ 今年是二零零五年。**Jīnnián shì èrlínglíngwǔ nián.** = *This year is the year 2005.*
■ 我祖父今年八十岁了。**Wǒ zǔfù jīnnián bāshí suì le.** = *My grandfather is eighty years old this year.*

jīntiān 今天 [modif: 今 *now* + 天 *day*] NOUN = today
■ 今天天气很好。**Jīntiān tiānqì hěn hǎo.** = *The weather's fine today.*
■ 我今天要上五节课。**Wǒ jīntiān yào shàng wǔ jié kè.** = *I have five classes today.*

jīn 斤 MEASURE WORD = *jin* (a traditional Chinese unit of weight equal to half a kilogram)
■ 这条鱼重八斤。**Zhè tiáo yú zhòng bā jīn.** = *This fish weighs eight jin.*
■ 妈妈买了两斤肉。**Māma mǎile liǎng jīn ròu.** = *Mom bought two jin of meat.*

jīn 金 NOUN
1 = gold (两 **liǎng**, ounce)
■ 这块金表价值极高，你要好好保存。**Zhè kuài jīn biǎo jiàzhí jí gāo, nǐ yào hǎohǎo bǎocún.** = *This gold watch is very valuable. You must keep it well.*
2 = money
■ 他每两周拿五百块退休金。**Tā měi liǎng zhōu ná wǔbǎi kuài tuìxiū jīn.** = *He gets five hundred dollars as pension money every fortnight.*
jīnzi 金子 = gold
jiǎngxuéjīn 奖学金 = scholarship
jiǎngjīn 奖金 = bonus, prize money
tuìxiū jīn 退休金 = superannuation, pension

jīnshǔ 金属 NOUN = metal
■ 金、银、铜、铁都是金属。**Jīn, yín, tóng, tiě dōu shì jīnshǔ.** = *Gold, silver, copper and iron are all metals.*

jǐn 仅 Trad 僅 ADVERB = only, merely
■ 她一个月的工资仅够付房租和吃饭。**Tā yí ge yuè de gōngzī jǐn gòu fù fángzū hé chīfàn.** = *Her monthly wages are only enough for rent and food.*
■ 小王是我在这个城市里仅有的朋友。**Xiǎo Wáng shì wǒ zài zhège chéngshì li jǐn yǒu de péngyou.** = *Xiao Wang is my only friend in this city.*

jǐnjǐn 仅仅 ADVERB = same as 仅 **jǐn**, but more emphatic.

jǐn 尽 Trad 盡 VERB = to the greatest extent
■ 这事要尽快办。**Zhè shì yào jǐn kuài bàn.**

= *This matter must be handled as soon as possible.*

jǐnguǎn 尽管
1 ADVERB = feel free to, not hesitate
■ 有什么问题，尽管和我联系。**Yǒu shénme wèntí, jǐnguǎn hé wǒ liánxì.** = *If you have any questions, do not hesitate to contact us.*
■ 你尽管吃，菜还多着呢！**Nǐ jǐnguǎn chī, cài hai duōzhe ne!** = *Eat to your heart's content. More dishes are coming.*
2 CONJUNCTION = even though
■ 尽管她很聪明，但是念书不用功，结果成绩不好。**Jǐnguǎn tā hěn cōngmíng, dànshì niànshū bú yònggōng, jiēguǒ chéngjì bùhǎo.** = *Even though she is quite intelligent, she does not study hard and consequently fails to get good results in exams.*

jǐn 紧 Trad 緊 ADJECTIVE = tight, taut
■ 今天的活动安排得比较紧。**Jīntiān de huódòng ānpái de bǐjiào jǐn.** = *Today's activities are scheduled rather tightly.*
■ 这件上衣肩部紧了一点。**Zhè jiàn shàngyī jiānbù jǐnle yìdiǎn.** = *The shoulders of the coat are a bit tight.*

jǐnzhāng 紧张 [compound: 紧 *tight* + 张 *tense*] ADJECTIVE = tense, nervous
■ 明天要考试了，我没有很好准备，心里很紧张。**Míngtiān yào kǎoshì le, wǒ méiyǒu hěn hǎo zhǔnbèi, xīnli hěn jǐnzhāng.** = *We're having an examination tomorrow. I'm not well prepared, and feel really nervous.*
■ 这个电影很紧张，看得我心直跳。**Zhège diànyǐng hěn jǐnzhāng, kàn de wǒ xīn zhí tiào.** = *This film was so nerve-racking that my heart beat violently.*

jìn 尽 Trad 盡 VERB = exhaust
■ 我已经尽了最大努力。**Wǒ yǐjīng jìnle zuì dà nǔlì.** = *I've already exhausted my energies [on this]. (→ I've done my very best.)*

jìnliàng 尽量 [v+obj: 尽 *exhaust* + 量 *amount*] ADVERB = do one's utmost, as far as possible
■ 对孩子你要尽量耐心一点。**Duì háizi nǐ yào jìnliàng nàixīn yìdiǎn.** = *In dealing with children you should try your best to be patient.*
■ 你们多商量商量，尽量取得一致的意见。**Nǐmen duō shāngliang-shāngliang, jìnliàng**

J

qǔdé yízhì de yìjiàn. = *You all should discuss the matter more and try your best to reach a unanimous view.*

jìn 进 Trad 進 VERB = move forward, enter
- 请进！**Qǐng jìn!** = *Please come in!* (or *Please go in!*)

jìnlai 进来 = come in, come into
- 进来吧，我们在等你呢！**Jìnlai ba, wǒmen zài děng nǐ ne!** = *Please come in. We've been waiting for you.*

jìnqu 进去 = go in, go into
- 他们在开会，请不要进去。**Tāmen zài kāihuì, qǐng bú yào jìnqu.** = *They're having a meeting. Please don't go in.*

jìnbù 进步

1 ADJECTIVE = progressive (antonym 落后 lòuhòu)
- 社会上的进步力量一定会取胜。**Shèhuì shang de jìnbù lìliàng yídìng huì qǔshèng.** = *The progressive forces in society will surely prevail.*

2 NOUN = progress
- 你们的中文学习有了很大进步。**Nǐmen de Zhōngwén xuéxí yǒule hěn dà jìnbù.** = *You have made very good progress in your Chinese studies.*

jìngōng 进攻 [compound: 进 advance + 攻 attack] VERB = advance and attack, attack
- 部队出发进攻敌人。**Bùduì chūfā jìngōng dírén.** = *The troops set out to attack the enemy forces.*

jìnhuà 进化 VERB = evolve, develop
- 人是从猴子进化来的，你信不信？**Rén shì cóng hóuzi jìnhuà lái de, nǐ xìng bú xìng?** = *Man evolved from the monkey. Do you believe this?*

jìnhuàlùn 进化论 = (Charles Darwin's) theory of evolution

jìnkǒu 进口 [v+obj: 进 enter + 口 the mouth] VERB = import (antonym 出口 chūkǒu)
- 这台机床是从德国进口的。**Zhè tái jīchuáng shì cóng Déguó jìnkǒu de.** = *This machine tool was imported from Germany.*
- 这个国家每年进口大量农产品。**Zhège guójiā měi nián jìnkǒu dàliàng nóngchǎnpǐn.**

= *This country imports large quantities of farm produce every year.*

jìnrù 进入 [compound: 进 enter + 入 enter] VERB = enter, enter into
- 狗不得进入商场。**Gǒu bùdé jìnrù shāngchǎng.** = *Dogs are not allowed to enter the shopping center.*
- 工程进入最后阶段。**Gōngchéng jìnrùle zuìhòu jiēduàn.** = *The project has entered into the last stage.*

jìnxíng 进行 [compound: 进 enter + 行 walk] VERB = conduct, carry out
- 孩子做错了事，应该进行教育。**Háizi zuò cuòle shì, yīnggāi jìnxíng jiàoyù.** = *When a child makes a mistake, he should be educated.*

NOTE: The object that 进行 **jìnxíng** takes must be a noun of two or more syllables. 进行 **jìnxíng** is used only in formal Chinese.

jìnxiū 进修 VERB = do advanced studies, undergo in-service advanced training
- 我们的中文老师要去北京进修半年。**Wǒmen de Zhōngwén lǎoshī yào qù Běijīng jìnxiū bànnián.** = *Our Chinese teacher will go to Beijing for half a year's advanced studies.*

jìnyíbù 进一步 [v+obj: 进 advance + 一步 one (more) step] ADVERB = advancing a step further, further, more deeply
- 对于这个问题，我们还要进一步研究。**Duìyú zhège wèntí, wǒmen hái yào jìnyíbù yánjiū.** = *We need to study this problem further.*
- 他们进一步提出了要求。**Tāmen jìnyíbù tíchūle yāoqiú.** = *They made further demands.*

jìn 近 ADJECTIVE = close to, close by (antonym 远 yuǎn)
- 商店很近，不用开车去。**Shāngdiàn hěn jìn, búyòng kāichē qù.** = *The store is close by. There is no need to drive.*

lí ... jìn 离 ... 近 = be close to
- 爸爸的办公室离家很近。**Bàba de bàngōngshì lí jiā hěn jìn.** = *Father's office is close to home.*

jìnlái 近来 NOUN = recently, nowadays, these days
- 他近来好事连连。**Tā jìnlái hǎoshì liánlián.**

= *These days good things are happening to him, one after another.*
■ 近来天气反常。**Jìnlái tiānqì fǎncháng.** = *The weather has been rather abnormal recently.*

jìn 劲 Trad 勁 NOUN = physical strength
■ 这位举重运动员真有劲! **Zhè wèi jǔzhòng yùndòngyuán zhēn yǒu jìn!** = *This weight lifter is really powerful!*
méijìn 没劲 = dull, boring, bored
■ 这日子过得真没劲! **Zhè rìzi guòde zhēn méijìn!** = *Life is so boring!*

jìn 禁 VERB = forbid

jìnzhǐ 禁止 [compound: 禁 *forbid* + 止 *stop*]
VERB = forbid, prohibit
■ 电影院内严格禁止使用手机。**Diànyǐngyuàn nèi yángé jìnzhǐ shǐyòng shǒujī.** = *Using the cell phone is strictly forbidden in the cinema.*
■ 外国人禁止入内。**Wàiguórén jìnzhǐ rùnèi.** = *Out of bounds to foreigners.*
■ 禁止吸烟。**Jìnzhǐ xīyān.** = *No smoking.*

jīng 京 NOUN = capital city

jīngjù 京剧 [modif: 京 *Beijing (Peking)* + 剧 *opera*] NOUN = Beijing (Peking) opera
■ 京剧有歌有舞, 还有武术, 真精彩! **Jīngjù yǒu gē yǒu wǔ, háiyǒu wǔshù, zhēn jīngcǎi!** = *Beijing opera contains singing, dancing and martial arts as well. It's really brilliant!*

jīng 经 Trad 經 VERB = pass through, experience

jīngcháng 经常 [compound: 经 *constant* + 常 *often*] ADVERB = often
■ 你经常迟到, 这样不好。**Nǐ jīngcháng chídào, zhèyàng bù hǎo.** = *You're often late, which is not good.*
■ 他们夫妻俩都讨厌做饭, 所以经常在外面吃。**Tāmen fūqī liǎ dōu tǎoyàn zuòfàn, suǒyǐ jīngcháng zài wàimian chī.** = *Both husband and wife hate cooking, so they often eat out.*

jīngguò 经过 [compound: 经 *go through* + 过 *pass*]
1 VERB = go through, pass
■ 我去学校去的路上, 要经过一座公园。**Wǒ**

qù xuéxiào de lùshang, yào jīngguò yí zuò gōngyuán. = *I pass by a park on my way to school.*
■ 没有亲自经过, 就不知道多难。**Méiyǒu qīnzì jīngguò, jiù bù zhīdào duō nán.** = *Without experiencing it personally, you wouldn't know how difficult it is.*
2 PREPOSITION = through, after
■ 经过这件事, 他变得聪明了。**Jīngguò zhè jiàn shì, tā biàn de cōngmíng le.** = *He was more sensible after this incident.*

jīngjì 经济 [compound: 经 *govern* + 济 *bring relief to*] NOUN = economy
■ 这个国家的经济不太好。**Zhège guójiā de jīngjì bú tài hǎo.** = *This country's economy is not in very good shape.*
■ 每个国家都在发展自己的经济。**Měi ge guójiā dōu zài fāzhǎn zìjǐ de jīngjì.** = *Every country is working hard to develop its economy.*
jīngjìxué 经济学 = economics
jīngjìxuéjiā 经济学家 = economist
shìchǎng jīngjì 市场经济 = market economy

jīnglǐ 经理 [compound: 经 *manage* + 理 *administrate*] NOUN = manager (位 **wèi**)
■ 他是管人力资源的经理。**Tā shì guǎn rénlì zīyuán de jīnglǐ.** = *He is the manager in charge of human resources.*
fùjīnglǐ 副经理 = deputy manager
shìchǎng jīnglǐ 市场经理 = marketing manager
zǒngjīnglǐ 总经理 = general manager, chief executive officer (CEO)

jīnglì 经历
1 VERB = experience, undergo
■ 这位老人经历了很多困难, 才获得幸福的晚年。**Zhè wèi lǎorén jīnglìle hěn duō kùnnan, cái huòdé xìngfú de wǎnnián.** = *This old man has experienced many troubles before enjoying blissful old age.*
2 NOUN = personal experience
■ 请你谈谈在美国学习和工作的经历。**Qǐng nǐ tántan zài Měiguó xuéxí hé gōngzuò de jīnglì.** = *Please tell us about your experience studying and working in the States.*

jīngyàn 经验 [compound: 经 *go through* + 验 *test*] NOUN = experience, lesson (learnt from experiences)

■ 这个经验对我很有价值。**Zhège jīngyàn duì wǒ hěn yǒu jiàzhí.** = *This experience is very valuable to me.*

qǔdé jīngyàn 取得经验 = acquire experience
yǒu jīngyàn 有经验 = experienced
■ 她是一位有经验的老师。**Tā shì yí wèi yǒu jīngyàn de lǎoshī.** = *She's an experienced teacher.*

jīng 惊 Trad 驚 VERB = be startled (See 吃惊 **chījīng**.)

jīng 睛 NOUN = the pupil of the eye (See 眼睛 **yǎnjing**.)

jīng 精 ADJECTIVE = choice

jīngcǎi 精彩 [compound: 精 *choice* + 彩 *colorful, brilliant*] ADJECTIVE = (of a theatrical performance or sports event) brilliant, thrilling, wonderful
■ 昨天的足球比赛真精彩啊！**Zuótiān de zúqiú bǐsài zhēn jīngcǎi a!** = *The football match yesterday was really wonderful!*
■ 他在会上的发言十分精彩，赢得了热烈的掌声。**Tā zài huì shang de fāyán shífēn jīngcǎi, yíngdéle rèliè de zhǎngshēng.** = *He made a stirring speech at the meeting and earned warm applause.*

jīnglì 精力 [compound: 精 *energy* + 力 *strength*] NOUN = energy, vigor
■ 我父亲年纪大了，精力不如以前了。**Wǒ fùqin niánjì dà le, jīnglì bùrú yǐqián le.** = *My father is getting old and is not so energetic as before.*

jīngshén 精神 [compound: 精 *essence* + 神 *spirit*] NOUN = vigor, vitality
■ 这位老人八十多岁了，但是精神很好。**Zhè wèi lǎorén bāshí duō suì le, dànshì jīngshén hěn hǎo.** = *This old man (or woman) is over eighty, but is energetic and alert.*
■ 不知道为什么，我今天没有精神。**Bù zhīdào wèishénme, wǒ jīntiān méiyǒu jīngshén.** = *I don't know why, but I'm in low spirits today.*
jīngshénbìng 精神病 = mental illness

jǐng 景 NOUN = view, scenery (See 风景 **fēngjǐng**, 情景 **qíngjǐng**.)

jǐng 警 VERB = warn

jǐngchá 警察 NOUN = policeman, police
■ 这里发生了交通事故，快叫警察！**Zhèli fāshēngle jiāotōng shìgù, kuài jiào jǐngchá!** = *A traffic accident has happened here. Call the police quickly!*

NOTE: In China the police bureau is called 公安局 **gōng'ānjú** = *Public Security Bureau*, which should be distinguished from 国安局 **guó'ānjú** = *Bureau of National Security*.

jìng 净 ADJECTIVE = clean (See 干净 **gānjing**.)

jìng 竞 Trad 競 VERB = compete

jìngsài 竞赛 [compound: 竞 *compete* + 赛 *contest*] VERB = compete, contest
■ 他们兄弟俩一直竞赛，看谁学习成绩好。**Tāmen xiōngdì liǎ yìzhí jìngsài, kàn shuí xuéxí chéngjì hǎo.** = *The two brothers have always been competing with each other to see who is the better student.*

jìng 竟 ADVERB = unexpectedly (See 究竟 **jiūjìng**.)

jìng 敬 VERB = respect

jìng'ài 敬爱 [compound: 敬 *respect* + 爱 *love*] VERB = respect and love
■ 有多少孩子敬爱自己的父母？**Yǒu duōshǎo háizi jìng'ài zìjǐ de fùmǔ?** = *How many children respect and love their parents?*

jìng 境 NOUN = boundary, place (See 环境 **huánjìng**.)

jìng 静 ADJECTIVE = quiet, peaceful, silent
■ 阅览室里很静，针掉在地上都听得见。**Yuèlǎnshì li hěn jìng, zhēn diào zài dìshang dōu tīng de jiàn.** = *The reading room is so quiet that one can hear a pin drop.*
■ 别管我，让我在这里静静地坐一会。**Bié guǎn wǒ, ràng wǒ zài zhèli jìngjìng de zuò yíhuì.** = *Please leave me alone and let me sit here quietly for a while.*
■ 请大家静一静，我要宣布一件事。**Qǐng dàjiā jìng yi jìng, wǒ yào xuānbù yí jiàn shì.** = *Be quiet, everybody. I have an announcement to make.*

jìng 镜 Trad 鏡 NOUN = mirror

jìngzi 镜子 [suffix: 镜 *mirror* + 子 nominal suffix] NOUN = mirror (面 **miàn**)
zhào jìngzi 照镜子 = look at oneself in a mirror
■ 她喜欢照镜子。**Tā xǐhuan zhào jìngzi.** = *She likes to look at herself in the mirror.*

jiū 究 VERB = investigate

jiūjìng 究竟 ADVERB = same as 到底 **dàodǐ**

jiū 纠 Trad 糾 VERB = rectify

jiūzhèng 纠正 [v+comp: 纠 *rectify* + 正 *correct*] VERB = rectify, correct
■ 我们应该及时纠正错误。**Wǒmen yīnggāi jíshí jiūzhèng cuòwù.** = *We should rectify our mistakes promptly.*

jiǔ 九 NUMERAL = nine
■ 九一一 **jiǔ-yāo-yāo** = 9/11, September 11
■ 九千九百九十九 **jiǔqiān jiǔbǎi jiǔshíjiǔ** = 9,999
■ 九九八十一 **jiǔjiǔ bāshíyī** = *Nine times nine is eighty-one.*

NOTE: See note on 一 **yī** regarding pronunciation of 一 as **yāo**.

jiǔ 久 ADJECTIVE = for a long time
■ 时间太久了，我记不清了。**Shíjiān tài jiǔ le, wǒ jìbuqīng le.** = *It was too long ago. I can't remember it clearly.*
■ 我等你等了很久了。**Wǒ děng nǐ děngle hěn jiǔ le.** = *I've been waiting for you for a long time.*
■ 日久见人心。**Rì jiǔ jiàn rén xīn.** = *As time goes on, you will know a person's nature.*

jiǔ 灸 NOUN = moxibustion (See 针灸 **zhēnjiǔ**.)

jiǔ 酒 NOUN = alcoholic beverage (种 **zhǒng**, 瓶 **píng**)
■ 这种酒，我不喜欢喝。**Zhè zhǒng jiǔ, wǒ bù xǐhuan hē.** = *I don't like this kind of alcoholic drink.*
■ 我不喝酒，我还要开车。**Wǒ bù hē jiǔ, wǒ háiyào kāichē.** = *No alcoholic drinks for me. I'll be driving.*
jiǔbā 酒吧 = (wine) bar, pub

jiǔdiàn 酒店 = wine shop, restaurant, hotel
báijiǔ 白酒 = colorless spirit distilled from grains
huángjiǔ 黄酒 = yellow rice wine

jiù 旧 Trad 舊 ADJECTIVE = (of things) old, second-hand (antonym 新 **xīn**)
■ 这件衣服不太旧，还可以穿。**Zhè jiàn yīfu bú tài jiù, hái kěyǐ chuān.** = *This jacket is not too old. It can still be worn.*
■ 他把旧车卖了一千块钱。**Tā bǎ jiù chē màile yìqiān kuài qián.** = *He sold his old car for one thousand dollars.*
■ 旧的不去，新的不来。**Jiù de bú qù, xīn de bù lái.** = *If the old doesn't go, the new won't come.* (→ *If you don't discard old stuff, you won't have new things.*)

jiù 救 VERB = save
■ 王医生及时动手术，救了他的命。**Wáng yīshēng jíshí dòng shǒushù, jiùle tā de mìng.** = *Dr Wang operated on him immediately and saved his life.*
■ 他在河中大叫，"救命！救命！" **Tā zài hé zhong dà jiào, "Jiù mìng! Jiù mìng!"** = *He cried out in the river, "Help! Help!"*
jiùhuǒ 救火 = put out a fire, fire fighting
jiùhuǒchē 救火车 = fire engine
jiùhùchē 救护车 = ambulance

jiù 就 1 PREPOSITION
1 = with regard to, concerning
■ 商业部长就物价问题发表谈话。**Shāngyè bùzhǎng jiù wùjià wèntí fābiǎo tánhuà.** = *The Minister of Commerce delivered a talk on prices.*
2 = as far as ... is concerned, in terms of
■ 就人口来说，中国是世界上第一大国。**Jiù rénkǒu láishuō, Zhōngguó shì shìjiè shang dì-yī dà guó.** = *In terms of population, China is the biggest country in the world.*

jiù 就 2 ADVERB = as early as ..., as soon as ... (used before a verb to emphasize that the action takes place very early, very quickly or only for a very short period of time)
■ 他今天早上六点钟就起床了。**Tā jīntiān zǎoshang liù diǎnzhōng jiù qǐchuáng le.** = *He got up as early as six o'clock this morning.*
■ 我马上就来。**Wǒ mǎshàng jiù lái.** = *I'll come immediately.* (→ *I'm coming.*)

J

yī ... jiù ... 一… 就 … = as soon as ...
■ 妈妈一下班就做晚饭。**Māma yí xiàbān jiù zuò wǎnfàn.** = *Mom prepared supper as soon as she got off work.*

jiùshì 就是 CONJUNCTION = even if
■ 我就是不睡觉，也要做完这个作业。**Wǒ jiùshì bú shuìjiào, yě yào zuòwán zhège zuòyè.** = *Even if I don't sleep, I must finish this assignment.*
■ 他们就是借钱，也要供儿子上大学。**Tāmen jiùshì jièqián, yě yào gòng érzi shàng dàxué.** = *They determined to put their son through university even if they have to borrow money.*

jū 居 VERB = occupy (See 邻居 línjū.)

jú 局 NOUN = office

júzhǎng 局长 [modif: 局 bureau + 长 chief]
NOUN = director/chief of a bureau
■ 一个部下面有几个局，所以一位部长下面有几位局长。**Yí ge bù xiàmiàn yǒu jǐ ge jú, suǒyǐ yí wèi bùzhǎng xiàmian yǒu jǐ wèi júzhǎng.** = *As there are several bureaus under a ministry, there are several bureau chiefs under a minister.*

jú 橘 NOUN = tangerine

júzi 橘子 [suffix: 橘 tangerine + 子 nominal suffix] NOUN = tangerine (只 zhī)
■ 苹果、香蕉、橘子，我都爱吃。**Píngguǒ, xiāngjiāo, júzi, wǒ dōu ài chī.** = *I like apples, bananas and tangerines.*

NOTE: 橘子 júzi can also be written 桔子 júzi.

jǔ 举 Trad 舉 VERB = hold high, raise, lift
■ 谁同意，请举手！**Shuí tóngyì, qǐng jǔ shǒu!** = *Those in favor [of the motion], please raise your hands.*
■ 举头望明月，低头思故乡 (李白) **Jǔ tóu wàng míng yuè, dī tóu sī gùxiāng (Lí Bái)** = *I raise my head to gaze at the bright moon and hang my head yearning for my hometown (Li Bai)* (lines from a poem by Li Bai)

jǔxíng 举行 VERB = hold (a meeting, a ceremony)
■ 下个月将举行国际会议，讨论这个问题。**Xiàge yuè jiāng jǔxíng guójì huìyì, tǎolùn zhège wèntí.** = *An international conference will be held next month to discuss this issue.*

jù 巨 ADJECTIVE = gigantic

jùdà 巨大 [compound: 巨 gigantic + 大 big]
ADJECTIVE = huge, gigantic, tremendous
■ 我们国家的经济发展取得了巨大的成绩。**Wǒmen guójiā de jīngjì fāzhǎn qǔdéle jùdà de chéngjì.** = *Our country has made tremendous achievements in economic development.*

jù 句 MEASURE WORD = (for sentences)
■ 一句话 **yí jù huà** = *one sentence*
■ 这句话 **zhè jù huà** = *this sentence*

jùzi 句子 [suffix: 句 sentence + 子 nominal suffix] NOUN = sentence (句 jù, 个 ge)
■ 张老师，这句句子什么意思？我看不懂。**Zhāng lǎoshī, zhè jù jùzi shénme yìsi? Wǒ kàn bu dǒng.** = *Teacher Zhang, what is the meaning of this sentence? I don't understand it.*
■ 这句句子语法不对。**Zhè jù jùzi yǔfǎ bú duì.** = *The grammar of this sentence is wrong.*

jù 拒 VERB = resist

jùjué 拒绝 VERB = refuse, reject
■ 她拒绝了他的邀请。**Tā jùjuéle tā de yāoqǐng.** = *She turned down his invitation.*
■ 他拒绝承认错误。**Tā jùjué chéngrèn cuòwù.** = *He refused to admit to any wrongdoing.*

jù 具 VERB = own, possess

jùbèi 具备 VERB = possess, be provided with
■ 这个小城市不具备建立大学的条件。**Zhège xiǎo chéngshì bú jùbèi jiànlì dàxué de tiáojiàn.** = *This small city does not possess the conditions necessary for establishing a university.*

jùtǐ 具体 ADVERB = specific, concrete
■ 你说他这个人不好，能不能说得具体些？**Nǐ shuō tā zhège rén bù hǎo, néng bù néng shuōde jùtǐ xiē?** = *You say he is not a good man. Can you be more specific?*
■ 请你举两三个具体的例子。**Qǐng nǐ jǔ liǎng-sān ge jùtǐ de lìzi.** = *Please give two or three concrete examples.*

jùyǒu 具有 VERB = have, possess, be provided with
- 这一事件具有重大的历史意义。**Zhè yí shìjiàn jùyǒu zhòngdà de lìshǐ yìyì.** = *This incident has major historic significance.*
- 中国文化具有哪些特点？ **Zhōngguó wénhuà jùyǒu nǎxiē tèdiǎn?** = *What characteristic features does Chinese culture have?*

jù 俱 ADVERB = together

jùlèbù 俱乐部 [modif: 俱 *together* + 乐 *joy* + 部 *department*] NOUN = club
- 这个俱乐部每年要交多少会费？ **Zhège jùlèbù měi nián yào jiāo duōshǎo huìfèi?** = *What are the annual dues of this club?*

jù 剧 NOUN = drama

jùchǎng 剧场 [modif: 剧 *drama* + 场 *site*] NOUN = theatre (座 **zuò**)
- 今晚在剧场里有精彩演出。**Jīnwǎn zài jùchǎng li yǒu jīngcǎi yǎnchū.** = *There will be a wonderful performance in the theatre this evening.*

jù 据 Trad 據 VERB = according to

jùshuō 据说 IDIOM = it is said, they say, rumor has it
- 据说王小姐现在在美国工作。**Jùshuō Wáng xiǎojiě xiànzài zài Měiguó gōngzuò.** = *It is said that Miss Wang is working in America.*
- 据说，一家外国公司就要买下我们工厂了。**Jùshuō, yì jiā wàiguó gōngsī jiù yào mǎixia wǒmen gōngchǎng le.** = *Rumor has it that a foreign company is going to buy our factory.*

jù 距 PREPOSITION = (an stretch of distance)

jùlí 距离 NOUN = distance
- 两地之间的距离有一百多公里。**Liǎngdì zhī jiān de jùlí yǒu yìbǎi duō gōnglǐ.** = *The distance between the two places is over a hundred kilometers.*
- 她和谁都保持一定距离。**Tā hé shuí dōu bǎochí yídìng jùlí.** = *She keeps a distance from everybody.* (→ *She gives everyone a wide berth.*)

juǎn 卷 VERB = roll up
- 他把地图卷起来，放在书架上。**Tā bǎ dìtú juǎn qǐlai, fàng zài shūjià shang.** = *He rolled the map up and placed it on the bookshelf.*

juàn 绢 Trad 絹 NOUN = silk (See 手绢 shǒujuàn.)

jué 决 ADVERB = definitely, under any circumstance (used before a negative word, e.g. 不 bù)
- 我决不做任何对社会有害的事。**Wǒ jué bù zuò rènhé duì shèhuì yǒuhài de shì.** = *I would never, ever, do anything that is harmful to society.*

juédìng 决定 [compound: 决 *determine* + 定 *decide*]
1 VERB = decide, determine, make up one's mind
- 你有没有决定买哪一辆汽车？ **Nǐ yǒu méiyǒu juédìng mǎi nǎ yí liàng qìchē?** = *Have you decided which car to buy?*
- 这件事实在很难决定。**Zhè jiàn shì shízài hěn nán juédìng.** = *This really is a difficult matter to decide.*
2 NOUN = decision
- 你们的决定是错误的。**Nǐmen de juédìng shì cuòwù de.** = *You've made a wrong decision.*
- 我希望你改变这个决定。**Wǒ xīwàng nǐ gǎibiàn zhège juédìng.** = *I hope you will change this decision.*
zuò juédìng 做决定 = make a decision
- 买哪一座房子，他们还没有做决定。**Mǎi nǎ yí zuò fángzi, tāmen hái méiyǒu zuò juédìng.** = *They haven't decided which house to buy.*

juéxīn 决心 [modif: 决 *determined* + 心 *heart*]
1 NOUN = determination
- 他的决心很大。**Tā de juéxīn hěn dà.** = *He is very determined.*
- 我们有决心，有信心，一定按时完成计划。**Wǒmen yǒu juéxīn, yǒu xìnxīn, yídìng ànshí wánchéng jìhuà.** = *We are determined, and we are confident, that we will fulfill the plan according to schedule.*
2 VERB = be determined, make up one's mind
- 我们决心按时完成计划。**Wǒmen juéxīn ànshí wánchéng jìhuà.** = *We are determined to fulfill the plan according to schedule.*

J

jué 觉 Trad 覺 VERB = feel

juéde 觉得 VERB = feel, find, think
- 我觉得你说的话很有道理。**Wǒ juéde nǐ shuō de huà hěn yǒu dàolǐ.** = *I think what you said is quite true* (or *reasonable*).
- 你觉得他的想法行不行? **Nǐ juéde tā de xiǎngfǎ xíng bu xíng?** = *Do you think his idea will work?*

jué 绝 Trad 绝 ADJECTIVE = absolute

juéduì 绝对 ADJECTIVE = absolute
- 我告诉你的消息绝对正确。**Wǒ gàosù nǐ de xiāoxi juéduì zhèngquè.** = *The news I told you is absolutely correct.*
- juéduì duōshù 绝对多数 = absolute majority

jūn 军 Trad 軍 NOUN = army, armed forces
- 中国人民解放军 **Zhōngguó Rénmín Jiěfàng Jūn** = *the Chinese People's Liberation Army*
- jūnhuǒ 军火 = arms and ammunition
- jūnrén 军人 = soldier
- jūnzhuāng 军装 = army uniform
- hǎijūn 海军 = navy
- kōngjūn 空军 = air force
- lùjūn 陆军 = army

jūnduì 军队 [modif: 军 *army* + 队 *rows of people*] NOUN = armed forces, troops
- 军队应该属于国家。**Jūnduì yīnggāi shǔyú guójiā.** = *The armed forces should belong to the state.*

jūnshì 军事 [modif: 军 *army* + 事 *affair*] NOUN = military affairs
- 军事上的事, 我不大懂。**Jūnshì shang de shì, wǒ bú dà dǒng.** = *I don't know much about military affairs.*

jūn 均 ADJECTIVE = equal (See 平均 **píngjūn**.)

jūn 菌 NOUN = fungus, bacterium (See 细菌 **xìjūn**.)

K

kāfēi 咖啡 NOUN = coffee (杯 **bēi**)
- 这种咖啡很好喝。**Zhè zhǒng kāfēi hěn hǎohē.** = *This kind of coffee is tastes good.*
- 从厨房飘来咖啡的香味。**Cóng chúfáng piāolai kāfēi de xiāngwèi.** = *The aroma of coffee floated in from the kitchen.*
- chōng kāfēi 冲咖啡 = make (instant) coffee
- zhǔ kāfēi 煮咖啡 = brew coffee

NOTE: 咖啡 **kāfēi** is one of the few transliterations (音译词 **yīnyìcí**) in Chinese vocabulary, as it represents more or less the sound of "coffee."

kǎ 卡 NOUN = card (张 **zhāng**)
- 这张卡很重要, 你要放好了。**Zhè zhǒng kǎ hěn zhòngyào, nǐ yào fànghǎo le.** = *This is a very important card. Keep it safely.*
- hèkǎ 贺卡 = greeting card
- jièshū kǎ 借书卡 = library card
- xìnyòng kǎ 信用卡 = credit card
- yínháng kǎ 银行卡 = banking card

kǎchē 卡车 NOUN = lorry, truck (辆 **liàng**)
- 开过来一辆卡车。**Kāi guòlái yì liàng kǎchē.** = *A truck is coming.*
- 我叔叔是个卡车司机。**Wǒ shūshu shì ge kǎchē sījī.** = *My uncle is a truck driver.*

NOTE: The composition of 卡车 **kǎchē** is semi-transliteration (半音译词 **bàn yīnyìcí**): 卡 **kǎ** represents the sound of the English word "car" and 车 **chē** means *vehicle*. See 咖啡 **kāfēi** for an example of transliteration.

kāi 开 Trad 開 VERB
1 = open, open up (antonym 关 **guān**)
- 开开门! **Kāikai mén!** = *Open the door, please!*
2 = turn on, switch on (antonym 关 **guān**)
- 天黑了, 开灯吧。**Tiān hēi le, kāi dēng ba.** = *It's dark. Let's turn on the light.*
3 = drive (a vehicle), pilot (a plane)
- 我会开汽车, 不会开飞机。**Wǒ huì kāi qìchē, bú huì kāi fēijī.** = *I can drive a car, but I can't pilot a plane.*
- kāiguān 开关 = switch
- 这个机器的开关坏了。**Zhège jīqì de kāiguān huài le.** = *The switch of this machine is out of order.*
- kāimén 开门 = open for business
- "这里的商店什么时候开门?" "九点钟开门。" **"Zhèlǐ de shāngdiàn shénme shíhou kāimén?" "Jiǔ diǎnzhōng kāimén."** = *"When*

do stores here open for business?" "Nine o'clock."

kāixué 开学 = begin (school)
■ 中国的学校九月一日开学。**Zhōngguó de xuéxiào Jiǔyuè yírì kāixué.** = *In China, schools begin on September 1 every year.*

kāi yèchē 开夜车 = burn the midnight oil
■ 明天要交作业，今天晚上我得开夜车。
Míngtiān yào jiāo zuòyè, jīntiān wǎnshang wǒ děi kāi yèchē. = *I must hand in my assignment tomorrow. I'll burn the midnight oil tonight.*

kāifā 开发 [compound: 开 *open* + 发 *develop*]
VERB = develop (resources, products, etc.)
■ 这个地区资源丰富，经济落后，需要开发。**Zhège dìqū zīyuán fēngfù, jīngjì luòhòu, xūyào kāifā.** = *This region is rich in natural resources but is backward economically. It needs developing.*
■ 我们公司花大量资金研究开发新产品。
Wǒmen gōngsī huā dàliàng zījīn yánjiū kāifā xīn chǎnpǐn. = *Our company spends large amounts of funds on researching and developing new products.*

kāifàng 开放 [compound: 开 *open* + 放 *release*] VERB = open, open up
■ 这个展览会从下周起对外开放。**Zhège zhǎnlǎnhuì cóng xià zhōu qǐ duìwài kāifàng.** = *This exhibition will open to the public next week.*

kāihuì 开会 [v+obj: 开 *open up* + 会 *meeting*]
VERB = attend a meeting, hold a meeting
■ 我们最好开个会，讨论一下这个问题。
Wǒmen zuìhǎo kāi ge huì, tǎolùn yíxià zhège wèntí. = *We'd best have a meeting to discuss this issue.*
■ 王老师在开会。**Wáng lǎoshī zài kāihuì.** = *Teacher Wang is at a meeting.*

kāipì 开辟 [compound: 开 *open up* + 辟 *open up*] VERB = open up, start
■ 这里要开辟成特别经济区。**Zhèli yào kāipì chéng tèbié jīngjìqū.** = *A special economic zone will be started here.*

kāishǐ 开始 [compound: 开 *open* + 始 *begin*]
1 VERB = begin, commence (antonym 结束 jiéshù)

■ 我从明年一月一日开始每天跑步半小时。
Wǒ cóng míngnián Yíyuè yírì kāishǐ měi tiān pǎobù bàn xiǎoshí. = *I'll begin jogging half an hour everyday from January 1 next year.*
■ 我进电影院的时候，电影已经开始了。**Wǒ jìn diànyǐngyuàn de shíhou, diànyǐng yǐjīng kāishǐ le.** = *The film had started by the time I entered the cinema.*
2 NOUN = beginning, start
■ 我开始觉得中文非常难，现在觉得不太难了。**Wǒ kāishǐ juéde Zhōngwén fēicháng nán, xiànzài juéde bú tài nán le.** = *At the beginning I found Chinese very difficult, but now I think it's not too difficult.*

kāi wánxiào 开玩笑 VERB = joke
■ 别开玩笑了！**Bié kāi wánxiào le!** = *Stop kidding!*
■ 这是很严肃的事，你不要开玩笑。**Zhè shì hěn yánsù de shì, nǐ bú yào kāi wánxiào.** = *This is a very serious matter. Don't joke about it. (→ This is no laughing matter.)*
gēn/hé ... kāi wánxiào 跟 / 和 ... 开玩笑 = joke with ..., make fun of ...
■ 他常常跟妹妹开玩笑。**Tā chángcháng gēn mèimei kāi wánxiào.** = *He often jokes with his younger sister.*

kāixué 开学 [v+obj: 开 *open* + 学 *school*] VERB
= start (school)
■ 中国的学校一般九月一日开学。你们国家的学校哪一天开学？**Zhōngguó de xuéxiào yìbān Jiǔyuè yírì kāixué. Nǐmen guójiā de xuéxiào nǎ yì tiān kāixué?** = *Schools in China usually start on September 1. On which day does school begin in your country?*

kāiyǎn 开演 [v+obj: 开 *open* + 演 *performance*] VERB = start (a performance, a film, etc.)
■ 电影什么时候开演？**Diànyǐng shénme shíhou kāiyǎn?** = *When does the film start?*

kāizhǎn 开展 [compound: 开 *open up* + 展 *fold*] VERB = launch, develop, expand
■ 他一当上经理，就积极开展业务。**Tā yí dāngshang jīnglǐ, jiù jījí kāizhǎn yèwù.** = *As soon as he became manager, he actively expanded the business.*

K

kǎn 砍 VERB = chop, hack
- 这棵树要砍掉。**Zhè kē shù yào kǎndiào.** = *This tree should be chopped down.*

kàn 看 VERB
1 = look, watch
- 我看看你的新衣服。**Wǒ kànkan nǐ de xīn yīfu.** = *Let me have a look at your new dress.*
2 = read
- "你每天看报吗？""我不每天看报。" **"Nǐ měi tiān kàn bào ma?" "Wǒ bù měi tiān kàn bào."** = *"Do you read newspapers everyday?" "No."*

kàn diànshì 看电视 = watch TV
kàn diànyǐng 看电影 = watch a film
kàn tǐyù bǐsài 看体育比赛 = watch a sport event

NOTE: See note on 看见 **kànjiàn**.

kànbìng 看病 [v + obj: 看 *see* + 病 *illness*]
VERB = see a doctor
- 我下午要请半天假，去看病。**Wǒ xiàwǔ yào qǐng bàn tiān jià, qù kànbìng.** = *I'll ask for half-day leave to see a doctor this afternoon.*

kànbuqǐ 看不起 VERB = look down upon, despise
- 我看不起这种不老实的人。**Wǒ kànbuqǐ zhè zhǒng bù lǎoshí de rén.** = *I despise such dishonest people.*

kàndeqǐ 看得起 = respect, hold in esteem

NOTE: In colloquial Chinese, 瞧不起 **qiáobuqǐ** can be used instead of 看不起 **kànbuqǐ**. Likewise 看得起 **kàndeqǐ** may be replaced by 瞧得起 **qiáodeqǐ**.

kànfǎ 看法 [modif: 看 *view* + 法 *way, method*]
NOUN
1 = way of looking at things, view
- 你的看法不一定对。**Nǐ de kànfǎ bù yídìng duì.** = *Your view is not necessarily correct.*
2 = negative opinion
- 他对我有看法。**Tā duì wǒ yǒu kànfǎ.** = *He has a negative opinion of me.*

kànjiàn 看见 [v+comp 看 *look* + 见 *see*] VERB
= see, get sight of
- 我朝山上看了很久，才看见一个人在爬山。**Wǒ cháo shān shang kànle hěn jiǔ, cái kànjiàn yí ge rén zài pá shān.** = *I looked at the hills for a long time before I saw a man climbing.*

kàn bu jiàn 看不见 = cannot see
kàn de jiàn 看得见 = can see
- "山上的人，你看得见吗？""看不见。" **"Shān shang de rén, nǐ kàn de jiàn ma?" "Kàn bu jiàn."** = *"Can you see the man (or people) on the hill?" "No, I can't."*

méi kànjiàn 没看见 = fail to see
- 我没看见他在图书馆里。**Wǒ méi kànjiàn tā zài túshūguǎn li.** = *I did not see him in the library.*

NOTE: While 看 **kàn** is *to look* or *to look at*, 看见 **kànjiàn** is *to see* or *to catch sight of*. For example:
- 我朝窗外看，没有看见什么。**Wǒ cháo chuāng wài kàn, méiyǒu kànjiàn shénme.** = *I looked out of the window and did not see anything.*

kànlái 看来 ADVERB = it looks as if, it seems as if
- 看来要下大雨了。**Kànlái yào xià dà yǔ le.** = *It seems that a downpour is coming our way.*
- 他看来很能干。**Tā kànlái hěn nénggàn.** = *He looks like a very able man.*

kànwàng 看望 [compound: 看 *see* + 望 *look*]
VERB = call on, pay a visit to
- 我每年过年都要看望中学时的老师。**Wǒ měi nián guònián dōu yào kànwàng zhōngxué shí de lǎoshī.** = *I pay a visit to my high school teacher every New Year's Day.*

kànyàngzi 看样子 ADVERB = same as 看来 **kànlái**

kāng 康 NOUN = good health (See 健康 **jiànkāng**.)

kàng 抗 VERB = resist (See 反抗 **fǎnkàng**.)

kǎo 考 VERB = examine, test
- 下星期二考中文。**Xià Xīngqī'èr kǎo Zhōngwén.** = *There will be an examination on Chinese next Tuesday.*
- 他不是不知道怎么回答，而是要考考你。**Tā bú shì bù zhīdào zěnme huídá, érshì yào kǎokao nǐ.** = *It is not that he did not know how to answer the question, but that he wanted to test you.*

kǎolǜ 考虑 VERB = think over carefully, consider, contemplate
- 我要好好考虑一下你的建议，明天给你回答。**Wǒ yào hǎohǎo kǎolǜ yíxià nǐ de jiànyì, míngtiān gěi nǐ huídá.** = *I need to consider your suggestion carefully. I will give you a reply tomorrow.*
- 他正在考虑转到另一个学校去。**Tā zhèngzài kǎolǜ zhuǎndào lìng yí ge xuéxiào qu.** = *He is contemplating transferring to another school.*

kǎoshì 考试 [compound: 考 examine, inquire + 试 test]
1 VERB = examine, test
- 我们明天考试。**Wǒmen míngtiān kiaoshì.** = *We're having an examination tomorrow.*
　kǎo de hǎo 考得好 = do well in an examination
　kǎo de bù hǎo 考得不好 = do poorly in an examination
- 我去年中文考得不好。**Wǒ qùnián Zhōngwén kǎo de bù hǎo.** = *I did not do well in the Chinese examination last year.*
2 NOUN = examination, test (次 cì)
- 这次考试太难了！**Zhè cì kǎoshì tài nán le!** = *This test was really difficult!*
- "你怕考试吗？""准备好了就不怕，没准备好就怕。" **"Nǐ pà kǎoshì ma?" "Zhǔnbèi hǎole jiù bú pà, méi zhǔnbèihǎo jiù pà."** = *"Are you afraid of examinations?" "Not when I'm prepared. If I weren't prepared, I'd be afraid."*
　gāoděng xuéxiào rùxué kǎoshì (gāokǎo) 高等学校入学考试 (高考) = university entrance examination
　Hànyǔ Shuǐpíng Kǎoshì 汉语水平考试 = Chinese Proficiency Test (HSK)

kǎo 烤 VERB = bake, roast
- 中国人很少吃烤牛肉。**Zhōngguórén hěn shǎo chī kǎo niúròu.** = *The Chinese rarely eat roast beef.*

kào 靠 VERB = rely on, depend on
- 这事全靠你了。**Zhè shì quán kào nǐ le.** = *This matter depends entirely on you.*
- 做事不能靠运气。**Zuòshì bù néng kào yùnqi.** = *You cannot rely on luck to get things done.*
　kàodezhù 靠得住 = trustworthy, reliable
　kàobuzhù 靠不住 = untrustworthy, unreliable

kē 科 NOUN = classification

kēxué 科学 [modif: 科 classification + 学 study] NOUN = science
- 科学能解决世界上所有的问题吗？**Kēxué néng jiějué shìjiè shang suǒyǒu de wèntí ma?** = *Can science solve all the problems in the world?*
- 我丈夫学科学，我学语言。**Wǒ zhàngfu xué kēxué, wǒ xué yǔyán.** = *My husband studies science, and I study languages.*
　kēxué yánjiū (kēyán) 科学研究 (科研) = scientific research
　kēxuéyuàn 科学院 = academy of science

kēxuéjiā 科学家 [modif: 科学 science + 家 nominal suffix] NOUN = scientist (位 wèi)
- 这座大学有几位世界著名的科学家。**Zhè zuò dàxué yǒu jǐ wèi shìjiè zhùmíng de kēxuéjiā.** = *This university has several world-renowned scientists.*

kē 棵 MEASURE WORD = (for plants)
- 三棵树 **sān kē shù** = *three trees*
- 一颗草 **yì kē cǎo** = *a blade of grass*

ké 咳 VERB = cough

késou 咳嗽 [compound: 咳 cough + 嗽 cough up] VERB = cough
- 这个病人每天夜里都咳嗽。**Zhège bìngrén měi tiān yèli dōu késou.** = *The patient coughs every night.*
- 你咳嗽很厉害，得去看病。**Nǐ késou hěn lìhai, děi qù kànbìng.** = *You've got a bad cough. You need to see a doctor.*
　késou yàoshuǐ 咳嗽药水 = cough syrup
　késou táng 咳嗽糖 = cough lozenge, cough drop

kě 可
1 ADVERB = indeed (used before an adjective for emphasis)
- 当父母可不容易呢！**Dāng fùmǔ kě bù róngyì ne!** = *Being a parent is indeed no easy job!*
- 她跳舞条跳得可美啦。**Tā tiàowǔ tiào de kě měi la.** = *She dances really beautifully!*
2 ADVERB = after all (used before a verb for emphasis)
- 我可找到你了！**Wǒ kě zhǎodào nǐ le!** = *I've found you after all.*

K

■ 他可出院了。**Tā kě chūyuàn le.** = *He was discharged from the hospital after all.*

3 ADVERB = be sure to (used in an imperative sentence for emphasis)

■ 可别忘了给他发一份电子邮件。**Kě bié wàngle gěi tā fā yí fèn diànzǐ yóujiàn!** = *Be sure not to forget to send him an e-mail. (→ Be sure to send him an e-mail.)*

■ 考试的时候可要看懂题目。**Kǎoshì de shíhou kě yào kàndǒng tímù.** = *During an examination, make sure that you understand the questions.*

4 CONJUNCTION = same as 可是 **kěshì**

NOTE: 可 **kě** is only used colloquially. When using 可 **kě** to emphasize an adjective or a verb, 啦 **la**, 呢 **ne** or 了 **le** is often used at the end of the sentence.

kě'ài 可爱 VERB = lovable, lovely

■ 这小女孩真可爱！ **Zhè xiǎo nǚhái zhēn kě'ài!** = *What a lovely little girl!*

kěkào 可靠 VERB = reliable, trustworthy

■ 很难找到可靠的人来管理秘密文件。**Hěn nán zhǎodào kěkào de rén lái guǎnlǐ mìmìwénjiàn.** = *It is difficult to find a trustworthy person to take care of confidential documents.*

■ 你这个消息可靠吗？ **Nǐ zhège xiāoxi kěkào ma?** = *Is your news reliable?*

kělián 可怜 ADJECTIVE = pitiful, pitiable

■ 这小孩的父母在交通事故中死了，真可怜！ **Zhè xiǎohái de fùmǔ zài jiāotōng shìgù zhong sǐ le, zhēn kělián!** = *Both his parents died in a road accident, the poor child!*

kěnéng 可能 [compound: 可 may + 能 can]

1 MODAL VERB = may, possible, possibly

■ 他两天没来上课，可能病了。**Tā liǎng tiān méi lái shàngkè, kěnéng bìng le.** = *He's been absent from class for two days. He may be ill.*

■ 他听了可能会生气。**Tā tīngle kěnéng huì shēngqì.** = *He may be offended when he hears this.*

2 NOUN = possibility

■ 这种可能是有的。**Zhè zhǒng kénèng shì yǒu de.** = *This is possible.*

(méi) yǒu kěnéng (没)有可能 = (im)possible, (im)possibly

■ "这件事有解决的可能吗？" "有可能。" **"Zhè jiàn shì yǒu jiějué de kěnéng ma?" "Yǒu kěnéng."** = *"Is it possible to solve this matter?" "Yes."*

kěkǒukělè 可口可乐 NOUN = Coca-Cola (瓶 **píng**)

■ 可口可乐有吗？ **Kěkǒukělè yǒu ma?** = *Do you have Coca-Cola?*

■ 我很渴，我想喝一瓶可口可乐。**Wǒ hěn kě, wǒ xiǎng hē yì píng kěkǒukělè.** = *I'm thirsty, I want to drink a bottle of Coca-Cola.*

bǎishìkělè 百事可乐 = Pepsi[-Cola]

NOTE: 可口可乐 **kěkǒukělè** is a transliteration of "Coca-Cola." It can be shortened into 可乐 **kělè**.

kěpà 可怕 ADJECTIVE = fearsome, frightening

■ 这种病很可怕，还没有药治。**Zhè zhǒng bìng hěn kěpà, hái méiyǒu yào zhì.** = *This disease is frightening, as there is still no medicine for it.*

kěshì 可是 CONJUNCTION = same as 但是 **dànshì**. Used colloquially.

kěyǐ 可以 MODAL VERB = giving permission, may, can, be allowed

■ "我可以走了吗？" "可以。" **"Wǒ kěyǐ zǒu le ma?" "Kěyǐ."** = *"May I leave now?" "Yes, you may."*

■ 你不可以把阅览室的书带回家。**Nǐ bù kěyǐ bá yuèlánshì de shū dàihuí jiā.** = *You are not allowed to take books home from the reading room.*

kě 渴 ADJECTIVE = thirsty

■ 我渴了，请给我一杯水。**Wǒ kě le, qǐng gěi wǒ yì bēi shuǐ.** = *I'm thirsty. Please give me a glass of water.*

kǒukě 口渴 = thirsty

■ 你口渴吗？ 这里有水。**Nǐ kǒu kě ma? Zhèli yǒu shuǐ.** = *Are you thirsty? Here's some water.*

NOTE: See note on 喝 **hē**.

kè 克 MEASURE WORD = gram

■ 五百克 **wǔbǎi kè** = *500 grams*

kèfú 克服 VERB = overcome, conquer
■ 我相信一定能克服这些暂时的困难。**Wǒ xiāngxìn yídìng néng kèfú zhèxiē zànshí de kùnnan.** = *I am convinced that we are surely able to overcome these temporary difficulties.*

kè 刻 1 VERB = carve
■ 他在石头上刻上自己的名字。**Tā zài shítou shang kè shang zìjǐ de míngzi.** = *He carved his name on the rock.*

kè 刻 2 MEASURE WORD = quarter of an hour
■ 一刻钟 **yí kè zhōng** = *a quarter of an hour; 15 minutes*
■ 三点一刻 **sān diǎn yí kè** = *a quarter past three*

kèkǔ 刻苦 ADJECTIVE = hardworking, assiduous, painstaking
■ 这位科学家刻苦研究十几年，终于找到了答案。**Zhè wèi kēxuéjiā kèkǔ yánjiū shí jǐ nián, zhōngyú zhǎodào le dá'àn.** = *The scientist researched arduously for a dozen years and finally found the answer.*

kè 客 NOUN = guest

kèqi 客气 [modif: 客 *guest* + 气 *manner*] ADJECTIVE
1 = polite, stand on ceremony
■ 您跟我们一起吃午饭吧，别客气。**Nín gēn wǒmen yìqǐ chī wǔfàn ba, bié kèqi.** = *Have lunch with us. Don't stand on ceremony.*
■ 他要请你帮忙的时候，就很客气。**Tā yào qǐng nǐ bāngmáng de shíhou, jiù hěn kèqi.** = *When he asks for your help, he's very polite.*
2 = modest
■ 你唱歌唱得这么好，还说不好，太客气了。**Nǐ chànggē chàng de zhème hào, hái shuō bù hǎo, tài kèqi le.** = *You sing so well but you still say you don't sing well. You're too modest.*

kèren 客人 NOUN = guest, visitor
■ 宴会八点钟开始，七点三刻客人陆续到来。**Yànhuì bā diǎnzhōng kāishǐ, qī diǎn sān kè kèren lùxù dàolai.** = *The banquet began at eight o'clock; guests arrived one after another at a quarter to eight.*

kè 课 Trad 課 NOUN = lesson, class, lecture
■ 今天的课你听懂没有？**Jīntiān de kè nǐ tīngdǒng méiyǒu?** = *Do you understand today's lesson?*
shàng kè 上课 = go to class
xià kè 下课 = finish class

kèběn 课本 [modif: 课 *lesson* + 本 *book*] NOUN = textbook, course book (本 **běn**)
■ 你知不知道哪一本中文课本比较好？**Nǐ zhī bu zhīdào nǎ yì běn Zhōngwén kèběn bǐjiào hǎo?** = *Do you know which Chinese textbook is relatively good? (→ Do you know of a good Chinese textbook?)*
■ 王老师打算编一本适合日本学生学中文的课本。**Wáng lǎoshī dǎsuàn biān yì běn shìhé Rìběn xuésheng xué Zhōngwén de kèběn.** = *Teacher Wang plans to compile a textbook suitable for Japanese students of Chinese.*

kèchéng 课程 [modif: 课 *lesson* + 程 *course*] NOUN = course, a program of study
■ 医学课程花的时间比其他课程长。**Yīxué kèchéng huā de shíjiān bǐ qítā kèchéng cháng.** = *A course in medicine takes more time than other courses.*
■ 我们的课程排得很满，没有多少时间搞课外活动。**Wǒmen de kèchéng pái de hěn mǎn, méiyǒu duōshǎo shíjiān gǎo kèwài huódòng.** = *Our timetable is very crowded and leaves little time for extracurricular activities.*

kèwén 课文 [modif: 课 *lesson* + 文 *writing*] NOUN = text (篇 **piān**)
■ 这篇课文写得真好。**Zhè piān kèwén xiě de zhēn hǎo.** = *This text is really well written.*
■ 我要多念几遍课文。**Wǒ yào duō niàn jǐ biàn kèwén.** = *I should read the text a few more times.*

kěn 肯 MODAL VERB = be willing to
■ 你肯不肯帮我着一件事？**Nǐ kěn bu kěn bāng wǒ zuò yí jiàn shì?** = *Are you willing to do something for me? (→ Would you do me a favor?)*
■ 中国的父母一般肯为孩子作出牺牲。**Zhōngguó de fù-mǔ yìbān kěn wèi háizi zuòchu xīshēng.** = *Generally speaking, Chinese parents are willing to make sacrifices for their children.*

K

kěndìng 肯定

1 VERB = confirm, acknowledge (antonym 否定 fǒudìng)
- 总公司充分肯定你们的成绩。**Zǒnggōngsī chōngfèn kěndìng nǐmen de chéngjì.** = *The company's head office fully acknowledges your achievements.*

2 ADJECTIVE = affirmative, positive, definite (antonym 否定 fǒudìng)
- "你支持我们的计划吗?" "我肯定支持。" **"Nǐ zhīchí wǒmen de jìhuà ma?" "Wǒ kèndìng zhīchí."** = *"Do you support our plan?" "I definitely support it."*
- 很抱歉，我不能给你一个肯定的回答。**Hěn bàoqiàn, wǒ bù néng gěi nǐ yí ge kèndìng de huídá.** = *I'm sorry, but I'm not in a position to give you a definite reply.*

kěn 恳 Trad 懇 ADJECTIVE = sincere (See 诚恳 chéngkěn.)

kōng 空 ADJECTIVE = empty
- 箱子是空的，里面什么也没有。**Xiāngzi shì kōng de, lǐmiàn shénme yě méiyǒu.** = *The suitcase is empty, there's nothing in it.*

kōngjiān 空间 NOUN = space, room
- 要给孩子留一些空间，让他做自己喜欢做的事。**Yào gěi háizi liú yìxiē kōngjiān, ràng tā zuò zìjǐ xǐhuan zuò de shì.** = *Leave a child room (or time) to let him do what he enjoys doing.*

kōngqì 空气 [modif: 空 empty + 气 vapor] NOUN = air
- 这里的空气真好! **Zhèlǐ de kōngqì zhēn hǎo!** = *The air here is really fresh.*
- 空气是由什么组成的? **Kōngqì shì yóu shénme zǔchéng de?** = *What is air composed of?*

kōngqián 空前 ADJECTIVE = unprecedented
- 这种经济增长的速度是空前的。**Zhè zhǒng jīngjì zēngzhǎng de sùdù shì kōngqián de.** = *This kind of economic growth rate is unprecedented.*

kōngzhōng 空中 NOUN = in the sky, in the air
- 他们在表演空中飞人的节目。**Tāmen zài biǎoyǎn kōngzhōng fēirén de jiémù.** = *They are performing on the flying trapeze.*

kǒng 孔 NOUN = aperture, hole
- 这座桥有三个孔。**Zhè zuò qiáo yǒu sān ge kǒng.** = *The bridge has three arches.*

kǒngbù 恐 VERB = fear

kǒngbù 恐怖 [compound: 恐 fear, dread + 怖 terrifying] ADJECTIVE = horrible, terrifying
- 这个电影太恐怖了，小孩子不能看。**Zhège diànyǐng tài kǒngbù le, xiǎo háizi bù néng kàn.** = *This film is too frightening for children to see.*
kǒngbù diànyǐng 恐怖电影 = horror movie
kǒngbù fènzi 恐怖分子 = terrorist
kǒngbù huódòng 恐怖活动 = terrorist activity
kǒngbù zhǔyì 恐怖主义 = terrorism

kǒngpà 恐怕 [compound: 恐 fear, dread + 怕 fear] ADVERB = I'm afraid, perhaps
- 他的病恐怕两三天好不了。**Tā de bìng kǒngpà liǎng-sān tiān hǎobuliǎo.** = *I'm afraid he won't recover in a couple of days.*
- 她恐怕已经回国了。**Tā kǒngpà yǐjīng huíguó le.** = *She has perhaps gone back to her home country.*

NOTE: 恐怕 **kǒngpà** and 也许 **yéxǔ** may both mean *perhaps*, but 恐怕 **kǒngpà** implies that what will perhaps happen is undesirable.

kòngzhì 控制 VERB = control
- 我们要控制人口的增长，提高人口的质量。**Wǒmen yào kòngzhì rénkǒu de zēngzhǎng, tígāo rénkǒu de zhìliàng.** = *We should control population growth and raise population quality.*
- 她控制不住自己的感情，大哭起来。**Tā kòngzhì bú zhù zìjǐ de gǎnqíng, dàkū qǐlai.** = *She couldn't control her emotions and began to cry loudly.*

kòng 空 NOUN = free time
- "你今天晚上有空吗?" "我今天晚上没有空，明天晚上有空。" **"Nǐ jīntiān wǎnshang yǒukòng ma?" "Wǒ jīntiān wǎnshang méiyǒu kòng, míngtiān wǎnshang yǒu kòng."** = *"Are you free this evening?" "No, I'm not. I'll be free tomorrow evening."*
- 你有空常来玩。**Nǐ yǒu kòng cháng lái wán.** = *Do come to visit us when you have time.*

K

kǒu 口

1 NOUN = mouth
- 病从口入。 **Bìng cóng kǒu rù.** = *Disease enters your body by the mouth.* (→ *Bad food causes disease.*)

2 MEASURE WORD = (for members of a family)
- 我家有四口人。 **Wǒ jiā yǒu sì kǒu rén.** = *There're four people in my family.*

kǒudài 口袋 NOUN = pocket (只 zhī)
- 他喜欢把手插在口袋里。 **Tā xǐhuan bǎ shǒu chā zài kǒudài li.** = *He likes to put his hands in his pockets.*

kǒuhào 口号 NOUN = slogan (条 tiáo)
- 这种政治口号已经没有人喊了。 **Zhè zhǒng zhèngzhì kǒuhào yǐjīng méiyǒu rén hǎn le.** = *Nobody shouts such political slogans any more.*

kǒuyǔ 口语 [modif: 口 the mouth + 语 speech] NOUN = spoken language, speech
- 我中文口语不行，很多话不会说。 **Wǒ Zhōngwén kǒuyǔ bù xíng, hěn duō huà bú huì shuō.** = *My oral Chinese is rather poor. There are many things I can't express.*
- 要学好口语，就要多听，多说。 **Yào xué hǎo kǒuyǔ, jiù yào duō tīng, duō shuō.** = *To learn the spoken language well, one should listen a lot and speak a lot.*
- 他喜欢找中国人说话练口语。 **Tā xǐhuan zhǎo Zhōngguórén shuōhuà liàn kǒuyǔ.** = *He likes to talk with Chinese to practice his oral Chinese.*

kū 哭 VERB = cry, weep, sob (antonym 笑 xiào)
- 别哭了，有话好好说。 **Bié kū le, yǒu huà hǎohǎo shuō.** = *Don't cry. Speak up if you have something to say.*
- 她难过得哭起来。 **Tā nánguó de kū qǐlai.** = *She was so sad that she cried.*
- 听了他的话，我哭笑不得。 **Tāngle tā de huà, wǒ kū-xiào bù dé.** = *Hearing what he said, I didn't know whether to laugh or cry.*

kǔ 苦 ADJECTIVE = bitter; (of life) hard, miserable
- 这杯咖啡太苦了，要放点儿糖。 **Zhè bēi kāfēi tài kǔ le, yào fàng diǎnr táng.** = *This coffee is too bitter. Put a bit of sugar in it.*
- 经济不好，不少人生活很苦。 **Jīngjì bù hǎo, bù shǎo rén shēnghuó hěn kǔ.** = *As the economy is not in good shape, many people's lives are very hard.*
- chīkǔ 吃苦 = suffer hardships, endure hardships

kù 裤 Trad 褲 NOUN = trousers

kùzi 裤子 [suffix: 裤 trousers + 子 nominal suffix] NOUN = trousers (条 tiáo)
- 这条裤子短了一点儿。 **Zhè tiáo kùzi duǎnle yìdiǎnr.** = *This pair of trousers is a bit too short.*
- 这个小孩会脱裤子，但还不会穿裤子。 **Zhège xiǎohái huì tuō kùzi, dàn hái bú huì chuān kùzi.** = *This child can take off his trousers, but still can't put them on.*

kuà 跨 VERB = take big strides
- 他再向前跨一步，就要滚下楼梯了。 **Tā zài xiàngqián kuà yí bù, jiùyào gǔnxia lóutī le.** = *If he took another step forward he would tumble down the staircase.*
- kuàguó gōngsī 跨国公司 = multinational company

kuài 快 ADJECTIVE = quick, fast (antonym 慢 màn)
- 快，公共汽车来了！ **Kuài, gōnggòng qìchē lái le!** = *Quick, the bus is coming!*
- 他跑得很快。 **Tā pǎo de hěn kuài.** = *He runs very fast.*
- kuài chē 快车 = express train

kuàilè 快乐 ADJECTIVE = joyful, happy
- 祝你生日快乐！ **Zhù nǐ shēngrì kuàilè!** = *Happy birthday!*
- 在这个快乐的节日里，人们暂时忘了生活中种种不愉快的事。 **Zài zhège kuàilè de jiérì li, rénmen zànshí wàngle shēnghuó zhōng zhǒng-zhǒng bù yúkuài de shì.** = *At this happy festival, people forget for the time being unpleasant things in life.*

kuài 块 Trad 塊 MEASURE WORD

1 = (for things that can be broken into lumps or chunks)
- 一块蛋糕 **yí kuài dàngāo** = *a piece/slice of cake*
- 两块面包 **liǎng kuài miànbāo** = *two pieces of bread*

2 = (for money) *yuan*, dollar (only in spoken Chinese)

K

■ 三块钱 **sǎn kuài qián** = *three yuan (or dollars)*

NOTE: See note on 元 **yuán**.

kuài 筷 NOUN = chopstick

kuàizi 筷子 [suffix: 筷 *chopstick* + 子 nominal suffix] NOUN = chopsticks (双 **shuāng** = *a pair*)
■ 你会用筷子吗？ **Nǐ huì yòng kuàizi ma?** = *Can you eat with chopsticks?*

kuān 宽 Trad 寬 ADJECTIVE = wide
■ 江面很宽，我游不过去。 **Jiāngmiàn hěn kuān, wǒ yóu bu guòqu.** = *The river is too wide for me to swim across.*

kuǎn 款 NOUN = sum of money (笔 **bǐ**)
■ 你可以用这张卡取款，或者存款。 **Nǐ kěyǐ yòng zhè zhāng kǎ qǔ kuǎn, huòzhě cún kuǎn.** = *You can withdraw or deposit money with this card.*
zìdòng qǔkuǎnjī 自动取款机 = automatic teller machine (ATM)

kuàng 况 NOUN = situation (See 情况 **qíngkuàng**, 状况 **zhuàngkuàng**.)

kuàng 矿 Trad 礦 NOUN = (coal, gold, etc.) mine (座 **zuò**)
■ 这座矿已经开了一百多年了。 **Zhè zuò kuàng yǐjīng kāile yìbǎi duō nián le.** = *This coal mine has been mined for over a century.*
kuànggōng 矿工 = miner
jīnkuàng 金矿 = gold mine
méikuàng 煤矿 = coal mine
yóukuàng 油矿 = oilfield

kuì 愧 ADJECTIVE = ashamed (See 惭愧 **cánkuì**.)

kùn 困 VERB = be stranded, be in a tough spot
■ 由于突然发大水，人们被困在那个小山村。 **Yóuyú tūrán fā dàshuǐ, rénmen bèi kùn zài nàge xiǎo shāncūn.** = *Because of a sudden flood, people were stranded in the small mountain village.*

kùnnan 困难 [compound: 困 *be stranded* + 难 *difficult*]
1 NOUN = difficulty
■ 困难是有的，但是没有关系。 **Kùnnan shì**

yǒu de, dànshì méiyǒu guānxi. = *There are difficulties, but it doesn't matter.*
■ 你不要怕困难，要想一想怎么办。 **Nǐ bú yào pà kùnnan, yào xiǎng yi xiǎng zénme bàn.** = *You mustn't be afraid of difficulties. You should think of what to do.*
2 ADJECTIVE = difficult
■ 我们现在的情况比较困难。 **Wǒmen xiànzài de qíngkuàng bǐjiào kùnnan.** = *Our situation is rather difficult.*
kèfú kùnnan 克服困难 = overcome difficulty

kuò 扩 Trad 擴 VERB = spread out

kuòdà 扩大 VERB = expand, enlarge
■ 这个城市的范围在不断扩大。 **Zhège chéngshì de fànwéi zài búduàn kuòdà.** = *The boundary of this city is constantly expanding.*
■ 他们打算扩大生产规模。 **Tāmen dǎsuàn kuòdà shēngchǎn guīmó.** = *They plan to expand the scale of production.*

kuò 括 VERB = include, embrace (See 概括 **gàikuò**.)

kuò 阔 ADJECTIVE = wide (See 广阔 **guǎngkuò**.)

L

lā 拉 VERB = pull
■ 请你拉这个门，别推这个门。 **Qǐng nǐ lā zhège mén, bié tuī zhège mén.** = *Please pull this door, not push it.*

lājī 垃圾 NOUN = rubbish, garbage
■ 请不要乱扔垃圾。 **Qǐng bú yào luàn rēng lājī.** = *Please do not litter.*
lājī chǔlǐ 垃圾处理 = rubbish disposal
lājī dài 垃圾袋 = rubbish bag
lājī xiāng 垃圾箱 = rubbish bin

la 啦 PARTICLE = (an exclamation indicating completion of an action and/or emergence of a new situation; 了 **le** + 啊 **a**)
■ 我们赢啦！ **Wǒmen yíng la!** = *We've won!*
■ 我做完作业啦！ **Wǒ zuòwán zuòyè la!** = *I've finished my assignment!*

NOTE: 啦 **la** is the combination of 了 **le** and 啊 **a**. It is always used at the end of a sentence. You can replace 啦 **la** with 了 **le** but then the strong emotive coloring of 啊 **a** is lost. Compare: 我赢啦! **Wǒ yíng la!** = *I won!* and 我们赢了。**Wǒmen yíng le** = *I won.*

lái 来 Trad 來 1 VERB = come, come to; move forward the speaker (antonym 去 **qù**)
- 王先生来了没有？ **Wáng xiānsheng láile méiyǒu?** = *Has Mr Wang come?*
- 他是三年前来新西兰的。**Tā shì sān nián qián lái Xīnxīlán de.** = *He came to New Zealand three years ago.*

lái 来 Trad 來 2 NUMERAL = approximately, more or less, close to (used after the number 10 or a multiple of 10 to indicate approximation)
- 十来辆车 **shí lái liàng chē** = *about ten cars*
- 五十来个学生 **wǔshí lái ge xuésheng** = *approximately fifty students*
- 三百四十来块钱 **sānbǎi sìshí lái kuài qián** = *about 340 yuan*

láibují 来不及 VERB = not enough time (to do something)
- 到那时候，哭都来不及。**Dào nà shíhou, kū dōu láibují.** = *Should such a moment come, there would even be no time to cry (→ it would be too late to regret).*
- 来不及吃早饭了。**Láibují chī zǎofàn le.** = *There is no time for breakfast.*

NOTE: The opposite is 来得及 **láidejí**, e.g.
- 还来得及吃早饭。**Hái láid jí chī zǎofàn.** = *There is still enough time to have breakfast.*

láixìn 来信 [modif: 来 *arriving* + 信 *letter*] NOUN = letter received, incoming letter
- 来信早已收到。**Láixìn zǎo yǐ shōudào.** = *I received your letter long ago.*

láizì 来自 VERB = come from
- 这个中文班的学生来自世界各国。**Zhège Zhōngwén bān de xuésheng láizì shìjiè gè guó.** = *The students of this Chinese class came from all over the world.*

lán 兰 Trad 蘭 NOUN = orchid (See 新西兰 **Xīnxīlán.**)

lán 拦 Trad 攔 VERB = stop, block, hold back
- 你要去就去，没人拦你。**Nǐ yào qù jiù qù, méi rén lán nǐ.** = *If you want to go, go ahead. Nobody is trying to stop you.*

lán 蓝 Trad 藍 ADJECTIVE = blue
- 天很蓝，因为空气很干净。**Tiān hěn lán, yīnwèi kōngqì hěn gānjing.** = *The sky is blue because the air is clean.*
- 蓝蓝的天上白云飘，多好看啊! **Lánlán de tiān shang báiyún piāo, duō hǎokàn a!** = *White clouds float in the blue sky. How beautiful!*

lán 篮 Trad 籃 NOUN = basket

lánqiú 篮球 [modif: 篮 *basket* + 球 *ball*] NOUN = basketball
- 他们在打篮球。**Tāmen zài dǎ lánqiú.** = *They're playing basketball.*
  lánqiú bǐsài 篮球比赛 = basketball match
  lánqiú duì 篮球队 = basketball team
  dǎ lánqiú 打篮球 = play basketball

lǎn 览 Trad 覽 VERB = view (See 游览 **yóulǎn**, 阅览室 **yuèlǎnshì**, 展览 **zhǎnlǎn**.)

lǎn 懒 Trad 懶 ADJECTIVE = lazy, indolent
- 你真太懒了，收到他来信两个星期了，还不回信。**Nǐ zhēn tài lǎn le, shōudào tā láixìn liǎng ge xīngqī le hái bù huíxìn.** = *You're really lazy. It's two weeks since you received his letter and you still haven't replied.*
  lǎn gútou 懒骨头 = lazy bone
  hào-chī-lǎn-zuò 好吃懒做 = like eating but hate working, be gluttonous and lazy

làn 烂 Trad 爛
1 VERB = go rotten, go bad
- 水果容易烂，运输是个问题。**Shuǐguǒ róngyì làn, yùnshū shì ge wèntí.** = *Fruit rots easily, and its transport is a problem.*
2 ADJECTIVE = rotten
- 这个苹果烂了，扔了吧。**Zhège píngguǒ làn le, rēng le ba.** = *This apple is rotten. Throw it away.*

láng 狼 NOUN = wolf (只 **zhī**)
- 狼是羊群的大敌。**Láng shì yángqún de dàdí.** = *Wolves are the great enemies of the sheep flock.*

L

pīzhe yángpí de láng 披着羊皮的狼 = a wolf in sheep's clothing
yì qún láng 一群狼 = a pack of wolves

lǎng 朗 ADJECTIVE = loud and clear

lǎngdú 朗读 [modif: 朗 *loud and clear* + 读 *read*] VERB = read in a loud and clear voice
■ 学外语，一定要朗读课文。**Xué wàiyǔ, yídìng yào lǎngdú kèwén.** = *To learn a foreign language, one should read texts aloud.*

làng 浪 NOUN = wave
■ 风急浪高，不能出海。**Fēng jí làng gāo, bù néng chūhǎi.** = *The winds are strong and the waves high. We can't go out to sea.*

làngfèi 浪费 VERB = waste
■ 浪费时间就是浪费生命。**Làngfèi shíjiān jiùshì làngfèi shēngmìng.** = *To waste time is to waste life.*

lāo 捞 Trad 撈 VERB = pull or drag out of water
■ 孩子们在小河里捞什么呢？ **Háizimen zài xiǎo hé li lāo shénme ne?** = *What are the children trying to scoop out of the stream?*
dǎlāo 打捞 = salvage (a sunken ship, etc.)

láo 劳 Trad 勞 VERB = toil

láodòng 劳动 [compound: 劳 *toil* + 动 *move*] VERB = do manual labor
■ 他夏天在父亲的农场劳动。**Tā xiàtiān zài fùqin de nóngchǎng láodòng.** = *In summer he works on his father's farm.*
láodòng jié 劳动节 = Labor Day (on May 1)
nǎolì láodòng 脑力劳动 = mental work
tǐlì láodòng 体力劳动 = physical (manual) labor

láojià 劳驾 IDIOM = May I trouble you to ..., Would you mind (doing ... for me)
■ 劳驾，请您让一下。**Láojià, qǐng nín ràng yíxià.** = *Excuse me, would you please make way?*

NOTE: 劳驾 **láojià** is a northern dialect expression. 对不起 **duìbuqǐ** is more widely used.

lǎo 老
1 ADJECTIVE = old, elderly
■ 爸爸老了，不能在农场劳动了。**Bàba lǎo le, bù néng zài nóngchǎng láodòng le.** = *Father is old and can't work on the farm.*
■ 他在帮一位老太太过马路。**Tā zài bāng yí wèi lǎo tàitai guò mǎlù.** = *He's helping an old lady cross the street.*
lǎo tàitai 老太太 = old lady, old woman
lǎo xiānsheng 老先生 = old gentleman, old man
2 ADJECTIVE = long-standing
■ 这个老问题一直没有办法解决。**Zhè ge lǎo wèntí yìzhí méiyǒu bànfǎ jiějué.** = *This perennial problem has remained unsolved for a long time.*
lǎo péngyou 老朋友 = long-standing friend
■ 我们在小学的时候就认识了，是老朋友。**Wǒmen zài xiǎoxué de shíhou jiù rènshi le, shì lǎo péngyou.** = *We've known each other since primary school. We're old friends.*
3 PREFIX = (added to numerals to indicate seniority among siblings)
lǎo dà 老大 = the eldest child
lǎo èr 老二 = the second child

NOTE: Chinese tradition values and respects old age. Today, people still attach 老 **lǎo** to a family name as a form of address to show respect and friendliness to an older person, e.g. 老李 **Lǎo Lǐ**, 老王 **Lǎo Wáng**. See note on 小 **xiǎo**.

lǎobǎixìng 老百姓 [modif: 老 *old* + 百 *hundred* + 姓 *family names*] NOUN = common people, ordinary folk
■ 老百姓对当官的有意见，怎么办呢？**Lǎobǎixìng duì dāngguānde yǒu yìjiàn, zénme bàn ne?** = *What should common people do when they have a complaint against an official?*

lǎobǎn 老板 NOUN
1 = boss
■ 他是我的老板，他要我做什么我就做什么。**Tā shì wǒ de lǎobǎn, tā yào wǒ zuò shénme wǒ jiù zuò shénme.** = *He is my boss; I do what he tells me to do.*
2 = owner of a store, a business, etc.
■ 老板不在，没人可以作主。**Lǎobǎn bú zài, méi rén kěyǐ zuòzhǔ.** = *As the owner is away, nobody can make a decision.*

L

lǎodàniáng 老大娘 NOUN = (a respectful form of address or reference to an old woman) (位 wèi)
■ 他把座位让给一位老大娘。**Tā bǎ zuòwèi rànggěi yí wèi lǎodàniáng.** = *He offered his seat to an old woman.*
■ 老大娘，您找谁？ **Lǎodàniáng, nín zhǎo shuí?** = *Who are you looking for, ma'am?*

NOTE: 老大娘 **lǎodàniáng** has a rustic flavor. It is normally not used in cities or among better-educated people. 老太太 **lǎotàitai** is a more appropriate word.

lǎodàye 老大爷 NOUN = (a respectful form of addresses or reference to an old man) (位 wèi)
■ 老大爷，请您让我看看您的票子。**Lǎodàye, qǐng nín ràng wǒ kànkan nín de piàozi.** = *Please show me your ticket, sir.*

NOTE: 老大爷 **lǎodàye** has a rustic flavor. It is normally not used in cities or among better-educated people. 老先生 **lǎoxiānsheng** is a more appropriate word.

lǎohǔ 老虎 [prefix: 老 nominal prefix + 虎 tiger] NOUN = tiger (头 tóu, 只 zhī)
■ 动物园里的老虎逃跑了！ **Dòngwùyuán li de lǎohǔ táopǎo le!** = *A tiger has escaped from the zoo!*

lǎorén 老人 [modif: 老 old + 人 person] NOUN = old person, elderly person (位 wèi)
■ 这位老人人老心不老，还在学中文和武术。**Zhè wèi lǎorén rén lǎo xīn bù lǎo, háizài xué Zhōngwén hé wǔshù.** = *This old person is young at heart. He (or She) is still learning Chinese and martial arts.*

lǎoshī 老师 [modif: 老 aged + 师 teacher, master] NOUN = teacher (位 wèi)
■ 我的中文老师是北京人。**Wǒ de Zhōngwén lǎoshì shì Běijīngrén.** = *My Chinese teacher is from Beijing.*
■ 我要问老师几个问题。**Wǒ yào wèn lǎoshī jǐ ge wèntí.** = *I want to ask the teacher some questions.*

NOTE: 老师 **lǎoshī**, usually prefixed by a family name, is the standard form of address to a teacher, e.g. 王老师 **Wáng Lǎoshī**. There is

no equivalent of 王老师 **Wáng Lǎoshī** in English. This dictionary uses the literal translation *Teacher Wang*.

lǎoshi 老是 ADVERB = always, constantly
■ 你怎么老是这么晚回家？ **Nǐ zěnme lǎoshi zhème wǎn huíjiā?** = *Why do you always come home so late?*
■ 他老是写错这个字。**Tā lǎoshi xiěcuò zhège zì.** = *He always writes this character wrongly.*

lǎoshi 老实 ADJECTIVE = honest
■ 说老实话，做老实人。**Shuō lǎoshi huà, zuò lǎoshi rén.** = *Speak the truth and be an honest person.*
■ 他太老实，容易受人欺骗。**Tā tài lǎoshi, róngyì shòurén qīpiàn.** = *He is too honest and is prone to be deceived.*
lǎoshi huà 老实话 = plain truth
lǎoshi rén 老实人 = honest person
lǎoshi shuō 老实说 = to be frank, to tell the truth
■ 老实说，你这种做法我并不赞成。**Lǎoshi shuō, nǐ zhè zhǒng zuòfǎ wǒ bìng bù zànchéng.** = *To tell the truth, I don't approve of your way of doing things.*

lǎotàitai 老太太 NOUN = (a respectful form of address or reference to an old woman) (位 wèi)
■ 老太太，您找谁？ **Lǎotàitai, nín zhǎo shuí?** = *Who are you looking for, ma'am?*
■ 他把座位让给一位老太太。**Tā bǎ zuòwèi rànggěi yí wèi lǎotàitai.** = *He offered his seat to an old lady.*

lǎotóur 老头儿 NOUN = old man (个 ge)
■ 几个老头儿在树下打牌。**Jǐ ge lǎotóur zài shù xia dǎpái.** = *Some old men were playing cards under the tree.*

NOTES: (1) 老头儿 **lǎotóur** is an impolite way of referring to an old man. As a form of address, 老头儿 **lǎotóur** is very rude. Instead, use the neutral term 老人 **lǎorén** or the polite terms 老先生 **lǎoxiānsheng** or 老大爷 **lǎodàyé**. (2) The corresponding impolite word for an old woman is 老太婆 **lǎotàipó**. Use 老太太 **lǎotàitai** or 老大娘 **lǎodàniáng** instead.

lǎoxiānsheng 老先生 [modif: 老 old, elderly + 先生 gentleman] NOUN = (a respectful form of address or reference to an old man) (位 wèi)

L

■ 老先生，请您让我看看您的票子。 **Lǎoxiānsheng, qǐng nín ràng wǒ kànkan nín de piàozi.** = *Please show me your ticket, sir.*

lè 乐 Trad 樂 ADJECTIVE = happy

lèguān 乐观 [modif: 乐 *happy* + 观 *view*]
ADJECTIVE = optimistic (antonym 悲观 **bēiguān**)
■ 他很乐观，相信世界会越变越好。 **Tā hěn lèguān, xiāngxìn shìjiè huì yuè biàn yuè hǎo.** = *He is optimistic, believing that the world is getting ever better.*
■ 根据乐观的估计，今年经济增长可以达到百分之五。 **Gēnjù lèguān de gǔjì, jīnnián jīngjì zēngzhǎng kěyǐ dádào bǎifēn zhī wǔ.** = *According to an optimistic estimate, the economy will grow by five percent this year.*

le 了 PARTICLE
1 = (used after a verb to indicate the completion of an action)
■ 我昨天写了三封信。 **Wǒ zuótiān xiěle sān fēng xìn.** = *I wrote three letters yesterday.*
■ 他吃了晚饭就上网玩游戏。 **Tā chīle wǎnfàn jiù shàngwǎng wán yóuxì.** = *As soon as he had eaten supper, he went online to play games.*
2 = (used at the end of a sentence to indicate the emergence of a new situation)
■ 秋天来了，树叶黄了。 **Qiūtiān lái le, shùyè huáng le.** = *Autumn has come and leaves have turned yellow.*
■ 我会说一点儿中文了。 **Wǒ huì shuō yidiǎnr Zhōngwén le.** = *I can speak a bit of Chinese now.*

léi 雷 NOUN = thunder
■ 昨天又打雷，又闪电，挺吓人的。 **Zuótiān yòu dǎ léi, yòu shǎndiàn, tǐng xiàrén de.** = *There was thunder and lightning yesterday. It was rather frightening.*
dǎ léi 打雷 = thunder
léi yǔ 雷雨 = thunderstorm

lèi 泪 Trad 淚 NOUN = teardrop, tear (See 眼泪 **yǎnlèi**.)

lèi 类 Trad 類 NOUN = kind, category, class
■ 这两类不同的情况，不要混为一谈。 **Zhè liǎng lèi bùtóng de qíngkuàng, bú yào hùnwéi yìtán.** = *These are two different situations. Don't lump them together.*

lèi 累 ADJECTIVE = exhausted, tired
■ "你劳动了半天，累不累？""不累，一点都不累。" **"Nǐ láodòngle bàntiān, lèi bu lèi?" "Bú lèi, yìdiǎn dōu bú lèi."** = *"Are you tired after doing manual labor for such a long time?" "No, I'm not the least tired."*

lěng 冷 ADJECTIVE = cold (antonym 热 **rè**)
■ 今天很冷。 **Jīntiān hěn lěng.** = *It's cold today.*
■ 他每天都洗冷水澡。 **Tā měi tiān dōu xǐ lěngshuǐ zǎo.** = *He takes a cold bath every day.*

lí 厘 MEASURE WORD = one thousandth of a foot

límǐ 厘米 MEASURE WORD = centimeter
■ 他身高178 厘米。 **Tā shēngāo yìbǎi qīshí bā límǐ.** = *He is 178 centimeters tall.*

lí 离 Trad 離
1 VERB = depart, leave
■ 他每天很早就离家，很晚才回家。 **Tā měi tiān hěn zǎo jiù lí jiā, hěn wǎn cái huí jiā.** = *He leaves home early and returns late every day.*
2 PREPOSITION = (indicating distance in space or time) away from, from
■ 加拿大离英国很远，离美国很近。 **Jiānádà lí Yīngguó hěn yuǎn, lí Měiguó hěn jìn.** = *Canada is far away from Britain, and close to the USA.*
■ 现在离寒假只有两个星期了。 **Xiànzài lí jiàqī zhǐyǒu liǎngge xīngqī le.** = *There are only two weeks before the winter holiday.*
lí ... jìn 离 … 近 = close to
lí ... yuǎn 离 … 远 = far away from

líhūn 离婚 [v+obj: 离 *separate* + 婚 *marriage*]
VERB = divorce
■ 他们终于离婚了。 **Tāmen zhōngyú líhūn le.** = *They eventually divorced.*
■ 她和丈夫离婚了。 **Tā hé zhàngfu líhūn le.** = *She and her husband are divorced.*

líkāi 离开 [compound: 离 *leave* + 开 *away from*] VERB
1 = depart, leave
■ 他十八岁的时候离开父母，到美国去念书。 **Tā shíbā suì de shíhou líkāi fùmǔ, dào Měiguó qù niànshū.** = *When he was eighteen he left his parents and went to America to study.*

■我离开一会儿，马上就回来。**Wǒ líkāi yíhuìr, mǎshàng jiù huílai.** = *Excuse me for a minute. I'll be back soon.*

2 = do without

líbukāi 离不开 = cannot do without

■孩子还小，离不开妈。**Háizi hái xiǎo, líbukāi mā.** = *The child is too young to be without his mother.*

lí 梨 NOUN = pear (只 **zhī**)

■这梨很甜，你尝尝。**Zhè lí hěn tián, nǐ chángchang.** = *This pear is very sweet. Try it.*

lí 璃 NOUN = glass (See 玻璃 **bōli**.)

Lǐ 李 NOUN = (a family name)

> NOTE: According to the latest census, 李 **Lǐ** is the most common family name in China.

lǐ 礼 Trad 禮 NOUN = rite

Lǐbàitiān 礼拜天 [modif: 礼拜 *worship* + 天 *day*] NOUN = same as 星期天 **Xīngqītiān**. A rather old-fashioned word.

lǐmào 礼貌 ADJECTIVE = polite, courteous

■礼貌待客。**Lǐmào dài kè.** = *Treat customers with courtesy.*

■盯着人家看，是不礼貌的。**Dīngzhe rénjiā kàn, shì bù lǐmào de.** = *It is impolite to stare at people.*

lǐtáng 礼堂 [modif: 礼 *ceremony, ritual* + 堂 *hall*] NOUN = auditorium, assembly hall (座 **zuò**)

■礼堂里正在举行一个大会。**Lǐtáng li zhèngzài jǔxíng yí ge dàhuì.** = *A rally is being held in the auditorium.*

lǐwù 礼物 [modif: 礼 *gift* + 物 *thing*] NOUN = gift, present (件 **jiàn**)

■这件小小的礼物，请您收下。**Zhè jiàn xiǎoxiǎo de lǐwù, qǐng nín shōuxia.** = *Please accept this small present.*

■今天是你的生日，我送你一件小礼物。**Jīntiān shì nǐ de shēngrì, wǒ sòng nǐ yí jiàn xiǎo lǐwù.** = *Today's your birthday. I'll give you a little gift.*

jiéhūn lǐwù 结婚礼物 = wedding present

shēngrì lǐwù 生日礼物 = birthday present

xīnnián lǐwù 新年礼物 = New Year present

> NOTE: Chinese modesty requires that you belittle your present, describing it as 一件小礼物 **yí jiàn xiǎo lǐwù** = *a small/insignificant gift*. Upon receiving a present, it is bad manners to open it immediately. The recipient is first supposed to say 不用不用 **búyòng búyòng** = *You didn't have to* and then express thanks for the gift, describing it as 这么好的礼物 **Zhème hǎo de lǐwù** = *such a nice gift*, e.g.
> ■谢谢你送给我这么好的礼物。**Xièxie nǐ sònggei wǒ zhème hǎo de lǐwù.** = *Thank you for giving me such a nice gift.*

lǐ 里 Trad 裏 **1** NOUN = inside (antonym 外 **wài**)

■房间里没有人。**Fángjiān li méiyǒu rén.** = *There is nobody in the room.*

■生活里总会出现种种麻烦。**Shēnghuó li zǒng huì chūxiàn zhǒng-zhǒng máfan.** = *You are bound to encounter various troublesome situations in life.*

lǐ 里 Trad 裏 **2** MEASURE WORD = (a traditional Chinese unit of distance equivalent to half a kilometer)

■从市中心到飞机场有二十里，也就是十公里。**Cóng shìzhōngxīn dào fēijīchǎng yǒu èrshí lǐ, yě jiù shì shí gōnglǐ.** = *From the city center to the airport it's twenty li, or ten kilometers.*

lǐbian 里边 [modif: 里 *inner* + 边 *side*] NOUN = inside, in (antonym 外边 **wàibian**)

■房子外边不好看，里边很舒服。**Fángzi wàibian bù hǎokàn, lǐbian hěn shūfu.** = *The outside of the house is not very attractive, but inside is quite comfortable.*

■箱子里边有什么？**Xiāngzi lǐbian yǒu shénme?** = *What's inside the box?*

lǐmiàn 里面 NOUN = same as 里边 **lǐbian**

lǐ 理 NOUN = pattern, reason

lǐfà 理发 [v+obj: 理 *tidy up* + 发 *hair*] VERB = have a haircut and shampoo, have one's hair done

■我半个月理一次发。**Wǒ bàn ge yuè lǐ yí cì fà.** = *I have a haircut every half a month.*

lǐfàdiàn 理发店 = barbershop, hair salon

lǐfàshī 理发师 = barber, hairdresser, hairstylist

L

NOTE: Instead of the straightforward word 理发店 **lǐfàdiàn**, many hair salons now give themselves fanciful names such as 美发厅 **měifàtīng**.

lǐjiě 理解 [compound: 理 *reason* + 解 *understand*] VERB = understand, comprehend
■ 这首古诗我不理解。 **Zhè shǒu gǔ shī wǒ bù lǐjiě.** = *I don't understand this classic poem.*
■ 我理解你的心情。 **Wǒ lǐjiě nǐ de xīnqíng.** = *I understand how you feel.*

lǐlùn 理论 [compound: 理 *reason* + 论 *theory*] NOUN = theory
■ 你用什么理论来解释这一现象？ **Nǐ yòng shénme lǐlùn lái jiěshì zhè yí xiànxiàng?** = *What theory are you going to apply to interpret this phenomenon?*

lǐxiǎng 理想 [compound: 理 *reason* + 想 *thought, wish*] NOUN = ideal, aspiration
■ 我小时候的理想是当个旅行家。 **Wǒ xiǎoshíhou de lǐxiǎng shì dāng ge lǚxíngjiā.** = *When I was a child, I dreamed of being a traveler.*
shíxiàn lǐxiǎng 实现理想 = realize an ideal
lǐxiǎng zhǔyì 理想主义 = idealism

lǐyóu 理由 [compound: 理 *reason* + 由 *origin, cause*] NOUN = reason, justification, ground, argument
■ 我们有充分的理由处分他。 **Wǒmen yǒu chōngfèn de lǐyóu chǔfèn tā.** = *We have sufficient reason to discipline him.*
■ 你有什么理由不来上班？ **Nǐ yǒu shénme lǐyóu bù lái shàngbān?** = *What reason can you give for being absent from work?*

lì 力 NOUN = strength, force, might
■ 他提出的理由很有力。 **Tā tíchū de lǐyóu hěn yǒulì.** = *He put forward forceful arguments.*
■ 我全身无力，恐怕生病了。 **Wǒ quánshēn wú lì, kǒngpà shēngbìng le.** = *I feel weak all over; I'm afraid I'm ill.*

lìliàng 力量 NOUN
1 = strength
■ 人多力量大。 **Rén duō lìliàng dà.** = *Strength lies in numbers.*

2 = efforts, ability
■ 我们尽最大的力量克服当前的困难。 **Wǒmen jìn zuì dà de lìliàng kèfú dāngqián de kùnnan.** = *We are making maximum efforts to overcome the present difficulties.*

lìqi 力气 VERB = physical strength
■ 没想到这个孩子力气这么大。 **Méi xiǎngdào zhège háizi lìqi zhème dà.** = *I did not expect this child to be so strong.*

lì 历 Trad 歷 NOUN = past experience

lìshǐ 历史 [compound: 历 *past experience* + 史 *recording*] NOUN = history
■ 中国的历史非常长，有三千多年。 **Zhōngguó de lìshǐ fēicháng cháng, yǒu sānqiān duō nián.** = *China has a very long history of over three thousand years.*
■ 你知道这个城市的历史吗？ **Nǐ zhīdào zhège chéngshì de lìshǐ ma?** = *Do you know the history of this city?*
lìshǐxuéjiā 历史学家 = historian

lì 立 VERB = stand
■ 你立在门口干什么？ **Nǐ lì zài ménkǒu gàn shénme?** = *Why are you standing by the door?*
zuò-lì-bù-ān 坐立不安 = on pins and needles, on tenterhooks, anxious

lìchǎng 立场 NOUN = position, standpoint
■ 站在公司的立场上，你就会同意这个措施是必要的。 **Zhàn zài gōngsī de lìchǎng shang, nǐ jiù huì tóngyì zhège cuòshī shì bìyào de.** = *From the company's standpoint, you would agree that this measure is necessary.*

lìfāng 立方 MEASURE WORD = (mathematics) cube
■ 三立方米／公尺 **sān lìfāng mǐ/gōngchǐ** = *3 cubic meters*

lìjí 立即 ADVERB = immediately, without delay
■ 王董事长要我立即飞往上海处理一件事。 **Wáng dǒngshìzhǎng yào wǒ lìjí fēiwǎng Shànghǎi chǔlǐ yí jiàn shì.** = *Chairman Wang wants me to fly to Shanghai immediately to handle an emergency.*

lìkè 立刻 [compound: 立 *immediately* + 刻 *a brief time*] ADVERB = at once, immediately

L

■ 我接到你的电话，立刻就来了。**Wǒ jiēdào nǐ de diànhuà, lìkè jiù lái le.** = *I came immediately after getting your call.*
■ 你要我立刻拿出这么多钱，办不到。**Nǐ yào wǒ lìkè náchū zhème duō qián, bàn bú dào.** = *You want me to produce such a large amount of money right away. I can't do it.*

lì 厉 Trad 厲 ADJECTIVE = severe, strict

lìhai 厉害 ADJECTIVE = severe, fierce, formidable
■ 这个人说话很厉害。**Zhège rén shuōhuà hěn lìhai.** = *This person has a sharp tongue.*
■ 她看样子厉害，其实没有用。**Tā kànyàngzi lìhai, qíshí méiyǒuyòng.** = *She looks formidable but actually is rather useless.*

NOTES: (1) 厉害 **lìhai** is often used with 得 **de** to indicate a very high degree, e.g.
■ 这两天热得厉害。**Zhèliǎngtiān rède lìhai.** = *These days are terribly hot.*
■ 情人节花儿贵得厉害。**Qíngrénjié huār guìde lìhai.** = *Flowers are terribly expensive on Valentine's Day.*
(2) 厉害 **lìhai** may be written as 利害 **lìhai**.

lì 丽 Trad 麗 ADJECTIVE = beautiful (See 美丽 **měilì**.)

lì 励 Trad 勵 VERB = encourage (See 鼓励 **gǔlì**.)

lì 利 NOUN = benefit

lìyì 利益 [compound: 利 *benefit* + 益 *benefit*] NOUN = benefit, interest
■ 每个人都为了个人利益而工作，但也要考虑社会的利益。**Měi gè rén dōu wèile gèrén de lìyì ér gōngzuò, dàn yě yào kǎolǜ shèhuì de lìyì.** = *Everybody works to their personal interest, but should also take into consideration the interests of society.*

lìyòng 利用 [compound: 利 *benefit* + 用 *use*] VERB = make use of, benefit from
■ 你应该好好利用时间。**Nǐ yīnggāi hǎohǎo lìyòng shíjiān.** = *You should make good use of your time.*
■ 我们要合理地利用自然资源。**Wǒmen yào hélǐ de lìyòng zìrán zīyuán.** = *We should make use of natural resources in a rational way.*

lì 例 NOUN = example

lìrú 例如 [compound: 例 *example* + 如 *same as*] CONJUNCTION = for example, such as
■ 有些汉字，例如"日"、"月"、"山"，是从图画变来的。**Yǒuxiē hànzì, lìrú "rì," "yuè," "shān," shì cóng túhuà biànlai de.** = *Some Chinese characters, such as 日, 月, 山, are derived from pictures.*

lìzi 例子 [suffix: 例 *example* + 子 nominal suffix] NOUN = example (个 **ge**)
■ 王老师举了很多例子，说明这个词的用法。**Wáng lǎoshī jǔle hěn duō lìzi, shuōmíng zhège cí de yòngfǎ.** = *Teacher Wang gave many examples to illustrate the way this word is used.*
jǔ lìzi 举例子 = give an example

lì 粒 MEASURE WORD = (for rice, pearls, etc.)
■ 一粒米 **yí lì mǐ** = *a grain of rice*

liǎ 俩 Trad 倆 NUMERAL = two people
■ 他们俩是好朋友，经常在一起玩。**Tāmen liǎ shì hǎo péngyou, jīngcháng zài yìqǐ wán.** = *The two of them are good friends. They often play together.*
■ 这件事你们夫妻俩好好商量一下。**Zhè jiàn shì nǐmen fūqī liǎ hǎohǎo shāngliang yíxià.** = *(To a couple) I hope you two will discuss this matter properly.*

lián 连 Trad 連
1 VERB = connect, join
■ 海洋把世界连成一片。**Hǎiyáng bǎ shìjiè lián chéng yípiàn.** = *Oceans and seas connect the entire world.*
2 ADVERB = in succession, repeated
■ 我连发了三份电子邮件给他，他都没有回。**Wǒ lián fāle sān fèn diànzǐ yóujiàn gěi tā, tā dōu méiyǒu huí.** = *I sent him three e-mail messages in succession but there has been no reply.*

lián ... dōu ... 连 ... 都 ... IDIOM = even
■ 连三岁小孩都知道。**Lián sān suì xiǎohái dōu zhīdào.** = *Even a toddler (← a three-year-old) knows this.*

L

■ 你连中文报纸都会看了！ **Nǐ lián Zhōngwén bàozhǐ dōu huì kàn le!** = *You can even read Chinese language newspapers!*

NOTES: (1) 连 ... 都 ... **lián ... dōu ...** is an emphatic expression, stressing the word after 连 **lián**. (2) 都 **dōu** may be replaced by 也 **yě**, i.e. 连 ... 也 ... **lián ... yě ...** is the same as 连 ... 都 ... **lián ... dōu ...**, for example: ■ 连三岁小孩也知道。**Lián sān suì xiǎohái yě zhīdào.** = *Even a toddler knows this.*

liánmáng 连忙 ADVERB = make haste, hasten without the slightest delay
■ 他踩了一位小姐的脚，连忙说"对不起，对不起。" **Tā cǎile yí wèi xiǎojiè de jiǎo, liánmáng shuō "duìbuqǐ, duìbuqǐ."** = *Stepping on a young lady's toes, he hastened to say, "I'm sorry, I'm sorry."*
■ 她听说老父亲跌倒了，连忙回家。**Tā tīngshuō lǎo fùqin diēdǎo le, liángmáng huíjiā.** = *Hearing that her old father had had a fall, she hastened back home.*

liánxù 连续 VERB = in succession, in a row
■ 他连续四天开夜车。**Tā liánxù sì tiān kāi yèchē.** = *He burned the midnight oil for four consecutive nights.*
■ 他连续喝了八瓶啤酒，终于醉倒了。**Tā liánxù hēle bā píng píjiǔ, zhōngyú zuìdǎo le.** = *He drank eight bottles of beer in succession and finally became drunk.*

lián 怜 Trad 憐 VERB = pity (See 可怜 **kělián**.)

lián 联 Trad 聯 VERB = connect

liánhé 联合 [compound: 联 *join* + 合 *merge*] VERB = unite, get together (to do something)
■ 两国要联合开发海洋资源。**Liǎng guó yào liánhé kāifā hǎiyáng zīyuán.** = *The two countries will jointly develop their ocean resources.*
Liánhé Guó 联合国 = the United Nations
Liánhé Guó bùduì 联合国部队 = United Nations troops

liánhuān 联欢 [modif: 联 *jointly* + 欢 *have a good time*] VERB = have a get-together, have a gala/party
■ 明天中外学生联欢，你表演什么节目？**Míngtiān zhōngwài xuésheng liánhuān, nǐ biǎoyǎn shénme jiémù?** = *At the gala for Chinese and overseas students tomorrow, what item will you be performing?*

liánxì 联系 [compound: 联 *connect* + 系 *tie, knot*]
1 VERB = get in touch, contact
■ 你有什么事，可以用电子邮件和张小姐联系。**Nǐ yǒu shénme shì, kěyǐ yòng diànzǐ yóujiàn hé Zhāng xiǎojiě liánxì.** = *You can contact Miss Zhang by email if you've any business.*
■ 如感兴趣，请与陈先生联系。**Rú gǎn xìngque, qǐng yú Chén xiānsheng liánxì.** = *If interested, please contact Mr Chen.*
2 NOUN = connection, being related
■ 这两件事有什么联系？**Zhè liǎng jiàn shì yǒu shénme liánxì?** = *What do these two matters have to do with each other?*

liǎn 脸 Trad 臉 NOUN = face (张 **zhāng**)
■ 我每天早上用冷水洗脸。**Wǒ měi tiān zǎoshang yòng léngshuǐ xǐ liǎn.** = *I wash my face in cold water every morning.*
■ 顾客来了，她总是笑脸相迎。**Gùkè lái le, tā zǒngshì xiào liǎn xiāngyíng.** = *When a customer comes, she always smiles a welcome.*
■ 出了这样的事，他觉得没脸见人。**Chūle zhèyang de shì, tā juéde méi liǎn jiàn rén.** = *After this event, he felt too ashamed to face anyone.*
diūliǎn 丢脸 = be disgraced, lose face

liàn 练 Trad 練 VERB = practice
■ 他早晨五点起床，先练武术，再练中文口语。**Tā zǎochén wǔ diǎn qǐchuáng, xiān liàn wǔshù, zài liàn Zhōngwén kǒuyǔ.** = *He gets up at five o'clock every morning, practices martial arts first and then oral Chinese.*

liànxí 练习 [compound: 练 *drill, train* + 习 *practice*]
1 VERB = exercise, train, drill
■ 你常常练习汉语口语吗？ **Nǐ chángcháng liànxí Hànyǔ kǒuyǔ ma?** = *Do you often practice oral Chinese?*
2 NOUN = exercise, drill
■ 我数学练习做好了，还有三道英文练习没有做。**Wǒ shùxué liànxí zuò hǎo le, hái yǒu sān dào Yīngwén liànxí méiyǒu zuò.** = *I've finished my mathematics exercises. I haven't done the three English exercises.*

liàn 炼 Trad 煉 VERB = smelt (See 锻炼 **duànliàn**, 训练 **xùnliàn**.)

liàn 恋 NOUN = infatuation

liàn'ài 恋爱 [compound: 恋 *infatuate* + 爱 *love*]
1 VERB = be in romantic love, be courting
■ 他们俩恋爱了两年，在上个月结婚了。
Tāmen liǎ liàn'ài le liǎngnián, zài shàng ge yuè jiéhūn le. = *They courted for two years and got married last month.*
2 NOUN = romantic love
■ 恋爱、婚姻是青年人的大事。**Liàn'ài, hūnyīn shì qīngniánrén de dàshì.** = *Falling in love and marriage are major events for young people.*
tán liàn'ài 谈恋爱 = in courtship, in love

liáng 良 ADJECTIVE = good

liánghǎo 良好 [compound: 良 *good* + 好 *good*] ADJECTIVE = good, fine, commendable
■ 这种药经过试验，证明效果良好。**Zhè zhǒng yào jīngguò shìyàn, zhèngmíng xiàoguǒ liánghǎo.** = *After testing, this medicine proved to have good effects.*

liáng 凉 ADJECTIVE = cool, chilly
■ 尽管中午很热，早上和夜里还是挺凉的。**Jǐnguǎn zhōngwǔ hěn rè, zǎoshang hé yèli háishì tǐng liáng de.** = *Even though it is hot at noon, it is still cool in the early morning and at night.*

liángkuai 凉快 [compound: 凉 *cool* + 快 *pleasant*] ADJECTIVE = pleasantly cool
■ 今天很热，但是树下挺凉快。**Jīntiān hěn rè, dànshì shù xià tǐng liángkuai.** = *It's hot today but it's rather cool under the tree.*

liáng 量 VERB = measure, take measurements
■ 你量一量，这个房间有多大。**Nǐ liáng yi liáng, zhège fángjiān yǒu duō dà.** = *Measure the room, find out how big it is.*

liáng 粮 Trad 糧 NOUN = grain

liángshí 粮食 [compound: 粮 *grain* + 食 *food*] NOUN = grain, cereal, staple food
■ 大米和小麦是中国的主要粮食。**Dàmǐ hé**

xiǎomài shì Zhōngguó de zhǔyào liángshí.** = *Rice and wheat are China's staple food.*

liáng 梁 Trad 樑 NOUN = beam (in structure) (See 桥梁 **qiáoliáng**.)

liǎng 两 1 MEASURE WORD = (a traditional Chinese unit of weight equivalent to 50 grams), ounce
■ 我买二两茶叶。**Wǒ mǎi èr liǎng cháyè.** = *I want two liang of tea.*

liǎng 两 2 NUMERAL
1 = two
■ 两个人 **liǎng ge rén** = *two people*
■ 两本书 **liǎng běn shū** = *two books*
2 = (as an approximation) a couple of, a few
■ 我来说两句话。**Wǒ lái shuō liǎng jù huà.** = *Let me say a few words.*

> NOTE: Both 两 **liǎng** and 二 **èr** may mean *two*, but are used differently. 二 **èr** must be used in mathematics or when saying the number 2 in isolation, e.g.:
> ■ 一、二、三、四 … **yī, èr, sān, sì ...** = 1, 2, 3, 4...
> ■ 二加三是五。**Èr jiā sān shì wǔ.** = 2 plus 3 is 5.
> Use 两 **liǎng** when referring to "two something," e.g.:
> ■ 两张桌子 **liǎng zhāng zhuōzi** = *two tables*
> ■ 两个小时 **liǎng ge xiǎoshí** = *two hours*
> The ordinal number *second* is 第二 **dì-èr**.

liàng 亮 ADJECTIVE = bright
■ 天亮了！**Tiān liàng le!** = *Day is breaking!*
■ 这个灯不太亮。**Zhège dēng bú tài liàng.** = *This lamp is not very bright.*

liàng 谅 Trad 諒 VERB = forgive (See 原谅 **yuánliàng**.)

liàng 辆 Trad 輛 MEASURE WORD = (for vehicles)
■ 一辆汽车 **yí liàng qìchē** = *a car*
■ 两辆自行车 **liǎng liàng zìxíngchē** = *two bicycles*

liàng 量 NOUN = quantity (See 产量 **chǎnliàng**, 大量 **dàliàng**, 分量 **fēnliàng**, 尽量 **jìnliàng**, 力量 **lìliàng**, 质量 **zhìliàng**, 重量 **zhòngliàng**.)

L

liáo 聊 VERB = chat

liáotiān 聊天 VERB = chat
- 奶奶常去邻居家聊天。**Nǎinai cháng qù línjū jiā liáotiān.** = *My granny often goes to her neighbor's home for a chat.*
- 我没空陪你聊天。**Wǒ méi kòng péi nǐ liáotiān.** = *I don't have the time to chat with you.*

liǎo 了 VERB = finish, be done with
- 这么多工作，一星期也做不了。**Zhème duō gōngzuò, yì xīngqī yě zuò bu liǎo.** = *So much work can't be finished even in a week.*

NOTE: 了 **liǎo**, together with 得 **de** or 不 **bu**, is often used after a verb as a complement to mean *can ...* or *cannot ...* For example:
- 这件事我干得了，那件事我干不了。**Zhè jiàn shì wǒ gàn de liǎo, nà jiàn shì wǒ gàn bu liǎo.** = *I can do this job, but I can't do that job.*

liǎobuqǐ 了不起 ADJECTIVE = wonderful, terrific
- 这个孩子门门功课第一名，真了不起！**Zhège háizi ménmén gōngkè dì-yī míng, zhēn liǎobuqǐ!** = *This child came out the first in all the subjects. How wonderful!*
- 你别自以为了不起。**Nǐ bié zì yǐwéi liǎobuqǐ.** = *Don't think yourself so terrific. (→ Don't think you're so hot.)*

liǎojiě 了解 [compound: 了 *see through* + 解 *analyze, comprehend*] VERB = know, understand, find out
- 我和他是老朋友，我很了解他。**Wǒ hé tā shì lǎo péngyou, wǒ hěn liǎojiě tā.** = *He and I are old friends. I know him very well.*
- 我来是要了解这一地区的市场情况。W6 **lái shì yào liǎojiě zhè yí dìqū de shìchǎng qíngkuàng.** = *I've come to find out the marketing situation in this region.*

liào 料 NOUN = material (See 材料 **cáiliào**, 塑料 **sùliào**, 原料 **yuánliào**, 资料 **zīliào**.)

liè 列 MEASURE WORD = (for trains)
- 一列火车 **yí liè huǒchē** = *a train*

liè 烈 ADJECTIVE = intense (See 激烈 **jīliè**, 热烈 **rèliè**.)

lín 邻 Trad 鄰 NOUN = neighbor

línjū 邻居 [modif: 邻 *neighboring* + 居 *residents*] NOUN = neighbor
- 和邻居保持良好的关系，很重要。**Hé línjū bǎochí liánghǎo de guānxi, hěn zhòngyào.** = *It is important to maintain good relations with the neighbors.*
- 我家左面的邻居是一对老夫妻。**Wǒ jiā zuǒmiàn de línjū shì yí duì lǎo fūqī.** = *My neighbors on the left are an old couple.*

lín 林 NOUN = wood, woods (See 森林 **sēnlín**, 树林 **shùlín**.)

lín 临 Trad 臨 VERB = arrive

línshí 临时 ADJECTIVE = tentative, provisional
- 这是临时措施，正式办法还要研究制定。**Zhè shì línshí cuòshī, zhèngshì bànfǎ hái yào yánjiū zhìdìng.** = *This is only a tentative measure. We need to study and devise formal measures.*

líng 灵 Trad 靈

línghuó 灵活 [compound: 灵 *agile* + 活 *alive*] ADJECTIVE = flexible, agile
- 他头脑灵活，能迅速对付各种不同的情况。**Tā tóunǎo línghuó, néng xùnsù duìfù gè zhǒng bùtóng de qíngkuàng.** = *He is quick-witted and can cope with various situations promptly.*

líng 零 NUMERAL = zero
- 一百零二 **yìbǎi líng èr** = *102*
- 四千零五 **sìqiān líng wǔ** = *4005*

NOTES: (1) No matter how many zeros there are between digits, only one 零 **líng** is used. For example, 4005 is 四千零五 **sìqiān líng wǔ**, not 四千零零五 **sìqiān líng líng wǔ**. (2) 零 **líng** can also be written as 〇, e.g 四千〇五 **sìqiān líng wǔ** = *4005*.

língqián 零钱 [modif: 零 *parts* + 钱 *money*] NOUN = allowance, pocket money, small change
- 我身上没有零钱。**Wǒ shēnshang méiyǒu língqián.** = *I don't have small change on me.*
- 一个月该给孩子多少零钱比较合适？**Yí ge yuè gāi gěi háizi duōshǎo língqián bǐjiào**

héshì? = *How much monthly allowance is appropriate for children?*

líng 铃 Trad 鈴 NOUN = bell
■门铃响了，看看是谁来了。**Mén líng xiǎng le, kànkan shì shéi lái le.** = *The doorbell is ringing. Go and see who's there.*
■上课铃响了，学生们陆续走进教室。**Shàngkè líng xiǎng le, xuéshengmen lùxù zǒujìn jiàoshì.** = *The bell rang for class and students entered the classroom one after another.*

líng 龄 Trad 齡 NOUN = age (See 年龄 **niánlíng**.)

líng 领 Trad 領 VERB = lead, take
■服务员领客人到他们预订的桌子。**Fúwùyuán líng kèrén dào tāmen yùdìng de zhuōzi.** = *The waiter led the customers to the table they had reserved.*

língdǎo 领导 [compound: 领 lead + 导 guide]
1 VERB = lead, provide leadership
■政府领导人民发展经济。**Zhèngfǔ língdǎo rénmín fāzhǎn jīngjì.** = *The government provides leadership for the people to develop the economy.*
2 NOUN = leader, the person in charge
■领导不在，你有什么事情请跟我说。**Língdǎo bú zài, nǐ yǒu shénme shìqíng qǐng gēn wǒ shuō.** = *The person in charge is not in. Please talk to me if you've any business.*
■我要找你们的领导。**Wǒ yào zhǎo nǐmen de língdǎo.** = *I want to see the person in charge here.*

NOTES: (1) 领导 **língdǎo** as a verb is somewhat pompous, appropriate only for grand occasions. (2) As a noun 领导 **língdǎo** is no longer very popular in China and has never been very popular in other Chinese-speaking communities. To refer to "the person in charge," many Chinese use 老板 **lǎobǎn** (*boss*) or specific terms such as 厂长 **chǎngzhǎng** (*factory manager*) or 校长 **xiàozhǎng** (*headmaster, school principal, university president*).

língxiù 领袖 NOUN = leader (位 **wèi**)
■他是这个国家的一位重要政治领袖。**Tā shì zhège guójiā de yí wèi zhòngyào zhèngzhì língxiù.** = *He is an important political leader of this country.*

lìng 令 VERB = command, cause (See 命令 **mìnglìng**.)

lìng 另 ADJECTIVE = same as 另外 **lìngwài**. Used before a monosyllabic verb.

lìngwài 另外 ADJECTIVE = other, another
■这个方法不行，得另外想办法。**Zhège fāngfǎ bù xíng, děi lìngwài xiǎng bànfǎ.** = *This method doesn't work. We've got to find another way.*
■除了小王以外，另外有没有人会用这台机器？**Chúle Xiǎo Wáng yǐwái, lìngwài yǒu méiyǒu rén huì yòng zhè tái jīqì?** = *Is there anybody other than Xiao Wang who can operate this machine?*

liú 流 VERB = flow
■河水慢慢地向东流去。**Hé shuǐ mànmàn de xiàng dōng liúqù.** = *The river flows slowly to the east.*

liúlì 流利 ADJECTIVE = fluent
■我什么时候才能流利地说中文呢？**Wǒ shénme shíhou cái néng liúlì de shuō Zhōngwén ne?** = *When will I be able to speak Chinese fluently?*

liú 留 VERB = remain (in the same place), stay behind
■你们先回家吧，我再留一会儿做完这件事。**Nǐmen xiān huíjiā ba, wǒ zài liú yíhuìr zuòwán zhè jiàn shì.** = *You go home first. I'll stay behind for a while to finish this job.*
■妈妈知道我爱吃鸡腿，总是把鸡腿留给我吃。**Māma zhīdào wǒ ài chī jītuǐ, zǒngshì bǎ jītuǐ liúgěi wǒ chī.** = *Mom knows I like to eat drumsticks. She always leaves them for me.*
■我留他吃饭，他说有事要办，就走了。**Wǒ liú tā chī fàn, tā shuō yǒu shì yào bàn, jiù zǒu le.** = *I asked him to stay for a meal, but he said he had something to attend to, and left.*

liúxué 留学 [compound: 留 stay + 学 study]
VERB = study abroad
■很多亚洲学生在美国留学。**Hěn duō Yàzhōu xuésheng zài Měiguó liúxué.** = *Many Asian students are studying in America.*

L

liúxuéshēng 留学生 = international students
(especially in a university)
■ 不少留学生星期日也在图书馆学习。
**Bùshǎo liúxuéshēng Xīngqīrì yě zài túshūguǎn
xuéxí.** = *Even on Sundays quite a few international students study in the library.*

liù 六 NUMERAL = six
■ 六十六 **liùshí liù** = *sixty-six*
■ 六十五岁 **liùshí wǔ suì** = *sixty-five years of
age*

lóng 龙 Trad 龍 NOUN = dragon (条 tiáo)
■ 中国人把自己称作"龙的传人"。
**Zhōngguórén bǎ zìjǐ chēngzuò "lóng de
chuánrén".** = *The Chinese call themselves "de-
scendants of the dragon."*

lóu 楼 Trad 樓 NOUN
1 = building with two or more stories (座 zuò)
■ 这座楼是去年建的。**Zhè zuò lóu shì qùnián
jiàn de.** = *This building was built last year.*
■ 她住在那座黄色的大楼里。**Tā zhù zài nà
zuò huángsè de dàlóu li.** = *She lives in that yellow building.*
2 = floor (层 céng)
■ 这一层楼有多少房间?**Zhè yì céng lóu yǒu
duōshǎo fángjiān?** = *How many rooms are
there on this floor?*
■ 老师的办公室在三楼。**Lǎoshī de
bàngōngshì zài sān-lóu.** = *Teachers' offices are
on the third floor.*
dàlóu 大楼 = a big building (especially a high-
rise building)
gāo lóu 高楼 = high-rise
lóu fáng 楼房 = multi-storied building (compare
平房 **píngfáng** = *one-story building, bungalow*)
lóu shang 楼上 = upstairs
lóu xia 楼下 = downstairs

NOTE: In naming floors, the Chinese system is
the same as the American system and different
from the British one, i.e. 一楼 **yī-lóu** is the
American *first floor*, and the British *ground
floor.*

lóutī 楼梯 [modif: 楼 *floor, story* + 梯 *steps*]
NOUN = stairs, stairway, staircase
■ 别站在楼梯上讲话,会妨碍别人上下。**Bié
zhàn zài lóutī shang jiǎnghuà, huì fáng'ài**

biérén shàng-xià. = *Do not stand talking on the
stairs. It'll obstruct people going up and down.*

lòu 漏 VERB = leak
■ 屋顶漏了,要找人修理。**Wūdǐng lòu le, yào
zhǎo rén xiūlǐ.** = *The roof leaks. We'll have to
find someone to fix it.*

lù 陆 Trad 陸 NOUN = land

lùxù 陆续 ADVERB = one after another, in
succession
■ 开会的代表陆续到达。**Kāihuì de dàibiǎo
lùxù dàodá.** = *Congress delegates arrived one
after another.*

lù 录 Trad 錄 VERB = record

lùxiàng 录像 [v+obj: 录 *record* + 像 *image*]
VERB = record with a video camera or video
recorder
■ 他们的婚礼全录像了。**Tāmen de hūnlǐ quán
lùxiàng le.** = *Their wedding ceremony was
videotaped.*
lùxiàngjī 录像机 = video recorder

lùyīn 录音 [v+obj: 录 *record* + 音 *sound*] VERB
= make a recording of sounds (e.g. music,
reading)
■ 这里在录音,请安静!**Zhèli zài lùyīn, qǐng
ānjìng!** = *Recording is in progress. Please be
quiet.*
■ 你有没有听过王老师读这篇课文的录音?
**Nǐ yǒu méiyǒu tīngguo Wáng lǎoshī dú zhè
piān kèwén de lùyīn?** = *Have you listened to
the recording of Teacher Wang's reading of this
text?*
lùyīnjī 录音机 = audio recorder, sound recorder

lù 路 NOUN = road (条 tiáo)
■ 这条路很长,一直通到山里。**Zhè tiáo lù
hěn cháng, yìzhí tōngdào shān li.** = *This road is
very long and leads all the way into the hills.*
■ 你认识去大学的路吗?**Nǐ rènshì qù dàxué
de lù ma?** = *Do you know the way to the
university?*
mǎlù 马路 = road (in a city)

lùshang 路上 NOUN
1 = on one's way (to)
■ 她去学校的路上,要经过一座公园。**Tā qù**

xuéxiào de lùshàng, yào jīngguò yí zuò **gōngyuán**. = *On her way to school, she passes by a park.*

2 = on the road
■ 路上车辆很多。**Lùshang chēliàng hěn duō.** = *There is lots of traffic on the road.*

lùxiàn 路线 [modif: 路 *road* + 线 *line*] NOUN = route, itinerary
■ 这是不是去那里最近的路线？ **Zhè shì bu shì qù nàli zuì jìn de lùxiàn.** = *Is this the shortest route to that place?*

lù 露 VERB = show, reveal
■ 她笑的时候，露出雪白的牙齿。 **Tā xiào de shíhou, lùchū xuěbái de yáchǐ.** = *When she smiles, white teeth show.*

lǚ 旅 VERB = travel

lǚguǎn 旅馆 [modif: 旅 *travel* + 馆 *house*] NOUN = hotel (座 **zuò**, 家 **jiā**)
■ 我上个月在那家旅馆订了房间。 **Wǒ shàng ge yuè zài nà jiā lǚguǎn dìngle fángjiān.** = *I booked a room in that hotel last month.*
qìchē lǚguǎn 汽车旅馆 = motel
wǔxīng lǚguǎn 五星旅馆 = five-star hotel

lǚkè 旅客 [modif: 旅 *traveling* + 客 *guest*] NOUN = hotel guest, passenger (of coach, train, plane, etc.)
■ 航空公司尽力保证旅客的安全。 **Hángkōng gōngsī jìnlì bǎozhèng lǚkè de ānquán.** = *The airline does all it can to guarantee the safety of the traveling public.*
■ 旅客们，欢迎你们乘坐本次列车。 **Lǚkèmen, huānyíng nǐmen chéngzuò běn cì lièchē.** = *Welcome aboard this train, everyone!*

lǚtú 旅途 [modif: 旅 *travel* + 途 *journey*] NOUN = journey, travels
■ 祝你旅途愉快！ **Zhù nǐ lǚtú yúkuài!** = *Have a pleasant journey!*
■ 他把旅途看到，听到的都写下来。 **Tā bǎ lǚtú kàndào, tīngdào de dōu xiě xiàlái.** = *He wrote down all he saw and heard on his travels.*

lǚxíng 旅行 [compound: 旅 *travel* + 行 *walk, go*] VERB = travel
■ 我在中国旅行的时候，学到不少知识。 **Wǒ**

zài Zhōngguó lǚxíng de shíhou, xuédào bùshǎo **zhīshi.** = *I gained a lot of knowledge when I traveled in China.*
■ 一个人在外国旅行，千万要注意安全。 **Yígerén zài wàiguó lǚxíng, qiānwàn yào zhùyì ānquán.** = *When you are travelling alone in a foreign country, you must always be mindful of personal safety.*
lǚxíngshè 旅行社 = travel agency
■ 我要去旅行社买去英国的飞机票。 **Wǒ yào qù lǚxíngshè mǎi qù Yīngguó de fēijī piào.** = *I'll go to the travel agency to buy an air ticket to Britain.*

lǚyóu 旅游 [compound: 旅 *travel* + 游 *play, holiday*] VERB = travel for pleasure
■ 我有了钱，就到国外去旅游。 **Wǒ yǒule qián, jiù dào guówài qù lǚyóu.** = *I'll go overseas for a holiday when I've got the money.*
lǚyóuchē 旅游车 = tour bus
lǚyóu gōngsī 旅游公司 = tourist company
lǚyóu lùxiàn 旅游路线 = tour itinerary
lǚyóutuán 旅游团 = tour group
lǚyóuzhě 旅游者 = tourist, holiday-maker

lǜ 率 NOUN = rate (See 效率 **xiàolǜ**.)

lǜ 绿 Trad 綠 ADJECTIVE = green
■ 春天到了，树木都绿了。 **Chūntian dào le, shùmù dōu lǜ le.** = *Spring has come; the trees are all green.*
■ 红花绿树，美极了。 **Hónghuā lǜshù, měi jíle.** = *Red flowers and green trees—they're so beautiful!*
lǜkǎ 绿卡 = green card (permanent residency permit in the USA and some other countries)
lǜdǎng 绿党 = the Green Party

lǜ 律 NOUN = law (See 法律 **fǎlǜ**, 规律 **guīlǜ**, 纪律 **jìlǜ**.)

lǜ 虑 Trad 慮 VERB = ponder (See 考虑 **kǎolǜ**.)

luàn 乱 Trad 亂 ADJECTIVE
1 = disorderly, chaotic (antonym 整齐 **zhěngqí**)
■ 我的房间很乱，要收拾一下。 **Wǒ de fángjiān hěn luàn, yào shōushi yíxià.** = *My room is in a mess and needs tidying up.*
2 = at will, random
■ 他总是乱花钱。 **Tā zǒngshì luàn huā qián.** = *He always spends money unwisely. (→ He*

L

always wastes his money.)
■ 你别乱说。**Nǐ bié luànshuō.** = *Do not talk irresponsibly.*

lüè 略 VERB = capture (See 侵略 **qīnlüè**.)

lún 轮 Trad 輪 NOUN = wheel

lúnchuán 轮船 [modif: 轮 *wheel* + 船 *boat, ship*] NOUN = steamship, ship
■ 现在很少人坐轮船旅行。**Xiànzài hěn shǎo rén zuò lúnchuán lǚxíng.** = *Few people travel by ship now.*

lùn 论 Trad 論 VERB = discuss

lùnwén 论文 [compound: 论 *treatise* + 文 *essay*] NOUN = dissertation, thesis, essay (篇 **piān**)
■ 张教授发表了多篇关于中国历史的论文。**Zhāng jiàoshòu fābiǎole duō piān guānyú Zhōngguó lìshǐ de lùnwén.** = *Professor Zhang has published several theses on Chinese history.*

luó 萝 Trad 蘿 NOUN = trailing plant

luóbo 萝卜 NOUN = turnip, radish, carrot (根 **gēn**, 个 **ge**)
■ 咱们做个萝卜汤吧。**Zánmen zuò ge luóbo tāng ba.** = *Let's prepare turnip soup.*
bái luóbo 白萝卜 = turnip
hóng luóbo 红萝卜 = radish
hú luóbo 胡萝卜 = carrot

luò 落 VERB = fall, drop
■ 秋天，树叶落了。**Qiūtiān, shùyè luò le.** = *In autumn, leaves fall.*

luòhòu 落后 ADJECTIVE = backward, outdated
■ 你这种观点太落后了。**Nǐ zhè zhǒng guāndiǎn tài luòhòu le.** = *Your views are outdated.*

M

mā 妈 Trad 媽 NOUN = ma, mom

māma 妈妈 NOUN = mom, mommy

■ 妈妈在辅导妹妹做作业。**Māma zài fúdǎo mèimei zuò zuòyè.** = *Mom is tutoring sister in her homework.*
■ 我想每个人都爱自己的妈妈。**Wǒ xiǎng měi ge rén dōu ài zìjǐ de māma.** = *I think everyone loves their mom.*

má 麻 NOUN = hemp

máfan 麻烦 [idiom]
1 VERB = bother
■ 这封信我能翻译，不用麻烦陈先生了。**Zhè fēng xìn wǒ néng fānyì, búyòng máfan Chén xiānsheng le.** = *I can translate this letter. We don't have to bother Mr Chen.*
■ 麻烦你把这封信交给王经理。**Máfan nǐ bǎ zhè fēng xìn jiāo gei Wáng jīnglǐ.** = *Would you mind delivering this letter to Mr Wang, the manager?*
2 ADJECTIVE = troublesome, complicated
■ 这件事很麻烦，我不一定能做好。**Zhè jiàn shì hěn máfan, wǒ bù yídìng néng zuò hǎo.** = *This matter is complicated. I'm not sure I can get it done well.*

NOTE: 麻烦您 **máfan nín** is a polite expression to request somebody's service or to ask a favor. More examples:
■ 麻烦您把盐递给我。**Máfan nín bǎ yán dì gei wǒ.** = *Please pass the salt [to me].*
■ 麻烦您查一下他的电话号码。**Máfan nín chá yíxià tā de diànhuà hàomǎ.** = *Would you mind finding out his telephone number for me?*

májiàng 麻将 NOUN = the game of mahjong, mahjong
■ 你不能每个星期天都打麻将啊！**Nǐ bù néng měi ge Xīngqītiān dōu dǎ májiàng a!** = *You mustn't play mahjong every Sunday!*
■ 打麻将好像挺有趣，你教教我，好吗？**Dǎ májiàng hǎoxiàng tǐng yǒuqù, nǐ jiāojiao wǒ, hǎoma?** = *Mahjong seems an interesting game. Would you teach me please?*

mǎ 马 Trad 馬 NOUN = horse
■ 你会骑马吗？**Nǐ huì qí mǎ ma?** = *Can you ride a horse?*
■ 马跑得快，还是狗跑得快？**Mǎ pǎo de kuài, háishì gǒu pǎo de kuài?** = *Which runs faster—the horse or the dog?*

L

mǎhu 马虎 ADJECTIVE = sloppy, careless
- 你这个作业作得太马虎了。**Nǐ zhège zuòyè zuò de tài mǎhu le.** = *You did this assignment carelessly.*

NOTE: 马马虎虎 **mǎ-ma-hū-hū** is a common idiomatic expression meaning *so-so, not too bad* or *just managing*. For example:
- "去年你考试成绩怎么样？""马马虎虎。" **"Qùnián nǐ kǎoshì chéngjì zénmeyàng?" "Mǎ-ma-hū-hū."** = *"How did you do in the exams last year?" "So-so."*

mǎlù 马路 [modif: 马 *horse* + 路 *road*] NOUN = street, avenue (条 **tiáo**)
- 这条马路从早到晚车很多。**Zhè tiáo mǎlù cóng-zǎo-dào-wǎn chē hěn duō.** = *This street has lots of traffic from morning till night.*
mǎlù shang 马路上 = in the street, on the road
- 你不能把车停在马路上。**Nǐ bù néng bǎ chē tíng zài mǎlù shang.** = *You can't park the car in the street.*
guò mǎlù 过马路 = walk across a street
- 过马路要特别小心。**Guò mǎlù yào tèbié xiǎoxīn.** = *One should be especially careful when crossing the street.*

mǎshàng 马上 [idiom] ADVERB = at once, immediately
- 好，我马上来！**Hǎo, wǒ mǎshàng lái!** = *OK, I'm coming!*
- 他要我们马上回信。**Tā yào wǒmen mǎshàng huíxìn.** = *He demands a prompt reply.*

mǎ 码 Trad 碼 VERB = stack

mǎtóu 码头 NOUN = dock, wharf
- 船马上要靠码头了。**Chuán mǎshàng yào kào mǎtóu le.** = *The ship will soon anchor at the dock.*
mǎtóu gōngrén 码头工人 = docker, longshoreman

mà 骂 Trad 罵 VERB = curse, swear
- 你怎么骂人？**Nǐ zěnme mà rén?** = *How can you swear at people?*

ma 嘛 PARTICLE = surely, that goes without saying (used at the end of a sentence to indicate that the truth of the statement is obvious)
- 农村的空气就是比城市干净嘛！**Nóngcūn de kōngqì jiùshì bǐ chéngshì gānjing ma!** = *The air in rural areas is surely cleaner than that in cities.*

ma 吗 Trad 嗎 PARTICLE = (used at the end of a sentence to turn it into a yes-or-no question)
- 你会说中文吗？**Nǐ huì shuō Zhōngwén ma?** = *Do you speak Chinese?*
- 你去过香港吗？**Nǐ qùguo Xiānggǎng ma?** = *Have you been to Hong Kong?*
- 这么简单的题目，你也不会做吗？**Zhème jiǎndān de tímù, nǐ yě bú huì zuò ma?** = *Can't you do such a simple question?*

mái 埋 VERB = bury
- 他把死狗埋在树下。**Tā bǎ sí gǒu mái zài shù xia.** = *He buried his dead dog under the tree.*

mǎi 买 Trad 買 VERB = buy
- 我要买一双鞋。**Wǒ yào mǎi yì shuāng xié.** = *I want to buy a pair of shoes.*
- 你这本书在哪儿买的？**Nǐ zhè běn shū zài nǎr mǎi de?** = *Where did you buy this book?*

mǎimài 买卖 [compound: 买 *buy* + 卖 *sell*] NOUN = trade, business
- 最近店里的买卖怎么样？**Zuìjìn diànli de mǎimài zěnmeyàng?** = *How is business at your shop recently?*
- 他在城里有个小卖买。**Tā zài chénglǐ yǒu ge xiǎo mǎimài.** = *He has a small business in town.*
zuò mǎimài 做买卖 = do business, be engaged in business
- 几乎每一家大公司都想跟中国做买卖。**Jīhū měi yì jiā dà gōngsī dòu xiǎng gēn Zhōngguó zuò mǎimài.** = *Almost every corporation wants to do business with China.*
- 他很会做买卖，几年工夫就发财了。**Tā hěn huì zuò mǎimài, jǐ nián gōngfu jiù fācái le.** = *He is very good at doing business, and has become prosperous just in a few years.*

mài 迈 Trad 邁 VERB = step forward
- 完成了这项任务，我们就朝工厂自动化迈了一大步。**Wánchéngle zhè xiàng rènwù, wǒmen jiù cháo gōngchǎng zìdònghuà màile yī dà bù.** = *After completing this project, we will have made a big stride towards automation of the factory.*

M

mài 麦 Trad 麥 NOUN = wheat (See 小麦 xiǎomài.)

mài 卖 Trad 賣 VERB = sell
- 他把汽车卖了。**Tā bǎ qìchē mài le.** = *He sold his car.*
- 你们这里卖水果吗? **Nǐmen zhè mài shuǐguǒ ma?** = *Do you sell fruit here?*

mài 脉 Trad 脈 NOUN = blood vessel (See 山脉 shānmài.)

mán 瞒 VERB = conceal truth from
- 这件事你不该瞒我。**Zhè jiàn shì nǐ bù gāi mán wǒ.** = *You shouldn't have hidden this matter from me.*

mán 馒 Trad 饅

mántou 馒头 [suffix: 馒 *steamed bun* + 头 *nominal suffix*] NOUN = steamed bun (只 **zhī**)
- 我早饭吃了两个馒头。**Wǒ zǎofàn chīle liǎng ge mántou.** = *I ate two steamed buns for breakfast.*

mǎn 满 ADJECTIVE = full, full to the brim
- 碗里的水满了。**Wǎn li de shuǐ mǎn le.** = *The bowl is full of water.*
- 房间里挤得满满的。**Fángjiān li jǐ de mǎnmǎn de.** = *The room is packed.*

mǎnyì 满意 [v+obj: 满 *make full* + 意 *wish, desire*] ADJECTIVE = satisfied, satisfactory
- 我们要让顾客高兴地来，满意地走。**Wǒmen yào ràng gùkè gāoxìng de lái, mǎnyì de zǒu.** = *We should make customers arrive happy and leave satisfied.*
- 我对你们的服务很不满意。**Wǒ duì nǐmen de fúwù hěn bù mǎnyì.** = *I'm very dissatisfied with your service.*
- duì ... mǎnyì 对 ... 满意 = be satisfied with

mǎnzú 满足 VERB = meet the needs of, satisfy
- 老师尽量满足学生的要求。**Lǎoshī jìnliàng mǎnzú xuésheng de yāoqiú.** = *The teacher tries his best to meet the demands of his students.*
- 我们要增加产量，满足市场的需要。**Wǒmen yào zēngjiā chǎnliàng, mǎnzú shìchǎng de xūyào.** = *We should increase output to satisfy the needs of the market.*

màn 慢 ADJECTIVE = slow (antonym 快 **kuài**)
- 我的表慢了五分钟。**Wǒ de biǎo mànle wǔ fēnzhōng.** = *My watch is five minutes slow.*
- 别着急，慢慢地走。**Bié zháojí, mànman de zǒu.** = *Don't be impatient. Walk slowly.*
- 你说得慢，我就听得懂。**Nǐ shuō de màn, wǒ jiù tīng de dǒng.** = *If you speak slowly, I can understand you.*
- mànxìngzi 慢性子 = slow or indolent person, slow coach

máng 忙 ADJECTIVE = busy
- 我最近很忙，没有空儿跟你去看电影。**Wǒ zuìjìn hěn máng, méiyǒu kòngr gēn nǐ qù kàn diànyǐng.** = *I'm busy these days, and don't have time to go to the movies with you.*
- 你在忙什么? **Nǐ zài máng shénme?** = *What are you busy with?*

NOTE: When friends meet in China, a common conversation opener is 你最近忙吗? **Nǐ zuìjìn máng ma?** = *Have you been busy lately?*

māo 猫 NOUN = cat (只 **zhī**)
- 我家有一只小白猫。**Wǒ jiā yǒu yì zhī xiǎo bái māo.** = *We keep a white kitten at home.*

máo 毛 1 NOUN = hair
- yángmáo 羊毛 = wool

máo 毛 2 MEASURE WORD = same as 角 **jiǎo 2** MEASURE WORD. Used colloquially.

máobìng 毛病 NOUN
1 = illness
- 我什么毛病也没有，身体健康得很。**Wǒ shénme máobìng yě méiyǒu, shēntǐ jiànkāng de hěn.** = *I have no complaints at all; I am in excellent health.*
2 = trouble, breakdown
- 洗衣机出毛病了。**Xǐyījī chū máobìng le.** = *The washing machine is out of order.*

máojīn 毛巾 NOUN = towel (条 **tiáo**)
- 他拿着一条大毛巾进浴室洗澡。**Tā názhe yì tiáo dà máojīn jìn yùshì xǐzǎo.** = *He went into the bathroom with a big towel to take a bath.*

M

máoyī 毛衣 [modif: 毛 *woolen* + 衣 *clothing*]
NOUN = woolen sweater, woolen pullover (件 jiàn)
■ 她给对象织了一件毛衣。**Tā gěi duìxiàng zhīle yí jiàn máoyī.** = *She knitted a woolen sweater for her fiancé.*

máo 矛 NOUN = spear

máodùn 矛盾 [compound: 矛 *spear* + 盾 *shield*]
1 NOUN = contradiction, disunity
■ 他们之间有很大的矛盾。**Támen zhījiān yǒu hěn dà de máodùn.** = *There is a big rift between them.*
2 ADJECTIVE = contradictory, inconsistent
zìxiāng máodùn 自相矛盾 = self-contradictory, inconsistent
■ 这篇文章前后自相矛盾。**Zhè piān wénzhāng qiánhòu zìxiāng máodùn.** = *This article is inconsistent in its argument.*

NOTE: 矛盾 **máodùn** is a colorful word derived from an ancient Chinese fable. A man who sold spears (矛 **máo**) and shields (盾 **dùn**) boasted that his spears were so sharp that they could penetrate any shield, and that his shields were so strong that no spear could ever penetrate them. As there seemed to be a contradiction there, 矛盾 **máodùn** came to mean *inconsistency* or *contradiction*.

mào 冒 VERB = emit, send forth, give off
■ 开水冒着热气。**Kāishuǐ màozhe rè qì.** = *Boiling water gives off steam.*

mào 帽 NOUN = hat, cap

màozi 帽子 [suffix: 帽 *hat, cap* + 子 nominal suffix] NOUN = hat, cap
■ 今天外面很冷，你要戴帽子。**Jīntiān wàimiàn hěn lěng. Nǐ yào dài màozi.** = *It's very cold outside. You'd better wear a hat.*
dài màozi 戴帽子 = put on/wear a hat (or a cap)
tuō màozi 脱帽子 = take off a hat (or a cap)

mào 贸 Trad 貿 NOUN = trade

màoyì 贸易 NOUN = trade, exchange
■ 搞制造和搞贸易，那个更赚钱？**Gǎo zhìzào hé gǎo màoyì, nǎge gèng zhuànqián?** =

Manufacturing or trade, which is more profitable?
duìwài màoyì 对外贸易 = foreign trade
guójì màoyì 国际贸易 = international trade
màoyì gōngsī 贸易公司 = trading company

mào 貌 NOUN = appearance (See 礼貌 lǐmào, 面貌 miànmào.)

me 么 Trad 麼 PARTICLE = (used to form certain words) (See 多么 duōme, 那么 nàme, 什么 shénme, 为什么 wèishénme, 怎么 zěnme, 怎么样 zěnmeyàng, 这么 zhème.)

méi 没 ADJECTIVE = same as 没有 méiyǒu
méi guānxi 没关系 = See 关系 guānxi.
méi yìsi 没意思 = See 意思 yìsi.

méishénme 没什么 IDIOM = nothing serious, it doesn't matter
■ "你不舒服吗？" "没什么，就是有点儿头疼。" **"Nǐ bù shūfu ma?" "Méishénme, jiùshì yǒudiǎnr tóuténg."** = *"Aren't you feeling well?" "Nothing serious, just a bit of headache."*
■ "对不起，我这么晚打电话给你。" "没什么，有什么事吗？" **"Duìbuqǐ, wǒ zhème wǎn dǎ diànhuà gei nǐ." "Méishénme, yǒu shénme shì ma?"** = *"I'm sorry for ringing you so late." "It doesn't matter. What can I do for you?"*

méiyòng 没用 ADJECTIVE = useless
■ 这本词典太旧，没用了。**Zhè běn cídiǎn tài jiù, méiyòng le.** = *That dictionary is too old and no longer useful.*
■ 他这个人太没用了，连一个小孩都对付不了。**Tā zhège rén tài méiyòng le, lián yí ge xiǎohái dōu duìfu bu liǎo.** = *That man is really useless. He can't even deal with a child.*

méiyǒu 没有 ADJECTIVE
1 = do not have
■ 我没有这么多钱。**Wǒ méiyǒu zhème duō qián.** = *I don't have that much money.*
■ 他没有兄弟，只有一个姐姐。**Tā méiyǒu xiōngdì, zhǐyǒu yí ge jiějie.** = *He has no brothers, only an elder sister.*
2 = there is/are no
■ 房间里没有人。**Fángjiān li méiyǒu rén.** = *There is nobody in the room.*
■ 这条街上没有饭店。**Zhè tiáo jiē shang**

M

méiyǒu fàndiàn. = *There is no restaurant on this street.*

3 = did not, have not (indicating negation of past experiences, usually used before a verb or at the end of a question)

■ 我没有学过这个字。**Wǒ méiyǒu xuéguo zhège zì.** = *I haven't learnt this Chinese character.*

■ "你去过中国没有?" "还没有。" **"Nǐ qùguo Zhōngguó méiyǒu?" "Hái méiyǒu."** = *"Have you ever been to China?" "Not yet."*

hái méiyǒu 还没有 = not yet

> NOTE: In spoken Chinese, 没有 **méiyǒu** is often shortened 没 **méi**. However, when 没有 **méiyǒu** is used at the end of a question, as in ■ 你去过中国没有? **Nǐ qùguo Zhōngguó méiyǒu?** = *Have you ever been to China?* it cannot be replaced by 没 **méi**.

méi 煤 VERB = coal

■ 这个国家不产煤。**Zhège guójiā bù chǎn méi.** = *This country does not produce coal.*

méikuàng 煤矿 = coal mine
méikuànggōng 煤矿工 = coal miner, collier
méiqì 煤气 = coal gas
méitián 煤田 = coalfield

měi 每

1 ADVERB = every, each

■ 我每隔三天游一次泳。**Wǒ měi gé sān tiān yóu yí cì yǒng.** = *I swim once every three days.*

■ 卡车司机每工作两天，休息一天。**Kǎchē sījī měi gōngzuò liǎng tiān, xiūxi yì tiān.** = *The truck drivers have a day off after working for two days.*

2 PRONOUN = every, each

■ 你每天都看电视新闻吗? **Nǐ měi tiān dōu kàn diànshì xīnwén ma?** = *Do you watch TV news everyday?*

■ 这条街每座房子都不一样。**Zhè tiáo jiē měi zuò fángzi dóu bù yíyàng.** = *Every house on this street is different from the other.*

> NOTE: Usage in Chinese requires that 每 **měi** is followed by 都 **dōu** = *all, without exception.*

měi 美 ADJECTIVE = beautiful

■ 这里的风景真美! **Zhèli de fēngjǐng zhēn měi!** = *The scenery here is truly beautiful!*

■ 她从小就是个美人儿。**Tā cóngxiǎo jiù shì ge měirénr.** = *She has been a beauty since childhood.*

Měiguó 美国 NOUN = America, the USA

■ 中国和美国离得很远。**Zhōngguó hé Měiguó lí de hěn yuǎn.** = *China and the US are far apart.*

měihǎo 美好 [compound: 美 *beautiful* + 好 *fine*] ADJECTIVE = (of abstract things) fine, beautiful

■ 我有一个美好的愿望。**Wǒ yǒu yí ge měihǎo de yuànwàng.** = *I have a beautiful aspiration.*

■ 世界上的事物并不都象人们希望的那样美好。**Shìjiè shang de shìwù bìng bù dōu xiàng rénmen xīwàng de nàyàng měihǎo.** = *Things in the world are not all as fine as people wish them to be.*

měilì 美丽 [compound: 美 *beautiful* + 丽 *beautiful*] ADJECTIVE = beautiful

■ 春天各种颜色的花儿都开放了，花园真美丽。**Chūntiān gè zhǒng yánsè de huār dōu kāifàng le, huāyuán zhēn měilì.** = *In spring with flowers of all colors in full bloom, the garden is beautiful.*

měimǎn 美满 [compound: 美 *beautiful* + 满 *full, totally satisfied*] ADJECTIVE = (of marriage, family, etc.) totally satisfactory, happy

■ 她有美满的家庭、成功的事业，真是太幸福了。**Tā yǒu měimǎn de jiātíng, chénggōng de shìyè, zhēnshì tài xìngfú le.** = *She has a happy family and a successful career. What a fortunate woman!*

měishù 美术 [modif: 美 *beautiful* + 术 *craft*] NOUN = fine arts

■ 她对美术非常感兴趣。**Tā duì měishù fēicháng gǎn xìngqù.** = *She has a great interest in the fine arts.*

měishùguǎn 美术馆 = gallery, art museum
měishùjiā 美术家 = artist

Měiyuán 美元 [modif: 美 *American* + 元 *dollar*] NOUN = US dollar, greenback

■ 我想换一些美元。**Wǒ xiǎng huàn yìxiē Měiyuán.** = *I want to change some money into American dollars.*

Měizhōu 美洲 [modif: 美 *America* + 洲 *continent*] NOUN = (continent of) America

mèi 妹 NOUN = younger sister

mèimei 妹妹 NOUN = younger sister
- 我妹妹还在念小学呢。**Wǒ mèimei háizài niàn xiǎoxué ne.** = *My younger sister is still in primary school.*
- 去年夏天我教妹妹游泳。**Qùnián xiàtiān wǒ jiāo mèimei yóuyǒng.** = *Last summer I taught my younger sister to swim.*

mén 门 Trad 門 1 NOUN = door, gate (道 **dào**)
- 我们学校的大门正对汽车站。**Wǒmen xuéxiào de dàmén zhèng duì qìchē zhàn.** = *There is a bus stop directly opposite the gate of our school.*
ménkǒu 门口 = doorway, by the door, by the gate
- 他站在门口等一个朋友。**Tā zhàn zài ménkǒu děng yí ge péngyou.** = *He's standing by the door, waiting for a friend.*
dàmén 大门 = gate

mén 门 Trad 門 2 MEASURE WORD = (for school subjects, languages, etc.)
- 你今年年念几门课？**Nǐ jīnnián niàn jǐ mén kè?** = *How many subjects do you study this year?*
- 要学会一门语言，非下功夫不可。**Yào xuéhuì yì mén yǔyán, fēi xià gōngfu bùkě.** = *To learn a language, you simply must make great efforts.*

men 们 Trad 們 SUFFIX = (indicating plural number)
- 学生们都很喜欢这位新老师。**Xuéshengmen dōu hěn xǐhuan zhè wèi xīn lǎoshī.** = *All the students like this new teacher.*

NOTE: As a plural number marker, 们 **men** is only used with nouns denoting people. It is not used when there are words indicating plurality, such as numerals or words like 一些 **yìxiē**, 很多 **hěn duō**. In many cases, the plural number of a personal noun is implicit without the use of 们 **men**. In the example sentence, 们 **men** is not obligatory, i.e. 学生都很喜欢这位新老师。**Xuésheng dōu hěn xǐhuan zhè wèi xīn lǎoshī.** = *All the students like this new teacher.* is correct and idiomatic.

mèng 梦 Trad 夢 NOUN = dream
- 我昨天夜里做了一个奇怪的梦。**Wǒ zuótiān yèli zuòle yí ge qíguài de mèng.** = *I had a strange dream last night.*
zuòmèng 做梦 = have a dream

mí 迷 VERB = be lost (See 昏迷 **hūnmí**.)

mǐ 米 1 MEASURE WORD = meter (colloquial)
- 一米 **yì mǐ** = *one meter*
- 三米半 **sān mǐ bàn** = *three and half meters.*

NOTE: The formal word for *meter* is 公尺 **gōngchǐ**.

mǐ 米 2 NOUN = rice, paddy rice (粒 **lì**)
- 在中国南方，很多农民种米。**Zài Zhōngguó nánfāng, hěn duō nóngmín zhòng mǐ.** = *In South China many farmers grow rice.*
mǐjiǔ 米酒 = rice wine

mǐfàn 米饭 [compound: 米 *rice* + 饭 *meal*] NOUN = cooked rice (碗 **wǎn**)
- 米饭煮好了，菜还没有做好。**Mǐfàn zhǔ hǎo le, cài hái méiyǒu zuò hǎo.** = *The rice is cooked, but the dishes are not ready yet.*
- 王家是南方人，每天都吃米饭。**Wáng jiā shì nánfāngrén, měi tiān dōu chī mǐfàn.** = *The Wangs are southerners. They eat rice every day.*
- 外国人煮的米饭，中国人往往不爱吃。**Wàiguórén zhǔ de mǐfàn, Zhōngguórén wǎngwǎng bú ài chī.** = *A Chinese person usually does not like the cooked rice prepared by a foreigner.*

NOTE: The staple food for southern Chinese (Chinese living south of the Yangtze River) is 米饭 **mǐfàn**, while northern Chinese mainly eat 面食 **miànshí** (*food made of wheat flour*), such as 面条儿 **miàntiáor** (*noodles*) and 馒头 **mántou** (*steamed buns*).

mì 秘 ADJECTIVE = secret

mìmì 秘密 [compound: 秘 *secret* + 密 *confidential*]
1 NOUN = secret
- "我告诉你一个秘密。""要是你能告诉我，那就不是秘密。" **"Wǒ gàosù nǐ yí ge mìmì." "Yàoshì nǐ néng gàosù wǔ, nà jiù bú shì mìmì."**

M

= "I'll tell you a secret." "If you can tell me, then it's not really a secret."

2 ADJECTIVE = secret, confidential
■ 她有一个秘密信箱。**Tā yǒu yí ge mìmì xìnxiāng.** = *She has a secret post office box.*
mìmì jǐngchá 秘密警察 = secret police
mìmì wénjiàn 秘密文件 = classified document

mìshu 秘书 NOUN = secretary
■ 要当秘书，一定要打字打得好。**Yào dāng mìshu, yídìng yào dǎzì dǎ de hǎo.** = *To be a secretary, one must have good typing skills.*
■ 他要秘书通知小王马上来见他。**Tā yào mìshu tōngzhī Xiǎo Wáng mǎshàng lái jiàn tā.** = *He wants his secretary to inform Xiao Wang to come and see him immediately.*
sīrén mìshu 私人秘书 = private secretary

mì 密 ADJECTIVE = close

mìqiè 密切 [compound: 密 *close* + 切 *intimate*] ADJECTIVE = close, intimate
■ 这家人家的兄弟姐妹关系很密切。**Zhè jiā rénjiā de xiōng-dì-jiě-mèi guānxì hěn mìqiè.** = *The siblings in this family are very close to each other.*
■ 公司各部门要密切配合，不能自行其是。**Gōngsī gè bùmén yào mìqiè pèihé, bù néng zì xíng qí shì.** = *The departments in a company should be closely coordinated, and not act as they think fit.*

mì 蜜 NOUN = honey

mìfēng 蜜蜂 [modif: 蜜 *honey* + 蜂 *wasp*] NOUN = bee (只 zhī)
■ 他养蜜蜂为生。**Tā yǎng mìfēng wéishēng.** = *He makes a living by beekeeping.*

mián 棉 NOUN = cotton

miánhuā 棉花 [modif: 棉 *cotton* + 花 *bloom*] NOUN = cotton
■ 中国是棉花进口国，还是棉花出口国？**Zhōngguó shì miánhuā jìnkǒuguó, háishì miánhuā chūkǒuguó?** = *Is China a cotton importer or cotton exporter?*

miǎn 免 VERB = avoid (See 避免 bìmiǎn.)

miǎn 勉 VERB = strive

miǎnqiǎng 勉强
1 ADJECTIVE = grudgingly, barely
■ 他勉强答应了我的要求。**Tā miǎnqiáng dāyìngle wǒ de yāoqiú.** = *He yielded to my demand grudgingly.*
■ 他的理由很勉强。**Tā de lǐyóu hěn miǎnqiáng.** = *His justifications are not at all convincing.*
2 VERB = force to do
■ 他不愿去，你就别勉强他。**Tā bú yuàn qù, nǐ jiù bié miǎnqiáng tā.** = *If he's unwilling to go, don't force him to.*
■ 你真的不想学下去，就别勉强了。**Nǐ zhēnde bù xiǎng xuéxiàqu, jiù bié miánqiǎng le.** = *If you really don't want to go on studying, then don't force yourself to.*

miàn 面 1 NOUN = face
■ 你们俩有矛盾，还是面对面地谈一下吧。**Nǐmen liǎ yǒu máodùn, háishì miàn-duì-miàn de tán yíxià ba.** = *If there is conflict between the two of you, you'd better discuss it face to face.*
miànzi 面子 = face, honor
diū miànzi 丢面子 = lose face
liú miànzi 留面子 = save face

miàn 面 2 MEASURE WORD = (for flat objects)
■ 一面镜子 **yí miàn jìngzi** = *a mirror*
■ 两面旗子 **liǎng miàn qízi** = *two flags*

miànbāo 面包 [modif: 面 *wheat flour* + 包 *lump*] NOUN = bread (只 zhī, 条 tiáo)
■ 新做的面包特别香。**Xīn zuò de miànbāo tèbié xiāng.** = *Freshly baked bread smells particularly good.*
miànbāo fáng 面包房 = bakery

miànjī 面积 NOUN = (mathematics) area
■ 这个房间的面积是二十平方公尺。**Zhège fángjiān de miànjī shì èrshí píngfāng gōngchǐ.** = *This room has an area of 20 square meters.*

miànmào 面貌 [compound: 面 *face* + 貌 *looks, appearance*] NOUN = appearance, state (of things)
■ 改革以来，社会上出现了新面貌。**Gǎigé yǐlái, shèhuì shang chūxiànle xīn miànmào.** = *Since the reform, society has taken on a new look.*

miànqián 面前 NOUN = in face of, in front of, before
- 在我们面前摆着两种选择。**Zài wǒmen miànqián bǎizhe liǎng zhǒng xuǎnzé.** = We are faced with two choices.

miàntiáor 面条儿 NOUN = noodles (碗 **wǎn**)
- 面条儿要热的才好吃。**Maàntiáor yào rè de cái hǎochī.** = Noodles must be eaten hot.
- 她是北方人，面条儿做得好，米饭做得不好。**Tā shì běifāngrén, miàntiáor zuò de hǎo, mǐfàn zuò de bù hǎo.** = She's a northerner. She makes good noodle meals, but doesn't cook rice well.
- 简单点，做碗面条儿就行。**Jiǎndān diǎn, zuò wǎn miàntiáor jiù xíng.** = Let's keep it simple. Making a bowl of noodles is good enough.

miáo 描 VERB = trace, copy

miáoxiě 描写 VERB = describe (in writing)
- 她在信中描写了那里的美丽风景。**Tā zài xìn zhōng miáoxiěle nàli de měilì fēngjǐng.** = In her letter she gives a description of the beautiful landscape there.

miǎo 秒 MEASURE WORD = (of time) second
- 我跑一百公尺要十四秒，你呢？**Wǒ pǎo yìbǎi gōngchǐ yào shísì miǎo, nǐ ne?** = It takes me 14 seconds to run 100 meters. How about you?

miào 妙 ADJECTIVE = wonderful, ingenious
- 你的主意真妙！**Nǐ de zhǔyi zhēn miào!** = What a wonderful idea!
  búmiào 不妙 = not good, unpromising
- 这两天情况不妙。**Zhè liǎngtian qíngkuàng búmiào.** = Things are not good these days.

miào 庙 Trad 廟 NOUN = temple (座 **zuò**)
- 在中国的名胜，常常有一座古庙。**Zài Zhōngguó de míngshèng, chángcháng yǒu yí zuò gǔ miào.** = In scenic spots in China, there is often an ancient temple.

miè 灭 Trad 滅 VERB = extinguish, put out, go out
- 火灭了。**Huǒ miè le.** = The fire was extinguished.
  mièhuǒqì 灭火器 = fire extinguisher

mín 民 NOUN = people

mínzhǔ 民主
1 NOUN = democracy
- 世界上发达国家都实行真正的政治民主。**Shìjiè shang fādá guójiā dōu shíxíng zhēnzhèng de zhèngzhì mínzhǔ.** = All the developed countries in the world practice genuine political democracy.
2 ADJECTIVE = democratic
- 没有民主的制度，不可能长期稳定。**Méiyǒu mínzhǔ de zhìdù, bù kěnéng chángqī wěndìng.** = There can be no long-term stability without a democratic system.

NOTE: 民主 **mínzhǔ** literally means the people rule. The word-formation is "subject + predicate," which is fairly uncommon.

mínzú 民族 [compound: 民 people + 族 clan] NOUN = ethnic group, nationality (个 **ge**)
- 汉民族是中国最大的民族。**Hàn mínzù shì Zhōngguó zuì dà de mínzú.** = The Hans are the biggest ethnic group in China.
- 你们国家有多少个民族？**Nǐmen guójiā yǒu duōshǎo ge mínzù?** = How many ethnic groups are there in your country?
  shǎoshù mínzú 少数民族 = minority ethnic group
  duō mínzú wénhuà 多民族文化 = multiculturalism

míng 名 1 NOUN
1 = name
- 你记得他家的那条街名吗？**Nǐ jìdé tā jiā de nà tiáo jiā míng ma?** = Do you remember the name of the street where his home is?
2 = (personal) given name
- 他们要给新生儿取个名。**Tāmen yào gěi xīnshēngér qǔ ge míng.** = They're going to name their newborn baby.
  chūmíng 出名 = become famous
  guómíng 国名 = name of a country

míng 名 2 MEASURE WORD = (used for people, especially those with a specific position or occupation)
- 一名军人 **yì míng jūnrén** = a soldier
- 两名学生 **liǎng míng xuésheng** = two students

M

mìngshèng 名胜 NOUN = famous scenic spot
■ 这个地区有很多名胜，每年吸引大批旅游者。**Zhège dìqū yǒu hěn duō míngshèng, měi nián xīyǐn dàpī lǚyóuzhe.** = *The area boasts many famous scenic spots and attracts large numbers of tourists every year.*

míngzi 名字 [compound: 名 *given name* + 字 *courtesy name*] NOUN = name, given name
■ 我的名字叫王小明。**Wǒ de míngzi jiào Wáng Xiǎo Míng.** = *My name is Wang Xiaoming.*
■ "你知道他的名字吗？" "不知道。" **"Nǐ zhīdào tā de míngzi ma?" "Bù zhīdào."** = *"Do you know his name?" "No."*

NOTE: To be exact, 名字 **míngzi** only means *given name*, but informally 名字 **míngzi** may also mean *full name* (family name + given name). The formal word for *full name* is 姓名 **xìngmíng**. See 姓 **xìng**.

míng 明 ADJECTIVE = bright

míngbai 明白 [compound: 明 *bright* + 白 *white*]
1 ADJECTIVE = clear, obvious
■ 对不起，我没有说明白。**Duìbuqǐ, wǒ méiyǒu shuō míngbai.** = *Sorry, I didn't make it very clear.*
2 VERB = understand, see the point
■ 老师又解释了一遍，我才明白了。**Lǎoshī yòu jiěshì yí biàn, wǒ cái míngbai le.** = *I only understood after the teacher explained it again.*
■ 我还不明白，能不能再说一遍。**Wǒ hái bù míngbai, néng bu néng zài shuō yí biàn?** = *I still don't understand. Could you say it again?*

míngnián 明年 [modif: 明 (in this context) *next* + 年 *year*] NOUN = next year
■ 明年我二十一岁了！**Míngnián wǒ èrshìyī suì le!** = *I'll be twenty-one next year!*

NOTE: 明年 **míngnián** is *next year* only to *this year* 今年 **jīnnián**. For the year after another year, we use 第二年 **dì-èr nián** or 下一年 **xià yì nián**. For example:
■ 他们在 2002 年结婚，第二年生了一个儿子。**Tāmen zài èr-líng-líng-èr nián jiéhūn, dì-èr nián shēngle yí ge érzi.** = *They married in 2002 and had a son the following year.*
It would be wrong to use 明年 **míngnián** in this example.

míngliàng 明亮 [compound: 明 *bright* + 亮 *bright*] ADJECTIVE = bright, well-lit
■ 这间房间很明亮，我很喜欢。**Zhè jiān fángjiān hěn míngliàng, wǒ hěn xǐhuan.** = *This room is very bright. I like it.*

míngquè 明确 [compound: 明 *clear* + 确 *definite, specific*]
1 ADJECTIVE = definite and explicit
■ 他说得很明确，本月十五日下午三点二十五分到达北京机场。**Tā shuō de hěn míngquè, běnyuè shíwǔ rì xiàwǔ sān diǎn èrshíwǔ fēn dàodá Běijīng jīchǎng.** = *He made it very clear—he will be arriving at Beijing Airport at 3:25 p.m. on the fifteenth of this month.*
2 VERB = make definite and explicit
■ 请你明确一下品种、数量和交货日期。**Qǐng nǐ míngquè yíxià pǐnzhǒng, shùliàng hé jiāohuò rìqī.** = *Please be definite about the product specifications, quantity and date of shipment.*

míngtiān 明天 [modif: 明 (in this context) *next* + 天 *day*] NOUN = tomorrow
■ "明天是几月几日？" "明天是六月二十一日。" **"Míngtiān shì jǐ yuè jǐ rì?" "Míngtiān shì Liùyuè èrshíyī rì."** = *"What date is tomorrow?" "It's June 21."*
■ 我想睡觉了，这些作业明天再做吧。**Wǒ xiǎng shuìjiào le, zhèxiē zuòyè míngtiān zài zuò ba.** = *I want to go to bed. I'll do these assignments tomorrow.*

míngxiǎn 明显 [compound: 明 *clear* + 显 *showing*] ADJECTIVE = obvious, apparent, evident
■ 你明显瘦了。**Nǐ míngxiǎn shòu le.** = *You've obviously lost weight.*
■ 价格没有明显变化。**Jiàgé méiyǒu míngxiǎn biànhuà.** = *There has been no apparent change in prices.*

mìng 命 NOUN = life

mìnglìng 命令
1 NOUN = order
■ 军人必须服从命令。**Jūnrén bìxū fúcóng mìnglìng.** = *A soldier must obey orders.*
2 VERB = order
■ 公司总部命令分公司立即关闭。**Gōngsī zǒngbù mìnglìng fēngōngsī lìjí guānbì.** = *The*

company's head office ordered immediate closure of the branch.

mìngyùn 命运 [compound: 命 *destiny* + 运 *luck*]

1 NOUN = fate, destiny
- 他总是怪自己命运不好。**Tā zǒngshì guài zìjǐ mìngyùn bù hǎo.** = *He always blames his bad luck (← poor fate).*
- 有些传统中国人相信出生的年、月、日、时决定一个人的命运。**Yǒuxiē chuántǒng de Zhōngguórén xiāngxìn chūshēng de nián, yuè, rì, shí juédìng yí ge rén de mìngyùn.** = *Some traditional Chinese believe that the year, month, date and hour of birth determines a person's fate.*

mō 摸 VERB = touch
- 请不要摸展览品。**Qǐng bú yào mō zhǎnlǎnpǐn.** = *Please do not touch the exhibits.*

mófǎng 模仿 [compound: 模 *mould* + 仿 *simulate*] VERB = imitate, ape, be a copycat
- 小明喜欢模仿爸爸讲话，而且模仿得很象。**Xiǎo Míng xǐhuan mófǎng bàba jiǎnghuà, érqiě mófǎng de hěn xiàng.** = *Xiao Ming likes to mimic his daddy, and he does it well.*

mótuōchē 摩托车 NOUN = motorcycle (辆 liàng)
- 开摩托车千万要小心，别开得太快。**Kāi mótuōchē qiānwàn yào xiǎoxīn, bié kāi de tài kuài.** = *You should be very, very careful when riding a motorcycle. Don't ride too fast.*

mò 末 NOUN = end (See 周末 zhōumò.)

mò 漠 NOUN = desert (See 沙漠 shāmò.)

mò 墨 NOUN = ink

mòshuǐ 墨水 [modif: 墨 *ink* + 水 *water*] NOUN = ink
- 电脑打字很费墨水。**Diànnǎo dǎzì hěn fèi mòshuǐ.** = *Computer printing takes lots of ink.*

mò 默 ADJECTIVE = silent (See 沉默 chénmò.)

mǒu 某 PRONOUN = certain (used to denote an indefinite person or thing, usually in writing)
- 在该国某地发生森林大火。**Zài gāiguó mǒu**

dì fāshēng sēnlín dàhuǒ. = *At a certain place in that country a forest fire broke out.*

mǔ 母 ADJECTIVE
1 = maternal, of a mother
- 孩子需要母爱。**Háizi xūyào mǔ'ài.** = *Children need maternal love.*
2 = female (of certain animals) (antonym 公 gōng)
- 他们养了八只公鸡，二十多只母鸡。**Tāmen yǎngle bā zhī gōngjī, èrshí duō zhī mǔ jī.** = *They keep eight roosters and over twenty hens.*
mǔxìng 母性 = maternal instinct
mǔyǔ 母语 = mother tongue
- 她英语说得这么好，真让人不相信英语不是她的母语。**Tā Yīngyǔ shuō de zhème hǎo, zhēn ràng rén bù xiāngxìn Yīngyǔ bú shì tā de mǔyǔ.** = *She speaks English so well that it's hard to believe that it isn't her mother tongue.*

mǔqin 母亲 [modif: 母 *mother* + 亲 *parent*] NOUN = mother
- 母亲在家照顾孩子。**Mǔqin zài jiā zhàogù háizi.** = *Mother takes care of her children at home.*
- 你常常给母亲打电话吗？**Nǐ chángcháng gěi mǔqin dǎ diànhuà ma?** = *Do you often give mother a call?*
mǔqin jié 母亲节 = Mother's Day

mǔ 亩 Trad 畝 MEASURE WORD = (a traditional Chinese unit of area, especially in farming; 1 *mu* is equivalent to $\frac{1}{15}$ hectare, about 667 square meters)
- 十亩地 (田) **shí mǔ dì (tián)** = *10 mu of ground (paddy fields/farmland)*

mù 木 NOUN
1 = same as 木头 mùtou
- 我喜欢木家具。**Wǒ xǐhuan mù jiājù.** = *I like wood furniture.*
2 = tree
- 独木不成林。**Dú mù bù chéng lín.** = *A single tree does not make a forest. (→ One swallow doesn't make a summer.)*

mùtou 木头 [suffix: 木 *wood* + 头 nominal suffix] NOUN = wood, timber
- 我喜欢木头家具。**Wǒ xǐhuan mùtou jiājù.** = *I like wooden furniture.*

M

mù 目 NOUN = eye

mùbiāo 目标 NOUN = target, objective, goal
- 她的目标是五年内存十万元。**Tā de mùbiāo shì wǔ nián nèi cún shíwàn yuán.** = *Her goal is to save a hundred thousand dollars in five years.*

mùdì 目的 NOUN = aim, purpose
- 我们做市场调查的目的是更好地为顾客服务。**Wǒmen zuò shìchǎng diàochá de mùdì shì gèng hǎo de wèi gùkè fúwù.** = *The purpose of our market investigation is to serve our customers more satisfactorily.*

mùqián 目前 NOUN = at present
- 目前的困难是暂时的。**Mùqián de kùnnan shì zànshí de.** = *The present difficulties are only temporary.*

mù 慕 VERB = admire (See 羡慕 **xiànmù**.)

N

ná 拿 VERB = hold, carry in hand
- 我手里拿着很多书，不能开门，请你帮帮我。**Wǒ shǒu li názhe hěn duō shū, bù néng kāi mén, qǐng nǐ bāngbang wǒ.** = *I'm holding lots of books and can't open the door. Please help me.*
ná zhǔyi 拿主意 = make a decision
- 这件事你得自己拿主意。**Zhè jiàn shì nǐ děi zìjǐ ná zhǔyi.** = *You've got to make a decision about this matter by yourself.*
ná zǒu 拿走 = take away, remove
- 他已经不在这个办公室工作了，不过东西还没拿走。**Tā yǐjīng bú zài zhège bàngōngshì gōngzuò le, búguò dōngxi hái méiyǒu názǒu.** = *He no longer works in this office, but he has not removed his things.*

nǎ 哪 PRONOUN
1 = which
- 哪辆自行车是你的？**Nǎ liàng zìxíngchē shì nǐ de?** = *Which bicycle is yours?*
- 这么多新车，你说哪辆最漂亮？**Zhème duō xīn chē, nǐ shuō nǎ liàng zuì piàoliang?** = *Of so many new cars, which do you think is the most attractive?*

2 = whatever, whichever
- 这些鞋子，我哪双都不喜欢。**Zhèxiē xiézi, wǒ nǎ shuāng dōu bù xǐhuan.** = *I don't like any of the shoes here.*
- 下星期我都在家，你哪天来都可以。**Xià xīngqī wǒ dōu zài jiā, nǐ nǎ tiān lái dōu kěyǐ.** = *I'll be home all next week. You may come any day.*

nǎli 哪里 [modif: 哪 *which* + 里 *place*] PRONOUN = where
- 你住在哪里？**Nǐ zhù zài nǎli?** = *Where do you live?*

NOTE: 哪里哪里 **nǎli nǎli** is an idiomatic expression used as a modest reply to a compliment, e.g.
- "你汉字写得真漂亮。" "哪里哪里。" **"Nǐ Hànzì xiě de zhēn piàoliang." "Nǎli, nǎli."** = *"You write beautiful Chinese characters." "Thank you."*

nǎpà 哪怕 CONJUNCTION = even if, even though
- 哪怕卖掉房子，王先生和王太太也要让孩子念大学。**Nǎpà màidiào fángzi, Wáng xiānsheng hé Wáng tàitai yěyào ràng háizi niàn dàxué.** = *Even if they have to sell the house, Mr and Mrs Wang will put their son through university.*
- 他总是完成每天的工作，哪怕要开夜车。**Tā zǒngshì wánchéng měi tiān de gōngzuò, nǎpà yào kāi yèchē.** = *He always finishes the day's work, even when he has to burn the midnight oil.*

NOTE: 哪怕 **nǎpà** introduces an exaggerated, rather unlikely situation to emphasize the statement of the sentence.

nǎr 哪儿 PRONOUN = same as 哪里 **nǎli**. Used colloquially.

nǎxiē 哪些 PRONOUN = the plural form of 哪 **nǎ**
- 你想看哪些书？**Nǐ xiǎng kàn nǎxiē shū?** = *Which books do you want to read?*

nà 那 PRONOUN
1 = that
- 这辆自行车是我的，那辆自行车是我弟弟的。**Zhè liàng zìxíngchē shì wǒ de, nà liàng zìxíngchē shì wǒ dìdi de.** = *This bike is mine. That one is my younger brother's.*

M

■ "麻烦你帮我租一套房子。""那不难。" **"Máfan nǐ bāng wǒ zū yí tào fángzi." "Nà bù nán."** = *"Would you mind renting a house for me?" "That won't be a problem."*
2 = same as 那么 **nàme** 2 CONJUNCTION

nàge 那个 [modif: 那 *that* + 个 *one*] PRONOUN = that one
■ 那个不是我的，我的在这里。 **Nàge bú shì wǒ de, wǒ de zài zhèlǐ.** = *That one is not mine. Mine's here.*

nàli 那里 [modif: 那 *that* + 里 *place*] PRONOUN = there, over there
■ 他在那里工作。 **Tā zài nàli gōngzuò.** = *He works there.*
■ 那里就是图书馆。 **Nàli jiù shì túshūguǎn.** = *Over there is the library.*

NOTES: (1) 那里 **nàli** is used after a personal noun or pronoun to make it a place word as a personal noun or pronoun cannot be used immediately after a preposition. For example, 我从张小姐听到这个消息。 **Wǒ cóng Zhāng xiǎojiě tīngdao zhège xiāoxi.** is incorrect. 那里 **nàli** must be added after 张小姐 **Zhāng xiǎojiě** (*Miss Zhang*): 我从张小姐那里听到这个消息。 **Wǒ cóng Zhāng xiǎojiě nàli tīngdao zhège xiāoxi.** = *I learnt the news from Miss Zhang.* In this case 张小姐那里 **Zhāng xiǎojiě nàli** becomes a place word which can occur after the preposition 从 **cóng**. (2) Colloquially, 那儿 **nàr** may replace 那里 **nàli**.

nàme 那么
1 PRONOUN = like that
■ 上海没有北京那么冷。 **Shànghǎi méiyǒu Běijīng nàme lěng.** = *Shanghai is not as cold as Beijing.*
■ 你那么做，她会不高兴。 **Nǐ nàme zuò, tā huì bù gāoxìng.** = *If you behave like that, she'll be unhappy.*
2 CONJUNCTION = in that case, then
■ 你不喜欢吃米饭，那么吃面包吧。 **Nǐ bù xǐhuan chī mǐfàn, nàme chī miànbāo ba.** = *You don't like rice; in that case eat bread.* (→ *Since you don't like rice, have bread instead.*)
■ "去北京的飞机票全卖完了。"" 那么，我们就乘火车去吧。" **"Qù Běijīng de fēijī piào quán màiwán le." "Nàme, wǒmen jiù chéng huǒchē qù ba."** = *"The air tickets to Beijing are sold out." "In that case, let's go by train."*

NOTE: Although 那么 **nàme** as a conjunction is glossed as *in that case, then*, Chinese speakers tend to use it much more than English speakers use "in that case" or "then." In colloquial Chinese 那么 **nàme** is often shortened to 那 **nà**, e.g.
■ 你不喜欢吃米饭，那吃面包吧。 **Nǐ bù xǐhuan chī mǐfàn, nà chī mianbāo ba.** = *You don't like rice; in that case eat bread.*

nàr 那儿 PRONOUN = same as 那里 **nàli**. Used colloquially.

nàxiē 那些 PRONOUN = those
■ 这些是中文书，那些是英文书。 **Zhèxiē shì Zhōngwén shū, nàxiē shì Yīngwén shū.** = *These are Chinese books. Those are English books.*

nàyàng 那样 PRONOUN = same as 那么 **nàme** 1 PRONOUN

nǎi 奶 NOUN = milk

nǎinai 奶奶 NOUN = paternal grandmother, granny
■ 奶奶，我上学去了！ **Nǎinai, wǒ shàngxué qù le!** = *Granny, I'm going to school!*

NOTE: The formal word for paternal grandmother is 祖母 **zǔmǔ** and that for maternal grandmother is 外祖母 **wàizǔmǔ**. While 奶奶 **nǎinai** is the colloquialism for 祖母 **zǔmǔ**, that for 外祖母 **wàizǔmǔ** is 姥姥 **lǎolao**, or 外婆 **wàipó**.

nài 耐 VERB = able to endure

nàifán 耐烦 [v+obj: 耐 *tolerate* + 烦 *irritation*] ADJECTIVE = patient
■ 尽管顾客东挑西拣，营业员也不能露出不耐烦的样子。 **Jǐnguǎn gùkè dōng-tiāo-xī-jiǎn, yíngyèyuán yě bù néng lùchu bú nàifán de yàngzi.** = *Even if the customer is very choosy, the shop assistant mustn't appear impatient.*

NOTE: 耐烦 **nàifán** is only used in its negative form, 不耐烦 **bú nàifán**.

nàixīn 耐心 [modif: 耐 *tolerate* + 心 *heart*]
1 ADJECTIVE = patient

N

■ 她对孩子很有耐心。**Tā duì háizi hěn yǒu nàixīn.** = *She is really patient with children.*
■ 除了耐心地等待，没有别的办法。**Chúle nàixīn de děngdài, méiyǒu biéde bànfǎ.** = *There is nothing you can do except wait patiently.*
2 NOUN = patience
■ 我看他快要没有耐心了。**Wǒ kàn tā kuài yào méiyǒu nàixīn le.** = *I think he will soon run out of patience.*

nàiyòng 耐用 ADJECTIVE = durable
■ 我们的产品很耐用。**Wǒmen de chǎnpǐn hěn nàiyòng.** = *Our products are durable.*
■ 这种牌子的手表很便宜，但是不耐用。**Zhè zhǒng páizi de shǒubiǎo hěn piányì, dànshì bú nàiyòng.** = *Watches of this brand are cheap but don't last long.*

nán 男 ADJECTIVE = (of humans) male (antonym 女 **nǚ**)
nán háizi 男孩子 = boy
■ 那个男孩子是王先生的小儿子。**Nàge nán háizi shì Wáng xiānsheng de xiǎo érzi.** = *That boy is Mr Wang's youngest son.*
nán qīngnián 男青年 = young man
■ 昨天有一个男青年来找你。**Zuótiān yǒu yíge nán qīngnián lái zhǎo nǐ.** = *A young man came to see you yesterday.*
nánshēng 男生 = male student/pupil
nánzǐhàn 男子汉 = man, men, hero

nánrén 男人 NOUN = man, men
■ 男人能做的事，女人也能做。**Nánrén néng zuò de shì, nǚrén yě néng zuò.** = *What men can do, women also can.*

nán 南 NOUN = south, southern
■ 很多老年人喜欢住在南方。**Hěn duō lǎoniánrén xǐhuan zhù zài nánfāng.** = *Many old people like to live in the south.*

nánbiān 南边 [modif: 南 *south* + 边 *side*] NOUN = south side, to the south, in the south
■ "新西兰的南边还有什么国家吗？" "没有了。" **"Xīnxīlán de nánbiān hái yǒu shénme guójiā ma?" "Méiyǒu le."** = *"Is there any country to the south of New Zealand?" "No, there isn't."*

nánfāng 南方 NON = the southern part, the south of a country

■ 中国的南方夏天一般很热。**Zhōngguó de nánfāng xiàtiān yìbān hěn rè.** = *In southern China, summer is generally very hot.*
náifāngrén 南方人 = southerner

nánmiàn 南面 NOUN = same as 南边 **nánbian**

nán 难 Trad 難 ADJECTIVE = difficult (antonym 容易 **róngyì**)
■ 这道练习太难了，我不会做。**Zhè dào liànxí tài nán le, wǒ bú huì zuò.** = *This exercise is too difficult. I can't do it.*
■ 在这个政府部门，人难见，事难办。**Zài zhège zhèngfǔ bùmén, rén nán jiàn, shì nán bàn.** = *In this government department, it is difficult to meet any officials or to get things done.*

nándào 难道 ADVERB = (used at the beginning of a sentence or before a verb to make it a rhetorical question).
■ 难道你不知道吗？**Nándào nǐ bù zhīdào ma?** = *Didn't you know?*
■ 他连旧车都买不起，难道还买得起新车吗？**Tā lián jiù chē dōu mǎi bu qǐ, nándào hái mǎi de qǐ xīn chē ma?** = *He even can't afford a second-hand car. How can he afford a new car?*

nánguò 难过 ADJECTIVE = sad, grieved (antonym 高兴 **gāoxìng**)
■ 听到这个不幸的消息，我们非常难过。**Tīngdào zhège búxìng de xiāoxi, wǒmen fēicháng nánguò.** = *Hearing this unfortunate news, we were all very sad.*

NOTE: 难过 **nánguò** is usually used as a predicate, and seldom as an attribute.

nánkàn 难看 ADJECTIVE = ugly (antonym 好看 **hǎokàn**)
■ 他穿这件衣服真难看。**Tā chuān zhè jiàn yīfu zhēn nánkàn.** = *He really looks ugly in that suit.*

nánshòu 难受 ADJECTIVE
1 = feel ill, uncomfortable
■ 他昨天晚上酒喝得太多，今天早上头疼难受。**Tā zuótiān wǎnshang jiǔ hē de tài duō, jīntiān zǎoshang tóuténg nánshòu.** = *He drank too much last night. This morning he had a headache and felt terrible (→ had a hangover).*

■ 这双新鞋小了点儿，穿着难受。**Zhè shuāng xīn xié xiǎole diǎnr, chuānzhe nánshòu.** = *The new shoes are too small, and are uncomfortable to wear.*
2 = feel sorry, feel bad, sad
■ 我的错误给公司带来损失，我心里很难受。**Wǒ de cuòwù gěi gōngsī dàilai sǔnshī, wǒ xīnli hěn nánshòu.** = *I feel bad that my mistake has caused loss to the company.*

nǎo 脑 Trad 腦 NOUN = brain

nǎodai 脑袋 [modif: 脑 *brain* + 袋 *bag*] NOUN = same as 头 **tóu**. Used only colloquially and in a derogative sense.

nǎozi 脑子 [suffix: 脑 *brain* + 子 nominal suffix] NOUN = brain, mind
■ 他怎么有这种想法？脑子出问题了吧？**Tā zěnme yǒu zhè zhǒng xiǎngfǎ? Nǎozi chū wèntí le ba?** = *How come he has such ideas? Something wrong with his mind? (or He must be out of his mind./He must be crazy.)*
　dòng nǎozi 动脑子 = use brains
■ 遇到难题，要多动脑子，总会找到解决的方法。**Yùdao nántí, yào duō dòng nǎozi, zǒnghuì zhǎodao jiějué de bànfǎ.** = *When confronted with difficulties, use your brains and you will always find a solution.*

nào 闹 Trad 鬧 VERB = make trouble, create a disturbance
■ 这几个孩子闹得我根本看不进书。**Zhè jǐ ge háizi nào de wǒ gēnběn kànbujìn shū.** = *These kids raised such a ruckus that I could not concentrate on reading at all.*
■ 别闹了，邻居该来提意见了。**Bié nào le, línjū gāilái tí yìjiàn le.** = *Stop making such a noise. The neighbors will come to complain.*
　nào xiàohua 闹笑话 = make a fool of oneself, cut a ridiculous figure
　nào píqi 闹脾气 = throw a tantrum

ne 呢 PARTICLE
1 = (used at the end of a question to soften the tone of enquiry)
■ 你打算明年做什么呢？**Nǐ dǎsuàn míngnián zuò shénme ne?** = *What do you intend to do next year?*
2 = How about…? Where is (are)…?
■ 你们明天出去旅游，孩子呢？**Nǐmen**

míngtiān chūqu lǚyóu, háizi ne? = *You're going on holiday tomorrow. How about the kids?*
■ "小明，你妈呢？" **"Xiǎo Míng, nǐ mā ne?"** = *"Xiao Ming, where is your mom?"*

nèi 那 same as 那 **nà**. Used colloquially.

nèi 内 NOUN = inside, within (antonym 外 **wài**)
■ 房间内外都很干净。**Fángjiān nèi wài dōu hěn gānjìng.** = *The home is clean both inside and out.*
■ 我一定在十天内还清借款。**Wǒ yídìng zài shí tiān nèi huánqīng jièkuǎn.** = *I will pay off the debt within ten days.*

nèibù 内部 NOUN = interior, inside
■ 展览会内部整理，暂停对外开放。**Zhǎnlǎnhuì nèibù zhěnglǐ, zàntíng duìwài kāifàng.** = *The exhibition is temporarily closed for reorganization.*
　nèibù zīliào 内部资料 = document for internal circulation (e.g. within a government department)

nèiróng 内容 [modif: 内 *inside* + 容 *contain*] NOUN = content, substance
■ 这本书的内容很丰富。**Zhè běn shū de nèiróng hěn fēngfù.** = *The book is rich in content.*
■ 他说了半天，但是没有什么内容。**Tā shuōle bàntiān, dànshì méiyǒu shénme nèiróng.** = *He talked for a long time but there wasn't much substance.*
■ 王董事长讲话的主要内容是什么？**Wáng dǒngshìzhǎng jiǎnghuà de zhǔyào nèiróng shì shénme?** = *What is the main idea of Chairman Wang's talk?*

nèn 嫩 ADJECTIVE = young and tender, tender
■ 请你把牛肉做得嫩一点。**Qǐng nǐ bǎ niúròu zuò de nèn yìdiǎn.** = *Please make the beef tender. (→ Don't overcook the beef.)*

néng 能 MODAL VERB = can, be able to
■ 我今天不舒服，不能去上班。**Wǒ jīntiān bù shūfu, bù néng qù shàngbān.** = *I'm unwell today and won't be able to go to work.*
■ 这辆车加满汽油，能跑多少公里？**Zhè liàng chē jiā mǎn qìyóu, néng pǎo duōshǎo gōnglǐ?** = *How many kilometers can this car run on a full tank?*

NOTE: See note on 会 **huì** MODAL VERB.

nénggàn 能干 ADJECTIVE = (of people) able, capable, efficient
■ 他非常能干，别人一星期做的工作，他三天就完成了。**Tā fēicháng nénggàn, biérén yì xīngqī zuò de gōngzuò, tā sān tiān jiù wánchéng le.** = *He is very efficient. He can finish in three days what takes others a week to do.*

nénggòu 能够 MODAL VERB = same as 能 **néng**

nénglì 能力 [compound: 能 *ability* + 力 *strength*] NOUN = ability
■ 他能力比一般人强，但是太骄傲了。**Tā nénglì bǐ yìbān rén qiáng, dànshì tài jiāo'ào le.** = *He is more capable than most people, but he is too conceited.*
■ 我们要求职工有使用电脑的能力。**Wǒmen yāoqiú zhígōng yǒu shǐyòng diànnǎo de nénglì.** = *We require that our staff have computer competence. (← We require that our staff have the ability to use computers.)*

néngyuán 能源 [modif: 能 *energy* + 源 *source, resource*] NOUN = energy resources
■ 石油和煤总有用完的一天，人类必须开发新能源。**Shíyóu hé méi zǒngyǒu yòngwán de yìtiān, rénlèi bìxū kāifā xīn néngyuán.** = *There will be a day when oil and coal are exhausted. Mankind must develop new energy resources.*

ng 嗯 INTERJECTION = (used after a question to reinforce questioning)
■ 你把自行车借给谁了，嗯？**Nǐ bǎ zìxíngchē jiègei shuí le, ng?** = *Who did you lend your bicycle to, eh?*

ní 泥 NOUN = mud
■ 他们在下雨天踢球，搞得身上都是泥。**Tāmen zài xiàyǔtiān tīqiú, gǎode shēnshang dōushì ní.** = *They played soccer in the rain and got themselves all covered with mud.*

nǐ 你 PRONOUN = you (singular)
■ 你是谁？**Nǐ shì shuí?** = *Who're you?*
■ 我不认识你。**Wǒ bú rènshi nǐ.** = *I don't know you.*

nǐmen 你们 [suffix: 你 *you* (singular) + 们 *suffix denoting a plural number*] PRONOUN = you (plural)
■ 你们都是我的朋友。**Nǐmen dōu shì wǒ de péngyou.** = *You all are my friends.*
■ 我告诉你们一个好消息。**Wǒ gàosu nǐmen yí ge hǎo xiāoxi.** = *I'll tell you a piece of good news.*

nián 年 NOUN = year (no measure word required)
■ 一年有十二个月。**Yì nián yǒu shí'èr ge yuè.** = *There're twelve months in a year.*
■ 我在美国住了两年。**Wǒ zài Měiguó zhùle liǎng nián.** = *I lived in the States for two years.*
jīnnián 今年 = this year
míngnián 明年 = next year
qùnián 去年 = last year

NOTE: No measure word is used with 年 **nián**, e.g. 一年 **yì nián** (*one year*), 两年 **liǎng nián** (*two years*), 三年 **sān nián** (*three years*).

niándài 年代 [compound: 年 *year* + 代 *age*] NOUN = a decade of a century
■ 我爸爸妈妈喜欢听(二十世纪)七十年代的歌。**Wǒ bàba māma xǐhuan tīng (èrshí shìjì) qīshí niándài de gē.** = *My dad and mom enjoy listening to songs of the seventies (of the twentieth century).*

niánjí 年级 [compound: 年 *year* + 级 *grade*] NOUN = grade (in school)
■ 这个年级有多少学生？**Zhège niánjí yǒu duōshǎo xuésheng?** = *How many students are there in this grade?*
■ 他们的女儿刚念一年级。**Tāmen de nǚ'ér gāng niàn yì niánjí.** = *Their daughter is only a first grade pupil.*

niánjì 年纪 [compound: 年 *year* + 纪 *number*] NOUN = age
■ 他虽然年纪小，但是很懂事。**Tā suīrán niánjì xiǎo, dànshì hěn dǒngshì.** = *Although he's very young, he's quite sensible.*
■ "老先生，您多大年纪了？""七十了。" **"Lǎo xiānsheng, nín duōdà niánjì le?" "Qīshí le."** = *"How old are you, sir?" "Seventy."*

NOTE: 您多大年纪了？**Nín duōdà niánjì le?** is an appropriate way to ask the age of an elderly person. To ask a young child his/her age, the question should be 你几岁了？ **Nǐ jǐ suì le?** For people who are neither children nor elderly, the question to use is 你多大岁数？ **Nǐ duō dà suìshù?**

niánlíng 年龄 [compound: 年 *year* + 龄 *age*]
NOUN = age (of a person or other living things)
■ 你别问别人的年龄，尤其别问女士的年龄。**Nǐ bié wèn biérén de niánlíng, yóuqí bié wèn nǚshì de niánlíng.** = *Do not ask about somebody's age, especially a lady's age.*
■ 这棵树的年龄比我爷爷还大。**Zhè kē shù de niánlíng bǐ wǒ yéye hái dà.** = *This tree is older than my grandpa.*

niánqīng 年轻 [modif: 年 *age* + 轻 *light*]
ADJECTIVE = young
■ 你还年轻，有些事你还不大懂。**Nǐ hái niánqīng, yǒuxiē shì nǐ hái bú dà dǒng.** = *You're still too young to understand some matters.*
■ 他年轻的时候可能干了！**Tā niánqīng de shíhou, kě nénggàn le!** = *He was a very capable man when he was young.*
niánqīngrén 年轻人 = young person

niàn 念 VERB
1 = read, read aloud
■ 你每天念中文课文吗？**Nǐ měi tiān niàn Zhōngwén kèwén ma?** = *Do you read your Chinese lessons everyday?*
2 = study (in a school)
■ 他们的大儿子在英国念大学，他念数学。**Tāmen de dà érzi zài Yīngguó niàn dàxué, tā niàn shùxué.** = *Their eldest son is studying in a university in the UK; he studies mathematics.*

NOTE: See note on 读 **dú.**

niáng 娘 NOUN = girl; mother (See 姑娘 **gūniang.**)

niǎo 鸟 Trad 鳥 NOUN = bird (只 **zhī**)
■ 两只鸟在花园里飞来飞去。**Liǎng zhī niǎo zài huāyuán li fēi-lái-fēi-qù.** = *Two birds darted here and there in the garden.*

nín 您 PRONOUN = you (honorific)

NOTE: 您 **nín** is the honorific form of 你 **nǐ.** Use 您 **nín** when respect or deference is called for. Normally, 您 **nín** does not have a plural form. 您们 **nínmen** is absolutely unacceptable in spoken Chinese, and only marginally so in written Chinese. To address more than one person politely, you can say 您两位 **nín liǎng wèi** (two people), 您三位 **nín sān wèi** (three people), or 您几位 **nín jǐ wèi** (several people).

niú 牛 VERB = cattle, ox, cow, calf, buffalo (头 **tóu**)
■ 牛在草地上吃草。**Niú zài cǎodì shang chī cǎo.** = *The cattle are grazing in the field.*
■ 西方人用狗放羊放牛，所以他们说狗是人最好的朋友。**Xīfāngrén yòng gǒu fàng yáng fàng niú, suǒyǐ tāmen shuō gǒu shì rén zuì hǎo de péngyou.** = *People in the West use dogs to herd cattle and sheep; that's why they say the dog is man's best friend.*
niúnǎi 牛奶 = cow's milk, milk
niúròu 牛肉 = beef
gōng niú 公牛 = bull
huángniú 黄牛 = ox
nǎiniú 奶牛 = cow
shuǐniú 水牛 = water buffalo
xiǎo niú 小牛 = calf

NOTE: In the Chinese context, the ox (黄牛 **huángniú**) and the water buffalo (水牛 **shuǐniú**) are more important than the milk cow (奶牛 **nǎiniú**).

nóng 农 Trad 農 NOUN = farming

nóngchǎng 农场 [modif: 农 *farming* + 场 *field, ground*] NOUN = farm
■ 这个农场真大！**Zhège nóngchǎng zhēn dà!** = *How big this farm is!*
■ 外国人可以在这里买农场吗？**Wàiguórén kěyǐ zài zhèli mǎi nóngchǎng ma?** = *Can a foreigner buy a farm here?*
nóngchǎngzhǔ 农场主 = farmer

nóngcūn 农村 [modif: 农 *farming* + 村 *village*] NOUN = farming area, rural area, countryside (antonym 城市 **chéngshì**)
■ 农村人口比较少，生活不太方便。**Nóngcūn rénkǒu bǐjiào shǎo, shēnghuó bú tài fāngbiàn.** = *In rural areas, the population is small and life is not very convenient.*

N

■在中国，农村很多地区还比较落后。**Zài Zhōngguó, nóngcūn hěn duō dìqū hái bǐjiào luòhòu.** = *Many regions in rural China are still rather backward.*

nóngmín 农民 [modif: 农 *farming* + 民 *people*] NOUN = peasant, farmer

■农民都很关心天气。**Nóngmín dōu hěn guānxīn tiānqì.** = *Farmers are all concerned about the weather.*
■这个村子的农民生活相当困难。**Zhège cūnzi de nóngmín shēnghuó xiāngdāng kùnnan.** = *The peasants in this village live a tough life.*
■她十年前和一位农民结婚，以后一直住在农村。**Tā shí nián qián hé yí wèi nóngmín jiéhūn, yǐhòu yìzhí zhù zài nóngcūn.** = *She married a farmer ten years ago and has since lived in rural areas.*

nóngyè 农业 [modif: 农 *farming* + 业 *industry*] NOUN = agriculture

■农业十分重要。**Nóngyè shífēn zhòngyào.** = *Agriculture is of great importance.*
■我们必须努力发展农业。**Wǒmen bìxū nǔlì fāzhǎn nóngyè.** = *We must work hard to develop agriculture.*

nóng 浓 Trad 濃 ADJECTIVE = (of gas or liquid) thick, dense (antonym 淡 **dàn**)

■今天早上有浓雾。**Jīntiān zǎoshang yǒu nóng wù.** = *There was dense fog this morning.*
■我不喝浓咖啡，不要冲得太浓。**Wǒ bù hē nóng kāfēi, bú yào chōng de tài nóng.** = *I don't drink strong coffee. Don't make it too strong.*

nòng 弄 VERB = do, manage, get ... done

■我弄饭，你去买点儿酒。**Wǒ nòng fàn, nǐ qù mǎi diǎnr jiǔ.** = *I'll do the cooking, you go and buy some wine.*
■这么多事儿，我今天弄不完。**Zhème duō shìr, wǒ jīntiān nòng bu wán.** = *There're so many things to do, I can't finish them all today.*

nǔ 努 VERB = work hard

nǔlì 努力 [compound: 努 *physical effort* + 力 *strength*] ADJECTIVE = making great efforts

■她是个很努力的学生，考试一定能取得好成绩。**Tā shì ge hěn nǔlì de xuésheng, kǎoshì yídìng néng qǔdé hǎo chéngjì.** = *She's a hard-working student, and will definitely get good results in the examinations.*
■我们大家努力工作，为了更好的明天。**Wǒmen dàjiā nǔlì gōngzuò, wèile gèng hǎo de míngtiān.** = *We all work hard for a better tomorrow.*
■他中文学习得很努力。**Tā Zhōngwén xuéxí de hěn nǔlì.** = *He studies Chinese very hard.*

nǔ 女 ADJECTIVE = (of humans) female (antonym 男 **nán**)

■请问，女洗手间在哪里？**Qǐngwèn, nǔ xǐshǒujiān zài nǎlǐ?** = *Excuse me, where is the women's toilet?*
nǔ háizi 女孩子 = girl
nǔ qīngnián 女青年 = young woman
nǔshēng 女生 = female student

nǔ'ér 女儿 NOUN = daughter

■他们的三个孩子都是女儿，没有儿子。**Tāmen de sān ge háizi dōu shì nǔ'ér, méiyǒu érzi.** = *All their three children are daughters; they don't have a son.*

nǔrén 女人 [modif: 女 *female human* + 人 *person*] NOUN = woman, adult woman (antonym 男人 **nánrén**)

■这条街都是卖女人穿的衣服，所以叫"女人街"。**Zhè tiáo jiē dōu shì mài nǔrén chuān de yīfu, suǒyǐ jiào "nǔrén jiē".** = *The shops along this street all sell women's clothes, so it is known as "Women's Street."*

nǔshì 女士 [modif: 女 *female human* + 士 *gentleman, gentlewoman*] NOUN = (respectful form of address or reference to a woman) Madam, Ms, lady, a woman

■王女士是我们城市的教育局局长。**Wáng nǔshì shì wǒmen chéngshì de jiàoyùjú júzhǎng.** = *Madam Wang is director of our city's education bureau.*
■女士们，先生们，请允许我代表市政府热烈欢迎大家。**Nǔshìmen, xiānshengmen, qǐng yúnxǔ wǒ dàibiǎo shì zhèngfǔ rèliè huānyíng dàjiā.** = *Ladies and gentlemen, allow me to extend you a warm welcome on behalf of the city government.*

nuǎn 暖 ADJECTIVE = warm

■在中国，一到四月天就暖了。**Zài Zhōngguó, yídào Sìyuè tiān jiù nuǎn le.** = *In*

China the weather becomes warm when April comes.

nuǎnhuo 暖和 [compound: 暖 *warm* + 和 (in this context) *mild*] ADJECTIVE = pleasantly warm
■ 春天的太阳不太热，很暖和。**Chūntiān de tàiyáng bú tài rè, hěn nuǎnhuo.** = *The sunshine in spring is not hot; it's warm.*
■ 她的话说得我心里很暖和。**Tā de huà shuō de wǒ xīnli hěn nuǎnhuo.** = *What she said warmed my heart.*

O

ō 噢 INTERJECTION = (used to indicate understanding or a promise)
■ 噢，我明白了。**Ō, wǒ míngbai le.** = *Oh, I see.*
■ 噢，我忘不了。**Ō, wǒ wàng bu liǎo.** = *Yes, I won't forget it.*

ōu 欧 Trad 歐 NOUN = Europe

Ōuyuán 欧元 [modif: 欧 *Europe* + 元 *dollar*] NOUN = Euro
■ 一百欧元可以换多少美元？**Yìbǎi Ōuyuán kěyǐ huàn duōshǎo Měiyuán?** = *How many US dollars can a hundred Euros be exchanged for?*

Ōuzhōu 欧洲 [modif: 欧 *Europe* + 洲 *continent*] NOUN = Europe
■ 我有了钱，就去欧洲旅游。**Wǒ yǒule qián, jiù qù Ōuzhōu lǚyóu.** = *When I have the money, I'll go to Europe for a holiday.*

ǒ 哦 INTERJECTION = (used to indicate doubt)
■ 哦，他还会说日本话？**Ǒ, tá hái huì shuō Rìběn huà?** = *Well, he also speaks Japanese?*

P

pá 爬 VERB = crawl, climb
■ 他们的儿子才一岁，还不会走路，只会在地上爬。**Tāmen de érzi cái yī suì, hái bú huì zǒulù, zhǐ huì zài dì shang pá.** = *Their son is*

only a year old, he still can't walk and can only crawl on the floor.
páxíng dòngwù 爬行动物 = reptile

pà 怕
1 VERB = fear, be afraid
■ 一个人住这么大的房子，我有点儿怕。**Yí ge rén zhù zhème dà de fángzi, wǒ yǒu diǎnr pà.** = *I'm a bit afraid to live alone in such a big house.*
■ 我怕他没接到我的信，又打了电话。**Wǒ pà tā méi jiēdao wǒ de xìn, yòu dǎle diànhuà.** = *I was afraid he might not get my letter, so I rang him.*
2 ADVERB = same as 恐怕 **kǒngpà**, but with less force.

pāi 拍 VERB = pat, clap
■ 孩子们拍手欢迎新老师。**Háizimen pāishǒu huānyíng xīn lǎoshī.** = *The children gave the new teacher a big hand.*
pāimài 拍卖 = auction, sell at a reduced price
pāishǒu 拍手 = clap, applaud
pāizhào 拍照 = take photos

pái 排
1 VERB = arrange in a definite order
■ 旅客排成一行，等待登机前检查。**Lǚkè pái chéng yì háng, děngdài dēngjī qián jiǎnchá.** = *The travelers stood in a line for the preflight inspection.*
2 NOUN = row, rank
■ "你的票是几排几座？" "七排四座。" **"Nǐ de piào shì jǐ pái jǐ zuò?" "Qī pái sì zuò."** = *"What is the seat and row in your ticket?" "Row 7, Seat 4."*
■ 我要坐在前排，后排听不请。**Wǒ yào zuòzài qián pái, hòu pái, tīng bu qǐng.** = *I want to sit in a front row. I can't hear clearly in the back seats.*
3 MEASURE WORD = (for things arranged in a row)
■ 一排椅子 **yì pái yǐzi** = *a row of chairs*
■ 两排战士 **liǎng pái zhànshì** = *two rows of soldiers*

páiqiú 排球 [modif: 排 *row* + 球 *ball*] NOUN = volleyball (只 **zhī**)
■ 夏天我们常常在海边打排球。**Xiàtiān wǒmen chángcháng zài hǎibiān dǎ páiqiú.** = *In summer we often play volleyball at the seaside.*

pái 牌 1 NOUN = playing cards (张 **zhāng**, 副 **fù**)
- 他在火车上和别的旅客一起打牌。**Tā zài huǒchē shang hé biéde lǚkè yìqǐ dǎpái.** = *He played cards with fellow passengers on the train.*
- 我不会打这种牌。**Wǒ bú huì dǎ zhè zhǒng pái.** = *I don't know how to play this card game.*

dǎpái 打牌 = play cards
fāpái 发牌 = deal cards
xǐpái 洗牌 = shuffle cards

NOTE: 扑克牌 **pūkèpái** is a more common word for *playing cards* (noun).

pái 牌 2 NOUN = brand name, brand
- 你买的汽车是什么牌的? **Nǐ mǎi de qìchē shì shénme pái de?** = *What brand of car did you buy?*

míngpái 名牌 = famous brand, name brand

páizi 牌子 [suffix: 牌 *signboard* + 子 *nominal suffix*] NOUN
1 = signboard (块 **kuài**)
- 他在门口放了一块牌子, "减价出售"。**Tā zài ménkǒu fàngle yí kuài páizi, "jiǎnjià chūshòu".** = *He put up a signboard at the gate: "Discount sale."*
2 = same as 牌 **pái** 2
- 这种牌子的衣服特别贵。**Zhè zhǒng páizi de yīfu tèbié guì.** = *Clothes of this brand name are extremely expensive.*

pài 派
1 VERB = dispatch
- 公司派我到上海开发市场。**Gōngsī pài wǒ dào Shànghǎi kāifā shìchǎng.** = *The company sent him to Shanghai to develop the market.*
2 VERB = assign (a job)
- 校长派我教三年级。**Xiàozhǎng pài wǒ jiāo sān-nián jí.** = *The principal assigned me to teach third grade.*
3 NOUN = faction, school (of thought)
- 在这个问题上有很多派。**Zài zhège wèntí shang yǒu hěn duō pài.** = *There are many schools of thought on this issue.*

pán 盘 Trad 盤 NOUN = dish, plate

pánzi 盘子 [suffix: 盘 *plate, dish* + 子 *nominal suffix*] NOUN = plate, dish, tray (只 **zhī**)
- 她在饭店里端盘子。**Tā zài fàndiàn li duān**

pánzi. = *She carries plates in a restaurant.* (→ *She is a waitress in a restaurant.*)

pàn 判 VERB = judge

pànduàn 判断 [compound: 判 *judge* + 断 *reach a verdict*]
1 VERB = judge, decide
- 他说的话是真是假, 你怎么判断? **Tā shuō de huà shì zhēn shì jiǎ, nǐ zěnme pànduàn?** = *How do you judge whether his statement is true or false?*
- 他判断是非的能力很强。**Tā pànduàn shì-fēi de nénglì hěn qiáng.** = *He is very good at telling right from wrong.*
2 NOUN = judgment, verdict
- 我的判断是这批货都是假的。**Wǒ de pànduàn shì zhè pī huò dōu shì jiǎ de.** = *My judgment is that this batch of goods is counterfeit.*

pàn 盼 VERB = expect

pànwàng 盼望 [compound: 盼 *expect* + 望 *look forward to*] VERB = look forward to, long for
- 母亲盼望孩子们都回家过春节。**Mǔqin pànwàng háizimen dōu huíjiā guò chūnjié.** = *The mother longed for the homecoming of all her children for Chinese New Year.*
- 我盼望不久就和你见面。**Wǒ pànwàng bùjiǔ jiù hé nǐ jiànmiàn.** = *I look forward to meeting you soon.*

páng 旁 NOUN = side
- 路旁都摆着各种各样的小摊子。**Lùpáng dōu bǎizhe gè-zhǒng-gè-yàng de xiǎo tānzi.** = *By the roadside are all kinds of stalls.*

pángguān 旁观 = look on
Pángguānzhě qīng 旁观者清 = The onlooker sees most of the game.

pángbiān 旁边 [modif: 旁 *aside* + 边 *side*] NOUN = side
- 王先生旁边那位先生是谁? **Wáng xiānsheng pángbiān nà wèi xiānsheng shì shéi?** = *Who is the man beside Mr Wang?*
- 小河旁边有一个农场。**Xiǎo hé pángbiān yǒu yí ge nóngchǎng.** = *There's a farm by the small river.*

pàng 胖 ADJECTIVE = fat, plump
- 现在胖的人越来越多了。**Xiànzài pàng de rén yuèlaiyuè duō le.** = *There are more and more fat people now.*

pàngzi 胖子 = fat person, "fatty"

pǎo 跑 VERB = run
- 我们比一比，看谁跑得快。**Wǒmen bǐ yi bǐ, kàn shéi pǎo de kuài.** = *Let's compete and see who runs faster.*

pǎodào 跑道 = runway, track (in a sports ground)

pǎobù 跑步 [modif: 跑 *run* + 步 *steps*] VERB = jog
- 每天早上很多人在公园里跑步。**Měi tiān zǎoshang hěn duō rén zài gōngyuán li pǎobù.** = *Many people jog in the park early every morning.*

pào 炮 NOUN = cannon, gun (门 mén, 座 zuò)
- 山顶上放着一门古炮。**Shāndǐng shang fàngzhe yì mén gǔ pào.** = *On top of the hill stands an old cannon.*

pàobīng 炮兵 = artillery man

péi 陪 VERB = accompany
- 他妻子上街买衣服，他陪她去。**Tā qīzi shàngjiē mǎi yīfu, tā péi tā qù.** = *His wife went out to buy clothes, and he went with her.*
- 我今天没有空陪你去看电影。**Wǒ jīntiān méiyǒu kòng péi nǐ qù kàn diànyǐng.** = *I don't have time to go to the movies with you.*

péi 赔 Trad 賠 VERB = compensate, pay for (damage, loss, etc.)
- 你借给我的书，我丢了。我赔你吧。**Nǐ jiè gei wǒ de shū, wǒ diū le. Wǒ péi nǐ ba.** = *I've lost the book you lent me. Let me pay for it.*

pèi 佩 VERB = wear

pèifu 佩服 VERB = admire
- 我佩服自学成才的人。**Wǒ pèifu zì-xué-chéng-cái de rén.** = *I admire those who become a success from being self-taught.*

NOTE: You can utter 佩服 **Pèifu** or 佩服! 佩服! **Pèifu! Pèifu!** to express great admiration for a feat or a remarkable achievement, for example:

- "你五门功课都是一百分？佩服！佩服！" **"Nǐ wǔ mén gōngkè dōu shì yībǎi fēn? Pèifu! Pèifu!"** = *"You got full marks for all the five subjects? Wow!"*

pèi 配 VERB = match

pèihé 配合 [compound: 配 *match* + 合 *cooperate*] VERB = cooperate, coordinate
- 各个部门都要相互配合。**Gè ge bùmén dōu yào xiānghù pèihé.** = *All the departments should cooperate with each other.*
- 病人要和医生密切配合，才能早日恢复健康。**Bìngrén yào hé yīshēng mìqiè pèihé, cáinéng zǎorì huīfù jiànkāng.** = *A patient should cooperate closely with his doctor so as to achieve a speedy recovery.*

pēn 喷 Trad 噴 VERB = sprinkle, spray
- 这棵树上有虫子，要喷点儿药。**Zhè kē shù shang yǒu chóngzi, yào pēn diǎnr yào.** = *This tree has insects on it and needs spraying.*

pén 盆 NOUN = basin, pot (个 ge)
péndì 盆地 = basin (geographical)
huāpén 花盆 = flower pot
xǐliǎnpén 洗脸盆 = washbasin

péng 朋 NOUN = companion

péngyou 朋友 [compound: 朋 *companion* + 友 *friend*] NOUN = friend
- 朋友之间应该互相帮助。**Péngyou zhī jiān yīnggāi hùxiāng bāngzhù.** = *Friends should help one another.*
- 他有很多朋友。**Tā yǒu hěn duō péngyou.** = *He has many friends.*

gēn/hé … jiāo péngyou 跟 / 和 … 交朋友 = make friends with …
- 他在中学的时候交了不少朋友。**Tā zài zhōngxué de shíhou jiāole bù shǎo péngyou.** = *He made quite a few friends in high school.*

nánpéngyou 男朋友 = boyfriend
nǚpéngyou 女朋友 = girlfriend

pěng 捧 VERB
1 = hold in both hands (with care, pride, etc.)
- 他捧着一盆花回家。**Tā pěngzhe yì péng huā huíjiā.** = *He came home with a pot of flowers in his hands.*

P

2 = sing somebody's praise (especially insincerely), flatter
■ 你别捧我，我知道自己有几斤几两。**Nǐ bié pěng wǒ, wǒ zhīdào zìjǐ yǒu jǐ jīn jǐ liǎng.** = *Don't flatter me. I know my worth.*

pèng 碰 VERB = bump into, touch
■ 别碰我，我手里拿着水呢! **Bié pèng wǒ, wǒ shǒu li názhe shuǐ ne!** = *Don't bump into me. I'm carrying water.*
pèngdao 碰到 = meet unexpectedly, run into
■ 我昨天在城里碰到一个老同学。**Wǒ zuótiān zài chénglǐ pèngdao yí ge lǎo tóngxué.** = *I ran into an old classmate in town yesterday.*

pī 批 MEASURE WORD = (for a batch of goods, and for things/people arriving at the same time)
■ 一批新书 **yì pī xīn shū** = *a batch of new books (published at about the same time)*
■ 两批旅游者 **liǎng pī lǚyóuzhě** = *two groups of tourists*

pīpíng 批评 [compound: 批 criticism + 评 comment]
1 VERB = criticize, scold (antonym 表扬 **biǎoyáng**)
■ 老师批评他常常迟到。**Lǎoshī pīpíng tā chángcháng chídào.** = *The teacher criticized him for being often late for class.*
2 NOUN = criticism
■ 你对他的批评很正确。**Nǐ duì tā de pīpíng hěn zhèngquè.** = *Your criticism of him is correct.*
■ 我接受你对我的批评。**Wǒ jiēshòu nǐ duì wǒ de pīpíng.** = *I accept your criticism.*

pīzhǔn 批准 [compound: 批 express opinion + 准 approve, permit] VERB = approve, ratify
■ 你的申请已经批准了。**Nǐ de shēnqǐng yǐjīng pīzhǔn le.** = *Your application has been approved.*

pī 披 VERB = drape over the shoulder
■ 他披着大衣，看孩子在雪地里玩。**Tā pīzhe dàyī, kàn háizi zài xuědì li wán.** = *With an overcoat draped over his shoulders, he watched the children play in the snow.*

pí 皮 NOUN = skin, leather
■ 她从自行车上摔下来，擦破了点皮。**Tā cóng zìxíngchē shang shuāi xiàlai, cāpóle diǎn**

pí. = *She fell off the bike and scraped her skin.*
píyī 皮衣 = fur coat

pífū 皮肤 [compound: 皮 skin + 肤 skin] NOUN = skin (human)
■ 她的皮肤又白又嫩。**Tā de pífū yòu bái yòu nèn.** = *Her skin is fair and tender.*
■ 在海边住了一个夏天，他的皮肤晒黑了。**Zài hǎibiān zhùle yí ge xiàtiān, tā de pífū shài hēi le.** = *After a summer by the sea, he was tanned.*

pí 疲 ADJECTIVE = fatigued

píláo 疲劳 ADJECTIVE = fatigued, tired
■ 我连续工作了六小时，实在疲劳。**Wǒ liánxù gōngzuòle liù xiǎoshí, shízài píláo.** = *I have been working nonstop for six hours. I am indeed tired.*

pí 啤 NOUN = beer

píjiǔ 啤酒 NOUN = beer (瓶 **píng**, 杯 **bēi**)
■ 这种啤酒很好喝。**Zhè zhǒng píjiǔ hěn hǎohē.** = *This beer tastes good.*
■ 爸爸每星期五买很多啤酒。**Bàba měi Xīngqīwǔ mǎi hěn duō píjiǔ.** = *Daddy buys lots of beer every Friday.*

NOTE: 啤酒 **píjiǔ** is an example of semi-transliteration: 啤 **pí** represents the sound of English word "beer" and 酒 **jiǔ** means *alcoholic drink*.

pí 脾 NOUN = spleen

píqi 脾气 NOUN = temper
■ 王医生脾气好，很少生气。**Wáng yīshēng píqi hǎo, hěn shǎo shēngqì.** = *Dr Wang is good-tempered; he rarely gets angry.*
fā píqi 发脾气 = throw a tantrum, lose one's temper
■ 他为什么发脾气? **Tā wèishénme fā píqi?** = *Why did he lose his temper?*
píqi huài 脾气坏 = have an irritable temper

pǐ 匹 MEASURE WORD = (for horses)
■ 一匹快马 **yì pǐ kuài mǎ** = *a fast horse*

pì 辟 Trad 闢 VERB = open up (See 开辟 **kāipì**.)

piān 偏 ADVERB = must (used to indicate that the action in question is contrary to one's expectation or wishes)
- 大家都要睡觉了，他偏把收音机开得很响。**Dàjiā dōu yào shuìjiào le, tā piān bǎ shōuyīnjī kāide hěn xiǎng.** = *When everybody else wanted to sleep, he must turn up the radio.*
- 明天有一个重要的考试，她偏今天病倒了。**Míngtiān yǒu yí ge zhòngyào de kǎoshì, tā piān jīntiān bìngdǎo le.** = *Just as there'll be an important exam tomorrow, what must she do but fall ill today?*
- 我正在洗澡，电话铃偏响了。**Wǒ zhèngzài xǐzǎo, diànhuàlíng piān xiǎng le.** = *The telephone must ring when I was taking a bath.*

NOTE: You can use 偏偏 **piānpian** instead of 偏 **piān**.

piān 篇 MEASURE WORD = (for a piece of writing)
- 一篇文章 **yì piān wénzhāng** = *an article/essay*

pián 便 ADJECTIVE = comfortable

piányi 便宜 ADJECTIVE = inexpensive, cheap (antonym 贵 **guì**)
- 这家商店东西很便宜。**Zhè jiā shāngdiàn dōngxi hěn piányi.** = *Things are cheap in this store.*
- 我想买便宜一点儿的衣服。**Wǒ xiǎng mǎi piányi yìdiǎnr de yīfu.** = *I want to buy less expensive clothes.*
piányi huò 便宜货 = cheap goods

piàn 片
1 NOUN = thin and flat piece
- 王太太做的肉片特别好吃。**Wáng tàitai zuò de ròupiàn tèbié hǎochī.** = *The meat slices cooked by Mrs Wang are particularly delicious.*
2 MEASURE WORD = (for thin, flat pieces)
- 一片面包 **yí piàn miànbāo** = *a slice of bread*

piànmiàn 片面 ADJECTIVE = one-sided, unilateral (antonym 全面 **quánmiàn**)
- 我们应该全面考虑问题，不要有片面的观点。**Wǒmen yīnggāi quánmiàn de kǎolǜ wèntí, bú yào yǒu piànmiàn de guāndiǎn.** = *We should approach an issue from all sides and do not have a one-sided view.*

piàn 骗 Trad 騙 VERB = deceive, fool
- 你受骗了！ **Nǐ shòu piàn le!** = *You've been duped!*
- 那个人骗我钱。 **= Nàge rén piàn wǒ qiǎn.** = *That man cheated me out of my money.*
piànzi 骗子 = swindler, con-man
piànjú 骗局 = hoax, fraud

piāo 飘 Trad 飄 VERB = flutter
- 彩旗飘飘。**Cǎiqí piāopiāo.** = *Colorful banners fluttered in the breeze.*

piào 票 NOUN = ticket (张 **zhāng**)
- 这场电影票全卖完了。**Zhè chǎng diànyǐng piào quán màiwán le.** = *Tickets are all sold out for this movie show.*
- 我买两张去香港的飞机票。**Wǒ mǎi liǎng zhāng qù Xiānggǎng de fēijī piào.** = *I want to buy two air tickets to Hong Kong.*
diànyǐng piào 电影票 = movie ticket
fēijī piào 飞机票 = air ticket
huǒchē piào 火车票 = train ticket
ménpiào 门票 = admission ticket (to a show, sporting event, etc.)
qìchē piào 汽车票 = bus/coach ticket

piào 漂 ADJECTIVE = pretty

piàoliang 漂亮 [idiom] ADJECTIVE = pretty, good-looking
- 这个小女孩真漂亮！ **Zhège xiǎo nǚhái zhēn piàoliang!** = *This little girl is really pretty. (→ What a pretty little girl!)*
- 她又买了好几件漂亮衣服。**Tā yòu mǎile hǎo jǐ jiàn piàoliang yīfu.** = *She bought some pretty clothes again.*
- 你的汉字写得真漂亮。**Nǐ de hànzi xiě de zhēn piàoliang.** = *Your Chinese characters are beautifully written.*

pīn 拼 VERB = fight bitterly

pīnmìng 拼命 [v+obj: 拼 *fight bitterly* + 命 *one's life*] VERB = do all one can, risk one's life
- 他拼命赚钱，都是为了什么呢？ **Tā pīnmìng zhuànqián, dōushì wèile shénme ne?** = *He does everything possible to earn money, but for what purpose?*

pǐn 品 NOUN = article

pǐnzhǒng 品种 [compound: 品 *article* + 种 *kind*] NOUN = variety, breed
■ 超级市场里的水果品种多得不得了，简直让人眼睛都看花了。**Chāojíshìchǎng li de shuǐguǒ pǐnzhǒng duō de bùdeliǎo, jiǎnzhí rang rén yǎnjing dōu kànhuā le.** = *There is a huge variety of fruits in the supermarket. It is simply dazzling.*

pīngpāngqiú 乒乓球 NOUN = table tennis, table tennis ball (只 **zhī**)
■ 很多中国人乒乓球打得很好。**Hěn duō Zhōngguórén pīngpāngqiú dǎ de hěn hǎo.** = *Many Chinese are good at table tennis.*

píng 平 ADJECTIVE = flat, level, smooth
■ 这张桌面不平。**Zhè zhāng zhuōmiàn bù píng.** = *This table surface is not level.*

píng'ān 平安 [compound: 平 *peace* + 安 *peace*] ADJECTIVE = safe and sound
■ 祝你一路平安！ **Zhù nǐ yílù píng'ān!** = *I wish you a safe journey! (→ Bon voyage!)*
■ 高高兴兴上班，平平安安回家。**Gāo-gāo-xìng-xìng shàngbān, píng-píng-ān-ān huíjiā .** = *Come to work in high spirits and return home safe and sound. (A Chinese slogan urging workers to observe occupational safety.)*

píngcháng 平常 [compound: 平 *flat* + 常 *usual*]
1 ADJECTIVE = ordinary, common
■ 这位世界冠军的父母都是平平常常的人。**Zhè wèi shìjiè guànjūn de fùmǔ dōushì píng-píng-cháng-cháng de rén.** = *The parents of this world champion are just ordinary people.*
■ 那是我一生中最不平常的一天。**Nà shì wǒ yìshéng zhong zuì bù píngcháng de yì tiān.** = *That was the most unusual day of my life.*
2 NOUN = ordinary time, usually, normally
■ 我平常不喝酒，只有节日的时候喝一点儿。**Wǒ píngcháng bù hē jiǔ, zhǐyǒu jiérì de shíhou hē yìdiǎnr.** *I normally don't drink. I only drink a little on festive occasions.*

píngděng 平等 [modif: 平 *flat* + 等 *grade*]
1 ADJECTIVE = equal (in status)
■ 法律面前人人平等。**Fǎlù miànqián rénren píngděng.** = *Everyone is equal in the eyes of the law.*
■ 尽管他是董事长，也应该平等待人。**Jǐnguǎn tā shì dǒngshìzhǎng, yě yīnggāi píngděng dàirén.** = *Even though he is chairman of the board, he should treat people as equals.*
■ 社会上还有很多不平等现象。**Shèhuì shang háiyǒu hěn duō bù píngděng xiàndàng.** = *There are still many cases of inequality in society.*
2 NOUN = equality
■ 夫妻之间的平等是现代婚姻的基础。**Fūqī zhījiān de píngděng shì xiàndài hūnyīn de jīchǔ.** = *Equality between husband and wife is the foundation of modern marriage.*

píngfāng 平方 NOUN = square (mathematics)
■ 三平方公尺 **sān píngfāng gōngchǐ** = *3 square meters*

píngjìng 平静 [compound: 平 *peace* + 静 *quiet*] ADJECTIVE = calm, quiet, uneventful
■ 没有一点风，大海十分平静。**Méiyǒu yìdiǎn fēn, dàhǎi shífēn píngjìng.** = *It is windless. The sea is perfectly calm.*
■ 老人平静的生活被这个消息打乱了。**Lǎorén píngjìng de shēnghuó bèi zhège xiāoxi dàluàn le.** = *The old man's peaceful life was shattered by this news.*

píngjūn 平均 ADJECTIVE = average
■ 这个城市的人平均收入是一年一万元。**Zhège chéngshì de rén píngjūn shōurù shì yì nián yíwàn yuán.** = *The average per capita income of this city is 10,000 yuan a year.*

píngshí 平时 [compound: 平 *ordinary* + 时 *time*] NOUN = ordinary time
■ 我平时六点半起床，周末八点多才起床。**Wǒ píngshì liù diǎnbàn qǐchuáng, zhōumò bā diǎn duō cái qǐchuáng.** = *I usually get up at half past six, but on weekends I get up after eight o'clock.*

píngyuán 平原 NOUN = flatland, plain
■ 中国东北地区是一个大平原。**Zhōngguó dōngběi dìqū shì yí ge dà píngyuán.** = *The northeast region of China is a huge plain.*

píng 评 Trad 評 VERB = comment (See 批评 **pīpíng**.)

píng 苹 Trad 蘋 NOUN = apple

píngguǒ 苹果 [modif: 苹 *apple* + 果 *fruit*]
NOUN = apple (个 **ge**)
■ 这种苹果多少钱一公斤? **Zhè zhǒng píngguǒ duōshǎo qián yì gōngjīn?** = *How much is a kilo of these apples?*
■ 这苹果太酸，我不爱吃。**Zhè píngguǒ tài suān, wǒ bú ài chī.** = *This apple is too sour. I don't like it.*
píngguǒ yuán 苹果园 = apple orchard

píng 瓶
1 NOUN = bottle (个 **ge**)
■ 给我一个空瓶子。**Gěi wǒ yí ge kōng píngzi.** = *Give me an empty bottle.*
píngzi 瓶子 = bottle
2 MEASURE WORD = a bottle of
■ 一瓶啤酒 **yì píng píjiǔ** = *a bottle of beer*
■ 两瓶可口可乐 **liǎng píng kěkǒukělè** = *two bottles of Coca-Cola.*

pō 坡 NOUN = slope
■ 骑自行车上坡很累。**Qí zìxíngchē shàng pō hěn lèi.** = *Cycling up a slope is very tiring.*

pō 泼 Trad 潑 VERB = sprinkle (See 活泼 **huópo**.)

pò 迫 VERB = compel

pòqiè 迫切 ADJECTIVE = urgent, pressing
■ 我们的迫切任务是了解商场情况。**Wǒmen de pòqiè rènwù shì liǎojiě shìchǎng qíngkuàng.** = *Our urgent task is to understand the market situation.*

pò 破
1 VERB = break, damage
■ 你的衣服破了。**Nǐ de yīfu pò le.** = *Your clothes are torn.*
2 ADJECTIVE = torn, damaged
■ 这件破衣服不能穿了。**Zhè jiàn pò yīfu bù néng chuān le.** = *This torn coat is no longer wearable.*
■ 花瓶打破了。**Huāpíng dǎpò le.** = *The vase is broken.*

pòhuài 破坏 [v+obj: 破 *break* + 坏 *bad*] VERB = sabotage, damage
■ 不准破坏公共财物。**Bù zhǔn pòhuài gōnggòng cáiwù.** = *Vandalism of public property is not allowed.*

pū 铺 Trad 鋪 VERB = spread, unfold
■ 桌子上铺这一块漂亮的桌布。**Zhuōzi shang pūzhe yí kuài piàoliang de zhuōbù.** = *A beautiful tablecloth was spread over the table.*

pútao 葡萄 NOUN = grape (颗 **kē**)
■ 这里的葡萄又大又甜。**Zhèli de pútao yòu dà yòu tián.** = *The grapes here are big and sweet.*
pútaojiǔ 葡萄酒 = grape wine
pútaoyuán 葡萄园 = vineyard

pǔ 朴 Trad 樸 ADJECTIVE = plain

pǔsù 朴素 ADJECTIVE = simple and plain
■ 她喜欢穿朴素的衣服。**Tā xǐhuan chuān pǔsù de yīfu.** = *She likes to dress simply.*

pǔ 普 ADJECTIVE = common

pǔbiàn 普遍 [compound: 普 *common* + 遍 *everywhere*] ADJECTIVE = widespread, commonplace
■ 在那个地方，少女母亲的现象很普遍。**Zài nàge dìfang, shàonǚ mǔqin de xiànxiàng hěn pǔbiàn.** = *In that area, teenage mothers are quite commonplace.*
■ 人们普遍认为这种做法是不对的。**Rénmen pǔbiàn rènwéi zhè zhǒng zuòfǎ shì bú duì de.** = *People generally think this kind of behavior is wrong.*

pǔjí 普及 VERB = popularize, make commonplace
■ 在这个地区电脑已经普及了，几乎每个家庭都有一台电脑。**Zài zhège dìqū diànnǎo yǐjīng pǔjí le, jīhū měi ge jiātíng dōu yǒu yì tái diànnǎo.** = *In this region computers have become commonplace; almost every household has one.*

pǔtōng 普通 ADJECTIVE = common, commonplace, ordinary
■ 在这个城市里一座普通的房子要多少钱? **Zài zhège chéngshìli yízuò pǔtōng de fángzi yào duōshǎo qián?** = *How much is an ordinary house in this city?*

Pǔtōnghuà 普通话 [modif: 普通 *common* + 话 *speech*] NOUN = Standard Modern Chinese, Mandarin, Putonghua

■ 大多数中国人都听得懂普通话。**Dàduōshù Zhōngguórén dōu tīng de dǒng Pǔtōnghuà.** = *Most Chinese people understand Putonghua.*
■ 你说普通话不太标准，也不要紧。**Nǐ shuō Pǔtōnghuà bú tài biāozhǔn, yě bú yàojǐn.** = *It doesn't matter if you don't speak perfect Putonghua.*

NOTE: Modern Standard Chinese is known as 普通话 **Pǔtōnghuà** in China, 国语 **Guóyǔ** in Taiwan and 华语 **Huáyǔ** in Singapore and other Southeast Asian countries. They refer to the same language, though slight differences do exist among them.

Q

qī 七 NUMERAL = seven
■ 七个小矮人 **qī ge xiǎo ǎirén** = *the seven dwarves*
■ 七百七十七 **qībǎi qīshíqī** = *seven hundred and seventy-seven*

qī 妻 NOUN = wife

qīzi 妻子 [suffix: 妻 *wife* + 子 nominal suffix] NOUN = wife
■ 丈夫和妻子应当互相爱护，互相尊重。**Zhàngfu hé qīzi yīngdāng hùxiāng àihu, hùxiāng zūnzhòng.** = *Husband and wife should care for and respect each other.*
■ 他对他妻子好吗？**Tā duì tā qīzi hǎo ma?** = *Is he nice to his wife?*

qī 期 NOUN = fixed time
àn qī 按期 = according to the schedule, on time
■ 贵公司订购的货物我们一定按期送到。**Guìgōngsī dìnggòu de huòwù wǒmen yídìng àn qī sòngdào.** = *We will certainly deliver on time the goods your company ordered.*
dàoqī 到期 = expire, due
guòqī 过期 = overdue, expired

qījiān 期间 NOUN = during the period of
■ 春节期间饭店的生意特别好。= **Chūnjié qījiān fàndiàn de shēngyi tèbié hǎo.** = *During the Chinese New Year holidays, restaurants have particularly good business.*

qīpiàn 欺骗 [compound: 欺 *cheat* + 骗 *deceive*] VERB = deceive
■ 这件事我完全了解，他无法欺骗我。**Zhè jiàn shì wǒ wánquán liǎojiě, tā wúfǎ qīpiàn wǒ.** = *I know this matter full well. There is no way he can deceive me.*

qí 齐 Trad 齊
1 ADJECTIVE = neat, in a straight line
■ 书架上的书放得很齐。**Shūjià shang de shū fàng de hěn qí.** = *The books in the bookshelf are neatly arranged.*
2 VERB = reaching to the same height
■ 树长得齐屋顶了。**Shù zhǎng de qí wūdǐng le.** = *The trees have grown as tall as the roof.*

qí 其 PRONOUN = this, that

qícì 其次 ADVERB = next, secondary, secondly
■ 他们离婚的原因首先是性格不合，其次是经济上有矛盾。**Tāmen líhūn de yuányīn shǒuxiān shì xìnggé bù hé, qícì shì jīngjì shang yǒu máodùn.** = *The first reason they gave for divorcing was incompatibility of disposition and the second reason was financial conflict.*

qítā 其他 PRONOUN = other
■ 我只要买一台笔记本电脑，其它的什么都不要。**Wǒ zhǐyào mǎi yì tái bǐjìběn diànnǎo, qítā de shénme dōu bú yào.** = *I only want to buy a notebook computer. I don't want anything else.*

qíyú 其余 PRONOUN = the rest, the remainder
■ 我付了学费以后把其余的钱存进了银行。**Wǒ fùle xuéfèi yǐhòu bǎ qíyú de qián cúnjìnle yínháng.** = *After paying the tuition fee, I deposited the remainder of the money in the bank.*

qízhōng 其中 NOUN = among them, in it
■ 北京有很多名胜古迹，故宫是其中之一。**Běijīng yǒu hěn duō míngshèng gǔjì, gùgōng shì qízhōng zhī yī.** = *There are many scenic spots and historical sites in Beijing. The Palace Museum is one of them.*

qí 奇 ADJECTIVE = strange

qíguài 奇怪 [compound: 奇 *strange* + 怪 *unusual*] ADJECTIVE = strange, unusual, odd
■ 他一年到头戴着一顶黄帽子，真奇怪。**Tā**

yì-nián-dào-tóu dàizhe yì dǐng huáng màozi, zhēn qíguài. = *It is really odd that he wears a yellow cap all year long.*
■ 对这种奇怪的现象，我不能解释。**Duì zhè zhǒng qíguài de xiànxiàng, wǒ bù néng jiěshì.** = *I cannot explain this strange phenomenon.*

qí 旗 NOUN = flag, banner

qízi 旗子 [suffix: 旗 *flag, banner* + 子 nominal suffix] NOUN = flag, banner (面 **miàn**)
■ 国旗是代表国家的旗子。**Guóqí shì dàibiǎo guójiā de qízi.** = *A national flag is one that symbolizes the country.*

qí 骑 Trad 騎 VERB = ride (a horse, bicycle etc.)
qí zìxíngchē 骑自行车 = ride a bicycle
■ 我每天骑自行车去上学。**Wǒ měi tiān qí zìxíngchē qù shàngxué.** = *I go to school by bike every day.*
qí mǎ 骑马 = ride a horse

qǐ 企 VERB = hope

qǐtú 企图
1 VERB = attempt, try
■ 恐怖分子企图破坏铁路和公路，制造大规模交通事故。**Kǒngbùfènzǐ qǐtú pòhuài tiělù hé gōnglù, zhìzào dà guīmó jiāotōng shìgù.** = *Terrorists attempted to sabotage railways and highways to cause large-scale traffic accidents.*
2 NOUN = attempt
■ 他们的企图失败了。**Tāmen de qǐtú shībài le.** = *Their attempt failed.*

NOTE: 企图 **qǐtú** is usually used for negative situations. For example, we usually do not say 他企图帮助我。**Tā qǐtú bāngzhù wǒ.** = *He tried to help me.* but 他企图欺骗我。**Tā qǐtú qīpiàn wǒ.** = *He tried to deceive me.*

qǐyè 企业 NOUN = enterprise (家 **jiā**)
■ 管理一个大型企业是极其复杂的。**Guǎnlǐ yí ge dàxíng qǐyè shì jíqí fùzá de.** = *To manage a large enterprise is an extremely complex undertaking.*
qǐyèjiā 企业家 = entrepreneur
guóyǒu qǐyè 国有企业 = state-owned enterprise
sīyǒu qǐyè 私有企业 = private enterprise

qǐ 启 Trad 啓 VERB = open

qǐfā 启发 [compound: 启 *open* + 发 *release*]
1 VERB = enlighten, arouse
■ 科学家常常从平常的自然现象得到启发。**Kēxuéjiā chángcháng cóng píngcháng de zìrán xiànxiàng dédào qǐfā.** = *Scientists are often enlightened by commonplace natural phenomena.*
2 NOUN = enlightenment, inspiration
■ 我们应该启发孩子的学习兴趣。**Wǒmen yīnggāi qǐfā háizi de xuéxí xìngqù.** = *We should arouse an interest to learn in children.*

qǐ 起 VERB = rise, get up
■ 快十点钟了，他还没起呢! **Kuài shí diǎnzhōng le, tā hái méi qǐ ne!** = *It's almost ten o'clock and he still isn't up!*
cóng ... qǐ 从 ... 起 = starting from...
■ 从晚上七点起，网吧就特别忙。**Cóng wǎnshang qī diǎn qǐ, wǎngbā jiù tèbié máng.** = *Starting from seven o'clock in the evening, the Internet cafe is particularly busy.*

NOTE: 起 **qǐ** is seldom used alone. To express *to get up*, 起床 **qǐchuáng** is more common than 起 **qǐ**. One can very well say 快十点钟了，他还没起床呢! **Kuài shí diǎnzhōng le, tā hái méi qǐ chuáng ne!** = *It's almost ten o'clock and he still isn't up!*

qǐchuáng 起床 VERB = get up (out of bed)
■ "你每天几点起床?""平时七点，周末就晚一点。" **"Nǐ měi tiān jǐ diǎn qǐchuáng?" "Píngshí qī diǎn, zhōumò jiù wǎn yì diǎn."** = *"When do you get up everyday?" "Seven o'clock usually, but a bit later on weekends."*

qǐlai 起来 VERB = get up (out of bed), stand up
■ 校长走进教室，大家都站起来。**Xiàozhǎng zǒujin jiàoshì, dàjiā dōu zhàn qǐlai.** = *When the principal entered the classroom, everybody stood up.*

NOTE: 起来 **qǐlai** is often used after a verb as a complement to express various meanings. Among other meanings, 起来 **qǐlai** may be used after a verb to mean *begin to ...*, e.g.
■ 我们不等爸爸了，吃起来吧。**Wǒmen bù děng bàba le, chī qǐlai ba.** = *We're not going to wait for daddy any longer. Let's start eating.*

qì 气 Trad 氣 VERB = be angry, make angry
■ 知道他一直在骗我，我气极了。**Zhīdào tā yìzhí zai piàn wǒ, wǒ qì jíle.** = *When I found*

Q

that he had been deceiving me all the time, I was very angry.
■ 你干吗说这种话气她？ **Nǐ gànmá shuō zhè zhǒng huà qì tā?** = *Why on earth did you say that and make her angry?*

qìhòu 气候 NOUN = climate
■ 地球上的气候在渐渐变暖。**Dìqiú shang de qìhòu zài jiànjiàn biàn nuǎn.** = *The climate on earth is gradually becoming warmer.*

qìwēn 气温 [modif: 气 *atmosphere* + 温 *temperature*] NOUN = atmospheric, temperature
■ 受寒流影响，今天夜里气温要下降十度左右。**Shòu hánliú yíngxiǎng, jīntiān yèlǐ qìwēn yào xiàjiàng shí dù zuǒyòu.** = *Owing to a cold current, the temperature will fall by about 10 degrees tonight.*
■ 今天最高气温十五度，最低气温八度。**Jīntiān zuì gāo qìwēn shíwǔ dù, zuì dī qìwēn bā dù.** = *Today's maximum temperature is 15 degrees, and the minimum is 8 degrees.*

qìxiàng 气象 NOUN = meteorological phenomena, weather
qìxiàng yùbào 气象预报 = weather forecast
■ 你听今天的气象预报了吗？ **Nǐ tīng jīntiān de qìxiàng yùbào le ma?** = *Have you heard today's weather forecast?*
qìxiàngtái 气象台 = meteorological observatory
qìxiàngxué 气象学 = meteorology

qì 汽 NOUN = vapor, steam

qìchē 汽车 [modif: 汽 *vapor* + 车 *vehicle*] NOUN = automobile, car (辆 **liàng**)
■ 我的汽车坏了。**Wǒde qìchē huài le.** = *My car has broken down.*
kāi qìchē 开汽车 = drive a car
■ 你会开汽车吗？ **Nǐ huì kāi qìchē ma?** = *Can you drive a car?*

NOTE: In everyday Chinese, 车 **chē** is often used instead of 汽车 **qìchē** to refer to a car, e.g.
■ 我可以把车停在这里吗？ **Wǒ kěyǐ ba chē tíng zài zhèlǐ ma?** = *May I park my car here?*

qìshuǐ 汽水 [modif: 汽 *vapor* + 水 *water*] NOUN = soda water, soft drink, soda, pop (瓶 píng, 杯 **bēi**)

■ 这瓶汽水是给你的。**Zhè píng qìshuǐ shì gěi ní de.** = *This bottle of soda water is for you.*
■ 我不喝汽水，我喝水。**Wǒ bù hē qìshuǐ, wǒ hē shuǐ.** = *I don't drink soft drinks. I drink water.*

qìyóu 汽油 NOUN = gasoline, petroleum
■ 我们的汽油快用完了，到前面的加油站要停下加油。**Wǒmen de qìyóu kuài yòngwán le, dào qiánmiàn de jiāyóuzhàn yào tíngxia jiāyóu.** = *We've almost run out of gas. We'll have to stop for gas at the next gas station.*

qì 弃 Trad 棄 VERB = abandon (See 放弃 **fàngqì**.)

qì 器 NOUN = utensil (See 机器 **jīqì**, 武器 **wǔqì**, 仪器 **yíqì**.)

qiān 千 NUMERAL = thousand
■ 一千零一夜 **yìqiān líng yí yè** = *a thousand and one nights*
■ 四千五百八十 **sìqiān wǔbǎi bāshí** = *four thousand, five hundred and eighty*

qiānwàn 千万 ADVERB = be sure to, must never (used in an imperative sentence for emphasis)
■ 你开车千万要小心！ **Nǐ kāichē qiānwàn yào xiǎoxīn!** = *Be very, very careful while driving.*
■ 明天的会你千万别迟到。**Míngtiān de huì nǐ qiānwàn bié chídào.** = *Be sure not to be late for tomorrow's meeting.*

qiān 签 Trad 簽 VERB = sign, autograph

qiāndìng 签订 VERB = sign (a treaty, an agreement, etc.)
■ 那家建筑公司和市政府签订了两份合同。**Nà jiā jiànzhù gōngsī hé shì zhèngfǔ qiāndìngle liǎng fèn hétóng.** = *The construction company has signed two contracts with the city government.*

qiān 铅 Trad 鉛 NOUN = lead

qiānbǐ 铅笔 [modif: 铅 *lead* + 笔 *pen*] NOUN = pencil (支 **zhī**)
■ 我的红铅笔哪儿去了？ **Wǒ de hóng qiānbǐ nǎlǐ qù le?** = *Where's my red pencil?*
■ 我可以用一下你的铅笔吗？ **Wǒ kěyǐ yòng**

yíxià nǐ de qiānbǐ ma? = *May I use your pencil for a while?*

qiānbǐ hé 铅笔盒 = pencil box

qiānbǐ dāo 铅笔刀 = pencil sharpener

qián 前 NOUN

1 = front, in front of (antonym 后 **hòu**)

■ 房子前有一块草地。**Fángzi qián yǒu yí kuài cǎodì.** = *In front of the house there's a lawn.*

■ 中国人的姓名，姓在前，名在后。**Zhōngguórén de xìngmíng, xìng zài qián, míng zài hòu.** = *In a Chinese person's name, the family name comes before the given name.*

2 = same as 以前 **yǐqián**

NOTE: In everyday Chinese, 前 **qián** is seldom used alone to mean *front* or *in front of*. Often it is better to use 前边 **qiánbian**.

qiánbian 前边 [modif: 前 *front* + 边 *side*]

NOUN = front (antonym 后边 **hòubiān**)

■ 房子前边便有一块草地。**Fángzi qiánbian yǒu yí kuài cǎodì.** = *In front of the house, there's a lawn.*

■ 中国人的姓名姓在前边，名在后边。**Zhōngguórén de xìngmíng, xìng zài qiánbian, míng zài hòubian.** = *In a Chinese person's name, the family name comes before the given name.*

qiánjìn 前进 [compound: 前 *advance* + 进 *advance*] VERB = advance (antonym 后退 **hòutuì**)

■ 我们的经济在过去一年又前进了一大步。**Wǒmen de jīngjì zài guòqu yì nián yòu qiánjìn le yí dà bù.** = *Last year our economy took a big stride forward.*

qiánmiàn 前面 NOUN = same as 前边 **qiánbian**

qiánnián 前年 NOUN = the year before last

■ 今年是2005年，前年是2003年。**Jīnnián shì èr-líng-líng-wǔ nián, qiánnián shì èr-líng-líng-sān nián.** = *This year is 2005 and the year before last was 2003.*

■ 前年我刚开始学中文。**Qiánnián wǒ gāng kāishǐ xué Zhōngwén.** = *I just began to learn Chinese the year before last.*

qiántiān 前天 NOUN = the day before yesterday

■ 他前天去中国，今天我收到了他从中国发来的电子邮件。**Tá qiántiān qù Zhōngguó, jīntiān wǒ shōudàole tā cóng Zhōngguó fālai de diànzǐ yóujiàn.** = *He left for China the day before yesterday, and today I got an e-mail he sent from China.*

qiántú 前途 [modif: 前 *in front* + 途 *journey*]

NOUN = future, prospects, future prospects

■ 一个青年连中学都没有毕业，不可能有什么前途。**Yí ge qīngnián lián zhōngxué dōu méiyǒu bìyè, bù kěnéng yǒu shénme qiántú.** = *A young man does not have much future prospects if he does not even finish high school.*

■ 这次计划的成败将决定公司的前途。**Zhè cì jìhuà de chéngbài jiāng juédìng gōngsī de qiántú.** = *The success or failure of this plan will determine the future prospects of the company.*

qián 钱 Trad 錢 NOUN = money (笔 **bǐ**)

■ 钱很重要，但不是万能的。**Qián hěn zhòngyào, dàn bú shì wànnéng de.** = *Money is important, but it is not all-powerful.*

■ 他在银行里有一大笔钱。**Tā zài yínháng li yǒu yí dà bǐ qián.** = *He has a big sum of money in the bank.*

■ 他从来不向人借钱，也不借钱给别人。**Tā cónglái bú xiàng rén jiè qián, yě bú jiè qián gei biéren.** = *He never borrows money, nor does he lend money to others.*

qiánbāo 钱包 = wallet, purse

qiǎn 浅 Trad 淺 ADJECTIVE

1 = shallow (antonym 深 **shēn**)

■ 这条河很浅，可以走过去。**Zhè tiáo hé hěn qiǎn, kěyǐ zǒu guòqù.** = *This river is shallow. You can wade across it.*

2 = easy, of low standard

■ 这本书太浅，你不用看。**Zhè běn shū tài qiǎn, nǐ bú yòng kàn.** = *This book is too easy for you; you don't have to read it.*

qiàn 欠 VERB = owe, be in debt to

■ 他欠我一百元。**Tā qiàn wǒ yìbǎi yuán.** = *He owes me a hundred yuan.*

qiàn rénqíng 欠人情 = owe a debt of gratitude

qiāng 枪 Trad 槍 NOUN = small arms, gun, pistol (支 **zhī**, 把 **bǎ**)

■ 在我们国家，老百姓有枪是犯法的。**Zài wǒmen guójiā, lǎobǎixìng yǒu qiāng shì fànfǎ**

de. = *In our country, it's against the law for ordinary citizens to own guns.*
shǒuqiāng 手枪 = handgun (revolver, pistol)

qiáng 强 ADJECTIVE = strong (antonym 弱 **ruò**)
■ 她中文口语很强，但是写汉字的能力比较弱。**Tā Zhōngwén kǒuyǔ hěn qiáng, dànshì xiě Hànzì de nénglì bǐjiào ruò.** = *She is strong in oral Chinese, but weak in writing characters.*

qiángdà 强大 [compound: 强 *strong* + 大 *big*]
ADJECTIVE = powerful (antonym 弱小 **ruòxiǎo**)
■ 谁都希望自己的祖国强大。**Shéi dōu xīwàng zìjǐ de zǔguó qiángdà.** = *Everybody wants their motherland to be a powerful country.*

qiángdào 强盗 NOUN = bandit, robber
■ 他十几岁的时候是个小偷，现在二十多岁成了一名强盗。**Tā shí jǐ suì de shíhou shì ge xiǎotōu, xiànzài èrshí duō suì chéngle yì míng qiángdào.** = *When he was a teenager he was a thief. Now in his twenties, he has become a robber.*

qiángdiào 强调 [modif: 强 *strong* + 调 *tone*]
VERB = emphasize, lay stress on
■ 王老师强调语音准确的重要性。**Wáng lǎoshī qiángdiào yǔyīn zhǔnquè de zhòngyàoxìng.** = *Teacher Wang emphasized the importance of correct pronunciation.*

qiángdù 强度 [modif: 强 *strong* + 度 *degree*]
NOUN = intensity, strength
■ 这种材料的强度还不够。**Zhè zhǒng cáiliào de qiángdù hái bú gòu.** = *This material does not have enough strength.*

qiángliè 强烈 [compound: 强 *strong* + 烈 *raging*] ADJECTIVE = strong, intense, violent
■ 顾客们强烈要求退货。**Gùkèmen qiángliè yāoqiú tuìhuò.** = *The customers firmly demanded a refund.*

qiáng 墙 Trad 墙 NOUN = wall (道 **dào**)
■ 墙上有一张世界地图。**Qiáng shang yǒu yì zhāng shìjiè dìtú.** = *There's a map of the world on the wall.*

qiǎng 抢 Trad 搶 VERB = seize, grab
■ 他的玩具手枪被一个大孩子抢走了。**Tā de**

wánjù shǒuqiāng bèi yí ge dà háizi qiǎngzuǒ le. = *His toy pistol was snatched away by a big boy.*

qiāo 悄 ADJECTIVE = quiet

qiāoqiāo 悄悄 ADVERB = quietly, on the quiet
■ 他悄悄对我说，"别在这里买，太贵了。" **Tā qiāoqiāo de duì wǒ shuō, "Bié zài zhèlǐ mǎi, tài guì le."** = *He whispered to me, "Don't buy it here, it's too expensive."*

qiāo 敲 VERB = knock
■ 有人敲门。**Yǒu rén qiāo mén.** = *Someone is knocking at the door.*

qiáo 桥 Trad 橋 NOUN = bridge (座 **zuò**)
■ 这座石桥历史很久。**Zhè zuò shíqiáo lìshǐ hěn jiǔ.** = *This stone bridge has a long history.*
■ 长江上有很多大桥。**Chángjiāng shang yǒu hěn duō dà qiáo.** = *There are many big bridges across the Yangtze River.*
guò qiáo 过桥 = cross a bridge

qiáoliáng 桥梁 NOUN = big bridge (座 **zuò**)
■ 他的专业是桥梁建造。**Tā de zhuānyè shì qiáoliáng jiànzào.** = *His special field is bridge construction.*

qiáo 瞧 VERB = same as 看 **kàn** VERB 1. Used only as a colloquialism.

qiǎo 巧 ADVERB
1 = coincidence
■ 真巧，我正要找他，他来了。**Zhēn qiǎo, wǒ zhèngyào zhǎo tā, tā láile.** = *What a happy coincidence, he came just when I wanted to see him.*
■ 你要买的书最后一本刚卖走，很不巧。**Nǐ yào mǎi de shū zuì hòu yì běn gāng màizǒu, hěn bù qiǎo.** = *Unfortunately, the last copy of the book you want has just been sold.*
2 = skilled, clever
■ 他们的儿子手巧，女儿嘴巧。**Tāmen de érzi shǒu qiǎo, nǚ'er zuí qiǎo.** = *Their son is clever with his hands and their daughter has the gift of the gab.*

qiǎomiào 巧妙 [compound: 巧 *skilled* + 妙 *wonderful*] ADJECTIVE = ingenious, very clever
■ 这台机器设计得巧妙。**Zhè tái jīqì shèjì de**

hěn qiǎomiào. = *This machine is ingeniously designed.*
■ 她的回答很巧妙。**Tā de huídá hěn qiǎomiào.** = *She gave a clever answer.*

qiě 且 CONJUNCTION = moreover (See 而且 érqie.)

qiè 切 VERB = cut, slice
■ 爸爸把西瓜切成四块。**Bàba bǎ xīguā qiē chéng sì kuài.** = *Dad cut the watermelon into four pieces.*

qīn 亲 Trad 親 NOUN = blood relation

qīn'ài 亲爱 [compound: 亲 *intimate* + 爱 *love*] ADJECTIVE = dear, beloved, darling
■ 我亲爱的祖母去年去世了，我难受了好久。**Wǒ qīn'ài de zǔmǔ qùnián qùshì le, wǒ nánshòu le hǎojiǔ.** = *My dear grandmother died last year; I was sad for a long time.*

NOTE: Although 亲爱 **qīn'ài** is glossed as *dear*, the Chinese reserve 亲爱(的) **qīn'ài (de)** for the very few people who are really dear and close to their hearts.

qīnqi 亲戚 NOUN = relative, relation
■ 他爸爸妈妈兄弟姐妹很多，所以他亲戚很多。**Tā bàba māma xiōngdì jiěmèi duō, suǒyǐ tā qīnqi hěnduō.** = *His parents have many siblings, so he has many relatives.*
qīnqi péngyou 亲戚朋友 = relatives and friends
zǒu qīnqi 走亲戚 = visit a relative

qīnqiè 亲切 ADJECTIVE = cordial
■ 过圣诞节的时候，朋友们给我发来电子贺卡，表示亲切的问候。**Guò shèngdànjié de shíhou, péngyǒumen gěi wǒ fālai diànzǐ hèkǎ, biǎoshì qīnqiè de wènhòu.** = *At Christmas, my friends sent me e-cards, conveying cordial greetings.*

qīnzì 亲自 ADVERB = by oneself
■ 李校长亲自来征求对教学的意见。**Lǐ xiàozhǎng qīnzì lái zhēngqiú duì jiàoxué de yìjiàn.** = *Mr Li, the principal, came himself to ask for our comments on teaching.*

qīn 侵 VERB = encroach

qīnlüè 侵略 VERB = invade (by force)
■ 侵略别国在国际上是不允许的。**Qīnlüè bié guó zài guójì shang shì bù yúnxǔ de.** = *Invading another country is not permitted internationally.*

qīng 青 ADJECTIVE = green
■ 在新西兰草地一年到头都是青青的。**Zài Xīnxīlán cǎodì yì-nián-dào-tóu dōu shì qīngqīng de.** = *In New Zealand the grass is green all year round.*

qīngwā 青蛙 [modif: 青 *green* + 蛙 *frog*] NOUN = frog (只 zhī)
■ 青蛙能够跳得很高。**Qīngwā nénggòu tiào de hěn gāo.** = *A frog can jump high.*

qīngnián 青年 [modif: 青 *green* + 年 *year*] NOUN = young person, young people, youth (especially male) (位 wèi, 个 ge)
■ 那位青年是我姐姐的男朋友。**Nà wèi qīngnián shì wǒ jiějie de nánpéngyou.** = *That young man is my elder sister's boyfriend.*
■ 青年工人往往没有多少经验。**Qīngnián gōngrén wǎngwǎng méiyǒu duōshǎo jīngyàn.** = *Young workers often don't have much experience.*

qīng 清 ADJECTIVE
1 = clear (water), clean
■ 过去这条河的水很清，能看到河底的小石头。**Guòqù zhè tiáo hé de shuǐ hěn qīng, néng kàndào hédǐ de xiǎo shítou.** = *In the past this river had very clear water and you could see the little stones on the riverbed.*
2 = (of matters) clear, easy to understand
■ 这件事没有人能说得清。**Zhè jiàn shì méiyǒu rén néng shuō de qīng.** = *Nobody can give a clear account of this matter.*

qīngchu 清楚 [compound: 清 *clear* + 楚 *clear-cut*] ADJECTIVE = clear (of speech or image)
■ 你的意思很清楚，我明白。**Nǐ de yìsi hěn qīngchu, wǒ míngbai.** = *Your meaning is clear. I understand it.*
■ 老师，黑板上的字我看不清楚。**Lǎoshī, hēibǎn shang de zì wǒ kàn bu qīngchu.** = *Teacher, I can't see the words on the blackboard clearly.*
■ 我说得清清楚楚，你怎么会误会呢？**Wǒ shuōde qīng-qīng-chǔ-chǔ, nǐ zénme huì wùhuì**

ne? = *I said it very clearly. How could you misunderstand it?*

qīng 轻 Trad 輕 ADJECTIVE
1 = light (of weight) (antonym 重 **zhòng**)
■ 油比水轻。**Yóu bǐ shuǐ qīng.** = *Oil is lighter than water.*
2 = low, soft (of voice)
■ 她说话很轻，要仔细听，才能听清楚。**Tā shuōhuà hěn qīng, yào zǐxì tīng, cái néng tīng qīngchu.** = *She speaks softly. Only if you listen attentively can you hear her clearly.*
3 = of a low degree
■ 对他的处分太轻了。**Duì tā de chǔfèn tài qīng le.** = *The disciplinary action against him was not severe enough.*
qīng yīnyuè 轻音乐 = light music

qīngsōng 轻松 [compound: 轻 *light* + 松 *loose*] ADJECTIVE = (of a job) easy, not requiring much effort
■ 这个工作很轻松，当然工资不高。**Zhège gōngzuò hěn qīngsōng, dāngrán gōngzī bù gāo.** = *This job is easy and requires no real effort; of course it is poorly paid.*
■ 上个周末我过得非常轻松愉快。**Shàng ge zhōumò wǒ guò de fēicháng qīngsōng yúkuài.** = *Last weekend I had a very relaxed and pleasant time.*

qíng 情 NOUN = circumstance

qíngjǐng 情景 [compound: 情 *situation* + 景 *scene*] NOUN = scene, occasion
■ 旅馆大楼在半夜着火了，人们从楼上跳下，真是可怕的情景。**Lǚguǎn dàlóu zài bànyè zháohuǒ le, rénmen cóng lóushang tiàoxia, zhēn shì kěpà de qíngjǐng.** = *When the hotel caught fire at midnight, people jumped from the upper floors. It was indeed a frightening scene.*

qíngkuàng 情况 [compound: 情 *circumstance* + 况 *situation*] NOUN = situation, circumstance
■ 他生病住院了，情况很严重。**Tā shēng bìng zhùyuàn le, qíngkuàng hěn yánzhòng.** = *He's been hospitalized. His condition is very serious.*
■ 我不大了解这个国家的情况。**Wǒ bú dà liǎojiě zhège guójiā de qíngkuàng.** = *I don't quite know the situation this country is in.*

qíngxíng 情形 [compound: 情 *situation* + 形 *shape*] NOUN = circumstances, situation
■ 两列火车马上要相撞，情形十分紧张。**Liǎng liè huǒchē mǎshàng yào xiāngzhuàng, qíngxíng shífēn jǐnzhāng.** = *The two trains were about to collide. It was an extremely nerve-racking situation.*

qíngxù 情绪 [compound: 情 *emotion* + 绪 *mood*] NOUN = mood, feelings
■ 天气会影响人们的情绪。**Tiānqì huì yǐngxiǎng rénmen de qíngxù.** = *The weather can affect people's moods.*
■ 他看来情绪不好，你知道为什么吗？**Tā kànlai qíngxù bù hǎo, nǐ zhīdào wèishénme ma?** = *He seems to be in a bad mood. Do you know why?*

qíng 晴 ADJECTIVE = fine, clear (of weather)
■ 今天上午晴，中午以后开始下雨了。**Jīntiān shàngwǔ qíng, zhōngwǔ yǐhòu kāishǐ xià yǔ le.** = *It was fine this morning. It began raining in the afternoon.*
■ 晴天比雨天舒服。**Qíngtiān bǐ yǔtiān shūfu.** = *A fine day is more comfortable than a rainy day.*

qǐng 请 Trad 請 VERB
1 = invite
■ 今天晚上我请你吃饭。**Jīntiān wǎnshang wǒ qǐng nǐ chīfàn.** = *I'll invite you to dinner tonight.*
2 = ask, request
■ 学生请老师再说一遍。**Xuésheng qǐng lǎoshī zài shuō yí biàn.** = *The students asked the teacher to repeat it.*
qǐng bìngjià 请病假 = ask for sick leave
qǐngjià 请假 = ask for leave
qǐng shìjià 请事假 = ask for leave of absence
qǐngwèn ... 请问... = Excuse me, ...
■ 请问，您是上海来的张先生吗？**Qǐngwèn, nín shì Shànghǎi lái de Zhāng xiānsheng ma?** = *Excuse me, are you Mr Zhang from Shanghai?*

NOTE: 请 **qǐng** is used to start a polite request, equivalent to *Please ...*, e.g.
■ 请您别在这里吸烟。**Qǐng nín bié zài zhèli xīyān.** = *Please don't smoke here.*
■ 请坐！**Qǐng zuò!** = *Sit down, please!*
■ 请喝茶！**Qǐng hē chá.** = *Have some tea, please!*

qǐngkè 请客 [v+obj: 请 *invite* + 客 *guest*] VERB
1 = invite to dinner
■ 张先生这个星期六在家里请客吃饭。**Zhāng xiānsheng zhège Xīngqīliù zài jiālǐ qǐngkè chīfàn.** = *This Saturday Mr Zhang will give a dinner party at home.*
2 = stand treat
■ 这次出去玩，车票、门票都是我请客。**Zhè cì chūqu wán, chēpiào, ménpiào dōu shì wǒ qǐngkè.** = *On this date, I'll pay for bus fares and admission tickets.*

qǐngqiú 请求 [compound: 请 *request* + 求 *beseech*]
1 VERB = request, ask for
■ 我请求你原谅我的错误。**Wǒ qǐngqiú nǐ yuánliàng wǒ de cuòwù.** = *I ask for your forgiveness of my mistake.*
2 NOUN = request
■ 你们的请求已交委员会考虑。**Nǐmen de qǐngqiú yǐ jiāo wěiyuánhuì kǎolù.** = *Your request has been submitted to the committee for consideration.*

qìng 庆 Trad 慶 VERB = celebrate

qìngzhù 庆祝 [compound: 庆 *celebrate* + 祝 *good wishes*]
1 VERB = celebrate
■ 英国大使馆昨天举行宴会，庆祝女王生日。**Yīngguó dàshǐguǎn zuótiān jǔxíng yànhuì, qìngzhù nǚwáng shēngrì.** = *The British embassy gave a dinner party yesterday to celebrate the Queen's birthday.*
2 NOUN = celebration
■ 下个月他们的女儿大学毕业。他们打算好好庆祝一下。**Xià ge yuè tāmen de nǚ'ér dàxué bìyè, tāmen dǎsuàn hǎohǎo qìngzhù yíxià.** = *Their daughter will graduate from university next month. They plan to have a big celebration.*

qióng 穷 Trad 窮 ADJECTIVE = poor, poverty-stricken
■ 她家里比较穷。**Tā jiālǐ bǐjiào qióng.** = *Her family is rather poor.*
■ 国家再穷也应该花足够的钱办教育。**Guójiā zài qióng yě yīnggāi huā zúgòu de qián bàn jiàoyù.** = *No matter how poor a country is, sufficient funds should be spent on education.*
qióngrén 穷人 = poor person, poor people

qiū 秋 NOUN = fall, autumn
■ 北京香山的秋景很美。**Běijīng Xiāngshān de qiū jǐng hěn měi.** = *The autumn scenery on Fragrance Hill in Beijing is very beautiful.*

qiūtiān 秋天 [modif: 秋 *autumn* + 天 *day*] NOUN = fall, autumn
■ 秋天不冷不热，十分舒服。**Qiūtiān bù lěng bú rè, shífēn shūfu.** = *Autumn is neither hot nor cold; it's very comfortable.*

qiú 求 VERB = beseech, beg, ask for humbly
■ 你只有求他帮忙。**Nǐ zhǐyǒu qiú tā bāngmáng.** = *You can only ask him for help.*
■ 我求你再考虑考虑。**Wǒ qiú nǐ zài kǎolù kǎolù.** = *I beg you to give it further consideration.*

qiú 球 NOUN
1 = ball (只 **zhī**)
■ 花园里有一只球，是谁的？**Huāyuán li yǒu yì zhī qiú, shì shéi de?** = *There's a ball in the garden. Whose is it?*
2 = ball game (场 **chǎng**)
■ 我们每星期六下午打一场球。**Wǒmen měi Xīngqīliù xiàwǔ dǎ yì chǎng qiú.** = *We have a ball game every Saturday afternoon.*
qiúchǎng 球场 = sports ground (especially where ball games are played)
qiúduì 球队 = (ball game) team
bǐ qiú 比球 = have a (ball game) match
bàngqiú 棒球 = baseball
dǎ qiú 打球 = play basketball or volleyball
kàn qiú 看球 = watch a ball game
lánqiú 篮球 = basketball
páiqiú 排球 = volleyball
tī qiú 踢球 = play soccer
zúqiú 足球 = soccer

qū 区 Trad 區 NOUN = district (urban)
■ 中国的城市一般分成几个区。**Zhōngguó de chéngshì yìbān fēnchéng jǐ ge qū.** = *A city in China is usually divided into several districts.*
shāngyè qū 商业区 = commercial area, business district
gōngyè qū 工业区 = industrial zone, industrial district

qūbié 区别
1 VERB = distinguish between, differentiate
■ 你能区别美国英语和英国英语吗？**Nǐ**

Q

néng qūbié Měiguó Yīngyǔ hé Yīngguó Yīngyǔ ma? = *Can you tell American English from British English?*

2 NOUN = difference

■ 这两个词的意义没有多大区别。**Zhè liǎng ge cí de yìyì méiyǒu duōdà qūbié.** = *There is not much difference in the meaning of the two words.*

qǔ 取 VERB = fetch, collect

■ 我要找一个自动取款机取点钱。**Wǒ yào zhǎo yí ge zìdòng qǔkuǎnjī qǔ diǎn qián.** = *I'm looking for an ATM to withdraw some money.*

qǔkuǎn 取款 = withdraw money

qǔdé 取得 [compound: 取 *obtain* + 得 *get*] VERB = obtain, achieve

■ 我们去年取得很大成绩。**Wǒmen qùnián qǔdé hěn dà chéngjì.** = *We made great achievements last year.*

qǔxiāo 取消 VERB = cancel

■ 明天的会议已经取消了。**Míngtiān de huìyì yǐjīng qǔxiāo le.** = *The meeting tomorrow has been called off.*

qù 去 VERB = leave for, go to (来 lái)

■ 你什么时候去中国？ **Nǐ shénme shíhou qù Zhōngguó?** = *When are you going to China?*

■ 他下星期到美国去。**Tā xià xīngqī dào Měiguó qù.** = *He's going to America next week.*

NOTE: 到 **dào** and 到 … 去 **dào…qù** have the same meaning and are normally interchangeable.

qùnián 去年 [modif: 去 *what has gone* + 年 *year*] NOUN = last year

■ 她去年才开始学中文。**Tā qùnián cái kāishǐ xué Zhōngwén.** = *She began learning Chinese only last year.*

qùshì 去世 [v+obj: 去 *leave* + 世 *the world*] NOUN = die, pass away

■ 他的祖父在上个月去世了。**Tā de zǔfù zài shànggeyuè qùshì le.** = *His grandfather passed away last month.*

NOTE: 去世 **qùshì** must be used when you want to show respect and/or love to the deceased. For instance, the normal word for

die, 死 **sǐ**, would be totally inappropriate in the example sentence.

qù 趣 NOUN = interest (See 兴趣 **xìngqù**, 有趣 **yǒuqù**.)

quān 圈 NOUN = circle, ring

■ 运动会的旗子上有五个圈。**Yùndònghuì de qízi shang yǒu wǔ ge quān.** = *There are five circles on the flag of the Games.*

quán 全 ADJECTIVE = whole, complete

■ 过圣诞节那天，全家人一块儿吃午饭。**Guò shèngdànjié nàtiān, quánjiārén yíkuàir chī wǔfàn.** = *On Christmas Day, the whole family has lunch together.*

■ 你的病还没全好，怎么能上班呢？ **Nǐ de bìng hái méi quán hǎo, zěnme néng shàngbān ne?** = *You haven't fully recovered. How can you go to work?*

■ 他说的不全是真话。**Tā shuō de bù quán shì zhēnhuà.** = *He did not tell the whole truth.*

quánguó 全国 = the whole country

quánshìjiè 全世界 = the entire world

quánbù 全部 [modif: 全 *whole* + 部 *part*] NOUN = all, without exception

■ 我爸爸全部的时间都放在工作上。**Wǒ bàba quánbù de shíjiān dōu fàng zài gōngzuò shang.** = *My father devotes all his time to work.*

quánmiàn 全面 [modif: 全 *all* + 面 *side*] ADJECTIVE = all-round, comprehensive

■ 对这个问题，我们要做全面的考虑。**Duì zhège wèntí, wǒmen yào zuò quánmiàn de kǎolù.** = *We will give thorough consideration to this issue.*

quántǐ 全体 [modif: 全 *whole* + 体 *body*] NOUN = all, each and every one (of a group of people)

■ 她代表全体学生向老师表示感谢。**Tā dàibiǎo quántǐ xuésheng xiàng lǎoshī biǎoshì gǎnxiè.** = *On behalf of all the students she expressed gratitude to the teacher.*

quàn 劝 Trad 勸 VERB = try to talk … into (or out of) doing something, advise

■ 他劝我不要把钱都存在那家银行。**Tā quàn wǒ bú yào bǎ qián dōu cún zài nà jiā yínháng.** = *He advised me not to put all my money in that bank.*

■ 我劝你改善和她的关系。**Wǒ quàn nǐ gǎishàn hé tā de guānxi.** = *I encourage you to improve your relationship with her.*

quē 缺 VERB = lack, be short of
■ 要买笔记本电脑，我还缺三百块钱。**Yào mǎi bǐjìběn diànnǎo, wǒ hái quē sānbǎi kuài qián.** = *I'm short of 300 yuan for the purchase of a notebook computer.*
quē rénshǒu 缺人手 = shorthanded

quēdiǎn 缺点 [v+obj: 缺 *lack* + 点 *point*] NOUN = shortcoming, defect
■ 你要克服粗心的缺点。**Nǐ yào kèfú cūxīn de quēdiǎn.** = *You should overcome the shortcoming of carelessness.*
■ 这种新产品还有一些缺点，需要改进。**Zhè zhǒng xīn chǎnpǐn háiyǒu yìxiē quēdiǎn, xūyào gǎijìn.** = *This new product still has some defects and needs improvement.*

quēfá 缺乏 VERB = be deficient in, lack
■ 他知识丰富，但是缺乏实际经验。**Tā zhīshi fēngfù, dànshì quēfá shíjì jīngyàn.** = *He has very rich knowledge but lacks practical experience.*
■ 人们往往缺乏道德勇气。**Rénmen wǎngwǎng quēfá dàodé yǒngqì.** = *People often lack moral courage.*

quēshǎo 缺少 VERB = be short of, lack
■ 我们缺少一名球员，你愿意参加比赛吗？**Wǒmen quēshǎo yì míng qiúyuán, nǐ yuànyì cānjiā bǐsài ma?** = *We're still short of one player. Are you willing to participate in the game?*

NOTE: 缺乏 **quēfá** and 缺少 **quēshǎo** are synonyms, but 缺乏 **quēfá** has abstract nouns as objects, while 缺少 **quēshǎo** takes as objects nouns denoting concrete persons or things.

què 却 ADVERB = unexpectedly, contrary to what may be normally expected, but, yet
■ 今天是星期天，他却起得比平时还早。**Jīntiān shì Xīngqītiān, tā què qǐ de bǐ píngshí hái zǎo.** = *It's Sunday today, but he got up earlier than on weekdays.*
■ 他很有钱，却并不幸福。**Tā hěn yǒuqián, què bìng bù xìngfú.** = *He is rich, but he is not happy.*

què 确 Trad 確 ADJECTIVE = certain

quèdìng 确定 [compound: 确 *true* + 定 *definite*] VERB = confirm, fix, determine
■ 他出国的日期已经确定。**Tā chūguó de rìqī yǐjīng quèdìng.** = *His date of departure overseas has been fixed.*
■ 谁当总经理还没有确定。**Shéi dāng zǒngjīnglǐ hái méiyǒu quèdìng.** = *Who the general manager will be is not yet confirmed.*

quèshí 确实 [compound: 确 *certain* + 实 *substantial*] ADJECTIVE = verified to be true, indeed
■ 这个消息不确实。**Zhège xiāoxi bú quèshí.** = *This news is not true.*
■ 你确实错了。**Nǐ quèshí cuò le.** = *You're indeed wrong.*

qún 裙 NOUN = skirt

qúnzi 裙子 [suffix: 裙 *skirt* + 子 nominal suffix] NOUN = skirt (条 tiáo)
■ 你穿白裙子很好看。**Nǐ chuān bái qúnzi hěn hǎokàn.** = *You look good in a white skirt.*

qún 群 Trad 群 MEASURE WORD = a crowd of, a group of (for people or animals)
■ 一群狗 **yìqún gǒu** = *a pack of dogs*
■ 一群鸟 **yìqún niǎo** = *a flock of birds*
■ 一群牛 **yìqún niú** = *a herd of cattle*
■ 一群小学生 **yìqún xiǎoxuéshēng** = *a group of schoolchildren*
■ 一群羊 **yìqún yáng** = *a flock of sheep*

qúnzhòng 群众 [compound: 群 *crowd* + 众 *multitude*] NOUN = the masses (people), the general public
■ 在群众的帮助下，警察很快抓到了强盗。**Zài qúnzhòng de bāngzhù xià, jǐngchá hěn kuài zhuādào le qiángdào.** = *With the help of the general public, the police soon caught the robber.*

R

rán 然 ADVERB = however

rán'ér 然而 CONJUNCTION = same as 但是 **dànshì**. Usually used in written Chinese.

ránhòu 然后 [idiom] CONJUNCTION =
afterwards, ... and then
xiān ... ránhòu ... 先 ... 然后 ... = first ... and
then...
■ 他每天早上先跑步，然后吃早饭。**Tā měi
tiān zǎoshang xiān pǎobù, ránhòu chī zǎofàn.** =
*Every morning he first jogs and then has
breakfast.*

rán 燃 VERB = burn

ránshāo 燃烧 [compound: 燃 *burn* + 烧 *burn*]
VERB = burn
■ 森林大火燃烧了三天三夜。**Sēnlín dàhuǒ
ránshāole sān tiān sān yè.** = *The forest fire
raged three days and nights.*

rǎn 染 VERB = dye
■ 有些年轻人喜欢染头发。**Yǒuxiē
niánqīngrén xǐhuan rǎn tóufa.** = *Some young
people like to dye their hair.*

rǎng 嚷 VERB = yell, shout
■ 别嚷了，有话好好说。**Bié rǎng le, yǒu huà
hǎohǎo shuō.** = *Stop yelling. Speak nicely if you
have something to say.*

ràng 让 Trad 讓 VERB
1 = let, allow
■ 你应该让那辆车先行。**Nǐ yīnggāi ràng nà
liàng chē xiānxíng.** = *You should let that vehicle go first. (→ You should give way to that
vehicle)*
■ 让我想一想。**Ràng wǒ xiǎng yi xiǎng.** = *Let
me think.*
■ 妈不让我告诉你这件事。**Mā bú ràng wǒ
gàosu nǐ zhè jiàn shì.** = *Mom didn't allow me to
tell you this.*
2 = make
■ 他的话让我明白了许多道理。**Tā de huà
ràng wǒ míngbaile xǔduō dàolǐ.** = *What he said
made me understand many things. (→ What he
said enlightened me.)*

rǎo 扰 Trad 擾 VERB = harass (See 打扰 **dǎrǎo.**)

rào 绕 Trad 繞 VERB = make a detour, bypass
■ 前面施工，车辆绕道。**Qiánmiàn shīgōng,
chēliàng rào dào.** = *Road works ahead. Vehicles must detour.*

rě 惹 VERB = cause (something undesirable),
invite (trouble etc.)
■ 别惹麻烦了。**Bié rě máfan le.** = *Don't ask for
trouble.*
■ 你和这种人交朋友会惹爸爸生气。**Nǐ hé
zhè zhǒng rén jiāo péngyou huì rě bàba
shēngqì.** = *It will make daddy angry if you
make friends with such people.*

rè 热 Trad 熱 VERB = hot (antonym 冷 **lěng**)
■ 香港的夏天很热。**Xiānggǎng de xiàtiān hěn
rè.** = *Summer in Hong Kong is very hot.*
■ 我想喝一杯热水，不要冷水。**Wǒ xiǎng hē
yì bēi rè shuǐ, bú yào lěng shuǐ.** = *I want to
drink a glass of hot water, not cold water.*
■ 你怎么能肯定当冠军？脑子发热吧？**Nǐ
zěnme néng kěndìng dāng guànjūn? Nǎozi fā rè
ba?** = *How can you be so sure that you will
definitely be the champion? Are you being
hotheaded?*

rè'ài 热爱 [modif: 热 *hot* + 爱 *love*] VERB =
love ardently, be in deep love with
■ 我热爱我的祖国。**Wǒ rè'ài wǒ de zǔguó.** = *I
love my motherland.*

rèliè 热烈 [compound: 热 *hot* + 烈 *intense*]
ADJECTIVE = warm, ardent
■ 热烈欢迎新同学。**Rèliè huānyíng xīn
tóngxué!** = *A warm welcome to the new
students!*

rènao 热闹 [compound: 热 *hot* + 闹 *noisy*]
ADJECTIVE = noisy and exciting in a pleasant
way, boisterous, bustling, lively (of a scene or
occasion)
■ 中国人过年非常热闹。**Zhōngguórén
guònián fēicháng rènao.** = *When the Chinese
celebrate their New Year's Day, it is a noisy
and exciting occasion.*
■ 周末的市场十分热闹。**Zhōumò de shìchǎng
shífēn rènao.** = *The shopping mall bustles with
activity on weekends.*

rèqíng 热情 [modif: 热 *hot* + 情 *emotion*]
ADJECTIVE = enthusiastic, warmhearted
■ 她对人很热情。**Tā duì rén hěn rèqíng.** =
She's warmhearted towards people.
■ 他常常热情地帮助朋友。**Tā chángcháng
rèqíng de bāngzhù péngyou.** = *He often helps
his friends enthusiastically.*

■ 他热情的态度让我很感动。**Tā rèqíng de tàidu ràng wǒ hěn gǎndòng.** = *His warmheartedness moved me greatly.*

rèshuǐpíng 热水瓶 [modfi: 热 hot + 水 *water* + 瓶 *bottle, flask*] NOUN = thermos, thermos flask (只 **zhī**)
■ 有了热水瓶很方便，什么时候都可以喝上热水。**Yǒule rèshuǐpíng hěn fāngbiàn, shénme shíhou dōu kěyǐ hēshang rè shuǐ.** = *A thermos flask is very handy. You can have hot water any time.*

rèxīn 热心 [modif: 热 *hot* + 心 *heart*] ADJECTIVE = warmhearted, enthusiastic
duì ... rèxīn 对 ... 热心 = be warmhearted towards, be enthusiastic about
■ 他对朋友很热心。**Tā duì péngyou hěn rèxīn.** = *He is warmhearted towards friends.*

rén 人 NOUN = human being, person
■ 你认识这个人吗？ **Nǐ rènshi zhège rén ma?** = *Do you know this person?*
■ 人和动物有什么区别？ **Rén hé dòngwù yǒu shénme qūbié?** = *What are the differences between humans and animals?*

réncái 人才 [modif: 人 *human* + 才 *talent*] NOUN = talented person, person of ability
■ 他自以为是个人才。**Tā zì yǐwéi shì ge réncái.** = *He thinks himself quite talented.*
■ 我们公司需要电脑人才。**Wǒmen gōngsī xūyào diànnǎo réncái.** = *Our company needs people with computer skills.*

rénjia 人家 PRONOUN
1 = other people
■ 人家能做到的，我也能做到。**Rénjia néng zuòdao de, wǒ yě néng zuòdao.** = *What others can achieve, I can too.*
2 = he, she, they (used to refer another person or other people)
■ 人家不愿意，你别勉强。**Rénjia bú yuànyì, nǐ bié miǎnqiáng.** = *If they aren't willing, don't force them to do it.*

rénkǒu 人口 [compound: 人 *human* + 口 *mouth*] NOUN = population (human)
■ 你们国家有多少人口？ **Nǐmen guójiā yǒu duōshǎo rénkǒu?** = *What is the population of your country?*

■ 很多发展中国家都在控制人口增长。**Hěn duō fāzhǎnzhōng guójiā dōu zài kòngzhì rénkǒu zēngzhǎng.** = *Many developing countries are controlling population increase.*

NOTE: It is interesting that the Chinese word for *population* is made up of 人 **rén** (*human*) and 口 **kǒu** (*the mouth*). It suggests that feeding people (mouths) has been the primary concern in China.

rénlèi 人类 [modif: 人 *human* + 类 *kind*] NOUN = humankind, mankind
■ 人类应该保护自然环境。**Rénlèi yīnggāi bǎohù zìrán huánjìng.** = *Mankind should protect the natural environment.*
rénlèixué 人类学 = anthropology

rénmen 人们 [suffix: 人 *person, people* + 们 suffix indicating plural number] NOUN = people, the public
■ 春节那几天，人们都比较客气，避免争吵。**Chūnjié nà jǐ tiān, rénmen dōu bǐjiào kèqi, bìmiǎn zhēngchǎo.** = *During the Chinese New Year, people are polite to each other to avoid quarrels.*
■ 人们都认为发展经济很重要。**Rénmen dǒu rènwéi fāzhǎn jīngjì hěn zhòngyào.** = *People think it is important to develop the economy.*

rénmin 人民 [compound: 人 *human beings* + 民 *the people*] NOUN = the people (of a state)
■ 人民是国家的主人。**Rénmín shì guójiā de zhǔrén.** = *The people are the masters of a country.*
■ 政府应该为人民服务。**Zhèngfǔ yīnggāi wèi rénmín fúwù.** = *The government should serve the people.*

Rénmíngbì 人民币 [modif: 人民 *the people* + 币 *currency, banknote*] NOUN = the Chinese currency, Renminbi (RMB)
■ 我想用美元换人民币。**Wǒ xiǎng yòng Měiyuán huàn Rénmínbì.** = *I want to change some US dollars to Renminbi.*

rénwù 人物 NOUN = well-known and important person, figure, personage (位 **wèi**)
■ 这位大学校长是世界著名人物。**Zhè wèi dàxué xiàozhǎng shì shìjiè zhùmíng rénwù.** = *This university president is a famous figure in the world.*

rényuán 人员 [compound: 人 *human* + 员 *staff*] NOUN = personnel, staff
- 我校有教学人员五十六名，其他人员十八名。**Wǒ xiào yǒu jiàoxué rényuán wǔshí liù míng, qítā rényuán shíbā míng.** = *This school has a teaching staff of 56 people and 18 other staff members.*

rénzào 人造 [modif: 人 *man* + 造 *make*] ADJECTIVE = man-made, artificial
- 第一颗人造卫星是哪一年上天的？ **Dì-yī kē rénzào wèixīng shì nǎ yì nián shàngtiān de?** = *In which year was the first man-made satellite launched?*

rěn 忍 VERB = endure, tolerate, put up with
- 你刚来，有的地方不习惯，还得忍一点。**Nǐ gāng lái, yǒude dìfang bù xíguàn, hái děi rěn yídiàn.** = *You're new here, so there may be things you're not used to and will have to put up with for a while.*
  rěn bu zhù 忍不住 = unable to bear, cannot help
- 她在电话里听到妈妈的声音，忍不住哭起来。**Tā zài diànhuà li tīngdao māma de shēngyīn, rěnbuzhù kū qǐlai.** = *Hearing mom's voice on the phone, she couldn't help crying.*
  rěn de zhù 忍得住 = can endure, can bear

rèn 认 Trad 認 VERB
1 = recognize
- 两年不见，我几乎认不出你了！**Liǎng nián bú jiàn, wǒ jīhū rèn bu chū nǐ le!** = *I haven't seen you for two years, and I can hardly recognize you.*
2 = identify
- 你认一下，这里这么多自行车，哪辆是你的？ **Nǐ rèn yíxià, zhèli zhème duō zìxíngchē, nǎ liàng shì nǐ de?** = *Among so many bicycles here, can you identify which one is yours?*

rènde 认得 VERB = same as 认识 **rènshi**

rènshi 认识 [compound: 认 *recognize* + 识 *know*] VERB = know, understand
- 我不认识这个人。**Wǒ bú rènshi zhège rén.** = *I don't know this person. (or I've never met this person before.)*
- 认识你，很高兴。**Rènshi nǐ, hěn gāoxìng.** = *I'm glad to make your acquaintance.*
- 你认识这个汉字吗？ **Nǐ rènshi zhège Hànzì ma?** = *Do you know this Chinese character?*

rènwéi 认为 [idiom] VERB = think, consider (normally followed by a clause)
- 我认为你说得不对。**Wǒ rènwéi nǐ shuōde bú duì.** = *I think what you said is incorrect.*
- 我不这么认为。**Wǒ bú zhème rènwéi.** = *I don't think so.*

rènzhēn 认真 [v+comp: 认 *consider* + 真 *real*] VERB = earnest, conscientious, serious
- 他是个认真的学生。**Tā shì ge rènzhēn de xuésheng.** = *She's a conscientious student.*
- 他是在开玩笑，你不要太认真。**Tā shì zài kāiwánxiào, nǐ bú yào tài rènzhēn.** = *He's joking. Don't take it too seriously.*
- 老老实实做人，认认真真做事。**Lǎo-lǎo-shí-shí zuòrén, rèn-rèn-zhēn-zhēn zuòshì.** = *Be an honest person and a conscientious worker.*

rèn 任 CONJUNCTION = no matter

rènhé 任何 [compound: 任 *no matter* + 何 *what*] PRONOUN = any, whatever
- 你任何时候都可以来找我。**Nǐ rènhé shíhou dōu kěyǐ lái zhǎo wǒ.** = *You can come to see me at any time.*
- 在任何情况下，都要遵守法律。**Zài rènhé qíngkuàng xia, dōu yào zūnshǒu fǎlǜ.** = *One should abide by the law under any circumstances.*
  rènhé rén 任何人 = anyone
- 任何人都不可以那样做。**Rènhé rén dōu bù kěyǐ nàyàng zuò.** = *No one is allowed to do that.*
  rènhé shì 任何事 = any matter, anything, everything
- 他做任何事都挺认真。**Tā zuò rènhé shì dōu tǐng rènzhēn.** = *He does everything conscientiously.*

rènwù 任务 [compound: 任 *mission* + 务 *work*] NOUN = assignment, mission
- 李经理要派你一个重要任务。**Lǐ jīnglǐ yào pài nǐ yí ge zhòngyào rènwù.** = *Mr Li, the manager, will give you an important assignment.*
- 这个任务很难，不可能在一个月内完成。**Zhège rènwù hěn nán, bù kěnéng zài yí ge yuè nèi wánchéng.** = *This is a difficult mission which cannot be accomplished in a month.*

R

rēng 扔 VERB = throw, toss
- 不要乱扔垃圾。**Bú yào luàn rēng lājī.** = *Do not discard rubbish everywhere. (→ Don't litter.)*

réng 仍 ADVERB = same as 仍然 **réngrán**

réngjiù 仍旧 ADVERB = same as 仍然 **réngrán**

réngrán 仍然 ADVERB = still, as before
- 他有这么多钱，仍然不满足。**Tā yǒu zhème duō qián, réngrán bù mǎnzú.** = *He has so much money but he is still not satisfied.*
- 我睡了十几个小时，仍然觉得累。**Wǒ shuìle shí jǐ ge xiǎoshí, réngrán juéde lèi.** = *I slept for over ten hours but still feel tired.*

rì 日 NOUN = date, day
- 三月二十四日 **Sānyuè èrshísì rì** = *the twenty-fourth of March*
- 九月一日 **Jiǔyuè yī rì** = *the first of September*

rìyè 日夜 = day and night
rìjì 日记 = diary
rìyòngpǐn 日用品 = daily necessities

NOTE: In writing, 日 **rì** is used for dates as shown above. However, in speech it is more common to say 号 **hào**. For example, to say *the twenty-fourth of March* 三月二十四号 **Sānyuè èrshí sì hào** is more natural than 三月二十四日 **Sānyuè èrshi sì rì**.

Rìběn 日本 NOUN = Japan
- 日本在中国东边。**Rìběn zài Zhōngguó dōngbian.** = *Japan lies to the east of China.*
- 你去过日本吗？**Nǐ qùguo Rìběn ma?** = *Have you ever been to Japan?*

rìcháng 日常 [compound: 日 *daily* + 常 *usual*] ADJECTIVE = daily, routine
- 他不希望有规律的日常生活被打乱。**Tā bù xīwàng yǒu guīlǜ de rìcháng shēnghuó bèi dǎluàn.** = *He does not want his regular everyday life to be upset.*
- 这是我的日常工作，一点都不麻烦。**Zhè shì wǒ de rìcháng gōngzuò, yìdiǎn dōu bù máfan.** = *It is part of my routine work. There is no trouble at all.*

rìchéng 日程 [modif: 日 *daily* + 程 *journey*] NOUN = daily schedule, schedule
- 我们开一个会，安排一下工作日程。**Wǒmen kāi yí ge huì, ānpái yíxià gōngzuò rìchéng.** = *Let's have a meeting to plan our work schedule.*
- 今天的日程排得很满。**Jīntiān de rìchéng pái de hěn mǎn.** = *We have a full schedule today.*

rìchéngbiǎo 日程表 = timetable (for a schedule)
yìshì rìchéng 议事日程 = agenda

rìjì 日记 [modif: 日 *daily* + 记 *record*] NOUN = diary (本 **běn**, 篇 **piān**)
jì rìjì 记日记 = keep a diary
- 我从十五岁生日那天开始记日记。**Wǒ cóng shíwǔ suì shēngrì nà tiān kāishǐ jì rìjì.** = *I have been keeping a diary since my fifteenth birthday.*

rìjì běn 日记本 = diary book

rìqī 日期 [compound: 日 *day* + 期 *fixed time*] NOUN = date (especially of an event)
- 你知道考试日期吗？**Nǐ zhīdào kǎoshì rìqī ma?** = *Do you know the date of the exam?*
- 请你查一下这批饼干的过期日期。**Qǐng nǐ chá yíxià zhè pī bǐnggān de guòqī rìqī.** = *Please check the "use by" date of this batch of biscuits.*

Rìwén 日文 [modif: 日 *Japanese* + 文 *writing*] NOUN = the Japanese language (especially the writing)

Rìyǔ 日语 [modif: 日 *Japan* + 语 *speech*] NOUN = the Japanese language
- 日语和汉语很不一样。**Rìyǔ hé Hànyǔ hěn bù yíyàng.** = *Japanese is very different from Chinese.*
- 你们学校教日语吗？**Nǐmen xuéxiào jiāo Rìyǔ ma?** = *Does your school teach Japanese?*

Rìyuán 日元 [modif: 日 *Japan* + 元 *dollar*] NOUN = Japanese currency, yen
- 十万美元是一大笔钱，十万日元不算一大笔钱。**Shíwàn Měiyuán shì yí dà bǐ qián, shí wàn Rìyuán bú suàn yí dà bǐ qián.** = *While a hundred thousand American dollars is a big sum of money, a hundred thousand Japanese yen is not.*

R

rìzi 日子 [suffix: 日 *day* + 子 *nominal suffix*]
NOUN
1 = day, date
- 今天这个日子对我来说特别重要。**Jīntiān zhège rìzi duì wǒ lái shuō tèbié zhòngyào.** = *Today is particularly important to me.*
- 今天是什么日子？为什么街上那么多人？**Jīntiān shì shénme rìzi? Wèishénme jiē shang nàme duō rén?** = *What day is today? Why are there so many people in the street?*
2 = life
- 我们家的日子比过去好多了。**Wǒmen jiā de rìzi bǐ guòqù hǎo duō le.** = *The life of my family is much better than before. (→ My family is better off now.)*
- 我只想安安静静地过日子。**Wǒ zhǐ xiǎng ān-ān-jìng-jìng de guò rìzi.** = *I only want to live a quiet and peaceful life.*

róng 荣 Trad 榮 ADJECTIVE = glorious (See 繁荣 **fánróng**, 光荣 **guāngróng**.)

róng 容 VERB = tolerate

róngyì 容易 [compound: 容 *tolerant* + 易 *easy*]
ADJECTIVE
1 = easy, not difficult (antonym 难 **nán**)
- 这件事很容易。**Zhè jiàn shì hěn róngyì.** = *This is easy to do.*
- 这么容易的问题，你都不会回答？**Zhème róngyì de wèntí, nǐ dōu bú huì huídá?** = *You even can't answer such an easy question?*
2 = having a tendency to, likely
- 年轻人容易受朋友的影响。**Niánqīngrén róngyì shòu péngyou de yǐngxiǎng.** = *Young people are susceptible to their friends' influence.*
- 刚到一个新地方，容易生病。**Gāngdào yí ge xīn dìfang, róngyì shēngbìng.** = *You're likely to fall ill when you first arrive in a new land.*

ròu 肉 NOUN = flesh, meat
- 在我们这儿肉比鱼便宜。**Zài wǒmen zhèr ròu bǐ yú piányì.** = *Pork is cheaper than fish.*
jīròu 鸡肉 = chicken meat
niúròu 牛肉 = beef
yángròu 羊肉 = mutton
yúròu 鱼肉 = fish meat
zhūròu 猪肉 = pork

NOTE: The most popular meat in China is pork. Unspecified, 肉 **ròu** often refers to pork.

rú 如 CONJUNCTION = same as 如果 **rúguǒ**. Used only in writing.

rúguǒ 如果 CONJUNCTION = if
- 如果明天下雨，我们就不去海边游泳。**Rúguǒ míngtiān xià yǔ, wǒmen jiù bú qù hǎibian yóuyǒng.** = *If it rains tomorrow, we won't go to the seaside to swim.*

NOTE: 如果 **rúguǒ** is usually used with 就 **jiù**.

rù 入 VERB = enter
- 病从口入。**Bìng cóng kǒu rù.** = *Disease enters the body by the mouth. (→ Bad food causes disease.)*
rù kǒu 入口 = entry, entrance

ruǎn 软 Trad 軟 ADJECTIVE = soft, supple (antonym 硬 **yìng**)
- 这张床太软。**Zhè zhāng chuáng tài ruǎn.** = *This bed is too soft.*

ruǎnjiàn 软件 [modif: 软 *soft* + 件 *article*]
NOUN = computer software, software
- 他除了买这台新电脑以外，还买了一些软件。**Tā chúle mǎi zhè tái xīn diànnǎo yǐwài, hái mǎile yìxiē ruǎnjiàn.** = *In addition to the new computer he also bought some software.*
- 他们设计了一个软件非常成功。**Tāmen shèjìle yí ge ruǎnjiàn fēicháng chénggōng.** = *They have designed a very successful software.*

ruì 锐 Trad 銳 ADJECTIVE = sharp (See 尖锐 **jiānruì**.)

ruò 弱 ADJECTIVE = weak, feeble (antonym 强 **qiáng**)
- 他年老体弱，不能在田里干活了。**Tā niánlǎo-tǐ-ruò, bù néng zài tián li gànhuó le.** = *He is old and feeble, and is unable to work in the fields.*
- 我使用电脑的能力比较弱，可是我的语言能力很强。**Wǒ shǐyòng diànnǎo de nénglì bǐjiào ruò, kěshì wǒ de yǔyán nénglì hěn qiáng.** = *I'm rather weak in computer skills, but strong in languages.*

R

S

să 洒 Trad 灑 VERB = sprinkle, spray
- 这片稻田有害虫，要洒一点儿药。**Zhè piàn dàotián yǒu hàichóng, yào sǎ yìdiǎnr yào.** = *This paddy field is infested. You need to spray some pesticide on it.*

sài 赛 Trad 賽 VERB = compete (See 比赛 **bǐsài,** 竞赛 **jìngsài.**)

sān 三 NUMERAL = three
- 十三 **shísān** = *thirteen*
- 三十 **sánshí** = *thirty*

sǎn 伞 Trad 傘 NOUN = umbrella (把 **bǎ**)
- 今天可能会下雨，带着伞吧。**Jīntiān kěnéng huì xià yǔ, dàizhe sǎn ba.** = *It may rain today. Take your umbrella with you.*
- 我的伞又丢了。**Wǒ de sǎn yòu diū le.** = *I've lost my umbrella again.*

sàn 散 VERB = disperse

sànbù 散步 [modif: 散 *random* + 步 *step*] VERB = take a short leisurely walk, stroll
- 这位老人常常在公园里散步。**Zhè wèi lǎorén chángcháng zài gōngyuán li sànbù.** = *This old man often takes a walk in the park.*
- 他俩沿着小河散步，直到天快黑了。**Tā liǎ yánzhe xiǎo hé sànbù, zhídào tiān kuài hēi le.** = *The two of them took a walk along the stream till it was almost dark.*

sǎng 嗓 NOUN = throat

sǎngzi 嗓子 [suffix: 嗓 *throat* + 子 nominal suffix] NOUN
1 = voice
- 她嗓子很尖。**Tā sǎngzi hěn jiān.** = *She has a high-pitched voice.* (or *Her voice is very shrill.*)
2 = throat
- 我嗓子疼。**Wǒ sǎngzi téng.** = *I have a sore throat.*

sǎo 扫 Trad 掃 VERB = sweep
- 秋天我得常常扫院子里的落叶。**Qiūtiān wǒ děi chángcháng sǎo yuànzi li de luòyè.** = *In autumn, I have to often sweep away the fallen leaves in my courtyard.*

sǎo 嫂 NOUN = elder brother's wife

sǎozi 嫂子 [suffix: 嫂 *elder brother's wife* + 子 nominal suffix] NOUN = elder brother's wife, sister-in-law
- 他父母去世以后，嫂子对他非常关心。**Tā fùmǔ qùshì yǐhòu, sǎozi duì tā fēicháng guānxīn.** = *After his parents' death, his sister-in-law was very concerned for him.*

NOTE: One's younger brother's wife is 弟妹 **dìmèi.**

sè 色 NOUN = color
- 那座白色的大楼就是医院。**Nà zuò báisè de dàlóu jiù shì yīyuàn.** = *That white building is the hospital.*
sèqíng 色情 = pornography

sēn 森 NOUN = forest

sēnlín 森林 [compound: 森 *forest* + 林 *woods*] NOUN = forest
- 防止火灾，保护森林。**Fángzhǐ huǒzái, bǎohù sēnlín.** = *Prevent fires, protect the forest.*

shā 杀 Trad 殺 VERB = kill
- 你敢杀鸡吗？**Nǐ gǎn shā jī ma?** = *Do you dare to kill chickens?*

shā 沙 NOUN = sand

shāfā 沙发 NOUN = upholstered chair, sofa, couch
- 他买了一对单人沙发和一个双人沙发。**Tā mǎile yí duì dānrén shāfā hé yí ge shuāngrén shāfā.** = *He bought a pair of upholstered chairs and a two-seat sofa.*

shāmò 沙漠 [modif: 沙 *sand* + 漠 *desert*] NOUN = desert
- 沙漠里最需要的是水。**Shāmò li zuì xūyào de shì shuǐ.** = *In a desert, what is most needed is water.*

shāzi 沙子 [suffix: 沙 *sand* + 子 nominal suffix] NOUN = sand, grit (粒 **lì**)
- 我右眼里恐怕有一粒沙子，难受极了。**Wǒ yòuyǎn li kǒngpà yǒu yí lì shānzi, nánshòu jíle.** = *I'm afraid there is a grain of sand in my right eye. It's so irritating!*

shǎ 傻 ADJECTIVE = foolish, stupid (antonym 聪
明 cōngmíng)
- 你别看他模样傻，其实一点儿也不傻。Nǐ
bié kàn tā móyàng shǎ, qíshí yìdiǎnr yě bù shǎ.
= He may look stupid, but he is actually not at
all stupid.
- 你怎么会相信他？真太傻了！Nǐ zěnme
huì xiāngxìn tā? Zhēn tài shǎ le! = How could
you have believed him? It was really foolish!

shài 晒 Trad 曬 VERB = dry in the sun, bask
shài tàiyang 晒太阳 = sunbathe
- 有的人喜欢在夏天晒太阳，这对皮肤有
害。Yǒude rén xǐhuan zài xiàtiān shài tàiyang,
zhè duì pífu yǒuhài. = In summer some people
like to sunbathe, which is harmful to the skin.

shān 山 NOUN = mountain, hill (座 zuò)
- 这座山真高啊！Zhè zuò shān zhēn gāo a! =
How high this mountain is!
- 这个美丽的小城，前面是大河，背后是青
山。Zhège měilì de xiǎochéng, qiánmian shì dà
hé, bèihòu shì qīng shān. = In front of this
beautiful town is a big river and behind it are
green hills.
páshān 爬山 = mountain climbing, mountaineering
- 星期六我们去爬山吧！Xīngqīliù wǒmen
qù páshān ba! = Let's go mountain climbing
this Saturday.
shānshuǐ 山水 = landscape
- 新西兰的山水很美。Xīnxīlán de shānshuǐ
hěn měi. = The landscape of New Zealand is
beautiful.
yóu-shān-wán-shuǐ 游山玩水 = go sightseeing
- 他有钱，又有时间，所以经常出国游山玩
水。Tā yǒu qián, yòu yǒu shíjiān, suǒyǐ
jīngcháng chūguó yóu-shān-wán-shuǐ. = He's
rich and he's got the time, so he often goes
sightseeing overseas.

shānmài 山脉 [modif: 山 mountain + 脉 veins
and arteries] NOUN = mountain range (条 tiáo)
- 世界上最大的山脉 – 喜马拉雅山脉 – 在中
国。Shìjiè shang zuì dà de shānmài – Xǐmǎlāyǎ
shānmài – zài Zhōngguó. = The biggest mountain range in the world—the Himalayas—is in
China.

shān 衫 NOUN = shirt (See 衬衫 chènshān.)

shǎn 闪 NOUN = flash

shǎndiàn 闪电 NOUN = lightning
- 昨天夜里又打雷，又闪电，真吓人。
Zuótiān yèli yòu dǎléi, yòu shǎndiàn, zhēn
xiàrén. = Last night thunder boomed and lightning flashed. It was really frightening.

shàn 扇 NOUN = fan (See 电扇 diànshàn.)

shàn 善 ADJECTIVE = good

shànyú 善于 VERB = be good at
- 他善于理解，不善于表达。Tā shànyú lǐjiě,
bú shànyú biǎodá. = He is good at understanding, but not good at expressing himself.

shāng 伤 Trad 傷
1 VERB = wound, injure, hurt
- 他踢球的时候伤了脚。Tā tīqiú de shíhou
shāngle jiǎo. = He injured his foot playing
football.
- 你这么做会伤他的感情。Nǐ zhènme zuò huì
shāng tā de gǎnqíng. = Doing that will hurt his
feelings.
2 NOUN = wound, injury
- 你的伤不重，很快就会好的。Nǐ de shāng
bú zhòng, hěn kuài jiù huì hǎo de. = Your injury is not serious and will heal soon.
shāngfēng 伤风 = catch a cold
shòushāng 受伤 = be wounded, be injured

shāngxīn 伤心 [v+obj: 伤 wound + 心 the
heart] ADJECTIVE = heartbreaking, heartbroken
- 听到这个伤心的消息，玛丽忍不住哭了。
Tīngdao zhège shāngxīn de xiāoxi, Mǎlì rén bu
zhù kū le. = Hearing this heartbreaking news,
Mary couldn't help weeping.
- 当她三岁的儿子死了，她伤心得不想活。
Dāng tā sān suì de érzi sǐ le, tā shāngxīn de bù
xiǎng huó. = When her three-year-old son died,
she was so heartbroken that she did not want to
live.

shāng 商 NOUN = commerce

shāngchǎng 商场 [modif: 商 commerce + 场
place] NOUN
1 = shopping center, mall (家 jiā, 座 zuò)
- 这座商场有近一百家大大小小的商店。Zhè
zuò shāngchǎng yǒu jìn yìbǎi jiā dà-dà-xiǎo-

xiǎo de **shāngdiàn**. = *This shopping center has nearly a hundred shops, big and small.*

2 = department store
■ 这家商场地处市中心，停车不方便。**Zhè jiā shāngchǎng dìchù shìzhōngxīn, tíng chē bù fāngbiàn.** = *This department store is in the city center. Parking is inconvenient.*

shāngdiàn 商店 NOUN = shop, store (家 **jiā**)
■ 这家商店是卖什么的？ **Zhè jiā shāngdiàn shì mài shénme de?** = *What does this store sell?*
■ 我常去那家商店买东西。**Wǒ cháng qù nàjiā shāngdiàn mǎi dōngxi.** = *I often shop at that store.*
kāi shāngdiàn 开商店 = open a shop, keep a shop

shāngliang 商量 [compound: 商 *discuss* + 量 *weigh*] VERB = discuss, consult
■ 有重要的事，先和好朋友商量再决定。**Yǒu zhòngyào de shì, xiān hé hǎo péngyou shāngliang zài juédìng.** = *When an important matter arises, discuss it with good friends before making a decision.*
■ 我想和你商量一件事，听听你的意见。**Wǒ xiǎng hé nǐ shāngliang yí jiàn shì, tīngtīng nǐ de yìjiàn.** = *There is something I'd like to consult you over and hear your advice.*

shāngpǐn 商品 [modif: 商 *commerce* + 品 *article*] NOUN = commodity (件 **jiàn**, 种 **zhǒng**)
■ 我们卖出的商品都有质量保证。**Wǒmen màichū de shāngpǐn dōu yǒu zhìliàng bǎozhèng.** = *All the goods we sell have a quality guarantee.*
■ 商品的价格是由什么决定的？ = **Shāngpǐn de jiàgé shì yóu shénme juédìng de?** = *What determines the price of commodities?*

shāngyè 商业 [modif: 商 *commerce* + 业 *industry*] NOUN = commerce, business
■ 这个城市商业十分发达。**Zhège chéngshì shāngyè shífēn fādá.** = *Commerce is very well developed in this city.*
shāngyè guǎnlǐ 商业管理 = business administration
shāngyè qū 商业区 = business district

shàng 上 1 NOUN
1 = on top of, on, above (antonym 下 **xià**)
■ 山上有一座白房子。**Shān shang yǒu yí zuò bái fángzi.** = *There's a white house on the hill.*

2 = previous, last
■ 上星期 **shàng xīngqī** = *last week*
■ 上一课 **shàng yì kè** = *the previous class (lesson)*

NOTE: 上 **shàng** is often used after a noun to form words of location. While its basic meaning is on top, 上 **shàng** may have various, often semi-idiomatic senses, e.g.
bàozhǐ shang 报纸上 = in the newspaper
dìshang 地上 = on the ground
gōngzuò shang 工作上 = in work
huì shang 会上 = at the meeting
shìjiè shang 世界上 = in the world
shǒu shang 手上 = in hand, in the hands of

shàng 上 2 VERB
1 = go upwards, ascend
shàng lóu 上楼 = go upstairs
■ 我坐电梯上楼。**Wǒ zuò diàntī shàng lóu.** = *I take the lift upstairs.*
shànglai 上来 = come up
■ 楼上有空房间，快上来吧！ **Lóu shang yǒu kòng fángjiān, kuài shànglai ba!** = *There's a vacant room upstairs, please come up!*
shàngqu 上去 = go up
■ 他们在楼上等你，快上去吧！ **Tāmen zài lóu shang děng nǐ, kuài shàngqu ba!** = *They're waiting for you upstairs. Please go upstairs.*
2 = get on (a vehicle), go aboard (a plane, ship)
■ 火车来了，准备上车吧！ **Huǒchē lái le, zhǔnbèi shàng chē ba!** = *The train is coming. Let's get ready to board.*
shàng chē 上车 = get into a vehicle
shàng chuán 上船 = board a ship
shàng feijī 上飞机 = get on the plane
3 = attend (school), go to (work)
shàngxué 上学 = go to school
■ 你弟弟上学了吗？ **Nǐ dìdi shàngxué le ma?** = *Has your younger brother started school yet?*
■ 我骑自行车上学。**Wǒ qí zìxíngchē shàngxué.** = *I go to school by bike.*
shàngbān 上班 = go to work
■ 我母亲每天九点上班，五点下班。**Wǒ mǔqin měi tiān jiǔ diǎn shàngbān, wǔ diǎn xiàbān.** = *Every day my mother goes to work at nine and finishes at five.*
shàngkè 上课 = go to class, have class
■ 明天放假，不上课。**Míngtiān fàngjià, bú shàngkè.** = *Tomorrow's a holiday. There're no classes.*

S

shàngdàng 上当 VERB = be fooled, be duped
- 他太老实了，容易上当受骗。**Tā tài lǎoshí le, róngyì shàngdàng shòupiàn.** = *He is too straightforward and easily duped.*
- 你怎么又上她的当了？**Nǐ zěnme yòu shàng tā de dàng le?** = *How is it that you got fooled by her again?*

shàngbian 上边 [modif: 上 *top, upper* + 边 *side*] NOUN = above, high up (antonym 下边 **xiàbian**)
- 从那座大楼的上边可以看见飞机场。**Cóng nà zuò dàlóu de shàngbian kěyǐ kànjiàn fēijīchǎng.** = *From the top of that high building, one can see the airport.*

Shànghǎi 上海 NOUN = Shanghai (the biggest city in China)

shàngjí 上级 [modif: 上 *up, above* + 级 *step, grade*] NOUN = higher authorities, superior
- 上级发来通知，六月三十日停课。**Shàngjí fālai tōngzhī, Liùyuè sānshí rì tíng kè.** = *The authorities have advised that school be closed on June thirtieth.*
- 你是我的上级，我当然要完成你分配的任务。**Nǐ shì wǒ de shàngjí, wǒ dāngrán yào wánchéng nǐ fēnpèi de rènwù.** = *You're my superior, so of course I will complete the task you assigned.*

shàngmiàn 上面 NOUN = same as 上边 **shàngbian**

shàngwǔ 上午 [modif: 上 *upper half* + 午 *noon*] NOUN = morning (usually from 8 a.m. to noon) (antonym 下午 **xiàwǔ**)
- 我们上午上三节课。**Wǒmen shàngwǔ shàng sān jié kè.** = *We have three classes in the morning.*
- 他一直睡到第二天上午十点左右。**Tā yìzhí shuìdao dì-èr tiān shàngwǔ shí diǎn zuǒyòu.** = *He slept until about ten o'clock the next morning.*

NOTE: 上午 **shàngwǔ** does not mean the whole morning. It denotes the part of morning from about eight or nine o'clock to noon. The period before eight or nine o'clock is 早晨 **zǎochén** or 早上 **zǎoshang**.

shàngwǎng 上网 [v+obj: 上 *get on* + 网 *Internet*] NOUN = get on the Internet, surf the Internet
- 他一般吃了晚饭，就上网半小时看看新闻。**Tā yìbān chīle wǎnfàn jiù shàngwǎng bàn xiǎoshí kànkan xīnwén.** = *After supper he usually gets on the Internet for half an hour to read the news.*
- 这几天我忙得没有时间上网。**Zhè jǐ tiān wǒ máng de méiyǒu shíjiān shàngwǎng.** = *These days I'm so busy that I haven't got the time to get on the Internet.*

shàngyī 上衣 [modif: 上 *upper* + 衣 *clothing*] NOUN = upper garment, jacket (件 **jiàn**)
- 你这件上衣很好看，在哪儿买的？**Nǐ zhè jiàn shàngyī hěn hǎokàn, zài nǎr mǎi de?** = *Your jacket looks good. Where did you buy it?*

shāo 稍 ADVERB = same as 稍微 **shāowēi**. Often used in written Chinese.

shāowēi 稍微 [compound: 稍 *slight* + 微 *tiny*] ADVERB = slightly, just a little bit
- 你能不能把电视机的声音开得稍微大一点？**Nǐ néng bu néng bǎ diànshìjī de shēngyin kāi de shāowēi dà yìdiǎn?** = *Could you turn the TV up a bit?*
- 我稍微有点儿头疼，休息一会儿就会好的。**Wǒ shāowēi yǒu diǎnr tóuténg, xiūxi yíhuìr jiù huì hǎo de.** = *I've a slight headache. I'll be all right after a short rest.*

shāo 烧 Trad 燒 VERB
1 = burn
- 市政府禁止烧垃圾。**Shìzhèngfǔ jìnzhǐ shāo lājī.** = *The city government bans the burning of rubbish.*
2 = cook
- 今天我给你们烧个鱼。**Jīntiān wǒ gěi nǐmen shāo ge yú.** = *Today I'll cook you a fish.*
3 = have fever
- 这孩子烧得厉害，得马上送医院！**Zhè háizi shāo de lìhai, děi mǎshàng sòng yīyuàn!** = *The child is running a very high fever. He must be sent to the hospital right now!*

sháo 勺 NOUN = spoon

sháozi 勺子 [suffix: 勺 *ladle* + 子 *nominal suffix*] NOUN = ladle, spoon (把 **bǎ**)

■ 她用勺子把汤分给大家。 **Tā yòng sháozi bǎ tāng fēn gei dàjiā.** = *She gave soup to everyone with a ladle.*

shǎo 少

1 ADJECTIVE = small amount, few, little (antonym 多 **duō**)
■ 新西兰人少地多。 **Xīnxīlán rén shǎo dì duō.** = *New Zealand has a small population and much land.*
2 ADJECTIVE = not often, seldom
■ 我们虽然在同一个学校，但是很少见面。 **Wǒmen suīrán zài tóng yí ge xuéxiào, dànshì hěn shǎo jiànmiàn.** = *Although we're in the same school, we seldom see each other.*
3 VERB = be short, be missing
■ 原来我有一百元，现在怎么少了二十元？ **Yuánlái wǒ yǒu yìbǎi yuán, xiànzài zěnme shǎole èrshí yuán?** = *I originally had one hundred dollars. How is it that I have twenty dollars less now?*
■ 要和他们比赛，我们还少一个人。 **Yào hé tāmen bǐsài, wǒmen hái shǎo yí ge rén.** = *We're still short of one person if we want to compete with them.*

shǎoshù 少数 [modif: 少 few, little + 数 number] NOUN = minority (antonym 多数 **duōshù**)
■ 少数服从多数，这是民主的一条基本原则。 **Shǎoshù fúcóng duōshù, zhè shì mínzhǔ de yì tiáo jīběn yuánzé.** = *The minority should submit to the majority—this is a fundamental principle of democracy.*
shǎoshù mínzú 少数民族 = minority nationality (non-Han ethnic group in China)

shàonián 少年 [modif: 少 young + 年 age] NOUN = young man (from around 10 to 16 years old), adolescent
■ 自古少年出英雄。 **Zìgǔ shàonián chū yīngxióng.** = *Ever since ancient times, heroes have emerged from the young.*

NOTES: (1) A young woman of around 10 to 16 years old is called 少女 **shàonǚ**. (2) The word 青少年 **qīngshàonián** is often used to mean young people collectively.

shào 绍 Trad 紹 VERB = connect (See 介绍 **jièshào**.)

shé 舌 NOUN = tongue

shétou 舌头 [suffix: 舌 the tongue + 头 nominal suffix] NOUN = the tongue
■ 医生：你舌头伸出来，我看看。 **Yīshēng: Nǐ shétou shēn chūlai, wǒ kànkan.** = *Doctor: Stick out your tongue and I'll have a look. (→ Show me your tongue.)*

shé 蛇 NOUN = snake (条 **tiáo**)
■ 她最怕蛇。 **Tā zuì pà shé.** = *She finds snakes the most frightening [of all animals].*

shè 设 Trad 設 VERB = equip

shèbèi 设备 VERB = equipment, installation
■ 这座医院设备良好。 **Zhè zuò yīyuàn shèbèi liánghǎo.** = *This hospital is well equipped.*
■ 这套实验室设备是从国外进口的。 **Zhè tào shíyànshì shèbèi shì cóng guówài jìnkǒu de.** = *This set of laboratory equipment was imported from overseas.*

shèjì 设计 [compound: 设 plan + 计 calculate]
1 VERB = design
■ 工程师正在设计一种不用汽油的汽车。 **Gōngchéshī zhèngzài shèjì yì zhǒng bú yòng qìyóu de qìchē.** = *Engineers are designing a car that does not use petrol.*
2 NOUN = design, plan
■ 我有一个叔叔，是搞建筑设计的。 **Wǒ yǒu yí ge shūshu, shì gǎo jiànzhù shèjì de.** = *I have an uncle engaged in architectural design.*

shè 社 NOUN = association

shèhuì 社会 [compound: 社 god of the earth + 会 gathering] NOUN = society
■ 我们每个人都应该关心社会。 **Wǒmen měi ge rén dōu yīnggāi guānxīn shèhuì.** = *Each of us should be concerned for society.*
■ 今天的中国是个什么样的社会？ **Jīntiān de Zhōngguó shì ge shénmeyàng de shèhuì?** = *What kind of society is China today?*
shèhuì shang 社会上 = in society
shèhuìxué 社会学 = sociology
shèhuì zhǔyì 社会主义 = socialism

shè 舍 NOUN = hut, shed (See 宿舍 **sùshè**.)

shè 摄 Trad 攝 VERB = photograph, shoot

S

shèyǐng 摄影 [v+obj: 摄 *take* + 影 *shadow*]
NOUN = photography
■ 这个电影的摄影十分成功。**Zhège diànyǐng de shèyǐng shífēn chénggōng.** = *The cinematography of this film is a spectacular success.*
shèyǐngjiā 摄影家 = accomplished photographer
shèyǐngshī 摄影师 = photographer
shèyǐng zuòpǐn 摄影作品 = a work of photography

shéi 谁 Trad 誰 PRONOUN = same as 谁 **shuí.**
Used colloquially.

shēn 伸 VERB = stretch out, extend
■ 火车开的时候，你千万不要把头伸出车窗。**Huǒchē kāi de shíhou, nǐ qiānwàn bú yào bǎ tóu shēnchū chēzhuāng.** = *Never stick out your head out of the window when the train is moving.*

shēn 身
1 NOUN = the human body
■ 他身高175公分。**Tā shēn gāo yìbǎi qīshí wǔ gōngfēn.** = *He is 175 centimeters tall.*
2 MEASURE WORD = (for clothes)
■ 一身新衣服 **yì shēn xīn yīfu** = *a suit of new clothes*

shēnbiān 身边 NOUN = close by one's side, on one's person
■ 我身边没有她的地址，我发电子邮件告诉你。**Wǒ shēnbiān méiyǒu tā de dìzhǐ, wǒ fā diànzǐ yóujiàn gàosu nǐ.** = *I don't have her address with me. I'll send it to you by email.*
■ 他出去身边总带着手机。**Tā chūqu shēnbiān zǒng dàizhe shǒujī.** = *He never goes anywhere without his cell phone.*

shēntǐ 身体 [compound: 身 *body* + 体 *physical*] NOUN
1 = human body
■ 少年儿童正处在长身体的时期。**Shàonián értóng zhèng chǔ zai zhǎng shēntǐ de shíqī.** = *Children and adolescents are at a stage of physical development.*
2 = health
■ 我爸爸年纪大了，但是身体还很好。**Wǒ bàba niánjì dà le, dànshì shēntǐ hái hěn hǎo.** = *My father is getting old, but is still in good health.*

■ 你要注意身体。**Nǐ yào zhùyì shēntǐ.** = *You should pay attention to your health.*

NOTE: Although its original meaning is the body, 身体 **shēntǐ** is often used in colloquial Chinese to mean health. Friends often ask about each other's health in greeting:
■ 你身体好吗？ **Nǐ shēntǐ hǎo ma?** = *How's your health?*
■ 你最近身体怎么样？ **Nǐ zuìjìn shēntǐ zěnmeyàng?** = *How's your health been recently?*

shēn 深 ADJECTIVE
1 = deep (antonym 浅 **qiǎn**)
■ 这条河深吗？ **Zhè tiáo hé shēn ma?** = *Is this river deep?*
2 = difficult to understand, profound
■ 这本书太深了，我看不懂。**Zhè běn shū tài shēn le, wǒ kàn bu dǒng.** = *This book is too difficult. I can't understand it.*
shēn-rù-qiǎn-chū 深入浅出 = explain complicated theories or phenomena in simple, easy-to-understand language.

shēnhòu 深厚 [compound: 深 *deep* + 厚 *thick*]
ADJECTIVE = deep, profound
■ 他对故乡有深厚的感情。**Tā duì gùxiāng yǒu shēnhòu de gǎnqíng.** = *He has deep feelings for his hometown.*

shēnkè 深刻 [modif: 深 *deep* + 刻 *carve*]
ADJECTIVE = incisive, insightful, profound
■ 这位老人经历十分丰富，对人性有深刻的认识。**Zhè wèi lǎorén jīnglì shífēn fēngfù, duì rénxìng yǒu shēnkè de rènshi.** = *This old man has had very rich experiences and has an incisive understanding of human nature.*

shēnrù 深入 [modif: 深 *deep* + 入 *enter, penetrate*] VERB = enter deeply into
■ 这一政策深入人心。**Zhè yí zhèngcè shēnrù rénxīn.** = *This policy enters deeply into people's hearts.* (→ *This policy is extremely popular.*)

shén 什 PRONOUN = what

shénme 什么 PRONOUN = what
■ 什么是语法？ **Shénme shì yǔfǎ?** = *What is grammar?*

■你要什么? **Nǐ yào shénme?** = *What do you want?*

■你要什么菜? **Nǐ yào shénme cài?** = *Which dish do you want?* (or *What would you like to order?*)

shénmede 什么的 PRONOUN = and so on, and so forth

■他们要了很多菜，有鱼、肉、蔬菜，什么的。**Tāmen yàole hěn duō cài, yǒu yú, ròu, shùcài shénmede.** = *They ordered lots of dishes, fish, meat, vegetables and so on.*

shén 神 NOUN = god(s)

■你相信神吗? **Nǐ xiāngxìn shén ma?** = *Do you believe in God?*

shénhuà 神话 = mythology

cáishényé 财神爷 = the god of money, Mammon

shénjīng 神经 NOUN

1 = nerve

■我牙神经疼。**Wǒ yá shénjīng téng.** = *My tooth nerve hurts.*

2 = the mind, mental state

■他神经有毛病。**Tā shénjīng yǒu máobìng.** = *There is something wrong with his mind.*

shénjīngbìng 神经病 = neuropathy, mental disorder

> NOTE: The formal word for mental disorder is 精神病 **jīngshénbìng**, hence 精神病人 **jīngshénbìngrén** (*patient suffering from mental illness*) and 精神病院 **jīngshénbìngyuàn** (*psychiatric hospital, mental hospital*).

shēng 升 VERB = rise, go up

■昨天股票升了百分之零点五。**Zuótiān gǔpiào shēngle bǎifēn zhī líng diǎn wǔ.** = *Shares rose by half a percent yesterday.*

shēng 生 1 VERB = give birth to, grow

■他妻子上星期生了一个女儿。**Tā qīzi shàng xīngqī shēng le yí ge nǚ'ér.** = *His wife gave birth to a girl baby last week.*

shēng 生 2 ADJECTIVE

1 = raw, not cooked

■我不敢吃生鱼。**Wǒ bù gǎn chī shēng yú.** = *I don't dare to eat raw fish.*

2 = unripe

■苹果还太生，要等一段时间才能吃。**Píngguǒ hái tài shēng, yào děng yí duàn shíjiān cái néng chī.** = *The apples are not ripe yet. It will be some time before they'll be edible.*

shēngchǎn 生产 [compound: 生 grow + 产 produce] VERB = produce, manufacture

■这家工厂去年生产一万辆汽车。**Zhè jiā gōngchǎng qùnián shēngchǎn yíwàn liàng qìchē.** = *This factory manufactured 10,000 automobiles last year.*

shēngcí 生词 [modif: 生 unfamiliar + 词 word] NOUN = new word (in a language lesson)

■这些生词你都记住了吗? **Zhèxiē shēngcí nǐ dōu jìzhù le ma?** = *Have you committed these new words to memory?*

■这个句子里有一个生词，我不认识，也不会念。**Zhège jùzi li yǒu yí ge shēngcí, wǒ bú rènshi, yě bú huì niàn.** = *There's a new word in the sentence. I don't know it, nor do I know how to say it.*

jì shēngcí 记生词 = memorize new words

shēngdòng 生动 [compound: 生 lively + 动 move] ADJECTIVE = vivid, lively

■她在信里生动有趣地描写了旅行经历。**Tā zài xìn li shēngdòng yǒuqù de miáoxiěle lǚxíng jīnglì.** = *In her letter she gives vivid and interesting accounts of her travel experiences.*

shēnghuó 生活 [compound: 生 living + 活 alive]

1 NOUN = life

■这位老人的生活很困难。**Zhè wèi lǎorén de shēnghuó hěn kùnnan.** = *This old man's life is difficult.* (→ *This old man lives a hard life.*)

■请您介绍一下中国大学生的生活。**Qǐng nín jièshào yíxià Zhōngguó dàxuéshēng de shēnghuó.** = *Please tell us something about the life of Chinese university students.*

2 VERB = live/lead (a life)

■我小时候生活得很愉快。**Wǒ xiǎoshíhou shēnghuó de hěn yúkuài.** = *I lived a happy life in childhood.* (→ *I had a happy childhood.*)

shēnghuó fèi 生活费 = living allowance, cost of living

shēnghuó shuǐpíng 生活水平 = living standards

rìcháng shēnghuó 日常生活 = daily life

S

shēngmìng 生命 [compound: 生 *living* + 命 *life*] NOUN = life (条 tiáo)
- 他的生命在危险中。**Tā de shēngmìng zài wēixiǎn zhōng.** = *His life is in danger.*
- 这只小猫也是一条生命，不能眼看它死去。**Zhè zhī xiǎo māo yě shì yì tiáo xiǎo shēngmìng, bù néng yǎnkàn tā sǐqu.** = *This kitten is also a life. We can't let it die without doing anything.*

shēngmìng kēxué 生命科学 = life science
shēngmìnglì 生命力 = life force

shēngqì 生气 VERB = get angry, be offended
- 别对他生气，他不是故意的。**Bié duì tā shēngqì, tā bú shì gùyì de.** = *Don't get angry with him. He did not mean it.*
- 你为了什么事生气？**Nǐ wèile shénme shì shēngqì?** = *What are you angry about?*

shēngrì 生日 [modif: 生 *birth* + 日 *day*] NOUN = birthday
- 你的生日是哪一天？ **Nǐ de shēngrì shì nǎ yì tiān?** = *Which date is your birthday? (→ When is your birthday?)*
- 我忘了今天是我妻子的生日！ **Wǒ wàngle jīntiān shì wǒ qīzi de shēngrì!** = *I forgot it's my wife's birthday today.*
- 祝你生日快乐! **Zhù nǐ shēngrì kuàilè!** = *I wish you a happy birthday!*

guò shēngrì 过生日 = celebrate a birthday
- 你今年打算怎么过生日？ **Nǐ jīnnián dǎsuàn zěnme guò shēngrì?** = *How are you going to celebrate your birthday this year?*

shēngrì hékǎ 生日贺卡 = birthday card
shēngrì lǐwù 生日礼物 = birthday present

shēngwù 生物 [modif: 生 *living* + 物 *thing*] NOUN = living things
- 生物一般分为动物和植物两大类。**Shēngwù yìbān fēnwéi dòngwù hé zhíwù liǎng dà lèi.** = *Living things are generally categorized into animals and plants.*

shēngwùxué 生物学 = biology
shēngwù huàxué 生物化学 = chemical biology, biochemistry

shēngyi 生意 NOUN = business, trade
- 他每天上网做生意。**Tā měi tiān shàngwǎng zuò shēngyi.** = *He does trading over the Internet every day.*
- 最近生意很不好。**Zuìjìn shēngyi hěn bù hǎo.** = *Business has been slack lately.*

shēngzhǎng 生长 [compound: 生 *living* + 长 *growing*] VERB = grow, grow up
- 我生长在一个大城市里。**Wǒ shēngzhǎng zài yí ge dà chéngshì li.** = *I grew up in a big city.*
- 这种植物在河边生长得很好。**Zhè zhǒng zhíwù zài hébiān shēngzhǎng de hěn hǎo.** = *This kind of plant grows well by the river.*

shēng 声 Trad 聲 NOUN = sound, noise, voice
- 机器声太大，我听不请你说什么。**Jīqì shēng tài dà, wǒ tīng bu qīng nǐ shuō shénme.** = *The noise from the machine is too loud; I can't hear what you're saying.*

shēngdiào 声调 [modif: 声 *voice* + 调 *tone*] NOUN = tone of a Chinese word
- 汉语的声调确实比较难学。**Hànyǔ de shēngdiào quèshí bǐjiào nánxué.** = *The tones of Chinese are really rather difficult to learn.*
- "这个字是哪个声调？""这个字读第二声。" **"Zhège zì shì nǎge shēngdiào?" "Zhège zì dú dì-èr shēng."** = *"Which tone should this character be read with? (or Which tone does this character have?)" "This character is read with the second tone."*

shēngyīn 声音 [compound: 声 *voice* + 音 *sound*] NOUN = voice, sound
- 我听见有人在楼下说话的声音。**Wǒ tīngjiàn yǒurén zài lóuxià shuōhuà de shēngyīn.** = *I heard the sounds of conversation downstairs.*
- 她的声音很好听。**Tā de shēngyīn hěn hǎotīng.** = *Her voice is pleasant.*
- 请你们说话声音轻一点。**Qǐng nǐmen shuōhuà shēngyīn qīng yìdiǎn.** = *Please talk softly. (or Please don't talk so loudly.)*

shēng 牲 NOUN = domesticated animal (See 牲 xīshēng.)

shéng 绳 Trad 繩 NOUN = string, rope

shéngzi 绳子 [suffix: 绳 *rope* + 子 nominal suffix] NOUN = rope, cord (根 gēn, 条 tiáo)
- 你拉一下这根绳子，窗子就会开。**Nǐ lā yíxià zhè gēn shéngzi, chuāngzi jiù huì kāi.** = *Pull this cord and the window will open.*

shěng 省

1 NOUN = province
- 中国一共有多少个省？ **Zhōngguó yígòng yǒu duōshǎo ge shěng?** = *How many provinces are there in China?*

shěnghuì 省会 = provincial capital

shěng 省

2 VERB = save, economize
- 发电子邮件，既省钱，又省时间。 **Fā diànzǐ yóujiàn, jì shěng qián, yòu shěng shíjiān.** = *Sending e-mail saves money and time.*
- 他用钱很省。 **Tā yòng qián hěn shěng.** = *He is very frugal with money.*

shèng 胜 Trad 勝 VERB = triumph (over), be victorious, defeat
- 上海队胜了北京队。 **Shànghǎi duì shèngle Běijīng duì.** = *The Shanghai team defeated the Beijing team.*

shènglì 胜利 [compound: 胜 triumph + 利 gain benefit]

1 VERB = win victory
- 我们胜利了！ **Wǒmen shènglì le!** = *We've won!*

2 NOUN = victory
- 我们的胜利来得不容易。 **Wǒmen de shènglì lái de bù róngyì.** = *Our victory was hard-won.*

shèng 剩 VERB = be left over, have as surplus
- 我原来有五百块钱，用了四百块，还剩一百块。 **Wǒ yuánlái yǒu wǔbǎi kuài qián, yòngle sìbǎi kuài, hái shèng yìbǎi kuài.** = *I originally had five hundred dollars; I've used four hundred dollars and now have one hundred dollars left.*

shèng cài 剩菜 = leftovers

shī 失 VERB = lose

shībài 失败 [compound: 失 lose + 败 be defeated]

1 VERB = be defeated, lose, fail (antonym 胜利 shènglì, 成功 chénggōng)
- 他们的计划失败了。 **Tāmen de jìhuà shībài le.** = *Their plan failed.*

2 NOUN = defeat, loss, failure
- 失败是成功之母。 **Shībài shì chénggōng zhī mǔ.** = *Failure is the mother of success.*

shīqù 失去 [compound: 失 lose + 去 go away]
VERB = lose (something valuable)
- 她渐渐对孩子失去耐心。 **Tā jiànjiàn duì háizi shīqù nàixīn.** = *She is running out of patience with the kids.*

shīwàng 失望 [v+obj: 失 lose + 望 hope]
ADJECTIVE = disappointed
- 你们没有完成上个月的生产计划，我非常失望。 **Nǐmen méiyǒu wánchéng shàng ge yuè de shēngchǎn jìhuà, wǒ fēicháng shīwàng.** = *I am bitterly disappointed that you failed to complete last month's production plan.*

duì … shīwàng 对 … 失望 = be disappointed with…
- 我知道，我哥哥和嫂子对他们的孩子很失望。 **Wǒ zhīdào, wǒ gēge hé sǎozi duì tāmende háizi hěn shīwàng.** = *I know my brother and his wife are disappointed with their children.*

shīyè 失业 [v+obj: 失 lose + 业 occupation, employment] VERB = lose one's job, become unemployed
- 经济情况不好，失业的人越来越多。 **Jīngjì qíngkuàng bù hǎo, shīyè de rén yuèláiyuè duō.** = *As the economy is weak, more and more people lose their jobs.*
- 我万一失业了，就再进大学念书。 **Wǒ wànyī shīyè le, jiù zài jìn dàxué niànshū.** = *If I lose my job, I will go back to university to study.*

shī 师 Trad 師 NOUN = master, teacher

shīfu 师傅 [compound: 师 teacher + 傅 tutor]
NOUN = master worker (位 wèi)
- 这位师傅技术很高。 **Zhè wèi shīfu jìshù hěn gāo.** = *This master worker is highly skilled.*
- 这个机器坏了，要请一位师傅来看看。 **Zhège jīqì huàile, yào qǐng yí wèi shīfu lái kànkan.** = *This machine is not working properly. We need to ask a master worker to come and have a look.*

NOTE: 师傅 **shīfu** is also a polite form of address to a worker. For example, an electrician or mechanic can be addressed as 师傅 **shīfu** or, if his family name is 李 **Lǐ**, 李师傅 **Lǐ shīfu**.

S

shī 诗 Trad 詩 NOUN = poem, poetry (首 **shǒu**)
■ 现在写诗、读诗的人越来越少了。**Xiànzài xiě shī, dú shī de rén yuèlaiyuè shǎo le.** = *Nowadays fewer and fewer people write or read poems.*
　shīrén 诗人 = poet
　shīgē 诗歌 = poem, poetry

shī 施 VERB = carry out, execute

shīgōng 施工 [v+obj: 施 *execute* + 工 *work*] VERB = (construction work) be underway, be in progress
■ 新教学大楼什么时候施工? **Xīn jiàoxué dàlóu shénme shíhou kāishǐ shīgōng?** = *When will construction of the new classroom building be underway?*
■ 前面施工，绕道通行。**Qiánmiàn shīgōng, rào dào tōngxíng.** = *Road works ahead. Detour.*

shī 狮 Trad 獅 NOUN = lion

shīzi 狮子 [suffix: 狮 *lion* + 子 nominal suffix] NOUN = lion (头 **tóu**)
■ 动物园里有两头非洲来的狮子。**Dòngwùyuán li yǒu liǎng tóu Fēizhōu lái de shīzi.** = *In the zoo there are two lions from Africa.*

shī 湿 Trad 濕 ADJECTIVE = damp, wet, (antonym 干 **gān**)
■ 昨夜下过雨，早上路面还湿着。**Zuóyè xiàguo yǔ, zǎoshang lùmian hái shīzhe.** = *It rained last night, so the roads were wet this morning.*

shí 十 NUMERAL = ten
■ 十五　**shíwǔ** = *fifteen*
■ 五十　**wǔshí** = *fifty*

shífēn 十分 [modif: 十 *ten* + 分 *point*] ADVERB = one hundred percent, totally, fully
■ 我十分满意。**Wǒ shífēn mǎnyì.** = *I'm totally satisfied.*
■ 我十分理解你们的心情。**Wǒ shífēn lǐjiě nǐmen de xīnqíng.** = *I understand your feelings completely.*

shí 石 NOUN = stone

shítou 石头 [suffix: 石 *stone, rock* + 头 nominal suffix] NOUN = stone, rock (块 **kuài**)
■ 这座山上石头太多，不适合种树。**Zhè zuò shān shang shítou tài duō, bú shìhé zhòng shù.** = *This hill is too rocky. It is not suitable for tree planting.*
■ 摸着石头过河。**Mōzhe shítou guò hé.** = *Cross a river by feeling for stones. (→ Make decisions as you go along, act without a premeditated plan.)*

shíyóu 石油 [modif: 石 *stone* + 油 *oil*] NOUN = petroleum, oil
■ 必须在石油用尽以前，开发出新的能源。**Bìxū zài shíyóu yòngjìn yǐqián, kāifāchū xīn de néngyuán.** = *New sources of energy must be developed before petroleum is exhausted.*

shí 识 Trad 識 VERB = know (See 认识 **rènshi**, 知识 **zhīshi**.)

shí 时 Trad 時 NOUN = same as 点钟 **diǎnzhōng**. Used only in writing.

shídài 时代 [compound: 时 *time* + 代 *generation*] NOUN = a historical period, epoch, age
■ 人类从石器时代到电脑时代，花了几千年的时间。**Rénlèi cóng shíqì shídài dào diànnǎo shídài, huāle jǐqiān nián de shíjiān.** = *It took mankind thousands of years to move from the Stone Age to the Computer Age.*

shíhou 时候 [compound: 时 *time* + 候 *a certain point in time*] NOUN = a certain point in time, (the time) when
■ 飞机什么时候开? **Fēijī shénme shíhou kāi?** = *When will the plane depart?*
■ 他来的时候，我正在打电话。**Tā lái de shíhou, wǒ zhèngzài dǎ diànhuà.** = *I was on the phone when he came.*

shíjiān 时间 [compound: 时 *time* + 间 *moment*] NOUN = a period of time
■ 时间不够，我没做完那道练习。**Shíjiān bú gòu, wǒ méi zuòwán nà dào liànxí.** = *As there wasn't enough time, I did not finish that exercise.*
■ 我没有时间写信。**Wǒ méiyǒu shíjiān xiě xìn.** = *I don't have time to write letters.*

shíkè 时刻 [compound: 时 *time* + 刻 *a point*]
NOUN = at a particular point in time
■ 在关键时刻，可以看出一个人的本性。**Zài guānjiàn shíkè, kěyǐ kànchū yí ge rén de běnxìng.** = *At critical moments, a person shows his true colors.*
  shíkèbiǎo 时刻表 = (railway, coach) timetable

shíqī 时期 [compound: 时 *time* + 期 *period*]
NOUN = period of time, stage
■ 他在少年时期受到良好的教育。**Tā zài shàonián shíqī shòudao liánghǎo de jiàoyù.** = *He received a very good education during his adolescence.*

shí 实 Trad 實 ADJECTIVE = real, true

shíjì 实际
1 NOUN = reality, actual situation
■ 这项政策脱离实际。**Zhè xiàng zhèngcè tuōlí shíjì.** = *This policy is out of touch with reality.*
■ 我们的停车场停不了这么多的车，这是一个实际问题。**Wǒmen de tíngchēchǎng ting bu liǎo zhème duō de chē, zhè shì yíge shíjì wèntí.** = *It is a real problem that our car park is too small to accommodate so many cars.*
2 ADJECTIVE = practical, realistic
■ 我们订计划要实际一点。**Wǒmen dìng jìhuà yào shíjì yìdiǎn.** = *We should be practical when drawing up a plan.*

shíjiàn 实践 [compound: 实 *fruit, fruition* + 践 *implement*]
1 VERB = put into practice, apply
■ 懂了这个道理，就要实践。**Dǒngle zhège dàolǐ, jiù yào shíjiàn.** = *After you've understood this principle, you should put it into practice.*
2 NOUN = practice
■ 实践出真知。**Shíjiàn chū zhēnzhī.** = *Practice leads to genuine knowledge.*
■ 多年的实践证明这一理论是正确的。**Duō nián de shíjiàn zhèngmíng zhè yì lǐlùn shì zhèngquè de.** = *Years of practical application have proved this theory correct.*

shíxiàn 实现 [compound: 实 *fruit, fruition* + 现 *materialize*] VERB = materialize, realize
■ 我一定要实现这个计划。**Wǒ yídìng yào shíxiàn zhège jìhuà.** = *I must realize this plan.*

■ 他终于实现了自己的理想。**Tā zhōngyú shíxiànle zìjǐ de lǐxiǎng.** = *He finally realized his aspirations.*

shíxíng 实行 VERB = put into practice, take effect, implement, carry out, institute
■ 有的大学实行一年三学期的制度。**Yǒude dàxué shíxíng yì nián sān xuéqī de zhìdù.** = *Some universities implement the system of three terms a year.*
■ 他的新年决心实行了多久？ **Tā de xīnnián juéxīn shíxíngle duōjiǔ?** = *How long did he put his New Year's resolutions into practice?*
■ 中国从上世纪八十年代开始实行"改革开放"政策。**Zhōngguó cóng shàng shìjì bāshí niándài kāishǐ shíxíng "gǎigé kāifàng" zhèngcè.** = *In the 80s of the last century China began to implement the policies of "reform and opening-up."*

shíyàn 实验 [modif: 实 *practical* + 验 *testing*]
NOUN = experiment, test (项 xiàng, 次 cì)
■ 学化学一定要做实验。**Xué huàxué yídìng yào zuò shíyàn.** = *To study chemistry, one must do experiments.*
■ 有人反对用动物做实验。**Yǒurén fǎnduì yòng dòngwù zuò shíyàn.** = *Some people oppose experiments on animals.*
  shíyànshì 实验室 = laboratory
  shíyànyuán 实验员 = laboratory technician

shíyòng 实用 [modif: 实 *practical* + 用 *use*]
ADJECTIVE = practical (for use), useful, handy
■ 这套工作服穿着不好看，但是十分实用。**Zhè tào gōngzuòfú chuānzhe bù hǎokàn, dànshì shífēn shíyòng.** = *This set of work clothes does not look beautiful, but it is very practical.*
■ 这本词典非常实用。**Zhè běn cídiǎn fēicháng shíyòng.** = *This dictionary is very useful.*

shízài 实在
1 ADJECTIVE = honest, truthful
■ 他说的话你听了可能不高兴，但却很实在。**Tā shuō de huà nǐ tīngle kěnéng bù gāoxìng, dàn què hěn shízài.** = *What he said may have made you unhappy, but it was truthful.*
2 ADJECTIVE = indeed, really
■ 我记不起你的名字了，实在抱歉。**Wǒ jì bu qǐ nǐ de míngzi le, shízài hěn bàoqiàn.** = *I'm really sorry I can't remember your name.*

S

shí 食 NOUN = food

shípǐn 食品 [modif: 食 *food* + 品 *article*] NOUN
= foodstuff (as commodities) (件 **jiàn**)
■ 新西兰生产的食品质量很高。**Xīnxīlán
shēngchǎn de shípǐn zhìliàng hěn gāo.** = *The
foodstuffs produced in New Zealand are of very
high quality.*
shípǐn gōngyè 食品工业 = food industry
shípǐn jiāgōng 食品加工 = food processing
shípǐn shāngdiàn 食品商店 = provision shop,
grocery

shítáng 食堂 [modif: 食 *food* + 堂 *hall*] NOUN
= dining hall
■ 吃饭的时候，食堂里人很多。**Chīfàn de
shíhou, shítáng li rén hěn duō.** = *At mealtimes,
there're many people in the dining hall.*

shíwù 食物 [modif: 食 *food* + 物 *things*] NOUN
= food
■ 空气、水和食物都是绝对必要的。**Kōngqì,
shuǐ hé shíwù dōu shì juéduì bìyào de.** = *Air,
water and food are absolutely indispensable.*

shí 拾 VERB = pick up (from the ground) (See 收
拾 **shōushi.**)

shǐ 史 NOUN = history (See 历史 **lìshǐ.**)

shǐ 使 VERB = make, enable
■ 这次旅行使我学到很多知识。**Zhè cì lǚxíng
shǐ wǒ xuédao hěn duō zhīshi.** = *This trip en-
abled me to gain a great deal of knowledge.*
■ 岁月使人老。**Suìyuè shǐ rén lǎo.** = *Time
makes one old.*

shǐyòng 使用 [compound: 使 *use* + 用 *use*]
VERB = use, apply
■ 你会使用这个电脑吗？ **Nǐ huì shǐyòng
zhège diànnǎo ma?** = *Do you know how to use
this computer?*
■ 这辆车是公司的，只有办公事才能使用。
**Zhè liàng chē shì gōngsī de, zhǐyǒu bàn
gōngshì cái néng shǐyòng.** = *This car belongs
to the company; you can use it on company
business only.*

shǐzhōng 始终 [compound: 始 *beginning* + 终
end] ADVERB = from beginning to end,
throughout, ever

■ 他始终爱着初恋的情人。**Tā shǐzhōng àizhe
chūliàn de qíngrén.** = *He loved his first love all
his life.*
■ 我始终不明白她为什么这么恨那个地方。
**Wǒ shǐzhōng bù míngbai tā wèishénme zhème
hèn nàge dìfang.** = *I have never understood
why she should hate that place so much.*

shì 士 NOUN = scholar, gentleman (See 护士
hùshi, 女士 **nǔshì**, 战士 **zhànshì.**)

shì 示 VERB = show, indicate (See 表示 **biǎoshì.**)

shì 世 NOUN = the world; generation

shìjì 世纪 [modif: 世 *generation* + 纪 *age*]
NOUN = century
■ 公元两千年，世界迎来了一个新世纪 - 二
十一世纪。**Gōngyuán liǎngqiān nián, shìjiè
yíngláile yí ge xīn shìjì – èrshíyī shìjì.** = *In the
year AD 2000, the world greeted a new century—the twenty-first century.*

shìjiè 世界 [compound: 世 *world* + 界
boundary] NOUN = the world
■ 世界每天都在变。**Shìjiè měi tiān duō zài
biàn.** = *The world is changing every day.*
shìjiè shang 世界上 = in the world
■ 世界上的事情都很复杂。**Shìjiè shang de
shìqing dōu hěn fùzá.** = *Everything in the
world is complicated.*

shì 市 NOUN = municipality, city
■ 下午我要到市里去。**Xiàwǔ wǒ yào dào shìli
qù.** = *I'm going to the city this afternoon.*

shìchǎng 市场 [modif: 市 *market* + 场
ground] NOUN = marketplace, market
■ 她在市场上买了一只活鸡，两条活鱼。**Tā
zài shìchǎng shang mǎile yì zhī huó jī, liǎng
tiáo huóyú.** = *She bought a live chicken and
two live fish from the market.*
■ 市场上需要什么，他们就生产什么。
**Shìchǎng shang xūyào shénme, tāmen jiù
shēngchǎn shénme.** = *They produce whatever
the market needs.*
cài shìchǎng 菜市场 = vegetable market, food
market
shìchǎng jīngjì 市场经济 = market economy

shì 式 NOUN = form, pattern (See 方式 **fāngshì**, 形式 **xíngshì**, 正式 **zhèngshì**.)

shì 事 NOUN = affair, matter (件 **jiàn**)
■ 这件事很重要，一定要办好。 **Zhè jiàn shì hěn zhòngyào, yídìng yào bànhǎo.** = *This is an important matter and must be done well.*
■ 大家都很关心这件事。 **Dàjiā dōu hěn guānxīn zhè jiàn shì.** = *Everybody is concerned over this matter.*

NOTE: In many cases, as in the two examples above, 事 **shì** may be replaced by 事情 **shìqing**. 事 **shì** or 事情 **shìqing** is a noun that can be applied widely, denoting any affair, matter or business to be done or considered. Here are more examples:
■ 我今天晚上没有事情做。 **Wǒ jīntiān wǎnshang méiyǒu shìqing zuò.** = *I've nothing to do this evening.*
■ 我跟你说一件事。 **Wǒ gēn nǐ shuō yí jiàn shì.** = *I want to tell you something.*
■ 他们在路上出事了。 **Tāmen zài lùshàng chūshì le.** = *They had an accident on the way.*

shìgù 事故 NOUN = accident, mishap (件 **jiàn**)
■ 昨天工厂发生了一件严重事故。 **Zuótiān gōngchǎng fāshēngle yí jiàn yánzhòng shìgù.** = *A serious accident took place in the factory yesterday.*
■ 有关部门正在调查事故的原因。 **Yǒuguān bùmén zhèngzài diàochá shìgù de yuányīn.** = *The departments concerned are investigating the cause of the accident.*
shìgù xiànchǎng 事故现场 = scene of an accident
gōngshāng shìgù 工伤事故 = industrial accident
jiāotōng shìgù 交通事故 = traffic accident, road accident

shìjiàn 事件 NOUN = (historic) event, incident
■ "九一一"是个可怕的事件。 **"Jiǔ-yāo-yāo" shì ge kěpà de shìjiàn.** = *9/11 was a terrible event.*

NOTE: 一 is pronounced as **yāo** here. See note on 一 **yī** for more information.

shìqing 事情 NOUN = see note on 事 **shì**

shìshí 事实 [compound: 事 *thing* + 实 *truth*] NOUN = fact (件 **jiàn**)
■ 我的报告是根据事实写的。 **Wǒ de bàogào shì gēnjù shìshí xiě de.** = *My report is based on facts.*
■ 你应该先调查事实，再作结论。 **Nǐ yīnggāi xiān diàochá shìshí, zài zuò jiélùn.** = *You should check the facts before drawing a conclusion.*
shìshí shang 事实上 = in fact, as a matter of fact

shìxiān 事先 NOUN = beforehand, in advance
■ 他上星期去中国工作了，事先没有告诉任何人。 **Tā shàng xīngqī qù Zhōngguó gōngzuò le, shìxiān méiyǒu gàosu rènhé rén.** = *He went to work in China last week. He had not told anybody beforehand.*

shìyè 事业 [compound: 事 *work* + 业 *cause*] NOUN
1 = career
■ 要事业，还是要家庭？她决定不了。 **Yào shìyè, háishì yào jiātíng? Tā juédìng bù liǎo.** = *She can't make up her mind whether to make a career or have a family.*
2 = cause, undertaking
■ 他为世界和平事业作出了巨大贡献。 **Tā wèi shìjiè hépíng shìyè zuòchū le jùdà gòngxiàn.** = *He made tremendous contributions to the cause of world peace.*

shì 视 Trad 視 VERB = watch (See 电视 **diànshì**, 重视 **zhòngshì**.)

shì 是 VERB
1 = be, yes
■ "你们的中文老师是不是北京人？""是的。" **"Nǐmen de Zhōngwén lǎoshī shì bu shì Běijīngrén?" "Shìde."** = *"Is your Chinese teacher from Beijing?" "Yes."*
■ "这本书是你的吗？""不是，不是我的。" **"Zhè běn shī shì nǐ de ma?" "Bú shì, bú shì wǒ de."** = *"Is this book yours?" "No."*
2 = (indicating existence of), (there) be
■ 小学旁边是一座公园。 **Xiǎoxué pángbian shì yí zuò gōngyuán.** = *There is a park by the primary school.*
■ 张教授的办公室里到处是书。 **Zhāng jiàoshòu de bàngōngshì li dàochù shì shū.** = *There are books everywhere in Professor Zhang's office.*
■ 电脑旁边是一台电话。 **Diànnǎo pángbiān shì yì tái diànhuà.** = *Beside the computer is a telephone.*

S

3 = (used to emphasize the words following it)
■ 那家饭店的菜是不错。**Nà jiā fàndiàn de cài shì búcuò.** = *That restaurant's food is indeed quite good.*
■ 他这么做是出于好心。**Tā zhème zuò shì chūyú hǎoxīn.** = *He did it out of kindness.*
■ 那个电话是谁打来的？ **Nàge diànhuà shì shéi dǎ lai de?** = *Who rang?*

shì 室 NOUN = room (See 办公室 **bàngōngshì**, 教室 **jiàoshì**, 浴室 **yùshì**.)

shì 柿 NOUN = persimmon (See 西红柿 **xīhóngshì**.)

shì 适 Trad 適 VERB = suit, fit

shìdàng 适当 [compound: 适 *suitable* + 当 *ought to*] ADJECTIVE = appropriate, suitable
■ 我会在适当的时候批评他。**Wǒ huì zài shìdàng de shíhou pīpíng tā.** = *I will criticize him at an appropriate moment.*
■ 在中国送钟给老年人当礼物，是不适当的，因为"送钟"和"送终"同音。**Zài Zhōngguó sòng zhōng gěi lǎoniánrén dāng lǐwù, shì bú shìdàng de, yīnwèi "sòngzhōng" hé "sòngzhōng" tóngyīn.** = *In China it is not appropriate to give an old person a clock as a gift because "give a clock" (sòng zhōng) is pronounced the same as "pay last tribute" (sòng zhōng).*

shìhé 适合 [compound: 适 *suit* + 合 *be harmonious*] VERB = suit, fit
■ 他善于交际，适合做生意。**Tā shànyú jiāojì, shìhé zuò shēngyi.** = *He is good at social dealings, and is suited to be a businessman.*

shìyìng 适应 VERB = be able to adapt to
■ 你已经适应新环境了吗？**Nǐ yǐjīng shìyìng xīn huánjìng le ma?** = *Have you been able to adapt to your new situation?*
■ 她以前是教书的，现在当翻译，一时还不适应。**Tā yǐqián shì jiāoshū de, xiànzài dāng fānyì, yìshí hái bú shìyìng.** = *She used to teach. Now she works as an interpreter and has not quite adapted to it.*

shìyòng 适用 [v+obj: 适 *suit* + 用 *use, application*] ADJECTIVE = applicable, suitable
■ 你的方法很先进，但是在这里不适用。**Nǐ**

de fāngfǎ hěn xiānjìn, dànshì zài zhèli bú shìyòng. = *Your method is very advanced, but it cannot be applied here.*

shì 试 Trad 試 VERB = test, try
■ 你的办法不行，试试我的办法。**Nǐ de bànfǎ bù xíng, shìshì wǒ de bànfǎ.** = *Your method didn't work. Try my method.*
■ 这种新药，病人试过没有？ **Zhè zhǒng xīnyào, bìngrén shìguo méiyǒu?** = *Has the patient tried this new drug?*
shìshì/shì yíxià 试试 / 试一下 = have a try

shìyàn 试验 [compound: 试 *test* + 验 *test*] VERB = test, experiment (项 **xiàng**, 次 **cì**)
■ 研究人员正在动物身上试验这种新药。**Yánjiū rényuán zhèngzài dòngwù shēnshang shìyàn zhè zhǒng xīn yào.** = *Researchers are testing this new medicine on animals.*

shì 势 Trad 勢 NOUN = power, force (See 形势 **xíngshì**.)

shì 释 Trad 釋 VERB = explain (See 解释 **jiěshì**.)

shi 匙 NOUN = spoon (See 钥匙 **yàoshi**.)

shōu 收 VERB
1 = receive, accept
■ 我昨天收到一 封信。**Wǒ zuótiān shōudao yì fēng xìn.** = *I received a letter yesterday.*
■ 请你收下这件小礼物。**Qǐng nǐ shōuxia zhè jiàn xiǎo lǐwù.** = *Please accept this small gift.*
2 = collect (fee), charge
■ 这种服务是要收费的。**Zhè zhǒng fúwù shì yào shōufèi de.** = *This service will incur a fee.*
shōudao 收到 = receive
shōuhuí 收回 = take back, recall
shōuxia 收下 = accept

shōuhuò 收获 [compound: 收 *collect* + 获 *gain*]
1 VERB = gather in crops, harvest
■ 今年这位农民收获了五千公斤小麦。**Jīnnián zhè wèi nóngmín shōuhuòle wǔqiān gōngjīn xiǎomài.** = *This year the farmer harvested five thousand kilograms of wheat.*
2 NOUN = gain (of work), achievement, reward
■ 这次试验取得了大量数据，收获很大。**Zhè cì shìyàn qǔdéle dàliàng shùjù, shōuhuò hěn dà.** = *A large amount of data has been obtained from the test, which is a big achievement.*

shōurù 收入 [compound: 收 *collect* + 入 *entry*]

1 VERB = earn, receive

■ 我不想告诉他我去年收入多少钱。**Wǒ bù xiǎng gàosu tā wǒ qùnián shōurù duōshǎo qián.** = *I didn't want to tell him how much I earned last year.*

2 NOUN = income

■ 去年这个国家的人平均收入是增加了，还是减少了？**Qùnián zhège guójiā de rén píngjūn shōurù shì zēngjiā le, háishì jiǎnshǎo le?** = *Did this country's average per capita income increase or decrease last year?*

shōushi 收拾 [compound: 收 *gather in* + 拾 *pick up*] VERB = put in order, tidy up

■ 桌子上的书和报纸太多，我要收拾一下。**Zhuōzi shang de shū hé bàozhǐ tài duō, wǒ yào shōushi yíxià.** = *There are too many newspapers and books on the table. I'll tidy it up.*

■ 她做完饭，总要收拾一下厨房。**Tā zuòwán fàn, zǒngyào shōushi yíxià chúfáng.** = *She will always tidy up the kitchen after cooking.*

shōuyīnjī 收音机 [modif: 收音 *receive sound* + 机 *machine*] NOUN = radio (台 **tái**, 架 **jià**)

■ 这台收音机还是我爷爷买的。**Zhè tái shōuyīnjī háishì wǒ yéye mǎide.** = *This radio was bought by my grandpa.*

shǒu 手 NOUN = hand (只 **zhī**, 双 **shuāng**)

■ 我的手不干净，要洗一下才能吃饭。**Wǒ de shǒu bù gānjing, yào xǐ yíxià cái néng chīfàn.** = *My hands are not clean. I have to wash them before eating my meal.*

shǒu shang 手上 = in the hand

■ 他手上拿着一本书。**Tā shǒu shang názhe yì běn shū.** = *He's holding a book in his hand.*

yòushǒu 右手 = the right hand

zuǒshǒu 左手 = the left hand

shǒubiǎo 手表 [modif: 手 *hand* + 表 *watch*] NOUN = wristwatch (块 **kuài**)

■ 我的手表慢了，你的手表几点？ **Wǒ de shǒubiǎo màn le, nǐ de shǒubiǎo jǐ diǎn?** = *My watch is slow. What time is it by your watch?*

NOTE: In everyday usage, 手表 **shǒubiǎo** is often shortened to 表 **biǎo**: 我的表慢了，你的表几点？ **Wǒ de biǎo màn le, nǐ de biǎo jǐ diǎn?** = *My watch is slow. What time is it by your watch?*

shǒuduàn 手段 NOUN = means, measure

■ 我不赞成使用不合理的手段来达到目的。**Wǒ bú zànchéng shǐyòng bù hélǐ de shǒuduàn lái dádào mùdì.** = *I don't endorse the use of unjustifiable means to achieve your ends.*

shǒugōng 手工 [modif: 手 *hand* + 工 *work*] NOUN = done by hand, made by hand, manual

■ 这件丝绸衬衫是手工做的，所以比较贵。**Zhè jiàn sīchóu chènshān shì shǒugōng zuòde, suǒyǐ bǐjiào guì.** = *This silk shirt was handmade, so it is rather expensive.*

shǒugōngyè 手工业 = handicraft industry

shǒugōngyìpǐn 手工艺品 = handicraft article

shǒujī 手机 [modif: 手 *hand* + 机 *machine*] NOUN = cell phone, mobile telephone (只 **zhī**)

■ 上飞机以前，要关上手机。**Shàng fēijī yǐqián, yào guānshang shǒujī.** = *Switch off your cell phone before boarding a plane.*

■ 他又换了一只手机。**Tā yòu huànle yì zhī shǒujī.** = *He changed his cell phone again.*

shǒujuàn 手绢 NOUN = handkerchief (块 **kuài**)

■ 手绢要每天换。**Shǒujuàn yào měi tiān huàn.** = *Handkerchiefs should be changed daily. (→ You have to use a clean handkerchief everyday.)*

shǒushù 手术 NOUN = operation

■ 外科主任亲自做这个手术。**Wàikē zhǔrèn qīnzì zuò zhè ge shǒushù.** = *The chief surgeon will perform the operation himself.*

shǒushùjiān 手术间 = operating room, surgery room

zuò shǒushù 做手术 = perform an operation, operate

shǒutào 手套 [modif: 手 *hand* + 套 *covering*] NOUN = glove (只 **zhī**, 副 **fù**)

■ 今天真冷，我戴了手套、帽子，还觉得冷！ **Jīntiān zhēn lěng, wǒ dàile shǒutào, màozi, hái juéde lěng!** = *It's really cold today. I'm wearing gloves and a hat, but still feel cold!*

shǒuxù 手续 NOUN = formalities, procedure

■ 买卖房子，要办法律手续。**Mǎimài fángzi, yào bàn fǎlǜ shǒuxù.** = *You will have to complete the legal formalities when you buy or sell a house.*

bàn shǒuxù 办手续 = go through the formalities

S

shǒuzhǐ 手指 NOUN = finger, thumb
■ 她的手指又细又长。**Tā de shǒuzhǐ yòu xì, yòu cháng.** = *Her fingers are slender and long.*

NOTE: In Chinese the thumb 拇指 **mǔzhǐ**, or 大拇指 **dàmǔzhǐ** is considered just one of the fingers. So it is correct to say 我有十个手指。**Wǒ yǒu shí ge shǒuzhǐ.** = *I have ten fingers.*

shǒu 守 VERB = observe, abide by (See 遵守 **zūnshǒu**.)

shǒu 首 MEASURE WORD = (for songs and poems)
■ 一首歌 **yì shǒu gē** = *a song*

shǒudū 首都 [modif: 首 *the head, first* + 都 *metropolis*] NOUN = capital city
■ 中国的首都是北京。**Zhōngguó de shǒudū shì Běijīng.** = *China's capital city is Beijing.*

shǒuxiān 首先 [compound: 首 *first* + 先 *before*] ADVERB = first, first of all
■ 首先，请允许我自我介绍一下。**Shǒuxiān, qǐng yǔnxǔ wǒ zìwǒ jièshào yíxià.** = *First of all, allow me to introduce myself.*

shòu 受 VERB = receive, accept
■ 每个人都有受教育的权利。**Měi ge rén dōu yǒu shòu jiàoyù de quánlì.** = *Everyone has the right to receive an education.*
■ 他因为上班迟到而受批评了。**Tā yīnwèi chídào ér shòu pīpíng le.** = *He was criticized for being late for work.*

shòu 瘦 ADJECTIVE = thin, lean
■ 她比以前瘦多了。**Tā bǐ yǐqián shòu duō le.** = *She is much thinner than before.*
■ 别以为越瘦越好看。**Bié yǐwéi yuè shòu yuè hǎokàn.** = *Do not think that the thinner you are, the more beautiful you become.*
shòuròu 瘦肉 = lean meat
■ 她只吃瘦肉，不吃肥肉。**Tā zhǐ chī shòuròu, bù chī féiròu.** = *She eats only lean meat, and does not eat fatty meat.*

shòu 售 VERB = sell

shòuhuòyuán 售货员 [suffix: 售 *sell* + 货 *goods* + 员 *nominal suffix*] NOUN = shop assistant, salesperson
■ 售货员帮我挑选皮鞋。**Shòuhuòyuán bāng**

wǒ tiāoxuǎn píxié. = *The shop assistant helped me choose a pair of shoes.*

shū 书 Trad 書 NOUN = book (本 **běn**)
■ 这本书很有意思，你看过没有？**Zhè běn shū hěn yǒu yìsi, nǐ kànguo méiyǒu?** = *This book is very interesting. Have you read it?*
■ 她常常去图书馆借书。**Tā chángcháng qù túshūguǎn jiè shū.** = *She often goes to the library to borrow books.*
shūmíng 书名 = title of a book
kàn shū 看书 = read, do reading
■ 我喜欢看书。**Wǒ xǐhuan kàn shū.** = *I like reading.*

shūbāo 书包 [modif: 书 *book* + 包 *bag*] NOUN = schoolbag (只 **zhī**)
■ 小学生的书包为什么这么重？**Xiǎoxuéshēng de shūbāo wèishénme zhème zhòng?** = *Why are children's schoolbags so heavy?*

shūdiàn 书店 [modif: 书 *book* + 店 *store, shop*] NOUN = bookstore, bookshop (家 **jiā**)
■ 你们这里哪家书店最好？**Nǐmen zhèli nǎ jiā shūdiàn zuì hǎo?** = *Which is the best bookshop here?*

shūjià 书架 [modif: 书 *book* + 架 *shelf*] NOUN = bookshelf
■ 王老师的办公室有一个大书架。**Wáng lǎoshī de bàngōngshì yǒu yí ge dà shūjià.** = *There is a big bookshelf in Teacher Wang's office.*

shū 叔 NOUN = father's younger brother

shūshu 叔叔 NOUN = father's younger brother, uncle
■ 我叔叔是设计电脑软件的。**Wǒ shūshu shì shèjì diànnǎo ruǎnjiàn de.** = *My father's younger brother designs computer software.*

NOTE: 叔叔 **shūshu** is a form of address used by a child for a man around his/her father's age. It is common to put a family name before 叔叔 **shūshu** e.g. 张叔叔 **Zhāng shūshu**. Also see note on 阿姨 **āyí**.

shū 殊 ADJECTIVE = different (See 特殊 **tèshū**.)

S

shū 舒 VERB = stretch, unfold

shūfu 舒服 [compound: 舒 *relaxing* + 服 *conceding*] ADJECTIVE = comfortable
■ 这把椅子很舒服，你坐下去就不想起来了。**Zhè bǎ yǐzi hěn shūfu, nǐ zuò xiàqu jiù bù xiǎng qǐlái le.** = *This chair is very comfortable. Sit on it and you don't want to get up.*
■ 他们不是非常有钱，但是生活过得挺舒服。**Tāmen bú shì fēicháng yǒu qián, dànshì shēnghuó guò de tǐng shūfu.** = *They are not wealthy, but they live comfortably.*
bù shūfu 不舒服 = (of a person) not very well, be under the weather
■ 我今天不舒服，想早点回家。**Wǒ jīntiān bù shūfu, xiǎng zǎo diǎn huíjiā.** = *I'm unwell today. I want to go home early.*

shū 蔬 NOUN = vegetable

shūcài 蔬菜 NOUN = vegetable
■ 多吃蔬菜，少吃肉，对健康有利。**Duō chī shùcài, shǎo chī ròu, duì jiànkāng yǒulì.** = *Eating lots of vegetables and little meat is good for your health.*

shū 输 Trad 輸 VERB = lose (a game, a bet) (antonym 赢 **yíng**)
■ 上回我们队输了，这回一定要赢！**Shàng huí wǒmen duì shū le, zhè huí yídìng yào yíng!** = *Our team lost the game the last time; this time we must win!*
■ 客队输了两个球。**Kèduì shūle liǎng ge qiú.** = *The visiting team lost two points.*

shú 熟 ADJECTIVE
1 = ripe, cooked
■ 苹果还没有熟，很酸。**Píngguǒ hái méiyǒu shú, hěn suān.** = *The apples are not yet ripe. They're sour.*
■ 肉熟了就可以吃饭。**Ròu shúle jiù kěyǐ chīfàn.** = *We can have our meal when the meat is done.*
2 = familiar with, know well
■ 这个城市我不熟。**Zhège chéngshì wǒ bù shú.** = *I don't know this city very well.*

shúliàn 熟练 [compound: 熟 *familiar with* + 练 *practiced*] ADJECTIVE = skilful, skilled
■ 我们工厂缺乏熟练工人。**Wǒmen**

gōngchǎng quēfá shúliàn gōngrén. = *Our factory is short of skilled workers.*

shúxi 熟悉 [compound: 熟 *familiar with* + 悉 *knowing*] ADJECTIVE = familiar with, know well
■ 他和熟悉的人在一起的时候话很多。**Tā hé shúxi de rén zài yìqǐ de shíhou huà hěn duō.** = *He is talkative in the company of the people he knows well.*
■ 我对这个地方不熟悉。**Wǒ duì zhège dìfang bù shúxi.** = *I am not familiar with this place.*

shǔ 数 Trad 數 VERB = count
■ 我来数一下，这里有多少人，一、二、三、… **Wǒ lái shǔ yíxiò, zhèlǐ yǒu duōshǎo rén, yī, èr, sān...** = *Let me count to see how many people there are here. One, two, three...*

shǔ 暑 NOUN = heat

shǔjià 暑假 [modif: 暑 *summer* + 假 *holiday, vacation*] NOUN = summer holiday, summer vacation
■ 你暑假有什么打算？ **Nǐ shǔjià yǒu shénme dǎsuàn?** = *What is your plan for the summer holiday?*

shǔ 属 Trad 屬 VERB = belong to

shǔyú 属于 VERB = belong to
■ 这些书不是我个人的，而是属于学校图书馆。**Zhèxiē shū bú shì wǒ gèrén de, érshì shǔyú xuéxiào túshūguǎn.** = *These books are not mine, but belong to the school library.*
■ 这块森林属于一家跨国公司。**Zhè kuài sēnlín shǔyú yī jiā kuàguó gōngsī.** = *This forest belongs to a multinational company.*

shù 术 Trad 術 NOUN = craft (See 技术 **jìshù**, 技术员 **jìshùyuán**, 美术 **měishù**, 手术 **shǒushù**, 武术 **wǔshù**, 艺术 **yìshù**.)

shù 束 NOUN = knot (See 结束 **jiéshù**.)

shù 述 VERB = narrate (See 复述 **fùshù**.)

shù 树 Trad 樹 NOUN = tree (棵 **kē**)
■ 这棵树又高又大，树下很凉快。**Zhè kē shù yòu gāo yòu dà, shù xia hěn liángkuai.** = *This tree is big and tall; it's cool under it.*

S

■ 我爸爸在花园里种了两棵树。**Wǒ bàba zài huāyuán li zhòngle liǎng kē shù.** = *My father planted two trees in the garden.*

shùlín 树林 [compound: 树 *tree* + 林 *wood*]
NOUN = wood, woods
■ 在树林里有很多种鸟。**Zài shùlín li yǒu hěn duō zhǒng niǎo.** = *There are many kinds of birds in the woods.*

shù 数 Trad 數 NOUN = number, figure
■ 说这种语言的人数在不断减少。**Shuō zhè zhǒng yǔyán de rénshù zài búduàn jiǎnshǎo.** = *The number of speakers of this language is on the decline.*

shùjù 数据 [modif: 数 *number* + 据 *evidence*]
NOUN = datum, data
■ "你能肯定这些数据是准确的吗?""能肯定。" **"Nǐ néng kěndìng zhèxiē shùjù shì zhǔnquè de ma?" "Néng kěndìng."** = *"Are you sure these data are accurate?" "Positive."*

shùliàng 数量 [compound: 数 *number* + 量 *quantity*] NOUN = quantity, amount
■ 电视节目的数量在增加,但质量怎么样呢? **Diànshì jiémù de shùliàng zài zēngjiā, dàn zhìliàng zěnmeyàng ne?** = *The quantity of TV programs is increasing, but how about their quality?*

shùxué 数学 [modif: 数 *number* + 学 *knowledge, study of*] NOUN = mathematics, math
■ 我看,数学和语文是学校里最重要的两门课。**Wǒ kàn, shùxué hé yǔwén shì xuéxiào li zuì zhòngyào de liǎng mén kè.** = *In my view, mathematics and language are the two most important subjects in schools.*
■ 我们明天考数学。**Wǒmen míngtiān kǎo shùxué.** = *We're having a mathematics examination tomorrow.*

shùzì 数字 [modif: 数 *number* + 字 *written word*] NOUN
1 = numeral (in writing)
■ 我认为写中文的时候,一般应该写中文数字,如"一"、"二"、"三"。**Wǒ rènwéi xiě Zhōngwén de shíhou, yìbān yīnggāi xiě Zhōngwén shùzì, rú "yī", "èr", "sān".** = *I think when we're writing Chinese, we should gener-*

ally use Chinese numerals, such as "一," "二" and "三."
2 = figure, number
■ 每个月都节省一点钱,几年以后就是一笔不小的数字。**Měi ge yuè dōu jiéshěng yìdiǎn qián, jǐ nián yǐhòu jiùshì yìbǐ bù xiǎo de shùzì.** = *If you save some money every month, years later you will have a quite large sum.*

shuā 刷 VERB = brush
■ 我每天睡觉前刷牙。**Wǒ měi tiān shuìjiào qián shuā yá.** = *I brush my teeth before going to bed every night.*

shuāi 摔 VERB
1 = fall, fumble
■ 她从自行车上摔下来,擦破了手。**Tā cóng zìxíngchē shang shuāi xiàlai, cāpòle shǒu.** = *She fell off the bicycle and scraped her hand.*
2 = fall and break, cause to fall and break
■ 我不小心把茶杯摔了。**Wǒ bù xiǎoxīn bǎ chábēi shuāi le.** = *I accidentally broke the teacup.*

shuāng 双 Trad 雙 MEASURE WORD = a pair of (shoes, chopsticks, etc.)
■ 一双鞋 **yì shuāng xié** = *a pair of shoes*
■ 两双筷子 **liǎng shuāng kuàizi** = *two pairs of chopsticks*

shuāngfāng 双方 [modif: 双 *both* + 方 *side, party*] NOUN = both sides, both parties
■ 双方同意加强合作。**Shuāngfāng tóngyì jiāqiáng hézuò.** = *Both parties agree to strengthen their cooperation.*

shuí 谁 Trad 誰 PRONOUN
1 = who, whom
■ 谁是你们的中文老师? **Shuí shì nǐmen de Zhōngwén lǎoshī?** = *Who's your Chinese teacher?*
■ 你找谁? **Nǐ zhǎo shuí?** = *Who are you looking for?*
2 = everyone, anybody, whoever, no matter who
■ 谁都希望生活过得幸福。**Shuí dōu xīwàng shēnghuó guò de xìngfú.** = *Everybody hopes to live a happy life.*
■ 谁也不能保证永远不犯错误。**Shuí yě bù néng bǎozhèng yǒngyuǎn bú fàn cuòwù.** = *Nobody can guarantee that he will never make a mistake.*

shuǐ 水 NOUN = water
- 我口渴，要喝水。**Wǒ kǒu ke, yào hē shuǐ.** = *I'm thirsty. I want to drink some water.*
zìláishuǐ 自来水 = running water, tap water
- 这里的自来水能喝吗？ **Zhèlǐ de zìláishuǐ néng hē ma?** = *Is the tap water here drinkable?*
kāishuǐ 开水 = boiled water

shuǐdào 水稻 [modif: 水 *water* + 稻 *paddy rice*] NOUN = paddy rice, rice
- 这些年，水稻产量有了相当大的提高。 **Zhèxiē nián shuǐdào chǎnliàng yǒule xiāngdāng dà de tígāo.** = *The yield of paddy rice has increased considerably in recent years.*

shuǐguǒ 水果 [modif: 水 *water* + 果 *fruit*] NOUN = fruit
- 水果人人都爱吃。**Shuǐguǒ rénrén duō ài chī.** = *Everybody loves to eat fruit.*
- 我要去商店买一些水果。**Wǒ yào qù shāngdiàn mǎi yìxiē shuǐguǒ.** = *I'll go to the store to buy some fruit.*
shuǐguǒ diàn 水果店 = fruit shop, fruiterer
shuǐguǒ dāo 水果刀 = penknife

shuǐní 水泥 [compound: 水 *water* + 泥 *mud*] NOUN = cement
- 我要买两袋优质水泥，多少钱？ **Wǒ yào mǎi liǎng dài yōuzhì shuǐní, duōshǎo qián?** = *I want two sacks of quality cement. How much is it?*

shuǐpíng 水平 NOUN
1 = level, standard
- 政府努力提高人民的生活水平。**Zhèngfǔ nǔlì tígāo rénmín de shēnghuó shuǐpíng.** = *The government is working hard to raise the people's living standard.*
2 = proficiency (in language)
- 我的中文水平不高，请您多多帮助。**Wǒ de Zhōngwén shuǐpíng bù gāo, qǐng nín duōduō bāngzhù.** = *My proficiency in Chinese is not very high. Please help me.*
tígāo ... shuǐpíng 提高 ... 水平 = raise the standard of ...
shēnghuó shuǐpíng 生活水平 = living standard
wénhuà shuǐpíng 文化水平 = cultural level, educational experience
- 这位老人的文化水平不高，但是说的话总是有道理。**Zhè wèi lǎorén de wénhuà shuǐpíng bù gāo, dànshì shuō de huà zǒngshì hěn yǒu**

dàolǐ. = *This old person is not very well educated, but what he says always has a lot of truth in it.*

shuì 税 NOUN = tax, duty
- 每个公民都有交税的义务。**Měi ge gōngmín dōu yǒu jiāo shuì de yìwù.** = *Every citizen has an obligation to pay taxes.*
guānshuì 关税 = tariff
shuìwùjú 税务局 = tax bureau, Inland Revenue Service

shuì 睡 VERB = sleep
- 爸爸睡了，你明天再跟他说吧。**Bàba shuì le, nǐ míngtiān zài gēn tā shuō ba.** = *Daddy's sleeping. Talk to him tomorrow.*
- 我一般夜里睡得挺好，可是昨天没睡好，因为心里有事。**Wǒ yìbān yèlǐ shuì de tíng hǎo, kěshì zuótiān méi shuì hǎo, yīnwèi xīnli yǒushì.** = *I usually sleep well at night, but I did not sleep well last night as I had something on mind.*
shuìzháo 睡着 = fall asleep
- 昨天我十点上床，到十二点左右才睡着。**Zuótiān wǒ shí diǎnzhōng shàngchuáng, dào shí'èr diǎn zuǒyòu cái shuì zháo.** = *I went to bed at ten yesterday and didn't fall asleep until about twelve o'clock.*
shuìyī 睡衣 = pajamas, dressing gown

shuìjiào 睡觉 [compound: 睡 *sleep* + 觉 *sleep*] VERB = sleep, go to bed
- "你每天什么时候睡觉？""十点钟以后。" **"Nǐ měi tiān shénme shíhou shuìjiào?" "Shí diǎnzhōng yǐhòu."** = *"When do you go to bed every day?" "After ten o'clock."*
- 这么晚了，你还不睡觉？ **Zhème wǎn le, nǐ hái bú shuìjiào?** = *It's so late. You're not going to bed?*

NOTES: (1) 睡 **shuì** and 睡觉 **shuìjiào** are often interchangeable with each other. (2) 觉 is pronounced **jiào** in 睡觉 **shuìjiào**, but **jué** in 觉得 **juéde**.

shùn 顺 Trad 順 ADJECTIVE = smooth

shùnbiàn 顺便 [compound: 顺 *smooth* + 便 *convenient*] ADVERB = in passing, incidentally
- 你回家的路上，顺便给我买一份晚报，好吗？ **Nǐ huíjiā de lùshang, shùnbiàn gěi wǒ**

mǎi yífèn wǎnbào, hǎo ma? = *Could you buy me an evening paper on your way home?*
■ 顺便说一句，下个月我要请两天假。 **Shùnbiàn shuō yíjù, xià ge yuè wǒ yào qǐng liǎngtiān jià.** = *Incidentally, I'm going to ask for a couple of days' leave next month.*

shùnlì 顺利 [compound: 顺 *smooth* + 利]
ADJECTIVE = smooth, without a hitch, successful
■ 我们的计划执行得很顺利。**Wǒmen de jìhuà zhíxíng de hěn shùnlì.** = *Our plan has been carried out smoothly.*
■ 他一生都很顺利。**Tā yìshēng dōu hěn shùnlì.** = *All his life has been plain sailing. (→ He has had an easy life).*

shuō 说 Trad 說 VERB
1 = say, speak
■ 他说今天晚上没有时间。**Tā shuō jīntiān wǎnshang méiyǒu shíjiān.** = *He said he did not have time this evening.*
■ 他说什么？ **Tā shuō shénme?** = *What did he say?*
2 = explain, tell
■ 你说说，这个菜怎么做？ **Nǐ shuōshuo, zhège cài zěnme zuò?** = *Will you tell me how to cook this dish?*
■ 她很聪明，老师一说她就懂。**Tā hěn cōngmíng, lǎoshī yì shuō tā jiù dǒng.** = *She is very bright. As soon as the teacher has explained, she understands.*
shuō xiàohua 说笑话 = tell a joke

shuōmíng 说明 [v+comp: 说 *say* + 明 *clear*]
1 VERB = explain
■ 我来说明一下，为什么我最近有时候迟到。**Wǒ lái shuōmíng yíxià, wèishénme wǒ zuìjìn yǒu shíhou chídào.** = *Let me explain why I've been sometimes late recently.*
2 VERB = prove, show
■ 你考试取得了好成绩，这说明你学习很努力。**Nǐ kǎoshì qǔdéle hǎo chéngjì, zhè shuōmíng nǐ xuéxí hěn nǔlì.** = *You got a good grade at the examination. This shows you studied very hard.*
3 NOUN = explanation, manual
■ 这个电脑怎么用，我要看一下说明。**Zhège diànnǎo zěnme yòng, wǒ yào kàn yíxià shuōmíng.** = *As to how to use this computer, I need to read the manual.*

sī 司 VERB = take charge of

sījī 司机 [v+obj: 司 *take charge* + 机 *machine*]
NOUN = (professional) automobile driver, train driver
■ 出租汽车司机态度很友好。**Chūzū qìchē sījī tàidu hěn yóuhǎo.** = *The taxi driver is very friendly.*

sī 私 ADJECTIVE = private

sīrén 私人 [modif: 私 *private* + 人 *person*]
NOUN
1 = private, personal
■ 私人财产受到法律保护。**Sīrén cáichǎn shòudào fǎlǜ bǎohù.** = *Private property is protected by the law.*
2 = personal relationship
■ 我和他只是同事，没有私人关系。**Wǒ hé tā zhǐshì tóngshì, méiyǒu sīrén guānxi.** = *He and I are colleagues only, we do not have any personal relationship.*

sī 思 VERB = think

sīxiǎng 思想 [compound: 思 *think* + 想 *think*]
NOUN = thought, thinking
■ 人们的思想是什么决定的？ **Rénmen de sīxiǎng shì shénme juédìng de?** = *What determines people's thought?*
■ 这个孩子怎么会有这种思想呢？ **Zhège háizi zěnme huì yǒu zhè zhǒng sīxiǎng ne?** = *How did the child have this kind of thinking?*
sīxiǎngjiā 思想家 = thinker

sī 丝 Trad 絲 NOUN = silk

sīchóu 丝绸 [compound: 丝 *silk* + 绸 *silk cloth*] NOUN = silk, silk cloth
■ 我要买一些丝绸产品，带回去送朋友。**Wǒ yào mǎi yìxiē sīchóu chǎnpǐn, dài huíqu sòng péngyou.** = *I want to buy some silk products to take home as gifts for friends.*

sǐ 死 VERB = die (antonym 活 huó)
■ 我家的狗昨天死了。**Wǒ jiā de gǒu zuótiān sǐ le.** = *Our family dog died yesterday.*
■ 人总有一死，谁都不能避免。**Rén zǒng yǒu yì sǐ, shuí dōu bù néng bìmiǎn.** = *People eventually die. No one can avoid this.*

S

NOTE: See note on 去世 **qùshì.**

sì 四 NUMERAL = four
- 四十四 **sìshí sì** = *forty-four*
- 四海为家 **sì hǎi wéi jiā** = *Make the four seas one's home* (–> *Make one's home wherever one is.*)

sì 似 VERB = seem

sìhū 似乎 ADVERB = it seems, as if
- 他们似乎对我们公司的产品很有兴趣。 **Tāmen sìhū duì wǒmen gōngsī de chǎnpǐn hěn yǒu xìngqù.** = *They seem to be interested in our company's products.*
- 他听了我的话，似乎不大高兴。 **Tā tīngle wǒ de huà, sìhū bú dà gāoxìng.** = *He seemed unhappy to hear what I had to say.*
- 我似乎在哪儿见到过他。 **Wǒ sìhū zài nǎr jiàndaoguo tā.** = *I seem to have met him before somewhere.*

sōng 松 Trad 鬆
1 ADJECTIVE = lax, weak (antonym 紧 **jǐn**)
- 这个学校对学生的要求太松。 **Zhège xuéxiào duì xuésheng de yāoqiú tài sōng.** = *This school demands too little of the students.* (–> *This school does not set a high standard for students.*)
2 VERB = loosen, slacken
- 带子太紧了，要松一下。 **Dàizi tài jǐn le, yào sōng yíxià.** = *The belt is too tight. It needs to be loosened.*

sòng 送 VERB
1 = give as a gift
- 去年圣诞节，爸爸送给他一辆自行车。 **Qùnián shèngdànjié, bàba sòng gei tā yí liàng zìxíngchē.** = *Last Christmas his father gave him a bike.*
2 = deliver
- 我们可以把你买的电脑送到你家。 **Wǒmen kěyǐ bǎ nǐ mǎi de diànnǎo sòngdào nǐ jiā.** = *We can deliver the computer you've bought to your home.*
3 = accompany, take, escort
- 天太晚了，我开车送你回家吧。 **Tiān tài wǎn le, wǒ kāi chē sòng nǐ huíjiā ba.** = *It's too late. Let me drive you home.*

sòng 诵 Trad 誦 VERB = chant, recite (See 背诵 **bèisòng.**)

sòu 嗽 NOUN = cough (See 咳嗽 **késou.**)

sù 诉 Trad 訴 VERB = tell (See 告诉 **gàosu.**)

sù 肃 Trad 肅 ADJECTIVE = solemn (See 严肃 **yánsù.**)

sù 速 NOUN = speed

sùdù 速度 [modif: 速 *speed* + 度 *degree*] NOUN = speed, velocity
- 以这样的速度，我们可以在两小时之内到达目的地。 **Yǐ zhèyàng de sùdù, wǒmen kěyǐ zài liǎng xiǎoshí zhīnèi dàodá mùdidì.** = *At this speed, we can reach our destination in two hours.*
- 你开车超过了限定的速度。 **Nǐ kāichē chāoguòle xiàndìng de sùdù.** = *You have exceeded the speed limit.*

sù 素 ADJECTIVE = plain, simple (See 朴素 **pǔsù.**)

sù 宿 VERB = stay overnight

sùshè 宿舍 [modif: 宿 *stay overnight* + 舍 *lodge*] NOUN = hostel, dormitory
- 我的书忘在宿舍里了！ **Wǒ de shū wàng zài sùshè li le!** = *I've left my book in the dormitory.*
xuésheng sùshè 学生宿舍 = students' hostel (dormitory)

sù 塑 VERB = mold

sùliào 塑料 NOUN = plastic
- 这种桌椅是用塑料做的，又轻又便宜。 **Zhè zhǒng zhuōyǐ shì yòng sùliào zuò de, yòu qīng yòu piányì.** = *These tables and chairs are made of plastic; they are light and inexpensive.*

suān 酸 ADJECTIVE = sour
- 我不喜欢吃酸的东西。 **Wǒ bù xǐhuan chī suān de dōngxi.** = *I don't like to eat sour food.*
- 这种酒太酸了一点儿。 **Zhè zhǒng jiǔ tài suānle yìdiǎr.** = *This wine is a bit too sour.*

suàn 算 VERB
1 = calculate

S

■我算一下这个星期花了多少钱。**Wǒ suàn yíxià zhège xīngqī huāle duōshǎo qián.** = *Let me calculate how much money I've spent this week.*
■完成这项工程需要多少人工，你算过没有？ **Wánchéng zhè xiàng gōngchéng xūyào duōshǎo réngōng, nǐ suànguo méiyǒu?** = *Have you calculated how many man-days will be needed to finish this project?*
2 = may be considered as
■今天不算冷，昨天才冷呢！ **Jīntiān bú suàn lěng, zuótiān cái lěng ne!** = *Today can't be considered cold. Yesterday was really cold.*

suī 虽 Trad 雖 CONJUNCTION = although

suīrán 虽然 CONJUNCTION = although, though
■虽然已经是秋天了，这两天天气还是很热。 **Suīrán yǐjīng shì qiūtiān le, zhè liǎng tiān tiānqì háishì hěn rè.** = *Although it's already autumn, it's still hot these days.*
■他虽然赚了很多钱，但是还不满足。 **Tā suīrán zhuànle hěn duō qián, dàn hái bù mǎnzú.** = *Although he's earned a lot of money, he is still dissatisfied.*

suí 随 Trad 隨 VERB = let (somebody do as he pleases), as you wish
■这件事和我没有关系，随你处理。 **Zhè jiàn shì hé wǒ méiyǒu guānxi, suí nǐ chǔlǐ.** = *This matter is none of my businesses. You can deal with it the way you like.*

suíbiàn 随便 ADJECTIVE = casual, informal
■中饭我们随便一点，晚上我请你到餐馆去好好吃一顿。 **Zhōngfàn wǒmen suíbiàn chī yìdiǎn, wǎnshang wǒ qǐng nǐ dào fàndiàn qu hǎohǎo chī yí dùn.** = *For lunch we'll have a casual meal. In the evening I'll take you to a restaurant for a square meal.*

NOTE: 随便 **suíbiàn** is often used in casual conversation to mean something like *as you wish, anything you like*, or *I have no objection whatsoever*. e.g.
■"你喝红茶还是绿茶？""随便。" **"Nǐ hē hóngchá háishì lùchá?" "Suíbiàn."** = *"Do you want to drink black tea or green tea?" "Anything's fine with me."*

suíshí 随时 ADVERB = whenever, at any moment

■你有问题，可以随时给我打电话。 **Nǐ yǒu wèntí, kěyǐ suíshí gěi wǒ dǎ diànhuà.** = *If you have a problem, you can call me anytime.*

suì 岁 Trad 歲 MEASURE WORD = year (of age)
■我小弟弟今年八岁。 **Wǒ xiǎo dìdi jīnnián bā suì.** = *My younger brother is eight years old.*

NOTE: See 年纪 **niánjì**.

suì 碎 ADJECTIVE = broken, fragmentary
■车窗的玻璃被一块石头打碎了。 **Chēchuāng de bōli bèi yí kuài shítou dǎ suì le.** = *The car window was shattered by a stone.*

sǔn 损 Trad 損 VERB = damage

sǔnshī 损失 [compound: 损 *damage* + 失 *loss*]
1 VERB = lose, suffer from damage and/or loss
■由于他的错误决定，公司损失了五十万元。 **Yóuyú tā de cuòwù juédìng, gōngsī sǔnshīle wǔshíwàn yuán.** = *Owing to his wrong decision, the company lost half a million yuan.*
2 NOUN = loss, damage
■这次水灾造成巨大损失。 **Zhè cì shuǐzāi zàochéng jùdà sǔnshī.** = *This flooding caused huge losses.*

suō 缩 Trad 縮 VERB = shrink
■棉布下水以后会缩。 **Miánbù xiàshuǐ yǐhòu huì suō.** = *Cotton cloth will shrink in the wash.*

suǒ 所 MEASURE WORD = (for houses or institutions housed in a building)
■一所医院 **yì suǒ yīyuàn** = *a hospital*
■两所大学 **liǎng suǒ dàxué** = *two universities*

suǒwèi 所谓 ADJECTIVE = what is called, so-called
■他所谓的"理由"完全站不住脚。 **Tā suǒwèi de "lǐyóu" wánquán zhàn bu zhù jiǎo.** = *His so-called "reason" does not have a leg to stand on.*

suǒyǐ 所以 [idiom] CONJUNCTION = therefore, so
■我上星期病了，所以没有来上班。 **Wǒ shàng xīngqī bìng le, suǒyǐ méiyǒu lái shàngbān.** = *I was sick last week, so I did not come to work.*
■因为家里有事，所以她今天没来上班。 **Yīnwèi jiā li yǒu shì, suǒyǐ tā jīntiān méi lái**

shàngbàn. = *There was an emergency in her family, therefore she did not come to work today.*

suǒyǒu 所有 [idiom] ADJECTIVE = all
■ 所有的朋友都反对他的计划。**Suǒyǒu de péngyu dōu fǎnduì tā de jìhuà.** = *All his friends are opposed to his plan.*

NOTES: 所有 **suǒyǒu** is (1) used only as an attribute, (2) always followed by 的 **de** and (3) often used together with 都 **dōu**.

suǒ 索 VERB = search (See 探索 **tànsuǒ**.)

T

tā 他 PRONOUN = he, him
■ "他是谁？" "他是我的同学。" **"Tā shì shéi?" "Tā shì wǒ de tóngxué."** = *"Who's he?" "He's my classmate."*
■ 我不喜欢他。**Wǒ bù xǐhuan tā.** = *I don't like him.*
■ 他的朋友都叫他小王。**Tā de péngyou dōu jiào tā Xiǎo Wáng.** = *His friends all call him Xiao Wang.*

tāmen 他们 [suffix: 他 he, him + 们 suffix denoting a plural number] PRONOUN = they, them
■ 他们有困难，我们要帮助他们。**Tāmen yǒu kùnnan, wǒmen yào bāngzhù tāmen.** = *As they're in difficulty, we should help them.*
■ 这是他们的问题，我们没有办法。**Zhè shì tāmen de wèntí, wǒmen méiyǒu bànfǎ.** = *This is their problem. There's nothing we can do.*

tā 它 PRONOUN = it
■ 它是我的小狗。**Tā shì wǒ de xiǎo gǒu.** = *It's my puppy.*

tāmen 它们 [suffix: 它 it + 们 suffix denoting a plural number] PRONOUN = (non-human) they, them (plural form of 它 **tā**)

tā 她 PRONOUN = she, her
■ 她是我班上的女同学。**Tā shì wǒ bānshang de nǚ tóngxué.** = *She's a girl student in my class.*

tāmen 她们 [suffix: 她 she, her + 们 suffix denoting a plural number] PRONOUN = (female) they, them

tǎ 塔 NOUN = pagoda, tower (座 **zuò**)
■ 在中国几乎每一个城市都有一座古塔。**Zài Zhōngguó jīhū měi yí ge chéngshì dōu yǒu yí zuò gǔ tǎ.** = *In China almost every town has an ancient tower.*

tái 台
1 NOUN = table, desk (张 **zhāng**)
■ 董事长坐在一张大写字台后面。**Dǒngshìzhǎng zuò zai yì zhāng dà xiězìtái hòumiàn.** = *The chairman of the board sat behind a large desk.*
2 MEASURE WORD = (for machines, big instruments, etc.)
■ 一台机器 **yì tái jīqì** = *a machine*

Táiwān 台湾 NOUN = Taiwan

tái 抬 Trad 擡 VERB = lift, raise
■ 来，咱们俩把桌子抬到外边去。**Lái, zánmen liǎ bǎ zhuōzi táidao wàibian qù.** = *Come on, let's move the table outside.*
■ 这几个小姑娘怎么抬得动这台电脑呢？**Zhè jǐ ge xiǎogūniang zěnme tái de dòng zhè tái diànnǎo ne?** = *How could these little girls carry this computer?*
táigāo 抬高 = raise (prices)

tài 太 ADVERB
1 = excessively, too
■ 今天我太累了，不去游泳了。**Jīntiān wǒ tài lèi le, bú qù yóuyǒng le.** = *Today I'm too tired to go swimming.*
■ 这个房间太小，坐不下二十个人。**Zhège fángjiān tài xiǎo, zuò bu xià èrshí ge rén.** = *This room is too small. It can't seat twenty people.*
2 = extremely, really
■ 太好了！**Tài hǎo le!** = *That's wonderful!*
■ 你们现在抬高物价，太不讲道理了。**Nǐmen xiànzài táigāo wùjià, tài bù jiǎng dàolǐ le.** = *It is extremely unreasonable of you to raise prices now.*

tàitai 太太 NOUN
1 = Mrs
■ 王先生和王太太常常在家里请客吃饭。

Wáng xiānsheng hé Wáng tàitai chángcháng zài jiā li qǐngkè chīfàn. = *Mr and Mrs Wang often give dinner parties in their home.*

2 = wife

■ 您太太刚才打电话来。**Nín tàitai gāngcái dǎ diànhuà lai.** = *Your wife called just now.*

■ 今天是我太太生日，我要早一点回家。**Jīntiān shì wǒ tàitai shēngrì, wǒ yào zǎo yìdiǎn huíjiā.** = *Today's my wife's birthday. I need go home earlier.*

NOTES: (1) While *Mrs* is used in English-speaking countries regardless of class or social status, 太太 **tàitai** is only used in middle-class or upper-class circles. Similarly, 太太 **tàitai** meaning *wife* is only used in middle-class or upper-class circles. (2) Although Chinese women often retain their family names after marriage, 太太 **tàitai** as a form of address must be prefixed by the husband's family name.

tàiyang 太阳 [modif: 太 *big, super* + 阳 *open, overt, masculine*] NOUN = the sun, sunshine

■ 今天的太阳真好。**Jīntiān de tàiyang zhēn hǎo.** = *The sunshine's beautiful today.*

NOTES: (1) Put together, 太 **tài** (meaning *big, great* in classical Chinese) and 阳 **yáng** (meaning *Yang* of ancient Chinese thought) mean *the ultimate Yang*, as the sun is the ultimate symbol of Yang. The ultimate symbol of Yin is the moon 月 **yuè**. (2) In 太阳 **tàiyang**, 阳 **yang** is pronounced in the neutral tone.

tài 态 Trad 態 NOUN = stance

tàidu 态度 [compound: 态 *stance* + 度 *appearance, bearing*] NOUN = attitude, approach

■ 这位服务员的服务态度不好。**Zhè wèi fúwùyuán de fúwù tàidu bù hǎo.** = *This attendant's work attitude is not good.*

■ 这孩子说话态度不好，常惹人生气。**Zhè háizi shuōhuà tàidu bù hǎo, cháng rě rén shēngqì.** = *This child's manner of speaking is bad, and is often offensive.*

NOTE: Though 态度 **tàidu** is glossed as *attitude* or *approach*, it is more commonly used in Chinese than its equivalents in English.

tān 摊 Trad 攤 NOUN = trader's stand, stall

■ 路两边摆了很多摊子，有卖吃的，也有卖工艺品的。**Lù liǎngbiān bǎile hěn duō tānzi, yǒu mài chī de, yě yǒu mài gōngyìpǐn de.** = *There are many stands on the two sides of the street; some sell food and others sell small handicraft articles.*

tán 谈 Trad 談 VERB = talk, discuss

■ 我想跟你谈一件事。**Wǒ xiǎng gēn nǐ tán yí jiàn shì.** = *I'd like to discuss something with you.*

tántiān 谈天 = chat

■ 上班的时候，不能谈天。**Shàngbān de shíhou, bù néng tántiān.** = *You are not supposed to chat during working hours.*

tán yíxià 谈一下 = talk briefly about, give a brief talk about

■ 请你谈一下去中国旅行的情况。**Qǐng nǐ tán yíxià qù Zhōngguó lǚxíng de qíngkuàng.** = *Please give a brief talk about your trip to China.*

tánhuà 谈话 [compound: 谈 *talk* + 话 *talk*] VERB = have a (serious, formal) talk

■ 校长找我谈话。**Xiàozhǎng zhǎo wǒ tánhuà.** = *The principal summoned me for a talk.*

tánpàn 谈判

1 VERB = negotiate

■ 双方正在为签订一项合同谈判。**Shuāngfāng zhèngzài wèi qiāndìng yí xiàng hétóng tánpàn.** = *The two sides are negotiating a contract.*

2 NOUN = negotiation (项 **xiàng**)

■ 这项谈判在进行了三个星期以后终于取得双方满意的结果。**Zhè xiàng tánpàn zài jìnxíngle sān ge xīngqī yǐhòu zhōngyú qǔdé shuāngfāng mǎnyì de jiéguǒ.** = *After three weeks the negotiations finally reached a conclusion that satisfied both parties.*

tǎn 毯 NOUN = same as 毯子 **tǎnzi**

tǎnzi 毯子 [suffix: 毯 *blanket* + 子 *nominal suffix*] NOUN = blanket (条 **tiáo**)

■ 中国人一般不用毯子，而用被子。**Zhōngguórén yìbān bú yòng tǎnzi, ér yòng bèizi.** = *The Chinese usually do not use blankets, but use quilts.*

tàn 探 VERB = explore

tànsuǒ 探索 [compound: 探 explore + 索 search] VERB = explore, seek, search for
- 这些年他都在探索人生的意义。**Zhèxiē nián tā dōu zài tànsuǒ rénshēng de yìyì.** = All these years he has been searching for the meaning of life.
- 医生们正在探索医治这种疾病的方法。**Yīshēngmen zhèngzài tànsuǒ yīzhì zhè zhǒng jíbìng de fāngfǎ.** = Doctors are searching for a way to cure this disease.

tāng 汤 Trad 湯 NOUN = soup (碗 **wǎn**)
- 妈妈做的汤真好喝。**Māma zuò de tāng zhēn hǎohē.** = The soup mom prepared is really delicious.
hē tāng 喝汤 = eat soup

táng 堂 NOUN = main room, hall (See 食堂 **shítáng**.)

táng 糖 NOUN = sugar, candy (块 **kuài**)
- "你的咖啡里要放糖吗?" "要，请放一块糖。" **"Nǐ de kāfēi li yào fàng táng ma?" "Yào, qǐng fàng yí kuài táng."** = "Do you want sugar in your coffee?" "Yes, a lump of sugar, please."
tángguǒ 糖果 = candy, sweets
- 小孩儿一般都喜欢吃糖果。**Xiǎo háir yìbān dòu xǐhuan chī tángguǒ.** = Children usually love candy.

tǎng 躺 VERB = lie
- 她喜欢躺在床上看书。**Tā xǐhuan tǎng zài chuángshang kànshū.** = She likes to lie on bed and read.
- 你既然醒了，就起床吧，别躺在床上了。**Nǐ jìrán xǐngle, jiù qǐchuáng ba, bié tǎng zài chuángshang le.** = Now that you've awake, you should get up. Don't lie in bed.

tàng 趟 MEASURE WORD = (for trips)
- 我去了两趟，都没找到他。**Wǒ qùle liǎng tàng, dōu méi zhǎodao tā.** = I made two trips but did not find him.

tàng 烫 Trad 燙 ADJECTIVE = boiling hot, scalding hot, burning hot
- 这碗汤太烫了，没法喝。**Zhè wǎn tāng tài tàng le, méifǎ hē.** = This bowl of soup is too hot to eat.

táo 逃 VERB = flee, run away (from danger, punishment, etc.)
- 警察来的时候，强盗已经逃走了。**Jǐngchá lái de shíhou, qiángdào yǐjīng táozǒu le.** = By the time the policemen arrived, the robbers had fled.

tǎo 讨 Trad 討 VERB = ask for

tǎolùn 讨论 [compound: 讨 explore + 论 discuss]
1 VERB = discuss
- 老师们在讨论明年的工作。**Lǎoshīmen zài tǎolùn míngnián de gōngzuò.** = The teachers are discussing next year's work.
2 NOUN = discussion (次 **cì**)
- 我们要讨论一下才能作出决定。**Wǒmen yào tǎolùn yíxià cái néng zuòchū juédìng.** = We must have a discussion before we can make a decision.
- 这次讨论对我们很有用。**Zhè cì tǎolùn duì wǒmen hěn yǒuyòng.** = This discussion is useful to us.

tǎoyàn 讨厌 [v+obj: 讨 ask for + 厌 boredom, vexation]
1 ADJECTIVE = vexing, disgusting
- 这种电视广告讨厌得很。**Zhè zhǒng diànshì guǎnggào tǎoyàn de hěn.** = This kind of TV commercial is disgusting.
2 VERB = find vexing, find disgusting
- 我讨厌连续下雨的天气。**Wǒ tǎoyàn liánxù xiàyǔ de tiānqì.** = I hate incessant rain.

tào 套 MEASURE WORD = set, suit, suite (for a collection of things)
- 一套衣服 **yí tào yīfu** = a suit of clothes
- 两套家具 **liǎng tào jiājù** = two sets of furniture

tè 特 ADVERB = particularly, especially

tèbié 特别 [compound: 特 special + 别 other, unusual] ADJECTIVE = special, especially
- 他病得很重，住在特别病房。**Tā bìng de hěn zhòng, zhù zài tèbié bìngfáng.** = He's seriously ill and stays in the special ward.
- 我特别喜欢吃新西兰的苹果。**Wǒ tèbié xǐhuan chī Xīnxīlán de píngguǒ.** = I especially like New Zealand apples.

T

tèdiǎn 特点 [modif: 特 *special* + 点 *point*]
NOUN = special features, characteristic
■ 中国文化有什么特点? **Zhōngguó wénhuà yǒu shénme tèdiǎn?** = *What are the special features of Chinese culture?*

tèshū 特殊 [compound: 特 *special* + 殊 *different*] ADJECTIVE = special, unusual, exceptional
■ 你只有在特殊情况下才能采取这一措施。**Nǐ zhǐyǒu zài tèshū qíngkuàng xia cái néng cǎiqǔ zhè yí cuòshī.** = *Only under special circumstances can you take this step.*
■ 每个公民都必须遵守法律，没有人可以特殊。**Měi ge gōngmín dōu bìxū zūnshǒu fǎlǜ, méiyǒu rén kéyǐ tèshū.** = *Every citizen must obey the law and nobody can be an exception.*

téng 疼 VERB
1 = ache, hurt
■ 我头疼，得躺一会儿。**Wǒ tóu téng, děi tǎng yíhuìr.** = *I have a headache. I have to lie down for a while.*
tóu téng 头疼 = headache, have a headache

NOTE: 疼 **téng** in the sense of *ache, hurt* is a colloquial word. You can use 痛 **tòng** instead of 疼 **téng** to mean *ache, hurt*.

2 = love dearly
■ 我小时候，我奶奶可疼我了。**Wǒ xiǎoshíhou, wǒ nǎinai kě téng wǒ le.** = *When I was a child, my granny really loved me dearly.*

tī 梯 NOUN = ladder, steps (See 电梯 **diàntī**, 楼梯 **lóutī**.)

tī 踢 VERB = kick
tī qiú 踢球 = play soccer
■ 一些男孩儿在操场上踢球。**Yìxiē nánháir zài cāochǎng shang tīqiú.** = *Some boys are playing soccer on the sports ground.*
tī zúqiú 踢足球 = play soccer

tí 提 VERB
1 = carry in the hand (with the arm down)
■ 我可以提这个小皮箱上飞机吗? **Wǒ kéyǐ tí zhège xiǎo píxiāng shàng fēijī ma?** = *Can I carry this small bag on board the plane?*
2 = mention
■ 你见到他的时候，别提这件事。**Nǐ jiàndao**

tā de shíhou, bié tí zhè jiàn shì. = *Don't mention this matter when you see him.*
tí jiànyì 提建议 = put forward a proposal, make a suggestion
tí wèntí 提问题 = raise a question

tíchàng 提倡 [compound: 提 *put forward* + 倡 *advocate*] VERB = advocate, recommend
■ 政府提倡一对夫妻只生一个孩子。**Zhèngfǔ tíchàng yí duì fūqī zhǐ shēng yí ge háizi.** = *The government recommends that every couple has only one child.*

tígāo 提高 [v+comp: 提 *raise* + 高 *high*] VERB = raise, advance
■ 我要提高自己的中文水平。**Wǒ yào tígāo zìjǐ de Zhōngwén shuǐpíng.** = *I want to raise my proficiency in Chinese.*
■ 我们不断提高产品的质量。**Wǒmen búduàn tígāo chǎnpǐn de zhìliàng.** = *We work constantly to improve the quality of our products.*

tígòng 提供 [compound: 提 *put forward* + 供 *supply*] VERB = provide, supply
■ 我们提供售后服务。**Wǒmen tígòng shòuhòu fúwù.** = *We provide after-sales service.*
■ 这项研究为决定政策提供了有力的数据。**Zhè xiàng yánjiū wèi juédìng zhèngcè tígòngle yǒulì de shùjù.** = *This research provided solid data for policy-making.*

tíqián 提前 [v+obj: 提 *put forward* + 前 *forward*] VERB = put ahead of schedule, advance
■ 长途汽车提前半小时到达。**Chángtú qìchē tíqián bàn xiǎoshí dàodá.** = *The coach arrived half an hour ahead of the schedule.*
■ 你知道吗? 考试提前两天举行。**Nǐ zhīdào ma? Kǎoshì tíqián liǎng tiān jǔxíng.** = *Do you know that the examination will be held two days earlier?*

tí 题 Trad 題 NOUN = question

tímù 题目 NOUN
1 = question for an examination, school exercises, etc. (道 **dào**)
■ 这次测验一共有十道题目。**Zhè cì cèyàn yígòng yǒu shí dào tímù.** = *There will be ten questions in this test.*

■ 这道数学题目太难了，我不会做。**Zhè dào shùxué tímù tài nán le, wǒ bú huì zuò.** = *This math problem is too difficult for me.*

2 = title, subject

■ 他要给文章取一个好题目。**Tā yào gěi wénzhāng qǔ yí ge hǎo tímù.** = *He will give his essay a good title.*

tǐ 体 Trad 體 ADJECTIVE = physical

tǐhuì 体会

1 VERB = learn, realize, gain intimate knowledge through personal experience

■ 他当了一年爸爸，体会到当父母是多么不容易。**Tā dāngle yì nián bàba, tǐhuì dào dāng fùmǔ shì duōme bù róngyì.** = *After being a father for a year, he realized how difficult parenting was.*

2 NOUN = personal understanding

■ 请你谈谈你在中国工作的体会。**Qǐng nǐ tántan nǐ zài Zhōngguó gōngzuò de tǐhuì.** = *Please tell us what you have learned from working in China.*

tǐjī 体积 NOUN = volume (mathematics)

■ 这个箱子体积不大，为什么这么重？**Zhège xiāngzi tǐjī bú dà, wèishénme zhème zhòng?** = *This box is not big. Why is it so heavy?*

tǐyù 体育 [modif: 体 *physical* + 育 *education*] NOUN = physical education, sports

■ 体育和学习，哪个更重要？**Tǐyù hé xuéxí, nǎge gèng zhòngyào?** = *Sports or study, which is more important?*

tǐyù kè 体育课 = physical education (PE) lesson

■ 今天下午上体育课，我不能穿皮鞋。**Jīntiān xiàwǔ shàng tǐyù kè, wǒ bù néng chuān píxié.** = *I'm having a PE class this afternoon, so I can't wear leather shoes today.*

tǐyùchǎng 体育场 [modif: 体育 *sports* + 场 *ground*] NOUN = stadium

■ 体育场里正在举行一场精彩的足球比赛。**Tǐyùchǎng li zhèngzài jǔxíng yì chǎng jīngcǎi de zúqiú bǐsài.** = *A thrilling football match is going on in the stadium.*

tǐyùguǎn 体育馆 [modif: 体育 *sports* + 馆 *building*] NOUN = gymnasium

■ 这个体育馆有多少座位？**Zhège tǐyùguǎn**

yǒu duōshǎo zuòwèi? = *How many seats are there in this gymnasium?*

tǐ 替 VERB

1 = replace, substitute

■ 万一他生病了，谁来替他呢？**Wànyī tā shēngbìng le, shuí lái tì tā ne?** = *If he falls ill, who will replace him?*

2 = same as 给 **gěi** PREPOSITION

tiān 天 NOUN

1 = sky, heaven

■ 秋天，天特别蓝。**Qiūtiān, tiān tèbié lán.** = *In autumn, the sky is especially blue.*

2 = day

■ 我在朋友家住了三天。**Wǒ zài péngyou jiā zhùle sān tiān.** = *I stayed with my friend for three days.*

■ 这位老人下雨天一般不出去。**Zhè wèi lǎorén xià yǔ tiān yìbān bù chūqu.** = *This old man normally does not go out in rainy days.*

3 = weather

■ 农民还是靠天吃饭。**Nóngmín háishì kào tiān chīfàn.** = *Peasants still depend on the weather to make a living.*

Lǎotiānyé 老天爷 = Heavens (a colloquial term that denotes "God" or "Nature")

■ 老天爷再不下雨，就要闹灾了。**Lǎotiānyé zài bú xià yǔ jiù yào nào zāi le.** = *If it does not rain, there'll be disaster.*

tiān shang 天上 = in the sky

tiāntiān 天天 = every day

tiān xià 天下 = under heaven, in the world, on earth

Tiān zhīdào! 天知道! = Only God knows!

tiānqì 天气 [compound: 天 *weather* + 气 *weather*] NOUN = weather

■ 天气变化很大。**Tiānqì biànhuà hěn dà.** = *The weather changes dramatically.*

■ 明天的天气怎么样？**Míngtiān de tiānqì zěnmeyàng?** = *How will the weather be tomorrow?*

tiānzhēn 天真 [compound: 天 *natural* + 真 *genuine*] ADJECTIVE

1 = simple and unaffected, ingenuous

■ 和天真的孩子说话，是一种享受。**Hé tiānzhēn de háizi shuōhuà, shì yì zhǒng xiǎngshòu.** = *Talking with innocent children is an enjoyment.*

2 = naive, gullible

■ 你怎么会相信这种广告？太天真了！ **Nǐ zěnme huì xiāngxìn zhè zhǒng guǎnggào? Tài tiānzhēn le!** = *How could you believe such advertisements? You're too naive!*

tiān 添 VERB = add

■ 你这么忙，我不想给你添麻烦。 **Nǐ zhème máng, wǒ bù xiǎng gěi nǐ tiān máfan.** = *You're so busy. I don't want to add to your trouble.*

tián 田 NOUN = farmland (especially paddy fields), fields

■ 他在田里干活。 **Tā zài tián li gànhuó.** = *He was working in the fields.*

zhòngtián 种田 = grow crops, farm

■ 在中国光靠种田，很难富。 **Zài Zhōngguó guāng kào zhòngtián, hěn nán fù.** = *In China, it's difficult to get rich simply by growing crops.*

tiányě 田野 [compound: 田 *fields, farmland* + 野 *old country*] NOUN = farmland and open country

■ 城里人有时候喜欢到田野走走。 **Chénglǐrén yǒushíhou xǐhua dào tiányě zǒuzǒu.** = *City people like to take an occasional walk in the open country.*

tián 填 VERB = fill in (a form, blanks as in an exercise)

■ 进入一个国家要填表，离开一个国家也要填表。 **Jìnrù yí ge guójiā yào tián biǎo, líkāi yí ge guójiā yě yào tián biǎo.** = *To enter a country you need to fill in a form, and to leave a country you need to fill in a form as well.*

tiāo 挑 VERB = take one's pick, choose, select

■ 商店里这么多鞋子，你还挑不到一双喜欢的？ **Shàngdiàn li zhème duō xiézi, nǐ hái tiāo bu dào yì shuāng xǐhuan de?** = *There are so many shoes in the store, and you still can't choose a pair you like?*

dōng-tiāo-xī-jiǎn 东挑西拣 = choose this and pick that, spend a long time choosing, be very choosy

tiāoxuǎn 挑选 [compound: 挑 *take one's pick* + 选 *select*] VERB = select

■ 董事会要从经理中挑选出一名总经理。 **Dǒngshìhuì yào cóng jīnglǐ zhong tiāoxuǎnchu yì míng zǒngjīnglǐ.** = *The board of directors will select a chief executive officer from the executives.*

■ 有时候可以挑选的东西太多，很难决定。 **Yǒushíhou kěyǐ tiāoxuǎn de dōngxi tài duō, hěn nán juédìng.** = *Sometimes when there are too many things to choose from, it's difficult to decide.*

tiáo 条 Trad 條 MEASURE WORD = (for things with a long, narrow shape)

■ 一条河 **yì tiáo hé** = *a river*
■ 两条鱼 **liǎng tiáo yú** = *two fish*

tiáojiàn 条件 [compound: 条 *item, piece* + 件 *item, piece*] NOUN

1 = condition

■ 这个地区的自然条件不好。 **Zhège dìqū de zìrán tiáojiàn bù hǎo.** = *The natural conditions of this region are rather poor.*

shēnghuó tiáojiàn 生活条件 = living conditions

■ 他们那里的生活条件比较差。 **Tāmen nàlǐ de shēnghuó tiáojiàn bǐjiào chà.** = *Their living conditions are rather poor.*

gōngzuò tiáojiàn 工作条件 = working conditions

■ 工人们要求改善工作条件。 **Gōngrénmen yāoqiú gǎishàn gōngzuò tiáojiàn.** = *Workers demand that their working conditions be improved.*

2 = requirement, prerequisite

■ 她找对象的条件非常高。 **Tā zhǎo duìxiàng de tiáojiàn fēicháng gāo.** = *She has very high requirements of a fiancé.*

■ 对方的条件太高，我们无法合作。 **Duìfāng de tiáojiàn tài gāo, wǒmen wúfǎ hézuò.** = *The other party's requirements are too high for us to work with them.*

■ 参加比赛有一个条件，参加比赛的人必须小于十八岁。 **Cānjiā bǐsài yǒu yí ge tiáojiàn, cānjiā bǐsài de rén bìxū xiǎoyú shíbā suì.** = *There is a requirement for participation in the competition: the participant must be under eighteen years.*

tiáoyuē 条约 [compound: 条 *article (of a treaty)* + 约 *agreement*] NOUN = treaty, pact (份 fèn)

■ 两国将签订条约，以加强合作。 **Liǎng guó jiāng qiāndìng tiáoyuē, yǐ jiāqiáng hézuò.** = *The two countries will sign a treaty in order to strengthen cooperation.*

tiáo 调 Trad 調 VERB = adjust

tiáozhěng 调整 [compound: 调 *adjust* + 整 *rectify*] VERB = adjust, rectify
■ 教育部打算调整中小学的师生比例。**Jiàoyùbù dǎsuàn tiáozhěng zhōng-xiǎoxué de shīshēng bǐlì.** = *The Ministry of Education plans to adjust the teacher-student ratio in schools.*

tiào 跳 VERB = jump
■ 他跳得很高, 所以篮球打得好。**Tā tiào de hěn gāo, suǒyǐ lánqiú dǎ de hǎo.** = *He can jump high, so he plays basketball well.*
tiào gāo 跳高 = high jump
tiào shéng 跳绳 = rope-skipping, rope-jumping
tiào shuǐ 跳水 = dive
tiào yuǎn 跳远 = long jump

tiàowǔ 跳舞 [compound: 跳 *jump* + 舞 *dance*] VERB = dance
■ 我可以请您跳舞吗? **Wǒ kěyǐ qǐng nín tiàowǔ ma?** = *May I have a dance with you?*
■ 她跳舞跳得很美。**Tā tiàowǔ tiào de hěn měi.** = *She dances beautifully.*

tiē 贴 Trad 貼 VERB = paste, stick
■ 他回到办公室, 发现门上贴了一张便条。**Tā huídào bàngōngshì, fāxiàn mén shang tiēle yì zhāng biàntiáo.** = *When he came back to the office he found a note stuck on the door.*

tiě 铁 Trad 鐵 NOUN = iron
■ 花园里的那条长椅是铁做的。**Huāyuán li de nà tiáo chángyǐ shì tiě zuò de.** = *The bench in the garden is made of iron.*

tiělù 铁路 [modif: 铁 *iron* + 路 *road*] NOUN = railway (条 tiáo)
■ 这条铁路伸进大山脉。**Zhè tiáo tiělù shēnjìn dà shānmài.** = *This railway extends all the way to the great mountain range.*

tīng 厅 Trad 廳 NOUN = hall (See 餐厅 cāntīng.)

tīng 听 Trad 聽 VERB
1 = listen
■ 他每天早上都听广播。**Tā měi tiān zǎoshang dōu tīng guǎngbō.** = *He listens to the radio early every morning.*
tīngjiàn 听见 = hear

■ 我听见有人在花园里叫我。**Wǒ tīngjiàn yǒu rén zài huāyuán li jiào wǒ.** = *I heard somebody calling me in the garden.*
2 = heed, obey
■ 你不听他的话, 会后悔的。**Nǐ bù tīng tā de huà, huì hòuhuǐ de.** = *You will be sorry if you don't heed his advice* (or *warning*).
tīnghuà 听话 = heed, be obedient
■ 中国家长喜欢听话的孩子。**Zhōngguó jiāzhǎng xǐhuan tīnghuà de háizi.** = *Chinese parents like obedient children.*
tīngshuō 听说 = hear of, people say
■ 听说张先生一家搬走了。**Tīngshuō Zhāng xiǎnsheng yìjiā bānzǒu le.** = *I've heard that Mr Zhang's family has moved.*
tīngxiě 听写 = dictation, do dictation

tíng 停 VERB = stop, park (a vehicle)
■ 路上车辆太多了, 我们停停开开, 花了一个小时才回到家。**Lùshang chēliàng tài duō le, wǒmen tíng tíng kāi kāi, huāle yí ge xiǎoshí cái huídao jiā.** = *Traffic was heavy. We were continually stopping and it took us one hour to arrive home.*
tíng chē 停车 = park (a car)
■ 我可以把车停在这里吗? **Wǒ kěyǐ ba qìchē tíng zai zhèli ma?** = *May I park my car here?*
tíngchēchǎng 停车场 = parking lot, car park
tíng xiàlai 停下来 = come to a stop
■ 前面是红灯, 车子要停下来。**Qiánmiàn shì hóngdēng, chēzi yào tíng xiàlai.** = *It's a red light in front. The car must stop.*

tíngzhǐ 停止 [compound: 停 *stop* + 止 *end*] VERB = stop, cease
■ 那家公司停止营业了, 那他们欠我们的钱怎么办呢? **Nà jiā gōngsī tíngzhǐ yíngyè le, nà tāmen qiàn wǒmen de qián zěnme bàn ne?** = *That company has gone out of business. Then what about the money they owe us?*
■ 请你们立即停止这种影响他人的行为。**Qǐng nǐmen lìjí tíngzhǐ zhè zhǒng yǐngxiǎng tārén de xíngwéi.** = *Stop such disruptive behavior immediately, please.*

tíng 庭 NOUN = front courtyard (See 家庭 jiātíng.)

tǐng 挺 ADVERB = very
■ 她学习挺认真。**Tā xuéxí tǐng rènzhēn.** = *She studies conscientiously.*

NOTE: 挺 **tǐng** and 很 **hěn** share the same meaning, but 挺 **tǐng** is a colloquial word.

tōng 通

1 VERB = (of roads, railways) lead to, go to
- 这条路通到哪里？ **Zhè tiáo lù tōngdào nǎlǐ?** = *Where does this road lead?*
- 条条大路通罗马。**Tiáotiáo dàlù tōng Luómǎ.** = *All roads lead to Rome.*

2 ADJECTIVE = (of language) grammatical, logical
- 这句话不通，但是我说不出错在哪里。**Zhè jù huà bù tōng, dànshì wǒ shuō bu chū cuò zài nǎlǐ.** = *This sentence is not quite right, but I can't identify where the mistake is.*

tōngguò 通过 [compound: 通 *go through* + 过 *pass*]

1 VERB = pass through
- 从我家到机场，要通过城里。**Cóng wǒ jiā dào jīchǎng, yào tōngguò chénglǐ.** = *Going from my home to the airport, one has to pass through the city center.*

2 PREPOSITION = through, as a result of
- 通过这次访问，我更了解中国了。**Tōngguò zhè cì fǎngwèn, wǒ gèng liǎojiě Zhōngguó le.** = *As a result of this visit, I understand China better.*

tōngxùn 通讯 [v+obj: 通 *communicate* + 讯 *message*] NOUN = communication

- 这几年通讯技术迅速发展，传真、电子邮件、手机等越来越普及。**Zhè jǐ nián tōngxùn jìshù xùnsù fāzhǎn, chuánzhēn, diànzǐ yóujiàn, shǒujī děng yuèláiyuè pǔjí.** = *In recent years communication technology has seen rapid development. Fax, e-mail, cell phones and so on are becoming more and more widely used.*

tōngzhī 通知

1 VERB = notify, inform
- 科长通知我们，明天上午开会。**Kēzhǎng tōngzhī wǒmen, míngtiān kāihuì.** = *The section head has informed us that there will be a meeting tomorrow morning.*
- 代表团什么时候来，请及时通知。**Dàibiǎotuán shénme shíhou lái, qǐng jíshí tōngzhī.** = *Please let us know promptly when the delegation will come.*

2 NOUN = notice
- 市政府在报上发了一个通知。**Shì zhèngfǔ**

zài bào shang fāle yí ge **tōngzhī.** = *The city government has published a notice in the paper.*

tóng 同

1 PREPOSITION = with, along with
- 同你在一起，我感到很愉快。**Tóng nǐ zài yìqǐ, wǒ gǎndao hěn yúkuài.** = *I find it a pleasure to be with you.*
- 我们正在同那家公司商量合办食品加工厂的计划。**Wǒmen zhèngzài tóng nà jiā gōngsī shāngliang hébàn shípǐn jiāgōngchǎng de jìhuà.** = *We are discussing a plan with that company to open a food-processing plant.*

2 CONJUNCTION = and
- 这件事已经分别通知了教育局长同卫生局长。**Zhè jiàn shì yǐjīng fēnbié tōngzhī le jiàoyù júzhǎng tóng wèishēng júzhǎng.** = *The director of the education bureau and the director of the public health bureau respectively have been informed of this matter.*

tóngqíng 同情 [modif: 同 *same* + 情 *emotion*]

1 VERB = sympathize with
- 我很同情这位在交通事故中失去儿子的母亲。**Wǒ hěn tóngqíng zhè wèi zài jiāotōng shìgù zhong shīqù érzi de mǔqin.** = *I sympathize with the mother who lost her son in the traffic accident.*

2 NOUN = sympathy
- 他的痛苦经历，引起了我的同情。**Tā de tòngkǔ jīnglì, yǐnqǐle wǒ de tóngqíng.** = *His painful experience aroused my sympathy.*

tóngshí 同时 [modif: 同 *same* + 时 *time*] NOUN = at the same time, simultaneously

- 我和她同时开始学中文。**Wǒ hé tā tóngshí kāishǐ xué Zhōngwén.** = *She and I began to learn Chinese at the same time.*
- 我再找找那本书，同时希望你也回家找找。**Wǒ zài zhǎozhǎo nà běn shū, tóngshí xīwàng nǐ yě huíjiā zhǎozhǎo.** = *I'll go on looking for the book; at the same time, I hope you'll search for it at home.*

tóngshì 同事 [modif: 同 *same* + 事 *job*] NOUN = colleague

- 同事之间要建立合作关系。**Tóngshì zhījiān yào jiànlì hézuò guānxi.** = *Colleagues should build a cooperative relationship among themselves.*

tóngwū 同屋 [modif: 同 *same* + 屋 *room*]
NOUN = roommate, flatmate
■ 他是我的同学，也是我的同屋。**Tā shì wǒ de tóngxué, yě shì wǒ de tóngwū.** = *He is my classmate, and my roommate as well.*

tóngxué 同学 [modif: 同 *together* + 学 *study*]
NOUN = classmate, schoolmate
■ 我的朋友大多是我的同学。**Wǒ de péngyou dàduō shì wǒ de tóngxué.** = *Most of my friends are my schoolmates.*
lǎotóngxué 老同学 = former schoolmate
■ 他利用老同学的关系，取得了那份合同。**Tā lìyòng lǎotóngxué de guānxi, qǔdéle nà fèn hétóng.** = *He got the contract through the connection of an old schoolmate.*

NOTE: In Chinese schools, teachers address students as 同学们 **tóngxuémen**, e.g.
■ 同学们，我们现在上课了。**Tóngxuémen, wǒmen xiànzài shàngkè le.** = *Class, we're starting class now.*

tóngyàng 同样 [modif: 同 *same* + 样 *way*]
ADJECTIVE = same
■ 他和妻子有同样的爱好，同样的理想。**Tā hé qīzi yǒu tóngyàng de àihào, tóngyàng de lǐxiǎng.** = *He and his wife share the same hobby and the same dream.*

tóngyì 同意 [modif: 同 *same* + 意 *opinion*]
VERB = agree, approve (antonym 反对 **fǎnduì**)
■ 我不同意你说的话。**Wǒ bù tóngyì nǐ shuō de huà.** = *I don't agree with what you said.*
■ 我不反对你的计划，但是不同意立即执行。**Wǒ bù fǎnduì nǐ de jìhuà, dànshì bù tóngyì lìjì zhíxíng.** = *I don't oppose your plan, but I don't agree to its immediate implementation.*

tóngzhì 同志 [compound: 同 *same* + 志 *aspiration*] NOUN = comrade

NOTE: 同志 **tóngzhì** used to be the most common form of address in China before 1980. Now it is seldom used. 同志 **tóngzhì** is almost never used between a Chinese and a foreigner. The common forms of address in China today are 先生 **xiānsheng** (to men) and 小姐 **xiǎojiě** (to women, especially young women). In some places 同志 **tóngzhì** has acquired the meaning *a fellow homosexual.*

tóng 铜 Trad 銅 NOUN = copper, bronze
■ 铜是一种重要金属。**Tóng shì yì zhǒng zhòngyào jīnshǔ.** = *Copper is an important metal.*

tóng 童 NOUN = child (See 儿童 **értóng**.)

tǒng 桶 NOUN = bucket, pail (只 **zhī**)
■ 他提了一桶水去洗汽车。**Tā tíle yì tǒng shuǐ qù xǐ qìchē.** = *He carried a bucket of water over to wash his car.*

tǒng 统 Trad 統 ADJECTIVE = together

tǒngyī 统一
1 VERB = unify, integrate
■ 关于这个问题，我们需要统一认识。**Guānyú zhège wèntí, wǒmen xūyào tǒngyī rènshi.** = *We need to reach a common understanding on this issue.*
2 ADJECTIVE = unified
■ 这些国家已经形成一个统一的市场。**Zhèxiē guójiā yǐjīng xíngchéng yí ge tǒngyī de shìchǎng.** = *These countries have already formed a common market.*

tǒngzhì 统治 [compound: 统 *lead* + 治 *govern*] VERB = rule
■ 这个党统治已经很多年了。**Zhège dǎng tǒngzhì yǐjīng hěn duō nián le.** = *This party has ruled the country for many years.*
tǒngzhì jiējí 统治阶级 = ruling class

tòng 痛 VERB = same as 疼 **téng** VERB 1

tòngkǔ 痛苦 [compound: 痛 *painful* + 苦 *bitter*] ADJECTIVE = painful, torturous
■ 他不想回忆那段痛苦的生活。**Tā bù xiǎng huíyì nà duàn tòngkǔ de shēnghuó.** = *He does not want to recall that painful period of his life.*

tòngkuai 痛快 [compound: 痛 *to one's heart's content* + 快 *delight*] ADJECTIVE = overjoyed, very delighted
■ 我在会上说了一直想说的话，心里很痛快。**Wǒ zài huìshang shuōle yìzhí xiǎng shuō de huà, xīnli hěn tòngkuai.** = *At the meeting I said that I'd been wanting to say, and felt extremely pleased.*
■ 上星期日我们玩得真痛快。**Shàng Xīngqīrì**

T

wǒmen wán de zhēn tòngkuai. = *We had a terrific time last Sunday.*

tōu 偷 VERB = steal, pilfer
- 我的钱包让人偷了！ **Wǒ de qiánbāo ràng rén tōu le!** = *My wallet's been stolen!*
- 在有些国家偷东西的人会被砍断手。 **Zài yǒuxiē guójiā tōu dōngxi de rén huì bèi kǎnduàn shǒu.** = *In some countries, those who steal have their hands chopped off.*

tōutōu 偷偷 ADVERB = stealthily, on the quiet
- 我看见一个人偷偷走进校长办公室。 **Wǒ kànjiàn yí ge rén tōutōu zǒujìn xiàozhǎng bàngōngshì.** = *I saw a figure walking stealthily into the principal's office.* (→ *I saw someone sneak into the principal's office.*)
- 孩子偷偷告诉我，他哥哥就躲在门背后。 **Háizi tōutōu gàosu wǒ, tā gēge jiù duǒ zài mén bèihòu.** = *The child furtively told me that his brother was hiding behind the door.*

tóu 头 Trad 頭
1 NOUN = the head
- 我头疼。 **Wǒ tóu téng.** = *My head aches.* (→ *I have a headache.*)
2 NOUN = foreman, chief
- 你们的头儿呢？我要找他说话。 **Nǐmen de tóur ne? Wǒ yào zhǎo tā shuōhuà.** = *Who's your foreman?* (or *Who's in charge here?*) *I want to talk to him.*
3 ADJECTIVE = first, first few
- 我刚来的头几个星期，几乎天天下雨。 **Wǒ gāng lái de tóu jǐge xīngqī, jīhū tiāntiān xiàyǔ.** = *The first few weeks after I arrived, it rained almost every day.*
4 MEASURE WORD = (for cattle or sheep)
- 一头牛 **yì tóu niú** = *a head of cattle* (or *buffalo/cow*)
- 两头羊 **liǎng tóu yáng** = *two sheep*

tóufa 头发 [modif: 头 head + 发 hair] NOUN = hair (of the human head) (根 gēn)
- 爸爸的头发渐渐白了。 **Bàba de tóufa jiànjiàn bái le.** = *Daddy's hair is turning gray.*

tóu 投 VERB = throw

tóurù 投入 [v+obj: 投 throw + 入 enter] VERB = put into, invest
- 他们在孩子的教育上投入很多钱。 **Tāmen**

zài háizi de jiàoyù shang tóurù hěn duō qián.** = *They put lots of money into their children's education.*

tòu 透
1 VERB = penetrate, pass through
- 月光透进房间。 **Yuèguāng tòujìn fángjiān.** = *Moonlight came into the room.*
2 ADJECTIVE = thorough
- 王老师把这个语法问题讲得很透。 **Wáng lǎoshī bǎ zhège yǔfǎ wèntí jiǎng de hěn tòu.** = *Teacher Wang explained this grammar point thoroughly.*

tū 突 ADJECTIVE = protruding

tūchū 突出 [compound: 突 protrude + 出 out]
1 VERB = give prominence, highlight, emphasize
- 他在这篇文章中突出市场调查的重要性。 **Tā zài zhè piān wénzhāng zhong tūchūle shìchǎng diàochá de zhòngyàoxìng.** = *In this article he emphasizes the importance of market research.*
2 ADJECTIVE = prominent, conspicuous
- 火车上只有他一个外国人，显得很突出。 **Huǒchē shang zhǐyǒu tā yí ge wàiguórén, xiǎnde hěn tūchū.** = *He is the only foreigner on the train and is very conspicuous.*

tūrán 突然 [suffix: 突 sudden + 然 adjective suffix] ADJECTIVE = sudden, suddenly
- 他没有给我打电话，也没有写信，昨天晚上突然来了。 **Tā méiyǒu gěi wǒ dǎ diànhuà, yě méiyǒu xiě xìn, zuótiān wánshang tūrán lái le.** = *He hadn't rung or written to me, but suddenly showed up yesterday evening.*
- 突然发生这件事，我真不知道怎么办。 **Tūrán fāshēng zhè jiàn shì, wó zhēn bù zhīdào zěnme bàn.** = *I really don't know what to do about this sudden incident.*

tú 图 Trad 圖 NOUN = picture, drawing, chart, diagram (张 zhāng)
- 他画了一张图，说明这种药不同成分的比例。 **Tā huàle yì zhāng tú, shuōmíng zhè zhǒng yào bùtóng chéngfèn de bǐlì.** = *He drew a chart to show the proportion of the various ingredients in this medicine.*

túshūguǎn 图书馆 [modif: 图书 books + 馆 building] NOUN = library (座 zuò)

■ 我们学校的图书馆没有多少中文书。 **Wǒmen xuéxiào de túshūguǎn méiyǒu duōshǎo Zhōngwén shū.** = *The library in our school doesn't have many Chinese books.*
■ 图书馆里不准吃东西。 **Túshūguǎn li bù zhǔn chī dōngxi.** = *Eating in the library is not allowed. (→ No food in the library.)*

tú 涂 Trad 塗 VERB = smear, spread on
■ 她在面包上涂了一层黄油。 **Tā zài miànbāo shang túle yì céng huángyóu.** = *She spread butter on the bread.*

tú 途 NOUN = way, route (See 前途 **qiántú**.)

tǔ 土 NOUN = soil, earth
■ 你鞋上怎么全是土? **Nǐ xié shang zěnme quán shì tǔ?** = *How come your shoes are covered with dirt?*

tǔdì 土地 [compound: 土 *soil* + 地 *land*] NOUN = land
■ 对农民来说，最重要的资源是土地。 **Duì nóngmín lái shuō, zuì zhòngyào de zīyuán shì tǔdì.** = *To farmers, the most important resource is land.*

tǔdòu 土豆 [modif: 土 *soil* + 豆 *bean*] NOUN = potato (只 **zhī**, 块 **kuài**)
■ "土豆烧牛肉" 是一道有名的西菜。 **"Tǔdòu shāo niúròu" shì yí dào yǒumíng de xīcài.** = *"Beef and potato stew"* (or *Hungarian goulash*) *is a famous Western dish.*

tǔ 吐 VERB = spit, exhale
■ 她吓得半天才吐出一口气。 **Tā xià de bàntiān cái tǔ chū yì kǒu qì.** = *She was so terrified that she held her breath.*

tù 吐 VERB = vomit
■ 他酒喝得太多，吐了。 **Tā jiǔ hē de tài duō, tù le.** = *He vomited because he drank too much.*
■ 我想吐。 **Wǒ xiǎng tù.** = *I want to vomit (→ I feel sick).*

tù 兔 NOUN = rabbit, hare

tùzi 兔子 [suffix: 兔 *rabbit, hare* + 子 nominal suffix] NOUN = rabbit, hare (只 **zhī**)
■ 我小时候养过两只兔子。 **Wǒ xiǎoshíhou**

yǎngguo liǎng zhī tùzi. = *When I was a child I once kept two rabbits.*

tuán 团 Trad 團 NOUN = (military) regiment; group, team
■ 你打算参加旅行团，还是自己一个人去中国? **Nǐ dǎsuàn cānjiā lǚxíngtuán, háishi zìjǐ yígerén qù Zhōngguó?** = *Do you plan to tour China in a tourist group or all by yourself?*
dàibiǎotuán 代表团 = delegation
lǚxíngtuán 旅行团 = tour group
gēwǔtuán 歌舞团 = song and dance troupe

tuánjié 团结 [compound: 团 *rally around* + 结 *tie up*] VERB = unite, be in solidarity with
■ 这一家的兄弟姐妹很团结。 **Zhè yì jiā de xiōng-dì-jiě-mèi hěn tuánjié.** = *The siblings in this family are united.*
■ 团结就是力量。 **Tuánjié jiù shì lìliàng.** = *Unity is strength.*

tuī 推 VERB = push
■ 你要推这个门，不要拉。 **Nǐ yào tuī zhège mén, bú yào lā.** = *You should push this door, not pull it.*
■ 他推着自行车上坡。 **Tā tuīzhe zìxíngchē shàng pō.** = *He pushed the bicycle up the slope.*

tuīdòng 推动 [v+obj: 推 *push* + 动 *move*] VERB = push forward, promote
■ 中国迅速的经济发展推动了中文教学。 **Zhōngguó xùnsù de jīngjì fāzhǎn tuīdòngle Zhōngwén jiàoxué.** = *China's rapid economic development has promoted teaching and learning of the Chinese language.*

tuīguǎng 推广 [v+comp: 推 *push* + 广 *wide*] VERB = popularize, spread
■ 中国大力推广普通话，已经取得了成功。 **Zhōngguó dàlì tuīguǎng Pǔtōnghuà, yǐjīng qǔdéle chénggōng.** = *China's tremendous efforts to popularize Putonghua have been successful.*

tuījiàn 推荐 [compound: 推 *push* + 荐 *recommend*] VERB = recommend
■ 王老师给我推荐一本汉英词典。 **Wáng lǎoshī gěi wǒ tuījiàn yì běn Hànyīng cídiǎn.** = *Teacher Wang recommended me a Chinese-English dictionary.*

T

■ 你能不能给我推荐一位会说英语的牙医? **Nǐ néng bu néng gěi wǒ tuījiàn yí wèi huì shuō Yīngyǔ de yáyī?** = *Could you recommend me a dentist who speaks English?*

tuǐ 腿 NOUN = leg (条 tiáo)
■ 他腿长，跑得快。**Tā tuǐ cháng, pǎo de kuài.** = *He's got long legs and runs fast.*

tuì 退 VERB = move back, retreat
■ 请你退到黄线后面。**Qǐng nǐ tuìdao huángxiàn hòumiàn.** = *Please step back behind the yellow line.*
■ 你对商品不满意，可以退款。**Nǐ duì shāngpǐn bù mǎnyì, kěyǐ tuìkuǎn.** = *If you are not satisfied with your purchase, you can ask for a refund.*
tuìkuǎn 退款 = refund, ask for refund

tuō 托 VERB = entrust, ask
■ 你进城吗? 我托你办一件事，行吗? **Nǐ jìnchéng ma? Wǒ tuō nǐ bàn yí jiàn shi, xíng ma?** = *Are you going to town? May I ask you to do something?*

tuō 拖 VERB = drag on, defer, procrastinate
■ 这件事不能再拖了，得马上决定。**Zhè jiàn shì bù néng zài tuō le, děi mǎshàng juédìng.** = *We cannot defer any longer but have to make an immediate decision on this matter.*

tuō 脱 VERB = take off (clothes, shoes, etc.)
tuō yīfu 脱衣服 = take off clothes
■ 这个小孩儿会自己脱衣服吗? **Zhège xiǎoháir huì zìjǐ tuō yīfu ma?** = *Can the child take off his clothes by himself? (→ Can this child undress himself?)*
tuō màozi 脱帽子 = take off one's hat
tuō xié 脱鞋 = take off one's shoes

tuōlí 脱离 [compound: 脱 get out of + 离 leave] VERB = break away from, sever
■ 此人已与本公司脱离一切关系。**Cǐ rén yǐ yú běn gōngsī tuōlí yíqiè guānxi.** = *This person has severed all ties with this company.*

W

wā 蛙 NOUN = frog (See 青蛙 qīngwā.)

wà 袜 Trad 襪 NOUN = stocking

wàzi 袜子 [suffix: 袜 stocking + 子 nominal suffix] NOUN = stocking, sock (只 zhī, 双 shuāng)
■ 我的袜子破了。**Wǒ de wàzi pò le.** = *My socks have holes.*
■ 你不穿袜子就穿鞋，不舒服吧? **Nǐ bù chuān wàzi jiù chuān xié, bù shūfu ba?** = *Don't you feel uncomfortable wearing shoes without socks?*
chuān wàzi 穿袜子 = put on socks, wear socks
tuō wàzi 脱袜子 = take off socks

wāi 歪 ADJECTIVE = not straight, askew, crooked
■ 这幅画挂歪了。**Zhè fú huà guà wāi le.** = *The picture hangs askew.*

wài 外 NOUN = outside (antonym 里 lǐ)
■ 墙外是一条安静的小街。**Qiáng wài shì yì tiáo ānjìng de xiǎo jiē.** = *Beyond the wall is a quiet by-street.*

wàibian 外边 [modif: 外 outside + 边 side] NOUN = outside (antonym 里边 lǐbian)
■ 外边凉快，我们到外边去吧。**Wàibian liángkuai, wǒmen dào wàibian qù ba.** = *It's cool outside. Let's go outside.*
■ 外边下雨呢，带着伞吧! **Wàibian xià yǔ ne, dàizhe sǎn ba!** = *It's raining outside. Bring an umbrella with you.*

wàidì 外地 [modif: 外 outside + 地 place] NOUN = parts of the country other than where one is (antonym 本地 běndì)
■ 他经常到外地去开会。**Tā jīngcháng dào wàidì qù kāihuì.** = *He often travels to other parts of the country to attend conferences.*
wàidìrén 外地人 = one who is from other parts of the country, not a native
■ 她的丈夫是外地人。**Tāde zhàngfu shì wàidìrén.** = *Her husband is from another part of the country.*

wàiguó 外国 [modif: 外 outside + 国 country] NOUN = foreign country
■ 你去过外国吗? **Nǐ qùguo wàiguó ma?** = *Have you ever been abroad?*
wàiguórén 外国人 = foreigner
wàiguóhuò 外国货 = foreign products, foreign goods

wàimiàn 外面 NOUN = same as 外边 **wàibian**

wàiwén 外文 [modif: 外 *foreign* + 文 *writing*]
NOUN = foreign language (especially its writing)
(门 **mén**)
■ 这封信是用外文写的，我看不懂。**Zhè fēn xìn shì yòng wàiwén xiě de, wǒ kàn bu dǒng.** = *This letter is written in a foreign language. I can't read it.*
■ 这本书已经翻译成多种外文。**Zhè běn shū yǐjīng fānyì chéng duō zhǒng wàiwén.** = *This book has been translated into many foreign languages.*

wàiyǔ 外语 [modif: 外 *foreign* + 语 *language*]
NOUN = foreign language (门 **mén**)
■ 懂一门外语很有用。**Dǒng yì mén wàiyǔ hěn yǒuyòng.** = *Knowing a foreign language is useful.*
■ 他本国语都没学好，还学什么外语？ **Tā běnguóyǔ dōu méi xuéhǎo, hái xué shénme wàiyǔ?** = *He hasn't even learnt his mother tongue properly. How can he learn a foreign language?*

wān 弯 Trad 彎 ADJECTIVE = curved, tortuous
■ 你这条线划得不直，划弯了。**Nǐ zhè tiáo xiàn huà de bù zhí, huà wān le.** = *You did not draw this line straight; it's curved.*

wān 湾 Trad 灣 NOUN = bay, gulf (See 台湾 **Táiwān**.)

wán 完 VERB = finish, end
■ 电影什么时候完？ **Diànyǐng shénme shíhou wán?** = *When will the movie end?*
chīwán 吃完 = finish eating, eat up
■ 我吃完饭就去开会。**Wǒ chīwán fàn jiù qù kāihuì.** = *I'm going to a meeting as soon as I finish my meal.*
kànwán 看完 = finish reading/watching
■ 我昨天看完电视已经十二点了。**Wǒ zuótiān kànwán diànshì yǐjīng shí'èr diǎn le.** = *It was already twelve o'clock when I finished watching TV last night.*
zuòwán 做完 = finish doing
■ 你什么时候可以做完作业？ **Nǐ shénme shíhou kěyǐ zuòwán zuòyè?** = *When can you finish your homework?*
yòngwán 用完 = use up

■ 我的钱用完了，我要到银行去取钱。**Wǒ de qián yòngwán le, wǒ yào dào yínháng qu qǔ qián.** = *I've used up my money. I'll go to the bank to get some cash.*

wánchéng 完成 [compound: 完 *finish* + 成 *accomplish*] VERB = accomplish, fulfill
■ 这个计划在明年六月完成。**Zhège jìhuà zài míngnián liùyuè wánchéng.** = *This plan will be fulfilled in June next year.*
■ 我们完成这个任务后要好好庆祝一下。**Wǒmen wánchéng zhège rènwù hòu yào hǎohǎo qìngzhù yíxià.** = *We will have a good celebration after we have accomplished this task.*

wánquán 完全 [compound: 完 *finished* + 全 *all*] ADJECTIVE = complete
■ 你提供的材料不完全。**Nǐ tígòng de cáiliào bù wánquán.** = *The data you have supplied are not complete.*
■ 你完全不懂我的意思。**Nǐ wánquán bù dǒng wǒ de yìsi.** = *You completely fail to see my point.*

wánzhěng 完整 [compound: 完 *complete* + 整 *whole*] ADJECTIVE = complete, integrated
■ 这一套书一共有二十册，现在只有十八册，不完整了。**Zhè yí tào shū yígòng yǒu èrshí cè, xiànzài zhǐyǒu shíbā cè, bù wánzhāng le.** = *This set of books has twenty volumes altogether. Now we have only eighteen volumes so the set is incomplete.*
■ 请你用一个完整的句子来回答。**Qǐng nǐ yòng yí ge wánzhěng de jùzi lái huídá.** = *Please answer in a complete sentence.*

wánr 玩儿 [suffix: 玩 *play* + 儿 suffix] VERB = play; have fun
■ 我们一块儿到公园去玩儿吧。**Wǒmen yíkuàir dào gōngyuán qù wánr ba.** = *Let's go to the park to have fun!*

NOTE: Though 玩儿 **wánr** is often glossed as *to play*, its basic meaning is *to have fun* or *to have a good time*. It can refer to many kinds of activities and therefore has a very wide application. More examples:
■ 我们常常到小明家去玩儿。**Wǒmen chángcháng dào Xiǎo Míng jiā qu wánr.** = *We often go to Xiao Ming's home to have a good*

W

time. (e.g. singing, dancing, playing cards, playing games or just chatting.)
■ 上星期天我们在海边玩儿得真高兴！ **Shàng Xīngqītiān wǒmen zài hǎibiān wánr de zhēn gāoxìng.** = *We had a wonderful time by the seaside last Sunday.*
■ 我想去香港玩儿。**Wǒ xiǎng qù Xiānggǎng wánr.** = *I want to have a holiday in Hong Kong.*

wǎn 晚 ADJECTIVE = late, not on time
■ 对不起，我来晚了。**Duìbuqǐ, wǒ lái wǎn le.** = *I'm sorry I'm late.*
■ 时间太晚了，我得走了。**Shíjiān tài wǎn le, wǒ děi zǒu le.** = *It's very late; I've got to go.*
wǎnnián 晚年 = old age

wǎnfàn 晚饭 [modif: 晚 *supper* + 饭 *meal*] NOUN = supper (顿 **dùn**)
■ 你们家一般什么时候吃晚饭？ **Nǐmen jiā yìbān shénme shíhou chī wǎnfàn?** = *When do you usually have supper at home?*
zuò wǎnfàn 做晚饭 = prepare supper

wǎnhuì 晚会 [modif: 晚 *evening* + 会 *assembly*] NOUN = evening party, an evening of entertainment
■ 很多重要的人要来参加今天的晚会。**Hěn duō zhòngyào de rén yào lái cānjiā jīntiān de wǎnhuì.** = *Many important people will attend today's evening party.*

wǎnshang 晚上 NOUN = evening
■ 你今天晚上打算做什么？ **Nǐ jīntiān wǎnshang dǎsuàn zuò shénme?** = *What do you plan to do this evening?*
■ 他往往晚上还要工作两三个小时。**Tā wǎngwǎng wǎnshang háiyào gōngzuò liǎng-sān ge xiǎoshí.** = *He usually has to work two or three hours in the evening.*
jīntiān wǎnshang (jīnwǎn) 今天晚上 (今晚) = this evening
zuótiān wǎnshang (zuówǎn) 昨天晚上 (昨晚) = yesterday evening

wǎn 碗 NOUN = bowl (只 **zhī**)
■ 中国人吃饭一般用碗，大碗放菜，小碗放米饭。**Zhōngguórén chīfàn yìbān yòng wǎn, dà wǎn fàng cài, xiǎo wǎn fàng mǐfàn.** = *Chinese people usually use bowls for meals: big bowls for dishes and small ones for cooked rice.*

... wǎnfàn ... 碗饭 = ... bowl(s) of rice
■ "你一顿吃几碗饭？" "两碗饭。" **"Nǐ yí dùn chī jǐ wǎn fàn?" "Liǎng wǎn fàn."** = *"How many bowls of rice do you have for one meal?" "Two."*
càiwǎn 菜碗 = a dish bowl, big bowl
fànwǎn 饭碗 = rice bowl; livelihood, job

wàn 万 Trad 萬 NUMERAL = ten thousand
■ 一万两千三百 **yíwàn liǎngqiān sānbǎi** = *twelve thousand and three hundred*
■ 二十万 **èrshí wàn** = *two hundred thousand*

NOTE: 万 **wàn** (*ten thousand*) is an important number in Chinese. While English has four basic digits (one, ten, hundred and thousand) Chinese has five (个 **gè** *one*, 十 **shí** *ten*, 百 **bǎi** *hundred*, 千 **qiān** *thousand*, 万 **wàn** *ten thousand*). The Chinese use 万 **wàn** to mean *ten thousand.* Therefore *a hundred thousand* is 十万 **shí wàn**. In Chinese-speaking communities in Southeast Asia, some people use 十千 **shíqiān** for *ten thousand*, e.g. 三十千 **sānshíqiān** = *30,000.* This is, however, not acceptable in standard Chinese.

Wáng 王 NOUN = (a family name)

wǎng 网 Trad 網 NOUN = net

wǎngbā 网吧 [modif: 网 *net, network* + 吧 *bar*] NOUN = Internet café (座 **zuò**, 家 **jiā**)
■ 这家网吧吸引很多年轻人。**Zhè jiā wǎngbā xīyǐn hěn duō niánqīngrén.** = *This Internet café attracts many young people.*
■ 他不在家，就在网吧。**Tā bú zài jiā, jiù zài wǎngbā.** = *If he is not home, then he must be at the Internet café.*

wǎngqiú 网球 [modif: 网 *net* + 球 *ball*] NOUN = tennis
■ 我们来打一场网球吧。**Wǒmen lái dǎ yì chǎng wǎngqiú ba.** = *Let's have a game of tennis.*
wǎngqiúchǎng 网球场 = tennis court

wǎngzhàn 网站 [modif: 网 *net, network* + 站 *station*] NOUN = Web site
■ 欢迎您访问我的个人网站。**Huānyíng nín fǎngwèn wǒ de gèrén wǎngzhàn.** = *You are welcome to visit my personal Web site.*

wǎng 往 PREPOSITION = towards, in the direction of
- 你往前走，到红绿灯的地方，往左拐，就可以到火车站。**Nǐ wǎng qián zǒu, dào hónglǜdēng de dìfang, wàng zuǒ guǎi, jiù kěyǐ dào huǒchēzhàn.** = *Walk straight on, and turn left at the traffic lights. Then you'll reach the railway station.*

wàng 忘 VERB = forget
- 别忘了寄这封信。**Bié wàngle jì zhè fēng xìn.** = *Don't forget to post this letter.*
- 他叫什么名字? 我忘了。**Tā jiào shénme míngzi? Wǒ wàngle.** = *What's his name? I've forgotten it.*

wàng 望 VERB = look at, gaze into the distance
- 举头望明月。**Jǔ tóu wàng míngyuè.** = *I look up to gaze at the bright moon.* (a line from a poem by Tang dynasty poet Li Bai)

wēi 危 ADJECTIVE = perilous

wēihài 危害 [compound: 危 *endanger* + 害 *damage*]
1 VERB = harm severely, jeopardize
- 降低农产品价格会危害农民的利益。**Jiàngdǐ nóngchǎnpǐn jiàgé huì wēihài nóngmín de lìyì.** = *Lowering produce prices will severely harm the farmer's interest.*
2 NOUN = severe harm, damage
- 森林面积的减少给环境造成很大危害。**Sēnlín miànji de jiǎnshǎo gěi huánjìng zàochéng hěn dà wēihài.** = *The reduction of forest areas causes great damage to the environment.*

wēijī 危机 [compound: 危 *perilous* + 机 *situation*] NOUN = crisis
- 要解决危机，先要了解危机是怎么发生的。**Yào jiějué wēijī, xiānyào liáojiě wēijī shì zěnme fāshēng de.** = *In order to resolve a crisis, one should first of all learn how it came into being.*

wēixiǎn 危险 [compound: 危 *perilous* + 险 *risky*]
1 ADJECTIVE = dangerous, in danger
- 下雪天开车比较危险。**Xià xuě tiān kāichē bǐjiào wēixiǎn.** = *It's dangerous to drive in snow.*

2 NOUN = danger, risk
- 我不怕危险。**Wǒ bú pà wēixiǎn.** = *I'm not afraid of danger.*
- 病人已经脱离危险。**Bìngrén yǐ tuōlí wēixiǎn.** = *The patient is out of danger.*

wēi 微 ADJECTIVE = small

wēixiào 微笑 [modif: 微 *small* + 笑 *smile, laugh*] VERB = smile
- 她微笑着说，"谢谢你了。" **Tā wēixiàozhe shuō, "Xièxie nǐ le."** = *She said, smiling, "Thank you."*

wéi 唯 ADVERB = only

wéiyī 唯一 [compound: 唯 *only* + 一 *one*] ADJECTIVE = the only one, sole
- 他唯一的爱好是打麻将，一有空就打。**Tā wéiyī de àihào shì dǎ májiàng, yì yǒukòng jiù dǎ.** = *His only hobby is playing mahjong. He plays mahjong whenever he has time.*

wéi 围 Trad 圍 VERB = enclose, surround
- 他建了一道墙，把自己的房子围起来。**Tā jiànle yí dào qiáng, bǎ zìjǐ de fángzi wéi qǐlai.** = *He built a wall to enclose his home.*

wéirào 围绕 [compound: 围 *enclose* + 绕 *around*] VERB
1 = move around, encircle
- 地球围绕太阳转。**Dìqiú wéirào tàiyang zhuàn.** = *The earth moves around the sun.*
2 = center on, focus on
- 请大家围绕这个问题谈，不要离题。**Qǐng dàjiā wéirào zhè ge wèntí tán, bú yào lítí.** = *Please focus on this question. Do not digress.*

wéi 维 Trad 維 VERB = preserve, safeguard

wéihù 维护 [compound: 维 *preserve* + 护 *protect*] VERB = safeguard, defend
- 为了维护国家安全，必须要有一支强大的军队。**Wèile wéihù guójiā ānquán, bìxū yào yǒu yì zhī qiángdà de jūnduì.** = *To ensure national security, we must maintain strong armed forces.*

wěi 尾 NOUN = tail, end

W

wěiba 尾巴 NOUN = tail (条 **tiáo**)
■ 狗摇尾巴，是表示高兴。**Gǒu yáo wěiba, shì biǎoshì gāoxìng.** = *When a dog wags its tail, it indicates happiness.*

wěi 委 VERB = entrust

wěiyuánhuì 委员会 NOUN = committee (个 **ge**)
■ 这个委员会的任务是制定教育政策。**Zhège wěiyuánhuì de rènwù shì zhìdìng jiàoyù zhèngcè.** = *This committee's mission is to set policies on education.*

wěi 伟 Trad 偉 ADJECTIVE = big

wěidà 伟大 [compound: 伟 *big* + 大 *big*]
ADJECTIVE = great
■ 孙中山是中国历史上的一位伟大人物。**Sūn Zhōngshān shì Zhōngguó lìshǐ shang de yí wèi wěidà rénwù.** = *Dr Sun Yat-sen is a great man in Chinese history.*

wèi 卫 Trad 衛 VERB = defend, protect

wèishēng 卫生 [v+obj: 卫 *defend* + 生 *life*]
NOUN = hygiene, sanitation
■ 保持个人卫生和公共卫生，有利于人民的身体健康。**Bǎochí gèrén wèishēng hé gōnggòng wèishēng, yǒulì yú rénmín de shēntǐ jiànkāng.** = *Maintaining good personal hygiene and public sanitation is beneficial to people's health.*
wèishēngjian 卫生间 = bathroom, (private) toilet
wèishēngjú 卫生局 = Health Department
gèrén wèishēng 个人卫生 = hygiene, personal hygiene
gōnggòng wèishēng 公共卫生 = sanitation, public sanitation
huánjìng wèishēng 环境卫生 = environmental sanitation

wèixīng 卫星 [modif: 卫 *encircling* + 星 *star*]
NOUN = satellite
■ 月球是地球的卫星。**Yuèqiú shì dìqiú de wèixīng.** = *The moon is a satellite of the earth.*
rénzào wèixīng 人造卫星 = man-made satellite

wèi 为 Trad 爲 VERB = (do, work) for the benefit of
■ 我为人人，人人为我。**Wǒ wèi rénrén, rénrén wèi wǒ.** = *I work for everybody else as*

everybody else works for me. (→ One for all and all for one.)
■ 你是为钱工作吗？**Nǐ shì wèi qián gōngzuò ma?** = *Do you work for money?*

wèile 为了 PREPOSITION = for the purpose of
■ 他这样辛辛苦苦地工作，都是为了孩子。**Tā zhèyàng xīn-xīn-kǔ-kǔ de gōngzuò, dōu shì wèile háizi.** = *He works so hard, all for his children.*
■ 为了健康，他不吸烟不喝酒，每天锻炼身体。**Wèile jiànkāng, tā bù xīyān bù hē jiǔ, měi tiān duànliàn shēntǐ.** = *In order to keep fit he does not smoke or drink, and exercises every day.*

NOTE: Both 为 **wèi** and 为了 **wèile** can be used as prepositions and have similar meanings, but 为了 **wèile** is more commonly used in everyday Chinese.

wèishénme 为什么 [v+obj: 为 *for* + 什么 *what*] ADVERB = why, what for
■ 你昨天为什么没有来上课？**Nǐ zuótiān wèishénme méiyǒu lái shàngkè?** = *Why didn't you come to school yesterday?*

wèi 未 ADJECTIVE = have not, did not
■ 他未婚以前，住在学校宿舍里。**Tā wèi hūn yǐqián, zhù zài xuéxiào shùshè li.** = *He lived in the school hostel before he married.*
■ 该生未经批准不来上课，将受处分。**Gāishēng wèi jīng pīzhǔn bù lái shàngkè, jiāng shòu chǔfèn.** = *This student was absent from class without permission and will be disciplined.*

NOTE: 未 **wèi** is only used in rather formal, written styles. In everyday Chinese, 没有 **méiyǒu** is used instead.

wèilái 未来 NOUN = future
■ 少年儿童是国家的未来。**Shàonián értóng shì guójiā de wèilái.** = *Teenagers and children are the future of a nation.*
■ 我们对未来有信心。**Wǒmen duì wèilái yǒu xìnxīn.** = *We have confidence in the future.*

wèi 位 MEASURE WORD = (a polite measure word used with people)

■ 一位老师 **yí wèi lǎoshī** = *a teacher*
■ 那位先生是谁? **Nà wèi xiānsheng shì shuí?** = *Who is that gentleman?*

wèizhi 位置 [compound: 位 *seat* + 置 *locate*] NOUN
1 = place, location
■ 没有人能确定沉船的位置。**Méiyǒu rén néng quèdìng chénchuán de wèizhi.** = *Nobody can determine the location of the sunken ship.*
2 = (abstract) position
■ 人力资源经理是公司里一个极其重要的位置。**Rénlì zīyuán jinglǐ shì gōngsī li yí ge jíqí zhòngyào de wèizhi.** = *The human resource manager holds an extremely important position in a company.*

wèi 味 NOUN = taste, flavor

wèidao 味道 NOUN = taste
■ 这个菜味道好极了。**Zhège cài wèidao hǎo jíle.** = *This dish is very delicious indeed.*
■ 我觉得这个菜味道太淡, 我喜欢味道浓一点的菜。**Wǒ juéde zhège cài wèidao tài dàn, wǒ xǐhuan wèidao nóng yìdiǎn de cài.** = *I find this dish too bland. I like strongly-flavored dishes.*

wèi 胃 NOUN = stomach
■ 我胃疼。**Wǒ wèi téng.** = *I have a stomachache.*
■ 她的胃不太好, 多吃一点儿就不舒服。**Tā de wèi bú tài hǎo, duō chī yìdiǎn jiù bù shūfu.** = *She has a weak stomach. If she eats a little too much she feels uncomfortable.*

wèi 谓 Trad 謂 VERB = be called (See 所谓 suǒwèi.)

wèi 慰 VERB = console (See 安慰 ānwèi.)

wèi 喂 1 INTERJECTION
1 = hey
■ 喂, 你的票呢? **Wèi, nǐ de piào ne?** = *Hey, where's your ticket?*
2 = hello, hi
■ 喂, 这里是大华公司, 您找谁? **Wèi, zhèlǐ shì Dàhuá Gōngsī, nín zhǎo shuí?** = *Hello, this is Dahua Company. Who would you like to speak to?*

NOTE: In telephone conversation 喂 **wèi** is equivalent to *hello*. In other contexts, 喂 **wèi** is a rude way of getting people's attention. It is more polite to say 对不起 **duìbuqǐ**, e.g.
■ 对不起, 先生, 您的票呢? **Duìbuqǐ, xiānsheng, nín de piào ne?** = *Excuse me, sir, where's your ticket?*

wèi 喂 2 VERB = feed
■ 她夜里起来给孩子喂奶。**Tā yèli qǐlai gěi háizi wèi něi.** = *Every night she gets up to feed her baby.*

wēn 温 ADJECTIVE = warm

wēndù 温度 [modif: 温 *warmth* + 度 *degree*] NOUN = temperature (atmospheric)
■ 今天温度比较低, 但是没有风, 所以不觉得怎么冷。**Jīntiān wēndù bǐjiào dī, dànshì méiyǒu fēng, suǒyǐ bù juéde zěnme lěng.** = *The temperature is rather low today but it is not windy. So you don't feel very cold.*

NOTES: (1) 温度 **wēndù** generally refers to atmospheric temperature only. For body temperature the expression is 体温 **tǐwēn**, e.g.
■ 人的正常体温是多少? **Rénde zhèngcháng tǐwēn shì duōshǎo?** = *What is the normal temperature of a human being?*
When a person has a fever, however, 热度 **rèdù** is used to refer to his/her temperature, e.g.
■ 他今天热度还很高。**Tā jīntiān rèdù hái hěn gāo.** = *He is still running a fever.*
(2) The Chinese use the centigrade system, which is called 摄氏 **shèshì**, e.g.
■ 今天最高温度摄氏二十八度。**Jīntiān zuì gāo wēndù shèshì érshí bā dù.** = *Today's maximum temperature is 28 degrees centigrade.*
In everyday usage, however, people usually omit 摄氏 **shèshì**.

wén 文 NOUN = culture

wénhuà 文化 NOUN = culture
■ 语言中有很多文化知识。**Yǔyán zhong yǒu hěn duō wénhuà zhīshi.** = *A language contains a great deal of cultural knowledge.*
■ 我对中国文化知道得不多。**Wǒ duì Zhōngguó wénhuà zhīdào de bù duō.** = *I don't know much about Chinese culture.*

W

wénjiàn 文件 NOUN = document (份 **fèn**)
■ 这个文件你保留在电脑里了吗？ **Zhège wénjiàn nǐ bǎoliú zài diànnǎo li le ma?** = *Have you saved this document in the computer?*

wénmíng 文明 [compound: 文 *culture* + 明 *enlightenment*]
1 NOUN = civilization, culture
■ 各种文明各有优点，各有缺点。 **Gè zhǒng wénmíng gé yǒu yōudiǎn, gè yǒu quēdiǎn.** = *Each of the civilizations has its merits and shortcomings.*
2 ADJECTIVE = civilized
■ 在文明社会不应该存在这种现象。 **Zài wénmíng shèhuì bù yīnggāi cúnzài zhè zhǒng xiànxiàng.** = *Such a phenomenon should not exist in a civilized society.*

wénxué 文学 NOUN = literature
■ 我姐姐在大学念英国文学。 **Wǒ jiějie zài dàxué niàn Yīngguó wénxué.** = *My elder sister studies English literature in university.*
wénxué jiā 文学家 = (great) writer

wényì 文艺 [compound: 文 *literature* + 艺 *art*] NOUN = literature and art; performing arts
■ 我妈妈喜欢文艺，我爸爸喜欢体育。 **Wǒ māma xǐhuan wényì, wǒ bàba xǐhuan tǐyù.** = *My mother likes literature and art while my father likes sports.*
wényì wǎnhuì 文艺晚会 = an evening of entertainment, soirée

wénzhāng 文章 [compound: 文 *writing* + 章 *chapter*] NOUN = essay, article (篇 **piān**)
■ 昨天晚报上有一篇很有意思的文章。 **Zuótiān wǎnbào shang yǒu yì piān hěn yǒu yìsi de wénzhāng.** = *There's an interesting article in yesterday's evening paper.*
■ 他文章写得又快又好。 **Tā wénzhāng xiě de yòu kuài yòu hǎo.** = *He writes good essays, and he writes them quickly.*

wénzì 文字 [compound: 文 *writing* + 字 *script*] NOUN = written language, script, character
■ 这本小说已经翻译成六种文字了。 **Zhè běn xiǎoshuō yǐjīng fānyì chéng liù zhǒng wénzì le.** = *This novel has been translated into six languages.*
wénzì chǔlǐ 文字处理 = word processing

wén 闻 Trad 聞 NOUN = what is heard (See 新闻 **xīnwén**.)

wén 蚊

wénzi 蚊子 [suffix: 蚊 *mosquito* + 子 nominal suffix] NOUN = mosquito (只 **zhī**)
■ 这里夏天有蚊子吗？ **Zhèli xiàtiān yǒu wénzi ma?** = *Are there mosquitoes here in summer?*

wěn 稳 Trad 穩 ADJECTIVE = steady, stable
■ 等车停稳了再下车。 **Děng chē tíng wěnle zài xià chē.** = *Do not get off the car* (or *bus*) *before it comes to a complete stop.*

wěndìng 稳定 [compound: 稳 *stable* + 定 *fixed*] ADJECTIVE = stable
■ 现在的形势十分稳定。 **Xiànzài de xíngshì shífēn wěndìng.** = *The present situation is very stable.*

wèn 问 Trad 問 VERB = ask (a question), inquire
■ 我可以问你一个问题吗？ **Wǒ kěyǐ wèn nǐ yí ge wèntí ma?** = *May I ask you a question?*
wèn lù 问路 = ask the way
wèn hǎo 问好 = ask after, give greetings to
■ 请代问您父母亲好。 **Qǐng dài wèn nín fùmǔqin hǎo.** = *Please give my regards to your parents.*

wènhòu 问候 VERB = give regards to, send regards to, ask after
■ 见到王老师，替我问候他。 **Jiàndào Wáng lǎoshī, tì wǒ wènhòu tā.** = *When you see Teacher Wang, please give him my regards.*
■ 我在信里问候她全家。 **Wǒ zài xìnli wènhòu tā quán jiā.** = *In the letter I sent my regards to his family.*

wèntí 问题 [compound: 问 *inquiry* + 题 *question*] NOUN = question (道 **dào**, for school examinations only)
■ "有什么问题吗？""有，我有一个问题。" **"Yǒu shénme wèntí ma?" "Yǒu, wǒ yǒu yí ge wèntí."** = *"Do you have any questions?" "Yes, I do."*
■ 考试的五道问题，你答对了三道，答错了两道。 **Kǎoshì de wǔ dào wèntí, nǐ dá duìle sān dào, dá cuòle liǎng dào.** = *Of the five questions*

W

in the examination, you answered three cor-rectly and two incorrectly.   •

wǒ 我 PRONOUN = I, me
- 我叫张明，我是中国人。**Wǒ jiào Zhāng Ming, wǒ shì Zhōngguórén.** = *My name is Zhang Ming. I'm Chinese.*

wǒmen 我们 [suffix: 我 *I, me* + 们 suffix denoting a plural number] PRONOUN = we, us
- 我们是学中文的学生。**Wǒmen shì xué Zhōngwén de xuésheng.** = *We're students of Chinese.*

wò 握 VERB = hold, grasp

wòshǒu 握手 [v+obj: 握 *hold* + 手 *hand*] VERB = shake hands
- 他和新认识的朋友握手。**Tā hé xīn rènshi de péngyou wòshǒu.** = *He shook hands with his new friends.*

wū 污 NOUN = filth

wūrǎn 污染 [compound: 污 *to soil* + 染 *to dye*]
1 VERB = pollute
- 这家化工厂严重污染环境，必须关闭。**Zhè jiā huàgōngchǎng yánzhòng wūrǎn huánjìng, bìxū guānbì.** = *This chemical plant is seriously polluting the environment and must be closed down.*
2 NOUN = pollution
- 工业污染影响了生活质量。**Gōngyè wūrǎn yǐngxiǎngle shēnghuó zhìliàng.** = *Industrial pollution affects the quality of life.*

wū 屋 NOUN = house, room

wūzi 屋子 [suffix: 屋 *house, room* + 子 nominal suffix] NOUN = room (间 **jiān**)
- 这个房子有几间屋子？ **Zhège fángzi yǒu jǐ jiān wūzi?** = *How many rooms are there in the house?*

NOTE: 屋子 **wūzi** in the sense of *room* is only used in north China. To southern Chinese 屋子 **wūzi** may mean *house*. To avoid ambiguity, it is better to use the word 房间 **fángjiān** for *room.*

wú 无 Trad 無 VERB = have no (antonym 有 **yǒu**)
- 我们无法解决这个问题。**Wǒmen wú fǎ jiějué zhège wèntí.** = *We have no way to solve this problem.*

wúlùn 无论 CONJUNCTION = same as 不管 **bùguǎn.** Tends to be used in writing.

wúshù 无数 [modif: 无 *no* + 数 *number*] ADJECTIVE = innumerable, countless
- 无数事实证明，那种社会制度是行不通的。**Wúshù shìshí zhèngmíng, nà zhǒng shèhuì zhìdù shì xíngbutōng de.** = *Innumerable facts have proven that kind of social system does not work.*

wǔ 五 NUMERAL = five
- 五五二十五。**Wǔ wǔ érshíwǔ.** = *Five times five is twenty-five.*
- 五星红旗 **wǔ xīng hóng qí** = *the five-star red flag* (the Chinese national flag)

wǔ 午 NOUN = noon

wǔfàn 午饭 [modif: 午 *noon* + 饭 *meal*] NOUN = lunch (顿 **dùn**)
- 我在学校吃午饭。**Wǒ zài xuéxiào chī wǔfàn.** = *I have lunch in school.*
- 工人有一小时的午饭时间。**Gōngrén yǒu yì xiǎoshí de wǔfàn shíjiān.** = *The workers have a one-hour lunch break.*

wǔ 武 NOUN = military

wǔqì 武器 [modif: 武 *military* + 器 *artifact*] NOUN = weapon (件 **jiàn**)
- 不准带任何武器上飞机。**Bù zhǔn dài rènhé wǔqì shàng fēijī.** = *It is forbidden to bring a weapon of any kind on board the plane.*
- dàguīmó shāshāng wǔqì 大规模杀伤武器 = weapon of mass destruction (WMD)

wǔshù 武术 [modif: 武 *martial* + 术 *arts*] NOUN = martial arts
- 他在中国学了三年武术。**Tā zài Zhōngguó xuéle sān nián wǔshù.** = *He studied martial arts in China for three years.*

wǔ 舞 NOUN = dance (See 鼓舞 **gǔwǔ**, 跳舞 **tiàowǔ**.)

W

wù 务 Trad 務 VERB = work (See 服务 fúwù, 服务员 fúwùyuán, 家务 jiāwù, 任务 rènwù, 义务 yìwù, 业务 yèwù, 医务室 yīwùshì.)

wù 物 NOUN = things, objects

wùjià 物价 [modif: 物 thing + 价 price] NOUN = price, commodity price
■ 最近的物价比较稳定。**Zuìjìn de wùjià bǐjiào wěndìng.** = *Prices have been quite stable recently.*

wùlǐ 物理 [modif: 物 things, objects + 理 pattern, rule] NOUN = physics
■ 我弟弟物理、数学都挺好。**Wǒ dìdi wùlǐ, shùxué dōu tíng hǎo.** = *My younger brother is good at physics and mathematics.*

wù 雾 Trad 霧 NOUN = fog, mist
■ 今天早上有大雾，很多人迟到。**Jīntiān zǎoshang yǒu dà wù, hěn duō rén chídào.** = *Many people were late for work this morning because of the heavy fog.*
■ 有雾天气，开车要特别小心。**Yǒu wù tiānqì, kāichē yào tèbié xiǎoxīn.** = *You should be particularly careful when driving in foggy weather.*

wù 误 Trad 誤 ADJECTIVE = erroneous

wùhuì 误会 [modif: 误 mistaken + 会 understanding]
1 VERB = misunderstand, misconstrue
■ 你误会了我的意思。**Nǐ wùhuìle wǒ de yìsi.** = *You've misconstrued my meaning.*
2 NOUN = misunderstanding
■ 我没有说清楚，造成了误会，很抱歉。**Wǒ méiyǒu shuō qīngchu, zàochéngle wùhuì, hěn bàoqiàn.** = *I did not make it clear, which has caused a misunderstanding. I apologize.*

X

xī 西 NOUN = west, western
■ 河东是一座小城，河西是一大片农场。**Hé dōng shì yí zuò xiǎo chéng, hé xī shì yí dà piàn nóngchǎng.** = *East of the river is a small town, and on the west is a big farm.*

xīběi 西北 [compound: 西 west + 北 north] NOUN = northwest, the Northwest
■ 中国正在努力开发大西北。**Zhōngguó zhèngzài nǔlì kāifā dà xīběi.** = *China is making efforts to develop her northwest region.*

xībian 西边 [modif: 西 west + 边 side] NOUN = west side, to the west, in the west
■ 太阳在西边下山。**Tàiyang zài xībian xiàshān.** = *The sun sets in the west.*

xīcān 西餐 [modif: 西 West + 餐 meal] NOUN = Western-style meal
■ 走，我请你吃西餐。**Zǒu, wǒ qǐng nǐ chī xīcān.** = *Let's go. I'll treat you to a Western-style meal.*
xīcānguǎn 西餐馆 = Western-style restaurant

xīfāng 西方 [modif: 西 West + 方 direction, part] NOUN = the West, Occident
■ 西方文明有什么重要特点？**Xīfāng wénmíng yǒu shénme zhòngyào tèdiǎn?** = *What are the major characteristics of Western Civilization?*

xīguā 西瓜 NOUN = watermelon (只 zhī)
■ 中国人夏天最喜欢吃西瓜。**Zhōngguórén xiàtiān zuì xǐhuan chī xīguā.** = *The Chinese people's favorite fruit in summer is the watermelon.*

xīhóngshì 西红柿 [modif: 西 Western + 红 red + 柿 persimmon] NOUN = tomato (只 zhī)
■ 我要买一公斤西红柿。**Wǒ yào mǎi yì gōngjīn xīhóngshì.** = *I want to buy a kilogram of tomatoes.*

xīnán 西南 [compound: 西 west + 南 south] NOUN = southwest, the Southwest
■ 中国西南地方有很多少数民族。**Zhōngguó xīnán dìfang yǒu hěn duō shǎoshù mínzú.** = *There are many national minorities in China's southwestern region.*

xī 吸 VERB = inhale, suck
xīyān 吸烟 = smoke, smoking
■ 这里不准吸烟。**Zhèlǐ bù zhǔn xīyān.** = *Smoking is not allowed here.*

xīshōu 吸收 [compound: 吸 suck + 收 receive] VERB = suck up, absorb

■ 我们要吸收别人的好经验。**Wǒmen yào xīshōu biérén de hǎo jīngyàn.** = *We should draw from other people's positive experiences.*

xīyǐn 吸引 [compound: 吸 *suck* + 引 *guide*]
VERB = attract
■ 我们想吸引更多的旅游者来我国游览。**Wǒmen xiǎng xīyǐn gèng duō de lǚyóuzhě lái wǒguó yóulǎn.** = *We want to attract more tourists to our country.*
xīyǐnlì 吸引力 = attraction
yǒu xīyǐnlì 有吸引力 = attractive

xī 希 VERB = wish

xīwàng 希望 [compound: 希 *wish* + 望 *look forward to*]
1 VERB = hope, wish
■ 我希望你常给我打电话。**Wǒ xīwàng nǐ cháng gěi wǒ dǎ diànhuà.** = *I hope you'll ring me often.*
■ 希望你旅行愉快！**Xīwàng nǐ lǚxíng yúkuài!** = *I wish you a happy journey. (→ Bon voyage!)*
2 NOUN = hope
■ 孩子是父母的希望。**Háizi shì fùmǔ de xīwàng.** = *Children are their parents' hope.*

xī 息 VERB = cease (See 消息 xiāoxi, 休息 xiūxi.)

xī 牺 Trad 犧 NOUN = sacrifice

xīshēng 牺牲
1 VERB = sacrifice, give up
■ 他们为子女牺牲了大量时间和金钱。**Tāmen wèi zǐnǚ xīshēngle dàliàng shíjiān hé jīnqián.** = *They gave up a great deal of time and money for their children.*
2 NOUN = sacrifice
■ 她为家庭作出了巨大牺牲。**Tā wèi jiātíng zuòchule jùdà xīshēng.** = *She made great sacrifices for the family.*

xī 悉 VERB = know (See 熟悉 shúxi.)

xí 习 Trad 習 VERB = practise

xíguàn 习惯 [compound: 习 *be familiar with* + 惯 *be accustomed to*]

1 NOUN = habit
■ 他有一个坏习惯，我希望他改掉。**Tā yǒu yí ge huài xíguàn, wǒ xīwàng tā gǎidiào.** = *He has a bad habit. I hope he'll get rid of it.*
2 VERB = be accustomed to, be used to
■ 很多中国人不习惯吃西餐。**Hěn duō Zhōngguórén bù xíguàn chī xīcān.** = *Many Chinese are not used to eating western-style meals.*
xíguàn shang 习惯上 = habitually

xí 席 NOUN = seat (See 出席 chūxí, 主席 zhǔxí.)

xǐ 洗 VERB = wash
■ 吃饭前要洗手。**Chīfàn qián yào xǐ shǒu.** = *You should wash your hands before having a meal.*
xǐshǒujiān 洗手间 = toilet, restroom, washroom
■ 请问，洗手间在哪里？**Qǐngwèn, xǐshǒujiān zài nǎli?** = *Excuse me, where's the washroom?*

NOTE: 洗手间 **xǐshǒujiān** is a common euphemism for *toilet*. The formal word for *toilet* is 厕所 **cèsuǒ**, e.g. 男厕所 **nán cèsuǒ** (*Men's room, Gents'*), 女厕所 **nǚ cèsuǒ** (*Ladies' room, Ladies'*).

xǐyījī 洗衣机 [modif: 洗衣 *wash clothes* + 机 *machine*] NOUN = washing machine (台 **tái**)
■ 洗衣机又坏了，得买一台新的了。**Xǐyījī yòu huàile, děi mǎi yì tái xīnde le.** = *The washing machine broke down again. We've got to buy a new one.*

xǐzǎo 洗澡 [compound: 洗 *wash* + 澡 *bath, take a bath*] VERB = take a bath, take a shower
■ 有人每天早上洗澡，有人每天晚上洗澡。**Yǒurén měi tiān zǎoshang xǐzǎo, yǒurén měi tiān wǎnshang xǐzǎo.** = *Some people take a bath early every morning, and others in the evening.*
■ 他习惯临睡前洗一个热水澡。**Tā xíguàn línshuì qián xǐ yí ge rèshuǐ zǎo.** = *He is used to taking a hot bath just before going to bed.*
xǐzǎojiān 洗澡间 = bathroom, shower room (Same as 浴室 yùshì.)

xǐ 喜 VERB = be fond of

xǐhuan 喜欢 [compound: 喜 *be fond of* + 欢 *pleasure*] VERB = like, be fond of

■ 你喜欢不喜欢中国音乐? **Nǐ xǐhuan bu xǐhuan Zhōngguó yīnyuè?** = *Do you like Chinese music?*

■ 他喜欢一边喝 啤酒，一边看体育节目。**Tā xǐhuan yìbiān hē píjiǔ, yìbiān kàn tǐyù jiémù.** = *He likes to drink beer while watching sports programs.*

xì 戏 Trad 戲 NOUN = drama, play (出 **chū**)

■ 今天晚上我们去看戏。**Jīntiān wǎnshang wǒmen qù kàn xì.** = *We're going to watch a play this evening.*

xì 系 NOUN = department (of a university)

■ 这座大学有十二个系，最大的是电脑系。**Zhè zuò dàxué yǒu shí'èr ge xì, zuì dà de shì diànnǎo xì.** = *This university has twelve departments; the biggest is the Computing Science Department.*

xì zhǔrèn 系主任 = chair of a (university) department

xìtǒng 系统 NOUN = a group of items serving a common purpose, system (套 **tào**)

■ 系统中只要有一个地方出毛病，整套系统就不能正常工作。**Xìtǒng zhōng zhǐyào yǒu yí ge dìfang chū máobìng, zhěngtào xìtǒng jiù bù néng zhèngcháng gōngzuò.** = *If only one part of a system goes wrong, the entire system will not be able to function properly.*

xì 细 Trad 細 ADJECTIVE = thin, slender (of objects shaped like a strip) (粗 **cū**)

■ 中国的面条又细又长，是我最喜欢吃的东西。**Zhōngguó de miàntiáo yòu xì yòu cháng, shì wǒ zuì xǐhuan chī de dōngxi.** = *Chinese noodles are thin and long; they are my favorite food.*

■ 他把计划的各个方面都考虑得很细。**Tā bǎ jìhuà de gè ge fāngmiàn dōu kǎolǜ de hěn xì.** = *He considered every single aspect of the plan very carefully.*

xìjūn 细菌 [modif: 细 *tiny* + 菌 *bacterium*] NOUN = bacterium, germ

■ 科学家还没有找到引起这种病的细菌。**Kēxuéjiā hái méiyǒu zhǎodào yínqǐ zhè zhǒng bìng de xìjūn.** = *Scientists have not identified the bacterium that causes this disease.*

xìxīn 细心 [modif: 细 *tiny* + 心 *the heart*] ADJECTIVE = very careful, meticulous

■ 她做完数学练习后总要细心地检查一遍。**Tā zuòwán shùxué liànxí hòu zǒngyào xìxīn de jiǎnchá yíbiàn.** = *After doing mathematics exercises she checks every question very carefully.*

xià 下 1 NOUN = below, under, underneath (antonym 上 **shàng**)

■ 树下很凉快。**Shù xià hěn liángkuài.** = *It's cool under the tree.*

shānxia 山下 = at the foot of a mountain or hills

xià 下 2 VERB = go/come down (antonym 上 **shàng**)

■ 他常常走下楼。**Tā chángcháng zǒu xià lóu.** = *He often walks downstairs.*

xiàbān 下班 = get off work

■ 我下班以后要去买菜。**Wǒ xiàbān yǐhòu yào qù mǎi cài.** = *I'll go and do grocery shopping after work.*

xiàchē 下车 = get off a vehicle

■ 到了，下车吧！**Dàole, xiàchē ba!** = *Here we are. Let's get off the car* (or *bus*).

xiàkè 下课 = finish class

■ 你们每天几点钟下课? **Nǐmen měi tiān jǐ diǎnzhōng xiàkè?** = *When does school finish everyday?*

xiàlai 下来 = come down

■ 晚饭做好了，快下来吃吧！**Wǎnfàn zuòhǎo le, kuài xiàlai chī ba!** = *Supper is ready. Come down and eat!*

xiàqu 下去 = go down

■ 时间不早了，我们(从山上)下去吧。**Shíjiān bù zǎo le, wǒmen (cóng shānshang) xiàqu ba.** = *It's quite late. Let's go down [the hill].*

xià 下 3 MEASURE WORD = (used with certain verbs to indicate the number of times the action is done)

■ 我试了几下，都不行。**Wǒ shìle jǐ xià, dōu bù xíng.** = *I tried several times, but it didn't work.*

... yíxià ... 一下 = (used after a verb to indicate the action is done briefly or tentatively)

■ 我看一下电视就去洗澡。**Wǒ kàn yíxià diànshì, jiù qù xǐzǎo.** = *I'll watch TV for a short while before taking a bath.*

xiàbian 下边 [modif: 下 *below, underneath* + 边 *side*] NOUN = below, under (antonym 上边 **shàngbian**)

X

■ 椅子下边有几本书，是谁的？**Yǐzi xiàbian yǒu jǐ běn shū, shì shéi de?** = *There are some books under the chair. Whose are they?*

xiàgǎng 下岗 [v+obj: 下 *leave* + 岗 *post, job*] VERB = be laid off, be unemployed
■ 张师傅下岗好几年了，生活很困难。**Zhāng shīfu xiàgǎng hǎo jǐ nián le, shēnghuó hěn kùnnan.** = *Master worker Zhang was laid off several years ago and has been living a hard life.*
xiàgǎng gōngrén 下岗工人 = worker who has been laid off, unemployed worker

xiàmiàn 下面 NOUN = same as 下边 **xiàbian**

xiàwǔ 下午 [modif: 下 *lower half* + 午 *noon*] NOUN = afternoon (antonym 上午 **shàngwǔ**)
■ 上午多云，下午天晴了。**Shàngwǔ duō yún, xiàwǔ tiān qíng le.** = *It was cloudy in the morning, but it cleared up in the afternoon.*

xià 吓 Trad 嚇 VERB
1 = frighten, scare
■ 我不是吓你，你父亲的病极其严重。**Wǒ bú shì xià nǐ, nǐ fùqin de bìng jíqí yánzhòng.** = *I don't want to frighten you, but your father's illness is extremely severe.*
2 = be frightened, be scared
■ 她看到强盗手里拿着刀，吓得尖叫起来。**Tā kàndao qiángdào shǒuli názhe dāo, xià de jiānjiào qǐlai.** = *When she saw the robber holding a knife in hand, she was so frightened that she screamed.*

xià 夏 NOUN = summer

xiàtiān 夏天 [modif: 夏 *summer* + 天 *days*] NOUN = summer
■ 北京的夏天热吗？**Běijīng de xiàtiān rè ma?** = *Is summer in Beijing hot?*
■ 我们夏天常常到海边去游泳。**Wǒmen xiàtiān chángcháng dào hǎibiān qù yóuyǒng.** = *We often go swimming by the seaside in summer.*

xiān 先 ADVERB = first (in time sequence) (antonym 后 **hòu**)
■ 他早上先跑步，再吃早饭。**Tā zǎoshang xiān pǎobù, zài chī zǎofàn.** = *Early in the morning he first jogs and then has breakfast.*

■ 您先请。**Nín xiān qǐng.** = *After you.*
xiān ... zài ... 先 ... 再 = first ... and then...

xiānhòu 先后 [compound: 先 *before* + 后 *later*] ADVERB = one after another, successively
■ 他们四个孩子大学毕业后先后离家。**Tāmen sì ge háizi dàxué bìyè hòu xiānhòu lí jiā.** = *After graduation from university their four sons and daughters left home one after another.*
■ 他的祖父和祖母在去年先后去世。**Tā de zǔfù hé zǔmǔ zài qùnián xiānhòu qùshì.** = *His grandfather and grandmother died one after another last year.*

xiānjìn 先进 [modif: 先 *in advance* + 进 *go forward*] ADJECTIVE = advanced
■ 这种照相机使用最用先进的技术。**Zhè zhǒng zhàoxiàngjī shǐyòng zuì xiānjìn de jìshù.** = *This camera uses the most advanced technology.*

xiānsheng 先生 [modif: 先 *first, before* + 生 *born*] NOUN
1 = Mr
■ 王先生，这位是 张先生。**Wáng xiānsheng, zhè wèi shì Zhāng xiānsheng.** = *Mr Wang, this is Mr Zhang.*
2 = sir, gentleman
■ 先生，有事吗？**Xiānsheng, yǒu shì ma?** = *Is there anything I can do for you, sir?*
■ 有一位先生要见你。**Yǒu yí wèi xiānsheng yào jiàn nǐ.** = *There's a gentleman wanting to see you.*
3 = husband
■ 您先生在哪儿工作？**Nín xiānsheng zài nǎr gōngzuò?** = *Where does your husband work?*

xiān 鲜 Trad 鮮 ADJECTIVE = fresh
■ 她买了几根鲜黄瓜回家做凉菜。**Tā mǎile jǐ gēn xiān huánggua huíjiā zuò liángcài.** = *She bought several fresh cucumbers and brought them home to prepare a cold dish.*

xiānhuā 鲜花 [modif: 鲜 *fresh* + 花 *flower*] NOUN = fresh flower, flower (朵 **duǒ**)
■ 他采了路边的一朵鲜花，送给女朋友。**Tā cǎile lùbiān de yì duǒ xiānhuā, sòng gei nǚpéngyou.** = *He picked a fresh flower by the roadside and gave it to his girlfriend.*

X

xiān 纤 Trad 纖

xiānwéi 纤维 NOUN = fiber
■ 有了化学纤维，衣服便宜多了。 **Yǒule huàxué xiānwéi, yīfu piányì duōle.** = With [the invention of] chemical fiber, clothes have become much cheaper.

xián 咸 Trad 鹹 ADJECTIVE = salty
■ 你盐放多了，这个菜太咸。 **Nǐ yán fàngduōle, zhège cài tài xián.** = You've put too much salt in the dish; it's too salty.

xián 闲 Trad 閑 ADJECTIVE = idle, unoccupied
■ 有的人挺忙，有的人闲着：分工不合理。 **Yǒude rén tǐng máng, yǒude rén xiánzhe: fēngōng bù hélǐ.** = While some are very busy, others are idle. The division of labor is irrational.
qīngxián 清闲 = leisurely, carefree
xiánhuà 闲话 = chat, small talk
xiánrén 闲人 = idler, uninvolved person
xiánshì 闲事 = matter that does not concern you
■ 别管闲事。 **Bié guǎn xiánshì.** = It's none of your business.

xiǎn 显 Trad 顯 VERB = appear, look

xiǎnde 显得 VERB = appear to be, seem to be
■ 他穿了黑衣服显得更瘦。 **Tā chuānle héi yīfu xiǎnde gèng shòu.** = Dressed in a black suit, he appeared all the thinner.

xiǎnrán 显然 ADJECTIVE = obvious, obviously
■ 这道题目显然答错了。 **Zhè dào tímù xiǎnrán dá cuò le.** = The answer to this question is obviously wrong.
■ 他的计划显然不可行。 **Tā de jìhuà xiǎnrán bù kě xíng.** = It's obvious that his plan is not feasible.

xiǎnzhù 显著 ADJECTIVE = remarkable, outstanding, notable
■ 今年我们公司在开发新产品方面取得了显著成就。 **Jīnnián wǒmen gōngsī zài kāifā xīn chǎnpǐn fāngmiàn qǔdéle xiǎnzhù chéngjiù.** = This year our company has made notable achievements in developing new products.

xiǎn 险 Trad 險 ADJECTIVE = dangerous (See 危险 wēixiǎn.)

xiàn 县 Trad 縣 NOUN = (rural) county
■ 中国有两千左右个县。 **Zhōngguó yǒu liǎngqiān zuǒyòu ge xiàn.** = China has around 2,000 counties.
xiànchéng 县城 = county town, county seat
xiànzhǎng 县长 = mayor of a county

xiàn 现 Trad 現

xiàndài 现代 [modif: 现 present + 代 generation] NOUN = modern times, the contemporary age
■ 我祖父不喜欢现代音乐。 **Wǒ zǔfù bù xǐhuan xiàndài yīnyuè.** = My grandfather does not like modern music.
■ 在这座古庙前，盖了这么一个现代建筑，很不合适。 **Zài zhè zuò gǔ miào qián, gàile zhème yí ge xiàndài jiànzhù, hěn bù héshì.** = It is inappropriate to put up such a modern building in front of this ancient temple.

xiàndàihuà 现代化

1 VERB = modernize
■ 我们的教学手段应该现代化。 **Wǒmen de jiàoxué shǒuduàn yīnggāi xiàndàihuà.** = Our means of teaching and learning should be modernized.
2 NOUN = modernization
■ 办公设备的现代化提高了工作效率。 **Bàngōng shèbèi de xiàndàihuà tígāole gōngzuò xiàolù.** = The modernization of office equipment has increased work efficiency.

xiànshí 现实 [compound: 现 present + 实 real]
1 NOUN = what is real, reality, actuality
■ 现实往往不那么美好。 **Xiànshí wǎngwǎng bù nàme měihǎo.** = The reality is often not so perfect.
2 ADJECTIVE = realistic
■ 这个计划不太现实。 **Zhège jìhuà bú tài xiànshí.** = This plan is not very realistic.

xiànxiàng 现象 NOUN = phenomenon
■ 有些自然现象还不能解释。 **Yǒuxiē zìrán xiànxiàng hái bù néng jiěshì.** = Some natural phenomena still cannot be explained.

xiànzài 现在 [compound: 现 present + 在 being] NOUN = the present time, now
■ 我现在没有时间，晚上再打电话给他。 **Wǒ xiànzài méiyǒu shíjiān, wǎnshang zài dǎ**

X

diànhuà gěi tā. = *I don't have time now, I'll ring him this evening.*
- 现在几点钟? **Xiànzài jǐ diǎn zhōng?** = *What time is it?*

xiàn 线 Trad 綫 NOUN = string, thread, wire (根 gēn)
- 这根线太短,有没有长一点的? **Zhè gen xiàn tài duǎn, yǒu méi yǒu cháng yìdiǎn de?** = *This string is too short. Do you have a longer one?*

xiàn 限 VERB = limit

xiànzhì 限制 [compound: 限 *limit* + 制 *control*] VERB = limit, restrict, confine
- 为了减肥,她限制自己一天吃两顿饭。 **Wèile jiǎnféi, tā xiànzhì zìjǐ yì tiān chī liǎng dùn fàn.** = *To reduce weight she restricted herself to two meals a day.*
- 政府限制进口汽车的数量。 **Zhèngfǔ xiànzhì jìnkǒu qìchē de shùliàng.** = *The government restricts the number of imported cars.*

xiàn 羡 VERB = admire, envy

xiànmù 羡慕 [compound: 羡 *envy* + 慕 *envy*] VERB = envy
- 她的家庭这么美满,真让人羡慕。 **Tā de jiātíng zhème měimǎn, zhēn ràng rén xiànmù!** = *Her perfectly happy family really makes one envious.*
- 我很羡慕记忆力好的人。 **Wǒ hěn xiànmù jìyìlì hǎo de rén.** = *I envy those who have a good memory.*

xiàn 献 Trad 獻 VERB = offer (See 贡献 gòngxiàn.)

xiāng 乡 Trad 鄉 NOUN = rural town
- 乡比县小,比村大。 **Xiāng bǐ xiàn xiǎo, bǐ cūn dà.** = *A rural town is smaller than a county, but bigger than a village.*

xiāngxia 乡下 NOUN = countryside, rural area
- 他的爷爷奶奶住在乡下。 **Tā de yéye nǎinai zhù zài xiāngxia.** = *His grandpa and grandma live in the country.*

xiāng 相 ADVERB = each other, mutually

xiāngdāng 相当
1 ADJECTIVE = suitable, appropriate
- 我在翻译的时候,常常想不出一个相当的词。 **Wǒ zài fānyì de shíhou, chángcháng xiǎng bu chū yí ge xiāngdáng de cí.** = *When I do translation I often cannot find a suitable word.*
2 ADVERB = fairly, rather, quite
- 他中文说得相当不错。 **Tā Zhōngwén shuō de xiāngdāng búcuò.** = *He speaks Chinese rather well.*

xiāngfǎn 相反 ADJECTIVE = opposite, contrary
- 不同的意见,甚至相反的意见也要听。 **Bùtóng de yìjiàn, shènzhì xiāngfǎn de yìjiàn dōu yào tīng.** = *We should hear out different, even opposing, opinions.*
- 相反相成。 **Xiāng fǎn xiāng chéng.** = *Two opposing things may also complement each other.*

xiānghù 相互 ADJECTIVE = mutual, each other
- 一对年轻人必须相互了解才能考虑婚姻。 **Yíduì niánqīngrén bìxū xiānghù liǎojiě cái néng kǎolǜ hūnyīn.** = *A young man and a young woman must know each other well before contemplating marriage.*

xiāngsì 相似 ADJECTIVE = similar to, be alike
- 你提出的方案和我的想法很相似。 **Nǐ tíchū de fāng'àn hé wǒ de xiǎngfǎ hěn xiāngsì.** = *Your plan is similar to my ideas.*
- 他们姐妹俩长得很相似,但是脾气性格不一样。 **Tāmen jiě-mèi liǎ zhǎng de hěn xiāngsì, dànshì píqi xìnggé bù yíyàng.** = *The two sisters resemble each other, but have different temperaments.*

xiāngtóng 相同 ADJECTIVE = identical, same
- 相同的年龄,相同的经历使他们有很多共同语言。 **Xiāngtóng de niánlíng, xiāngtóng de jīnglì shǐ tāmen yǒu hěn duō gòngtóng yǔyán.** = *The same age and the same experiences give them lots of common language.*

xiāngxìn 相信 [modif: 相 *each other* + 信 *trust*] VERB = believe, believe in
- 我不相信他会做这种事。 **Wǒ bù xiāngxìn tā huì zuò zhè zhǒng shì.** = *I don't believe that he would do such a thing.*
- 你相信鬼故事吗? **Nǐ xiāngxìn guǐ gùshi ma?** = *Do you believe ghost stories?*

X

xiāng 香 ADJECTIVE = fragrant, sweet-smelling, aromatic
- 这花真香！**Zhè huā zhēn xiāng!** = *How sweet this flower smells!*
- 我闻到烤肉的香味。**Wǒ wéndao kǎoròu de xiāngwèi.** = *I smell the delicious aroma of roast beef.*

xiāngcháng 香肠 [modif: 香 *savory* + 肠 *intestine*] NOUN = sausage (根 **gēn**)
- 中国的香肠和西方的香肠味道不一样。**Zhōngguó de xiāngcháng hé xīfāng de xiāngcháng wèidao bù yíyàng.** = *Chinese sausages and Western sausages taste very different.*

xiāngjiāo 香蕉 [modif: 香 *fragrant* + 蕉 *banana*] NOUN = banana (根 **gēn**)
- 这些香蕉还没有熟，过两天再吃吧。**Zhèxiē xiāngjiāo hái měiyǒu shú, guò liǎngtiān zài chī ba.** = *These bananas are not ripe yet. Let's wait a few days before eating them.*
- 你饿了，就吃一根香蕉。**Nǐ è le, jiù chī yì gēn xiāngjiāo.** = *Have a banana first if you're hungry.*

Xiānggǎng 香港 [modif: 香 *fragrant* + 港 *harbor*] NOUN = Hong Kong
- 香港是买东西的好地方。**Xiānggǎng shì mǎi dōngxi de hǎo dìfang.** = *Hong Kong is a good place for shopping.*

xiāngzào 香皂 [modif: 香 *fragrant* + 皂 *soap*] NOUN = toilet soap, bath soap (块 **kuài**)
- 这块香皂很好闻。**Zhè kuài xiāngzào hěn hǎowén.** = *This soap smells nice.*

xiāng 箱 NOUN = box, chest

xiāngzi 箱子 [suffix: 箱 *trunk* + 子 *nominal suffix*] NOUN = trunk, chest, box, suitcase
- 这个箱子是她奶奶传给她的。**Zhège xiāngzi shì tā nǎinai chuán gei tā de.** = *This trunk was passed down to her from her grandmother.*

xiáng 详 Trad 詳 ADJECTIVE = detailed

xiángxì 详细 [compound: 详 *in detail* + 细 *tiny*] ADJECTIVE = in detail, detailed
- 我只知道大概的情况，详细情况不清楚。

Wǒ zhǐ zhīdào dàgài de qíngkuàng, xiángxì qíngkuàng bù qīngchu. = *I only know the general situation and am not clear about the details.*
- 他详细说明了全部经过。**Tā xiángxì shuōmíngle quánbù jīngguò.** = *He told the whole story in detail.*

xiǎng 享 VERB = enjoy

xiǎngshòu 享受 [compound: 享 *enjoy* + 受 *experience*] VERB = enjoy
- 在有些方面现代人享受的比古代皇帝还多。**Zài yǒuxiē fāngmiàn xiàndàirén xiǎngshòu de bǐ gǔdài huángdì hái duō.** = *In some respects a modern man enjoys more things than an emperor did in ancient times.*
- 忙了半个月，今天可以享受一下清闲了。**Mángle bàn ge yuè, jīntiān kěyǐ xiǎngshòu yíxià qīngxián le.** = *After half a month's busy work, I can enjoy carefree leisure today.*

xiǎng 响 Trad 響 ADJECTIVE = loud, noisy
- 教室里在考试，你们说话声音别这么响。**Jiàoshì li zài kǎoshì, nǐmen shuōhuà shēngyīn bié zhènme xiǎng.** = *There's an examination in progress in the classroom. Don't talk so loudly.*

xiǎng 想 VERB = think
- 这个问题我要想想。**Zhège wèntí wǒ yào xiǎngxiǎng.** = *I need to think over this problem.*
- 我想这个手续不会太麻烦。**Wǒ xiǎng zhè shǒuxù bú huì tài máfan.** = *I don't think this procedure will be very complicated.*
- xiǎng yíxià 想一下 = think for a while, give ... some thought
- 明天晚上跟不跟他一块儿去看电影？让我想一下。**Míngtiān wǎnshang gēn bu gēn tā yíkuàir qù kàn diànyǐng? Ràng wǒ xiǎng yì xiǎng.** = *Shall I go to the movie with him tomorrow evening? Let me think it over.*
- xiǎng bànfǎ 想办法 = think of a way (to do something)
- 没关系，我来想办法。**Méiguānxi, wǒ lái xiǎng bànfǎ.** = *It's OK. I'll think of a way.*

xiǎngfǎ 想法 [modif: 想 *thinking* + 法 *way, method*] NOUN = what one thinks, idea, opinion
- 你有什么想法，尽管谈。**Nǐ yǒu shénme xiǎngfǎ, jìnguǎn tán.** = *Feel free to say whatever you have in mind.*

X

■ 老师想了解一下学生对开口语课的想法。 **Lǎoshī xiǎng liáojiě yíxià xuésheng duì kāi kǒuyǔ kè de xiǎngfǎ.** = *The teacher wants to find out what the students think of introducing an oral Chinese class.*

xiǎngniàn 想念 [compound: 想 *think* + 念 *miss (someone)*] VERB = miss, remember with longing
■ 祖母去世两年了，我还非常想念她。 **Zǔmǔ qùshì liǎng nián le, wǒ hái fēicháng xiǎngniàn tā.** = *It's over two years since Granny died, but I still miss her very much.*

xiǎngxiàng 想象 [v+obj: 想 *think* + 象 *image*] VERB = imagine
■ 小女孩常常想象自己是一位美丽的舞蹈演员。 **Xiǎonǚhái chángcháng xiǎngxiàng zìjǐ shì yí wèi měilì de wǔdǎo yǎnyuán.** = *The little girl often imagines herself to be a beautiful dancer.*
■ 我不能想象，没有音乐，怎么生活。 **Wǒ bù néng xiǎngxiàng, méiyǒu yīnyuè, zěnme shēnghuó.** = *I cannot imagine how one can live without music.*

xiàng 项 Trad 項 MEASURE WORD = item of something (for things that are composed of items or things considered to be component)
■ 一项任务 **yí xiàng rènwù** = *a mission*
■ 两项文件 **liǎng xiàng wénjiàn** = *two documents*

xiàngmù 项目 [compound: 项 *item* + 目 *item*] NOUN = item
■ 他负责一个重要的研究项目。 **Tā fùzé yíge zhòngyào de yánjiū xiàngmù.** = *He is in charge of an important research project.*

xiàng 象 NOUN = elephant (头 **tóu**)
■ 小孩子都喜欢大象。 **Xiǎoháizi dōu xǐhuan dàxiàng.** = *Children are all fond of elephants.*

NOTE: Chinese often fondly refer to elephants as 大象 **dàxiàng**.

xiàng 像
1 VERB = resemble, bear resemblance to, be like
■ 她很像妈妈。 **Tā hěn xiàng māma.** = *She takes after her mother.*
■ 他的脾气一点也不像他爸爸。 **Tā de píqì**

yìdiǎn yě bú xiàng tā bàba. = *His temperature is not at all like his father's.*
2 NOUN = likeness of (a human being), portrait
■ 墙上挂着祖父的像。 **Qiáng shang guàzhe zǔfù de xiàng.** = *On the wall hangs a portrait of their grandfather.*

xiàng 向
1 PREPOSITION = in the direction of, towards
■ 中国的长江，黄河都向东流。 **Zhōngguó de Chángjiāng, Huánghé dōu xiàng dōng liú.** = *China's Yangtze River and Yellow River flow to the east.*
2 VERB = face
■ 这个房间有两个窗子，一个向南，一个向东。 **Zhège fángjiān yǒu liǎng ge chuāngzi, yí ge xiàng nán, yí ge xiàng dōng.** = *There are two windows in the room. One faces south and the other faces east.*

xiāo 消 VERB = vanish

xiāofèi 消费 VERB = consume
■ 生活水平提高了，人们消费的商品就越来越多。 **Shēnghuó shuǐpíng tígāole, rénmen xiāofèi de shāngpǐn jiù yuèláiyuè duō.** = *As people's living standard rises, they consume more and more goods.*
xiāofèipǐn 消费品 = consumer commodities, consumer goods
xiāofèizhě 消费者 = consumer

xiāohuà 消化 [compound: 消 *eliminate* + 化 *exterminate*] VERB = digest
■ 我中饭还没有消化呢，不想吃晚饭。 **Wǒ zhōngfàn hái méiyǒu xiāohuà ne, bù xiǎng chī wǎnfàn.** = *I still haven't digested my lunch. I don't want to eat supper.*
■ 今天老师讲了这么多，我还没有完全消化。 **Jīntiān lǎoshī jiǎngle zhème duō, wǒ hái méiyǒu wánquán xiāohuà.** = *The teacher gave us so much information today, I haven't entirely digested it.*

xiāomiè 消灭 [compound: 消 *eliminate* + 灭 *exterminate*] VERB = eliminate, wipe out
■ 这种害虫在本地区基本消灭。 **Zhè zhǒng hàichóng zài běn dìqū jīběn xiāomiè.** = *This pest has been mainly exterminated in this region.*

X

xiāoshī 消失 [compound: 消 *vanish* + 失 *lose*]
VERB = disappear, vanish
■ 太阳出来以后，雾渐渐消失了。**Tàiyang chūlai yǐhòu, wù jiànjiàn xiāoshī le.** = *As the sun came out, the fog dissipated.*

xiāoxi 消息 [compound: 消 *information* + 息 *news*] NOUN = news (条 **tiáo**)
■ 今天报上有什么消息? **Jīntiān bàoshang yǒu shénme xiāoxi?** = *What's the news in today's paper?*
■ 我告诉你一个好消息。**Wǒ gàosu nǐ yí ge hǎo xiāoxi.** = *I'll tell you a piece of good news.*
■ 一有关于他的消息，请马上告诉我。**Yì yǒu guānyú tā de xiāoxi, qǐng mǎshàng gàosu wǒ.** = *Please let me know as soon as you've got news about him.*

xiǎo 小 ADJECTIVE
¹ = small, little (antonym 大 **dà**)
■ 这双鞋太小了，有没有大一点儿的? **Zhè shuāng xié tài xiǎo le, yǒu méiyǒu dà yìdiǎnr de?** = *This pair of shoes is too small. Do you have a bigger size?*
xiǎobiàn 小便 = urine, urinate
xiǎofèi 小费 = tip, gratuity
xiǎoqì 小气 = stingy, miserly
xiǎozǔ 小组 = group
² = young
■ 我小时候，放暑假的时候，常常住在奶奶家。**Wǒ xiǎo shíhou, fàng shǔjià de shíhou, chángcháng zhù zai nǎinai jiā.** = *When I was a child, I often stayed with granny during the summer holidays.*
■ 我姓李，您就叫我小李吧。**Wǒ xìng Lǐ, nín jiù jiào wǒ Xiǎo Lǐ ba.** = *My family name is Li. You can call me Xiao Li.*

NOTE: " 小 **xiǎo** + family name," like 小李 **Xiǎo Lǐ**, is a casual, friendly form of address to a person younger than oneself. See note on 老 **lǎo** for forms of address like 老李 **Lǎo Lǐ**.

xiǎoháir 小孩儿 [suffix: 小孩 *young child* + 儿 *diminutive nominal suffix*] NOUN = same as 孩子 **háizi**

xiǎohuǒzi 小伙子 NOUN = young man, lad
■ 这些农村来的小伙子又老实又肯干。
Zhèxiē nóngcūn lái de xiǎohuǒzi yòu lǎoshí yòu kěngàn. = *These country lads are honest and hardworking.*

NOTE: See note on 姑娘 **gūniang**.

xiǎojiě 小姐 [compound: 小 *young* + 姐 *elder sister*] NOUN = young lady; Miss
■ 有一位小姐要见你。**Yǒu yí wèi xiǎojiě yào jiàn nǐ.** = *There's a young lady wanting to see you.*
■ 王先生，王太太和他们的女儿王小姐都在美国旅行。**Wáng xiānsheng, Wáng tàitai hé tāmen de nǚ'ér Wáng xiǎojiě dōu zài Měiguó lǚxíng.** = *Mr and Mrs Wang, with their daughter Miss Wang, are all travelling in the United States.*

NOTE: 小姐 **xiǎojiě** is a common form of address to a young (or not so young) woman. If her family name is not known, just use 小姐 **xiǎojiě**. 小姐 **xiǎojiě** is also the form of address for a waitress or female attendant, e.g.
■ 小姐，请给我一杯水。**Xiǎojiě, qǐng gěi wǒ yì bēi shuǐ.** = *Please give me a glass of water.*

xiǎomài 小麦 NOUN = wheat
■ 在中国北方粮食以小麦为主。**Zài Zhōngguó běifang liángshi yǐ xiǎomài wéi zhǔ.** = *In northern China, wheat is the main cereal crop.*

xiǎopéngyou 小朋友 NOUN = (a friendly form of address or reference to a child)
■ 小朋友，你们校长办公室在哪里? **Xiǎopéngyou, nǐmen xiàozhǎng bàngōngshì zài nǎlǐ?** = *Where's your headmaster's office, children?*

xiǎoshí 小时 [modif: 小 *small* + 时 *time*] NOUN = hour
■ 我等你等了一个半小时了。**Wǒ děng nǐ děngle yí ge bàn xiǎoshí le.** = *I've been waiting for you for an hour and a half.*
bàn xiǎoshí 半小时 = half an hour

xiǎoshuō 小说 [modif: 小 *small* + 说 *talk*] NOUN = novel (本 **běn**, 篇 **piān**)
■ 这本小说的作者有丰富的生活经历。**Zhè běn xiǎoshuō de zuòzhě yǒu fēngfù de shēnghuó jīnglì.** = *The author of this novel has had rich life experiences.*
■ 这篇小说语言优美，但是没有多大意思。**Zhè piān xiǎoshuō yǔyán yōuměi, dànshì méiyǒu duō dà yìsi.** = *The language of this*

story is beautiful but it is not very meaningful.
àiqíng xiǎoshuō 爱情小说 = romance novel
chángpiān xiǎoshuō 长篇小说 = novel
duǎnpiān xiǎoshuō 短篇小说 = short story, story
lìshǐ xiǎoshuō 历史小说 = historical novel
xiǎoshuōjiā 小说家 = (accomplished) novelist

xiǎotōu 小偷 [modif: 小 *small, petty* + 偷 *thief*] NOUN = thief
■ 抓小偷！抓小偷！ **Zhuō xiǎotōu! Zhuō xiǎotōu!** = *Stop thief! Stop thief!*

xiǎoxīn 小心 [modif: 小 *small* + 心 *the heart*] ADJECTIVE = careful, cautious
■ 他说话、做事都很小心。 **Tā shuōhuà, zuòshì dōu hěn xiǎoxīn.** = *He is cautious in speech and action.*
■ 今天有雾，开车要特别小心。 **Jīntiān yǒu wù, kāichē yào tèbié xiǎoxīn.** = *It's foggy today. You need to be particularly careful while driving.*

xiǎoxué 小学 [modif: 小 *small* + 学 *school*] NOUN = primary school (座 **zuò**, 所 **suǒ**)
■ 这座小学操场太小，孩子没地方玩。 **Zhè zuò xiǎoxué cāochǎng tài xiǎo, háizi méi dìfang wán.** = *This primary school's sports ground is too small and the children have nowhere to play.*

xiǎo 晓 Trad 曉 VERB = know

xiǎode 晓得 VERB = same as 知道 **zhīdào**. Only used in colloquial Chinese.

xiào 效 NOUN = effect

xiàoguǒ 效果 [compound: 效 *effect* + 果 *result*] NOUN = effect, result
■ 对孩子太严格，往往效果不好。 **Duì háizi tài yángé, wǎngwǎng xiàoguǒ bù hǎo.** = *Being too strict with children often gives poor results.*
■ 这种新方法效果怎么样？ **Zhè zhǒng xīn fāngfǎ xiàoguǒ zěnmeyàng?** = *How effective is this new method?*

xiàolǜ 效率 [modif: 效 *effect* + 率 *rate*] NOUN = efficiency
■ 我们必须不断提高工作效率。 **Wǒmen bìxū búduàn tígāo gōngzuò xiàolǜ.** = *We must constantly increase work efficiency.*

xiào 校 NOUN = school

xiàozhǎng 校长 [modif: 校 *school* + 长 *chief*] NOUN = headmaster, principal, university president, university vice chancellor
■ 这位校长得到大多数教师的拥护。 **Zhèwèi xiàozhǎng dédào dàduōshù jiàoshī de yōnghù.** = *This principal enjoys the support of most of the teachers.*
■ 在中文里，小学、中学、大学的负责人都叫"校长"。 **Zài Zhōngwén li, xiǎoxué, zhōngxué, dàxué de fùzérén dōu jiào "xiàozhǎng".** = *In Chinese, people in charge of primary schools, high schools or universities are all called "xiaozhang."*

NOTES: (1) While in Chinese the chief of any school is called 校长 **xiàozhǎng**, different terms are required in English. (2) In an English-system university, the vice-chancellor is its chief executive officer. *Vice-chancellor* should therefore be translated as 校长 **xiàozhǎng** while *chancellor*, being largely an honorary position, should be 名誉校长 **míngyù xiàozhǎng**.

xiào 笑 VERB = laugh, smile (antonym 哭 **kū**)
■ 他笑着和我握手。 **Tā xiàozhe hé wǒ wòshǒu.** = *He shook my hand, smiling.*
■ 你笑什么？ **Nǐ xiào shénme?** = *What are you laughing at?*
■ 笑一笑，十年少。 **Xiào yi xiào, shí nián shào.** = *Laugh and you'll be ten years younger.* (→ *Laughter is the best medicine.*)
dàxiào 大笑 = laugh

xiàohua 笑话 [modif: 笑 *laughing* + 话 *talk*]
1 NOUN = joke
■ 我来讲个笑话。 **Wǒ lái jiǎng ge xiàohua.** = *I'll tell you a joke.*
■ 他很会讲笑话。 **Tā hěn huì jiǎng xiàohua.** = *He is good at telling jokes.*
2 VERB = laugh at
■ 我中文讲得不好，你们别笑话我。 **Wǒ Zhōngwén jiǎng de bù hǎo, nǐmen bié xiàohua wǒ.** = *I don't speak Chinese very well. Please don't laugh at me.*

xiē 些 MEASURE WORD = some, a few, a little
■ 午饭我吃了一些面包。 **Wǔfàn wǒ chīle yìxiē miànbāo.** = *I had some bread for lunch.*

hǎoxiē 好些 = quite a few, lots of
■ 昨天晚上他和老朋友谈了很久，喝了好些酒。**Zuótiān wǎnshang tā hé lǎo péngyou tánle hěn jiǔ, hēle hǎoxiē jiǔ.** = *Yesterday evening he chatted with his old friends for a long time and drank lots of wine.*

xiē 歇 VERB = take a rest
■ 我走不动了，歇会儿吧。**Wǒ zǒu bu dòng le, xiē huìr ba.** = *I can't walk any further. Let's take a break.*

xié 斜 ADJECTIVE = oblique, slanting
■ 他斜穿过马路。**Tā xié chuānguo mǎlù.** = *He crossed the street diagonally.*

xié 鞋 NOUN = shoe (只 **zhī**, 双 **shuāng**)
■ 他总是穿一双黑鞋。**Tā zǒngshi chuān yì shuāng hēi xié.** = *He always wears a pair of black shoes.*
xié dài 鞋带 = shoelace, shoestring
liáng xié 凉鞋 = sandals
pí xié 皮鞋 = leather shoes
tuō xié 拖鞋 = slippers
yǔ xié 雨鞋 = rubber boots
yùndòng xié 运动鞋 = sports shoes

xiě 血 NOUN = same as 血 **xuè**. Used only in colloquial Chinese.

xiě 写 Trad 寫 VERB = write, write with a pen
■ 这个汉字怎么写？**Zhège Hànzì zěnme xiě?** = *How do you write this Chinese character?*
■ 他在写一篇经济学论文。**Tā zài xiě yì piān jīngjìxué lùnwén.** = *He is writing a thesis on economics.*
■ 我经常用电脑，不大写字。**Wǒ jīngcháng yòng diànnǎo, búdà xiě zì.** = *I often use computers and seldom write with a pen.*

xiè 谢 Trad 謝 VERB = thank

xièxie 谢谢 VERB = thank
■ "谢谢你。""不客气。" **"Xièxie nǐ." "Bú kèqi."** = *"Thank you." "You're welcome."*
■ 你给我这么大帮助，我不知道怎样谢谢你才好。**Nǐ gěi wǒ zhème dà bāngzhù, wǒ bù zhīdào zěnyàng xièxie nǐ cái hǎo.** = *You've given me so much help. I don't know how to thank you.*

NOTE: There are many ways of replying to 谢谢你 **xièxie nǐ**, e.g.
■ 不客气。**Bú kèqi.** = *You don't have to be so polite.*
■ 不用谢。**Bú yòng xiè.** = *You don't have to thank me.*
■ 没关系。**Méi guānxi** = *It doesn't matter.*

xiè 械 NOUN = tool (See 机械 **jīxiè**.)

xīn 心 NOUN = the heart
■ 这个人心真好！**Zhège rén xīn zhēn hǎo!** = *This person is really kindhearted.*
yòngxīn 用心 = apply oneself to
■ 你学习不太用心。**Nǐ xuéxí bú tài yòngxīn.** = *You don't really apply yourself to studying.*
fàngxīn 放心 = feel relieved, be assured, at ease
■ 你一个人去爬山，我不放心。**Nǐ yí ge rén qù páshān, wǒ bú fàngxīn.** = *I'd be worried if you go mountain-climbing all by yourself.*
kāixīn 开心 = be joyous
tòngxīn 痛心 = pained, agonized
shāngxīn 伤心 = heartbroken

xīnqíng 心情 [compound: 心 *the heart* + 情 *emotion*] NOUN = state of mind, mood
■ 她孩子又生病了，她心情怎么会好？**Tā háizi yòu shēngbìng le, tā xīnqíng zěnme huì hǎo?** = *Her child has fallen ill again. How can she be in a good mood?*

xīnzàng 心脏 [modif: 心 *the heart* + 脏 *human organ*] NOUN = the heart (as a medical term)
■ 经过检查，医生确定他有心脏病。**Jīngguò jiǎnchá, yīshēng quèdìng tā yǒu xīnzàng bìng.** = *After examination, the doctor confirmed that he had heart trouble.*

xīn 辛 ADJECTIVE = spicy hot

xīnkǔ 辛苦 [compound: 辛 *spicy hot* + 苦 *bitter*]
1 ADJECTIVE = hard and toilsome (job)
■ 这个工作很辛苦。**Zhège gōngzuò hěn xīnkǔ.** = *This is a tough job.*
■ 你们辛苦了。**Nǐmen xīnkǔ le.** = *You've been working hard.*
2 ADJECTIVE = harsh, difficult (life)
■ 很多农民的生活很辛苦。**Hěn duō nóngmín de shēnghuó hěn xīnkǔ.** = *Many peasants live a hard life.*

X

3 VERB = (used to request somebody's service)
■ 辛苦你把这几只箱子搬到楼上去。**Xīnkǔ nǐ bǎ zhè jǐ zhī xiāngzi bān dào lóu shang qù.** = *Would you please carry these suitcases upstairs?*

NOTE: 你们辛苦了! **Nǐmen xīnkǔ le.** is used by a superior to express appreciation of hard work done by subordinate(s). When somebody has done you a service, you can say 辛苦你了! **Xīnkǔ nǐ le!**

xīn 新 ADJECTIVE = new (antonym 旧 jiù)
■ 你觉得我这件新衣服 怎么样? **Nǐ juéde wǒ zhè jiàn xīn yīfu zěnmeyàng?** = *What do you think of my new dress?*
■ 旧的不去, 新的不来。**Jiù de bú qù, xīn de bù lái.** = *If old stuff doesn't go away, new stuff won't come. (→ If you don't discard old things, you won't be able to use new things.)*

Xīnjiāpō 新加坡 NOUN = Singapore
■ 大多数新加坡人会说华语。**Dàduōshù Xīnjiāpōrén huì shuō Huáyǔ.** = *Most Singaporeans can speak Chinese.*

xīnnián 新年 [modif: 新 new + 年 year] NOUN = New Year
■ 新年好! **Xīnnián hǎo!** = *Happy New Year!*
■ 祝您新年快乐! **Zhù nín xīnnián kuàile!** = *I wish you a happy New Year!*
Xīnnián hèkǎ 新年贺卡 = New Year card

xīnwén 新闻 [modif: 新 new + 闻 what is heard] NOUN = news (of current affairs) (条 tiáo)
■ 你是怎么样得到新闻的 — 读报纸, 听广播, 还是看电视? **Nǐ shì zěnmeyàng dédào xīnwén de—dú bàozhǐ, tīng guǎngbō, háishì kàn diànshì?** = *How do you get news—by reading newspapers, listening to radio or watching television?*
■ 他每天一边吃晚饭, 一边看电视新闻。**Tā měi tiān yìbiān chī wǎnfàn, yìbiān kàn diànshì xīnwén.** = *Everyday he watches TV news while having supper.*

Xīnxīlán 新西兰 NOUN = New Zealand
■ 每年很多外国人到新西兰去旅游。**Měi nián hěn duō wàiguórén dào Xīnxīlán qù lǚyóu.** = *Every year many foreigners go to New Zealand on holiday.*

xīnxiān 新鲜 [compound: 新 new + 鲜 fresh]
ADJECTIVE = fresh
■ 我们每天都要吃新鲜蔬菜。**Wǒmen měi tiān dōu yào chī xīnxiān shūcài.** = *We should eat fresh vegetables everyday.*
■ 这条鱼不新鲜了。**Zhè tiáo yú bù xīnxiān le.** = *This fish is no longer fresh.*

xìn 信 1 VERB = believe
■ 我不信他一天能干这么多活。**Wǒ bú xìn tā yì tiān néng gàn zhème duō huó.** = *I don't believe he could have done so much work in a day.*

xìn 信 2 NOUN = letter
■ 现在人们很少写信。**Xiànzài rénmen hěn shǎo xiě xìn.** = *People don't often write letters now.*
xìnfēng 信封 = envelope
jì xìn 寄信 = post a letter
jièshàoxìn 介绍信 = letter of recommendation, reference
shōudào xìn 收到信 = receive a letter
zhùhèxìn 祝贺信 = letter of congratulation

xìnrèn 信任 [compound: 信 trust + 任 entrust]
1 VERB = trust, have confidence in
■ 你既然请他做这么重要的工作, 一定很信任他。**Nǐ jìrán qǐng tā zuò zhème zhòngyào de gōngzuò, yídìng hěn xìnrèn tā.** = *Since you've asked him to do such an important job, you must really trust him.*
2 NOUN = trust, confidence
■ 他得到董事会的信任, 到外地去开展业务。**Tā dédào dǒngshìhuì de xìnrèn, dào wàidì qù kāizhǎn yèwù.** = *He earned the trust of the board and has gone to other parts of the country to develop the company business.*

xìnxī 信息 [compound: 信 message + 息 news, tiding] NOUN = information
■ 这台电脑处理信息十分迅速。**Zhè tái diànnǎo chǔlǐ xìnxī shífēn xùnsù.** = *This computer processes information rapidly.*
■ 你有关于他的信息吗? **Nǐ yǒu guānyú tā de xìnxī ma?** = *Do you have any information about him?*

xìnxīn 信心 [modif: 信 believe + 心 the heart]
NOUN = confidence
■ 我对公司的前途充满信心。**Wǒ duì gōngsī**

X

de qiántú chōngmǎn xìnxīn. = *I have full confidence in the company's future.*
- 他对自己缺乏信心。**Tā duì zìjǐ quēfá xìnxīn.** = *He lacks self-confidence.*

xīng 兴 Trad 興 ADJECTIVE = flourishing

xīngfèn 兴奋 [compound: 兴 *flourishing* + 奋 *excited*] ADJECTIVE = excited, overjoyed
- 她们得了冠军, 兴奋得跳了起来。**Tāmen déle guànjūn, xīngfèn de tiàole qǐlai.** = *When they got the championship, they were so overjoyed that they jumped.*
- 不要在兴奋的时候, 做任何决定。**Bú yào zài xīngfèn de shíhou, zuò rènhé juédìng.** = *Don't make decisions when you are excited.*

xīng 星 NOUN = star (颗 **kē**)
- 太阳系有九大行星。**Tàiyangxì yǒu jiǔ dà xíngxīng.** = *There are nine planets in the solar system.*
xīngxīng 行星 = planet

> NOTE: In everyday Chinese 星星 **xīngxīng** is normally used instead of 星 **xīng**, e.g.
> - 今天晚上的星星真亮。**Jīntiān wǎnshang de xīngxing zhēn liàng.** = *Tonight the stars are really bright.*

xīngqī 星期 NOUN = week
- 一年有五十二个星期。**Yì nián you wǔshí èr ge xīngqī.** = *There're fifty-two weeks in a year.*
Xīngqīyī 星期一 = Monday
Xīngqī'èr 星期二 = Tuesday
Xīngqīsān 星期三 = Wednesday
Xīngqīsì 星期四 = Thursday
Xīngqīwǔ 星期五 = Friday
Xīngqīliù 星期六 = Saturday
Xīngqīrì 星期日 = Sunday
Xīngqītiān 星期天 = Sunday
shang xīngqī 上星期 = last week
xià xīngqī 下星期 = next week

xíng 行
1 VERB = all right, OK, (that) will do
- "我可以用一下你的词典吗?" "行。" **"Wǒ kěyǐ yòng yíxià nǐ de cídiǎn ma?" "Xíng."** = *"May I use your dictionary?" "OK."*
- 学中文不学汉字不行。**Xué Zhōngwén bù xué hànzì bù xíng.** = *It won't do to learn Chinese without learning Chinese characters.*

2 ADJECTIVE = competent, capable
- 你又赢了, 真行! **Nǐ yòu yíng le, zhēn xíng!** = *You've won again. You're really great!*
- 我踢足球不行, 打篮球还可以。**Wǒ tī zúqiú bù xíng, dǎ lánqiú hái kěyǐ.** = *I'm not good at soccer but I'm not too bad at basketball.*

xíngdòng 行动 [compound: 行 *work* + 动 *move*]
1 VERB = move around
- 老人行动不便, 不愿多外出。**Lǎorén xíngdòng búbiàn, bú yuàn duō wàichū.** = *The old man has difficulty moving about and is reluctant to go out very often.*
2 NOUN = action, behavior
- 不但要听他说什么, 而且要看他的行动。**Búdàn yào tīng tā shuō shénme, érqiě yào kàn tā de xíngdòng.** = *We should not only listen to what he says but also look at what he does.*

xíngli 行李 NOUN = luggage, baggage (件 **jiàn**)
- 你有几件行李? **Nǐ yǒu jǐ jiàn xíngli?** = *How many pieces of luggage do you have?*
- 你的行李超重了, 要付一百元。**Nǐ de xíngli chāozhòng le, yào fù yìbǎi yuán.** = *Your luggage is overweight. You need to pay 100 yuan.*

xíng 形 NOUN = form, shape

xíngchéng 形成 [v+obj: 形 *form* + 成 *become*] VERB = take shape, form
- 习惯形成以后, 就很难改变。**Xíguàn xíngchéng yǐhòu, jiù hěn nán gǎibiàn.** = *After a habit is formed, it is difficult to break.*

xíngróng 形容 VERB = describe
- 我形容不出来那个小偷长的样子。**Wǒ xíngróng bu chūlái nà ge xiǎotōu zhǎng de yàngzi.** = *I can't describe what the thief looks like.*

xíngshì 形式 [compound: 形 *shape* + 式 *manner*] NOUN = form, shape (antonym 内容 **nèiróng**)
- 道歉是必要的, 用什么形式还要考虑。**Dàoqiàn shì bìyào de, yòng shénme xíngshì háiyào kǎolǜ.** = *While an apology is necessary, we need to think over the form it should take.*

X

xíngshì 形势 [compound: 形 *shape* + 势 *force*] NOUN = situation
- 目前的形势对我们有利。**Mùqián de xíngshì duì wǒmen yǒulì.** = *The present situation is in our favor.*

xíngxiàng 形象 [compound: 形 *shape* + 象 *image*] NOUN = image
- 公司要注意公共关系，改善社会形象。**Gōngsī yào zhùyì gōnggòng guānxi, gǎishàn shèhuì xíngxiàng.** = *The company should pay attention to public relations and improve its public image.*

xíngzhuàng 形状 [compound: 形 *shape* + 状 *shape*] NOUN = appearance, shape, form
- 这座山的形状象一只猴子，因此人们就叫它猴山。**Zhè zuò shān de xíngzhuàng xiàng yì zhī hóuzi, yīncǐ rénmen jiù jiào tā hóushān.** = *The hill has the shape of a monkey and is therefore called Monkey Hill.*

xíng 型 NOUN = model, type (See 大型 **dàxíng**.)

xǐng 醒 VERB = wake, wake up
- 我今天很早就醒了。**Wǒ jīntiān hěn zǎo jiù xǐng le.** = *I woke up very early this morning.*
shuìxǐng 睡醒 = have enough sleep
- 睡醒了没有？ **Shuì xǐngle méiyǒu?** = *Have you had enough sleep?*
jiàoxǐng 叫醒 = wake somebody up
- 你明天早上五点钟叫醒我，好吗？ **Nǐ míngtiān zǎoshang wǔ diǎnzhōng jiàoxǐng wǒ, hǎo ma?** = *Could you wake me up tomorrow morning at five?*

xìng 兴 Trad 興 ADJECTIVE = joyful

xìngqù 兴趣 [compound: 兴 *joy* + 趣 *interest*] NOUN = interest
- 这孩子对动物很感兴趣。**Zhè háizi duì dòngwù hěn gǎn xìngqù.** = *This child is very interested in animals.*
- 我对别人的私事没有兴趣。**Wǒ duì biéren de sīshì méiyǒu xìngqù.** = *I'm not interested in other people's private matters.*
duì ... gǎn xìngqù 对 ... 感兴趣 = be interested in ...
duì ... yǒu xìngqù 对 ... 有兴趣 = be interested in ...
duì ... bù gǎn xìngqù 对 ... 不感兴趣 = be uninterested in ...
duì ... méiyǒu xìngqù 对 ... 没有兴趣 = be uninterested in ...

xìng 性 NOUN = nature, character

xìnggé 性格 NOUN = person's character, disposition, temperament
- 她性格很坚强。**Tā xìnggé hěn jiānqiáng.** = *She has a strong character.*

xìngzhì 性质 [compound: 性 *nature* + 质 *substance*] NOUN = nature (of a matter, an event, etc.), basic quality
- 这一事件的性质是新旧力量之间的一场政治斗争。**Zhè yí shìjiàn de xìngzhì shì xīn jiù lìliang zhījiān de yì chǎng zhèngzhì dòuzhēng.** = *This incident is in nature a political struggle between the new and old forces.*

xìng 幸 NOUN = good fortune

xìngfú 幸福 [compound: 幸 *good fortune* + 福 *happiness*] ADJECTIVE = happy, fortunate
- 多么幸福的家庭！**Duōme xìngfú de jiātíng!** = *What a happy family!*
- 她实现了自己的理想，感到很幸福。**Tā shíxiàn le zìjǐ de lǐxiǎng, gǎndao hěn xìngfú.** = *She feels happy as she has realized her aspiration.*

NOTE: 幸福 **xìngfú** is used in a sublime sense, denoting a profound and almost perfect happiness. So it has a much more limited use than its English equivalents *happy* or *fortunate*. The usual Chinese word for *happy*, as in "I'm happy to hear the news," is 高兴 **gāoxìng**, e.g.
- 听到这个消息，我很高兴。**Tīngdào zhège xiāoxi, wǒ hěn gāoxìng.** = *I'm happy to hear the news.*

xìng 姓 NOUN = family name
- 中国人最常用的三个姓是李、王、张。**Zhōngguórén zuì chángyòng de sān ge xìng shì Lǐ, Wáng, Zhāng.** = *The three most common family names of the Chinese are Li, Wang and Zhang.*
guìxìng 贵姓 = your family name (polite usage, normally in a question)

X

■ "您贵姓？" "我姓王。" **"Nín guìxìng?" "Wǒ xìng Wáng."** = *"What's your family name?" "Wang."*

NOTE: The character 姓 **xìng** has the signific graph of 女 **nǚ**, meaning *female*, an indication that the Chinese once had a matriarchal society.

xìngmíng 姓名 [compound: 姓 *family name* + 名 *given name*] NOUN = full name
■ 请你在这里写上自己的姓名。**Qǐng nǐ zài zhèlǐ xiěshang zìjǐ de xìngmíng.** = *Please write down your full name here.*

xiōng 兄 NOUN = elder brother

xiōngdì 兄弟 [compound: 兄 *elder brother* + 弟 *younger brother*] NOUN = brother(s)
■ 他们兄弟之间关系很好，一人有事，大家帮忙。**Tāmen xiōngdì zhījiān guānxi hěn hǎo, yì rén yǒu shì, dàjiā bāngmáng.** = *The brothers have a very good relationship—when one of them is in difficulty, the others will come to help him.*

xiōng 胸 NOUN = the chest, thorax
■ 医生，我胸口疼。**Yīshēng, wǒ xiōngkǒu téng.** = *Doctor, I have a pain in the chest.*

xióng 雄 ADJECTIVE = male (of animals) (antonym 雌 **cí**)
■ 雄狮子比雌狮子大得多。**Xióng shīzi bǐ cí shīzi dà de duō.** = *Male lions are much bigger than female ones.*

xióngwěi 雄伟 [compound: 雄 *male* + 伟 *great*] ADJECTIVE = grand, magnificent
■ 这个城市有很多雄伟的建筑。**Zhège chéngshì yǒu hěn duō xióngwěi de jiànzhù.** = *This city boasts many grand buildings.*

xióng 熊 NOUN = bear (只 **zhī**)

xióngmāo 熊猫 [compound: 熊 *bear* + 猫 *cat*] NOUN = panda, giant panda (只 **zhī**)
■ 熊猫只吃竹子。**Xióngmāo zhǐ chī zhúzi.** = *Pandas eat only bamboo.*

xiū 修 VERB
1 = same as 修理 **xiūlǐ**

2 = build, construct (a building, bridge, road, etc.)
■ 这条江上还要修一座大桥。**Zhè tiáo jiāng shang háiyào xiū yí zuò dà qiáo.** = *A big bridge will be built across this river.*

xiūgǎi 修改 [compound: 修 *repair* + 改 *alter*] VERB = amend, revise
■ 这份报告要修改一下，再送董事会。**Zhè fèn bàogào yào xiūgǎi yíxià, zài sòng dǒngshìhuì.** = *This report needs some revision before being submitted to the board of directors.*

xiūlǐ 修理 VERB = repair, fix
■ 自行车坏了，你会修理吗？**Zìxíngchē huài le, nǐ huì xiūlǐ ma?** = *The bike is broken. Can you fix it?*
■ 这台机器很旧了，不值得再修理了。**Zhè tái jīqì hěn jiù le, bù zhídé zài xiūlǐ le.** = *This machine is very old and is not worth repairing any more.*

xiū 休 NOUN = leisure

xiūxi 休息 [compound: 休 *leisure* + 息 *pause*] VERB = rest, take a rest, have a day off
■ 我们工作了两个小时了，休息一会儿吧。**Wǒmen gōngzuòle liǎng ge xiǎoshí le, xiūxi yíhuìr ba.** = *We've been working for over two hours. Let's take a break.*
■ 我感到很疲劳，需要休息几天。**Wǒ gǎndao hěn píláo, xūyào xiūxi jǐtiān.** = *I feel worn out. I need a few days' rest.*

xiù 秀 ADJECTIVE = elegant (See 优秀 **yōuxiù**.)

xiù 袖 NOUN = sleeve (See 领袖 **lǐngxiù**.)

xū 须 Trad 須 MODAL VERB = must (See 必须 **bìxū**.)

xū 虚 ADJECTIVE = void

xūxīn 虚心 [modif: 虚 *empty* + 心 *the heart*] ADJECTIVE = open-minded and modest
■ 我们虚心地请您提意见。**Wǒmen xūxīn de qǐng nín tí yìjian.** = *We sincerely request your comments.*
■ 他很不虚心，总是认为自己了不起。**Tā hěn bù xūxīn, zǒngshi rènwéi zìjǐ liǎobuqǐ.** = *He is very arrogant, always thinking himself terrific.*

X

xū 需 VERB = need

xūyào 需要 [compound: 需 *need* + 要 *want*]
VERB = need, be in need of
■ 我需要一本中文词典。**Wǒ xūyào yì běn Zhōngwén cídiǎn.** = *I need a Chinese dictionary.*
■ "你有什么需要，可以跟我说。" "谢谢，没有什么需要。" **"Nǐ yǒu shénme xūyào, kěyǐ gēn wǒ shuō." "Xièxie, méiyǒu shénme xūyào."** = *"If there's anything you need, let me know." "Thank you, but there's nothing I need."*

xǔ 许 Trad 許 VERB = same as **允许 yúnxǔ**

xǔduō 许多 [compound: 许 *approximate* + 多 *many, much*] ADJECTIVE = many, much
■ 妈妈买回来许多好吃的东西。**Māma mǎi huílai xǔduō hǎochī de dōngxi.** = *Mom bought lots of delicious food.*

xù 序 NOUN = sequence, order (See 秩序 **zhìxù.**)

xù 续 Trad 續 VERB = continue (See 继续 **jìxù,** 连续 **liánxù,** 陆续 **lùxù,** 手续 **shǒuxù.**)

xù 绪 Trad 緒 NOUN = mood (See 情绪 **qíngxù.**)

xuān 宣 VERB = declare

xuānbù 宣布 VERB = declare, announce
■ 校长在大会上宣布了对他的处分。**Xiàozhǎng zài dàhuì shang xuānbùle duì tā de chǔfèn.** = *At the assembly the principal announced the disciplinary action against him.*

xuānchuán 宣传 [compound: 宣 *announce* + 传 *spread*]
1 VERB = disseminate, publicize
■ 卫生部正在大力宣传吸烟的害处。**Wèishēngbù zhèngzài dàlì xuānchuán xīyān de hàichu.** = *The Ministry of Health is making efforts to disseminate information regarding the harm that smoking does.*
2 NOUN = dissemination of information, propaganda
■ 这完全是宣传，不能相信。**Zhè wánquán shì xuānchuán, bù néng xiāngxìn.** = *This is propaganda, pure and simple. You mustn't believe it.*

xuǎn 选 Trad 選 VERB
1 = same as 选举 **xuǎnjǔ**
2 = select, choose
■ 不同牌子的电视机都差不多，很难选。**Bùtóng páizi de diànshìjī dōu chàbuduō, hěn nán xuǎn.** = *TV sets of different brands are more or less the same; it is difficult to select one.*

xuǎnjǔ 选举 [compound: 选 *select* + 举 *recommend*]
1 VERB = elect, vote
■ 我们下午选举班长。**Wǒmen xiàwǔ xuǎnjǔ bānzhǎng.** = *We're going to elect a class monitor this afternoon.*
2 NOUN = election, voting
■ 参加大会的代表必须由选举产生。**Cānjiā dàhuì de dàibiǎo bìxū yóu xuǎnjǔ chǎnshēng.** = *The delegates to the congress must be chosen by election.*

xuǎnzé 选择 [compound: 选 *select* + 择 *choose*]
1 VERB = select, choose
■ 人生的道路要自己选择。**Rénshēng de dàolù yào zìjǐ xuǎnzé.** = *One should decide for oneself what kind of life to lead.*
2 NOUN = choice
■ 我们除此以外，别无选择。**Wǒmen chú cǐ yǐwài, bié wú xuǎnzé.** = *We have no choice but to do this.*

xué 学 Trad 學 VERB = learn, study
■ "你在大学学什么？" "学电脑。" **"Nǐ zài dàxué xué shénme?" "Xué diànnǎo."** = *"What do you study at university?" "Computing science."*
■ 活到老，学到老。**Huó dào lǎo, xué dào lǎo.** = *One should keep learning as long as one lives.*

xué fèi 学费 [modif: 学 *study* + 费 *fee*] NOUN = tuition, tuition fee
■ 你们学校国际学生的学费是多少？**Nǐmen xuéxiào guójì xuésheng de xué fèi shì duōshǎo?** = *How much is the tuition fee for international students in your school?*

xuéqī 学期 [modif: 学 *study* + 期 *period*] NOUN = semester, term
■ 中国的学校一般分上学期和下学期两个学

X

期。**Zhōngguó de xuéxiào yìbān fēn shàng xuéqī he xià xuéqī liǎng ge xuéqī.** = *Chinese schools generally have two terms: the first term and the second term.*

xuésheng 学生 [modif: 学 *study* + 生 *scholar*]
NOUN = student, pupil (个 ge, 名 míng)
■ "这个班有多少学生?" "三十二个。"
"Zhège bān yǒu duōshǎo xuésheng?"
"Sānshí'èr ge." = *"How many students are there in this class?" "Thirty-two."*

xuéwèn 学问 [compound: 学 *study* + 问 *ask*]
NOUN = learning, knowledge
■ 这位老教授很有学问。**Zhè wèi lǎo jiàoshòu hěn yǒu xuéwèn.** = *This old professor has a great deal of learning.*

xuéxí 学习 [compound: 学 *learn* + 习 *practice*]
1 VERB = study, learn
■ 年轻的时候，应该多学习些知识。
Niánqíng de shíhou, yīnggāi duō xuéxí xiē zhīshi. = *One should learn lots of knowledge when young.*
■ 学生不但从书本中学习，而且在社会上学习。**Xuésheng búdan cóng shūběn zhong xuéxí, érqiě zài shèhuì shang xuéxí.** = *A student learns not only from books but also from society.*
xiàng ... xuéxí 向 ... 学习 = learn from ..., emulate ...
■ 你工作很认真，我要向你学习。**Nǐ gōngzuò hěn rènzhēn, wǒ yào xiàng nǐ xuéxí.** = *You work conscientiously. I must emulate you.*
2 NOUN = study
■ 学生应该把学习放在第一位。**Xuésheng yīnggāi bǎ xuéxí fàng zai dì-yī wèi.** = *Students should give priority to their studies.*

xuéxiào 学校 [compound: 学 *study* + 校 *school*] NOUN = school (座 zuò)
■ 王老师每天八点前就到学校来了。**Wáng lǎoshī měi tiān bā diǎn qián jiù dào xuéxiào lái le.** = *Teacher Wang comes to school before eight o'clock every day.*
■ 市政府去年新建了两座学校。**Shì zhèngfǔ qùnián xīn jiànle liàng zuò xuéxiào.** = *The city government built two schools last year.*

xuéyuàn 学院 [compound: 学 *study* + 院 *place (for certain activities)*] NOUN = college, institute
■ 在中国有些高等学校叫"学院"，例如"教育学院"。**Zài Zhōngguó yǒuxiē gāoděng xuéxiào jiào "xuéyuàn", lìrú "jiàoyù xuéyuàn".** = *In China some institutions of higher learning are called "college," for example "college of education."*

xuě 血 NOUN = blood
■ 流了一点血，不要紧。**Liúle yìdiǎn xuě, bú yàojǐn.** = *It's just a little bleeding, nothing serious.*

xuěyè 血液 [modif: 血 *blood* + 液 *liquid*] NOUN = blood (as a technical term)
■ 你要化验血液。**Nǐ yào huàyàn xuěyè.** = *You should have your blood tested.*

xuě 雪 NOUN = snow
■ "香港冬天下雪吗?" "不下。" **"Xiānggǎng dōngtiān xià xuě ma?" "Bú xià."** = *In Hong Kong, does it snow in winter?" "No."*
xuě bái 雪白 = snow-white
xià xuě 下雪 = to snow

xún 寻 Trad 尋 VERB = seek

xúnzhǎo 寻找 [compound: 寻 *seek* + 找 *look for*] VERB = look for, seek
■ 他家的猫不见了，他们正在到处寻找。**Tā jiā de māo bú jiàn le, tāmen zhèngzài dàochù xúnzhǎo.** = *Their cat has disappeared, and they are looking for it everywhere.*

xùn 讯 Trad 訊 NOUN = message (See 通讯 tōngxùn.)

xùn 迅 ADJECTIVE = rapid

xùnsù 迅速 [compound: 迅 *rapid, speedy* + 速 *swift*] ADJECTIVE = rapid, speedy, swift
■ 这件事很急，要迅速处理。**Zhè jiàn shì hěn jí, yào xùnsù chǔlǐ.** = *This is an urgent matter, and should be dealt with without delay.*

xùn 训 Trad 訓 VERB = train

xùnliàn 训练 [compound: 训 *train* + 练 *practice*] VERB = train

X

■全国运动会快开了，运动员正在紧张训练。**Quánguó yùndònghuì kuài kāi le, yùndàngyuán zhèngzài jǐnzhāng xùnliàn.** = *The national games will be held soon. Athletes are engaged in intense training.*

Y

yā 压 Trad 壓 VERB = press, push down
■这纸盒不能压。**Zhè zhǐhé bù néng yā.** = *This paper box mustn't be crushed.*
yājià 压价 = undersell
yālì 压力 = pressure

yāpò 压迫 [compound: 压 *press* + 迫 *force, compel*]
1 VERB = oppress
■在有些国家，妇女仍然受到压迫。**Zài yǒuxiē guójiā, fùnǚ réngrán shòudao yāpò.** = *In some countries, women still suffer from oppression.*
2 NOUN = oppression
■有压迫，就有反抗。**Yǒu yāpò, jiùyǒu fǎnkàng.** = *Where there is oppression, there is resistance.*

yā 呀 INTERJECTION = oh, ah (expressing surprise)
■呀，这不是约翰吗，没想到在这里见到你！**Yā, zhè bú shì Yuēhàn ma, méi xiǎngdào zài zhèli jiàndào nǐ!** = *Oh, isn't it John? Fancy seeing you here!*
■呀，你还会说上海话！**Yā, nǐ hái huì shuō Shànghǎi huà!** = *Oh, you also speak the Shanghai dialect!*

yá 牙 NOUN = tooth, teeth
■我牙疼。**Wǒ yá téng.** = *I have a toothache.*
yáyī 牙医 = dentist

yágāo 牙膏 [modif: 牙 *tooth* + 膏 *paste, cream*] NOUN = toothpaste
■有这么多种牙膏，不知道该选哪一种。**Yǒu zhème duō zhǒng yágāo, bù zhīdào gāi xuǎn nǎ yì zhǒng.** = *There are so many brands of toothpaste, I don't known which one to choose.*

yáshuā 牙刷 [modif: 牙 *tooth* + 刷 *brush*] NOUN = toothbrush (把 **bǎ**)
■我忘了带牙刷，要买一把。**Wǒ wàngle dài yáshuā, yào mǎi yì bǎ.** = *I forgot to bring my toothbrush. I need to buy one.*

yà 亚 Trad 亞

Yàzhōu 亚洲 [modif: 亚 *Asia* + 洲 *continent*] NOUN = Asia
■亚洲是世界上最大的一个洲。**Yàzhōu shì shìjiè shang zuì dà de yí ge zhōu.** = *Asia is the largest continent in the world.*

ya 呀 PARTICLE = same as **ā** 啊 2 PARTICLE. Used after *a, e, i, o, u.*
■这个苹果真大呀！**Zhège píngguǒ zhēn dà ya!** = *How big this apple is!*

yán 严 Trad 嚴 ADJECTIVE = strict, severe

yángé 严格
1 ADJECTIVE = strict, stringent, rigorous
■在中国的传统中，一位严格的老师才是好老师。**Zài Zhōngguó de chuántǒng zhong, yí wèi yángé de lǎoshī cái shì hǎo lǎoshī.** = *In the Chinese tradition, only a strict teacher was a good one.*
2 VERB = make ... strict, make ... stringent
■工厂决定严格产品质量检查制度。**Gōngchǎng juédìng yángé chǎnpǐn zhìliàng jiǎnchá zhìdù.** = *The factory has decided to make the product quality control system more stringent.*

yánsù 严肃 [compound: 严 *severe* + 肃 *solemn*] ADJECTIVE = serious, solemn
■李校长为什么总是这么严肃？**Lǐ xiàozhǎng wèishénme zǒngshì zhème yánsù?** = *Why does Mr Li, the principal, always look so serious?*

yánzhòng 严重 [compound: 严 *severe* + 重 *weighty*] ADJECTIVE = serious, critical
■这是一个严重的问题，必须认真对付。**Zhè shì yí ge yánzhòng de wèntí, bìxū rènzhēn duìfu.** = *This is a serious problem and must be dealt with earnestly.*
■她的病情很严重。**Tā de bìngqíng hěn yánzhòng.** = *She is critically ill.*

yán 延 VERB = extend

yáncháng 延长 [v+comp: 延 *extend* + 长 *long*] VERB = prolong, extend
■ 会议延长两天。**Huìyì yáncháng liǎng tiān.** = *The conference was extended two more days.*

yán 言 NOUN = speech (See 语言 **yǔyán**.)

yán 沿 PREPOSITION = along
■ 沿街有很多小商店。**Yán jiē yǒu hěn duō xiǎo shāngdiàn.** = *There are numerous small shops along the street.*
■ 你沿着公园一直走，就到市中心了。**Nǐ yánzhe gōngyuán yì zhí zǒu, jiù dào shìzhōngxīn le.** = *Walk along the park and you will get to the city center.*

yán 研 VERB = study, research

yánjiū 研究 [compound: 研 *research* + 究 *investigate*]
1 VERB = research, study, consider carefully
■ 科学家们正在研究一种新药。**Kēxuéjiāmen zhèngzài yánjiū yì zhǒng xīn yào.** = *Scientists are researching a new medicine.*
■ 公司已经研究了你的计划，认为是可行的。**Gōngsī yǐjīng yánjiūle nǐ de jìhuà, rènwéi shì kěxíng de.** = *The company has considered your plan carefully and believes it is feasible.*
2 NOUN = research, study
■ 这个问题需要好好研究。**Zhège wèntí xūyào hǎohǎo yánjiū.** = *A great deal of study is needed on this problem.*
yánjiūshēng 研究生 = graduate student, post-graduate student
yánjiūshēng yuàn 研究生院 = graduate school (of a university)
yánjiū suǒ 研究所 = research institute, research unit
yánjiūyuàn 研究院 = research institute

yán 盐 Trad 鹽 NOUN = salt
■ 我吃得比较淡，你菜里少放点盐。**Wǒ chī de bǐjiào dàn, nǐ cài li shǎo fàng diǎn yán.** = *I prefer my food to be bland. Please don't put too much salt in the dish.*

yán 颜 NOUN = complexion

yánsè 颜色 [compound: 颜 *complexion* + 色 *color*] NOUN = color
■ "你最喜欢什么颜色？""蓝颜色。" **"Nǐ zuì**

xǐhuan shénme yánsè?" "Lán yánsè."** = *"What's your favorite color?" "Blue."*
■ 我们有各种颜色的墙纸。**Wǒmen yǒu gè zhǒng yánsè de qiángzhǐ.** = *We have wallpaper in various colors.*

yǎn 眼 NOUN = eye
yǎnkē yīshēng 眼科医生 = ophthalmologist
zuǒyǎn 左眼 = the left eye
yòuyǎn 右眼 = the right eye

yǎnjìng 眼镜 [modif: 眼 *eye* + 镜 *mirror*] NOUN = glasses, spectacles (副 **fù**)
■ 那位戴眼镜的先生是谁？**Nà wèi dài yǎnjìng de xiānsheng shì shuí?** = *Who is the gentleman wearing glasses over there?*
yǎnjìngdiàn 眼镜店 = optician's shop
yǎnjìnghé 眼镜盒 = glasses case
tàiyang yǎnjìng 太阳眼镜 = sunglasses

yǎnjing 眼睛 [compound: 眼 *eye* + 睛 *eyeball*] NOUN = eye
■ 打电脑的时间太长，我的眼睛累了。**Dǎ diànnǎo de shíjiān tài cháng, wǒ de yǎnjing lèi le.** = *I've been working on the computer for too long; my eyes are tired.*

yǎnlèi 眼泪 [modif: 眼 *eye* + 泪 *tear*] NOUN = tear (滴 **dī**)
■ 她用手绢擦眼泪。**Tā yòng shǒujuàn cā yǎnlèi.** = *She wiped the tears away with her handkerchief.*

yǎnqián 眼前 NOUN
1 = before one's eyes
■ 那件交通事故就发生在他眼前。**Nà jiàn jiāotōng shìgù jiù fāshēng zài tā yǎnqián.** = *The road accident happened right in front of him.*
2 = at present, at this moment
■ 眼前我们有些困难，但很快能克服的。**Yǎnqián wǒmen yǒuxiē kùnnan, dàn hěn kuài néng kèfú de.** = *At present we have some difficulties, but they can be overcome very soon.*

yǎn 演 VERB
1 = act, perform, show
■ 他很会演戏。**Tā hěn huì yǎn xì.** = *He is good at acting.*
2 = show (a film)
■ 今天电影院演什么电影？**Jīntiān**

Y

diànyǐngyuàn yǎn shénme diànyǐng? = *What movies are being shown at the cinema today?*

yǎnchū 演出

1 VERB = put on a theatrical performance, perform
■ 这次音乐会有两位有名的歌唱家演出。**Zhè cì yīnyuèhuì yǒu liǎng wèi yǒumíng de gēchàngjiā yǎnchū.** = *Two well-known singers will perform at the concert.*
■ 他们将在全国各大城市演出。**Tāmen jiāng zài quánguó gè dà chéngshì yǎnchū.** = *They will perform in big cities throughout the country.*
2 NOUN = theatrical performance
■ 他们的演出精彩极了！ **Tāmen de yǎnchū jīngcǎi jíle.** = *How wonderful their performance was!*
■ 昨天晚上的演出让人失望。**Zuótiān wǎnshang de yǎnchū ràng rén shīwàng.** = *The performance last night was disappointing.*

yǎnyuán 演员 [modif: 演 *act* + 员 *person*]
NOUN = actor, actress
■ 在中国要当演员一定要会说标准的普通话。**Zài Zhōngguó yào dāng yǎnyuán yídìng yào huì shuō biāozhǔn de Pǔtōnghuà.** = *In China if one wants to be an actor one must be able to speak standard Putonghua.*

yàn 厌 Trad 厭 VERB = detest (See 讨厌 tǎoyàn.)

yàn 咽 VERB = swallow
■ 我要喝一点水，才能把药片咽下去。**Wǒ yào hē yìdiǎn shuǐ, cái néng bǎ yàopiàn yàn xiàqu.** = *I must drink a bit of water to be able to swallow the pill.*

yàn 宴 NOUN = feast

yànhuì 宴会 [modif: 宴 *feast* + 会 *meet*] NOUN
= banquet, feast
■ 他们回国以前，举行了告别宴会。**Tāmen huíguó yǐqián, jǔxíngle gàobié yànhuì.** = *Before returning to their country, they gave a farewell banquet.*
■ 明天晚上我要去参加朋友的结婚宴会。**Míngtiān wǎnshang wǒ yào qù cānjiā péngyou de jiéhūn yànhuì.** = *Tomorrow night I'll be attending a friend's wedding banquet.*

cānjiā yànhuì 参加宴会 = attend a banquet
gàobié yànhuì 告别宴会 = farewell banquet.
huānyíng yànhuì 欢迎宴会 = welcome banquet
jiéhūn yànhuì 结婚宴会 = wedding banquet

yàn 验 Trad 驗 VERB = examine (See 测验 cèyàn, 经验 jīngyàn, 实验 shíyàn, 试验 shìyàn.)

yáng 羊 NOUN = sheep, goat, lamb (头 tóu)
■ 春天是生小羊的时候。**Chūntián shì shēng xiǎoyáng de shíhou.** = *Spring is the lambing season.*
yángmáo 羊毛 = wool
yángpí 羊皮 = sheepskin
shānyáng 山羊 = goat
xiǎoyáng 小羊 = lamb
yángròu 羊肉 = mutton

yáng 阳 Trad 陽 NOUN = what is open, overt, masculine, the sun

yángguāng 阳光 [modif: 阳 *the sun* + 光 *light*] NOUN = sunshine, sunlight
■ 这里的阳光太强了。**Zhèli de yángguāng tài qiáng le.** = *The sunshine here is too intense.*

yáng 扬 Trad 揚 VERB = raise, make known (See 表扬 biǎoyáng, 发扬 fāyáng.)

yáng 洋 NOUN = ocean (See 大洋洲 Dàyángzhōu, 海洋 hǎiyáng.)

yǎng 养 Trad 養 VERB
1 = provide for, support
■ 爸爸妈妈辛辛苦苦地工作，把我养大。**Bàba māma xīn-xīn-kǔ-kǔ de gōngzuò, bǎ wǒ yǎng dà.** = *Dad and mom worked hard to provide for me.*
2 = raise, keep as pet
■ 我一直想养一只狗。**Wǒ yìzhí xiǎng yǎng yì zhī gǒu.** = *I have always wanted to have a dog.*

yàng 样 Trad 樣 MEASURE WORD = kind, category, type
■ 他做了几样菜，招待朋友。**Tā zuòle jǐ yàng cài, zhāodài péngyou.** = *He prepared several dishes to entertain his friends.*

yàngzi 样子 NOUN = appearance, manner
■ 几年不见，你还是以前的样子。**Jǐ nián bú**

Y

jiàn, nǐ hái shì yǐqián de yàngzi. = *It's been years since I last saw you and you still look the same as before.*

yāoqiú 要求 [compound: 要 ask + 求 request]

1 VERB = ask, demand, require
■ 老师要求我们每天都读课文。**Lǎoshī yāoqiú wǒmen měi tiān dōu dù kèwén.** = *The teacher requires us to read the texts everyday.*
■ 市场要求我们不断开发新产品。**Shìchǎng yāoqiú wǒmen búduàn kāifā xīn chǎnpǐn.** = *The market demands that we constantly develop new products.*

2 NOUN = demand, requirement
■ 我想提两个要求，可以吗？ **Wǒ xiǎng tí liǎng ge yāoqiú, kěyǐ ma?** = *May I make two demands?*
■ 我们尽量满足顾客的要求。**Wǒmen jìnliàng mǎnzú gùkè de yāoqiú.** = *We try our best to meet our clients' demands.*

yāo 腰 NOUN = waist, small of the back
■ 她胖得没有腰。**Tā pàng de méiyǒu yāo.** = *She is so fat that she has no waist.*

yāo 邀 VERB = invite

yāoqǐng 邀请 [compound: 邀 invite + 请 ask]

1 VERB = invite
■ 他邀请很多朋友来参加他的二十一岁生日宴会。**Tā yāoqǐng hěn duō péngyou lái cānjiā tā de èrshíyī suì shēngrì yànhuì.** = *He invited many friends to his twenty-first birthday dinner party.*

2 NOUN = invitation
■ 我昨天发出了邀请，他们大约明天会收到。**Wǒ zuótiān fāchūle yāoqǐng, tāmen dàyuē míngtiān huì shōudao.** = *I sent the invitation yesterday, and they'll probably receive it tomorrow.*
yāoqǐngxìn 邀请信 = letter of invitation

yáo 摇 VERB = shake, wave
■ 点头表示同意，摇头表示反对。**Diǎntóu biǎoshì tóngyì, yáo tóu biǎoshì bù tóngyì.** = *Nodding the head indicates agreement and shaking the head signals disagreement.*

yǎo 咬 VERB = bite
■ 我给蚊子咬了一口。**Wǒ gěi wénzi yǎole yì kǒu.** = *I was bitten by a mosquito.*

yào 药 Trad 藥 NOUN = medicine, drug
■ 这种药你一天吃两次，每次吃一片。**Zhè zhǒng yào nǐ yì tiān chī liǎng cì, měi cì chī yí piàn.** = *You should take this medicine twice a day, one pill each time.*
■ 现在还没有药治这种病。**Xiànzài hái méiyǒu yào zhì zhè zhǒng bìng.** = *At present there is no medicine that cures this disease.*
yàofáng 药房 = pharmacist's, pharmacy
yàopiàn 药片 = pill
yàoshuǐ 药水 = liquid medicine
cǎoyào 草药 = herbal medicine
chī yào 吃药 = take medicine
xīyào 西药 = western medicine
zhōngyào 中药 = traditional Chinese medicine

yào 要 VERB

1 VERB = want, would like
■ 我要一间安静的房间。**Wǒ yào yì jiān ānjìng de fángjiān.** = *I want a quiet room.*

2 VERB = ask (somebody to do something)
■ 我哥哥要我问你好。**Wǒ gēge yào wǒ wèn nǐ hǎo.** = *My brother asked me to give you his regards.*

3 MODAL VERB = should, must
■ 你想学好中文，就要多听，多讲。**Nǐ xiǎng xuéhǎo Zhōngwén, jiù yào duō tīng, duō jiǎng.** = *If you want to learn Chinese well, you should listen more and speak more.*

yàojǐn 要紧 ADJECTIVE = important, urgent, serious
■ 考试的时候，最要紧的是看清考题。**Kǎoshì de shíhou, zuì yàojǐn de shì kànqīng kǎotí.** = *The most important thing at examinations is to understand the question clearly.*
búyàojǐn 不要紧 = it doesn't matter
■ "对不起。""不要紧。" **"Duìbuqǐ." "Búyàojǐn."** = *"I'm sorry." "It doesn't matter."*

yàoshì 要是 CONJUNCTION = if
■ 要是你明天不能来，请给我打个电话。**Yàoshì nǐ míngtiān bù néng lái, qǐng gěi wǒ dǎ ge diànhuà.** = *If you're not able to come tomorrow, please give me a call.*

NOTE: Both 如果 **rúguǒ** and 要是 **yàoshì** mean *if*. While 如果 **rúguǒ** is for general use, 要是 **yàoshì** is a colloquialism.

yào 钥 Trad 鑰

yàoshi 钥匙 NOUN = key (把 bǎ)
- 钥匙一定要放好。**Yàoshi yídìng yào fànghǎo.** = *You must keep the keys in a safe place.*

yé 爷 Trad 爺 NOUN = paternal grandfather

yéye 爷爷 NOUN = same as 祖父 **zǔfù**. Used in colloquial Chinese.

yě 也 ADJECTIVE
1 = also, too
- 我喜欢打球，也喜欢游泳。**Wǒ xǐhuan dǎ qiú, yě xǐhuan yóuyǒng.** = *I like ball games, and I also like swimming.*
- 你想去北京学习，我也想去北京学习。**Nǐ xiǎng qù Běijīng xuéxí, wǒ yě xiǎng qù Běijīng xuéxí.** = *You want to study in Beijing, so do I.*
2 = neither, nor
- 你没有看过这个电影，我也没看过这个电影。**Nǐ méiyǒu kànguo zhège diànyǐng, wǒ yě méi kànguo zhège diànyǐng.** = *You haven't seen this movie, nor have I.*

yěxǔ 也许 ADVERB = perhaps, maybe
- 天上有大块的云，也许会下雨。**Tiān shang yǒu dà kuài de yún, yěxǔ huì xiàyǔ.** = *It's very cloudy. Perhaps it'll rain.*
- "他今天会给我们发电子邮件吗？""也许。"**"Tā jīntiān huì gěi wǒmen fā diànzǐ yóujiàn ma?" "Yěxǔ."** = *"Will he send us an e-mail today?" "Perhaps."*

NOTE: See note on 恐怕 **kǒngpà**.

yě 野 ADJECTIVE = open country (See 田野 **tiányě**.)

yè 业 Trad 業 NOUN = industry

yèwù 业务 [compound: 业 *occupation* + 务 *business*] NOUN
1 = professional work, vocational work
- 她业务水平很强。**Tā yèwù shuǐpíng hěn qiáng.** = *She is very efficient professionally.*
2 = business
- 公司的业务开展很顺利。**Gōngsī de yèwù kāizhǎn hěn shùnlì.** = *The business of the company has developed smoothly.*

yèyú 业余 ADJECTIVE = spare time, amateur
- 你业余时间做什么？**Nǐ yèyú shíjiān zuò shénme?** = *What do you do in your spare time?*
- 他是一位中学老师，也是业余音乐家。**Tā shì yí wèi zhōngxué lǎoshī, yě shì yèyú yīnyuèjiā.** = *He is a high school teacher and also an amateur musician.*

yè 叶 Trad 葉 NOUN = leaf

yèzi 叶子 [suffix: 叶 *leaf* + 子 nominal suffix] NOUN = leaf (片 **piàn**)
- 秋天，叶子都黄了。**Qiūtiān, yèzi dōu huáng le.** = *In autumn, leaves turn yellow.*

yè 页 Trad 頁 NOUN = page
- 这本词典有三百多页。**Zhè běn cídiǎn yǒu sānbǎi duō yè.** = *This dictionary has over three hundred pages.*
- 请把书翻到二十页。**Qǐng bǎ shū fān dào èrshí yè.** = *Please turn to page twenty of your book.*

yè 夜 NOUN = night, evening
- 他昨夜十一点钟才回家。**Tā zuó yè shíyī diǎnzhōng cái huíjiā.** = *Last night she returned home as late as eleven o'clock.*
- yèbān 夜班 = night shift
- yèchē 夜车 = night train
- bànyè 半夜 = midnight

yèli 夜里 NOUN = at night
- 这条大街也车辆不断。**Zhè tiáo dàjiē yèli yě chēliàng bú duàn.** = *There is constant traffic on this main street even at night.*
- 这个人喜欢白天睡觉，夜里工作，是个"夜猫子"。**Zhège rén xǐhuan báitiān shuìjiào, yèli gōngzuò, shì ge "yè māozi".** = *This person likes sleeping in the day and working at night, just like an owl.*

yèwǎn 夜晚 NOUN = same as 夜里 **yèlǐ**

yè 液 NOUN = liquid, fluid (See 血液 **xuèyè**.)

yī 一 NUMERAL = one
- 一万一千一百十一 **yíwàn yìqiān yìbǎi shíyī** = *eleven thousand, one hundred and eleven*

NOTES: (1) 一 undergoes tone changes (tone sandhi). When standing alone, 一 is pronounced with the first tone, i.e. **yī**. When followed by a sound in the fourth tone, 一

changes to the second tone, e.g. 一定 **yídìng**.
一 is pronounced in the fourth tone in all other
circumstances, e.g. 一般 **yìbān**, 一同 **yìtóng**,
一起 **yìqǐ**. Pay attention to the various tones
of 一 here and in following words. (2) When
saying a number (e.g. a telephone number)
people pronounce 一 as **yāo** for clarity, e.g.
■ 我的电话号码是五八一三九。**Wǒ de
diànhuà hàomá shì wǔ-bā-yāo-sān-jiǔ.** = *My
telephone number is 58139.*

yī … jiù … 一 … 就 … CONJUNCTION = as soon
as, no sooner … than …
■ 妈妈一回家, 就做晚饭。**Māma yì huíjiā, jiù
zuò wǎnfàn.** = *Mom cooks supper as soon as
she gets back home.*
■ 我一上火车, 车就开了。**Wǒ yí shàng
huǒchē, chē jiù kāi le.** = *No sooner did I board
the train than it started.*

yī 衣 NOUN = clothing

yīfu 衣服 [compound: 衣 *clothing* + 服
clothing] NOUN = clothes, a piece of clothing
(件 jiàn)
■ 她每年化很多钱买衣服。**Tā měi nián huā
hěn duō qián mǎi yīfu.** = *She spends lots of
money every year buying clothes.*
■ 她很会穿衣服。**Tā hěn huì chuān yīfu.** = *She
has good dress sense.*

NOTE: 衣服 **yīfu** may denote *clothes* or *a piece
of clothing*. 一件衣服 **yí jiàn yīfu** may be a
jacket, a coat, a dress or a sweater, but not a
pair of trousers, which is 一条裤子 **yì tiáo
kùzi.**

yī 医 Trad 醫 VERB = heal, cure

yīshēng 医生 [modif: 医 *medicine* + 生
scholar] NOUN = medical doctor (位 wèi)
■ 你要听医生的话。**Nǐ yào tīng yīshēng de
huà.** = *You should follow the doctor's advice.*
■ 我们的家庭医生是张医生。**Wǒmen de
jiātíng yīshēng shì Zhāng yīshēng.** = *Our family physician is Dr Zhang.*

yīwùshì 医务室 [modif: 医 *medical* + 务
affair + 室 *room*] NOUN = clinic (in a school,
factory, etc.)
■ 我们学校的医务室只有一位护士。**Wǒmen**

xuéxiào de yīwùshì zhǐyǒu yí wèi hùshi. =
There is only a nurse in our school clinic.

yīxué 医学 [modif: 医 *medical* + 学 *study*]
NOUN = medical science, medicine
■ 医学正在经历一场革命。**Yīxué zhèngzài
jīnglì yì chǎng gémìng.** = *Medical science is
experiencing a revolution.*
yīxuéyuàn 医学院 = medical school

yīyuàn 医院 [modif: 医 *medicine* + 院 *place
(for certain activities)*] NOUN = hospital (座
zuò)
■ 马上送医院! **Mǎshàng sòng yīyuàn!** = *Take
him to the hospital right now!*
■ 请问, 最近的医院在哪儿? **Qǐng wèn, zuì
jìn de yīyuàn zài nǎr?** = *Excuse me, where is
the nearest hospital?*
sòng … qù yīyuàn 送 … 去医院 = take … to the
hospital
zhù (yī) yuàn 住(医)院 = be hospitalized
■ 他病得很重, 得住医院。**Tā bìng de hěn
zhòng, děi zhù yīyuàn.** = *He's seriously ill and
has to be hospitalized.*

yī 依 VERB = rely on

yīkào 依靠 [compound: 依 *rely on* + 靠 *lean
on*] VERB = rely on, depend on
■ 公司的成功依靠全体职工的努力。**Gōngsī
de chénggōng yào yīkào quántǐ zhígōng de
nǔlì.** = *The success of the company depends on
the efforts of all staff.*

yíbàn 一半 NOUN = half, one half
■ 他一半时间念书, 一半时间做工。**Tā yíbàn
shíjiān niànshū, yíbàn shíjiān zuògōng.** = *He
spends half his time studying and the other half
working.*

yídào 一道 ADVERB = same as 一起 **yìqǐ**

yídìng 一定 ADJECTIVE
1 = fixed, specified
■ 他吃饭没有一定的时间。**Tā chīfàn méiyǒu
yídìng de shíjiān.** = *He has no fixed mealtimes.*
2 = to a certain degree, fair, limited
■ 你的中文已经达到了一定水平。**Nǐ de
Zhōngwén yǐjīng dádàole yídìng shuǐpíng.** =
*You've already reached a certain level of profi-
ciency in Chinese.*

3 = certainly, definitely
- 我们的目标一定能达到。**Wǒmen de mùbiāo yídìng néng dádào.** = *We can certainly reach our goal.*

yígòng 一共 ADJECTIVE = in all, total, altogether
- 你们学校一共有多少学生？ **Nǐmen xuéxiào yígòng yǒu duōshǎo xuésheng?** = *How many students are there altogether in your school?* (→ *What is the total number of students in your school?*)
- 我们去年一共学了五百二十个汉字。 **Wǒmen qùnián yígòng xuéle wǔbǎi érshí ge Hànzì.** = *Last year we learned 520 Chinese characters in total.*

yíhuìr 一会儿 ADVERB = in a very short time, in a moment
- 不用麻烦倒茶，我一会儿就走。 **Bú yòng máfan dào chá, wǒ yíhuìr jiù zǒu.** = *Please don't bother making tea. I'll be leaving in a moment.*
- 他只休息了一会儿，就又干起来了。 **Tā zhǐ xiūxile yíhuìr, jiù yòu gàn qǐlai le.** = *He took only a brief break and started working again.*
- 昨天的电视我只看了一会儿。 **Zuótiān de diànshì wǒ zhǐ kànle yíhuìr.** = *Yesterday I watched TV for a very short time only.*

yíkuàir 一块儿 ADVERB = same as 一起 **yìqǐ.** Tends to be used in colloquial Chinese.

yíqiè 一切
1 ADJECTIVE = all, every and each without exception
- 一切工作都做完了，才能放假。 **Yíqiè gōngzuò dōu zuòwánle, cái néng fàngjià.** = *You can have your holiday only all the work is done.*
- 出国的一切手续都办完，要多长时间？ **Chūguó de yíqiè shǒuxù dōu bànwán yào duō cháng shíjiān?** = *How long will it take to go through all the formalities for going abroad?*
2 PRONOUN = all, everything
- 我了解她的一切。 **Wǒ liáojiě tā de yíqiè.** = *I know everything about her.*
- 他做的一切都是为了赚更多的钱。 **Tā zuò de yíqiè dōushì wèile zhuàn gèng duō de qián.** = *Everything he does, he does to make more money.*

yíxià 一下 ADVERB = (used after a verb to indicate the action is done briefly or casually)
- 请您等一下，王先生马上就来。 **Qǐng nín děng yíxià, Wáng xiānsheng mǎshàng jiù lái.** = *Please wait for a while. Mr Wang will be here in a moment.*

NOTE: It is very common in spoken Chinese to use 一下 **yíxià** after a verb, especially as an informal request. Some Northern Chinese speakers use 一下儿 **yíxiàr** instead of 一下 **yíxià**. More examples:
- 请您来一下儿。 **Qǐng nín lái yíxiàr.** = *Please come over for a while.*
- 我们在这里停一下儿吧。 **Wǒmen zài zhèli tíng yíxiàr ba.** = *Let's stop here for a while.*
- 让我想一下儿再回答。 **Ràng wǒ xiǎng yíxiàr zài huídá.** = *Let me think a while before I answer.*

yíxiàzi 一下子 ADVER = all at once, all at a sudden
- 这么多事一下子做不完，明天再做吧。 **Zhème duō shì yíxiàzi zuò bu wán, míngtiān zài zuò ba.** = *We can't finish so many things at once. Let's continue tomorrow.*

yíyàng 一样 ADJECTIVE = same, identical
- "一下"和"一下儿"是一样的。 **"Yíxià" hé "yíxiàr" shì yíyàng de.** = *"Yixia" and "Yixiar" are the same.*
- 你今天去，明天去，都一样。 **Nǐ jīntiān qù, míngtiān qù, dōu yíyàng.** = *It's all the same whether you go today or tomorrow.*

yízhì 一致 ADJECTIVE = unanimous, identical
- 会上没有取得一致的意见。 **Huìshang méiyǒu qǔdé yízhì de yìjiàn.** = *No consensus of opinion was reached at the meeting.*
- 双方提出的数据是一致的。 **Shuāngfāng tíchū de shùjù shì yízhì de.** = *The two parties presented identical data.*

yí 仪 Trad 儀 NOUN = instrument

yíqì 仪器 [compound: 仪 *instrument* + 器 *utensil*] NOUN = instrument (件 **jiàn**)
- 做这个试验需要很多仪器。 **Zuò zhège shìyàn xūyào hěn duō yíqì.** = *This test requires many instruments.*

Y

yí 宜 ADJECTIVE = suitable (See 便宜 **piányi**.)

yí 移 VERB = move, shift
- 窗前的阳光太强，我要把桌子往边上移。 **Chuāngqián de yángguāng tài qiáng, wǒ yào bǎ zhuōzi wàng biānshang yí.** = *The sunshine is too strong by the window. I want to move my desk to the side.*

yímín 移民 = immigrate, emigrate; immigrant, emigrant; immigration

yídòng 移动 [compound: 移 *move* + 动 *move*] VERB = move, shift
- 强冷空气正在向东移动。 **Qiáng lěng kōngqì zhèngzài xiàng dōng yídòng.** = *Strong cold air is moving eastward.*

yídòng diànhuà 移动电话 = cordless telephone

yí 疑 VERB = doubt

yíwèn 疑问 [compound: 疑 *doubt* + 问 *inquire*] NOUN = doubt
- 这个计划一定要实现，这是毫无疑问的。 **Zhège jìhuà yídìng yào shíxiàn, zhè shì háowú yíwèn de.** = *It is beyond any doubt that this plan will materialize.*

yí 遗 Trad 遺 VERB = leave behind

yíhàn 遗憾
1 VERB = regret
- 部长非常遗憾，不能接受你们的邀请。 **Bùzhǎng fēicháng yíhàn, bù néng jiēshòu nǐmen de yāoqǐng.** = *The Minister regrets he is unable to accept your invitation.*
2 ADJECTIVE = regretful
- 我错过了那场音乐会，真是很遗憾。 **Wǒ cuòguole nà chǎng yīnyuèhuì, zhēn shì hěn yíhàn.** = *It is a pity that I missed the concert.*

yǐ 已 ADJECTIVE = same as 已经 **yǐjīng**. Used in written Chinese.

yǐjīng 已经 ADJECTIVE = already
- 我已经学了三年中文了。 **Wǒ yǐjīng xuéle sān nián Zhōngwén le.** = *I've already been studying Chinese for three years.*
- 她已经三十五岁了，还没有结婚。 **Tā yǐjīng sānshíwǔ suì le, hái méiyǒu jiéhūn.** = *She is already thirty-five years old and is not married yet.*

yǐ 以 1 PREPOSITION
1 = with, in the manner of
- 我们要以高标准严格要求自己。 **Wǒmen yào yǐ gāo biāozhǔn yángé yāoqiú zìjǐ.** = *We should set high standards for ourselves.*
2 = for, because of
- 这个地方以风景优美著名。 **Zhège dìfang yǐ fēngjǐng yōuměi zhùmíng.** = *This place is famous for its beautiful scenery.*

yǐ 以 2 CONJUNCTION = in order to, so as to
- 应该推广新技术以提高工作效率。 **Yīnggāi tuīguǎng xīn jìshù yǐ tígāo gōngzuò xiàolǜ.** = *We should promote new technology so as to increase efficiency.*

yǐhòu 以后 NOUN = after, later (antonym 以前 **yǐqián**)
- 做完作业以后，要检查一下。 **Zuòwán zuòyè yǐhòu, yào jiǎnchá yíxià.** = *After you've done an assignment, you should check it [for mistakes].*
- 这个问题我们以后再谈。 **Zhège wèntí wǒmen yǐhòu zài tán.** = *We'll discuss this problem later.*

yǐjí 以及 CONJUNCTION = same as 和 **hé** 1 CONJUNCTION, used in formal Chinese.

yǐlái 以来 PARTICLE = since, in the past ...
- 今年以来，天气一直不正常。 **Jīnnián yǐlái, tiānqì yìzhí bú zhèngcháng.** = *Since the beginning of this year the weather has been quite abnormal.*
- 三个月以来，你的中文口语有了很大进步。 **Sān ge yuè yǐlái, nǐ de Zhōngwén kǒuyǔ yǒule hěn dà jìnbù.** = *In the past three months you have made good progress in spoken Chinese.*

yǐnèi 以内 NOUN = within, during
- 三天以内我一定把报告交给你。 **Sān tiān yǐnèi wǒ yídìng bǎ bàogào jiāo gei nǐ.** = *I will definitely submit my report to you in three days.*

yǐqián 以前 NOUN = before, some time ago (antonym 以后 **yǐhòu**)
- 回答问题以前，先要想一下。 **Huídá wèntí yǐqián, xiān yào xiǎng yíxià.** = *Before you answer a question, you should think first.*
- 他不久以前身体不大好。 **Tā bùjiǔ yǐqián**

Y

shēntǐ bú dà hǎo. = *He was in poor health not long ago.*
  bùjiǔ yǐqián 不久以前 = not long ago

yǐshàng 以上 NOUN = over, more than
■ 中国人口百分之七十以上住在农村。**Zhōngguó rénkǒu bǎifēn zhī qíshí yǐshàng zhù zài nóngcūn.** = *Over seventy percent of China's population lives in rural areas.*

yǐwài 以外 NOUN = beyond, outside, other than
■ 八小时以外你可以做自己喜欢做的事。**Bā xiǎoshí yǐwài nǐ kěyǐ zuò zìjǐ xǐhuan zuò de shì.** = *You can do what you enjoy doing outside the eight working hours.*

yǐwéi 以为 VERB = think (usually incorrectly)
■ 呀，你还在工作？我以为你已经回家了。**Yǎ, nǐ háizài gōngzuò? Wǒ yǐwéi nǐ yǐjīng huíjiā le.** = *Oh, you're still working. I thought you'd gone home.*
■ 我一直以为他是日本人，现在才知道他是中国人。**Wǒ yìzhí yǐwéi tā shì Rìběnrén, xiànzài cái zhīdào tā shì Zhōngguórén.** = *I always thought he was Japanese; only now I know he is Chinese.*

yíxià 以下 NOUN = below, less than
■ 他们的年收入在一万元以下。**Tāmen de nián shōurù zài yíwàn yuán yǐxià.** = *Their annual income is less than 10,000 yuan.*

yǐ 椅 NOUN = chair

yǐzi 椅子 [suffix: 椅 *chair* + 子 nominal suffix] NOUN = chair (把 **bǎ**)
■ 房间里有一张桌子和四把椅子。**Fángjiān li yǒu yì zhāng zhuōzi hé sì bǎ yǐzi.** = *There are a table and four chairs in the room.*

yìbān 一般 ADJECTIVE
1 = generally speaking, ordinarily
■ 每星期一上午我们一般都开会。**Měi Xīngqīyī shàngwǔ wǒmen yìbān dōu kāihuì.** = *We usually have a meeting every Monday morning.*
2 = average, commonplace
■ 他的学习成绩一般。**Tā de xuéxí chéngjì yìbān.** = *His school record is average.*
3 = same as, as...as
■ 哥哥长得和爸爸一般高了。**Gēge zhǎng de**

hé bàba yìbān gāo le. = *My elder brother is now as tall as Daddy.*

yìbiān 一边 NOUN = one side
■ 在这场争论中，我站在你们一边。**Zài zhè chǎng zhēnglùn zhōng, wǒ zhàn zài nǐmen yìbiān.** = *In this debate I am on your side.*

yìbiān ... yìbiān ... 一边 ... 一边 ... CONJUNCTION = while ..., at the same time
■ 不少大学生一边学习一边工作。**Bùshǎo dàxuéshēng yìbiān xuéxí yìbiān gōngzuò.** = *Quite a few university students study and work at the same time.*

NOTE: 一边 ... 一边 ... **yìbiān ... yìbiān ...** links two verbs to indicate that the two actions denoted by the verbs take place simultaneously. Another example:
■ 他常常一边做作业一边听音乐。**Tā chángcháng yìbiān zuò zuòyè yìbiān tīng yīnyuè.** = *He often does his homework while listening to music.*
When the verbs are monosyllabic, 边 ... 边 ... **biān ... biān ...** may be used instead of 一边 ... 一边 ... **yìbiān ... yìbiān ... ,** e.g.
■ 孩子们边走边唱。**Háizimen biān zǒu biān chàng.** = *The children sang while walking.*
■ 我们边吃边谈吧。**Wǒmen biān chī biān tán ba.** = *Let's carry on the conversation while eating.*

yìdiǎnr 一点儿 NOUN = a tiny amount, a bit
■ 那个菜不好吃，我只吃了一点儿。**Nàge cài bù hǎo chī, wǒ zhǐ chīle yìdiǎnr.** = *That dish is not tasty. I ate only a tiny bit of it.*

yìfāngmiàn ... yìfāngmiàn ... 一方面 ... 一方面 ... CONJUNCTION = on the one hand ... on the other hand ...
■ 我们一方面要发展经济，一方面要保护环境。**Wǒmen yìfāngmiàn yào fāzhǎn jīngjì, yìfāngmiàn yào bǎohù huánjìng.** = *We should on the one hand develop the economy and on the other hand protect the environment.*

yìqí 一齐 ADVERB = same as 一起 **yìqǐ**

yìqǐ 一起 ADVERB = together
■ 我们一起去吃饭吧。**Wǒmen yìqǐ qù chīfàn ba.** = *Let's have a meal together.*

■他们夫妻俩在同一公司工作，常常一起上班，一起回家。**Tāmen fūqī liǎ zài tóng yì gōngsī gōngzuò, chángcháng yìqǐ shàngbān, yìqǐ huíjiā.** = *That couple work in the same company, so they often go to work together and come home together.*

yìshēng 一生 NOUN = all one's life, lifetime
■这位老人一生都住在这个山区。**Zhè wèi lǎorén yìshēng dōu zhù zài zhège shānqū.** = *This old man has lived in this mountainous area all his life.*

yìshí 一时 NOUN = for the time being, momentarily
■这个字我认识，但是一时记不起来了。**Zhège zì wǒ rènshi, dànshì yìshí jì bu qǐlái le.** = *I do know the word, but I just don't remember at this moment.*

yìtóng 一同 ADVERB = same as 一起 **yìqǐ**

yìxiē 一些 MEASURE WORD = a small amount of, a bit of
■请你在我的茶里放一些糖。**Qǐng nǐ zài wǒ de chá li fàng yìxiē táng.** = *Please put a little sugar in my tea.*
■我这里有一些书，你看看还有没有用。**Wǒ zhèli yǒu yìxiē shū, nǐ kànkan hái yǒu méiyǒu yòng.** = *I have a few books here. Have a look to see if they are still useful.*

yìzhí 一直 ADVERB = always, all the time
■我一直住在这个城市。**Wǒ yìzhí zhù zài zhège chéngshì.** = *I've always been living in this city.*
■他一直很关心你，常打听你的消息。**Tā yìzhí hěn guānxīn nǐ, cháng dǎtīng nǐ de xiāoxi.** = *He is always concerned for you and asks after you.*

yì 义 Trad 義 ADJECTIVE = righteous

yìwù 义务 NOUN = duty, obligation
■交税是每一个公民的义务。**Jiāo shuì shì měi yi ge gōngmín de yìwù.** = *Paying taxes is the duty of every citizen.*
■先生，我们没有义务为您提供这种服务。**Xiānsheng, wǒmen méiyǒu yìwù wèi nín tígòng zhè zhǒng fúwù.** = *We are not obligated to provide you with this service, sir.*

yìwù gōngzuò (yìgōng) 义务工作（义工） = voluntary work
yìwù jiàoyù 义务教育 = compulsory education

yì 亿 Trad 億 NUMERAL = one hundred million
■中国有十三亿人口。**Zhōngguó yǒu shísān yì rénkǒu.** *China has a population of 1.3 billion.*
shíyì 十亿 = billion

yì 艺 Trad 藝 NOUN = art

yìshù 艺术 [modif: 艺 *art* + 术 *craft, skill*] NOUN = art
■我不大懂现代艺术。**Wǒ bú dà dǒng xiàndài yìshù.** = *I don't quite understand modern art.*
■他是搞艺术的。**Tā shì gǎo yìshù de.** = *He is engaged in art.* (→ *He is an artist.*)
yìshùjiā 艺术家 = (accomplished, recognized) artist
yìshù zuòpǐn 艺术作品 = a work of art

yì 忆 Trad 憶 VERB = recall (See 回忆 **huíyì**, 记忆 **jìyì**.)

yì 异 Trad 異 ADJECTIVE = different

yìcháng 异常 [v+obj: 异 *differ from* + 常 *the usual*] ADJECTIVE = abnormal, unusual
■环境遭到破坏，造成天气异常。**Huánjìng zāodào pòhuài, zàochéng tiānqì yìcháng.** = *As the environment is damaged, abnormal weather results.*

yì 译 Trad 譯 VERB = translate (See 翻译 **fānyì**.)

yì 易 See 好容易 **hǎo róngyì**, 容易 **róngyì**, 贸易 **màoyì**.

yì 益 NOUN = benefit (See 利益 **lìyì**.)

yì 谊 Trad 誼 NOUN = friendship (See 友谊 **yǒuyì**.)

yì 意 NOUN = idea, meaning

yìjiàn 意见 [compound: 意 *idea* + 见 *viewpoint*] NOUN
1 = opinion, view (条 **tiáo**)
■对这个问题你有什么意见？**Duì zhège wèntí nǐ yǒu shénme yìjiàn?** = *What is your opinion on this issue?*

■ 在这个问题上我们已经取得了一致的意见。**Zài zhège wèntí shang wǒmen yǐjīng qǔdéle yízhì de yìjiàn.** = *We have reached consensus on this issue.*

2 = complaint, objection

■ 我对他处理这件事的方法很有意见。**Wǒ duì tā chǔlǐ zhè jiàn shì de fāngfǎ hěn yǒu yìjiàn.** = *I have objections to the way he dealt with this matter.*

■ 他只想到自己，我对他有意见。**Tā zhǐ xiǎngdao zìjǐ, wǒ duì tā yǒu yìjiàn.** = *My complaint against him is that he thinks only about himself.*

tí yìjiàn 提意见 = make a comment (on an issue, a proposal etc.), make a complaint

yìsi 意思 [compound: 意 *meaning* + 思 *thought*] NOUN = meaning

■ 这个字是什么意思？ **Zhège zì shì shénme yìsi?** = *What's the meaning of this character?*

■ 这句话的意思不清楚。**Zhè jù huà de yìsi bù qīngchu.** = *The meaning of this sentence is not clear.*

■ 他的意思是你最好别去。**Tā de yìsi shì nǐ zuìhǎo bié qù.** = *What he meant is that you'd better not go.*

yìwài 意外

1 ADJECTIVE = unexpected, unforeseen

■ 这个消息很意外。**Zhège xiāoxi hěn yìwài.** = *This is unexpected news.*

■ 她平时常常迟到，今天这么早就来了，让人感到意外。**Tā píngshí chángcháng chídào, jīntiān zhème zǎo jiù lái le, ràng rén gǎndao yìwài.** = *She is usually late for work, but she came so early today. It's quite unexpected.*

2 NOUN = mishap, accident

■ 我们要采取安全措施，以防止意外。**Wǒmen yào cǎiqǔ ānquán cuòshī, yǐ fángzhǐ yìwài.** = *We should take safety measures to prevent accidents.*

yìyì 意义 [compound: 意 *meaning* + 义 *meaning*] NOUN = significance

■ 这件事有很大的历史意义。**Zhè jiàn shì yǒu hěn dà de lìshǐ yìyì.** = *This event has great historical significance.*

■ 生活的意义是什么？ **Shēnghuó de yìyì shì shénme?** = *What is the meaning of life?*

yìzhì 意志 [compound: 意 *will* + 志 *aspiration*] NOUN = will

■ 这位运动员意志坚强，受了伤还每天锻炼。**Zhè wèi yùndòngyuán yìzhì jiānqiáng, shòule shāng hái měi tiān duànliàn.** = *This athlete is strong-willed. He trains everyday despite his injury.*

yì 议 Trad 議 VERB = discuss

yìlùn 议论 [compound: 议 *discuss* + 论 *comment*] VERB = comment, discuss, talk

■ 我从来不在背后议论别人。**Wǒ cónglái bú zài bèihòu yìlùn biéren.** = *I never talk about people behind their backs.*

■ 我看你别议论政治了，挺危险的。**Wǒ kàn nǐ bié yìlùn zhèngzhì le, tǐng wēixiǎn de.** = *I suggest you stop commenting on politics. It is rather dangerous.*

yīn 因 CONJUNCTION = because

yīncǐ 因此 CONJUNCTION = therefore, so

■ 这种产品质量极好，因此价格比较高。**Zhè zhǒng chǎnpǐn zhìliàng jí hǎo, yīncǐ jiàgé bǐjiào gāo.** = *This product is of excellent quality and is therefore rather expensive.*

yīn'ér 因而 CONJUNCTION = same as 因此 yīncǐ

yīnsù 因素 NOUN = factor, element

■ 坚强的意志是事业成功的因素。**Jiānqiáng de yìzhì shì shìyè chénggōng de yīnsù.** = *A strong will is an important factor for a successful career.*

■ 目前的这种情况，是由很多因素造成的。**Mùqián de zhè zhǒng qíngkuàng, shì yóu hěn duō yīnsù zàochéng de.** = *The present situation was brought about by many factors.*

yīnwèi 因为 CONJUNCTION = because

■ 因为没有时间，所以我很少去看朋友。**Yīnwèi méiyǒu shíjiān, suǒyǐ wǒ hěnshǎo qù kàn péngyou.** = *I seldom go visiting friends because I don't have the time.*

■ 因为大多数人都反对，所以这个计划放弃了。**Yīnwèi dàduōshù rén dōu fǎnduì, suǒyǐ zhège jìhuà fàngqì le.** = *Because the majority opposed the plan, it was abandoned.*

Y

NOTE: 因为 **yīnwèi** is usually followed by 所以 **suǒyǐ**: 因为 … 所以 … **yīnwèi…suǒyǐ…**

yīn 阴 Trad 陰 ADJECTIVE = cloudy, overcast
■ 昨天上午天晴，下午阴天，晚上下雨。**Zuótiān shàngwǔ tiānqíng, xiàwǔ yīntiān, wánshang xiàyǔ.** = *Yesterday it was fine in the morning, cloudy in the afternoon and it rained in the evening.*
yīntiān 阴天 = cloudy day
yīnxìng 阴性 = (of medical test) negative (antonym 阳性 **yángxìng**)

yīn 姻 NOUN = marriage (See 婚姻 **hūnyīn**.)

yīn 音 NOUN = sound

yīnyuè 音乐 [compound: 音 *sound* + 乐 *music*] NOUN = music
■ 星期天我常常跟朋友一块儿听音乐。**Xīngqītiān wǒ chángcháng gēn péngyou yíkuàir tīng yīnyuè.** = *I often listen to music with my friends on Sundays.*
■ 你喜欢什么样的音乐？ **Nǐ xǐhuan shénmeyàng de yīnyuè?** = *What kind of music do you like?*
yīnyuè huì 音乐会 = concert
yīnyuè jiā 音乐家 = musician
yīnyuè xuéyuàn 音乐学院 = conservatoire
qīng yīnyuè 轻音乐 = light music

yín 银 Trad 銀 NOUN = silver
■ 银是一种贵金属。**Yín shì yì zhǒng guì jīnshǔ.** = *Silver is a precious metal.*

yínháng 银行 [modif: 银 *silver, money* + 行 *firm*] NOUN = bank (家 **jiā**)
■ 他打算到银行去借钱。**Tā dǎsuàn dào yínháng qù jiè qián.** = *He plans to ask for a loan from the bank.*
■ 这里的银行几点钟开始营业？ **Zhèli de yínháng jǐ diǎnzhōng kāishǐ yíngyè?** = *What time do the banks here open for business.*

yín 引 VERB = lead, provoke

yínqǐ 引起 VERB = give rise to, lead to, cause, arouse
■ 连续三天大雨，引起了水灾。**Liánxù sān tiān dà yǔ, yǐnqǐle shuǐzāi.** = *Three days of incessant heavy rain caused flooding.*

yìn 印 VERB = print
■ 这张照片，我想印三份。**Zhè zhāng zhàopiàn, wǒ xiǎng yìn sān fèn.** = *I want three prints of this photo.*
yìngyìn 影印 = photocopy
yìngyìnjī 影印机 = photocopier

yìnshuā 印刷 [compound: 印 *print* + 刷 *brush*] VERB = print (books, pamphlets, etc.)
■ 本店印刷各类文件。**Běn diàn yìnshuā gè lèi wénjiàn.** = *This shop prints all kinds of documents.*
yìnshuāchǎng 印刷厂 = print shop
yìnshuājī 印刷机 = printing machine, press
yìnshuāpǐn 印刷品 = printed matter

yìnxiàng 印象 [compound: 印 *print* + 象 *image*] NOUN = impression
■ 这个展览会给我留下深刻印象。**Zhège zhǎnlǎnhuì gěi wǒ liúxià shēnkè yìnxiàng.** = *This exhibition has left a deep impression on me.*
gěi … liúxià yìnxiàng 给 … 留下印象 = leave an impression on ...

yīng 应 Trad 應 MODAL VERB = same as 应该 **yīnggāi**

yīngdāng 应当 MODAL VERB = same as 应该 **yīnggāi**

yīnggāi 应该 MODAL VERB = should, ought to
■ 你的朋友有困难的时候，你应该帮助他们。**Nǐ de péngyou yǒu kùnnan de shíhou, nǐ yīnggāi bāngzhù tāmen.** = *When your friends are in difficulty, you should help them.*
■ 你应该早一点告诉我。**Nǐ yīnggāi zǎo yìdiǎn gàosu wǒ.** = *You should have told me earlier.*
■ 不用谢，这是我应该做的。**Búyòng xiè, zhè shì wǒ yīnggāi zuò de.** = *Don't mention it. This is what I should do.*

yīng 英 ADJECTIVE = heroic

Yīngguó 英国 NOUN = England, Britain, the UK
■ 英国一年中夏天最好。**Yīngguó yì nián zhōng xiàtiān zuì hǎo.** = *In England, summer is the best season of the year.*

yīngtèwǎng 英特网 [modif: 英特 *Internet* + 网 *net*] NOUN = same as 互联网 **hùliánwǎng**

Y

Yīngwén 英文 [modif: 英 *English* + 文 *writing*] NOUN = the English language (especially the writing)

yīngxióng 英雄 NOUN = hero
■ 是英雄创造历史，还是历史产生英雄？ **Shì yīngxióng chuàngzào lìshǐ, háishì lìshǐ chǎnshēng yīngxióng?** = *Do heroes create history or does history produce heroes?*

Yīngyǔ 英语 [modif: 英 *English* + 语 *language*] NOUN = the English language
■ 你用英语说吧，大家都听得懂。**Nǐ yòng Yīngyǔ shuō ba, dàjiā dōu tīng de dǒng.** = *You can say it in English. Everybody here understands it.*
■ 英语是世界上最常用的国际语言。**Yīngyǔ shì shìjiè shang zuì chángyòng de guójì yǔyán.** = *English is the world's most widely used international language.*

yíng 迎 VERB = meet

yíngjiē 迎接 [compound: 迎 *meet* + 接 *receive*] VERB = meet, greet
■ 今天下午我们要去机场迎接外国客人。**Jīntiān xiàwǔ wǒmen yào qù jīchǎng yíngjiē wàiguó kèren.** = *This afternoon we are going to the airport to meet visitors from overseas.*

yíng 营 Trad 營 VERB = operate

yíngyǎng 营养 NOUN = nutrition, nourishment
■ 这种水果营养特别丰富。**Zhè zhǒng shuǐguǒ yíngyǎng tèbié fēngfù.** = *This fruit is particularly rich in nutrition.*

yíngyè 营业 VERB = (of a commercial or service establishment) do business
■ 本店营业范围广泛。**Běn diàn yíngyè fànwéi guǎngfàn.** = *This shop has an extensive range of business interests.*
yíngyèyuán 营业员 = shop assistant, salesperson
yíngyè shíjiān 营业时间 = business hours

yíng 蝇 Trad 蠅 NOUN = fly (See 苍蝇 **cāngying**.)

yíng 赢 VERB = win (a game), beat (a rival)
■ 昨天的球赛谁赢了？ **Zuótiān de qiúsài shéi yíng le?** = *Who won the ball game yesterday?*

■ 他买彩票赢了一千块钱。**Tā mǎi cǎipiào yíngle yìqiān kuài qián.** = *He won 1000 yuan in the lottery.*

yǐng 影 NOUN = shadow

yǐngxiǎng 影响 [compound: 影 *shadow* + 响 *sound*]
1 VERB = influence, affect
■ 经济发展慢，影响了生活水平的提高。**Jīngjì fāzhǎn màn, yǐngxiǎngle shēnghuó shuǐpíng de tígāo.** = *Slow economic development affects the improvement of living standards.*
2 NOUN = influence
■ 中学生受谁的影响大－父母，还是朋友？ **Zhōngxuéshēng shòu shuí de yǐngxiǎng dà － fù-mǔ, háishì péngyou?** = *Who has more influence on high school students—parents or friends?*
■ 她今年常常生病，影响了工作和学习。**Tā jīnnián chángcháng shēngbìng, yǐngxiǎngle gōngzuò hé xuéxí.** = *She has been sick quite often this year. This has affected her work and study.*

yìng 应 Trad 應 VERB = respond

yìngyòng 应用 VERB = apply
■ 这项新技术还不能应用在工业上。**Zhè xiàng xīn jìshù hái bù néng yìngyòng zài gōngyè shang.** = *This new technology cannot be applied in industry yet.*
yìngyòng kēxué 应用科学 = applied science

yìng 映 VERB = reflect (See 反映 **fǎnyìng**.)

yìng 硬 ADJECTIVE = (of substance) hard, tough (antonym 软 **ruǎn**)
■ 这种材料非常硬。**Zhè zhǒng cáiliào fēicháng yìng.** = *This material is very hard.*

yōng 拥 Trad 擁 VERB = embrace

yōngbào 拥抱 [compound: 拥 *embrace* + 抱 *hold in arms*] VERB = embrace, hug
■ 中国人一般不习惯和人拥抱。**Zhōngguórén yìbān bù xíguàn hé rén yōngbào.** = *The Chinese are generally unaccustomed to hugging.*

yǒng 永 ADVERB = forever

Y

yǒngyuǎn 永远 [compound: 永 *forever* + 远 *remote*] ADVERB = forever
- 我们永远是朋友。**Wǒmen yǒngyuǎn shì péngyou.** = *We'll be friends forever.*
- 他永远不会做对家庭有害的事。**Tā yǒngyuǎn bú huì zuò duì jiātíng yǒuhài de shì.** = *He would never do anything that may harm his family.*

yǒng 勇 NOUN = courage

yǒnggǎn 勇敢 [compound: 勇 *bold* + 敢 *daring*] ADJECTIVE = brave, bold, fearless
- 他勇敢地从大火中救出两个孩子。**Tā yǒnggǎn de cóng dà huǒ zhōng jiùchū liǎng ge háizi.** = *He bravely saved two children from the fire.*

yǒngqì 勇气 [modif: 勇 *courage* + 气 *quality*] NOUN = courage
- 你要有勇气承认错误。**Nǐ yào yǒu yǒngqì chéngrèn cuòwù.** = *You should have the courage to admit your mistake.*

yǒng 泳 VERB = swim (See 游泳 **yóuyǒng**.)

yòng 用 VERB = use, (do something) with
- 我可以用一下你的自行车吗？ **Wǒ kěyǐ yòng yíxià nǐ de zìxíngchē ma?** = *May I use your bicycle?*
- 我会用电脑写汉字。**Wǒ huì yòng diànnǎo xiě Hànzì.** = *I can use a computer to write Chinese characters.*

yòngbuzháo 用不着
1 = there is no need to
- 这点小事，用不着请别人帮忙。**Zhè diǎn xiǎo shì, yòngbuzháo qǐng biéren bāngmáng.** = *This is a trivial matter and there is no need to ask for help.*
2 = useless
- 用不着的书别放在书架上。**Yòngbuzháo de shū bié fàng zài shūjià shang.** = *Don't put useless books on the bookshelf.*

yòngchu 用处 [modif: 用 *use* + 处 *place*] VERB = use
- 这东西用处不大，就别买了。**Zhè dōngxi yòngchu bú dà, jiù bié mǎi le.** = *This isn't of much use. Let's not buy it.*

yònggōng 用功 [v+obj: 用 *use* + 功 *efforts*] ADJECTIVE = hardworking, diligent (student)
- 她学习非常用功。**Tā xuéxí fēicháng yònggōng.** = *She studies diligently.*
- 这学期我没有好好学习，下学期要用功点。**Zhè xuéqī wǒ méiyǒu hǎohǎo xuéxí, xià xuéqī yào yònggōng diǎn.** = *I did not study well this semester. I will work harder in the next semester.*

yònglì 用力 [v+obj: 用 *use* + 力 *strength*] VERB = exert oneself (physically)
- 他用力把桌子推到一边。**Tā yònglì bǎ zhuōzi tuīdao yìbiān.** = *He made an effort to push the desk to the side.*

yōu 优 Trad 優 ADJECTIVE = excellent

yōudiǎn 优点 [modif: 优 *excellent* + 点 *point*] NOUN = strong point, merit (antonym 缺点 **quēdiǎn**)
- 每个人都有优点和缺点。**Měi ge rén dōu yǒu yōudiǎn hé quēdiǎn.** = *Everybody has their strong points and weak points.*
- 这个产品有什么优点? **Zhège chǎnpǐn yǒu shénme yōudiǎn?** = *What are the merits of this new product?*

yōuliáng 优良 [compound: 优 *excellent* + 良 *good*] ADJECTIVE = fine, good
- 政府正在推广小麦优良品种。**Zhèngfǔ zhèngzài tuīguǎng xiǎomài yōuliáng pǐnzhǒng.** = *The government is promoting a fine variety of wheat.*
- 她的儿子年年考试成绩优良。**Tā de érzi niánnián kǎoshì chéngjì yōuliáng.** = *Her son gets good examination results every year.*

yōuměi 优美 [compound: 优 *excellent* + 美 *beautiful*] ADJECTIVE = beautiful, graceful
- 这里优美的风景吸引大批游览者。**Zhèli yōuměi de fēngjǐng xīyǐn dàpī yóulǎnzhě.** = *The beautiful landscape here attracts large numbers of tourists.*

yōuxiù 优秀 [compound: 优 *excellent* + 秀 *elegant*] ADJECTIVE = outstanding, excellent
- 这位青年是我们公司的优秀人才。**Zhè wèi qīngnián shì wǒmen gōngsī de yōuxiù réncái.** = *This young man is an outstanding talent of our company.*

yōu 悠 ADJECTIVE = remote

yōujiǔ 悠久 [compound: 悠 *remote* + 久 *long*]
ADJECTIVE = very long, long-standing, time-honored
■ 中国历史悠久，人口众多。**Zhōngguó lìshǐ
yōujiǔ, rénkǒu zhòngduō.** = *China has a long
history and a large population.*

yóu 尤 ADVERB = especially

yóuqí 尤其 ADVERB = especially
■ 新西兰的天气很舒服，尤其是夏天。
Xīnxīlán de tiānqì hěn shūfu, yóuqí shì xiàtiān.
= *The weather in New Zealand is very
pleasant, especially in summer.*
■ 我喜欢吃中国菜，尤其喜欢吃广东菜。**Wǒ
xǐhuan chī Zhōngguó cài, yóuqí xǐhuan chī
Guǎngdōng cài.** = *I love Chinese food, especially Cantonese food.*

yóu 由 PREPOSITION
1 = (introducing the agent of an action), by
■ 技术问题由你们解决。**Jìshù wèntí yóu
nǐmen jiějué.** = *Technical problems will be
solved by you.* (→ *You are responsible for solv-
ing technical problems.*)
2 = (introducing manner or cause of an action),
with
■ 很多交通事故都是由车速太快造成的。
**Hěn duō jiāotōng shìgù dōu shì yóu chēsù tài
kuài zàochéng de.** = *Many road accidents are
caused by speeding.*

yóuyú 由于
1 PREPOSITION = because of, owing to, due to
■ 由于家庭她不得不放弃事业。**Yóuyú jiātíng
tā bùdébù fàngqì shìyè.** = *She had no choice
but give up her career because of her family.*
2 CONJUNCTION = because
■ 由于丈夫身体不好，她不能出国工作。
**Yóuyú zhàngfu shēntǐ bù hǎo, tā bù néng
chūguó gōngzuò.** = *She was not able to go
abroad to work because her husband was in
poor health.*

yóu 邮 Trad 郵 NOUN = post

yóujú 邮局 [modif: 邮 *post* + 局 *office*] NOUN =
post office
■ 请问，附近有没有邮局？ **Qǐngwèn, fùjìn**

yǒu méiyǒu yóujú? = *Excuse me, is there a
post office nearby?*
■ 由于电脑的广泛使用，邮局已经没有以前
那么重要了。**Yóuyú diànnǎo de guǎngfàn
shǐyòng, yóujú yǐjīng méiyǒu yǐqián nàme
zhòngyào le.** = *Thanks to extensive use of the
computer, the post office is no longer as important as before.*

yóupiào 邮票 [modif: 邮 *post* + 票 *ticket*]
NOUN = postal stamp (张 **zhāng**)
■ 这封信寄到台湾，要多少邮票？ **Zhè fēng
xìn jìdao Táiwān, yào duōshǎo yóupiào?** =
*How much is the postage for this letter to
Taiwan?*
■ 我买十块钱邮票。**Wǒ mǎi shí kuài qián
yóupiào.** = *I want to buy ten yuan worth of
stamps.*

yóu 犹 Trad 猶

yóuyù 犹豫 ADJECTIVE = hesitant, wavering,
procrastinating
■ 去不去国外找工作，我还有点犹豫。**Qù bu
qù guówài zhǎo gōngzuò, wǒ hái yǒudiǎn
yóuyù.** = *I'm still wavering over going job
hunting abroad.*
■ 不能犹豫了，得马上决定。**Bú néng yóuyù
le, děi mǎshàng juédìng.** = *You can't hesitate
any more. You've got to decide right now.*

yóu 油
1 NOUN = oil
■ 油比水轻。**Yóu bǐ shuǐ qīng.** = *Oil is lighter
than water.*
2 ADJECTIVE = greasy (food)
■ 这个菜太油了，我不能吃。**Zhège cài tài
yóu le, wǒ bù néng chī.** = *This dish is too
greasy. I can't eat it.*
yóutián 油田 = oilfield
shíyóu 食油 = edible oil, cooking oil
shíyóu 石油 = petroleum, oil

yóu 游 VERB = play

yóulǎn 游览 [compound: 游 *play* + 览 *see*]
VERB = go sightseeing, tour for pleasure
■ 每年很多人去香港游览。**Měi nián hěn duō
rén qù Xiānggǎng yóulǎn.** = *Every year many
people go to Hong Kong on holiday.*
yóulǎnzhě 游览者 = tourist

yóuyǒng 游泳 [compound: 游 *swim* + 泳 *swim*] VERB = swim
- 他游泳游得很好。**Tā yóuyǒng yóu de hén hǎo.** = *He swims very well.*
- 我一星期游两次泳。**Wǒ yì xīngqī yóu liǎng cì yǒng.** = *I swim twice a week.*

yóuyǒngchí 游泳池 = swimming pool
yóuyǒng kù 游泳裤 = swimming trunks
yóuyǒng yī 游泳衣 = swimsuit
shìnèi yóuyǒngchí 室内游泳池 = indoor swimming pool

yóuxì 游戏 [modif: 游 *play* + 戏 *have fun*] NOUN = game
- 我们来做游戏！**Wǒmen lái zuò yóuxì!** = *Let's play a game!*

yóuxìjī 游戏机 = (computer) play station, (electronic game) console
diànnǎo yóuxì 电脑游戏 = computer game

yǒu 友 NOUN = friend

yǒuhǎo 友好 [compound: 友 *friendly* + 好 *amiable*] ADJECTIVE = friendly
- 她对所有的人都很友好。**Tā duì suǒyǒu de rén dōu hěn yǒuhǎo.** = *She is friendly to everyone.*
- 你这么做不大友好。**Nǐ zhème zuò bú dà yǒuhǎo.** = *It's not friendly of you to do so.*
- 他寄来贺卡是友好的表示。**Tā jì lai hèkǎ shì yǒuhǎo de biǎoshì.** = *His sending a card is a friendly gesture.*

yǒuyì 友谊 [compound: 友 *friendly* + 谊 *congeniality*] NOUN = friendship
- 我希望我们能发展我们之间的友谊。**Wǒ xīwàng wǒmen néng fāzhǎn wǒmen zhī jiān de yǒuyì.** = *I hope we will be able to develop the friendship between us.*
- 友谊天长地久。**Yǒuyì tiān-cháng-dì-jiǔ.** = *Our friendship will last forever.*

yǒu 有 VERB
1 = possess, have
- 他们有一座房子，一辆汽车，在银行里还有一些钱。**Tāmen yǒu yí zuò fángzi, yí liàng qìchē, zài yínháng li háiyǒu yìxiē qián.** = *They have a house, a car and some money in the bank.*
2 = exist, there is (are)
- 世界上有多少国家？**Shìjiè shang yǒu duōshǎo guójiā?** = *How many countries are there in the world?*
- 我们学校有三个电脑室。**Wǒmen xuéxiào yǒu sān ge diànnǎo shì.** = *There are three computer labs in our school.*

méiyǒu 没有 = do not possess, have no; do not exist, there is no
- 我没有汽车。**Wǒ méiyǒu qìchē.** = *I don't have a car.*
- 教室里没有人。**Jiàoshì li méiyǒu rén.** = *There is nobody in the classroom.*

yǒude 有的 PRONOUN = some
- 有的人喜欢体育，有的人喜欢艺术，也有的人什么也不喜欢。**Yǒude rén xǐhuan tǐyù, yǒude rén xǐhuan yìshù, yě yǒude rén shénme yě bù xǐhuan.** = *Some people are fond of sports, others are fond of the arts and still others are not fond of anything.*

yǒudeshì 有的是 VERB = be plenty of, be abundant, not in short supply
- 大学毕业生有的是。**Dàxué bìyèshēng yǒudeshì.** = *There are plenty of university graduates.*

yǒu(yì)diǎnr 有(一)点儿 ADVERB = slightly, a little, somewhat
- 我今天有点儿累了，明天再谈吧。**Wǒ jīntiān yǒudiǎnr lèi le, míngtiān zài tán ba.** = *I'm a bit tired today. Let's talk tomorrow.*
- 他这么回答，她有一点失望。**Tā zhème huídá, tā yǒuyìdiǎn shīwàng.** = *She is somewhat disappointed at his reply.*

NOTE: 有点 **yǒudiǎn**, 有点儿 **yǒudiǎnr**, 有一点 **yǒuyìdiǎn**, 有一点儿 **yǒuyìdiǎnr** mean the same thing. 有点儿 **yǒudiǎnr** and 有一点儿 **yǒuyìdiǎnr** are only used in colloquial Chinese.

yǒuguān 有关 VERB = have bearing on, have something to do with, be related to (antonym 无关 **wúguān**)
- 这件事与你有关。**Zhè jiàn shì yú nǐ yǒuguān.** = *This matter has something to do with you.* (→ *This matter concerns you.*)
- 一个人的性格和事业成功与否有关。**Yí ge rén de xìnggé hé shìyè chénggōng yúfǒu yǒuguān.** = *A person's disposition has a bearing on whether his career is successful or not.*

yǒulì 有力 [v+obj: 有 *have* + 力 *force*]
ADJECTIVE = forceful, powerful, strong
■ 我们要采取有力措施节水节电。**Wǒmen yào cǎiqǔ yǒulì cuòshī jié shuǐ jié diàn.** = *We should take strong measures to save water and electricity.*

yǒulì 有利 [v+obj: 有 *have* + 利 *benefit*]
ADJECTIVE = favorable, advantageous (antonym 不利 **búlì**)
■ 我们要在那里发展业务有有利条件，也有不利条件。**Wǒmen yào zài nàli fāzhǎn yèwù yǒu yǒulì tiáojiàn, yě yǒu búlì tiáojiàn.** *There are both favorable and unfavorable conditions for our developing our business there.*

yǒumíng 有名 [v+obj: 有 *have* + 名 *name, fame*] ADJECTIVE = famous, well-known
■ 这座大学很有名。**Zhè zuò dàxué hěn yǒumíng.** = *This is a famous university.*
■ 这是一本很有名的小说。**Zhè shì yì běn hěn yǒumíng de xiǎoshuō.** = *This is a well-known novel.*

yǒuqián 有钱 [v+obj: 有 *have* + 钱 *money*]
ADJECTIVE = rich, wealthy
■ 他爸爸很有钱，但是他从来不乱花钱。**Tā bàba hěn yǒuqián, dànshì tā cónglai bù luàn huā qián.** = *His father is very wealthy, but he is quite frugal*
■ 她想找一个有钱人结婚。**Tā xiǎng zhǎo yí ge yǒu qián rén jiéhūn.** = *She wants to find a rich man to marry.*

NOTE: See note on 富 **fù**.

yǒuqù 有趣 [v+obj: 有 *have* + 趣 *fun*]
ADJECTIVE = interesting, amusing
■ 我给你讲一个有趣的故事。**Wǒ gěi nǐ jiǎng yí ge yǒuqù de gùshi.** = *I'll tell you an interesting story.*
■ 他在旅行的时候，遇到很多有趣的事。**Tā zài lǚxíng de shíhou, yùdao hěn duō yǒuqù de shì.** = *He had many interesting experiences on his journey.*

yǒushí 有时 ADVERB = same as 有时候 **yǒushíhou**

yǒushíhou 有时候 ADVERB = sometimes
■ 爸爸有时候忙，有时候不那么忙。**Bàba**

yǒushíhou máng, yǒushíhou bú nàme máng. = *Sometimes my father is busy, sometimes he isn't so busy.*
■ 他工作一般都很认真，但有时候也会马虎。**Tā gōngzuò yìbān dōu hěn rènzhēn, dàn yǒushíhou yě huì mǎhu.** = *He is generally a conscientious worker, but he can be careless sometimes.*

yǒuxiào 有效 [v+obj: 有 *have* + 效 *effect*]
ADJECTIVE
1 = effective, efficacious
■ 王老师教我们记生词的办法很有效。**Wáng lǎoshī jiāo wǒmen jì shēngcí de bànfǎ hěn yǒuxiào.** = *Teacher Wang taught us an effective method of memorizing new words.*
2 = valid
■ 我的护照还有效。**Wǒ de hùzhào hái yǒuxiào.** = *My passport is still valid.*
yǒuxiàoqī 有效期 = term of validity, expiry date

yǒuxiē 有些 PRONOUN = same as 有的 **yǒude**

yǒu yìsi 有意思 [v+obj: 有 *have* + 意思 *meaning*] ADJECTIVE = meaningful, interesting
■ 这本书很有意思，每个人都应该看。**Zhè běn shū hěn yǒu yìsi, měi ge rén dōu yīnggāi kàn.** = *This book is very meaningful. Everybody should read it.*
■ 董事长讲话的最后几句很有意思。**Dǒngshìzhǎng jiǎnghuà de zuì hòu jǐ jù hěn yǒu yìsi.** = *The last few sentences in the Chairman's speech are rather meaningful.*
méiyǒu yìsi 没有意思 = uninteresting, meaningless
■ 那个电影没有意思。**Nàge diànyǐng méiyǒu yìsi.** = *That movie isn't interesting.*

yǒuyòng 有用 [v+obj: 有 *have* + 用 *use*]
ADJECTIVE = useful
■ 我相信中文会越来越有用。**Wǒ xiāngxìn Zhōngwén huì yuèláiyuè yǒuyòng.** = *I believe the Chinese language will be more and more useful.*
■ 这本词典很有用。**Zhè běn cídiǎn hěn yǒuyòng.** = *This dictionary is very useful.*
méiyǒu yòng 没有用 = useless
■ 这本书太旧了，没有什么用了。**Zhè běn shū tài jiù le, méiyǒu shénme yòng le.** = *This book is too outdated, and is not of much use.*

Y

yòu 右 NOUN = the right side (antonym 左 **zuǒ**)
- 你右边的那座房子就是图书馆。**Nǐ yòubian de nà zuò fángzi jiù shì túshūguǎn.** = *The building on your right is the library.*

yòubian 右边 [modif: 右 *right* + 边 *side*] NOUN = the right side, the right-hand side
- 超级市场的右边是一个停车场。**Chāojí shìchǎng de yòubian shì yí ge tíngchēchǎng.** = *On the right side of the supermarket is a car park.*

yòu 又 ADVERB
1 = again
- 电脑昨天刚修好，今天又坏了。**Diànnǎo zuótiān gāng xiūhǎo, jīntiān yòu huài le.** = *The computer was fixed yesterday, but it broke down again today.*
- 晴了半天，又下雨了。**Qíngle bàntiān, yòu xià yǔ le.** = *After just half a day's fine weather, it rained again.*
2 = moreover, additionally
- 这个菜味道好，营养又丰富。**Zhège cài wèidao hǎo, yíngyǎng yòu fēngfù.** = *This dish is tasty and also very nutritious.*
- 吸烟很花钱，又对身体有害。**Xīyān hěn huāqián, yòu duì shēntǐ yǒuhài.** = *Smoking is costly and, moreover, harmful to your health.*
yòu … yòu … 又 … 又 … = … and also …, both … and …
- 他们的小女儿又聪明又可爱。**Tāmen de xiǎo nǚ'ér yòu cōngmíng yòu kě'ài.** = *Their young daughter is bright and lovely.*

NOTE: See note on 再 **zài**.

yú 于 Trad 於 PREPOSITION = in, at (only used in written Chinese)
- 他生于一九七零年。**Tā shēng yú yī-jiǔ-qī-líng nián.** = *He was born in 1970.*

yúshì 于是 CONJUNCTION = as a result, consequently
- 他爸爸在上海找到了工作，于是全家搬到上海去了。**Tā bàba zài Shànghǎi zhǎodao le gōngzuò, yúshì quán jiā bāndao Shànghǎi qù le.** = *His father found a job in Shanghai; as a result the family moved to Shanghai.*

yú 余 Trad 餘 VERB = spare (See 其余 **qíyú**, 业余 **yèyú**.)

yú 鱼 Trad 魚 NOUN = fish (条 **tiáo**)
- 河里有鱼吗？**Hé li yǒu yú ma?** = *Is there any fish in the river?*

yú 愉 NOUN = pleasure

yúkuài 愉快 [compound: 愉 *pleasant* + 快 *delightful*] ADJECTIVE
1 = pleasant, joyful
- 祝你假期愉快！**Zhù nǐ jiàqī yúkuài!** = *I wish you a joyful holiday.*
- 和你一起工作是很愉快的。**Hé nǐ yìqǐ gōngzuò shì hěn yúkuài de.** = *Working with you is very pleasant.*
- 我永远不会忘记那段愉快的经历。**Wǒ yóngyuǎn bú huì wàngji zhè duàn yúkuài de jīnglì.** = *I will never forget that pleasant experience.*
2 = pleased, happy
- 听到这句话，我很不愉快。**Tīngdào zhè jù huà, wǒ hěn bù yúkuài.** = *I feel displeased to hear this.*

yǔ 与 Trad 與 Same as 和 **hé** and 跟 **gēn**. Only used in written Chinese.

yǔ 雨 NOUN = rain
- 这里夏天多雨。**Zhèli xiàtiān duō yǔ.** = *It often rains here in summer.*
- 我看马上要下雨了。**Wǒ kàn mǎshàng yào xià yǔ le.** = *It seems to me that it's going to rain soon.*
yǔtiān 雨天 = rainy day
yǔyī 雨衣 = raincoat
xià yǔ 下雨 = to rain

yǔ 羽 NOUN = feather

yǔmáoqiú 羽毛球 [modif: 羽毛 *feather* + 球 *ball*] VERB = badminton, shuttlecock (只 **zhī**)
- 我常常跟朋友在体育馆打羽毛球。**Wǒ chángcháng gēn péngyou zài tǐyùguǎn dǎ yǔmáoqiú.** = *I often play badminton with my friends in the gym.*

yǔ 语 Trad 語 NOUN = language

yǔdiào 语调 [modif: 语 *speech* + 调 *tune*] NOUN = intonation
- 中文的声调不容易掌握，语调也很难。**Zhōngwén de shēngdiào bù róngyì zhǎngwò,**

yǔdiào yě hěn nán. = *While it is not easy to have a good command of Chinese tones, Chinese intonation is also difficult.*

yǔfǎ 语法 [modif: 语 *language* + 法 *law, rule*] NOUN = grammar
■ 我不大懂汉语语法，我想学一点儿。**Wǒ bú dà dǒng Hànyǔ yǔfǎ, wǒ xiǎng xué yìdiǎnr.** = *I don't quite understand Chinese grammar; I want to learn a bit.*

yǔqì 语气 [modif: 语 *speech* + 气 *quality*] NOUN = tone, manner of speaking
■ 同样一句话，语气不同，听了感觉就不同。**Tóngyàng yí jù huà, yǔqì bùtóng, tīngle gǎnjué jiù bùtóng.** = *Saying the same sentence in different tones of the voice produces different feelings in the hearers.*

yǔyán 语言 [compound: 语 *language* + 言 *speech*] NOUN = language (门 **mén**, 种 **zhǒng**)
■ 要了解一个民族，就要学它的语言。**Yào liǎojiě yí ge mínzú, jiù yào xué tā de yǔyán.** = *If you want to understand an ethnic group, you should study its language.*
■ 学一门语言，就是多一个观察世界的窗户。**Xué yì mén yǔyán, jiù shì duō yí ge guānchá shìjiè de chuānghu.** = *To learn a language is to have one more window from which to look at the world.*

yù 玉 NOUN = jade

yùmǐ 玉米 [modif: 玉 *jade* + 米 *rice*] NOUN = corn, maize (根 **gēn**)
■ 肚子饿了，先吃一根玉米吧。**Dùzi è le, xiān chī yì gēn yùmǐ ba.** = *If you're hungry, eat some corn first.*

yù 育 VERB = educate, nurture (See 教育 **jiàoyù**, 体育 **tǐyù**, 体育场 **tǐyùchǎng**, 体育馆 **tǐyùguǎn**.)

yù 浴 VERB = bathe

yùshì 浴室 [modif: 浴 *bathe* + 室 *room*] NOUN = bathroom (间 **jiān**)
■ 这套房子很大，有两间浴室。**Zhè tào fángzi hěn dà, yǒu liǎng jiān yùshì.** = *This is a big flat with two bathrooms.*

yù 遇 VERB = encounter

yùdào 遇到 VERB = encounter, come across
■ 我在国外旅行的时候，遇到不少好心人。**Wǒ zài guówài lǚxíng de shíhou, yùdào bùshǎo hǎoxīnrén.** = *When I traveled overseas, I came across many kindhearted people.*
■ 在工作中总会遇到困难。**Zài gōngzuò zhōng zǒng huì yùdào kùnnan.** = *One is bound to encounter difficulties in work.*

yùjiàn 遇见 VERB = meet (someone) unexpectedly, come across, run into
■ 我昨天在超级市场遇见一个老同学。**Wǒ zuótiān zài chāojí shìchǎng yùjiàn yí ge lǎo tóngxué.** = *I ran into an old classmate of mine in the supermarket yesterday.*

yù 预 Trad 預 ADVERB = in advance

yùbào 预报 [modif: 预 *in advance* + 报 *report*] NOUN = forecast, prediction
■ 你听过今天的天气预报吗？**Nǐ tīngguo jīntiān de tiānqì yùbào ma?** = *Have you listened to the weather forecast for today?*

yùbèi 预备 [modif: 预 *in advance* + 备 *prepare*] VERB = prepare, get ready
■ 他们在春节前一个星期，就开始预备春节时的饭菜了。**Tāmen zài chūnjié qián yí ge xīngqī, jiù kāishǐ yùbèi chūnjié shí de fàncài le.** = *They began preparing the food for the Spring Festival a week before.*
yùbèi huìyì 预备会议 = preparatory meeting
yùbèi xuéxiào 预备学校 = preparatory school

yùxí 预习 [modif: 预 *preparatory* + 习 *study*] VERB = prepare lessons before class, preview
■ 明天上语法课，我要想预习一下。**Míngtiān shàng yǔfǎ kè, wǒ yào xiǎn yùxí yíxià.** = *Tomorrow there'll be a grammar lesson, and I'll prepare for it.*

yù 豫 NOUN = comfort (See 犹豫 **yóuyù**.)

yuán 元 MEASURE WORD = (the basic unit of Chinese currency: 1 元 **yuán** = 10 角 **jiǎo**/ 毛 **máo** =100 分 **fēn**), yuan, dollar
Měiyuán 美元 = US dollar
Rìyuán 日元 = Japanese yen

Y

NOTE: 元 **yuán** is the formal word for the basic unit of Chinese currency. In spoken Chinese 块 **kuài** is more common. For instance, the sum of 50 yuan is usually written as 五十元 **wǔshí yuán**, but spoken of as 五十块 **wǔshí kuài** or 五十块钱 **wǔshí kuài qián**.

yuán 员 Trad 員 NOUN = member (See 党员 **dǎngyuán**, 服务员 **fúwùyuán**, 官员 **guānyuán**, 技术员 **jìshùyuán**, 教员 **jiàoyuán**, 人员 **rényuán**, 售货员 **shòuhuòyuán**, 委员会 **wěiyuánhuì**, 演员 **yǎnyuán**, 运动员 **yùndòngyuán**.)

yuán 园 Trad 園 NOUN = garden (See 动物园 **dòngwùyuán**, 公园 **gōngyuán**, 花园 **huāyuán**.)

yuán 原 ADJECTIVE = original, former

yuánlái 原来 ADJECTIVE = original, former
■ 她原来的计划是去英国工作一段时间。**Tā yuánlái de jìhuà shì qù Yīngguó gōngzuò yí duàn shíjiān.** = *Her original plan was to go to England and work there for a period of time.*
■ 古建筑遭到破坏，不能恢复原来的样子。**Gǔ jiànzhù zāodao pòhuài, bù néng huīfú yuánlái de yàngzi.** = *The ancient building is damaged and cannot be restored to its former appearance.*

yuánliàng 原谅 VERB = pardon, excuse, forgive
■ 我今天上午没有能到飞机场去接你，请多原谅。**Wǒ jīntiān shàngwǔ méiyǒu néng dào fēijīchǎng qù jiē nǐ, qǐng duō yuánliàng.** = *Please forgive me for not having been able to meet you at the airport this morning.*
■ 你这么做，我不能原谅。**Nǐ zhème zuò, wǒ bù néng yuánliàng.** = *I can't forgive you for such behavior.*

yuánliào 原料 [modif: 原 *original* + 料 *material*] NOUN = raw material
■ 原料价格又涨了。**Yuánliào jiàgē yòu zhǎng le.** = *The price of raw materials has risen again.*

yuányīn 原因 [modif: 原 *origin* + 因 *cause*] NOUN = cause, reason
■ 出了问题，一定要找出原因。**Chūle wèntí,**

yídìng yào zhǎochū yuányīn. = *When something has gone wrong we must identify the cause.*

yuánzé 原则 NOUN = principle
■ 不管发生什么，我都不会放弃原则。**Bùguǎn fāshēng shénme, wǒ dōu bú huì fàngqì yuánzé.** = *I will not abandon my principles, no matter what.*
■ 有时候坚持原则是不容易的。**Yǒushíhou jiānchí yuánzé shì bù róngyì de.** = *Sometimes it is not easy to adhere to one's principles.*

yuán 圆 Trad 圓 ADJECTIVE = round, circular
■ 在古代，人们不知道地球是圆的。**Zài gǔdài rénmen bù zhīdào dìqiú shì yuán de.** = *In ancient times people did not know that the earth was round.*

yuán 援 VERB = help (See 支援 **zhīyuán**.)

yuán 源 NOUN = source (See 能源 **néngyuán**, 资源 **zīyuán**.)

yuǎn 远 Trad 遠 ADJECTIVE = far, distant, remote (antonym 近 **jìn**)
■ "这里离火车站有多远？" "大概两公里。" **"Zhèli lí huǒchēzhàn yǒu duō yuǎn?" "Dàgài liǎng gōnglǐ."** = *"How far is it from here to the railway station?" "About two kilometers."*
… lí … yuǎn … 离 … 远 = … *is far from* …
■ 我家离学校不远。**Wǒ jiā lí xuéxiào bù yuǎn.** = *My home is not far from school.*

yuàn 院 NOUN = courtyard

yuànzi 院子 [suffix: 院 *courtyard* + 子 nominal suffix] NOUN = courtyard, compound
■ 下午四点钟以后就有孩子在院子里玩。**Xiàwǔ sì diǎnzhōng yǐhòu hěn duō háizi zài yuànzi li wán.** = *After four o'clock many children will play in the courtyard.*

yuàn 愿 VERB = wish, hope

yuànwàng 愿望 [compound: 愿 *wish* + 望 *hope*] NOUN = wish, aspiration, desire
■ 我的愿望终于实现了。**Wǒ de yuànwàng zōngyú shíxiàn le.** = *My wish has come true at last!*
■ 谁也不能满足他的愿望。**Shuí yě bù néng**

mǎngzú tā de **yuànwàng**. = *Nobody can satisfy his desire.*

yuànyì 愿意 [compound: 愿 *wish* + 意 *desire*]

1 MODAL VERB = be willing, will
- 我愿意帮助你。**Wǒ yuànyì bāngzhù nǐ.** = *I'm willing to help you.*
- 你愿意去就去，你不愿意去就别去。**Nǐ yuànyì qù jiù qù, nǐ bú yuànyì qù jiù bié qù.** = *If you're willing to go, you can go; if you're not willing to go, you don't have to go.*

2 VERB = wish, want
- 父母都愿意自己的孩子幸福。**Fù-mǔ dōu yuànyì zìjǐ de háizi xìngfú.** = *All parents want their children to be happy.*

yuē 约 Trad 約 ADVERB = same as 大约 dàyuē. Used in written Chinese.

yuēhuì 约会 [v+obj: 约 *arrange* + 会 *meeting*]

NOUN = (social) appointment, engagement, date
- 她今天打扮得这么漂亮，看来有约会。**Tā jīntiān dǎbàn de zhème piàoliang, kànlai yǒu yuēhuì.** = *She dressed up beautifully today, she probably has a date.*

yuè 月 NOUN

1 = month
- 我在那里住了八个月。**Wǒ zài nàli zhùle bā ge yuè.** = *I stayed there for eight months.*

2 = the moon
- 明月当空。**Míng yuè dāng kōng.** = *The bright moon shines in the sky.*

yuèliang 月亮 = the moon
- 今天晚上的月亮真好！**Jīntiān wǎnshang de yuèliang zhēn hǎo!** = *What a fine moon it is, tonight!*

yuèqiú 月球 = the Moon (as a scientific term)

Yīyuè 一月 = January

Sānyuè 三月 = February

Wǔyue 五月 = May

Shí'èryuè 十二月 = December

yuè 乐 Trad 樂 NOUN = music (See 音乐 yīnyuè.)

yuè 越 ADVERB = even more

yuèlaiyuè 越来越 ADVERB = more and more
- 学中文的人越来越多。**Xué Zhōngwén de**

rén **yuèlaiyuè duō**. = *More and more people are learning Chinese.*
- 这孩子长得越来越象他爸爸了。**Zhè háizi zhǎngde yuèlaiyuè xiàng tā bàba le.** = *This child is becoming more and more like his father.*

yuè ... yuè ... 越⋯越⋯ ADVERB = the more ... the more ...
- 我越学越对中文感兴趣。**Wǒ yuè xué yuè duì Zhōngwén gǎn xìngqù.** = *The more I study the more interested I am in Chinese.*
- 你真是越活越年轻了。**Nǐ zhēn shì yuè huó yuè niánqīng le.** = *You seem to get younger and younger.*
- 天气越热，她越怕上街。**Tiānqì yuè rè, tā yuè pà shàngjiē.** = *The hotter the weather, the more she dislikes to go shopping.*
- 学生越用功，老师越高兴。**Xuésheng yuè yònggōng, lǎoshī yuè gāoxìng.** = *The harder students study, the more delighted their teachers.*

yuè 阅 Trad 閱 VERB = read

yuèdú 阅读 [compound: 阅 *read* + 读 *read*]

VERB = read seriously
- 总经理每天花很多时间阅读各部门的报告。**Zǒngjīnglǐ měi tiān huā hěn duō shíjiān yuèdú gè bùmén de bàogào.** = *The general manager spends a lot of time every day reading reports submitted by various departments.*

yuèlǎnshì 阅览室 [modif: 阅览 *read, browse* + 室 *room*] NOUN = reading room (间 jiān)
- 阅览室里的图书杂志不能带出室外。**Yuèlǎnshì li de túshū zázhì bù néng dàichū shìwài.** = *You are not allowed to take books and periodicals out of the reading room.*

yuè 跃 Trad 躍 VERB = leap (See 活跃 huóyuè.)

yún 云 Trad 雲 NOUN = cloud
- 蓝天白云，好看极了！**Lán tiān bái yún, hǎokàn jíle!** = *White clouds in the blue sky, how beautiful!*

duōyún 多云 = cloudy
- 今天多云。**Jīntiān duōyún.** = *It's cloudy today.*

yǔn 允 VERB = allow

Y

yǔnxǔ 允许 [compound: 允 *allow* + 许 *permit*]
VERB = allow, permit
■ 这里不允许停车。**Zhèlǐ bù yǔnxǔ tíng chē.** = *Parking is not allowed here.*
■ 我们不允许任何反社会行为。**Wǒmen bù yǔnxǔ rènhé fǎn shèhuì xíngwéi.** = *We do not allow any anti-social behavior.*

yùn 运 Trad 運 VERB = transport, carry
■ 中国主要靠火车运货。**Zhōngguó zhǔyào kào huǒchē yùn huò.** = *China mainly uses trains to transport cargo.*

yùndòng 运动 [compound: 运 *move* + 动 *move*]
1 VERB = do physical exercises
■ 你经常运动吗？**Nǐ jīngcháng yùndòng ma?** = *Do you exercise often?*
2 NOUN = physical exercises
■ "你每天做什么运动？" "我有时候打球，有时候跑步。" **"Nǐ měi tiān zuò shénme yùndòng?" "Wǒ yǒushíhou dǎ qiú, yǒushíhou pǎobù."** = *"What physical exercises do you do every day?" "Sometimes I play ball games and sometimes I jog."*
■ 生命在於运动。**Shēngmìng zài yú yùndòng.** = *Life lies in physical exercise.*
yùndòngxié 运动鞋 = sport shoes

yùndònghuì 运动会 [modif: 运动 *sports* + 会 *meeting*] NOUN = sports meet, games
■ 这个中学每年十月举行运动会。**Zhège zhōngxué měi nián Shíyuè jǔxíng yùndònghuì.** = *This high school holds a sports meet every October.*

yùndòngyuán 运动员 [modif: 运动 *sports* + 员 *person*] NOUN = athlete, sportsman, sportswoman
■ 我叔叔年轻的时候是一名长跑运动员。**Wǒ shūshu niánqīng de shíhou shì yì míng chángpǎo yùndòngyuán.** = *When young, my uncle was a long-distance runner*

yùnshū 运输 [compound: 运 *transport* + 输 *transport*]
1 VERB = transport, carry
■ 你们用什么把煤运输到港口？**Nǐmen yòng shénme bǎ méi yùnshū dào gǎngkǒu?** = *How do you transport coal to the port?*
2 NOUN = transportation

■ 修建了这条铁路，运输问题就基本解决了。**Xiūjiànle zhè tiáo tiělù, yùnshū wèntí jiù jīběn jiějué le.** = *When this railway is built, transportation problems will be basically solved.*

yùnyòng 运用 VERB = use, apply, put into use
■ 我们现在运用电脑控制生产过程。**Wǒmen xiànzài yùnyòng diànnǎo lái kòngzhì shēngchǎn guòchéng.** = *Now we use computers to control the production process.*

Z

zá 杂 Trad 雜 ADJECTIVE = miscellaneous, sundry, all sorts of
■ 我还有些杂事要办完才能回家。**Wǒ hái yǒu xiē zá shì yào bànwán cái néng huí jiā.** = *I still have some miscellaneous things to deal with before I can go home.*
záfèi 杂费 = sundry charges

zájì 杂技 [modif: 杂 *miscellaneous* + 技 *skills*] NOUN = acrobatics
■ 听说中国的杂技很有名。**Tīngshuō Zhōngguó de zájì hěn yǒumíng.** = *I've heard people say that Chinese acrobatics are very famous*
zájìtuán 杂技团 = acrobatics troupe
zájì yǎnyuán 杂技演员 = acrobat

zázhì 杂志 [modif: 杂 *miscellaneous* + 志 *record*] NOUN = magazine (本 **běn**, 种 **zhǒng**)
■ 他订了两种杂志。**Tā dìngle liǎng zhǒng zázhì.** = *He subscribes to two magazines.*

zāi 灾 Trad 災 NOUN = disaster, calamity
■ 中国每年都有地方受灾。**Zhōngguó měi nián dōu yǒu dìfang shòu zāi.** = *Every year there are places in China that are hit by calamities.*
huǒzāi 火灾 = fire
shuǐzāi 水灾 = flooding, floods

zāihài 灾害 [compound: 灾 *disaster* + 害 *damage*] NOUN = disaster, calamity
■ 由于各种灾害，全国每年损失几十亿元。**Yóuyú gè zhǒng zāihài, quánguó měi nián sǔnshī jǐ shí yì yuán.** = *Owing to disasters of*

Y

all kinds the country loses billions of dollars every year.
zìrán zāihài 自然灾害 = natural disaster

zài 再 ADVERB = again
■ 我没听清楚，请您再说一遍。**Wǒ méi tīng qīngchu, qǐng nín zài shuō yí biàn.** *I did not hear it clearly. Please say it again.*
■ 你的电脑修好了，要是再坏，我就没有办法了。**Nǐ de diànnǎo xiūhǎo le, yàoshì zài huài, wǒ jiù méiyǒu bànfǎ le.** = *Your computer has been repaired. If it breaks down again, there'll be nothing I can do.*

NOTE: 再 **zài** and 又 **yòu** are both glossed as *again*, but they have different usage: 又 **yòu** is used in the context of a past situation while 再 **zài** is used for a future situation. Here is another pair of examples:
■ 她昨天又迟到了。**Tā zuótiān yòu chídào le.** = *She was late* (for work, school, etc.) *again yesterday.*
■ 明天你不要再迟到了。**Míngtiān nǐ bú yào zài chídào le.** = *Please do not be late again tomorrow.*

zàijiàn 再见 [modif: 再 *again* + 见 *see*] VERB = see you again, goodbye
■ "我回家了，再见！" "再见，明天见。" **"Wǒ huíjiā le, zàijiàn!" "Zàijiàn, míngtiān jiàn."** = *"I'm going home, goodbye!" "Bye! See you tomorrow."*

zài 在 1
1 PREPOSITION = in, on, at
■ 在新加坡很多人会说中文。**Zài Xīnjiāpō hěn duō rén huì shuō Zhōngwén.** = *In Singapore many people speak Chinese.*
■ 我在两年以前开始学中文。**Wǒ zài liǎngnián yǐqián kāishǐ xué Zhōngwén.** = *I began to learn Chinese two years ago.*
2 VERB = be in
■ "你爸爸在家吗？他不在家。" **"Nǐ bàba zài jiā ma?" "Tā bú zài jiā."** = *"Is your father home?" "No, he isn't."*
■ "小明在哪里？" "他在操场上。" **"Xiǎo Míng zài nǎlǐ?" "Tā zài cāochǎng shang."** = *"Where's Xiao Ming?" "He's on the sports ground."*
zài ... li 在 ... 里 = in
■ 他在房间里休息。**Tā zài fángjiān li xiūxi.** = *He's taking a rest in the room.*

zài ... shang 在 ... 上 = on
■ 在桌子上有两本书。**Zài zhuōzi shang yǒu liǎng běn shū.** = *There are two books on the desk.*
zài ... xia 在 ... 下 = under ...
■ 在床下有一双鞋。**Zài chuáng xia yǒu yì shuāng xié.** = *There's a pair of shoes under the bed.*
zài ... zhī jiān 在 ... 之间 = between
■ 我要在这两棵树之间种一些花。**Wǒ yào zài zhè liǎng kē shù zhī jiān zhòng yìxiē huā.** = *I'm going to plant some flowers between the two trees.*

zài 在 2 ADVERB = (used to indicate an action in progress)
■ "你在做什么？" "我在找东西。" **"Nǐ zài zuò shénme?" "Wǒ zài zhǎo dōngxi."** = *"What are you doing?" "I'm looking for something."*

zán 咱 PRONOUN = same as 咱们 **zámen**

zánmen 咱们 [suffix: 咱 *we, us* + 们 suffix denoting a plural number] PRONOUN = we, us (including the person or persons spoken to)
■ 你在学中文，我也在学中文，咱们都在学中文。**Nǐ zài xué Zhōngwén, wǒ yě zài xué Zhōngwén, zánmen dōu zài xué Zhōngwén.** = *You're learning Chinese, I'm learning Chinese. We're both learning Chinese.*
■ 咱们去吃饭吧！**Zánmen qù chīfàn ba!** = *Let's go and have our meal.*

NOTE: 咱们 **zánmen** is only used in colloquial Chinese, and has a northern dialect flavor. You can always just use 我们 **wǒmen**, even to include the person(s) spoken to. The following examples are perfectly acceptable:
■ 你在学中文，我也在学中文，我们都在学中文。**Nǐ zài xué Zhōngwén, wǒ yě zài xué Zhōngwén, wǒmen dōu zài xué Zhōngwén.** = *You're learning Chinese. I'm learning Chinese. We're both learning Chinese.*
■ 我们去吃饭吧！**Wǒmen qù chīfàn ba!** = *Let's go and have a meal.*

zàn 暂 Trad 暫 ADJECTIVE = temporary

zànshí 暂时 [compound: 暂 *temporary* + 时 *time*] ADJECTIVE = temporary, for the time being
■ 你暂时在这里住一下，大房间一空出来就可以搬进去。**Nǐ zànshí zài zhèli zhù yíxià, dà**

fángjiān yí kòng chūlai jiù kěyǐ bān jìnqu. = *Please stay here for the time being. You can move to the bigger room as soon as it is vacated.*

zàn 赞 Trad 贊 VERB = support

zànchéng 赞成 VERB = approve of, support, be in favor of
■ 我不赞成他代表我们公司去参加会议。**Wǒ bú zànchéng tā dàibiǎo wǒmen gōngsī qù cānjiā huìyì.** = *I don't approve his being our company representative at the conference.*
■ 赞成的，请举手! **Zànchéng de, qǐng jǔshǒu!** = *Those in favor, please raise your hands.*

zāng 脏 Trad 髒 ADJECTIVE = dirty (antonym 干净 **gānjìng**)
■ 这些衣服脏了，要洗一下。**Zhèxiē yīfu zàng le, yào xǐ yíxià.** = *These clothes are dirty and need washing.*

zàng 脏 Trad 臟 NOUN = internal organs (See 心脏 **xīnzàng**.)

zāo 遭 VERB = meet with (misfortune)

zāodào 遭到 VERB = suffer, encounter, meet with
■ 公用电话常常遭到破坏。**Gōngyòng diànhuà chángcháng zāodào pòhuài.** = *Public telephones are often vandalized.*

zāoshòu 遭受 VERB = suffer, be subjected to
■ 去年这个地区连续遭受自然灾害。**Qùnián zhège dìqū liánxù zāoshòu zìrán zāihài.** = *Last year this area suffered repeated natural disasters.*

zāo 糟 ADJECTIVE = messy

zāogāo 糟糕 [modif: 糟 *messy* + 糕 *cake*]
1 ADJECTIVE = in a mess, terrible, very bad
■ 我这次考试很糟糕。**Wǒ zhè cì kǎoshì hěn zāogāo.** = *I did very poorly in the exam.*
■ 情况很糟糕。**Qíngkuàng hěn zāogāo.** = *The situation is in a shambles.*
2 INTERJECTION = How terrible! What bad luck!
■ 真糟糕，我的钥匙丢了。**Zhēn zāogāo, wǒ de yàoshi diū le.** = *How terrible! I've lost my keys!*

zǎo 早 ADJECTIVE = early
■ 现在才三点钟，还早呢! **Xiànzài cái sān diǎnzhōng, hái zǎo ne!** = *It's only three o'clock. It's still early!*
■ 李先生每天很早上班，很晚下班。**Lǐ xiānsheng měi tiān hěn zǎo shàngbān, hěn wǎn xiàbān.** = *Every day Mr Li goes to work early and comes off work late.*

NOTE: A common greeting among the Chinese when they meet in the morning is 早 **zǎo** or 你早 **Nǐ zǎo**.

zǎochén 早晨 [modif: 早 *early* + 晨 *early morning*] NOUN = early morning (approximately 6–9 a.m.)
■ 他早晨六点半起床。**Tā zǎochén liù diǎn bàn qǐchuáng.** = *He gets up at half past six in the morning.*
■ 很多人喜欢在早晨锻炼身体。**Hěn duō rén xǐhuan zài zǎochén duànliàn shēntǐ.** = *Many people like to exercise in the early morning.*

zǎofàn 早饭 [modif: 早 *early* + 饭 *meal*] NOUN = breakfast (顿 **dùn**)
■ 我今天起得太晚了，没有时间吃早饭。**Wǒ jīntiān qǐ de tài wǎn le, méiyǒu shíjiān chī zǎofàn.** = *I got up too late today and didn't have time for breakfast.*

zǎoshang 早上 NOUN = same as 早晨 **zǎochén**

zǎo 澡 NOUN = bath (See 洗澡 **xǐzǎo**.)

zào 皂 NOUN = soap (See 香皂 **xiāngzào**.)

zào 造 VERB = make, build
■ 中国人在公元一世纪就会造纸。**Zhōngguórén zài gōngyuán yī shìjì jiù huì zào zhǐ.** = *The Chinese knew how to make paper as early as in the first century.*
zàochéng 造成 = result in, give rise to
■ 不幸的童年造成他性格上的很多缺点。**Búxìng de tóngnián zàochéng tā xìnggé shang de hěn duō quēdiǎn.** = *An unhappy childhood gave rise to many faults in his character.*
zàojù 造句 = make sentences, sentence-making

zào 燥 ADJECTIVE = dry (See 干燥 **gānzào**.)

zé 则 Trad 則 CONJUNCTION = in that case, then
■ 不进则退。**Bú jìn zé tuì.** = *If you don't make progress, then you'll fall behind.*
■ 如果一切顺利，则工厂可在明年开工。 **Rúguǒ yíqiè shùnlì, zé gōngchǎng kě zài míngnián kāigōng.** = *If everything goes well, then the factory can start production next year.*

NOTE: 则 **zé** is only used in formal Chinese. In everyday Chinese, use 那 **nà** or 那么 **nàme** instead. See note on 那么 **nàme**.

zé 责 Trad 責 NOUN = duty

zérèn 责任 NOUN
1 = responsibility, duty
■ 教育孩子是父母的责任。**Jiàoyù háizi shì fù-mǔ de zérèn.** = *It is the parents' responsibility to educate their children.*
2 = responsibility for a fault or mistake
■ 这次交通事故责任主要在开快车的那一方。**Zhè cì jiāotōng shìgù zérèn zhǔyào zài kāi kuàichē de nà yì fāng.** = *The person who was speeding is mainly to blame for this traffic accident.*
zérènɡǎn 责任感 = sense of responsibility
■ 这个男人缺点很多，但是责任感很强，很顾家。**Zhège nánrén quēdiǎn hěn duō, dànshì zérènɡǎn hěn qiáng, hěn gù jiā.** = *This man may have many shortcomings, but he has a strong sense of responsibility and cares for his family.*

zé 择 Trad 擇 VERB = choose (See 选择 **xuǎnzé**.)

zěnme 怎么 PRONOUN
1 = how, in what manner
■ 这个汉字怎么写？ **Zhège Hànzi zěnme xiě?** = *How do you write this Chinese character?*
■ 对不起，请问去北京大学怎么走？ **Duìbuqǐ, qǐng wèn qù Běijīng Dàxué zěnme zuò?** = *Excuse me, could you please tell me how to get to Beijing University?*
2 = no matter how (used with 都 **dōu** or 也 **yě**)
■ 是这把钥匙吗？我怎么都开不开这个门。 **Shì zhè bǎ yàoshi ma? Wǒ zěnme dōu kāi bu kāi zhège mén.** = *Is this the right key? No matter how I tried, I couldn't open the door.*
■ 他怎么也找不到那本书。**Tā zěnme yě zhǎo bu dào nà běn shū.** = *No matter how hard he tried, he couldn't find the book.*

3 = why, how come
■ 你怎么又迟到了？ **Nǐ zěnme yòu chídào le?** = *Why are you late again?*
■ 她今天怎么这么高兴？ **Tā jīntiān zěnme zhème gāoxìng?** = *Why is she so happy today?*
4 = how can ...
■ 这么多作业，我今天怎么做得完？ **Zhème duō zuòyè, wǒ jīntiān zěnme zuò de wán?** = *How can I finish so many assignments today?*
■ 你说这种话，妈妈怎么会不生气？ **Nǐ shuō zhè zhǒng huà, māma zěnme huì bù shēngqì?** = *How would mom not feel angry, when you had said such things?*
zěnmebàn 怎么办 = what's to be done?
■ 要是飞机票卖完了，怎么办？ **Yàoshi fēijīpiào màiwán le, zěnmebàn?** = *What should we do if the air tickets are sold out?*
zěnmele 怎么了 = what happened?
■ 怎么了，她怎么哭了？ **Zěnmele, tā zěnme kū le?** = *What happened? Why is she crying?*

zěnmeyàng 怎么样 PRONOUN
1 = same as **zěnme 怎么** PRONOUN 1
2 = how
■ 你今天觉得怎么样？ **Nǐ jīntiān juéde zěnmeyàng?** = *How are you feeling today?*
■ 他使用电脑的能力怎么样？ **Tā shǐyòng diànnǎo de nénglì zěnmeyàng?** = *How competent is he in using the computer?*
3 = how's that? is it OK?
■ 我们每个人讲一个故事，怎么样？ **Wǒmen měi ge rén jiǎng yí ge gùshi, zěnmeyàng?** = *We each tell a story, how about that?*
■ 我晚上开车来接你，怎么样？ **Wǒ wǎnshang kāichē lái jiē nǐ, zěnmeyàng?** = *I'll pick you up this evening. Is it OK?*

zěnyàng 怎样 PRONOUN = same as 怎么样 **zěnmeyàng**. Used in writing.

zēng 增 VERB = increase

zēngjiā 增加 [compound: 增 *increase* + 加 *add*] VERB = increase
■ 去年他家的收入增加了两千元。**Qùnián tā jiā de shōurù zēngjiāle liǎngqiān yuán.** = *Last year his family income increased by 2,000 yuan.*

zēngzhǎng 增长 [compound: 增 *increase* + 长 *grow*] VERB = increase, grow

Z

■旅行增长知识。**Lǚxíng zēngzhǎng zhīshi.** =
Travelling increases one's knowledge.
■大学生人数在五年中增长百分之三十以
上。**Dàxuéshēng rénshù zài wǔ nián zhong
zēngzhǎng bǎifēn zhi sānshí yǐ shàng.** = *In the
past five years the number of university students has grown by more than thirty percent.*

zhāi 摘 VERB = pick, pluck
■星期天跟我们一起去果园摘苹果吧。
**Xīngqītiān gēn wǒmen yìqǐ qù guǒyuán zhāi
píngguǒ ba.** = *Do go to the orchard with us on
Sunday to pick apples.*

zhǎi 窄 ADJECTIVE = narrow (antonym 宽 kuān)
■这条街太窄, 汽车开不进去。**Zhè tiáo jiē
tài zhǎi, qìchē kāi bu jìnqu.** = *This street is too
narrow for a car to enter.*

zhǎn 展 VERB = display

zhǎnchū 展出 [v+comp: 展 show + 出 out]
VERB = be on show, put on display
■这两天商场展出最新夏装。**Zhè liǎngtiān
shāngchǎng zhǎnchū zuì xīn xiàzhuāng.** =
*These days the latest summer wear is on dis-
play in the shopping center.*

zhǎnkāi 展开 VERB = carry out, launch
■政府将要展开交通安全的活动。**Zhèngfǔ
jiāngyào zhǎnkāi jiāotōng ānquán de huódòng.**
= *The government will carry out activities to
promote traffic safety.*

zhǎnlǎn 展览 [modif: 展 display + 览 view]
1 VERB = put on display, exhibit
■这个画儿画得真好, 可以去展览。**Zhège
huàr huà de zhēn hǎo, kěyǐ qù zhǎnlǎn.** = *This
picture is done so well that it can be put on
display.*
2 NOUN = exhibition, show
■我上个星期参观了一个很有意思的展览。
**Wǒ shàngge xīngqī cānguānle yí ge hěn yǒu
yìsi de zhǎnlǎn.** = *Last week I visited a very interesting exhibition.*
zhǎnlǎnhuì 展览会 = same as 展览 2 NOUN

zhàn 占 VERB = occupy
■你一个人不能占两个座位。**Nǐ yí ge rén bù
néng zhàn liǎng ge zuòwèi.** = *You're only one
person and can't take two seats.*

zhàn 战 Trad 戰 VERB = battle

zhànshèng 战胜 [v+comp: 战 fight + 胜
victorious] NOUN = triumph over, defeat
■人不可能战胜自然。**Rén bù kěnéng
zhànshèng zìrán.** = *It is impossible for man to
triumph over nature.*

zhànshi 战士 [modif: 战 fighting + 士 person]
NOUN = soldier, fighter
■不管天冷天热, 战士们坚持军事训练。
**Bùguǎn tiān-lěng-tiān-rè, zhànshimen jiānchí
jūnshì xùnliàn.** = *The soldiers persist in military training regardless of the weather
conditions.*

zhànzhēng 战争 [compound: 战 fight + 争
strife] NOUN = war
■在二十一世纪, 人类能避免大规模战争吗?
**Zài èrshíyī shìjì, rénlèi néng bìmiǎn dà guīmó
zhànzhēng ma?** = *Can mankind avoid large-
scale wars in the twenty-first century?*

zhàn 站 1 VERB = stand
■房间里有些人站着, 有些人坐着。**Fángjiān
li yǒuxiē rén zhànzhe, yǒuxiē rén zuòzhe.** = *In
the room some people are standing, and others
are seated.*
■站在高山上, 可以看得很远。**Zhàn zài
gāoshān shang, kěyǐ kàn de hěn yuǎn.** = *Standing on a high mountain, one can see very far.*
zhàn qǐlai 站起来 = stand up
■老师走进教室, 学生们都站起来。**Lǎoshī
zǒujìn jiàoshi, xuéshengmen dōu zhàn qǐlai.** =
*When the teacher came into the classroom, all
the students stood up.*

zhàn 站 2 NOUN = station, stop
■我要一辆出租车去火车站。**Wǒ yào yí liàng
chūzū qìchē qù huǒchē zhàn.** = *I want a taxi to
go to the railway station.*
zhànzhǎng 站长 = railway/coach stationmaster
chūzū qìchē zhàn 出租汽车站 = taxi stand
huǒchē zhàn 火车站 = railway station
qìchē zhàn 汽车站 = coach/bus station; bus stop

zhāng 张 Trad 張 1 MEASURE WORD = (for paper,
bed, table etc.)
■一张纸 **yì zhāng zhǐ** = *a piece of paper*
■两张床 **liǎng zhāng chuáng** = *two beds*
■三张桌子 **sān zhāng zhuōzi** = *three tables/desks*

Zhāng 张 Trad 張 2 NOUN = a common family name

- 张先生 / 太太 / 小姐 **Zhāng xiānsheng/ tàitai/xiǎojiě** = *Mr/Mrs/Miss Zhang*

zhāng 章 NOUN = chapter (See 文章 **wénzhāng.**)

zhǎng 长 Trad 長 VERB

1 = grow

- 孩子长高了。**Háizi zhǎnggāo le.** = *The child has grown taller.*
- 孩子长大成人，父母也老了。**Háizi zhǎngdà chéngrén, fù-mǔ yě lǎo le.** = *The parents will be old when their children are grown up.*

2 = grow to be, look

- 他们的女儿长得很漂亮。**Tāmen de nǚ'ér zhǎng de hěn piàoliang.** = *Their daughter is very pretty.*
- 今年的庄稼长得真好。**Jīnnián de zhuāngjia zhǎng de zhēn hǎo.** = *The crops this year are really good.*

zhǎng 涨 Trad 漲 VERB = rise, go up

- 水涨船高。**Shuǐ zhǎng chuán gāo.** = *When the river rises the boat goes up.* (→ *When the general situation improves, particular things improve.*)
- 上周股票涨了很多。**Shàng zhōu gǔpiào zhǎngle hěn duō.** = *Last week shares rose greatly.*

zhǎng 掌 NOUN = hand, palm

zhǎngwò 掌握 [compound: 掌 *be in charge* + 握 *take ... in one's hands*] VERB = have a good command of, know well

- 要掌握一门外语是不容易的。**Yào zhǎngwò yì mén wàiyǔ shì bù róngyi de.** = *It is not easy to gain a good command of a foreign language.*

zhàng 丈 NOUN = senior

zhàngfu 丈夫 NOUN = husband (antonym 妻子 qīzi)

- 你认识她的丈夫吗？ **Nǐ rènshi tā de zhàngfu ma?** = *Do you know her husband?*

zhāo 招 VERB = beckon, attract

zhāodài 招待 VERB = receive or entertain (a guest)

- 他们用好酒好菜招待客人。**Tāmen yòng hǎo jiǔ hǎo cài zhāodài kèren.** = *They entertained their guests with good wine and good food.*

zhāodàihuì 招待会 = reception

zhāohu 招呼 [compound: 招 *beckon* + 呼 *call*] VERB = call, shout at

- 马路对面有人在招呼我。**Mǎlù duìmiàn yǒurén zài zhāohu wǒ.** = *There's someone calling me on the other side of the road.*

dǎ zhāohu 打招呼

1 = greet

- 他进屋就跟大家打招呼。**Tā jìn wū jiù gēn dàjiā dǎ zhāohu.** = *He greeted everybody when he came into the room.*

2 = inform casually, tell

- 他没跟我打招呼就把我自行车骑走了。**Tā méi gēn wǒ dǎ zhāohu jiù bǎ wǒ de zìxíngchē qízǒu le.** *He rode off on my bicycle without telling me.*

zháo 着 VERB = catch

zháojí 着急 VERB = be anxious, be worried

- 已经十二点了，女儿还没有回家，妈妈很着急。**Yǐjīng shí'èr diǎn le, nǚ'ér hái méi huíjiā, māma hěn zháojí.** = *It was almost twelve o'clock and her daughter was still not home. The mother felt very worried.*
- 你着急有什么用呢？慢慢想办法吧。**Nǐ zháojí yǒu shénme yòng ne? Mànman xiǎng bànfǎ ba.** = *What's the use of being worried? Let's think of a plan.*

bié zháojí 别着急 = don't worry

zhǎo 找 VERB = look for, search for

- "你在找什么?""我在找我的手表。" **"Nǐ zài zhǎo shénme?" "Wǒ zài zhǎo wǒ de shǒubiǎo."** = *"What are you looking for?" "I'm looking for my watch."*
- 你真的关心她，就帮她找个对象吧。**Nǐ zhēn de guānxīn tā, jiù bāng tā zhǎo ge duìxiàng ba.** = *If you are really concerned for her, help her to find a fiancé.*

zhǎodào 找到 = find

- 我姐姐在香港找到了一个好工作。**Wǒ jiějie zài Xiānggǎng zhǎodàole yí ge hǎo**

Z

gōngzuò. = *My elder sister has found a good job in Hong Kong.*

zhào 召 VERB = summon

zhàokāi 召开 [compound: 召 *summon* + 开 *open*] VERB = convene (a conference)
■ 下星期校长要召开全体教师会议，讨论明年工作安排。**Xià xīngqī xiàozhǎng yào zhàokāi quántǐ jiàoshī huìyì, tǎolùn míngnián gōngzuò ānpái.** = *Next week the [high school] principal will convene a meeting of all teaching staff to discuss next year's work.*

zhào 照 1 VERB
1 = take a photo
■ 麻烦您给我们照一张相。**Máfan nín gěi wǒmen zhào yí zhāng xiàng.** = *Would you please take a photo of us?*
■ 这儿风景不错，我想照一张相。**Zhèr fēngjǐng bú cuò, wǒ xiǎng zhào yì zhāng xiàng.** = *The scenery is good here. I'd like to have a picture taken.*
2 = look in a mirror
■ 他们的小男孩从来不照镜子，小女孩老是照镜子。**Tāmen de xiǎo nánhái cónglái bú zhào jìngzi, xiǎo nǚhái lǎoshì zhào jìngzi.** = *Their little boy never looks in the mirror but their little girl always looks in the mirror.*
3 = shine, light up
■ 冬天的太阳照在脸上，暖暖的，很舒服。**Dōngtiān de tàiyang zhào zài liǎnshang, nuǎnnuǎn de, hěn shūfu.** = *In winter when the sun shines on your face you feel warm and comfortable.*

zhào 照 2 PREPOSITION = according to, in the manner of
■ 我们还是照以前的方法付款。**Wǒmen háishì zhào yǐqián de fāngfǎ fùkuǎn.** = *We will pay in the same way as before.*
■ 照我说的去办，肯定不会错。**Zhào wǒ shōude qù bàn, kěndìng bú huì cuò.** = *Do as I say and you will definitely not go wrong.*

zhàocháng 照常 [v+obj: 照 *according to* + 常 *usual*] ADJECTIVE = as usual
■ 本店春节照常营业。**Běn diàn chūnjié zhàocháng yíngyè.** = *Business as usual during the Spring Festival.*

zhàogu 照顾 [compound: 照 *look after* + 顾 *attend to*] VERB = look after, care for
■ 他每个星期六到老人院去照顾老人。**Tā měi ge Xīngqīliù dào lǎorényuàn qù zhàogu lǎorén.** = *Every Saturday afternoon she goes to a senior citizens' home to look after the senior citizens there.*
■ 我在阿姨家过暑假的时候，她一家对我照顾得很好。**Wǒ zài āyí jiā guò shǔjià de shíhou, tā yìjiā duì wǒ zhàogu de hěn hǎo.** = *When I stayed with my aunt's family for the summer holidays, they took good care of me.*

zhàopiàn 照片 NOUN = photograph, picture, snapshot (张 **zhāng**)
■ 申请签证，要交三张照片。**Shēnqǐng qiānzhèng, yào jiāo sān zhāng zhàopiàn.** = *To apply for visa, you need to submit three photos.*
■ 老人常常看看老照片，回忆过去的生活。**Lǎorén chángcháng kànzhe lǎo zhàopiàn, huíyì guòqù de shēnghuó.** = *The old man (or woman) often looks at old photos, recalling life in the past.*

zhàoxiàng 照相 [v+obj: 照 *illuminate* + 相 *photograph*] VERB = take a picture
■ 请你给我们照个相。**Qǐng nǐ gěi wǒmen zhào ge xiàng.** = *Please take a picture of us.*
■ 人们喜欢站在那幅画前照相。**Rénmen xǐhuan zhàn zài nà fù huà qián zhàoxiàng.** = *People like to take photos standing in front of that painting.*
zhàoxiàngguǎn 照相馆 = photographic studio
zhàoxiàngjī 照相机 = camera
■ 明天出去玩，别忘了带照相机！**Míngtiān chūqu wán, bié wàngle dài zhàoxiàngjī!** = *Don't forget to bring a camera with you on your outing tomorrow!*

zhé 折
1 VERB = convert to, amount to
■ 一美元折多少日元？**Yì Měiyuán zhé duōshǎo Rìyuán?** = *How many Japanese yen does an American dollar amount to?*
2 NOUN = discount, reduction (in price)
■ 这些书现在打八折。**Zhèxiē shū xiànzài dǎ bā zhé.** = *These books are under a twenty percent discount now.*

zhé 哲 ADJECTIVE = wise

zhéxué 哲学 NOUN = philosophy
- 我对东方哲学感兴趣。 **Wǒ duì dōngfāng zhéxué gǎn xìngqù.** = *I am interested in Eastern philosophy.*
  zhéxuéjiā 哲学家 = philosopher

zhě 者 SUFFIX = (a nominal suffix denoting a person or people) (See 读者 dúzhě, 记者 jìzhě, 作者 zuòzhě.)

zhè 这 Trad 這 PRONOUN = this
- 这是什么？ **Zhè shì shénme?** = *What's this?*
- 这也不行，那也不行，你到底要我怎么办。 **Zhè yě bù xíng, nà yě bù xíng, nǐ dàodǐ yào wǒ zěnmebàn?** = *This won't do and that won't do either. What do you expect me to do?*

zhège 这个 [modif: 这 this + 个 one] PRONOUN = this one, this
- 这个太大，给我小一点儿的。 **Zhège tài dà, gěi wǒ xiǎo yìdiǎnr de.** = *This one is too big. Give me a smaller one.*
- 你为了这个生气，值得吗？ **Nǐ wèile zhège shēngqì, zhídé ma?** = *Is it worth getting angry over this?*

zhèli 这里 PRONOUN = this place, here
- 你在这里住了几年了？ **Nǐ zài zhèli zhùle jǐ nián le?** = *How long have you been living here?*
- 我刚来的时候，不习惯这里的天气。 **Wǒ gāng lái de shíhou, bù xíguàn zhèli de tiānqì.** = *When I first came, I wasn't used to the weather here.*

NOTE: In spoken Chinese 这里 **zhèli** can be replaced by 这儿 **zhèr.**

zhème 这么 PRONOUN = like this, in this manner, so
- 这件衣服这么贵，我没想到。 **Zhè jiàn yīfu zhème guì, wǒ méi xiǎngdào.** = *I did not expect this dress to be so expensive.*
- 你这么快就把文章写好了，佩服佩服！ **Nǐ zhème kuài jiù bǎ wénzhāng xiě hǎo le, pèifu pèifu!** = *It is simply admirable that you wrote the article so fast!*

zhèxiē 这些 PRONOUN = these
- 这些书你都看过吗？ **Zhèxiē shū nǐ dōu kànguo ma?** = *Have you read all these books?*

zhèyàng 这样 PRONOUN
1 = same as 这么 **zhème.** Used only in writing.
2 = such
- 他就是这样的一个人，根本靠不住。 **Tā jiùshì zhèyàng de yí ge rén, gēnběn kào bu zhù.** = *He is just such a person (→ That's just typical of him). He is not reliable at all.*

zhe 着 PARTICLE = (used after a verb to indicate the action or state is going on)
- 门开着，灯亮着，可是房间里没有人。 **Mén kāizhe, dēng liàngzhe, kěshì fángjiān li méiyǒu rén.** = *The door was open and the light was on but there was no one in the room.*

zhèi 这 Trad 這 PRONOUN = same as 这 **zhè.** Used colloquially.

zhēn 真 1 ADVERB = real, really, true, truly, indeed
- 中国真大呀！ **Zhōngguó zhēn dà ya!** = *China is really big!*
- 我真不愿意去参加那个晚会。 **Wǒ zhēn bú yuànyì qù cānjiā nàge wǎnhuì.** = *I really don't want to attend that evening party.*

zhēn 真 2 ADJECTIVE = true, real (antonym 假 jiǎ)
- 这个电影是根据真人真事编写的。 **Zhège diànyǐng shì gēnjù zhēn rén zhēn shì biānxiě de.** = *This movie is based on a real-life story.*
  zhēnhuà 真话 = truth
- 这家报纸很少说真话。 **Zhè jiā bàozhǐ hěn shǎo shuō zhēnhuà.** = *This newspaper rarely tells the truth.*
  zhēnkōng 真空 = vacuum
  zhēnxīn 真心 = sincerity

zhēnlǐ 真理 [modif: 真 true + 理 reasoning, principle] NOUN = truth
- 真理往往掌握在少数人手里。 **Zhēnlǐ wǎngwǎng zhǎngwò zài shǎoshù rén shǒuli.** = *Truth is very often in the hands of the minority.*

zhēnshí 真实 [compound: 真 real + 实 substance] ADJECTIVE = true, real, authentic
- 到底发生了什么？没有人知道真实的情况。 **Dàodǐ fāshēngle shénme? Méiyǒu rén zhīdào zhēnshí de qíngkuàng.** = *What on earth happened? Nobody knows the true situation.*

Z

zhēnzhèng 真正 [compound: 真 *neat* + 正 *orderly*] ADJECTIVE = true, real, genuine
- 真正的友谊是天长地久的。**Zhēnzhèng de yǒuyì shì tiān-cháng-dì-jiǔ de.** = *Genuine friendship is everlasting.*
- 他在农村各地旅行了一年多，才真正了解中国。**Tā zài nóngcūn gèdì lǚxíngle yì nián duō, cái zhēnzhèng liǎojiě Zhōngguó.** = *It was only after he traveled in various parts of rural China for over a year that he really came to understand China.*

zhēn 针 Trad 針 NOUN
1 = needle (根 gēn)
- 我要一根缝衣针。**Wǒ yào yì gēn féngyī zhēn.** = *I want a sewing needle.*
2 = injection
- 护士给他打了一针。**Hùshi gěi tā dǎ le yì zhēn.** = *The nurse gave him an injection.*
dǎzhēn 打针 = give an injection, get an injection
- 她打针吃药半个月病才好。**Tā dǎzhēn chīyào bàn ge yuè bìng cái hǎo.** = *She had injections and took medicine for half a month before she recovered.*

zhēnduì 针对 VERB = aim at, be aimed at
- 这次反吸烟运动主要针对青少年。**Zhè cì fǎn xīyān yùndòng zhǔyào zhēnduì qīngshàonián.** = *This anti-smoking campaign is mainly aimed at teenagers.*
- 厂长的话是针对经常迟到的工人说的。**Chǎngzhǎng de huà shì zhēnduì jīngcháng chídào de gōngrén shuō de.** = *The factory manager's words are directed at workers who often come late for work.*

zhēnjiǔ 针灸 [compound: 针 *needle* + 灸 *moxibustion*]
1 NOUN = acupuncture and moxibustion
- 他学中文的目的是为了研究针灸。**Tā xué Zhōngwén de mùdì shì wèile yánjiū zhēnjiǔ.** = *His purpose of learning Chinese is to study acupuncture and moxibustion.*
2 VERB = give or receive acupuncture and moxibustion treatment
- 他针灸了几次，肩就不疼了。**Tā zhēnjiǔle jǐ cì, jiān jiù bú tòng le.** = *After a few sessions of acupuncture and moxibustion, his shoulder no longer hurts.*

zhèn 阵 Trad 陣 MEASURE WORD = (for an action or event that lasts for some time)
- 雨下了一阵停了。**Yǔ xiàle yí zhèn tíng le.** = *The rain stopped after a while.*
- 刮了一阵大风，院子里满是落叶。**Guāle yí zhèn dà fēng, yuànzi li mǎnshì luòyè.** = *A strong wind blew for a while and the courtyard was full of fallen leaves.*
zhènyǔ 阵雨 = shower

zhēng 争 VERB = argue
- 别争了，争到明天也争不出结果来。**Bié zhēng le, zhēng dào míngtiān yě zhēng bu chū jiéguǒ lai.** = *Stop arguing. Even if you argue till tomorrow there will be no conclusion.*

zhēnglùn 争论 [compound: 争 *argue* + 论 *comment*] VERB = dispute, debate
- 他喜欢和朋友争论哲学问题。**Tā xǐhuan hé péngyou zhēnglùn zhéxué wèntí.** = *He likes to debate philosophical issues with his friends.*

zhēngqǔ 争取 [compound: 争 *strive* + 取 *obtain*] VERB = strive for, fight for
- 我们争取提前完成计划。**Wǒmen zhēngqǔ tíqián wánchéng jìhuà.** = *We strive to fulfill the plan ahead of schedule.*

zhēng 征 Trad 徵 VERB = solicit

zhēngqiú 征求 [compound: 征 *solicit* + 求 *request*] VERB = solicit, ask for
- 老师征求学生对教学的意见。**Lǎoshī zhēngqiú xuésheng duì jiàoxué de yìjiàn.** = *The teachers solicit students' comments on their teaching.*

zhēng 睁 VERB = open (the eyes)
- 奇怪，这个人怎么睁着眼睛睡觉？**Qíguài, zhège rén zěnme zhēngzhe yǎnjing shuìjiào?** = *Strange, how is it that this person sleeps with his eyes open?*
- 对这种行为，不能睁一只眼，闭一只眼。**Duì zhè zhǒng xíngwéi, bù néng zhēng yì zhī yǎn, bì yì zhī yǎn.** = *We must not turn a blind eye to such behavior.*

zhěng 整 ADJECTIVE = whole, full, entire
- 她昨天整夜没睡。**Tā zuótiān zhěngyè méi shuì.** = *She didn't sleep the entire night.*
- 他整天都在写那份报告。**Tā zhěngtiān dōu**

zài xiě nà fèn bàogào. = *He spent the whole day writing that report.*
■ 雨下了整整两天两夜。**Yǔ xiàle zhěngzhěng liǎng tiān liǎng yè.** = *It rained incessantly for two days and two nights.*

zhěngge 整个 ADJECTIVE = whole, entire
■ 整个工程都是他负责。**Zhěngge gōngchéng dōu shì tā fùzé.** = *He is in charge of the entire project.*

zhěnglǐ 整理 [compound: 整 *put in order* + 理 *tidy up*] VERB = put in order, tidy up
■ 客人来前，整理一下房间。**Kèren lái qián, zhěnglǐ yíxià fángjiān.** = *Tidy up the rooms before guests arrive.*

zhěngqí 整齐 [compound: 整 *neat* + 齐 *orderly*] ADJECTIVE = in good order, neat and tidy (antonym 乱 **luàn**)
zhěng-zhěng-qí-qí 整整齐齐 = an emphatic form of 整齐 **zhěngqí**
■ 十几双鞋排得整整齐齐。**Shí jǐ shuāng xié páide zhěng-zhěng-qí-qí.** = *Over a dozen pairs of shoes were arranged in a very orderly way.*

zhèng 正
1 ADJECTIVE = straight, upright (antonym 歪 **wāi**, 斜 **xié**)
■ 帮我看看，这幅画挂得正不正？**Bāng wǒ kànkan, zhè fú huà guà de zhèng bu zhèng?** = *Have a look to see if this picture is hung straight.*
2 ADVERB = same as 正在 **zhèngzài**

zhèngcháng 正常 [compound: 正 *normal* + 常 *usual*] ADJECTIVE = normal, regular (antonym 反常 **fǎncháng**)
■ 这几天，车间里一切正常。**Zhè jǐ tiān, chējiān li yíqiè zhèngcháng.** = *Everything is normal in the workshop these days.*
■ 在正常的情况下，他一周给父母发一份电子邮件。**Zài zhèngcháng de qíngkuàng xià, tā yì zhōu gěi fù-mǔ fā yí fèn diànzǐ yóujiàn.** = *Under normal circumstances he sends his parents an e-mail once a week.*

zhènghǎo 正好 [modif: 正 *just* + 好 *good*] ADJECTIVE
1 = just right
■ 我穿这双鞋正好。**Wǒ chuān zhè shuāng xié**

zhènghǎo. = *These shoes are just the right size for me.*
■ 你来得正好，我正要找你呢。**Nǐ lái de zhènghǎo, wǒ zhèngyào zhǎo nǐ ne.** = *You've come at the right moment; I was just looking for you.*
2 = chance to, by coincidence
■ 我正好那天下午没课，可以陪她进城。**Wǒ zhènghǎo nà tiān xiàwǔ méi kè, kěyǐ péi tā jìnchéng.** = *It happened that I did not have class that afternoon, so I could go to town with her.*

zhèngquè 正确 [compound: 正 *proper* + 确 *true*] ADJECTIVE = correct, accurate (antonym 错误 **cuòwù**)
■ 你的回答不正确。**Nǐ de huídá bú zhèngquè.** = *Your answer is not correct.*
■ 你要听各方面的意见，才能形成正确的观点。**Nǐ yào tīng gè fāngmiàn de yìjiàn, cáinéng xíngchéng zhèngquè de guāndiǎn.** = *You can form the correct viewpoint only after hearing out opinions from all sides.*

zhèngshì 正式 [modif: 正 *formal* + 式 *manner*] ADJECTIVE = formal, official
■ 公司正式通知职工，明年一月起工资提高百分之十。**Gōngsī zhèngshì tōngzhī zhígōng, míngnián Yīyuè qǐ gōngzī tígāo bǎifēn zhī shí.** = *The company has formally informed the staff that they will get a ten-percent raise starting next January.*

zhèngzài 正在 ADVERB = (used before a verb to indicate the action is in progress)
■ 他正在看电视。**Tā zhèngzài kàn diànshì.** = *He's watching TV.*
zhèngzài ... ne 正在 … 呢 = same as 正在 **zhèngzài** but with a casual, friendly tone

zhèng 证 Trad 證 NOUN = proof

zhèngmíng 证明 [v+comp: 证 *prove* + 明 *clear*]
1 VERB = prove, testify
■ 事实证明，他的想法行不通。**Shìshí zhèngmíng, tā de xiǎngfǎ xíng bu tōng.** = *Facts have proven that his ideas do not work.*
2 NOUN = certificate
■ 你要请医生开一张病假证明。**Nǐ yào qǐng yīshēng kāi yì zhāng bìngjià zhèngmíng.** = *You*

should ask your doctor to issue a certificate for medical leave.

chūshēng zhèngmíng 出生证明 = birth certificate

jiéhūn zhèngmíng 结婚证明 = marriage license, marriage certificate

chū zhèngmíng 出证明 = issue a certificate

zhèng 政 NOUN = governance

zhèngcè 政策 [modif: 政 government + 策 policy] NOUN = government policy
■ 政府的移民政策可能会变化。**Zhèngfǔ de yímín zhèngcè kěnéng huì biànhuà.** = *The government immigration policy may change.*

zhèngfǔ 政府 [modif: 政 governance + 府 building] NOUN = government
■ 政府有关部门正在研究这个问题。**Zhèngfǔ yǒuguān bùmén zhèngzài yánjiū zhège wèntí.** = *The government departments concerned are studying this issue.*

zhèngzhì 政治 [compound: 政 governance + 治 administering] NOUN = politics, governance
■ 我对这个国家的政治情况了解不多。**Wǒ duì zhège guójiā de zhèngzhì qíngkuàng liǎojiě bù duō.** = *I don't know much about the political situation in this country.*
■ 现代政治一定是民主的政治。**Xiàndài zhèngzhì yídìng shì mínzhǔ de zhèngzhì.** = *Modern governance must be democratic.*

zhī 之 PARTICLE = same as 的 de. Used in written Chinese or certain set expressions.
zhī hòu 之后 = after, behind
■ 他退休之后，要搬到故乡去住。**Tā tuìxiū zhī hòu, yào bāndào gùxiāng qù zhù.** = *After retirement he will move to his hometown.*
zhī jiān 之间 = between
■ 两座大楼之间有一座小公园。**Liǎng zuò dàlóu zhī jiān yǒu yí zuò xiǎo gōngyuán.** = *There is a small park between the two buildings.*
■ 我们之间存在着一些误会。**Wǒmen zhījiān cúnzàizhe yìxiē wùhuì.** = *There is some misunderstanding between us.*
zhī qián 之前 = before
■ 你在六月之前给我回信。**Nǐ yào zài Liùyuè zhī qián gěi wǒ huíxìn.** = *You should give me a reply before June.*

zhī wài 之外 = outside, apart from
■ 地球之外，还有其他地方有生命吗？**Dìqiú zhī wài, háiyǒu qítā dìfang yǒu shēngmìng ma?** = *Apart from Earth, is there life anywhere else?*
zhī xià 之下 = below, under
■ 三层楼之下是一个大餐厅。**Sāncéng lóu zhī xià shì yí ge dà cāntīng.** = *Below the third floor is a large restaurant.*
zhī yī 之一 = one of
■ 杭州是中国名胜之一。**Hángzhōu shì Zhōngguó míngshèng zhī yī.** = *Hangzhou is one of China's tourist attractions.*
zhī zhōng 之中 = between, among
■ 她的朋友之中，没有人会说中文。**Tā de péngyou zhī zhōng, méiyou rén huì shuō Zhōngwén.** = *There is none among her friends who speaks Chinese.*

zhī 支 MEASURE WORD = (for stick-like things)
■ 一支笔 **yì zhī bǐ** = *a pen*

zhīchí 支持 [compound: 支 prop up, support + 持 hold] VERB = support
■ 同事之间要相互合作，相互支持。**Tóngshì zhī jiān yào xiānghù hézuò, xiānghù zhīchí.** = *Colleagues should cooperate and support each other.*

zhīyuán 支援 [compound: 支 prop up, support + 援 aid]
1 VERB = support, aid
■ 全国支援受灾地区。**Quánguó zhīyuán shòuzāi dìqū.** = *The whole country aided the disaster-stricken region.*
2 NOUN = aid, support
■ 感谢你们给我们的宝贵支援。**Gǎnxiè nǐmen gěi wǒmen de bǎoguì zhīyuán.** = *Our thanks for your precious aid.*

zhī 只 MEASURE WORD = (used with certain nouns denoting animals or utensils, or objects normally occurring in pairs)
■ 一只手 **yì zhī shǒu** = *a hand*
■ 两只狗 **liǎng zhī gǒu** = *two dogs*

zhī 知 VERB = know

zhīdào 知道 VERB = know
■ 我不知道这件事。**Wǒ bù zhīdào zhè jiàn shì.** = *I don't know about this matter.*

■ 你知道这家公司的传真号码吗？ **Nǐ zhīdào zhè jiā gōngsī de chuánzhēn hàomǎ ma?** = *Do you know the fax number of this company?*

zhīshi 知识 NOUN = knowledge
■ 旅行使人学到知识。**Lǚxíng shǐ rén xuédao zhīshi.** = *Travelling enables one to learn knowledge.*
■ 他这一方面的知识很丰富。**Tā zhè yì fāngmiàn de zhīshi hěn fēngfù.** = *He has rich knowledge in this aspect.*
　zhīshi jīngjì 知识经济 = knowledge economy

zhī 织 Trad 織 VERB = weave (See 纺织 **fǎngzhī**, 组织 **zǔzhī**.)

zhí 执 Trad 執 VERB = grasp, persist

zhíxíng 执行 VERB = carry out, implement, execute
■ 坚决执行上级交给我们的任务。**Jiānjué zhíxíng shàngjí jiāo gei wǒmen de rènwù.** = *We will resolutely carry out the mission entrusted to us by the higher authorities.*
■ 这个计划很难执行。**Zhège jìhuà hěn nán zhíxíng.** = *This plan is difficult to implement.*

zhí 直
1 ADJECTIVE = straight (antonym 弯 **wān**)
■ 用尺划一条直线。**Yòng chǐ huà yì tiáo zhí xiàn.** = *Draw a straight line using a ruler.*
2 ADVERB = straight, directly
■ 这班航机直飞香港，中间不停。**Zhè bān hángjī zhí fēi Xiānggǎng, zhōngjiān bù tíng.** = *This airliner flies direct to Hong Kong without any stopover.*

zhídào 直到 [modif: 直 *straight* + 到 *arrive*] PREPOSITION = until, till
■ 孩子们在花园里玩，直到天黑。**Háizimen zài huāyuán li wán, zhídào tiānhēi.** = *The children played in the garden till it was dark.*
■ 他一直住在家乡，直到念完中学。**Tā yìzhí zhù zai jiāxiāng, zhídào niànwán zhōngxué.** = *He lived in his hometown until finishing high school.*

zhíjiē 直接 [modif: 直 *direct* + 接 *join*] ADJECTIVE = direct
■ 你可以直接找房东，不用通过中间人。**Nǐ kěyǐ zhíjiē zhǎo fángdōng, bú yòng tōngguò zhōngjiānrén.** = *You can make direct contact with the landlord without going through the middleman.*

zhí 值 NOUN = value

zhíde 值得 VERB = be worth
■ 为了这件小事生气，不值得。**Wèile zhè jiàn xiǎoshì shēngqì, bù zhíde.** = *Such a small matter is not worth getting angry over.*
■ 这本词典虽然不便宜，还是值得买。**Zhè běn cídiǎn suīrán bù piányì, háishì zhíde mǎi.** = *Although this dictionary is not cheap, it is worth buying.*

zhí 职 Trad 職 NOUN = job

zhígōng 职工 [compound: 职 *clerk* + 工 *worker*] NOUN = staff (of a factory, a company, an enterprise, etc.), employee(s)
■ 我们公司总共有一千八百五十名职工。**Wǒmen gōngsī zǒnggòng yǒu yìqiān bābǎi wǔshí míng zhígōng.** = *Our company has 1,850 employees in total.*

zhíyè 职业 [compound: 职 *job* + 业 *occupation*] NOUN = occupation, profession, vocation
■ 他的职业是医生，也是一位业余作家。**Tā de zhíyè shì yīshēng, yě shì yí wèi yèyú zuòjiā.** = *He is a doctor by profession but he is also a writer in his spare time.*
　zhíyèbìng 职业病 = occupational disease
　zhíyè jièshàosuǒ 职业介绍所 = employment agency

zhí 植 VERB = plant, grow

zhíwù 植物 [modif: 植 *plant* + 物 *thing*] NOUN = plant, flora
■ 这种植物很少见，应该受到保护。**Zhè zhǒng zhíwù hěn shǎojiàn, yīnggāi shòudào bǎohù.** = *This plant is rare and should be protected.*
　zhíwùxué 植物学 = botany
　zhíwùxuéjiā 植物学家 = botanist
　zhíwùyuán 植物园 = botanical garden

zhǐ 止 VERB = stop (pain, cough, thirst, etc.)
■ 这个止痛药有没有副作用？ **Zhège zhǐ tòng yào yǒu méiyǒu fùzuòyòng?** = *Does this painkiller have any side effects?*

Z

zhǐ 只 ADVERB = only

■ 我只有一个弟弟，没有哥哥，也没有姐妹。**Wǒ zhǐ yǒu yí ge dìdi, méiyǒu gēge, yě méiyǒu jiě-mei.** = *I've only got a younger brother. I don't have an elder brother or sister.*
■ 她只喝水，不喝酒。**Tā zhǐ hē shuǐ, bù hē jiǔ.** = *She only drinks water and does not drink wine.*

zhǐhǎo 只好 ADVERB = have no choice but

■ 他自行车坏了，只好走路去上学。**Tā zìxíngchē huài le, zhǐhǎo zǒu lù qù shàngxué.** = *His bicycle has broken down, so he has to walk to school.*
■ 飞机票全卖完了，我们只好坐火车去。**Fēijī piào quán màiwánle, wǒmen zhǐhǎo zuò huǒchē qù.** = *As air tickets were sold out we had no choice but go by train.*

zhǐshì 只是 ADVERB = only, just

■ 她只是想学几句旅游中文。**Tā zhǐshì xiǎng xué jǐ jù lǚyóu Zhōngwén.** = *She only wants to learn some Chinese for sightseeing.*
■ 他在饭店打工，只是因为一时找不到更合适的工作。**Tā zài fàndiàn dǎgōng, zhǐshì yīnwèi yìshí zhǎo bu dào gèng héshì de gōngzuò.** = *He worked in a restaurant only because he could not find a more suitable job at that time.*
■ 我很想认真了解中国的历史，只是没有时间。**Wǒ hěn xiǎng rènzhēn liǎojiě Zhōngguó de lìshǐ, zhǐshì méiyǒu shíjiān.** = *I'd like to learn Chinese history earnestly, it's just that I don't have the time.*
■ 她很想去听音乐会，只是买不起门票。**Tā hěn xiǎng qù tīng yīnyuèhuì, zhǐshì mǎi buqǐ ménpiào.** = *She wants to go to the concert badly, but unfortunately she can't afford the ticket.*

zhǐyào 只要 CONJUNCTION = so long as, provided that, if only

■ 只要身体好，就能享受生活。**Zhǐyào shēntǐ hǎo, jiù néng xiǎngshòu shēnghuó.** = *As long as you are in good health, you can enjoy life.*
■ 只要打一个电话，饭店就会马上把菜送来。**Zhǐyào dǎ yí ge diànhuà, fàndiàn jiù huì mǎshàng bǎ cài sònglai.** = *You only need give the restaurant a call and they will deliver your order immediately.*

zhǐyǒu 只有

1 ADVERB = can only, have no choice but
■ 既然答应帮助他，只有尽力而为了。**Jìrán dāyìng bāngzhù tā, zhǐyǒu jìn lì ér wéi le.** = *Now that I've promised to help him, I can only do my best.*
2 CONJUNCTION = only, only if
■ 只有认真地学，才能学好中文。**Zhǐyǒu rènzhēn de xué, cáinéng xuéhǎo Zhōngwén.** = *Only if you study in earnest, can you gain a good command of Chinese.*
■ 只有经理亲自道歉，顾客才会满意。**Zhǐyǒu jīnglǐ qīnzì dàoqiàn, gùkè cáihuì mǎnyì.** = *Only if the manager himself apologizes, will the customer be satisfied.*

zhǐ 纸 Trad 紙 NOUN = paper (张 zhāng)

■ 请给我几张纸。**Qǐng gěi wǒ jǐ zhāng zhǐ.** = *Please give me some paper.*
■ 纸是古代中国人发明的。**Zhǐ shì gǔdài Zhōngguórén fāmíng de.** = *Paper was invented by the ancient Chinese.*

zhǐ 址 NOUN = location (See 地址 dìzhǐ.)

zhǐ 指 VERB

1 = point at, point to
■ 你不知道那东西叫什么，就用手指。**Nǐ bù zhīdào nà dōngxi jiào shénme, jiù yòng shǒu zhǐ.** = *If you don't know what it's called, just point to it with your finger.*
■ 他指着自己的鼻子说，"就是我。" **Tā zhǐzhe zìjǐ de bízi shuō, "Jiù shì wǒ."** = *Pointing at his own nose, he said, "It's me."*
2 = refer to, allude to, mean
■ 他说有人工作不负责，不知道是指谁。**Tā shuō yǒuxiē rén gōngzuò bú fùzé, bù zhīdào shì zhǐ shuí.** = *I don't know to whom he was referring when he said some people were not responsible in their work.*

zhǐchū 指出 [v+obj: 指 point + 出 out] VERB = point out

■ 老师指出了我发音中的问题。**Lǎoshī zhǐchūle wǒ fāyīn zhōng de wèntí.** = *The teacher pointed out the problems in my pronunciation.*
■ 这篇文章指出，社会必须照顾弱者。**Zhè piān wénzhāng zhǐchū, shèhuì bìxū zhàogù ruòzhě.** = *This article points out that the society must take care of the weak.*

Z

zhǐdǎo 指导 [compound: 指 *point* + 导 *guide*]
VERB = guide, direct, supervise
■ 工程师指导技术员修理机器。
Gōngchéngshī zhǐdǎo jìshùyuán xiūlǐ jīqì. =
The engineer supervised technicians in repairing the machine.
zhǐdǎoyuán 指导员 = political instructor (in the Chinese People's Liberation Army)
zhǐdǎo sīxiǎng 指导思想 = guiding principle

zhì 至 VERB = to, until (only used in written Chinese)
■ 银行营业时间是上午九时至下午五时。
Yínháng yíngyè shíjiān shì shàngwǔ jiǔ shí zhì xiàwǔ wǔ shí. = *The business hours of the bank are from nine o'clock in the morning till five o'clock in the afternoon.*

zhìjīn 至今 [v+obj: 至 *to, until* + 今 *today*]
ADVERB = till now, to this day, so far
■ 至今已有七十多人报名学习中文。**Zhìjīn yǐ yǒu qīshí duō rén bàomíng xuéxí Zhōngwén.** = *So far over seventy people have applied to study Chinese.*
■ 我至今还不明白她为什么突然离家。**Wǒ zhìjīn hái bù míngbai tā wèishénme tūrán líjiā.** = *To this day I still do not understand why she left home all of a sudden.*

zhìshǎo 至少 ADVERB = at least
■ 我今年学了至少三百个汉字。**Wǒ jīnnián xuéle zhìshǎo sānbǎi ge hànzì.** = *I have learnt at least 300 Chinese characters this year.*
■ 孩子至少懂得了为什么不应该说假话。**Háizi zhìshǎo dǒngdele wèishénme bù yīnggāi shuō jiǎhuà.** = *At least the child has understood why one should not tell lies.*

zhì 志 Trad 誌 NOUN = record (See 杂志 zázhì.)

zhì 致 VERB = reach (See 一致 yízhì.)

zhì 治 VERB = treat (disease)
■ 医生的责任是治病救人。**Yīshēng de zérèn shì zhì bìng jiù rén.** = *It is the responsibility of a doctor to treat disease and save lives.*
■ 他的病恐怕治不好了。**Tā de bìng kǒngpà zhì bu hǎo le.** = *I'm afraid his disease cannot be cured.*

zhì 制 Trad 製 VERB = make, work out

zhìdìng 制定 [compound: 制 *work out* + 定 *decide*] VERB = lay down, draw up
■ 他们在每年年底制定第二年的计划。**Tāmen zài měi nián niándǐ zhìdìng dì-èr nián de jìhuà.** = *They draw up the plan for the next year at the end of a year.*

zhìdù 制度 NOUN = system
■ 目前的教育制度存在很多问题。**Mùqián de jiàoyù zhìdù cúnzài hěn duō wèntí.** = *There are many problems in the current educational system.*

zhìzào 制造 [compound: 制 *make* + 造 *make*]
VERB = make, manufacture
■ "中国制造"的商品越来越多。**"Zhōngguó zhìzào" de shāngpǐn yuèláiyuè duō.** = *There are more and more goods labeled "Made in China."*
■ 五年以前这家工厂制造自行车，现在制造摩托车。**Wǔ nián yǐqián zhè jiā gōngchǎng zhìzào zìxíngchē, xiànzài zhìzào mótuōchē.** = *Five years ago this factory made bicycles, and now it manufactures motorcycles.*
zhìzàoyè 制造业 = manufacturing industry

zhì 质 Trad 質 NOUN = nature, character

zhìliàng 质量 NOUN = quality (antonym 数量 shùliàng)
■ 这个牌子的汽车质量好，价格又便宜。**Zhège páizi de qìchē zhìliàng hǎo, jiàgé yòu piányi.** = *Cars of this make are of good quality and inexpensive.*
■ 你觉得这种产品的质量如何？= **Nǐ juéde zhè zhǒng chǎnpǐn de zhìliàng rúhé?** = *How do you find the quality of this product?*

zhì 秩 NOUN = order, rank

zhìxù 秩序 [compound: 秩 *order* + 序 *order*]
NOUN = order, proper sequence
■ 运动场内秩序良好。**Yùndòngchǎng nèi zhìxù liánghǎo.** = *In the stadium the audience maintains good order.*

zhì 置 VERB = place (See 位置 wèizhi.)

Z

zhōng 中

1 NOUN = center, middle
- 东南西北中 **dōng, nán, xī, běi, zhōng** = *the east, the south, the west, the north and the center*

2 ADJECTIVE = middle, medium

zhōngcān 中餐 [modif: 中 *Chinese* + 餐 *meal*]

NOUN = Chinese cuisine, Chinese food
- 我们用中餐招待客人。**Wǒmen yòng zhōngcān zhāodài kèren.** = *We entertain guests with Chinese food.*

zhōngcānguǎn 中餐馆 = Chinese restaurant
zhōngcāntīng 中餐厅 = Chinese restaurant (in a hotel, etc.)

Zhōngguó 中国 [modif: 中 *middle, central* + 国 *kingdom, country*] NOUN = China

- 中国历史长，人口多。**Zhōngguó lìshǐ cháng, rénkǒu duō.** = *China has a long history and a large population.*

Zhōnghuá 中华 NOUN = China, Chinese

- 中华文明对东亚各国有很大影响。**Zhōnghuá wénmíng duì Dōng-Yà gè guó yǒu hěn dà yíngxiǎng.** = *Chinese civilization has had great influence on countries in East Asia.*

NOTE: Both 中国 **Zhōngguó** and 中华 **Zhōnghuá** may refer to China, but 中华 **Zhōngghuá** has historical and cultural connotations

zhōngjiān 中间 NOUN = center, middle, among

- 花园的中间有一棵大树。**Huāyuán de zhōngjiān yǒu yì kē dà shù.** = *In the center of the garden there is a very big tree.*
- 我的朋友中间，他体育最好。**Wǒ de péngyou zhōngjiān, tā tǐyù zuì hǎo.** = *Among my friends he is the best athlete.*

Zhōngwén 中文 [modif: 中 *China* + 文 *writing*] NOUN = the Chinese language (especially the writing)

- 世界上有十几亿人用中文。**Shìjiè shang yǒu shí jǐ yì rén yòng Zhōngwén.** = *Over a billion people in the world use Chinese.*

NOTE: See note on 汉语 **Hànyǔ**.

zhōngwǔ 中午 [modif: 中 *middle* + 午 *noon*]

NOUN = noon
- 我们中午休息一个小时。**Wǒmen zhōngwǔ xiūxi yì ge xiǎoshí.** = *We have a one-hour break at noon.*

zhōngxīn 中心 [modif: 中 *central* + 心 *the heart*] NOUN = central part, center

- 城市的中心是一座大公园。**Chéngshì de zhōngxīn shì yí zuò dà gōngyuán.** = *There is a big park in the center of the city.*
- 他讲话的中心思想是必须保证产品的质量。**Tā jiǎnghuà de zhōngxīn sīxiǎng shì bìxū bǎozhèng chǎnpǐn de zhìliàng.** = *The central idea of his speech is that product quality must be guaranteed.*

shìzhōngxīn 市中心 = city center
yánjiū zhōngxīn 研究中心 = research center

zhōngxué 中学 [modif: 中 *middle* + 学 *school*] NOUN = secondary school, high school, middle school (座 zuò, 所 suǒ)

- 这座城市有十多所中学。**Zhè zuò chéngshì yǒu shí duō suǒ zhōngxué.** = *This city has over ten secondary schools.*
- 在中国，中学分初中、高中两部分。**Zài Zhōngguó, zhōngxué fēn chūzhōng, gāozhōng liǎng bùfen.** = *In China, high schools are divided into junior high and senior high.*

zhōngyào 中药 [modif: 中 *Chinese* + 药 *medicine, drug*] NOUN = traditional Chinese medicine (e.g. herbs)

- 很多常见的植物都是重要的中药。**Hěn duō chángjiàn de zhíwù dōu shì zhòngyào de zhōngyào.** = *Many common plants are an important part of traditional Chinese medicine.*

zhōngyī 中医 [modif: 中 *Chinese* + 医 *medicine, medical science*] NOUN

1 = traditional Chinese medicine
- 中医和古代哲学思想有关。**Zhōngyī hé gǔdài zhéxué sīxiǎng yǒuguān.** = *Traditional Chinese medicine is related to ancient Chinese philosophical thought.*

2 = traditional Chinese medical doctor
- 你这个病可以请一位中医看看。**Nǐ zhège bìng kěyǐ qǐng yí wèi zhōngyī kànkan.** = *You can consult a traditional Chinese doctor on your illness.*

Z

zhōng 钟 Trad 鐘 NOUN = clock (座 zuò)
■ 这座钟慢了三分钟。**Zhè zuò zhōng mànle sān fēnzhōng.** = *This clock is three minutes slow.*
zhōnglóu 钟楼 = clock tower

zhōngtóu 钟头 NOUN = same as 小时 xiǎoshí. Used in spoken Chinese.

zhōng 终 NOUN = end, finish

zhōngyú 终于 ADVERB = finally, in the end
■ 他终于实现了自己的愿望。**Tā zhōngyú shíxiànle zìjǐ de yuànwàng.** = *He finally realized his aspirations.*
■ 我终于找到了他的家。**Wǒ zhōngyú zhǎodaole tā de jiā.** = *I finally found his home.*

zhǒng 种 Trad 種 MEASURE WORD = kind, sort, type
■ 这里有三种酒，你想喝哪一种？ **Zhèli yǒu sān zhǒng jiǔ, nǐ xiǎng hē nǎ yì zhǒng?** = *Here are three kinds of wine. Which one would you like to drink?*
■ 你最喜欢吃哪种水果？ **Nǐ zuì xǐhuan chī nǎ zhǒng shuǐguǒ?** = *What kind of fruit do you like best?*
gè zhǒng gè yàng 各种各样 = all sorts of, all kinds of

zhǒngzi 种子 [suffix: 种 seed + 子 nominal suffix] NOUN = seed
■ 这家公司向农民提供各类优质种子。**Zhè jiā gōngsī xiàng nóngmín tígòng gè léi yōuzhí zhǒngzi.** = *This company provides farmers with all kinds of high quality seeds.*

zhòng 众 Trad 衆 NOUN = crowd (See 观众 guānzhòng, 群众 qúnzhòng.)

zhòng 种 Trad 種 VERB = plant
■ 爸爸在我家小花园里种了一些花。**Bàba zài wǒ jiā xiǎo huāyuán li zhòngle yìxiē huā.** = *Dad planted some flowers in our little garden.*

zhòng 重 ADJECTIVE = heavy (antonym 轻 qīng)
■ 这个机器太重了，我们两个人搬不动。**Zhège jīqì tài zhòng le, wǒmen liǎng ge rén bān bu dòng.** = *This machine is too heavy for the two of us to move.*
■ 他把钱看得太重。**Tā bǎ qián kànde tài zhòng.** = *He attaches too much importance to money.*

zhòngdà 重大 [compound: 重 weighty + 大 big] ADJECTIVE = major, great
■ 去年国际上有哪些重大事件？ **Qùnián guójì shang yǒu nǎxiē zhòngdà shìjiàn?** = *What were the major international events last year?*
■ 他在决定政策方面起重大作用。**Tā zài juédìng zhèngcè fāngmiàn qǐ zhòngdà zuòyòng.** = *He played a major role in policy making.*

zhòngdiǎn 重点 [compound: 重 weighty + 点 point] NOUN = main point, focal point, emphasis
■ 中文一年级的学习重点应该是发音和口语。**Zhōngwén yī niánjí de xuéxí zhòngdiǎn yīnggāi shì fāyīn hé kǒuyǔ.** = *The emphasis in first-year Chinese studies should be on pronunciation and spoken Chinese.*
■ 我今年要把重点放在学习语法上。**Wǒ jīnnián yào bǎ zhòngdiǎn fang zai xuéxí yǔfǎ shang.** = *This year I will put stress on the study of Chinese grammar.*

zhòngliàng 重量 [modif: 重 heavy + 量 amount] NOUN = weight
■ 称一下这件行李的重量。**Chēng yíxià zhè jiàn xíngli de zhòngliàng.** = *Weigh this piece of luggage to see how heavy it is.*

zhòngshì 重视 [modif: 重 weighty + 视 view] VERB = attach importance to, value
■ 老年人一般比较重视身体健康。**Lǎoniánrén yìbān bǐjiào zhòngshì shēntǐ jiànkāng.** = *Old people generally value good health.*
■ 中国人一般重视子女的教育－主要是知识教育。**Zhōngguórén yìbān zhòngshì zǐnǔ de jiàoyù－zhǔyào shì zhīshi jiàoyù.** = *Generally speaking, Chinese people attach much importance to their children's education—mainly knowledge education.*

zhòngyào 重要 [compound: 重 heavy + 要 (in this context) important] ADJECTIVE = important
■ 这件事非常重要，你别忘了！ **Zhè jiàn shì fēicháng zhòngyào, nǐ bié wàng le!** = *This matter is very important. Don't you forget it!*
■ 我有一个重要的消息告诉你。**Wǒ yǒu yí ge zhòngyào de xiāoxi gàosu nǐ.** = *I have important news to tell you.*

Z

zhōu 周 NOUN = week
- "你们学校寒假放几周?" "三周。" **"Nǐmen xuéxiào hánjià fàng jǐ zhōu?" "Sān zhōu."** = *"How many weeks of winter holiday does your school have?" "Three weeks."*

NOTES: (1) 周 **zhōu** and 星期 **xīngqī** both mean *week*, but 周 **zhōu** is usually used in writing only. Normally 星期 **xīngqī** is the word to use. (2) 周 **zhōu** is not used with any measure word.

Zhōu 周 NOUN = a common family name
- 周先生 / 太太 / 小姐 **Zhōu xiānsheng/tàitai/ xiǎojiě** = *Mr/Mrs/Miss Zhou*

zhōudào 周到 [modif: 周 *circumference, all sides* + 到 *reach*] ADJECTIVE = thorough, thoughtful
- 这个旅馆的服务很周到。**Zhège lǚguǎn de fúwù hěn zhōudào.** = *This hotel provides thoughtful service.*
- 你们都准备好了, 想得真周到。**Nǐmen dōu zhǔnbèi hǎole, xiǎngde zhēn zhōudào.** = *It is really thoughtful of you to get everything ready.*
- 你接受新工作以前, 要考虑得周到一点。**Nǐ jiēshòu xīn gōngzuò yǐqián, yào kǎolǜ de zhōudào yìdiǎn.** = *You should think very carefully before you accept a new job.*

zhōumò 周末 [modif: 周 *week* + 末 *end*] NOUN = weekend
- 这个周末我要进城买衣服和鞋子。**Zhège zhōumò wǒ yào jìnchéng mǎi yīfu hé xiézi.** = *This weekend I'll go to town to buy clothes and shoes.*
- "上个周末你过得好吗?" "过得很愉快。" **"Shàng ge zhōumò nǐ guòde hǎo ma?" "Guò de hěn yúkuài."** = *"Did you have a good time last weekend?" "Yes, I had a very pleasant time."*

zhōuwéi 周围 [compound: 周 *circuit* + 围 *encircle*] NOUN = surrounding area, all around
- 新西兰周围都是大海。**Xīnxīlán zhōuwéi dōu shì dàhǎi.** = *All around New Zealand is the sea.*

zhōu 洲 NOUN = continent (See 大洋洲 **Dàyángzhōu**, 欧洲 **Ōuzhōu**, 亚洲 **Yàzhōu**.)

zhū 猪 NOUN = pig (头 **tóu**)
- 这家农民养了十头猪。**Zhè jiā nóngmín yǎngle shí tóu zhū.** = *This peasant household keeps ten pigs.*
- 中国人一般吃猪肉, 不大吃牛肉、羊肉。**Zhōngguórén yìbān chī zhūròu, bú dà chī niúròu, yángròu.** = *The Chinese normally eat pork and don't eat much beef or mutton.*

zhú 竹 NOUN = bamboo

zhúzi 竹子 [suffix: 竹 *bamboo* + 子 nominal suffix] NOUN = bamboo (棵 **kē**)
- 院子里的一角种了几棵竹子。**Yuànzi li de yì jiǎo zhòngle jǐ kē zhúzi.** = *There is some bamboo planted in a corner of the courtyard.*
- 古代中国人特别喜爱竹子。**Gǔdài Zhōngguórén tèbié xǐ'ài zhúzi.** = *The ancient Chinese were particularly fond of bamboo.*

zhú 逐 ADVERB = successive

zhúbù 逐步 [modif: 逐 *successive* + 步 *step*] ADVERB = step by step, progressively, gradually
- 我们的中文水平在逐步提高。**Wǒmen de Zhōngwén shuǐpíng zài zhúbù tígāo.** = *Our Chinese proficiency is progressively improving.*

zhújiàn 逐渐 [compound: 逐 *successive, one by one* + 渐 *gradual*] ADVERB = gradually, step by step
- 地球正在逐渐变暖。**Dìqiú zhèngzài zhújiàn biàn nuǎn.** = *The Earth is gradually warming up.*
- 他逐渐能听懂中文广播了。**Tā zhújiàn néng tīngdǒng Zhōngwén guǎngbō le.** = *Gradually he could understand Chinese broadcasts.*

zhǔ 主 NOUN = master, owner

zhǔdòng 主动 [modif: 主 *self* + 动 *act*] ADJECTIVE = of one's own accord, taking the initiative
- 他主动提出帮助我们。**Tā zhǔdòng tíchū bāngzhù wǒmen.** = *He offered to help us without being asked.*
- 在谈恋爱的时候, 一般是小伙子主动一点。**Zài tán liàn'ài de shíhou, yìbān shì xiǎohuǒzi zhǔdòng yìdiǎn.** = *Normally young men take the initiative in courtship.*

Z

zhǔguān 主观 [modif: 主 *subjective* + 观 *view*] ADJECTIVE = subjective
■ 你这种说法只是建立在你个人的经历上，所以比较主观。**Nǐ zhè zhǒng shuōfǎ zhǐshì jiànlì zài nǐ gérén de jīnglì shang, suǒyǐ bǐjiào zhǔguān.** = *Your arguments are rather subjective because they are only based on your personal experiences.*

zhǔrén 主人 [modif: 主 *master* + 人 *person*] NOUN
1 = host (antonym 客人 **kèren**)
■ 客人都来了，主人呢？**Kèren dōu lái le, zhǔrén ne?** = *The guests have all arrived, but where is the host?*
2 = owner, proprietor
■ 我是这辆车的主人，你们为什么把车拖走？**Wǒ shì zhè liàng chē de zhǔrén, nǐmen wèishénme bǎ chē tuōzǒu?** = *I'm the owner of this car. Why did you tow it away?*

zhǔrèn 主任 [modif: 主 *principal* + 任 *appointed*] NOUN = chairman (of a committee), director (of a department)
■ 这个委员会的主任由一位教授担任。**Zhège wěiyuánhuì de zhǔrèn yóu yí wèi jiàoshòu dānrèn.** = *The chair of this committee was held by a professor.*
zhǔrèn yīshēng 主任医生 = chief physician, chief surgeon
bàngōngshì zhǔrèn 办公室主任 = office manager
chējiān zhǔrèn 车间主任 = head of a workshop (in a factory)

zhǔxí 主席 [modif: 主 *principal* + 席 *seat*] NOUN = chairman, chairperson
■ 中华人民共和国的主席是中国的国家元首。**Zhōnghuá Rénmín Gònghéguó de zhǔxí shì Zhōngguó de guójiā yuánshǒu.** = *The Chairman of the People's Republic of China is the head of state of China.*
dàhuì zhǔxí 大会主席 = chairperson of an assembly

zhǔyào 主要 [compound: 主 *advocate* + 要 (in this context) *important*] ADJECTIVE = major, chief, main
■ 这不是主要的问题，可以以后再讨论。**Zhè bú shì zhǔyào de wèntí, kěyǐ yǐhòu zài tǎolùn.** = *This is not a major issue. We can discuss it later.*

■ 纠正错误是主要的，谁该负责以后再说。**Jiūzhèng cuòwù shì zhǔyào de, shuí gāi fùzé yǐhòu zài shuō.** = *Rectifying the mistake is the main thing. The question of who is to blame can wait till later.*

zhǔyi 主意 [compound: 主 *major* + 意 *idea*] NOUN = definite view, idea
■ 这件事我没有什么主意，你看呢？**Zhè jiàn shì wǒ méiyǒu shénme zhǔyi, nǐ kàn ne?** = *I don't have any definite views on this matter. What do you think?*
■ 他打定主意要去北京学中文。**Tā dǎdìng zhǔyi yào qù Běijīng xué Zhōngwén.** = *He has made up his mind to go to Beijing to learn Chinese.*

zhǔzhāng 主张
1 VERB = advocate, stand for
■ 我主张立即恢复谈判。**Wǒ zhǔzhāng lìjì huīfù tánpàn.** = *I advocate resuming negotiations immediately.*
■ 她不主张借钱买车。**Tā bù zhǔzhāng jiè qián mǎi chē.** = *She does not favor borrowing to buy a car.*
2 NOUN = proposition, idea, what one stands for
■ 你的主张很有道理，但是恐怕很难实行。**Nǐ de zhǔzhāng hěn yǒu dàolǐ, dànshì kǒngpà hěn nán shíxíng.** = *Your idea is very reasonable but I'm afraid it's difficult to implement.*

zhǔ 煮 VERB = boil, cook
■ 这块牛肉至少要煮一小时才能吃。**Zhè kuài niúròu zhìshǎo yào zhǔ yì xiǎoshí cáinéng chī.** = *This piece of beef should be boiled for at least one hour before it is edible.*

zhǔ 嘱 Trad 囑 VERB = advise

zhǔfu 嘱咐 [compound: 嘱 *advice* + 咐 *tell*] VERB = exhort, tell (somebody to do something) earnestly, advise
■ 老人去世前，嘱咐子女要互相爱护，互相照顾。**Lǎorén qùshì qián, zhǔfu zǐnǚ yào hùxiāng àihu, hùxiāng zhàogu.** = *Before his death the old man exhorted his children to love each other and care for each other.*

zhù 住 VERB = live, stay
■ "你住在哪里？""我住在学校附近。" **"Nǐ zhù zài nǎlǐ?" "Wǒ zhù zài xuéxiào fùjìn."** =

"Where do you live?" "I live near the school.
zhùyuàn 住院 = be hospitalized

zhù 助 VERB = assist (See 帮助 bāngzhù.)

zhù 注 VERB = add, pour

zhùyì 注意 VERB = pay attention to, take notice of
■ 说话的时候，要注意语法。**Shuōhuà de shíhou, yào zhùyì yǔfǎ.** = One should pay attention to grammar when speaking.
■ 请大家注意！明天张老师要开一个重要的会，所以不上课。**Qǐng dàjiā zhùyì! Míngtiān Zhāng lǎoshī yào kāi yí ge zhòngyào de huì, suǒyǐ bú shàngkè.** = Attention, please! Tomorrow Teacher Zhang will be attending an important meeting, so there will be no class.

zhù 祝 VERB = express good wishes, wish
■ 祝你生日快乐！**Zhù nǐ shēngrì kuàilè!** = I wish you a happy birthday!

zhùhè 祝贺 [compound: 祝 wish well + 贺 congratulate] VERB = congratulate
■ 祝贺你大学毕业！**Zhùhè nǐ dàxué bìyè!** = Congratulations on your graduation!

zhù 著 VERB = write

zhùmíng 著名 ADJECTIVE = famous, well-known
■ 我们的中文老师是一位著名的小说家。**Wǒmen de Zhōngwén lǎoshī shì yí wèi zhùmíng de xiǎoshuōjiā.** = Our Chinese teacher is a famous novelist.

zhùzuò 著作 [v+obj: 著 write + 作 (literary) work] NOUN = writings, (literary) work
■ 他的著作被翻译为十多种语言。**Tā de zhùzuò bèi fānyìwéi shí duō zhǒng yǔyán.** = His works have been translated into a dozen foreign languages.

zhù 筑 Trad 築 VERB = build, construct (See 建筑 jiànzhù.)

zhuā 抓 VERB = grab, seize
■ 他抓住小偷的胳膊。**Tā zhuāzhù xiǎotōu de gēbo.** = He grabbed the thief by the arm.

zhuājǐn 抓紧 [v+obj: 抓 grab + 紧 tight] VERB = grasp firmly
■ 你要抓紧时间，在下星期一前写完报告。**Nǐ yào zhuājǐn shíjiān, zài xià Xīngqīyī qián xiě wán bàogào.** = You should make the best use of your time and write up the report before next Monday.

zhuān 专 Trad 專 ADJECTIVE = concentrated, focused

zhuānjiā 专家 [modif: 专 specialist + 家 expert] NOUN = expert, specialist
■ 他是计算机专家，关于计算机的事没有不知道的。**Tā shì jìsuànjī zhuānjiā, guānyú jìsuànjī de shì tā méiyǒu bù zhīdào de.** = He is a computer expert and knows everything there is to know about computers.

zhuānmén 专门 ADJECTIVE = specialized, specialist
■ 他发表过很多语言学专门著作。**Tā fābiǎoguo hěn duō yǔyánxué zhuānmén zhùzuò.** = He has published many specialist works on linguistics.

zhuānxīn 专心 [modif: 专 concentrate + 心 the heart] ADJECTIVE = concentrate on, be absorbed in
■ 妹妹正在专心地做数学练习。**Mèimei zhèngzài zhuānxīn de zuò shùxué liànxí.** = My younger sister is absorbed in doing her mathematics exercises.
■ 他做事不专心，所以一事无成。**Tā zuòshì bù zhuānxīn, suǒyǐ yí shì wú chéng.** = He does everything half-heartedly and, as a result, has accomplished nothing.

zhuānyè 专业 [modif: 专 specialist + 业 profession] NOUN = specialist field of study, specialty
■ 他的专业是中国农村经济。**Tā de zhuānyè shì Zhōngguó nóngcūn jīngjì.** = His specialist field is Chinese rural economics.

zhuǎn 转 Trad 轉 VERB
1 = turn, change
■ 今天下午雨转晴。**Jīntiān xiàwǔ yǔ zhuǎn qíng.** = This afternoon it'll change from a rainy day to a fine day.

Z

2 = pass on, forward
■ 我已经把他的电子邮件转给他姐姐了。**Wǒ yǐjīng bǎ tá de diànzǐ yóujiàn zhuān gei tā jiějie le.** = *I have forwarded his e-mail message to his sister.*
zhuǎnchē 转车 = transfer to another train (or bus)
zhuǎnxué 转学 = transfer to another school

zhuǎnbiàn 转变 [compound: 转 *turn* + 变 *change*] VERB = change, transform (usually for the better)
■ 他从一个小偷转变成一个对社会有用的公民。**Tā cóng yí ge xiǎotōu zhuǎnbiàn chéng yí ge duì shèhuì yǒuyòng de gōngmín.** = *He has transformed from a thief to a useful member of society.*
■ 她的态度转变了 – 从怀疑到信任。**Tā de tàidù zhuǎnbiàn le – cóng huáiyí dào xìnrèn.** = *Her attitude changed—from doubt to trust.*

zhuǎngào 转告 [modif: 转 *transfer* + 告 *tell*] VERB = pass along (word)
■ 请你把这个消息转告全班同学。**Qǐng nǐ bǎ zhège xiāoxi zhuǎngào quán bān tóngxué.** = *Please pass on the news to all your classmates.*

zhuàn 赚 Trad 賺 VERB = make money, make a profit
■ 现在赚钱不容易。**Xiànzài zhuàn qián bù róngyì.** = *It is not easy to make any money now.*
■ 这家小小的西餐馆去年赚了五万多。**Zhè jiā xiǎoxiǎo de xīcānguǎn qùnián zhuànle wǔwàn duō.** = *This small Western-style restaurant made a profit of over 50,000 yuan last year.*

zhuāng 庄 Trad 莊 NOUN = village

zhuāngjiā 庄稼 NOUN = crop
■ 光种庄稼，很难富起来。**Guāng zhòng zhuāngjiā, hěn nán fù qǐlai.** = *It is difficult to get rich raising crops only.*
zhuāngjiārén 庄稼人 = farmer (especially one that grows crops)
zhuāngjiādì 庄稼地 = farmland

zhuāng 装 Trad 裝 VERB = pretend
■ 她不想跟他说话，所以装着没看见。**Tā bù xiǎng gēn tā shuōhuà, suǒyǐ zhuāngzhe méi kànjiàn.** = *She did not want to talk to him, so she pretended not to see him.*

■ 不懂就是不懂，你干吗装懂！ **Bù dǒng jiù shì bù dǒng, gànmá zhuāng dǒng?** = *It's all right if you don't understand. Why do you pretend to understand?*

zhuàng 状 Trad 狀 NOUN = form, shape

zhuàngkuàng 状况 [compound: 状 *shape (of things)* + 况 *situation*] NOUN = shape (of things), situation, condition
■ 目前全国的经济状况很好。**Mùqián quánguó de jīngjì zhuàngkuàng hěn hǎo.** = *At present the national economy is in good shape.*
■ 你爷爷的身体状况怎么样？ **Nǐ yéye de shēntǐ zhuàngkuàng zěnmeyàng?** = *How is your grandpa's health?*

zhuàngtài 状态 [compound: 状 *shape (of things)* + 态 *condition*] NOUN = state (of affairs), appearance
■ 运动员的精神状态非常重要。**Yùndòngyuán de jīngshén zhuàngtài fēicháng zhòngyào.** = *It is important for an athlete to be in a good mental state.*

zhuàng 撞 VERB = bump against, collide
■ 两辆汽车相撞，造成重大交通事故。**Liǎng liàng qìchē xiāng zhuàng, zàochéng zhòngdà jiāotōng shìgù.** = *The two cars collided and caused a major road accident.*

zhuī 追 VERB = chase, run after
■ 孩子们在操场上你追我，我追你。**Háizimen zài cāochǎng shang nǐ zhuī wǒ, wǒ zhuī nǐ.** = *Children chased one another on the playing ground.*
zhuīshang 追上 = catch up with, catch
■ 我追不上他。**Wǒ zhuī bu shang tā.** = *I can't catch up with him.*

zhǔn 准 Trad 準 ADJECTIVE = accurate, exact
■ 电子手表一般都很准。**Diànzǐ shǒubiǎo yìbān dōu hěn zhǔn.** = *Electronic watches are usually quite accurate.*

zhǔnbèi 准备
1 VERB = prepare
■ 明天考试，你们准备好了吗？ **Míngtiān kǎoshì, nǐmen zhǔnbèi hǎo le ma?** = *There'll be an examination tomorrow. Are you well prepared?*

Z

■ 他正在准备在下午会议上的发言。**Tā zhèngzài zhǔnbèi zài xiàwǔ huìyì shang de fāyán.** = *He is preparing the speech to be delivered at this afternoon's meeting.*
zhǔnbèi hǎo 准备好 = be well prepared
2 NOUN = preparation
■ 老师上课前要做很多准备。**Lǎoshī shàngkè qián yào zuò hěn duō zhǔnbèi.** = *The teacher needs to do a lot of preparation before class.*

zhǔnquè 准确 [compound: 准 *accurate* + 确 *verified*] ADJECTIVE = accurate, exact
■ 发音不准确，有时候会闹笑话。**Fāyīn bù zhǔnquè, yǒushíhou huì nào xiàohua.** = *Inaccurate pronunciation can sometimes have comical effects.*
■ 你的计算不够准确。**Nǐ de jìsuàn bú gòu zhǔnquè.** = *Your calculation is not accurate enough.*

zhùnshí 准时 ADJECTIVE = punctual, on time
■ 这里的火车非常准时。**Zhèli de huǒchē fēicháng zhǔnshí.** = *The trains here are very punctual.*
■ 我从小养成了准时的习惯。**Wǒ cóngxiǎo yǎngchéngle zhǔnshí de xíguàn.** = *In my childhood I formed the habit of being punctual.*
■ 他每天准时九点钟到达办公室。**Tā měi tiān zhǔnshí jiǔ diǎnzhōng dàodá bàngōngshì.** = *Every day he arrives at his office punctually at nine o'clock.*

zhuō 捉 VERB = catch, capture
■ 你怎么捉得住猫？**Nǐ zěnme zhuō de zhu māo?** = *How can you catch a cat?*

zhuōzi 桌子 [suffix: 桌 *table* + 子 nominal suffix] NOUN = table, desk (张 **zhāng**)
■ 桌子上有几本书和一个杯子。**Zhuōzi shang yǒu jǐ běn shū hé yí ge bēizi.** = *There are some books and a cup on the table.*

zī 资 Trad 資 NOUN = money, property

zīběn 资本 [compound: 资 *capital* + 本 *principal*] NOUN = capital
■ 他开工厂的资本是从银行借来的。**Tā kāi gōngchǎng de zīběn shì cóng yínháng jièlai de.** = *The capital with which he opened his factory was borrowed from the bank.*
zīběn zhǔyì 资本主义 = capitalism

zījīn 资金 [compound: 资 *capital* + 金 *gold, fund*] VERB = fund
■ 学校向教育局申请建造教室的资金。**Xuéxiào xiàng jiàoyùjú shēnqǐng jiànzào jiàoshì de zījīn.** = *The school applied to the education bureau for funds to build new classrooms.*

zīliào 资料 [compound: 资 *capital* + 料 *material*] NOUN
1 = material, data
■ 王老师从北京带回来很多中文教学的参考资料。**Wáng lǎoshī cóng Běijīng dài huílai hěn duō Zhōngwén jiàoxué de cānkǎo zīliào.** = *Teacher Wang brought back from Beijing a great deal of reference materials for teaching and learning Chinese.*
2 = means (of production)
■ 生产资料公有，是社会主义的特点。**Shēngchǎn zīliào gōngyǒu, shì shèhuì zhǔyì de tèdiǎn.** = *Public ownership of the means of production is a special feature of socialism.*

zīyuán 资源 [modif: 资 *capital* + 源 *source*] NOUN = natural resources
■ 我们要开发海洋资源。**Wǒmen yào kāifā hǎiyáng zīyuán.** = *We will develop the natural resources of seas and oceans.*

zǐ 仔 ADJECTIVE = careful

zǐxì 仔细 ADJECTIVE = very careful, paying attention to details
■ 考试的时候一定要仔细看清题目。**Kǎoshì de shíhou yídìng yào zǐxì kànqīng tímù.** = *At an examination be sure to read the questions very, very carefully.*

zǐ 紫 ADJECTIVE = purple
■ 他冻得脸都发紫了。**Tā dòng de liǎn dōu fā zǐ le.** = *He was so cold that his face turned purple.*

zì 自 PREPOSITION = same as 从 **cóng**. Only used in written Chinese.

zìcóng 自从 [compound: 自 *from* + 从 *from*] PREPOSITION = from, since
■ 自从 2001 年 9 月 11 日，世界各地的飞机场都加强了行李检查。**Zìcóng èr-líng-líng-yī nián Jiǔyuè shíyī rì, shìjiè gèdì de fēijīchǎng**

dōu jiāqiángle xíngli jiǎnchá. = *Since September 11, 2001, airports all over the world have strengthened their luggage check system.*
■ 自从认识他以来，我渐渐对他产生了好感。**Zìcóng rènshi tā yǐlái, wǒ jiànjiàn duì tā chǎnshēngle hǎogǎn.** = *Since I came to know him, I have gradually grown fond of him.*

zìdòng 自动 [modif: 自 *self* + 动 *act*] ADJECTIVE = automatic
■ 这台机器会自动关闭。**Zhè tái jīqì huì zìdòng guānbì.** = *This machine will turn off automatically.*
zìdònghuà 自动化 = automatic, automation

zìfèi 自费 [modif: 自 *self* + 费 *cost*] ADJECTIVE = self-supporting, paid by myself
■ 我不明白，他们怎么有钱送孩子去国外自费留学？**Wǒ bù míngbái, tāmen zěnme yǒu qián sòng háizi qù guówài zìfèi liúxué?** = *I don't understand how they could afford to send their child overseas as a self-supporting student.*
zìfèi liúxuéshēng 自费留学生 = self-supporting foreign student, fee-paying foreign student

zìjué 自觉 [modif: 自 *self* + 觉 *conscious, aware*] ADJECTIVE = being aware of, being conscious of, voluntary, conscientious
■ 孩子自觉帮助做家务。**Háizi zìjué bāngzhù zuò jiāwù.** = *The child helps with the household chores voluntarily.*
■ 他犯这个错误不是自觉的。**Tā fàn zhège cuòwù bú shì zìjué de.** = *He made the mistake without being aware of it.*

zìjǐ 自己 PRONOUN = self, one's own
■ 自己的工作自己做。**Zìjǐ de gōngzuò zìjǐ zuò.** = *Each must do their own work.*
■ 你不能只想到自己。**Nǐ bù néng zhǐ xiǎngdao zìjǐ.** = *You mustn't think of yourself only.*
nǐ zìjǐ 你自己 = yourself
nǐmen zìjǐ 你们自己 = yourselves
tā zìjǐ 他自己 = himself
tāmen zìjǐ 他们自己 = themselves
wǒ zìjǐ 我自己 = myself
wǒmen zìjǐ 我们自己 = ourselves

zìrán 自然
1 NOUN = nature

■ 哲学问题之一就是人和自然的关系。**Zhéxué wèntí zhī yī jiù shì rén hé zìrán de guānxi.** = *One philosophical issue is the relationship between humankind and nature.*
2 ADJECTIVE = natural
■ 父母爱子女是自然的。**Fù-mǔ ài zǐnǚ shì zìrán de.** = *It is only natural that parents love their children.*
■ 她说话的样子很不自然。**Tā shuōhuà de yàngzi hěn bú zìrán.** = *The way she speaks is quite affected.*

zìxíngchē 自行车 [modif: 自 *self* + 行 *walking* + 车 *vehicle*] NOUN = bicycle (辆 **liàng**)
■ 我会骑自行车，但是不会修自行车。**Wǒ huì qí zìxíngchē, dànshì bú huì xiū zìxíngchē.** = *I can ride a bicycle, but I can't fix it.*

zìxué 自学 [modif: 自 *self* + 学 *study*] VERB = study independently, teach oneself
■ 他自学日语三年，已经能看懂日文书了。**Tā zìxué Rìyǔ sān nián, yǐjīng néng kàndǒng Rìwén shū le.** = *He taught himself Japanese for three years and is now able to read Japanese books.*
■ 我佩服自学成才的人。**Wǒ pèifu zìxué chéngcái de rén.** = *I admire those who have made themselves useful through self-study.*

zìyóu 自由
1 NOUN = freedom, liberty
■ 那个国家缺乏新闻自由，受到人们的普遍批评。**Nàge guójiā quēfá xīnwén zìyóu, shòudao rénmen de pǔbiàn pīpíng.** = *That country lacks freedom of the press and is widely criticized.*
■ 他不愿意结婚，因为他喜欢自由。**Tā bú yuànyì jiéhūn, yīnwèi tā xǐhuan zìyóu.** = *He is unwilling to marry because he enjoys his freedom.*
2 ADJECTIVE = free, unrestrained
■ 他觉得和父母住在一起不自由。**Tā juéde hé fù-mǔ zhù zài yìqǐ bú zìyóu.** = *Living with his parents, he does not feel free.*

zì 字 NOUN = Chinese character
■ 中国字很有意思。**Zhōngguó zì hěn yǒu yìsi.** = *Chinese characters are very interesting.*
■ 这个字是什么意思？怎么念？**Zhège zì shì shénme yìsi? zěnme niàn?** = *What is the mean-*

Z

ing of this Chinese character? How is it pronounced?

Hànzì 汉字 = Chinese character

zi 子 PARTICLE = (a nominal suffix) (See 杯子 bēizi, 被子 bèizi, 本子 běnzi, 鼻子 bízi, 脖子 bózi, 叉子 chāzi, 虫子 chóngzi, 村子 cūnzi, 刀子 dāozi, 电子 diànzi, 儿子 érzi, 房子 fángzi, 个子 gèzi, 孩子 háizi, 盒子 hézi, 猴子 hóuzi, 胡子 húzi, 饺子 jiǎozi, 橘子 júzi, 句子 jùzi, 裤子 kùzi, 筷子 kuàizi, 例子 lìzi, 帽子 màozi, 脑子 nǎozi, 牌子 páizi, 盘子 pánzi, 妻子 qīzi, 旗子 qízi, 裙子 qúnzi, 日子 rìzi, 嗓子 sǎngzi, 嫂子 sǎozi, 沙子 shāzi, 勺子 sháozi, 绳子 shéngzi, 狮子 shīzi, 毯子 tǎnzi, 兔子 tùzi, 袜子 wàzi, 蚊子 wénzi, 屋子 wūzi, 箱子 xiāngzi, 小伙子 xiǎohuǒzi, 样子 yàngzi, 叶子 yèzi, 一下子 yíxiàzi, 椅子 yǐzi, 院子 yuànzi, 种子 zhǒngzi, 竹子 zhúzi, 桌子 zhuōzi.)

zǒng 总 Trad 總 ADVERB = always, invariably
■ 他总觉得自己正确。**Tā zǒng juéde zìjǐ zhèngquè.** = *He always thinks himself correct.*
■ 你为什么总这么晚起床？ **Nǐ wèishénme zǒng zhème wǎn qǐchuáng?** = *Why do you always get up so late?*

zǒngjié 总结 [modif: 总 general + 结 conclude, conclusion]
1 VERB = sum up, do a review of one's past work or life experiences
■ 每年年底，公司都要总结一年的工作。**Měi nián niándǐ, gōngsī dōuyào zǒngjié yì nián de gōngzuò.** = *At the end of every year the company does a general review of the work done.*
2 NOUN = summary, a general view of one's past work or life experiences
■ 这个计划已经完成，我们应该做一个总结了。**Zhège jìhuà yǐjīng wánchéng, wǒmen yīnggāi zuò yí ge zǒngjié le.** = *Now that this plan is fulfilled, we should do a general review.*

zǒnglǐ 总理 [modif: 总 general + 理 administer] NOUN = premier, prime minister
■ 中国的国务院总理是政府首脑。**Zhōngguó de guówùyuàn zǒnglǐ shì zhèngfǔ shǒunǎo.** = *The premier of the Chinese State Council is China's head of government.*

zǒngshì 总是 ADVERB = same as 总 **zǒng**

zǒngtǒng 总统 [modif: 总 general + 统 rule, command] NOUN = president (of a country)
■ 美国每四年举行总统选举。**Měiguó měi sì nián jǔxíng zǒngtǒng xuǎnjǔ.** = *The USA holds its presidential election every four years.*

zǒu 走 VERB = walk; leave
■ 我家离学校很近，我每天走到学校。**Wǒ jiā lí xuéxiào hěn jìn, wǒ měi tiān zǒudao xuéxiào.** = *My home is close to the school. I walk to school everyday.*
■ 时间不早了，我们得走了。**Shíjiān bù zǎo le, wǒmen děi zǒu le.** = *It's quite late. We've got to go.*

zú 足 NOUN = foot

zúqiú 足球 [modif: 足 foot + 球 ball] NOUN = soccer
■ 我爸爸年轻的时候，常常踢足球，现在还爱看足球比赛。**Wǒ bàba niánqīng de shíhou, chángcháng tī zúqiú, xiànzài hái ài kàn zúqiú bǐsài.** = *My father often played soccer when he was young, and now he still enjoys watching soccer games.*
tī zúqiú 踢足球 = play soccer

zú 族 NOUN = clan, nationality (See 民族 mínzú.)

zǔ 祖 NOUN = ancestor

zǔfù 祖父 [modif: 祖 ancestor + 父 father] NOUN = grandfather
■ 我祖父七十多岁了，还每天锻炼身体。**Wǒ zǔfù qīshí duō suì le, hái měi tiān duànliàn shēntǐ.** = *My grandfather is over seventy and still does physical exercise every day.*

zǔguó 祖国 [modif: 祖 ancestor + 国 country] NOUN = motherland, fatherland
■ 我爱祖国。**Wǒ ài zǔguó.** = *I love my motherland.*
■ 他虽然住在国外，但深深地关心祖国。**Tā suīrán zhù zai guówài, dàn shēnshēn de guānxīn zǔguó.** = *Although living in a foreign country, he is still deeply concerned for his motherland.*

zǔmǔ 祖母 [modif: 祖 ancestor + 母 mother] NOUN = grandmother
■ 我祖母一个人住，我们常去看她。**Wǒ**

zǔmǔ yígerén zhù, wǒmen cháng qù kàn tā. = *My grandmother lives by herself. We often go to see her.*

zǔ 组 Trad 組 NOUN = group
■ 老师把全班分为三个组，练习口语。 **Lǎoshī bǎ quán bān fēn wéi sān ge zǔ, liànxí kǒuyǔ.** = *The teacher divided the class into three groups for oral Chinese practice.*

zǔzhī 组织 [compound: 组 *to group* + 织 *to weave*]
1 VERB = organize
■ 学校正在组织去北京旅游。 **Xuéxiào zhèngzài zǔzhī qù Běijīng lǚyóu.** = *The school is organizing a trip to Beijing.*
2 NOUN = organization
■ 我父亲不参加任何组织。 **Wǒ fùqin bù cānjiā rènhé zǔzhī.** = *My father did not join any organization.*

zuān 钻 Trad 鑽 NOUN = drill

zuānyán 钻研 [compound: 钻 *drill, bore into* + 研 *study, research*] VERB = study in great depth, study intensively
■ 这位科学家有时候钻研一个问题而忘了吃饭。 **Zhè wèi kēxuéjiā yǒushíhou zuānyán yí ge wèntí ér wàngle chīfàn.** = *Sometimes this scientist studies a problem so intensively that he forgets his meals.*

zuǐ 嘴 NOUN = mouth
■ 不要用嘴呼吸，要用鼻子呼吸。 **Bú yào yòng zuǐ hūxī, yào yòng bízi hūxī.** = *Breathe through the nose, not the mouth.*

zuì 最 ADVERB = most (used before an adjective to indicate the superlative degree)
■ 中国是世界上人口最多的国家。 **Zhōngguó shì shìjiè shang rénkǒu zuì duō de guójiā.** = *China is the most populous country in the world.*
■ 我最讨厌电视广告。 **Wǒ zuì tǎoyàn diànshì guǎnggào.** = *I detest TV commercials most.*

zuìchū 最初 NOUN = the initial stage, initially
■ 最初我不习惯那里的生活。 **Zuìchū wǒ bù xíguàn nàli de shēnghuó.** = *Initially I was not used to the life there.*

zuìhǎo 最好 [modif: 最 *most* + 好 *good*]
ADVERB = had better
■ 你最好常去看望奶奶。 **Nǐ zuìhǎo cháng qù kànwàng nǎinai.** = *You'd better visit your grandma often.*

zuìhòu 最后 NOUN = the final stage, finally
■ 笑得最后，才笑得最好。 **Xiào de zuìhòu, cái xiào de zuìhǎo.** = *He who laughs last laughs best.*
■ 最后他同意了我们的观点。 **Zuìhòu tā tóngyìle wǒmen de guāndiǎn.** = *Finally, he accepted our views.*

zuìjìn 最近 NOUN = recently, recent time
■ 我最近特别忙。 **Wǒ zuìjìn tèbié máng.** = *I'm particularly busy these days.*
■ 你最近看过什么好电影吗？ **Nǐ zuìjìn kànguo shénme hǎo diànyǐng ma?** = *Have you seen any good movies lately?*

zuì 醉 VERB = get drunk, be intoxicated
■ 我没醉，我还能喝。 **Wǒ méi zuì, wǒ hái néng hē.** = *I'm not drunk. I can drink more.*
■ 他昨天晚上喝醉了，今天头疼。 **Tā zuótiān wǎnshang hē zuì le, jīntiān tóuténg.** = *He was drunk last night and this morning he has a headache.*

zūn 尊 VERB = respect

zūnjìng 尊敬 [compound: 尊 *respect* + 敬 *respect*] VERB = respect, honor
■ 中国的传统是尊敬老人。 **Zhōngguó de chuántǒng shì zūnjìng lǎorén.** = *A tradition of the Chinese is to respect the aged.*

zūn 遵 VERB = obey

zūnshǒu 遵守 [compound: 遵 *obey* + 守 *abide by*] VERB = observe, abide by
■ 你既然在这个学校学习，就要遵守学校的各项规定。 **Nǐ jìrán zài zhège xuéxiào xuéxí, jiù yào zūnshǒu xuéxiào de gè xiàng guīdìng.** = *Since you are studying in this school, you should observe its regulations.*

zuó 昨 NOUN = yesterday

zuótiān 昨天 [modif: 昨 *past* + 天 *day*] NOUN = yesterday

Z

■ 你昨天晚上去哪里了? **Nǐ zuótiān wǎnshang qù nǎli le?** = *Where were you yesterday evening?*

zuǒ 左 NOUN = the left side
■ 我弟弟用左手吃饭，写字。**Wǒ dìdi yòng zuǒshǒu chīfàn, xiězì.** = *My younger brother eats and writes with the left hand.*

zuǒbian 左边 [modif: 左 *left* + 边 *side*] NOUN = the left side, the left-hand side
■ 坐在李先生左边的那位小姐是谁? **Zuò zai Lǐ xiānsheng zuǒbian de nà wèi xiǎojiě shì shuí?** = *Who is the young lady sitting on the left of Mr Li?*

zuǒyòu 左右 [compound: 左 *left* + 右 *right*] ADVERB = approximately, nearly, about
■ 今天最高温度二十度左右。**Jīntiān zuìgāo wēndù èrshí dù zuǒyòu.** = *Today's maximum temperature is about twenty degrees.*

zuò 坐 VERB = sit
■ 请坐! **Qǐng zuò!** = *Sit down, please!*
■ 她正坐在窗边看书。**Tā zhèng zuò zài chuāngbiān kànshū.** = *She's sitting by the window, reading.*

zuò 作 VERB = same as 做 **zuò**

NOTE: 做 **zuò** and 作 **zuò** have the same pronunciation and often the same meaning, but 做 **zuò** is much more commonly used while 作 **zuò** occurs only in certain set expressions.

zuòjiā 作家 [modif: 作 *create* + 家 *expert*] NOUN = writer (especially of literary works, e.g. novels, stories)
■ 在过去，作家是很受人尊敬的。**Zài guòqu, zuòjiā shì hěn shòu rén zūnjìng de.** = *In the past writers were very much respected.*

zuòpǐn 作品 [modif: 作 *create* + 品 *article*] NOUN = literary or artistic work
■ 这位作家又有新作品了。**Zhè wèi zuòjiā yòu yǒu xīn zuòpǐn le.** = *This writer has written another work.*

zuòwén 作文 [modif: 作 *create* + 文 *writing*] NOUN = (student's) composition
■ 她的作文经常得到老师的表扬。**Tā de**

zuòwén jīngcháng dédào lǎoshī de biǎoyáng. = *Her compositions are often commended by the teacher.*

zuòyè 作业 NOUN = school assignment, homework
■ 中国的中小学生每天要做很多作业。**Zhōngguó de zhōng-xiǎo xuésheng měi tiān yào zuò hěn duō zuòyè.** = *School children in China have lots of homework to do every day.*

zuòyòng 作用 [compound: 作 *work* + 用 *use*] NOUN = function, role
■ 他在这次谈判中起了很大作用。**Tā zài zhè cì tánpàn zhong qǐle hěn dà zuòyòng.** = *He played a major role in the negotiations.*
zài ... zhōng qǐ zuòyòng 在 ... 中起作用 = play a role in ..., perform a function in ...

zuòzhě 作者 [suffix: 作 *create* + 者 nominal suffix] NOUN = author
■ 这本书的作者是一位女作家。**Zhè běn shū de zuòzhé shì yí wèi nǚ zuòjiā.** = *The author of this book is a woman writer.*

zuò 座 MEASURE WORD = (for large and solid objects, such as a large building)
■ 一座大楼 **yí zuò dàlóu** = *a big building*
■ 一座山 **yí zuò shān** = *a mountain, a hill*
■ 一座工厂 **yí zuò gōngchǎng** = *a factory*
■ 一座大学 **yí zuò dàxué** = *a university*
■ 一座桥 **yí zuò qiáo** = *a bridge*
■ 一座城市 **yí zuò chéngshì** = *a city*

zuòtán 座谈 [compound: 座 *seat* + 谈 *talk*] VERB = have a informal discussion, have an informal meeting
■ 校长今天下午和一年级学生座谈。**Xiàozhǎng jīntiān xiàwǔ hé yī niánjí xuésheng zuòtán.** = *The principal will have an informal discussion with first-year students this afternoon.*
zuòtánhuì 座谈会 = an informal discussion, forum

zuòwèi 座位 [compound: 座 *seat* + 位 *seat*] NOUN = seat
■ 请你给我留一个座位，我马上就到。**Qǐng nǐ gěi wǒ liú yí ge zuòwèi, wǒ mǎshàng jiù dào.** = *Please save a seat for me. I'll be there soon.*

Z

■ 这个座位有人吗？ **Zhège zuòwèi yǒu rén ma?** = *Is this seat taken?*

zuò 做 VERB

1 = do

■ 这件事我不会做。 **Zhè jiàn shì wǒ bú huì zuò.** = *I don't know how to do this.*

■ "你会做这个作业吗？" "会，我已经做好了。" **"Nǐ huì zuò zhège zuòyè ma?" "Huì, wǒ yǐjīng zuòhǎo le."** = *"Can you do this assignment?" "Yes, I can. I've already done it."*

2 = make

■ 这张桌子是我爸爸做的。 **Zhè zhāng zhuōzi shì wǒ bàba zuò de.** = *This table was made by my father.*

■ 中国酒是用米做的。 **Zhōngguó jiǔ shì yòng mǐ zuò de.** = *Chinese wine is made from rice.*

zuògōng 做工 = do manual work, work

■ 今年夏天你要去哪里做工？ **Jīnnián xiàtiān nǐ yào qù nǎlǐ zuògōng?** = *Where are you going to work this summer?*

zuòfàn 做饭 = cook

■ "你们家里谁做饭？" "我，经常是我做饭。" **"Nǐmen jiāli shuí zuòfàn?" "Wǒ, jīngcháng shì wǒ zuòfàn."** = *"Who does the cooking in your family?" "I do. I usually do the cooking."*

zuòkè 做客 = be a guest, visit

zuòmèng 做梦 = dream

zuòfǎ 做法 [modif: 做 do + 法 method] NOUN = way of doing things, method, practice

■ 他这种做法不讲原则，我不赞成。 **Tā zhè zhǒng zuòfǎ bù jiǎng yuánzé, wǒ bú zànchéng.** = *This kind of practice of his is unprincipled and I don't approve of it.*

Z

English-Chinese Word Finder

A

(the) abovementioned **gāi** 该 69

abandon **fàngqì** 放弃 63

abdomen **dùzi** 肚子 53

abide by **zūnshǒu** 遵守 287

ability **běnlǐng** 本领 10, **běnshì** 本事 10, **lìliàng** 力量 138, **nénglì** 能力 160

able (person) **nénggàn** 能干 160

able to **huì** 会 97, **néng** 能 159, **nénggòu** 能够 160

abnormal **yìcháng** 异常 252

about **dàyuē** 大约 40, **guānyú** 关于 81, **zuǒyòu** 左右 288

above **shàng** 上 187, **shàngbian** 上边 188, **shàngmiàn** 上面 188

absolute **juéduì** 绝对 124

absorb **xīshōu** 吸收 226

absorbing (adj.) **hǎokàn** 好看 88

abstract **chōuxiàng** 抽象 30

abundant **chōngfèn** 充分 30, **fēngfù** 丰富 66

(be) abundant **yǒudeshì** 有的是 258

academy of science **kēxuéyuàn** 科学院 127

accept **jiēshòu** 接受 114, **shòu** 收 198, **shōuxia** 收下 198, **shòu** 受 200

accident **shìgù** 事故 197, **yìwài** 意外 253

accompany **péi** 陪 165, **sòng** 送 205

accomplish **wánchéng** 完成 219

accord with **fúhé** 符合 67

according to **àn** 按 3, **ànzhào** 按照 3, **gēnjù** 根据 74, **zhào** 照 270

according to schedule **àn qī** 按期 170

account for **jiěshì** 解释 116

accumulate **jīlěi** 积累 101

accurate **zhèngquè** 正确 273, **zhǔn** 准 283, **zhǔnquè** 准确 284

(be) accustomed to **xíguàn** 习惯 227

ache (v.) **tòng** 痛 215

achieve **dádào** 达到 37, **qǔdé** 取得 178

achievement **chéngguǒ** 成果 28, **chéngjì** 成绩 28, **shōuhuò** 收获 198

achievement (great) **chéngjiù** 成就 28

acknowledge **chéngrèn** 承认 28, **kěndìng** 肯定 130

acquire experience **qǔdé jīngyàn** 取得经验 120

acrobat **zájì yǎnyuán** 杂技演员 264

acrobatics **zájì** 杂技 264

act (v.) **yǎn** 演 244

action **xíngdòng** 行动 238

active **huóyuè** 活跃 99, **jījí** 积极 101

activity **huódòng** 活动 99

actor, actress **yǎnyuán** 演员 245

actuality **xiànshí** 现实 230

acupuncture and moxibustion **zhēnjiǔ** 针灸 272

AD (*anno Domini*) **gōngyuán** 公元 77

add **jiā** 加 105, **tiān** 添 202

additionally **yòu** 又 260

address (n.) **dìzhǐ** 地址 47

adequate **chōngfèn** 充分, **chōngzú** 充足 30

adjust **tiánzhěng** 调整 213

administer **guǎnlǐ** 管理 82

administration charge **guǎnlǐ fèi** 管理费 64

admire **pèifu** 佩服 165

admission ticket **ménpiào** 门票 167

admit (mistake, error, etc.) **chéngrèn** 承认 28

adolescent **shàonián** 少年 189

adopt **cǎiqǔ** 采取 21

adult (n., colloquial) **dàren** 大人 39

advance (v.) **cùjìn** 促进 36, **qiánjìn** 前进 173, **tígāo** 提高 210, **tíqián** 提前 210

advanced (adj.) **gāojí** 高级 72, **xiānjìn** 先进 229

advantageous **yǒulì** 有利 259

advertisement **guǎnggào** 广告 84

advise **quàn** 劝 178, **zhǔfu** 嘱咐 281

advocate (v.) **tíchàng** 提倡 210, **zhǔzhāng** 主张 281

affair **shì** 事, **shìqing** 事情 197

affect **guānxi** 关系 81, **yǐngxiǎng** 影响 255

affection **gǎnqíng** 感情 71

affirmative **kěndìng** 肯定 130

after **jīngguò** 经过 119, **yǐhòu** 以后 250, **zhī hòu** 之后 274

after all **kě** 可 127

afternoon **xiàwǔ** 下午 229

afterwards **hòulái** 后来 92, **ránhòu** 然后 180

(be) afraid **pà** 怕 163

again **chóng** 重 30, **chóngxīn** 重新 30, **yòu** 又 260, **zài** 再 265

age (n.) **niánjì** 年纪 160, **niánlíng** 年龄 161

agenda **yìshì rìchéng** 议事日程 183

agile **línghuó** 灵活 142

agonized (adj.) **bēitòng** 悲痛 9, **tòngxīn** 痛心 236

agree **tóngyì** 同意 215

agreement **hétóng** 合同 90

agriculture **nóngyè** 农业 162

ah **ā** 啊 1, **yā** 呀 243

aid **zhīyuán** 支援 274

aim (n.) **mùdì** 目的 156

aim at **zhēnduì** 针对 272

air (n.) **kōngqì** 空气 130

air force **kōngjūn** 空军 124

air ticket **fēijī piào** 飞机票 167

airline **hángkōng gōngsī** 航空公司 87

airplane **fēijī** 飞机 63

airport **fēijī chǎng** 飞机场 63, **jīchǎng** 机场 100

airport tax **jīchǎng fèi** 机场费 64

(be) alarmed **chījīng** 吃惊 29

alcoholic beverage **jiǔ** 酒 121

(be) alive **huó** 活 99

all **dàjiā** 大家 38, **dōu** 都 52, **fánshì** 凡是 60, **quánbù** 全部 178, **quántǐ** 全体 178, **suǒyǒu** 所有 207, **yíqiè** 一切 249

all around **zhōuwéi** 周围 280

all kinds of **gè zhǒng** 各种 74

all kinds/sorts of **gè zhǒng gè yàng** 各种各样 279

all right **hǎo** 好 88

all sorts of **zá** 杂 264

all the time **yìzhí** 一直 252

all-round **quánmiàn** 全面 178

alleviate **jiǎnqīng** 减轻 108

allocate **fēnpèi** 分配 65

allow **ràng** 让 180, **yǔnxǔ** 允许 264

allowance **língqián** 零钱 142

(be) allowed **kěyǐ** 可以 128

allude to **zhǐ** 指 276

almost **chàbuduō** 差不多 24, **chàdiǎnr** 差点儿 24, **jīhū** 几乎 100

alone **dú** 独 53

along **yán** 沿 244

along with **tóng** 同 214

already **yǐjīng** 已经 250

also **yě** 也 247

alter **gǎi** 改 69

although **suīrán** 虽然 206

altitude **gāodù** 高度 72

altogether **gòng** 共 78, **yígòng** 一共 249

always **cónglái** 从来 35, **lǎoshi** 老是 134, **yìzhí** 一直 252, **zǒng** 总 286, **zǒngshì** 总是 286

amateur (adj.) **yèyú** 业余 247

ambassador **dàshǐ** 大使 39

ambulance **jiùhùchē** 救护车 121

ameliorate **gǎishàn** 改善 69

amelioration **gǎishàn** 改善 69

amend **xiūgǎi** 修改 240

America **Měiguó** 美国 150

among **zhī zhōng** 之中 274

among **zhōngjiān** 中间 278

among them **qízhōng** 其中 170

amount **shùliàng** 数量 202

ample **chōngfèn** 充分 30

amusing **yǒuqù** 有趣 259

analysis, analyze **fēnxī** 分析 65

ancient **gǔ** 古 79

ancient **gǔlǎo** 古老 79

ancient times **gǔdài** 古代 79

and **bìngqiě** 并且 15, **hé** 和 90, **jí** 及 101, **tóng** 同 214, **yǐjí** 以及 250

anger (v.) **qì** 气 171

angle (fish) **diào** 钓 50

angry **fènnù** 愤怒 65

(be) angry **qì** 气 171, **shēngqì** 生气 192

animal **dòngwù** 动物 52

announce **xuānbù** 宣布 241

another **lìngwài** 另外 143

answer (n.) **dá'àn** 答案 37

answer (v.) **dāying** 答应 37, **dá** 答 37, **huídá** 回答 97, **jiědá** 解答 115

answer a telephone call **tīng diànhuà** 听电话 48

anthropology **rénlèixué** 人类学 181

anxious **jí** 急 102, **zuò-lì-bù-ān** 坐立不安 138, **zháojí** 着急 269

any **rènhé** 任何 182

anybody **shuí** 谁 202

anyone **rènhé rén** 任何人 182

anything **rènhé shì** 任何事 182

apart from **zhī wài** 之外 274

apart from that **cǐwài** 此外 35

ape (v.) **mófǎng** 模仿 155

aperture **kǒng** 孔 130

apologetic **bàoqiàn** 抱歉 8

apologize **dàoqiàn** 道歉 44

apparent **míngxiǎn** 明显 154

appeal (v.) **hàozhāo** 号召 89

appear **chūxiàn** 出现 31

appear to be **xiǎnde** 显得 230

appearance **miànmào** 面貌 152, **xíngzhuàng** 形状 239, **yàngzi** 样子 245, **zhuàngtài** 状态 283

applaud **gǔzhǎng** 鼓掌 80, **pāishǒu** 拍手 163

apple **píngguǒ** 苹果 169

applicable **shìyòng** 适用 198

applied science **yìngyòng kēxué** 应用科学 255

apply **shíjiàn** 实践 195, **shǐyòng** 使用 196, **yìngyòng** 应用 255, **yùnyòng** 运用 264

appointment (social) **yuēhuì** 约会 263

appraisal **gūjì** 估计 79

approach (n.) **tàidu** 态度 208

appropriate **héshì** 合适 90, **shìdàng** 适当 198, **xiāngdāng** 相当 231

approve **pīzhǔn** 批准 166, **tóngyì** 同意 215

approve of **zànchéng** 赞成 266

approximately **dàyuē** 大约 40, **lái** 来 133, **zuǒyòu** 左右 288

Arabic (language) **Ālābówén** 阿拉伯文, **Ālābóyǔ** 阿拉伯语 1

architect **jiànzhùshī** 建筑师 109

architecture **jiànzhù** 建筑 109

ardent **rèliè** 热烈 180

area **dìfang** 地方 46, **dìqū** 地区 47

area (mathematics) **miànjī** 面积 152

area nearby **fùjìn** 附近 68

argue **zhēng** 争 272

arid **gāncuì** 干脆 70

arm (n.) **gēbo** 胳膊 73

armed forces **jūn** 军, **jūnduì** 军队 124

arms and ammunition **jūnhuǒ** 军火 124

army **bùduì** 部队 20, **jūn** 军 124, **lùjūn** 陆军 124

army uniform **jūnzhuāng** 军装 124

aromatic **xiāng** 香 232

arouse **qǐfā** 启发 171, **yǐnqǐ** 引起 254

arrange **ānpái** 安排 2, **bǎi** 摆 4, **cuò** 措 36, **pái** 排 163

arrive **dào** 到, **dàodá** 到达 43

arrogant **jiāo'ào** 骄傲 112

arrow **jiàn** 箭 110

art **yìshù** 艺术 252

art museum **měishùguǎn** 美术馆 150

article **wénzhāng** 文章 224

artificial **rénzào** 人造 182

artificial leg **jiǎtuǐ** 假腿 106

artillery man **pàobīng** 炮兵 165

artist **huàjiā** 画家 95, **měishùjiā** 美术家 150, **yìshùjiā** 艺术家 252

artistic work **zuòpǐn** 作品 288

as **jì** 既 104, **jìrán** 既然 104

as a matter of fact **shìshí shang** 事实上 197

as a result **yúshì** 于是 260

as before **hái** 还, **háishì** 还是 86

as before **réng** 仍, **réngjiù** 仍旧, **réngrán** 仍然 183

as if **sìhū** 似乎 205

as soon as **jiù** 就 121

as soon as **yī ... jiù ...** 一 ... 就 ... 248

as usual **zhàocháng** 照常 270

as well **cǐwài** 此外 35

as you wish **suí** 随 206

as...as **yìbān** 一般 251

ascend **shàng** 上 187

ashamed **cánkuì** 惭愧 22

Asia **Yàzhōu** 亚洲 243

ask **dǎtīng** 打听 37

ask **qǐng** 请 176, **tuō** 托 278, **wèn** 问 224, **yāoqiú** 要求 246, **yào** 要 246

ask after **wènhòu** 问候 224

ask for **qǐngqiú** 请求 177

ask for **zhēngqiú** 征求 272

askew **wāi** 歪 218

aspect **dìfang** 地方 47, **fāngmiàn** 方面 62

aspiration **lǐxiǎng** 理想 138, **yuànwàng** 愿望 262

assemble **jíhé** 集合 102

assembly **dàhuì** 大会 38

assembly hall **lǐtáng** 礼堂 137

assiduous **kèkǔ** 刻苦 129

assign (a job) **pài** 派 164

assignment **rènwù** 任务 182

assignment (in school) **zuòyè** 作业 288

assist **bāng** 帮, **bāngzhù** 帮助 6

assistance **bāngzhù** 帮助 6

at **zài** 在 265

(be) at ease **fàngxīn** 放心 63

at first **běnlái** 本来 10

at least **zhìshǎo** 至少 277

at once **mǎshàng** 马上 147

at present **dāngqián** 当前 42

at present **mùqián** 目前 156

at will **luàn** 乱 145

athlete **yùndòngyuán** 运动员 264

atlas **dìtú cè** 地图册 47

atmospheric **qìwēn** 气温 172

attach importance to **zhòngshì** 重视 279

attack **jìngōng** 进攻 118

attempt (n.) **qǐtú** 企图 171

attempt (v.) **qǐtú** 企图 171

attend **cānjiā** 参加 22

attend (meeting, trial, etc.) **chūxí** 出席 31

attend (school) **dú** 读 53, **shàng** 上 187
attend a meeting **kāihuì** 开会 125
attend to **gù** 顾 80
attendant **fúwùyuán** 服务员 67
attitude **tàidu** 态度 208
attract **xīyǐn** 吸引 227
attraction **xīyǐnlì** 吸引力 227
attractive **yǒu xīyǐnlì** 有吸引力 227
auction **pāimài** 拍卖 163
audience **guānzhòng** 观众 82
audio recorder **lùyīnjī** 录音机 144
audio tape **cídài** 磁带 34
auditorium **lǐtáng** 礼堂 137
aunt **āyí** 阿姨 1, **bómǔ** 伯母 16, **gūgu** 姑姑 79
authentic **zhēnshí** 真实 271
author **zuòzhě** 作者 288
automatic **zìdòng** 自动, **zìdònghuà** 自动化 285
automatic teller machine (ATM) **zìdòng qǔkuǎnjī** 自动取款机 132
automation **zìdònghuà** 自动化 285
automobile **qìchē** 汽车 172
autumn **qiū** 秋, **qiūtiān** 秋天 177
avenue **mǎlù** 马路 147
average **píngjūn** 平均 168, **yìbān** 一般 251
aviation **hángkōng** 航空 87
avoid **bì** 避, **bìmiǎn** 避免 12
awake **xǐng** 醒 239
awaken **jiàoxǐng** 叫醒 239
award (n., v.) **jiǎng** 奖 110
away from **lí** 离 136

B

back (n.) **hòu** 后, **hòubian** 后边, **hòumiàn** 后面 92
backward **luòhòu** 落后 146
bacterium **xìjūn** 细菌 228
bad **huài** 坏 95
badminton **yǔmáoqiú** 羽毛球 260
bag (n.) **bāo** 包, **dài** 袋 6, 41
baggage **xíngli** 行李 238
bake **kǎo** 烤 127
bakery **miànbāo fáng** 面包房 152
ball, ball game **qiú** 球 177
ballroom dancing **jiāojìwǔ** 交际舞 111
bamboo **zhúzi** 竹子 280
banana **xiāngjiāo** 香蕉 232
bandit **qiángdào** 强盗 174
bank (financial) **yínháng** 银行 254
bank (river) **àn** 岸 3

banking card **yínháng kǎ** 银行卡 124
banner **qízi** 旗子 171
banquet **yànhuì** 宴会 245
barber **lǐfàshī** 理发师 137
barbershop **lǐfàdiàn** 理发店 137
barely **gāng** 刚 72
base (n.) **jīchǔ** 基础 101
baseball **bàngqiú** 棒球 177
basic **gēnběn, jīběn** 根本, 基本 74, 101
basic quality **xìngzhì** 性质 239
basically **jīběn shang** 基本上 101
basin **pén** 盆 165
basis **gēnjù** 根据 74
basketball **lánqiú** 篮球 133
bath (v.) **xǐzǎo** 洗澡 227
bath soap **xiāngzào** 香皂 232
bathroom **wèishēngjian** 卫生间 222, **xǐzǎojiān** 洗澡间 227, **yùshì** 浴室 261
BC **gōngyuán qián** 公元前 77
be **shì** 是 197
be alike **xiāngsì** 相似 231
bean curd **dòufu** 豆腐 53
bear resemblance to **xiàng** 像 233
beard **húzi** 胡子 92
(have) bearing on **yǒuguān** 有关 258
beautiful **měi** 美, **měihǎo** 美好, **měilì** 美丽 150
beautiful **yōuměi** 优美 256
because **yīnwèi** 因为 253, **yóuyú** 由于 257
because of **yóuyú** 由于 257
become **chéng** 成 27, **chéngwéi** 成为 28
become famous **chéng míng** 成名 27
become unemployed **shīyè** 失业 193
bed (n.) **chuáng** 床 33
bee **mìfēng** 蜜蜂 152
beef **niúròu** 牛肉 161, 184
beer **píjiǔ** 啤酒 166
before **miànqián** 面前 153, **yǐqián** 以前 250, **zhī qián** 之前 274
beforehand **shìxiān** 事先 197
beg **qiú** 求 177
begin **kāishǐ** 开始 125
begin construction **dònggōng** 动工 52
begin school **kāixué** 开学 125
begin work **dòngshǒu** 动手 52
beginning (n.) **chū** 初 32, **kāishǐ** 开始 125
behavior **xíngdòng** 行动 238
behind **zhī hòu** 之后 274
Beijing (Peking) **Běijīng** 北京 9
Beijing opera **jīngjù** 京剧 119
believe **xiāngxìn** 相信 231, **xìn** 信 237

believe in **xiāngxìn** 相信 231

bell **líng** 铃 143

belly **dùzi** 肚子 53

belong to **shǔyú** 属于 201

belongings **cáichǎn** 财产 21

beloved (adj.) **qīn'ài** 亲爱 175

below **xià** 下 228

below **xià** 下 228, **xiàbian** 下边 228, **xiàmiàn** 下面 229, **yíxià** 以下 251, **zhī xià** 之下 274

(be) beneficial to **duì ... yǒu hǎochù** 对...有好处 88

benefit (n.) **hǎochu** 好处 88, **lìyì** 利益 139

benefit from **lìyòng** 利用 139

beseech **qiú** 求 177

besides **chúle ... (yǐwài), cǐwài** 除了 ... (以外), 此外 32, 35

between **zhī jiān** 之间, **zhī zhōng** 之中 274

beyond **yǐwài** 以外 251

bicycle **zìxíngchē** 自行车 285

bid farewell to **gàobié** 告别 73

big **dà** 大 38

big shot **dà rénwù** 大人物 38

billion **shíyì** 十亿 252

biochemistry **shēngwù huàxué** 生物化学 192

biology **shēngwùxué** 生物学 192

bird **niǎo** 鸟 161

birth certificate **chūshēng zhèng** 出生证, **chūshēng zhèngmíng** 出生证明 31, 274

birth date **chūshēng rìqī** 出生日期 31

birthday **shēngrì** 生日 192

birthday card **shēngrì hèkǎ** 生日贺卡 91, 192

birthday present **shēngrì lǐwù** 生日礼物 137, 192

birthplace **chūshēng dì** 出生地 31

biscuit **bǐnggān** 饼干 15

(a) bit **diǎn** 点 48, **yìdiǎnr** 一点儿 251

(a) bit of **yìxiē** 一些 252

bitch (n.) **mǔ gǒu** 母狗 78

bite (v.) **yǎo** 咬 246

bitter **kǔ** 苦 131

black **hēi** 黑 91

black tea **hóngchá** 红茶 91

blackboard **hēibǎn** 黑板 91

blame (v.) **guài** 怪 81

bland **dàn** 淡 42

blanket (n.) **bèizi** 被子 9, **tǎnzi** 毯子 208

block (v.) **dǎng** 挡 43, **dǔ** 堵 53, **lán** 拦 133

blood **xuě** 血, **xuěyè** 血液 242

blow (v.) **chuī** 吹 34, **guā** 刮 80

blue **lán** 蓝 133

boast (v.) **chuīniú** 吹牛 34

boat **chuán** 船 33

boil (v.) **zhǔ** 煮 281

boiled water **kāishuǐ** 开水 203

boisterous **rènao** 热闹 180

bold **dàdǎn** 大胆 38, **yǒnggǎn** 勇敢 256

bone **gǔtou** 骨头 79

bonus **jiǎngjīn** 奖金 110

book (n.) **shū** 书 200

book (v.) **dìng** 订 50

book a table/seat **dìng zuò** 订座 51

book a ticket **dìng piào** 订票 50

bookshelf **shūjià** 书架 200

bookshop, bookstore **shūdiàn** 书店 200

border **biān** 边 12

boring (adj.) **méijìn** 没劲 119

(be) born **chūshēng** 出生 31

borrow **jiè** 借 116

boss (n.) **lǎobǎn** 老板 134

botanical garden **zhíwùyuán** 植物园 275

botanist **zhíwùxuéjiā** 植物学家 275

botany **zhíwùxué** 植物学 275

both **dōu** 都 52

both sides **shuāngfāng** 双方 202

both ... and ... **yòu ... yòu ...** 又 ... 又 ... 260

bother (v.) **máfan** 麻烦 146

bottle **píng** 瓶 169

bowl (n.) **wǎn** 碗 220

box (n.) **hézi** 盒子 90, **xiāngzi** 箱子 232

boy **nán háizi** 男孩子 158

boyfriend **nánpéngyou** 男朋友 165

brag (v.) **chuīniú** 吹牛 34

brain **nǎozi** 脑子 159

branch (of company) **fēn gōngsī** 分公司 77

brand (n.) **pái** 牌, **páizi** 牌子 164

brave **yǒnggǎn** 勇敢 256

bread **miànbāo** 面包 152

break (v.) **duàn** 断 54, **pò** 破 169

break a rule **fàn guī** 犯规 61

break down **huài** 坏 95

break off **duàn** 断 54

break the law **wéifàn fǎlǜ** 违反法律 59

breakdown **máobìng** 毛病 148

breakfast (n.) **zǎofàn** 早饭 266

breathe **hūxī** 呼吸 92

breed (n.) **pǐnzhǒng** 品种 168

brew coffee **zhǔ kāfēi** 煮咖啡 124

bribe **hóngbāo** 红包 91

bridge (n.) **qiáo** 桥 174

bright (clever) **cōngmíng** 聪明 35
bright (radiant) **guāngmíng** 光明 83, **liàng** 亮 141, **míngliàng** 明亮 154
brilliance **guānghuī** 光辉 83
brilliant **guānghuī** 光辉 83
bring **dài** 带 41
brisk **huóyuè** 活跃 99
Britain **Yīngguó** 英国 254
broadcast, broadcasting **guǎngbō** 广播 83
broadcasting company **guǎngbō gōngsī** 广播公司 83
broken **suì** 碎 206
bronze **tóng** 铜 215
brother (elder) **gēge** 哥哥 73
brother (younger) **dìdi** 弟弟 47
brother(s) **xiōngdì** 兄弟 240
brush (v.) **shuā** 刷 202
bucket **tǒng** 桶 215
buffalo **niú** 牛 161
build **zào** 造 266
build (n.) **gèzi** 个子 74
build (v.) **jiàn** 建, **jiànshè** 建设, **jiànzhù** 建筑 109, **xiū** 修 240
build up **jīlěi** 积累 101
building (n.) **guǎn** 馆 82, **jiànzhù** 建筑 109, **lóu** 楼 144
bull **gōng niú** 公牛 161
bump against **zhuàng** 撞 283
bump into **pèng** 碰 166
bun (steamed) **mántou** 馒头 148
bun (steamed, stuffed) **bāozi** 包子 7
bungalow **píngfáng** 平房 62
bungler **hútu chóng** 糊涂虫 93
bureau chief/director **júzhǎng** 局长 122
burn (v.) **ránshāo** 燃烧 180, **shāo** 烧 188
burn the midnight oil **kāi yèchē** 开夜车 125
bury **mái** 埋 147
bus (long-distance) **chángtú qìchē** 长途汽车 25
bus (public) **gōnggòng qìchē** 公共汽车 76
bus station **qìchē zhàn** 汽车站 268
bus stop **chēzhàn** 车站 26
bus/coach ticket **qìchē piào** 汽车票 167
business **mǎimài** 买卖 147, **shāngyè** 商业 187, **shēngyi** 生意 192, **yèwù** 业务 247
business administration **shāngyè guǎnlǐ** 商业管理 82, 187
business district **shāngyè qū** 商业区 177, 187
business hours **yíngyè shíjiān** 营业时间 255
bustling **rènao** 热闹 180
busy **máng** 忙 148

but **dànshì** 但是 42, **ér** 而 57, **què** 却 179, **rán'ér** 然而 179
butter (n.) **huángyóu** 黄油 96
buy (v.) **mǎi** 买 147
by (introducing agent) **bèi** 被 9, **yóu** 由 257
by and by **jiànjiàn** 渐渐 109
bypass (v.) **rào** 绕 180

C

cabbage **báicài** 白菜 4
cadre (communist) **gànbù** 干部 71
cake (n.) **dàngāo** 蛋糕 42
calamity **zāi, zāihài** 灾, 灾害 264
calculate **jìsuàn** 计算 103, **suàn** 算 205
calf **niú, xiǎo niú** 牛, 小牛 161
call (v.) **chēng** 称 27, **jiào** 叫 112, **zhāohu** 招呼 269
call on **kànwàng** 看望 126
call upon **hàozhào** 号召 89
calm (adj.) **píngjìng** 平静 168
camera **zhàoxiàngjī** 照相机 270
can (modal v.) **huì** 会 97, **kěyǐ** 可以 128, **néng** 能 159, **nénggòu** 能够 160
can (n.) **guàntou** 罐头 83
Canada **Jiānádà** 加拿大 105
cancel **qǔxiāo** 取消 178
candy **táng, tángguǒ** 糖, 糖果 209
canned food **guàntou shípǐn** 罐头食品 83
cannon **pào** 炮 165
cannot help but **rěn bu zhù** 忍不住 182
cap (n.) **màozi** 帽子 149
capability **běnlǐng** 本领, **běnshì** 本事 10
capable **nénggàn** 能干 160, **xíng** 行 238
capital **zīběn** 资本 284
capital (money) **běn** 本 10
capital city **jīng** 京 119, **shǒudū** 首都 200
capitalism **zīběn zhǔyì** 资本主义 284
capture (v.) **zhuō** 捉 284
car **qìchē** 汽车 172
car park **tíngchēchǎng** 停车场 26, 213
card (v.) **kǎ** 卡 124
cards (playing) **pái** 牌 164
care for **gù** 顾 80, **guānxīn** 关心 81, **zhàogù** 照顾 270
career **shìyè** 事业 197
carefree **qīngxián** 清闲 230
careful **xiǎoxīn** 小心 235
careless **mǎhu** 马虎 147
carrot **luóbo, hú luóbo** 萝卜, 胡萝卜 146
carry **duān** 端 54, **yùn** 运 264, **yùnshū** 运输 264

conversation **huìhuà** 会话 98

cook (v.) **shāo** 烧 188, **zhǔ** 煮 281, **zuòfàn** 做饭 289

cooked (adj.) **shú** 熟 201

cooked rice **fàn** 饭 61

cookie **bǐnggān** 饼干 15

cooking oil **shíyóu** 食油 257

cool (adj.) **liáng** 凉, **liángkuai** 凉快 141

cooperate **hézuò** 合作 90, **pèihé** 配合 165

cooperation **hézuò** 合作 90

coordinate **pèihé** 配合 165

cope with **duìfu** 对付 55

copper **tóng** 铜 215

copy by hand **chāo** 抄 25, **chāoxiě** 抄写 26

cord **shéngzi** 绳子 192

cordial (adj.) **qīnqiè** 亲切 175

cordless telephone **yídòng diànhuà** 移动电话 250

corn **yùmǐ** 玉米 261

corner (n.) **jiǎo** 角 112

corporation **gōngsī** 公司 77

correct (adj.) **búcuò** 不错 17, **duì** 对 55, **zhèngquè** 正确 273

correct (v.) **gǎi** 改 69, **jiūzhèng** 纠正 121

correct a mistake **jiūzhèng cuòwù** 纠正错误 36

correspondent **jìzhě** 记者 104

cost (n.) **fèiyòng** 费用 64

cost (v.) **fèi** 费 64, **huā** 花 94

cost of living **shēnghuó fèiyòng** 生活费用 64, **shēnghuó fèi** 生活费 191

cottage (thatched) **cǎofáng** 草房 62

cotton **miánhuā** 棉花 152

couch **shāfā** 沙发 185

cough **késou** 咳嗽 127

count (v.) **shǔ** 数 201

counterfeit goods **jiǎhuò** 假货 106

countless **wúshù** 无数 225

country **guó, guójiā** 国, 国家 85

countryside **nóngcūn** 农村 161, **xiāngxia** 乡下 231

county (rural) **xiàn** 县 230

(a) couple of **liǎng** 两 141

courage **yǒngqì** 勇气 256

courageous **dàdǎn** 大胆 38

course **kèchéng** 课程 129

courteous **lǐmào** 礼貌 137

courtyard **yuànzi** 院子 262

cow **niú** 牛, **nǎiniú** 奶牛 161

crawl **pá** 爬 163

create **chuàngzào** 创造 34

create (art, literature) **chuàngzuò** 创作 34

creativity **chuàngzàoxìng** 创造性 34

credit card **xìnyòng kǎ** 信用卡 124

crisis **wēijī** 危机 221

crisp (adj.) **cuì** 脆 36

criterion **biāozhǔn** 标准 13

critical **yánzhòng** 严重 243

criticism, criticize **pīpíng** 批评 166

crooked **wāi** 歪 218

crop (n.) **zhuāngjiā** 庄稼 283

cross (a water body) **dù** 渡 54

cross (v.) **guò** 过 85, **jǐ** 挤 103

crowd of **qún** 群 179

crowded **jǐ** 挤 103

crown (of head) **tóudǐng** 头顶 50

cry (v.) **kū** 哭 131

cube (mathematics) **lìfāng** 立方 138

cucumber **huángguā** 黄瓜 96

cultural level **wénhuà shuǐpíng** 文化水平 203

culture **wénhuà** 文化 223, 文明 224

cup **bēi** 杯, **bēizi** 杯子 9

cup (as prize) **jiǎngbēi** 奖杯 110

curse (v.) **mà** 骂 147

curved (adj.) **wān** 弯 219

custom **fēngsú** 风俗 66

customer **gùkè** 顾客 80

customs (duty) **hǎiguān** 海关 86

customs inspection **hǎiguān jiǎnchá** 海关检查 86

customs officer **hǎiguān rényuán** 海关人员 86

cut (v.) **gē** 割 73, **jiàngdī** 降低 111, **qiè** 切 175

cut (v., with scissors) **jiǎn** 剪 108

cut off **duàn** 断 54

D

daddy **ā bà** 阿爸 1, **bàba** 爸爸 3

daily **rìcháng** 日常 183

daily life **rìcháng shēnghuó** 日常生活 191

daily necessities **rìyòngpǐn** 日用品 183

daily schedule **rìchéng** 日程 183

damage (n.) **sǔnshī** 损失 206, **wēihài** 危害 221

damage (v.) **pò** 破, **pòhuài** 破坏 169

damaged (adj.) **pò** 破 169

damp **shī** 湿 194

dance (v.) **tiàowǔ** 跳舞 213

danger, dangerous **wēixiǎn** 危险 221

dare **gǎn** 敢 71

dark **àn** 暗 3, **hēi** 黑 91, **hēi'àn** 黑暗 91

darkroom **ànshì** 暗室 3

darling (adj.) **qīn'ài** 亲爱 175

data **cáiliào** 材料 21, **shùjù** 数据 202, **zīliào** 资料 204

date (n.) **rì** 日 183, **rìzi** 日子 184, **yuēhuì** 约会 263

date (of event) **rìqī** 日期 183

datum **shùjù** 数据 202

daughter **nǚ'ér** 女儿 162

day **rì** 日 183, **rìzi** 日子 184, **tiān** 天 211

daytime **báitiān** 白天 4

deal cards **fāpái** 发牌 164

deal with **chǔlǐ** 处理 32, **dài** 待 41, **duì** 对, **duìfu** 对付 55

dear (adj.) **qīn'ài** 亲爱 175

debate **zhēnglùn** 争论 272

decade (of a century) **niándài** 年代 160

deceive **piàn** 骗 167, **qīpiàn** 欺骗 170

decide **dìng** 定 50, **juédìng** 决定 123, **pànduàn** 判断 164

decide on **ná zhǔyi** 拿主意 156

decision **juédìng** 决定 123

decisive **gāncuì** 干脆 70

declare **xuānbù** 宣布 241

decorate **bùzhì** 布置 20

deduct **jiǎn** 减 108

deep **shēn** 深, **shēnhòu** 深厚 190

defeat (n.) **shībài** 失败 193

defeat (v.) **shèng** 胜 193, **zhànshèng** 战胜 268

(be) defeated **bài** 败 4, **shībài** 失败 193

defect **quēdiǎn** 缺点 179

defend **bǎowèi** 保卫 7, **wéihù** 维护 221

defer **tuō** 拖 218

definite **kěndìng** 肯定 130

definite and explicit **míngquè** 明确 154

definite view **zhǔyi** 主意 281

definitely **jué** 决 123, **yídìng** 一定 249

degree **chéngdù** 程度 29, **dù** 度 54

degree of difficulty **nándù** 难度 53

delay **dānwù** 耽误 41

delegation **dàibiǎotuán** 代表团 217

deliberate (adj.) **gùyì** 故意 80

delicious **hǎochī** 好吃 88

delighted (adj.) **gāoxìng** 高兴 72

deliver **sòng** 送 205

demand **yāoqiú** 要求 246

democracy **mínzhǔ** 民主 153

democratic **mínzhǔ** 民主 153

demolish **chāi** 拆 24

demonstrate **biǎomíng** 表明 14

dense (gas/liquid) **nong** 浓 162

dentist **yáyī** 牙医 243

dentures **jiǎyá** 假牙 106

deny **fǒudìng** 否定 66

depart **lí, líkāi** 离, 离开 136

department **bùmén** 部门 20

department (of university) **xì** 系 228

department store **shāngchǎng** 商场 187

depend on **kào** 靠 127, **yīkào** 依靠 248

deputy (adj.) **fù** 副 68

deputy manager **fùjīnglǐ** 副经理 119

describe **xíngróng** 形容 238

describe (in writing) **miáoxiě** 描写 153

desert (n.) **shāmò** 沙漠 185

design **shèjì** 设计 189

desire (n.) **yuànwàng** 愿望 262

desk **tái** 台 207, **zhuōzi** 桌子 284

desk lamp **táidēng** 台灯 45

despise **kànbuqǐ** 看不起 126

destiny **mìngyùn** 命运 155

detailed **xiángxì** 详细 232

determination **juéxīn** 决心 123

determine **juédìng** 决定 123, **quèdìng** 确定 179

determined (adj.) **jiānjué** 坚决 107

(be) determined **juéxīn** 决心 123

detour (v.) **rào** 绕 180

develop **fā** 发 58, **fāyáng** 发扬, **fāzhǎn** 发展 59

develop **jìnhuà** 进化 118, **kāifā** 开发 125, **kāizhǎn** 开展 125

developed (adj.) **fādá** 发达 58

developing country **fāzhǎnzhōng guójiā** 发展中国家 59

diagram **tú** 图 216

dialogue **duìhuà** 对话 55

diary **rìjì** 日记 183

dictation **tīngxiě** 听写 213

dictionary **cídiǎn** 词典 34

did not **méiyǒu** 没有 150, **wèi** 未 222

die **qùshì** 去世 178, **sǐ** 死 204

difference **qūbié** 区别 178

different **bùtóng** 不同 19

differentiate **qūbié** 区别 177

difficult **jiānkǔ** 艰苦 107, **kùnnan** 困难 132, **nán** 难 158

difficult (life) **xīnkǔ** 辛苦 236

difficulty **kùnnan** 困难 132

digest (v.) **xiāohuà** 消化 233

diligent (student) **yònggōng** 用功 256

dim **àn** 暗 3

dime **jiǎo** 角 112

dime (colloquial) **máo** 毛 148

dining hall **shítáng** 食堂 196

during **yǐnèi** 以内 250
during the period of **qījiān** 期间 170
dusk **bàngwǎn** 傍晚 6
duty **shuì** 税 203, **yìwù** 义务 252, **zérèn** 责
  任 267
dye **rán** 染 180
dynasty **dài** 代 40

E

e-card **diànzǐ hèkǎ** 电子贺卡 49, 90
e-mail **diànzǐ yóujiàn** 电子邮件 49
each **gè** 各 74, **měi** 每 150
each other **hùxiāng** 互相 93, **xiānghù** 相互
  231
ear **ěrduō** 耳朵 58
early **zǎo** 早 266
early morning **zǎochén** 早晨 266
earn **shōurù** 收入 199
earnest **rènzhēn** 认真 182
earth **tǔ** 土 217
earth (planet) **dìqiú** 地球 47
(the) earth's surface **dìmiàn** 地面 47
east **dōng** 东 51
east side **dōngbian** 东边, **dōngmiàn** 东面 51
eastern **dōng** 东 51
(the) East **dōngfāng** 东方 51
easy **qiǎn** 浅 173, **róngyì** 容易 184
easy (job) **qīngsōng** 轻松 176
easy to understand **qīng** 清 175
eat **chī** 吃 29
eat up **chīdiao** 吃掉 49
economics **jīngjìxué** 经济学 119
economist **jīngjìxuéjiā** 经济学家 119
economize **jiéyuē** 节约 115, **shěng** 省 193
economy **jīngjì** 经济 119
edifice **jiànzhù** 建筑 109
educate, education **jiàoyù** 教育 113
educator **jiàoyùjiā** 教育家 106
effect **xiàoguǒ** 效果 235
effective **yǒuxiào** 有效 259
efficacious **yǒuxiào** 有效 259
efficiency **xiàolǜ** 效率 235
efficient (of people) **nénggàn** 能干 160
effort **gōngfu** 工夫 75, **gōngfu** 功夫 77
efforts **lìliàng** 力量 138
egg (n.) **dàn** 蛋 42
egg (of chicken) **jīdàn** 鸡蛋 101
eight **bā** 八 3
elder brother **gēge** 哥哥 73
elder sister **jiějie** 姐姐 115
elderly **lǎo** 老 134

elect, election **xuǎnjǔ** 选举 241
electric fan **diànshàn** 电扇 49
electric light **diàndēng** 电灯 45, 48
electric pole **diànxiàn gān** 电线杆 70
electricity **diàn** 电 48
electron **diànzǐ** 电子 49
electronic game **diànzǐ yóuxì** 电子游戏 49
electronics **diàn** 电 48
electronics industry **diànzǐ gōngyè** 电子工业 49
element **yīnsù** 因素 253
elementary **chūjí** 初级 32
elementary school **chūjí xiǎoxué, chūxiǎo** 初级
  小学 32
elephant **xiàng** 象 233
elevator **diàntī** 电梯 49
eliminate **xiāomiè** 消灭 233
emancipate, emancipation **jiěfàng1** 解放 116
embassy **dàshǐguǎn** 大使馆 39
embrace **bào** 抱 8, **yōngbào** 拥抱 255
emerge **chūxiàn** 出现 31
emerge from **chū** 出 31
emigrate, emigrant **yímín** 移民 250
emit **fāchū** 发出 58, **mào** 冒 149
emotion **gànqíng** 感情 71
emperor **huángdì** 皇帝 96
emphasis **zhòngdiǎn** 重点 279
emphasize **qiángdiào** 强调 174, **tūchū** 突出
  216
employ **cǎiyòng** 采用 21
employee(s) **zhígōng** 职工 275
employment agency **zhíyè jièshàosuǒ** 职业介绍
  所 275
empty (adj.) **kōng** 空 130
emulate ... **xiàng ... xuéxí** 向...学习 242
enable **shǐ** 使 196
encircle **wéirào** 围绕 221
enclose **wéi** 围 221
encounter (v.) **yùdào** 遇到 261, **zāodào** 遭到
  266
encourage **gǔlì** 鼓励 79
end (v.) **jiéshù** 结束 115, **wán** 完 219
end class **xià kè** 下课 129
endure **rěn** 忍 182
endure hardship **chīkǔ** 吃苦 131
enemy **dírén** 敌人 46
energy **jīnglì** 精力 120
energy resources **néngyuán** 能源 160
engagement **yuēhuì** 约会 263
engineer (n.) **gōngchéngshī** 工程师 75
engineering **gōngchéng** 工程 75
England **Yīngguó** 英国 254

English (language) **Yīngwén** 英文, **Yīngyǔ** 英语 255

enjoy **xiǎngshòu** 享受 232

enlarge **fàngdà** 放大 63, **kuòdà** 扩大 132

enlighten, enlightenment **qǐfā** 启发 171

enough **chōngzú** 充足 30, **gòu** 够 78

enraged (adj.) **fènnù** 愤怒 65

enter **jìn** 进 118, **jìnrù** 进入 118, **rù** 入 184

enterprise **qǐyè** 企业 171

entertain (a guest) **zhāodài** 招待 269

entertainment expense **jiāojìfèi** 交际费 111

enthusiasm **jījíxìng** 积极性 101

enthusiastic **jījí** 积极 101, **rèqíng** 热情 180, **rèxīn** 热心 181

entire **zhěng** 整 272, **zhěngge** 整个 273

entrance **rù kǒu** 入口 184

entrepreneur **qǐyèjiā** 企业家 171

entrust **tuō** 托 218

entry **rù kǒu** 入口 184

envelope **xìnfēng** 信封 237

environment **huánjìng** 环境 95

envy **xiànmù** 羡慕 231

epoch **shídài** 时代 194

equal (in status) **píngděng** 平等 168

(be) equal to **děngyú** 等于 46

equality **píngděng** 平等 168

equipment **shèbèi** 设备 189

erroneous **cuòwù** 错误 36

error **cuòwù** 错误 36

escort (v.) **sòng** 送 205

especially **tèbié** 特别 209, **yóuqí** 尤其 257

essay (n.) **lùnwén** 论文 146, **wénzhāng** 文章 224

essence **gēnběn** 根本 74

essential **gēnběn** 根本 74

establish **chénglì** 成立 28, **jiànlì** 建立 109

estimate **gūjì** 估计 79

et cetera, etc. **děng** 等 46

ethics **dàodé** 道德 44

ethnic group **mínzú** 民族 153

Euro **Ōuyuán** 欧元 163

Europe **Ōuzhōu** 欧洲 163

evade **bì** 避 12

even (adv.) **lián ... dōu ...** 连... 都... 139

even if **jiùshì** 就是 122, **nǎpà** 哪怕 156

even more **gèng** 更, **gèngjiā** 更加 75

even though **jǐnguǎn** 尽管 117

even when **nǎpà** 哪怕 156

evening **wǎnshang** 晚上 220, **yè** 夜 247

evening party **wǎnhuì** 晚会 220

event (historic) **shìjiàn** 事件 197

event (sports) **bǐsài xiàngmù** 比赛项目 11

ever **cónglái** 从来 35, **shǐzhōng** 始终 196

every **fánshì** 凡是 60, **gè** 各 74, **měi** 每 150

everybody **dàjiā** 大家 38

everybody (colloquial) **dàhuǒr** 大伙儿 38

everyday **tiāntiān** 天天 211

everyone **shuí** 谁 202

everything **rènhé shì** 任何事 182, **yíqiè** 一切 249

everywhere **dàochù** 到处 43

evident **míngxiǎn** 明显 154

evolve **jìnhuà** 进化 118

exact **zhǔn** 准 283, **zhǔnquè** 准确 284

examination **cèyàn** 测验 23, **kǎoshì** 考试 127

examination result **chéngjì** 成绩, **kǎoshì chéngjì** 考试成绩 28

examine **jiǎnchá** 检查 108, **kǎo** 考 126, **kǎoshì** 考试 127

example **lìzi** 例子 139

example (positive) **bǎngyàng** 榜样 6

exceed **chāoguò** 超过 26

excellent **yōuxiù** 优秀 256

except **chúle ... (yǐwài)** 除了 ... (以外) 32

exceptional **gèbié** 个别 74, **tèshū** 特殊 210

excessively **tài** 太 207

exchange **diào** 调 50, **jiāohuàn** 交换, **jiāoliú** 交流 111

excited **jīdòng** 101, **xīngfèn** 激动, 兴奋 238

exciting **jīdòng** 激动 101

excuse (v.) **yuánliàng** 原谅 262

Excuse me, ... **qǐngwèn ...** 请问... 176

execute (v.) **zhíxíng** 执行 275

exercise (n., v.) **liànxí** 练习 140

exercise (physical) **yùndòng** 运动 264

exert **yònglì** 用力 256

exhale **tǔ** 吐 217

exhaust (v.) **jìn** 尽 117

exhausted **lèi** 累 136

exhibit (v.) **zhǎnlǎn** 展览 268

exhibition **zhǎnlǎn** 展览, **zhǎnlǎnhuì** 展览会 268

exhort **zhǔfu** 嘱咐 281

exist **cúnzài** 存在 36

exist (there is/are) **yǒu** 有 258

exit (n.) **chūkǒu** 出口 31

expand **kāizhǎn** 125, **kuòdà** 开展, 扩大 132

expense **fèiyòng** 费用 64

expensive **guì** 贵 84

experience (n.) **jīngyàn** 经验 119

experience (personal) **jīnglì** 经历 119

experience (v.) **jīnglì** 经历 119

experienced (adj.) **yǒu jīngyàn** 有经验 120
experiment (n.) **shíyàn** 实验 195
experiment (v.) **shìyàn** 试验 198
expert (n.) **zhuānjiā** 专家 282
expire **dàoqī** 到期 170
expired **guòqī** 过期 170
expiry date **yǒuxiàoqī** 有效期 259
explain **jiědá** 解答 115, **jiěshì** 解释 116, **shuō** 说 204, **shuōmíng** 说明 204
explanation **jiěshì** 解释 116, **shuōmíng** 说明 204
explore **tànsuǒ** 探索 209
export (v.) **chūkǒu** 出口 31
express thoughts/emotions **biǎodá** 表达 14
express train **kuài chē** 快车 131
expressway **gāosù gōnglù** 高速公路 77
extend **shēn** 伸 190, **yáncháng** 延长 244
extensive **guǎngdà** 广大, **guǎngfàn** 广泛 83
extent **dù** 度 53
extinguish **miè** 灭 153
extremely **jí** 极, **jíle** 极了, **jíqí** 极其 102
extremely **tài** 太 207
eye (n.) **yǎn** 眼, **yǎnjing** 眼睛 244
eyeglass case **yǎnjìnghé** 眼镜盒 244

F

face (n.) **liǎn** 脸 140, **miàn** 面 152, **miànzi** 面子 152
face (v.) **cháo** 朝 26, **xiàng** 向 233
fact **shìshí** 事实 197
faction **pài** 派 164
factor **yīnsù** 因素 253
factory **gōngchǎng** 工厂 75
fail **shībài** 失败 193
failure **shībài** 失败 193
fairly **xiāngdāng** 相当 231
fake (goods) **jiǎhuò** 假货 106
fall (season) **qiū** 秋, **qiūtiān** 秋天 177
fall (v.) **dǎo** 倒 43, **diào** 掉 49, **diē** 跌 50, **jiàng** 降 110, **luò** 落 146, **shuāi** 摔 202
fall asleep **shuìzháo** 睡着 203
fall ill **bìng** 病, **shēngbìng** 生病 16
fall unconscious **hūnmí** 昏迷 98
false **jiǎ** 假 106
familiar with **shú** 熟, **shúxi** 熟悉 201
family **jiā** 家 105, **jiātíng** 家庭 106
family name **xìng** 姓 239
(your) family name **guìxìng** 贵姓 84
famous **yǒumíng** 有名 259, **zhùmíng** 著名 282

(become) famous **chéng míng** 成名 27, **chūmíng** 出名 153
famous brand **míngpái** 名牌 164
far **yuǎn** 远 262
far away from **lí … yuǎn** 离 … 远 136
farewell banquet **gàobié yànhuì** 告别宴会 245
farewell party **huānsònghuì** 欢送会 95
farm (n.) **nóngchǎng** 农场 161
farm (v.) **zhòngtián** 种田 212
farmer **nóngchǎngzhǔ** 农场主 161, **nóngmín** 农民 162, **zhuāngjiārén** 庄稼人 283
farming area **nóngcūn** 农村 161
farmland **tián** 田 212, **zhuāngjiādì** 庄稼地 283
fast (adj.) **kuài** 快 131
fat (adj.) **féi** 肥 64, **pàng** 胖 165
fat person **pàngzi** 胖子 165
fate **mìngyùn** 命运 155
father **fùqin** 父亲 67
father's sister **gūgu** 姑姑 79
fatherland **zǔguó** 祖国 286
fatigued **píláo** 疲劳 166
fattened **féi** 肥 64
favorable **yǒulì** 有利 259
fax (n.) **chuánzhēn** 传真 33
fear (v.) **hàipà** 害怕 87, **pà** 怕 163
fearless **yǒnggǎn** 勇敢 256
fearsome **kěpà** 可怕 128
feast (n.) **yànhuì** 宴会 245
fee **fèi** 费 64
feeble **ruò** 弱 184
feed (v.) **wèi** 喂 223
feel **gǎndào** 感到 71, **gǎnjué** 感觉 71, **juéde** 觉得 124
feel bad **nánshòu** 难受 159
feel free to **jǐnguǎn** 尽管 117
feel sorry **nánshòu** 难受 159
feeling (n.) **gǎnjué** 感觉 71
feelings **gǎnqíng** 感情 71, **qíngxù** 情绪 176
female (animal) **cí** 雌 34
female (human) **nǚ** 女 162
ferry (boat) **dùlún** 渡轮 54
festival **jié** 节 114
fetch **qǔ** 取 178
few **shǎo** 少 189
(a) few **xiē** 些 235
fiancé(e) **duìxiàng** 对象 56
fiber **xiānwéi** 纤维 230
field **chǎng** 场 25
fields **tián** 田 212
fierce **jīliè** 激烈 101, **jiānruì** 尖锐 107, **lìhai** 厉害 139

fight **dòuzhēng** 斗争 53, **fèndòu** 奋斗 65

fight back **fǎnkàng** 反抗 60

fight for **zhēngqǔ** 争取 272

fighter **zhànshi** 战士 268

fill in (form, blanks) **tián** 填 212

finally **dàodǐ** 到底 44, **jiéguǒ** 结果 115, **zhōngyú** 终于 279, **zuìhòu** 最后 287

find (v.) **zhǎodào** 找到 269

find out **fāxiàn** 发现 59

fine (adj.) **liánghǎo** 良好 141, **měihǎo** 美好 150, **yōuliáng** 优良 256

fine (weather) **qíng** 晴 176

fine arts **měishù** 美术 150

finger **shǒuzhǐ** 手指 200

finish (v.) **liǎo** 了 142, **wán** 完 219

finish class **xià kè** 下课 129

fire (n.) **huǒ** 火 99

fire (disaster) **huǒzāi** 火灾 264

fire engine **jiùhuǒchē** 救火车 121

fire extinguisher **mièhuǒqì** 灭火器 153

fire fighting **jiùhuǒ** 救火 121

fire prevention **fánghuǒ** 防火 62

firm (n.) **gōngsī** 公司 77

firm (v.) **gǒnggù** 巩固 78, **jiāndìng** 坚定 107

first **shǒuxiān** 首先 200, **tóu** 头 216

first (in time sequence) **xiān** 先 229

first ... and then... **xiān ... ránhòu ...** 先...然后... 180

(the) first **dì-yī** 第一 47

fish (n.) **yú** 鱼 260

fish meat **yúròu** 鱼肉 184

fit (v.) **shìhé** 适合 198

five **wǔ** 五 225

five-star hotel **wǔxīng lǚguǎn** 五星旅馆 145

fix (v.) **dìng** 定 50, **quèdìng** 确定 179, **xiū** 修 240, **xiūlǐ** 修理 240

fixed (adj.) **yídìng** 一定 248

flag (n.) **qízi** 旗子 171

flat (adj.) **biǎn** 扁 13, **píng** 平 168

flatter **pěng** 捧 166

flee **táo** 逃 209

flesh **ròu** 肉 184

flexible **línghuó** 灵活 142

flimsy **báo** 薄 7

float (v.) **fú** 浮 67

flood (disaster) **shuǐzāi** 水灾 264

floor (level) **céng** 层 23, **lóu** 楼 144

flora **zhíwù** 植物 275

flow (v.) **liú** 流 143

flower (n.) **huā** 花 93, **xiānhuā** 鲜花 229

flower pot **huāpén** 花盆 165

fluent **liúlì** 流利 143

fluorescent lamp **rìguāngdēng** 日光灯 45

(be) flustered **huāng** 慌 96

flutter (v.) **piāo** 飘 167

fly (v.) **fēi** 飞 63

focal point **zhòngdiǎn** 重点 279

focus (v.) **jízhōng** 集中 102

focus on **wéirào** 围绕 221

focused (adj.) **jízhōng** 集中 103

fog (n.) **wù** 雾 226

follow **gēn** 跟 75

following (prep.) **cóng** 从 35

(be) fond of **hào** 好 89, **xǐhuan** 喜欢 227

food **shíwù** 食物 196

food industry **shípǐn gōngyè** 食品工业 196

food market **cài shìchǎng** 菜市场 196

food processing **shípǐn jiāgōng** 食品加工 105, 196

foodstuff **shípǐn** 食品 196

fool (v.) **piàn** 骗 167

(be) fooled **shàngdàng** 上当 188

foolish **dāi** 呆 40, **shǎ** 傻 186

foot (measurement) **yīngchǐ** 英尺 30

foot (n.) **jiǎo** 脚 112

for **gěi** 给 74, **tì** 替 211, **yǐ** 以 250

for example **bǐrú** 比如 11, **lìrú** 例如 139

for free **bái** 白 4

for the time being **yìshí** 一时 252

forbid **jìnzhǐ** 禁止 119

force (n.) **lì** 力 138

force (v.) **miǎnqiǎng** 勉强 152

forceful **yǒulì** 有力 259

forecast (n.) **yùbao** 预报 261

foreign country **wàiguó** 外国 218

foreign language **wàiwén** 外文, **wàiyǔ** 外语 219

foreign trade **duìwài màoyì** 对外贸易 149

foreigner **wàiguórén** 外国人 218

foreman **tóur** 头儿 216

forest **sēnlín** 森林 185

forever **yǒngyuǎn** 永远 256

forget **wàng** 忘 49, **wàngdiao** 忘掉 221

(be) forgetful **diū-sān-là-sì** 丢三落四 51

forgive **yuánliàng** 原谅 262

fork (n.) **chāzi** 叉子 23

form (n.) **biǎo** 表 14

form (n.) **xíngshì** 形式 238, **xíngzhuàng** 形状 239

form (v.) **gòuchéng** 构成 78, **xíngchéng** 形成 238

formal **zhèngshì** 正式 273

formalities **shǒuxù** 手续 199

former **yuánlái** 原来 262

formerly **céngjīng** 曾经 23

formidable **lìhai** 厉害 139

fortunate **xìngfú** 幸福 239

forum **zuòtánhuì** 座谈会 288

forward (v.) **zhuǎn** 转 283

foul (in sports) **fàn guī** 犯规 61

found **jiàn** 建 109

foundation **jīchǔ** 基础 101

fountain pen **gāngbǐ** 钢笔 72

four **sì** 四 205

fragmentary **suì** 碎 206

fragrant **xiāng** 香 232

France **Fǎguó** 法国 59

fraud **piànjú** 骗局 167

free (adj.) **zìyóu** 自由 285

free time **kòng** 空 130

freedom **zìyóu** 自由 285

freeze **dòng** 冻 52

freezing cold **hánlěng** 寒冷 87

French (language) **Fǎwén** 法文, **Fǎyǔ** 法语 59

fresh **xiān** 鲜 229, **xīnxiān** 新鲜 237

Friday **Xīngqīwǔ** 星期五 238

friend **péngyou** 朋友 165

friendly **yǒuhǎo** 友好 258

friendship **yǒuyì** 友谊 258

frighten, be frightened **xià** 吓 229

frightening **kěpà** 可怕 128

frog **qīngwā** 青蛙 175

from **cóng** 从 35, **lí** 离 136, **zìcóng** 自从 284

from now on **jīnhòu** 今后 116

from… till… **cóng … dào…** 从…到… 35

front **qiánbiān** 前边, **qiánmiàn** 前面 173

frozen meat **dòngròu** 冻肉 52

(be) frugal **jiéshěng** 节省 114

fruit **shuǐguǒ** 水果 203

fruit jelly **shuǐguǒ dòng** 水果冻 52

fruit shop **shuǐguǒ diàn** 水果店 203

fulfill **wánchéng** 完成 219

full **bǎo** 满 8, **mǎn** 整 148, **zhěng** 饱 272

full name **xìngmíng** 姓名 240

full of **chōngmǎn** 充满 30

fully **shífēn** 十分 194

fun **hǎowánr** 好玩儿 89

function (n.) **zuòyòng** 作用 288

fund **zījīn** 资金 284

fundamental **gēnběn** 根本 74, **jīběn** 基本 101

fur coat **píyī** 皮衣 166

furniture **jiājù** 家具 106

further (adv.) **jìnyíbù** 进一步 118

future (n.) **wèilái** 未来 173, **qiántú** 前途 222

(the) future **jiānglái** 将来 110

future prospects **qiántú** 前途 173

G

gallery **měishùguǎn** 美术馆 150

galoshes **yǔxié** 雨鞋 236

game **yóuxì** 游戏 258

garbage **lājī** 垃圾 132

garbage bin **lājī xiāng** 垃圾箱 132

garbage disposal **lājī chùlǐ** 垃圾处理 132

garden **huāyuán** 花园 94

gasoline **qìyóu** 汽油 172

gate **mén** 门, **dàmén** 大门 151

gather together **jíhé** 集合 102

gaze (v.) **dīng** 盯 50

general (adj.) **dàgài** 大概 38

general manager **zǒngjīnglǐ** 总经理 119

(the) general public **qúnzhòng** 群众 179

generally speaking **yìbān** 一般 251

generation **dài** 代 40

gentleman **xiānsheng** 先生 229

genuine **zhēnzhèng** 真正 272

germ **xìjūn** 细菌 228

German (language) **Déwén** 德文, **Déyǔ** 德语 45

Germany **Déguó** 德国 45

get **dé** 得 45, **huòdé** 获得 100

get in touch **liánxì** 联系 140

get in touch (with) **jiēchù** 接触 113

get on (a vehicle) **shàng** 上 187

get on the Internet **shàngwǎng** 上网 188

get ready **yùbèi** 预备 261

get rid of **chú** 除 32

get up **qǐ** 起 171

get up (out of bed) **qǐchuáng** 起床, **qǐlai** 起来 171

get … done **nòng** 弄 162

ghost **guǐ** 鬼 84

gift **lǐwù** 礼物 137

gigantic **jùdà** 巨大 122

girl **gūniang** 姑娘 79, **nǚ háizi** 女孩子 162

girlfriend **nǚpéngyou** 女朋友 165

give **gěi** 给 74

give an example **jǔ lìzi** 举例子 139

give as a gift **sòng** 送 205

give birth to **shēng** 生 191

give off **fāchū, mào** 发出, 冒 58, 149

give rise to **yǐnqǐ** 引起 254

give rise to **zàochéng** 造成 267

give up **xīshēng** 牺牲 227

glass **bōli** 玻璃 16

glass (n., cup) **bēi, bēizi, bōli bēi** 杯，杯子，玻璃杯 9, 9, 16

glasses **yǎnjìng** 眼镜 244

glasses case **yǎnjìnghé** 眼镜盒 244

glorious **guāngróng** 光荣 83

glove **shǒutào** 手套 199

gluttonous **hào chī** 好吃 89

go aboard (a plane, ship) **shàng** 上 187

go abroad/overseas **chūguó** 出国 31

go ashore **shàng àn** 上岸 3

go back **huí** 回 96

go in **jìnqu** 进去 118

go out **chūqu** 出去 31

go over **guòqu** 过去 85

go to **qù, tōng** 去，通 178, 214

go to class **shàng kè** 上课 129

go to work **shàngbān** 上班 5

go up **shēng, zhàng** 升，涨 191, 269

go upwards **shàng** 上 187

go/come down **xià** 下 228

goal **mùbiāo** 目标 156

goat **yáng, shānyáng** 羊，山羊 245

god(s) **shén** 神 191

gold **jīn, jīnzi** 金，金子 117

gold mine **jīnkuàng** 金矿 132

good **hǎo** 好 88, **liánghǎo** 良好 141, **yōuliáng** 优良 256

(be) good at **shànyú** 善于 186

good-looking **hǎokàn** 好看 88, **piàoliang** 漂亮 167

goodbye **zàijiàn** 再见 265

goods **huò** 货 100

goose (n.) **é** 鹅 57

gourd **guā** 瓜 80

governance **zhèngzhì** 政治 274

government **zhèngfǔ** 政府 274

government office **jīguān** 机关 100

government official **guān** 官 82

government policy **zhèngcè** 政策 274

grab **qiǎng** 抢 174, **zhuā** 抓 282

graceful **yōuměi** 优美 256

grade (in school) **niánjí** 年级 160

grade (n.) **děng** 等 46, **jí** 级 102

gradually **jiànjiàn** 渐渐 109, **zhúbù** 逐步 280, **zhújiàn** 逐渐 280

graduate (from school) **bìyè** 毕业 12

graduate school (of university) **yánjiūshēng yuàn** 研究生院 244

graduate student **yánjiūshēng** 研究生 244

grain **liángshí** 粮食 141

gram **kè** 克 128

grammar **yǔfǎ** 语法 261

grammatical **tōng** 通 214

grand **xióngwěi** 雄伟 240

grandfather (paternal) **yéye** 爷爷 247, **zǔfù** 祖父 286

grandmother (maternal) **wàizǔmǔ** 外祖母 157

grandmother (paternal) **nǎinai** 奶奶 157, **zǔmǔ** 祖母 286

granny (maternal) **ā pó** 阿婆 1, **lǎolao** 姥姥 157, **wàipó** 外婆 157

grape **pútao** 葡萄 169

grasp firmly **zhuājǐn** 抓紧 282

grass **cǎo** 草 22

grassland **cǎoyuán** 草原 23

(be) grateful **gǎnxiè** 感谢 71

(be very) grateful **gǎnjī** 感激 71

gratuity **xiǎofèi** 小费 234

gray **huī** 灰 96

greasy (food) **yóu** 油 257

great **wěidà** 伟大 222, **zhòngdà** 重大 279

great achievement **chéngjiù** 成就 28

(the) Great Wall **chángchéng** 长城 25

green (adj.) **lǜ** 绿 145, **qīng** 青 175

greenback **Měiyuán** 美元 150

greet **dǎzhāohu** 打招呼 269

greeting card **hèkǎ** 贺卡 90, 124

grieved (adj.) **bēitòng** 悲痛 9, **nánguò** 难过 158

grit (n.) **shāzi** 沙子 185

grocery **shípǐn shāngdiàn** 食品商店 196

ground (n.) **chǎng** 场 25

grounds **gēnjù** 根据 74

group (n.) **tuán** 团 217, **xiǎozǔ** 小组 234, **zǔ** 组 287

grow **shēng** 生 191, **shēngzhǎng** 生长 192, **zēngzhǎng** 增长 268, **zhǎng** 长 269

grow up **chéngzhǎng** 成长 28

grow up **shēngzhǎng** 生长 192

grown-up (n., colloquial) **dàren** 大人 39

grudging **miǎnqiǎng** 勉强 152

guarantee (n., product quality) **chǎnpǐn bǎozhèng shū** 产品保证书 7

guarantee **bǎozhèng** 保证 7

guard against **fáng** 防，**fángzhǐ** 防止 62

guess **cāi** 猜 20

guest **bīn** 宾 15, **kèren** 客人 129

guest room **kèfáng** 客房 62

guesthouse **bīnguǎn** 宾馆 15

guide (v.) **zhǐdǎo** 指导 277

guiding principle **zhǐdǎo sīxiǎng** 指导思想 277

highly **jí** 极, **jíqí** 极其 102
highway **gōnglù** 公路 77
hill **shān** 山 186
him **tā** 他 207
himself **tā zìjǐ** 他自己 285
hinder **fáng'ài** 妨碍 62
historian **lìshǐxuéjiā** 历史学家 138
historic site **gǔjì** 古迹 79
historical novel **lìshǐ xiǎoshuō** 历史小说 235
historical period **shídài** 时代 194
history **lìshǐ** 历史 138
hit (v.) **dǎ** 打 37
hoax (n.) **piànjú** 骗局 167
hobby **àihào** 爱好 1
hold (in both hands) **pěng** 捧 165
hold (meeting/ceremony) **jǔxíng** 举行 122
hold (v.) **ná** 拿 156
hold a meeting **kāihuì** 开会 125
hold back **lán** 拦 133
hole **dòng** 洞 52, **kǒng** 孔 130
holiday period **jiàqī** 假期 106
home **jiā** 家 105
home village **gùxiāng** 故乡 80
hometown **gùxiāng** 故乡 80, **jiāxiāng** 家乡 106
homework **gōngkè** 功课 77, **zuòyè** 作业 288
honest **chéngshí** 诚实 29, **lǎoshi** 老实 135, **shízài** 实在 195
honey **mì** 蜜 152
Hong Kong **Xiānggǎng** 香港 232
honor (n.) **miànzi** 面子 152
honor (v.) **zūnjìng** 尊敬 287
honorable **guāngróng** 光荣 83
hope **xīwàng** 希望 227
horrible **bùdéliǎo** 不得了 18, **kǒngbù** 恐怖 130
horror movie **kǒngbù diànyǐng** 恐怖电影 130
horse **mǎ** 马 146
hospital **yīyuàn** 医院 248
(be) hospitalized **zhù (yī) yuàn** 住(医)院 248, 282
host (n.) **zhǔrén** 主人 281
hostel **sùshè** 宿舍 205
hot **rè** 热 180
hot (scalding) **tàng** 烫 209
hotel **fàndiàn** 饭店 61, **jiǔdiàn** 酒店 121, **lǚguǎn** 旅馆 145
hour **xiǎoshí** 小时 234, **zhōngtóu** 钟头 279
house (n.) **fáng** 房 62, **fángzi** 房子 63
housefly **cāngying** 苍蝇 22
household **jiā** 家 105
household chores **jiāwù** 家务 106

housework **jiāwù** 家务 106
housing (n.) **fángzi** 房子 63
how **zěnme** 怎么, **zěnmeyàng** 怎么样 267
how ...! **duō** 多 56
how ...? **duō** 多 56
how about…? **ne** 呢 159
how can ... **zěnme** 怎么 267
how many **duōshǎo,** 多少 56, **jǐ** 几 103
how much **duōshǎo** 多少 56
how much is ...? **... duōshǎo qián** ... 多少钱... 56
how…! **hǎo** 好 88
how…! (colloquial) **duōme** 多么 56
hug **bào** 抱 8, **yōngbào** 拥抱 255
huge **jùdà** 巨大 122
hum (v.) **hēng** 哼 91
human being **rén** 人 181
human body **shēn** 身, **shēntǐ** 身体 190
human population **rénkǒu** 人口 181
humankind **rénlèi** 人类 181
hundred **bǎi** 百 4
hundred million **yì** 亿 252
hungry **è** 饿 57
hurried (adj.) **jímáng** 急忙 102
hurry **cuī** 催 36
hurry up **gǎn** 赶 70
hurt **shāng** 伤 186, **tòng** 痛 215
husband **xiānsheng** 先生 229, **zhàngfu** 丈夫 269
hygiene **wèishēng** 卫生 222
hyperactive **hào dòng** 好动 89

I

I **wǒ** 我 225
I'm sorry **duìbuqǐ** 对不起 55
ice **bīng** 冰 15
ice-skating **huábīng** 滑冰 94
idea **xiǎngfǎ** 想法 232, **zhǔyi** 主意 281, **zhǔzhāng** 主张 281
ideal **lǐxiǎng** 理想 138
idealism **lǐxiǎng zhǔyì** 理想主义 138
identical **xiāngtóng** 相同 231, **yíyàng** 一样 249, **yízhì** 一致 249
identify **rèn** 认 182
idle **xián** 闲 230
idler **xiánrén** 闲人 230
if **rúguǒ** 如果 184, **yàoshì** 要是 246
if only **zhǐyào** 只要 276
if… **... de huà** ... 的话 45
(be) ill **bìng** 病 16
illness **bìng** 病 16, **máobìng** 毛病 148

image **xíngxiàng** 形象 239
imagine **xiǎngxiàng** 想象 233
imitate **mófǎng** 模仿 155
immediately **jíshí** 及时 102, **lìjí** 立即 138, **mǎshàng** 马上 147, **lìkè** 立刻 138
immigrate, immigrant **yímín** 移民 250
immoral **bú dàodó** 不道德 44
impatient/impetuous person **jíxìngzi** 急性子 102
implement (v.) **guànchè** 贯彻 82, **shíxíng** 实行 195, **zhíxíng** 执行 275
implement a plan **zhíxíng jìhuà** 执行计划 103
import (v.) **jìnkǒu** 进口 118
important **yàojǐn** 要紧 246, **zhòngyào** 重要 279
important matter **dàshì** 大事 38
impossible **méi yǒu kěnéng** 没有可能 128
impression **gǎnjué** 感觉 71, **yìnxiàng** 印象 254
impressions **gǎnxiǎng** 感想 71
improve **gǎijìn** 改进 69
improvement **gǎijìn** 改进, **gǎishàn** 改善 69
in **lǐbian** 里边 137, **zài** 在 265
in a moment **yíhuìr** 一会儿 249
in accordance with **àn** 按, **ànzhào** 按照 3
in addition **jiāyǐ** 加以 105
in advance **shìxiān** 事先 197
(be) in charge **fùzé** 负责 68
in fact **shìshí shang** 事实上 197
in front of **miànqián** 面前 153, **qián** 前 173
in order to **yǐ** 以 250
in passing **shùnbiàn** 顺便 203
in succession **liánxù** 连续 140, **lùxù** 陆续 144
in that case **nà** 那 157, **zé** 则 267
in the end **dàodǐ** 到底 44
in the past **cóngqián** 从前 35
in vain **bái** 白 4
incessantly **búduàn** 不断 17, **bùtíng** 不停 19
inch (n.) **yingcùn** 英寸 36
incidentally **shùnbiàn** 顺便 203
incisive **shēnke** 深刻 190
include **bāokuò** 包括 7
income **shōurù** 收入 199
incoming letter **láixìn** 来信 133
inconsistent **máodùn** 矛盾 149
increase **zēngjiā** 增加, **zēngzhǎng** 增长 267
indeed **kě** 可 127, **quèshí** 确实 179, **shízài** 实在 195, **zhēn** 真 271
(be) independent **dúlì** 独立 53
indicate **dàibiǎo** 代表 40
individual (adj.) **gèbié** 个别 74

individual (n.) **gèrén** 个人 74
indolent **lǎn** 懒 133
industrial accident **gōngshāng shìgù** 工伤事故 197
industrial zone/district **gōngyè qū** 工业区 177
industry (manufacturing) **gōngyè** 工业 76
inevitable **bìrán** 必然 12
inexpensive **piányi** 便宜 167
influence **yǐngxiǎng** 影响 255
inform **gào** 告, **gàosu** 告诉 73, **guānzhào** 关照 81, **tōngzhī** 通知 214
inform casually **dǎzhāohu** 打招呼 269
informal **suíbiàn** 随便 206
information **xìnxī** 信息 237
ingenious **miào** 妙 153, **qiǎomiào** 巧妙 174
ingenuous **tiānzhēn** 天真 211
ingredient **chéngfèn** 成分 27
inhale **xī** 吸 226
initial (adj.) **chūbù** 初步, **chūjí** 初级 32
initially **zuìchū** 最初 287
initiative **jījíxìng** 积极性 101
inject **dǎzhēn** 打针 38
(be) injected **dǎzhēn** 打针 38
injection **zhēn** 针 272
injure **shāng** 伤 186
(be) injured **shòushāng** 受伤 186
injury **shāng** 伤 186
ink **mòshuǐ** 墨水 155
ink stain **mò diǎn** 墨点 48
Inland Revenue Service (IRS) **shuìwùjú** 税务局 203
innumerable **wúshù** 无数 225
inquire **dǎtīng** 打听 37, **wèn** 问 224
insect **chóngzi** 虫子 30
insert (v.) **chā** 插 23
inside **lǐ** 里, **lǐbian** 里边, **lǐmiàn** 里面 137
inside **nèi** 内, **nèibù** 内部 159
insightful **shēnke** 深刻 190
inspect **jiǎnchá** 检查 108
inspiration **qǐfā** 启发 171
inspire **gǔwǔ** 鼓舞 80
instant noodles **fāngbiàn miàn** 方便面 62
institute (n.) **xuéyuàn** 学院 242
institute (v.) **shíxíng** 实行 195
instruct **fēnfù** 吩咐 65
instrument **yíqì** 仪器 249
integrate **jiéhé** 结合 115, **tǒngyī** 统一 215
integrated (adj.) **wánzhěng** 完整 219
intelligent **cōngmíng** 聪明 35
intense **jīliè** 激烈 101, **qiángliè** 强烈 174
intensity **qiángdù** 强度 174

intentional **gùyì** 故意 80
interest (n.) **àihào** 爱好 1, **lìyì** 利益 139,
　　xìngqù 兴趣 239
(be) interested (in) **gǎn xìngqù** 感兴趣 71
interesting **yǒu yìsi** 有意思 259
interior **nèibù** 内部 159
international **guójì** 国际 85
international students **liúxuéshēng** 留学生 144
international trade **guójì màoyì** 国际贸易 149
(the) Internet **hùliánwǎng** 互联网 93,
　　yīngtèwǎng 英特网 254
Internet café **wǎngbā** 网吧 220
interpret **fānyì** 翻译 60
interpretation **jiěshì** 解释 116
interpreter **fānyì** 翻译 60
interrupt **dǎrǎo** 打扰 37
interview **fǎngwèn** 访问 63
intimate **mìqiè** 密切 152
intonation **yǔdiào** 语调 260
(be) intoxicated **zuì** 醉 287
introduce **jièshào** 介绍 116
invade **qīnlüè** 侵略 175
invariably **zǒng** 总, **zǒngshì** 总是 286
invent **fāmíng** 发明 58
invention **fāmíng** 发明 58
invest **tóurù** 投入 216
investigate, investigation **diàochá** 调查 50
invitation **yāoqǐng** 邀请 246
invite **qǐng** 请 176, **yāoqǐng** 邀请 246
invite (trouble etc.) **rě** 惹 180
iron (n.) **tiě** 铁 213
iron and steel **gāngtiě** 钢铁 72
island **dǎo** 岛 43
isolate **gélí** 隔离 73
isolation ward **gélí bìngfáng** 隔离病房 73
issue a certificate **chū zhèngmíng** 出证明 274
it **tā** 它 207
item **xiàngmù** 项目 233
itinerary **lùxiàn** 路线 145

J

jacket **shàngyī** 上衣 188
Japan **Rìběn** 日本 183
Japanese (language) **Rìwén** 日文, **Rìyǔ** 日语
　　183
jellied meat **ròudòng** 肉冻 52
jelly (with fruit) **shuǐguǒ dòng** 水果冻 52
jeopardize **wēihài** 危害 221
job **fànwǎn** 饭碗 61, **gōngzuò** 工作 76,
　　fànwǎn 饭碗 220
job (colloquial) **huór** 活儿 99

jog **pǎobù** 跑步 165
join **cānjiā, lián** 参加, 连 22, 139
jointly **gòng** 共 78
joke (n.) **xiàohua** 笑话 235
joke (v.) **kāi wánxiào** 开玩笑 125
journalist **xīnwén jìzhě** 新闻记者 104
journey (n.) **lǚtú** 旅途 145
judge (v.) **pànduàn** 判断 164
judgment **pànduàn** 判断 164
jump **tiào** 跳 213
junior high school **chūzhōng** 初中 32
just (adv.) **cá** 才 20, **gāncuì** 干脆 70, **gāng** 刚
　　72, **zhǐshì** 只是 276
just (n.) **gāngcái** 刚才 72
just a little bit **shāowēi** 稍微 188
just right **zhènghǎo** 正好 273
justification **lǐyóu** 理由 138

K

keep (v.) **bǎochí** 保持, **bǎocún** 保存 7, **cún** 存
　　36
keep a shop **kāi shāngdiàn** 开商店 187
keep as pet **yǎng** 养 245
kettle **hú** 壶, **shuǐhú** 水壶 92
key (n.) **yàoshi** 钥匙 247
kick (v.) **tī** 踢 210
kill (v.) **shā** 杀 185
kilogram **gōngjīn** 公斤 76
kilometer **gōnglǐ** 公里 77
kind (category) **yàng** 样 245, **zhǒng** 种 279
kind (n.) **lèi** 类 136
kindhearted **hǎoxīn** 好心 88
kitchen **chúfáng** 厨房 32
knife (n.) **dāo** 刀, **dāozi** 刀子 43
knock (v.) **qiāo** 敲 174
know **liǎojiě** 了解 142, **rènde** 认得 182,
　　rènshi 认识 182, **zhīdào** 知道 274
know how to **huì** 会 97
know well **shú** 熟 201, **shúxi** 熟悉 201,
　　zhǎngwò 掌握 269
knowledge **xuéwèn** 学问 242, **zhīshi** 知识
　　275
knowledge economy **zhīshi jīngjì** 知识经济 275
(be) known as **chēng** 称 27, **jiàozuo** 叫做 112
kung fu **gōngfu** 功夫 77
(the) Kuomintang **guómíndǎng** 国民党 85

L

labor **láodòng** 劳动 134
Labor Day (May 1st) **láodòng jié** 劳动节 134

laboratory **huàyàn shì** 化验室 94, **shíyànshì** 实验室 195

laboratory technician **huàyàn yuán** 化验员 94, **shíyànyuán** 实验员 195

laboratory test **huàyàn** 化验 94

lack **chà** 差 24, **quē** 缺, **quēfá** 缺乏, **quēshǎo** 缺少 179

lad **xiǎohuǒzi** 小伙子 234

ladle (n.) **sháozi** 勺子 188

(be) laid off **xiàgǎng** 下岗 229

lake **hú** 湖 93

lakeside **húbiān** 湖边 93

lamb **yáng** 羊, **xiǎoyáng** 小羊 245

lamp **dēng** 灯 45

lamplight **dēngguāng** 灯光 83

land (n.) **tǔdì** 土地 217

landscape (n.) **fēngjǐng** 风景 66, **shānshuǐ** 山水 186

language **yǔyán** 语言 261

large **dà** 大 38

large-scale **dàxíng** 大型 39

lass **gūniang** 姑娘 79

last year **qùnián** 去年 178

late **wǎn** 晚 220

(be) late **chídào** 迟到 29

later **huítóu** 回头 97, **yǐhòu** 以后 250

later on **hòulái** 后来 92

laugh (v.), laugh at **xiào** 笑 235

launch (a campaign) **fādòng** 发动 58

launch **kāizhǎn** 开展 125, **zhǎnkāi** 展开 268

law **fǎlù** 法律 59, **guīlù** 规律 84

lawn **cǎodì** 草地 22

lawyer **lùshī** 律师 59

lax **sōng** 松 205

lay down **zhìdìng** 制定 277

lazy **lǎn** 懒 133

lead (a life) **shēnghuó** 生活 191

lead (v.) **lǐng** 领, **lǐngdǎo** 领导 143

lead to **chǎnshēng** 产生 24, **tōng** 通 214, **yǐnqǐ** 引起 254

leader **bānzhǎng** 班长 5, **lǐngdǎo** 领导 143, **lǐngxiù** 领袖 143

leaf (n.) **yèzi** 叶子 247

leak (v.) **lòu** 漏 144

lean (adj.) **shòu** 瘦 200

lean meat **shòuròu** 瘦肉 200

learn **tǐhuì** 体会 211, **xué** 学 241, **xuésheng** 学生 242

learn from ... **xiàng ... xuéxí** 向...学习 242

learning **xuéwèn** 学问 242

leather **pí** 皮 166

leave (v.) **lí** 离 136, **líkāi** 离开 136, **zǒu** 走 286

leave application **jiàtiáo** 假条 107

leave for **qù** 去 178

leave work **xiàbān** 下班 5

lecture (n.) **jiǎngzuò** 讲座 110, **kè** 课 129

lecture (v.) **jiàoxùn** 教训 113

left hand **zuǒshǒu** 左手 199

(be) left over **shèng** 剩 193

left side **zuǒ** 左, **zuǒbian** 左边 288

leftovers **shèng cài** 剩菜 193

leg (n.) **tuǐ** 腿 218

leisurely **qīngxián** 清闲 230

lend **jiè** 借 116

less than **yíxià** 以下 251

lesson **kè** 课 129

lesson (from experience) **jiàoxùn** 教训 113, **jīngyàn** 经验 119

let **ràng** 让 180, **suí** 随 206

letter **xìn** 信 237

letter of invitation **yāoqǐngxìn** 邀请信 246

letter received **láixìn** 来信 133

level (adj.) **píng** 平 168

level (floor) **céng** 层 23

level (n.) **chéngdù** 程度 29, **shuǐpíng** 水平 203

lewd **hào sè** 好色 89

liberate, liberation **jiěfàng** 解放 116

liberty **zìyóu** 自由 285

library **túshūguǎn** 图书馆 82, 216

library card **jièshū kǎ** 借书卡 124

license plate (on vehicle) **chē pái** 车牌 26

lie (n.) **jiǎhuà** 假话 106

lie (v.) **tǎng** 躺 209

life **rìzi** 日子 184, **shēnghuó** 生活 191, **shēngmìng** 生命 192

lifestyle **shénghuó fāngshì** 生活方式 62

lifetime **yìshēng** 一生 252

lift (v.) **jǔ** 举 122, **tái** 抬 207

light (n.) **diàndēng** 电灯 45, **guāng** 光 83, **guāngxiàn** 光线 83

light (of weight) **qīng** 轻 176

light music **qīng yīnyuè** 轻音乐 176

light refreshments **diǎnxīn** 点心 48

light up **zhào** 照 270

lighten **jiǎnqīng** 减轻 108

lighting (n.) **dēng** 灯 45

lightning **shǎndiàn** 闪电 186

like (v.) **ài** 爱, **àihào** 爱好 1, **xǐhuan** 喜欢 227

(be) like **fǎngfú** 仿佛 63, **xiàng** 像 233

like that **nàme** 那么 157

like this **zhème** 这么, **zhèyàng** 这样 271
likely **róngyì** 容易 184
likeness of (a human being) **xiàng** 像 233
limit (n.) **dù** 度 53
limit (v.) **xiànzhì** 限制 231
limited (adj.) **yídìng** 一定 248
limits (n.) **fànwéi** 范围 61
line (measurement) **háng** 行 87
lion **shīzi** 狮子 194
liquid medicine **yàoshuǐ** 药水 246
listen **tīng** 听 213
literary work **zhùzuò** 著作 282, **zuòpǐn** 作品 288
literature **wénxué** 文学 224
little **shǎo** 少 189, **xiǎo** 小 234
　(a) little **diǎn** 点 48, **xiē** 些 235, **yǒu(yì) diǎnr** 有(一)点儿 258
little girl **xiǎo gūniang** 小姑娘 79
live (life) **guò** 过, **guò rìzi** 过日子 85, **shēnghuó** 生活 191
live (v.) **zhù** 住 281
livelihood **fànwǎn** 饭碗 220
lively **huópo** 活泼 99, **shēngdòng** 生动 191
lively (scene, occasion) **rènao** 热闹 180
liver (n.) **gān** 肝 70
living allowance **shēnghuó fèi** 生活费 191
living conditions **shēnghuó tiáojiàn** 生活条件 212
living expenses **shēnghuó fèiyòng** 生活费用 64
living standard **shēnghuó shuǐpíng** 生活水平 191, 203
living things **shēngwù** 生物 192
local (n.) **dāngdì rén** 当地人 42
local time **dāngdì shíjiān** 当地时间 42
location **chù** 处 33, **dìfang** 地方 46, **wèizhi** 位置 223
lofty **chónggāo** 崇高 30
logical **hélǐ** 合理 90
long (adj.) **cháng** 长 25
long distance **chángtú** 长途 25
long distance running **chángpǎo** 长跑 25
long for **pànwàng** 盼望 164
long jump **tiào yuǎn** 跳远 213
long-distance bus/coach **chángtú qìchē** 长途汽车 25
long-standing **lǎo** 老 134, **yōujiǔ** 悠久 257
longshoreman **mǎtóu gōngrén** 码头工人 147
look (v.) **kàn** 看 126
look after **guānzhào** 关照 81, **zhàogù** 照顾 270
look at **wàng** 望 221
look for **xúnzhǎo** 寻找 242, **zhǎo** 找 269

look forward to **pànwàng** 盼望 164
look on **pángguān** 旁观 164
loosen **sōng** 松 205
lorry **kǎchē** 卡车 124
lose **diū** 丢, **diūshī** 丢失 51, **shībài** 失败 193, **sǔnshī** 损失 206
lose (game/bet) **shū** 输 201
lose (something valuable) **shīqù** 失去 193
lose face **diūliǎn** 丢脸 51, **diū miànzi** 丢面子 152
lose one's job **shīyè** 失业 193
lose one's temper **fāhuǒ** 发火 58, **fā píqi** 发脾气 167
loss **shībài** 失败 193, **sǔnshī** 损失 206
lots of **dàpī** 大批 39
loud (color) **huār** 花儿 94
loud (sound) **xiǎng** 响 232
loudly **dàshēng** 大声 39
lovable **kě'ài** 可爱 128
love (n.) **gǎnqíng** 感情 71
love (romantic) **àiqíng** 爱情 2, **liàn'ài** 恋爱 141
love (v.) **ài** 爱 1
love ardently **rè'ài** 热爱 180
love dearly **téng** 疼 210
low **dī** 低 46
lower (v.) **dī** 低 46, **jiàng** 降, **jiàngdī** 降低 110
lozenge (for cough) **késou táng** 咳嗽糖 127
luggage **xíngli** 行李 238
lunch (n.) **wǔfàn** 午饭 225
lung(s) **fèi** 肺 64

M

machine **jīqì** 机器, **jīxiè** 机械 100
machine tool **jīchuáng** 机床 100
machinery **jīxiè** 机械 100
magazine **zázhì** 杂志 264
magnetic tape **cídài** 磁带 34
magnificent **xióngwěi** 雄伟 240
magnifying glass **fàngdàjìng** 放大镜 63
mahjong **májiàng** 麻将 146
mail (v.) **jì** 寄 105
mailbag **yóubāo** 邮包 6
main **zhǔyào** 主要 281
main point **zhòngdiǎn** 重点 279
main room **táng** 堂 209
main street **dàjiē** 大街 39
mainland **dàlù** 大陆 39
maintain **bǎochí** 保持 7
maize **yùmǐ** 玉米 261

major (adj.) **zhòngdà** 重大 279, **zhǔyào** 主要 281

majority **dàduōshù** 大多数 38, **duōshù** 多数 57

make (instant) coffee **chōng kāfēi** 冲咖啡 124

make (v.) **ràng** 让 180, **shǐ** 使 196, **zào** 造 266

make (v.) **zhìzào** 制造 277, **zuò** 作 288, **zuò** 做 289

make a speech **fāyán** 发言 59

make a decision **zuò juédìng** 做决定 123, **ná zhǔyi** 拿主意 156

make a fortune **fācái** 发财 58

make a mistake **fàn cuòwù** 犯错误 36, 61

make a telephone call **dǎ diànhuà** 打电话 37

make a turn **guǎi** 拐 80

make arrangement **ānpái** 安排 2

make clear **biǎomíng** 表明 14

make friends with … **gēn/hé … jiāo péngyou** 跟／和…交朋友 165

make known **bàogào** 报告 8, **fābiǎo** 发表 58, **fǎnyìng** 反映 61

make money/profit **zhuàn** 赚 283

make notes (while reading) **zuò bǐjì** 做笔记 12

make public **gōngkāi** 公开 76

make reservations **dìng zuò** 订座 51

make sentences **zàojù** 造句 267

make trouble **nào** 闹 159

make up **dǎbàn** 打扮 37, **gòuchéng** 构成 78

make up one's mind **juédìng** 决定 123

make use of **lìyòng** 利用 139

male (animal) **gōng** 公 76, **xióng** 雄 240

male (human) **nán** 男 158

mall **shāngchǎng** 商场 186

Mammon **cáishényé** 财神爷 191

man (n.) **nánrén** 男人, **nánzǐhàn** 男子汉 158

man-made **rénzào** 人造 182

manage **bàn** 办 5, **guǎnlǐ** 管理 82, **nòng** 弄 162

manager **jīnglǐ** 经理 119

Mandarin (language) **Pǔtōnghuà** 普通话 169

mankind **rénlèi** 人类 181

manner **fāngshì** 方式 62, **yàngzi** 样子 245

manner of speaking **yǔqì** 语气 261

manual (n.) **shǒugōng** 手工 199, **shuōmíng** 说明 204

manufacture **shēngchǎn** 生产 191

manufacture **zhìzào** 制造 277

manufacturing industry **gōngyè** 工业 76, **zhìzàoyè** 制造业 277

many **bùshǎo** 不少 19, **dàliàng** 大量 39, **duō** 多 56

many **hǎo** 好, **hǎo duō** 好多 88, 好些 89, **xǔduō** 许多 241

map (n.) **dìtú** 地图 47

mark (n.) **fēn** 分 64

market (n.) **shìchǎng** 市场 25, 196

market economy **shìchǎng jīngjì** 市场经济 119, 196

marketing manager **shìchǎng jīnglǐ** 市场经理 119

marketplace **shìchǎng** 市场 196

marriage **hūnyīn** 婚姻 98

marriage certificate/license **jiéhūn zhèngmíng** 结婚证明 274

marriage partner **duìxiàng** 对象 56

marry **jià** 嫁 106, **jiéhūn** 结婚 115

martial arts **gōngfu** 功夫 77, **wǔshù** 武术 225

(the) masses (people) **qúnzhòng** 群众 179

master worker **shīfu** 师傅 193

matchbox **huǒchái hé** 火柴盒 99

matchmaker **jièsháo rén** 介绍人 116

matchstick **huǒchái** 火柴 99

material **cáiliào** 材料 21, **zīliào** 资料 284

material incentive **wùzhì gǔlì** 物质鼓励 79

materialize **shíxiàn** 实现 195

maternal **mǔ** 母 155

maternal granny **ā pó** 阿婆 1

maternal instinct **mǔxìng** 母性 155

mathematics **shùxué** 数学 202

matter (n.) **shì** 事, **shìqing** 事情 197

mature **chéngshú** 成熟 28

may **kěnéng** 可能, **kěyǐ** 可以 128

maybe **yěxǔ** 也许 247

mayor of a county **xiànzhǎng** 县长 230

me **wǒ** 我 225

meager **bó** 薄 16

(a) meal **cān** 餐 22, **fàn** 饭 61

meals **huǒshí** 伙食 99

mean (v.) **zhǐ** 指 276

meaning (n.) **yìsi** 意思 253

meaningful **yǒu yìsi** 有意思 259

meaningless **méiyǒu yìsi** 没有意思 259

means (n.) **shǒuduàn** 手段 199

means (of production) **zīliào** 资料 284

measure (n.) **cuòshī** 措施 36, **shǒuduàn** 手段 199

measure (v.) **liáng** 量 141

measurements **chǐcùn** 尺寸 29

meat **ròu** 肉 184

medical certificate **bìngjiàtiáo** 病假条 107

medical doctor **yīshēng** 医生 248

medical school **yīxuéyuàn** 医学院 248

medical science **yīxué** 医学 248

medicine **yào** 药 246, **yīxué** 医学 248

medium (adj.) **zhōng** 中 278

meet (someone) unexpectedly **yùjiàn** 遇见 261

meet (v.) **jiànmiàn** 见面 108, **yíngjiē** 迎接 255

meet (v., formal) **huìjiàn** 会见 98

meet the needs of **mǎnzú** 满足 148

meet unexpectedly **pèngdao** 碰到 166

meeting (n.) **huì** 会 97, **huìyì** 会议 98

melodious **hǎotīng** 好听 89

melon **guā** 瓜 80

melt **huà** 化 94

memorize **jìyì** 记忆 104

memorize new words **jì shēngcí** 记生词 191

memory **huíyì** 回忆 97, **jìyì** 记忆 104

mend **bǔ** 补 17

mental disorder **shénjīngbìng** 神经病 191

mental illness **jīngshénbìng** 精神病 120

mental state **shénjīng** 神经 191

mental work **nǎolì láodòng** 脑力劳动 134

mention (v.) **tí** 提 210

merely **jǐn** 仅, **jǐnjǐn** 仅仅 117

merit **yōudiǎn** 优点 256

message (informal, written) **biàntiáo** 便条 13

metal **jīnshǔ** 金属 117

meteorological observatory **qìxiàngtái** 气象台 172

meteorological phenomena **qìxiàng** 气象 172

meteorology **qìxiàngxué** 气象学 172

meter (measurement) **gōngchǐ** 公尺 30, 76

method **bànfǎ** 办法 5, **fāngfǎ** 方法 62, **zuòfǎ** 做法 289

meticulous **xìxīn** 细心 228

Mid-Autumn Festival (Moon Festival) **zhōngqiūjié** 中秋节 114

middle **zhōng** 中, **zhōngjiān** 中间 278

middle school **zhōngxué** 中学 278

midnight **bànyè** 半夜 6, 247

might (n.) **lì** 力 138

military affairs **jūnshì** 军事 124

military regiment **tuán** 团 217

milk (from cow) **niú nǎi** 牛奶 161

(the) mind **nǎozi** 脑子 159, **shénjīng** 神经 191

mine (n., coal, gold etc.) **kuàng** 矿 132

miner **kuànggōng** 矿工 132

minister (government) **bùzhǎng** 部长 20

minority ethnic group/nationality **shǎoshù mínzú** 少数民族 153, 189

minuend **bèi jiǎnshù** 被减数 108

minute (n.) **fēn** 分 64, **fēnzhōng** 分钟 65

minutes (of meeting) **huìyì jìlù** 会议记录 104

mirror (n.) **jìngzi** 镜子 121

mirror (v.) **fǎnyìng** 反映 61

miscellaneous **zá** 杂 264

misconstrue **wùhuì** 误会 226

miserable (life) **kǔ** 苦 131

miserly **xiǎoqì** 小气 234

Miss **xiǎojiě** 小姐 234

miss (v.) **xiǎngniàn** 想念 233

mission **rènwù** 任务 182

mist (n.) **wù** 雾 226

mistake (n.) **cuòwù** 错误 36

misunderstand, misunderstanding **wùhuì** 误会 226

mix up (v.) **hùn** 混 98

mobile telephone **shǒujī** 手机 199

modern times **xiàndài** 现代 230

modernize, modernization **xiàndàihuà** 现代化 230

modest **kèqi** 客气 129

mom, mommy **māma** 妈妈 146

(in a) moment **yíhuìr** 一会儿 249

momentarily **yìshí** 一时 252

Monday **Xīngqīyī** 星期一 238

money **jīn** 金 117, **qián** 钱 173

monkey (n.) **hóuzi** 猴子 91

month **yuè** 月 263

mood **qíngxù** 情绪 176, **xīnqíng** 心情 236

(the) moon **yuè** 月, **yuèliang** 月亮 263

moonlight **yuèguāng** 月光 83

moral **dàodé** 道德 44

moral encouragement **jīngshén gǔlì** 精神鼓励 80

more **duō** 多 56

more and more **yuèláiyuè** 越来越 263

more or less **dàgài** 大概 38

more than **yǐshàng** 以上 251

moreover **bìngqiě** 并且 15, **érqiě** 而且 57, **jiāyǐ** 加以 105, **yòu** 又 260

morning (6–9 a.m.) **zǎochén** 早晨, **zǎoshang** 早上 266

morning (after 9 a.m.) **shàngwǔ** 上午 188

mosquito **wénzi** 蚊子 224

most (superlative) **zuì** 最 287

most of **dà bùfen** 大部分 20

mostly **dàduō** 大多 38

motel **qìchē lǚguǎn** 汽车旅馆 145

mother (n.) **mǔqin** 母亲 155

mother tongue **mǔyǔ** 母语 155

Mother's Day **mǔqin jié** 母亲节 155

mother's sister **āyí** 阿姨 1

noodles (instant) **fāngbiàn miàn** 方便面 62

noon **zhōngwǔ** 中午 278

nor **yě** 也 247

normal **hǎohǎor** 好好儿 88, **zhèngcháng** 正常 273

normally **píngcháng** 平常 168

north **běi** 北 9

North Pole **běijí** 北极 9

north side **běibian** 北边, **běimiàn** 北面 9

North Star **běijíxīng** 北极星 9

northeast **dōngběi** 东北 51

northern **běi** 北 9

northern region **běibian** 北方 9

northwest **xīběi** 西北 226

nose (n.) **bízi** 鼻子 10

not **bù** 不 18

not allowed **bùxíng** 不行 19, **bùxǔ** 不许 20

not as...as **bùrú** 不如 19

not at all **háo bù** 毫不 88

not bad **búcuò** 不错 17

not enough time (to do something) **láibují** 来不及 133

not many **méiyǒu duōshǎo** 没有多少 56

not much **búdà** 不大 17, **méiyǒu duōshǎo** 没有多少 56

not only **búdàn** 不但 17, **bùjǐn** 不仅 19

not permitted **bùxǔ** 不许 19

not very **búdà** 不大 17

not yet **hái méiyǒu** 还没有 150

notable **xiǎnzhù** 显著 230

notebook **běnzi** 本子 10, **bǐjì běn** 笔记本 12

notes (class, reading) **bǐjì** 笔记 11

notice (n.) **tōngzhī** 通知 214

notify **guānzhào** 关照 81, **tōngzhī** 通知 214

notion **gàiniàn** 概念 70

nourishment **yíngyǎng** 营养 255

novel (n.) **xiǎoshuō** 小说 234, **chángpiān xiǎoshuō** 长篇小说 235

novelist **xiǎoshuōjiā** 小说家 235

now **dāngqián** 当前 42, **jīn** 今 116, **xiànzài** 现在 230

now that **jì** 既 104, **jìrán** 既然 105

nowadays **jìnlái** 近来 118

number (n.) **shù** 数, **shùzì** 数字 202

numeral (in writing) **shùzì** 数字 202

nurse (n.) **hùshi** 护士 93

nutrition **yíngyǎng** 营养 255

O

o'clock **diǎn** 点, **diǎnzhōng** 点钟 48

(be) obedient **tīnghuà** 听话 213

obey **fúcóng** 服从 66

object (v.) **fǎnduì** 反对 60

objection **yìjiàn** 意见 253

objective (n.) **mùbiāo** 目标 156

obligation **yìwù** 义务 252

oblique **xié** 斜 236

oblong **chángfāng** 长方 61

observe **guānchá** 观察 82

observe a festival **guò jié** 过节 85

observer (at conference) **guāncháyuán** 观察员 82

obtain **dé** 获 45, **huòdé** 获得 100, **qǔdé** 取得 178

obvious **míngbai** 明白 154, **míngxiǎn** 明显 154, **xiǎnrán** 显然 230

obviously **xiǎnrán** 显然 230

occasion **qíngjǐng** 情景 176

(the) Occident **xīfāng** 西方 226

occupation **zhíyè** 职业 275

occupy **zhàn** 占 268

ocean **hǎiyáng** 海洋 86

Oceania **Dàyángzhōu** 大洋洲 40

odd **guài** 怪 80, **qíguài** 奇怪 170

odd number **dānshù** 单数 41

of course **dāngrán** 当然 42

offend **fàn** 犯 61

(be) offended **shēngqì** 生气 192

office **bàngōngshì** 办公室 5

office building **bàngōng dàlóu** 办公大楼 5

office hours **bàngōng shíjiān** 办公时间 5

office manager **bàngōngshì zhǔrèn** 办公室主任 281

official (adj.) **guān** 官 82, **zhèngshì** 正式 273

official (n.) **guānyuán** 官员 82

official (n., communist) **gànbù** 干部 71

often **cháng** 常, **chángcháng** 常常 25, **jīngcháng** 经常 119

oh **ā** 啊 1, **ō** 噢 163, **yā** 呀 243

oil (n.) **shíyóu** 石油 194, **yóu** 油 257

oil painting **yóuhuà** 油画 94

oilfield **yóukuàng** 油矿 132, **yóutián** 油田 257

OK **xíng** 行 238

old **lǎo** 老 134

old (things) **jiù** 旧 121

old age **wǎnnián** 晚年 220

old person **lǎorén** 老人 134

on **guānyú** 关于 81, **shàng** 上 187, **zài** 在 265

(be) on holiday **fàngjià** 放假 63

on purpose **gùyì** 故意 80

on the one hand ... on the other hand ...
  yìfāngmiàn ... yìfāngmiàn ... 一方面 ... 一
  方面 ... 251
on the whole **jībĕn shang** 基本上 101
on time **ànshí** 按时 3, **àn qī** 按期 170,
  zhŭnshí 准时 284
on top of **shàng** 上 187
once again **chóng** 重, **chóngxīn** 重新 30
once upon a time **cóngqián** 从前 36
one **yī** 一 247
one after another **lùxù** 陆续 144, **xiānhòu** 先后
  229
one another **hùxiāng** 互相 93
one of **zhī yī** 之一 274
one-sided **piànmiàn** 片面 167
only **cái** 才 20, **guāng** 光 83, **jǐn** 仅, **jǐnjǐn** 仅
  仅 117
only **zhǐ** 只, **zhǐshì** 只是, **zhǐyŏu** 只有 276
open (adj.) **gōngkāi** 公开 76
open (the eyes) **zhēng** 睁 272
open (v.) **kāi** 开 124, **kāifàng** 开放 125
open a shop **kāi shāngdiàn** 开商店 187
open a window **dăkāi chuānghu** 打开窗户 33
operate (surgically) **zuò shŏushù** 做手术 199
operating room **shŏushùjiān** 手术间 199
operation (surgical) **shŏushù** 手术 199
ophthalmologist **yănkē yīshēng** 眼科医生 244
opinion **xiăngfă** 想法 232, **yìjiàn** 意见 252
opportunity **jīhuì** 机会 100
oppose **fănduì** 反对 60
opposite **duìmiàn** 对面 55, **făn** 反 60,
  xiāngfăn 相反 231
(the) Opposition **fănduì dăng** 反对党 60
oppress, oppression **yāpò** 压迫 243
optician's shop **yănjìngdiàn** 眼镜店 244
optimistic **lèguān** 乐观 136
or **bùrán** 不然 19, **fŏuzé** 否则 66, **háishì** 还
  是 86, **huò** 或, **huòzhě** 或者 99
order (command) **mìnglìng** 命令 154
order (dish in restaurant) **diăn cài** 点菜 22
order (sequence) **zhìxù** 秩序 277
ordinarily **yìbān** 一般 251
ordinary **píngcháng** 平常 168, **pŭtōng** 普通 169
ordinary folk **lăobăixìng** 老百姓 134
organize, organization **zŭzhī** 组织 287
(the) Orient **dōngfāng** 东方 51
original **bĕnlái** 本来 10, **yuánlái** 原来 262
originally **bĕnlái** 本来 10
other **biéde** 别的 15, **lìngwài** 另外 143, **qítā**
  其他 170
(the) other party **duìfāng** 对方 55

other people **biérén** 别人 15, **rénjia** 人家 181
other than **yǐwài** 以外 251
otherwise **bùrán** 不然 19, **fŏuzé** 否则 66
ought to **gāi** 该 68, **yīnggāi** 应该 254
ounce **liăng** 两 141
ourselves **wŏmen zìjǐ** 我们自己 285
(be) out of order **huài** 坏 95
outdated **luòhòu** 落后 146
output (of production) **chănliàng** 产量 24
outside **wài** 外, **wàibian** 外边 218
outside **wàimian** 外面 219, **yǐwài** 以外 251,
  zhī wài 之外 274
outstanding **xiănzhù** 显著 230, **yōuxiù** 优秀
  256
over **duō** 多 56, **yǐshàng** 以上 251
over there **nàli** 那里, **nàr** 那儿 157
overcast **yīn** 阴 254
overcoat **dàyī** 大衣 40
overcome **kèfú** 克服 129
overcome difficulty **kèfú kùnnan** 克服困难 132
overdue **guòqī** 过期 170
overheads **bàngōng fèiyòng** 办公费用 64
overjoyed **tòngkuai** 痛快 215, **xīngfèn** 兴奋
  238
overtake **chāoguò** 超过 26
owe **qiàn** 欠 173
owing to **yóuyú** 由于 257
owner **zhŭrén** 主人 281
owner (of store, business) **lăobăn** 老板 134
ox **niú** 牛, **huángniú** 黄牛 161

P

pact **tiáoyuē** 条约 212
paddy fields **tián** 田 212
paddy rice **mǐ** 米 151, **shuǐdào** 水稻 203
page (n.) **yè** 页 247
pagoda **tă** 塔 207
pail **tŏng** 桶 215
pained **tòngxīn** 痛心 236
painful **tòngkŭ** 痛苦 215
painstaking **kèkŭ** 刻苦 129
paint (v., art) **huà** 画 94
paintbrush (for art) **huàbǐ** 画笔 11
painter (art) **huàjiā** 画家 95, 106
pair (n.) **duì** 对 55, **shuāng** 双 202
pajamas **shuìyī** 睡衣 203
pan (n.) **guō** 锅 85
panda **xióngmāo** 熊猫 240
panic **huāng** 慌 96
papa **bàba** 爸爸 3
paper **zhǐ** 纸 276

parcel **bāo** 包 6
pardon (v.) **yuánliàng** 原谅 262
park (a vehicle) **tíng** 停, **tíng chē** 停车 213
park (n.) **gōngyuán** 公园 77
parking lot **tíngchēchǎng** 停车场 26, 213
part (n.) **bùfen** 部分 20
part of **dìfang** 地方 47
part with **fēnbié** 分别 64, **gàobié** 告别 73
participate **cānjiā** 参加 22
partition (v.) **gé** 隔 73
party (political) **dǎng** 党 43
party member **dǎngyuán** 党员 43
pass (something) on **chuán** 传 33
pass (v.) **guò** 过 85, **jígé** 及格 102, **jīngguò** 经过 119
pass along (word) **zhuǎngào** 转告 283
pass away **qùshì** 去世 178
pass on **zhuǎn** 转 283
pass through **tōngguò** 通过 214, **tòu** 透 216
passenger (coach, train, plane etc.) **lǚkè** 旅客 145
passport **hùzhào** 护照 93
past **cóngqián** 从前 35
paste (v.) **tiē** 贴 213
pasture **cǎoyuán** 草原 23
pat **pāi** 拍 163
patch (v.) **bǔ** 补 17
paternal grandfather **yéye** 爷爷 247
paternal grandmother **nǎinai** 奶奶 157
path **dàolù** 道路 44
patience **nàixīn** 耐心 158
patient (adj.) **nàifán** 耐烦, **nàixīn** 耐心 157
patient (n.) **bìngrén** 病人 16
pay (v.) **fù** 付 67, **jiāo** 交 111
pay attention to **zhùyì** 注意 282
pay fees **jiāo fèi** 交费 64
pay for (damage, loss, etc.) **péi** 赔 165
payphone **gōngyòng diànhuà** 公用电话 77
peaceful **ān** 安, **ānjìng** 安静 2, **jìng** 静 120
peak (mountain) **shāndǐng** 山顶 50
peak (n.) **dǐng** 顶 50
pear **lí** 梨 137
peasant **nóngmín** 农民 162
pedestrian street **bùxíng jiē** 行街 114
Peking opera **jīngjù** 京剧 119
pen **bǐ** 笔 11
pencil **bǐ** 笔 11, **qiānbǐ** 铅笔 173
pencil drawing **qiānbǐ huà** 铅笔画 94
pencil sharpener **qiānbǐ dāo** 铅笔刀 43
penetrate **tòu** 透 216
penetrating (adj.) **jiānruì** 尖锐 107

penknife **shuǐguǒ dāo** 水果刀 43, 203
pension **tuìxiū jīn** 退休 117
people **rénmen** 人们 181
(the) people (of a state) **rénmin** 人民 181
Pepsi[-Cola] **bǎishìkělè** 百事可乐 128
perceive **jiàn** 见 108
... percent **bǎi fēnzhī** ... 百分之 ... 64
percentage **bǐlì** 比例 11
perfect (adj.) **biāozhǔn** 标准 14
perform **biǎoxiàn** 表现, **biǎoyǎn** 表演 14, **yǎn** 演 244, **yǎnchū** 演出 245
perform an operation **zuò shǒushù** 做手术 199
performance **biǎoyǎn** 表演 14
performance (theatrical) **yǎnchū** 演出 245
performing arts **wényì** 文艺 224
perhaps **kǒngpà** 恐怕 130, **yěxǔ** 也许 247
period **jiēduàn** 阶段 113
period of time **shíjiān** 时间 194, **shíqī** 时期 195
permit (v.) **yǔnxǔ** 允许 264
persist **jiānchí** 坚持 107
person **rén** 人 181
person in charge **fùzérén** 负责人 68
personage **rénwù** 人物 181
personal **sīrén** 私人 204
personal experience **jīnglì** 经历 119
personal hygiene **gèrén wèishēng** 个人卫生 222
personal understanding **tǐhuì** 体会 211
personnel **rényuán** 人员 182
perspiration **hàn** 汗 87
perspire **chūhàn** 出汗 87
pessimistic **bēiguān** 悲观 9
pest (insect) **hàichóng** 害虫 87
petroleum **qìyóu** 汽油 172, **shíyóu** 石油 194
pharmacy **yàofáng** 药房 246
phenomenon **xiànxiàng** 现象 230
philosopher **zhéxuéjiā** 哲学家 271
philosophy **zhéxué** 哲学 271
photocopier **yǐngyìnjī** 影印机 254
photocopy **yǐngyìn** 影印 254
photograph (n.) **zhàopiàn** 照片 270
photograph (v.) **pāizhào** 拍照 163
photographer **shèyǐngshī** 摄影师 190
photographic studio **zhàoxiàngguǎn** 照相馆 270
photography **shèyǐng** 摄影 190
physical education **tǐyù** 体育 211
physical strength **lìqi** 力气 138
physics **wùlǐ** 物理 226
pick (v.) **cǎi** 采 21, **zhāi** 摘 268
pictorial **huàbào** 画报 94
picture (n.) **huàr** 画儿 94, **tú** 图 216, **zhàopiàn** 照片 270

pig **zhū** 猪 280

pile up **duī** 堆 54

pilfer **tōu** 偷 216

pill **yàopiàn** 药片 246

pilot (a plane) **kāi** 开 63, **kāi fēijī** 开飞机 124

pinch (v.) **jiā** 夹 105

pistol **qiāng** 枪 173

pitiful **kělián** 可怜 128

place (n.) **chù** 处 33, **dìfang** 地方 46, **wèizhi** 位置 223

place (v.) **bǎi, gē** 摆, 搁 4, 73

plain (n.) **píngyuán** 平原 168

plain boiled water **báikāishuǐ** 白开水 4

plan (n.) **fāng'àn** 方案 61, **jìhuà** 计划 103, **shèjì** 设计 189

plan (v.) **ānpái** 安排 2, **dǎsuàn** 打算 37, **jìhuà** 计划 103

planet **xíngxīng** 行星 238

plant (n.) **zhíwù** 植物 275

plant (v.) **zhòng** 种 279

plastic **sùliào** 塑料 205

plate (n.) **pánzi** 盘子 164

plateau **gāoyuán** 高原 72

play (n.) **xì** 戏 228

play (v.) **wánr** 玩儿 219

play basketball **dǎ lánqiú** 打篮球 133

play cards **dǎpái** 打牌 164

playground **cāochǎng** 操场 22, 25

playing cards (n.) **pái** 牌 164

pleasant **yúkuài** 愉快 260

pleasantly warm **nuǎnhuo** 暖和 163

pleased **yúkuài** 愉快 260

pledge **bǎozhèng** 保证 7

pluck (v.) **cǎi** 采 21, **zhāi** 摘 268

plump **pàng** 胖 165

plus **jiā** 加 105

pocket (n.) **kǒudài** 口袋 41, 131

pocket money **língqián** 零钱 142

poem **shī** 诗, **shīgē** 诗歌 194

poet **shīrén** 诗人 194

poetry **shī** 诗, **shīgē** 诗歌 194

point (n.) **diǎn** 点 47, **fēn** 分 64

point at/to **zhǐ** 指 276

point out **zhǐchū** 指出 276

pointed (adj.) **jiān** 尖 107

Polaris **běijíxīng** 北极星 9

pole **gān** 杆 70

police (n.) **jǐngchá** 警察 120

policeman **gōng'ān rényuán** 公安人员 76, **jǐngchá** 警察 120

policy **fāngzhēn** 方针 62

polite **kèqi** 客气 129, **lǐmào** 礼貌 137

political instructor **zhǐdǎoyuán** 指导员 277

politics **zhèngzhì** 政治 274

pollute, pollution **wūrǎn** 污染 225

poor **chà** 差 24, **qióng** 穷 177

pop (soft drink) **qìshuǐ** 汽水 172

popularize **pǔjí** 普及 169, **tuīguǎng** 推广 217

population (human) **rénkǒu** 人口 181

pork **zhūròu** 猪肉 184

pornography **sèqíng** 色情 185

port **gǎng** 港, **gǎngkǒu** 港口 72

portion **bùfen** 部分 20

portrait **xiàng** 像 233

position **dìwèi** 地位 47, **lìchǎng** 立场 138

positive **jījí** 积极 101, **kěndìng** 肯定 130

positive result **chéngguǒ** 成果 28

possess **jùbèi** 具备 122, **jùyǒu** 具有 123, **yǒu** 有 258

possibility **kěnéng** 可能 128

possible, possibly **kěnéng** 可能 128

post (a letter) **jì** 寄 105, **jìxìn** 寄信 237

post office **yóujú** 邮局 257

postgraduate student **yánjiūshēng** 研究生 244

pot (n.) **guō** 锅 85, **pén** 盆 165

potato **tǔdòu** 土豆 217

pour (water) **dào** 倒 44

poverty-stricken **qióng** 穷 177

power (electricity) **diàn** 电 48

powerful **qiángdà** 强大 174, **yǒulì** 有力 259

practical **shíjì** 实际, **shíyòng** 实用 195

practice (n.) **shíjiàn** 实践 195, **zuòfǎ** 做法 289

practice (v.) **liàn** 练 140

praise **chēngzàn** 称赞 27

praise (v.) **biǎoyáng** 表扬 14

precious **bǎoguì** 宝贵 7

prediction **yùbao** 预报 261

premier **zǒnglǐ** 总理 286

preparation **zhǔnbèi** 准备 284

preparatory school **yùbèi xuéxiào** 预备学校 261

prepare **yùbèi** 预备 261, **zhǔnbèi** 准备 283

prepare lessons **yùxí** 预习 261

prerequisite **tiáojiàn** 条件 212

present (n.) **lǐwù** 礼物 137

(at) present **yǎnqián** 眼前 244

president (of country) **zǒngtǒng** 总统 286

president (of university) **xiàozhǎng** 校长 235

press (n.) **yìnshuājī** 印刷机 254

press (v.) **yā** 压 243

press conference **jìzhě zhāodàihuì** 记者招待会 104

pressing (adj.) **pòqiè** 迫切 169

pressure **yālì** 压力 243

pretend (v.) **zhuāng** 装 283

pretty **hǎokàn** 好看 88, **piàoliang** 漂亮 167

prevent **fáng** 防, **fángzhǐ** 防止 62

previous **shàng** 上 187

price (n.) **jiàgé** 价格, **jiàqián** 价钱 106, **wùjià** 物价 226

prick (v.) **cì** 刺 35

primary school **xiǎoxué** 小学 235

prime minister **zǒnglǐ** 总理 286

principal (money) **běn** 本 10

principal (n.) **xiàozhǎng** 校长 235

principle **dàolǐ** 道理 44, **yuánzé** 原则 262

print (v.) **yìn** 印, **yìnshuā** 印刷 254

printed matter **yìnshuāpǐn** 印刷品 254

private **sīrén** 私人 204

private enterprise **sīyǒu qǐyè** 私有企业 171

private secretary **sīrén mìshu** 私人秘书 152

prize (n.) **jiǎng** 奖 110

prize money **jiǎngjīn** 奖金 110

probably **dàgài** 大概 38, **huì** 会 97

procedure **shǒuxù** 手续 199

process (n.) **guòchéng** 过程 85

process (v.) **jiāgōng** 加工 105

procrastinate **tuō** 拖 218

produce (v.) **chǎnshēng** 产生 24, **fāchū** 发出 58, **shēngchǎn** 生产 191

product **chǎnpǐn** 产品 24

profession **zhíyè** 职业 275

professional work **yèwù** 业务 247

professor (at university) **jiàoshòu** 教授 112

proficiency (in language) **shuǐpíng** 水平 203

profound **shēn** 深, **shēnhòu** 深厚, **shēnke** 深刻 190

program (n.) **jiémù** 节目 114

progress (n.) **jìnbù** 进步 118

progressive **jìnbù** 进步 118

progressively **zhúbù** 逐步 280

prohibit **jìnzhǐ** 禁止 119

prolong **yáncháng** 延长 244

prominent **tūchū** 突出 216

promise **dāying** 答应 37

promote **cùjìn** 促进 36, **tuīdòng** 推动 217

promptly **jíshí** 及时 102

pronunciation **fāyīn** 发音 59

propaganda **xuānchuán** 宣传 241

propagate **chuánbō** 传播 33

property **cáichǎn** 财产 21

propose **jiànyì** 建议 109, **tí jiànyì** 提建议 210

proposition **zhǔzhāng** 主张 281

proprietor **zhǔrén** 主人 281

prospects **qiántú** 前途 173

protect **bǎo, bǎohù** 保，保护 7

proud **jiāo'ào** 骄傲 111

prove **shuōmíng** 说明 204, **zhèngmíng** 证明 273

provide **gěi** 给 74, **gōngjǐ** 供给 77, **tígòng** 提供 210

provide for **yǎng** 养 245

provided that **zhǐyào** 只要 276

province **shěng** 省 193

provincial capital **shěnghuì** 省会 193

provision shop **shípǐn shāngdiàn** 食品商店 196

provisional **línshí** 临时 142

pub **jiǔbā** 酒吧 121

public **gōnggòng** 公共, **gōngkāi** 公开 76

(the) public **rénmen** 人们 181

public road **gōnglù** 公路 77

public sanitation **gōnggòng wèishēng** 公共卫生 222

public security **gōng'ān** 公安 76

public telephone **gōngyòng diànhuà** 公用电话 77

public toilet **gōnggòng cèsuǒ** 公共厕所 23

publicize **fābiǎo** 发表 58, **xuānchuán** 宣传 241

publish **chūbǎn** 出版 31

publish (in newspaper, journal, etc.) **dēng** 登 45

puff (v.) **chuī** 吹 34

pull (v.) **lā** 拉 132

pullover (woolen) **máoyī** 毛衣 149

punctual **zhǔnshí** 准时 284

punctuation mark **biāodiǎn** 标点 13

pupil **xuésheng** 学生 242

puppy **xiǎo gǒu** 小狗 78

purple **zǐ** 紫 284

purpose **mùdì** 目的 156

purse **qiánbāo** 钱包 6, 173

push (v.) **tuī** 推 217

push down **yā** 压 243

put **bǎi** 摆 4, **fàng** 放 63, **gē** 搁 73

put in order **zhěnglǐ** 整理 273

put into **tóurù** 投入 216

put into practice **shíjiàn** 实践, **shíxíng** 实行 195

put on **chuān** 穿 33, **dài** 戴 41

put on a hat/cap **dài màozi** 戴帽子 149

put out (fire) **miè** 灭 153

put up with **rěn** 忍 182

put upside down **dào** 倒 44

Q

quality **zhìliàng** 质量 277

quantity **shùliàng** 数量 202
quarantine (v.) **gélí** 隔离 73
quarrel (v.) **chǎo** 吵 26
quarter of an hour **kè** 刻 129
question (n.) **tímù** 题目 210, **wèntí** 问题 224
queue **háng** 行 87
quick (adj.) **kuài** 快 131
quiet (adj.) **ānjìng** 安静 2, **jìng** 静 120,
　　píngjìng 平静 168
quietly **qiāoqiāo** 悄悄 174
quilt **bèizi** 被子 9
quite **bǐjiào** 比较 11, **xiāngdāng** 相当 231

R

rabbit **tùzi** 兔子 217
radiance **guānghuī** 光辉 83
radio **shōuyīnjī** 收音机 199
radio station **diàntái** 电台 49, **guǎngbō diàntái**
　　广播电台 83
radish **luóbo** 萝卜, **hóng luóbo** 红萝卜 146
railway **tiělù** 铁路 213
railway station **chēzhàn** 车站 26, **huǒchē zhàn**
　　火车站 268
rain (n.) **yǔ** 雨 260
rain (v.) **xià yǔ** 下雨 260
raincoat **yǔyī** 雨衣 260
raise **yǎng** 养 245
raise (prices) **táigāo** 抬高 207
raise (v.) **jǔ** 举 122, **tái** 抬 207, **tígāo** 提高
　　210
rally (n.) **dàhuì** 大会 38, 97
random **luàn** 乱 145
range (n.) **fànwéi** 范围 61
rank (n.) **děng** 等 46, **jí** 级 102
rapid **xùnsù** 迅速 242
rather **xiāngdāng** 相当 231
ratify **pīzhǔn** 批准 166
raw **shēng** 生 191
raw material **yuánliào** 原料 262
ray (of light) **guāngróng** 光荣 83
reach (v.) **dádào** 达到 37, **dàodá** 到达 43
reaction **fǎnyìng** 反应 60
reactionary **fǎndòng** 反动 60
read **dú** 读, **dúshū** 读书 53, **kàn** 看 126,
　　niàn 念 161, **kànshū** 看书 200
read aloud **niàn** 念 161
read aloud clearly **lǎngdú** 朗读 134
read seriously **yuèdú** 阅读 263
reader **dúzhě** 读者 53
reading room **yuèlǎnshì** 阅览室 263

real **zhēn** 真 271, **zhēnshí** 真实 271,
　　zhēnzhèng 真正 272
realistic, reality **shíjì** 实际 195, **xiànshí** 现实
　　230
realize **shíxiàn** 实现 195, **tǐhuì** 体会 211
really **díquè** 的确 46, **shízài** 实在 195, **tài** 太
　　207, **zhēn** 真 271
rear (n.) **hòu** 后, **hòubian** 后边, **hòumiàn** 后面
　　92
reason (n.) **dàolǐ** 道理 44, **lǐyóu** 理由 138,
　　yuányīn 原因 262
reasonable **yǒu dàolǐ** 有道理 44, **hélǐ** 合理 90
reasonable (person) **jiǎng dàolǐ** 讲道理 44
rebel (v.) **fǎnkàng** 反抗 60
rebuild **gǎizào** 改造 69
rebuilding (n.) **gǎizào** 改造 70
recall (v.) **huíyì** 回忆 97, **jì** 记 103, **shōuhuí**
　　收回 198
receive **jiē** 接 113, **shōu** 收, **shōudao** 收到
　　198, **shōurù** 收入 199, **shòu** 受 200
receive (guest/visitor) **huìkè** 会客 98, **jiēdài** 接
　　待 113, **zhāodài** 招待 269
recently **jìnlái** 近来 118, **zuìjìn** 最近 287
reception **zhāodàihuì** 招待会 269
reckon **gūjì** 估计 79
recognize **chéngrèn** 承认 28, **rèn** 认 182
recollect, recollection **huíyì** 回忆 97
recommend **tíchàng** 提倡 210, **tuījiàn** 推荐 217
record (n.) **jìlù** 记录 104
record (v.) **jì** 记 103, **jìlù** 记录 104
record (v., sounds) **lùyīn** 录音 144
record (v., video) **lùxiàng** 录像 144
recover **huīfù** 恢复 96
rectangular **chángfāng** 长方 61
rectify **gǎizhèng** 改正 70, **jiūzhèng** 纠正 121,
　　tiáozhěng 调整 213
red **hóng** 红 91
reduce **jiǎnshǎo** 减少 108, **jiàngdī** 降低 111
reduction (in price) **zhé** 折 270
refer to **zhǐ** 指 276
reference **jièshàoxìn** 介绍信 237
reflect **fǎnyìng** 反映 61
reflections **gǎnxiǎng** 感想 71
reform (n.) **gǎigé** 改革 69
reform (v.) **gǎigé** 改革, **gǎizào** 改造 69
refrigerator **bīngxiāng** 冰箱, **diàn bīngxiāng** 电
　　冰箱 15
refund **tuìkuǎn** 退款 218
refuse (v.) **jùjué** 拒绝 122
regard as **dàng** 当, **dàngzuò** 当做 43
regarding **duì** 对 55, **duìyú** 对于 56

regiment (military) **tuán** 团 217

region **dìqū** 地区 47

register (at a hospital) **guàhào** 挂号 80

register (v.) **bàodào** 报到 8, **dēngjì** 登记 45

registration fee **guàhào fèi** 挂号费 80

registration office **guàhào chù** 挂号处 80

regret (v.) **hòuhuǐ** 后悔 92, **yíhàn** 遗憾 250

regret deeply **hèn** 恨 91

regretful **bàoqiàn** 抱歉 8, **yíhàn** 遗憾 250

regular **zhèngcháng** 正常 273

regular pattern **guīlù** 规律 84

regulation **guīdìng** 规定 84

reinforce **jiāqiáng** 加强 105

reject (v.) **jùjué** 拒绝 122

(be) related to **yǒuguān** 有关 258

relation, relative **qīnqi** 亲戚 175

relatively **bǐjiào** 比较 11

release (v.) **fā** 发 58

reliable **kàodezhù** 靠得住 127, **kěkào** 可靠 128

rely on **kào** 靠 127, **yīkào** 依靠 248

remain **liú** 留 143

(the) remainder **qíyú** 其余 170

remarkable **xiǎnzhù** 显著 230

remember **jì** 记 103, **jìyì** 记忆 104

remote **yuǎn** 远 262

remove **ná zǒu** 拿走 156

Renminbi (RMB) **Rénmíngbì** 人民币 181

rent (v.) **chūzū** 出租 31

repair (v.) **xiū** 修, **xiūlǐ** 修理 240

repeat **chóngfù** 重复 30, **fùshù** 复述 68

repeat from memory **bèisòng** 背诵 9

repeated **lián** 连 139

repeatedly **fǎnfù** 反复 60

replace **dàitì** 代替 40, **huàn** 换 96, **tì** 替 211

reply (n.) **huíxìn** 回信 97

reply (v.) **dá** 答, **dāying** 答应 37, **huídá** 回答 97

report (n.) **bàogào** 报告 8

report (of laboratory test) **huàyàn bàogào** 化验报告 94

report (v.) **bàogào** 报告 8, **fǎnyìng** 反映 61

report (v., news) **bàodào** 报道 8

report for duty **bàodào** 报到 8

reporter (news) **xīnwén jìzhě** 新闻记者 104

represent **dàibiǎo** 代表 40

representative (n.) **dàibiǎo** 代表 40

reptile **páxíng dòngwù** 爬行动物 163

republic **gònghéguó** 共和国 78

request (n.) **qǐngqiú** 请求 177

request (v.) **qǐng** 请 176, **qǐngqiú** 请求 177

require **yāoqiú** 要求 246

requirement **tiáojiàn** 条件 212, **yāoqiú** 要求 246

research **yánjiū** 研究 244

research center **yánjiū zhōngxīn** 研究中心 278

research institute/unit **yánjiū suǒ** 研究所, **yánjiūyuàn** 研究院 244

resemble **hǎoxiàng** 好像 89, **xiàng** 像 233

reserve (v.) **bǎoliú** 保留 7

resist **fǎnkàng** 反抗 60

resolute **jiānjué** 坚决 107

resourceful **yǒu bànfǎ** 有办法 5

respect (v.) **kàndeqǐ** 看得起 126, **zūnjìng** 尊敬 287

respect and love **jìng'ài** 敬爱 120

response **fǎnyìng** 反应 60

(be) responsible **fùzé** 负责 68

responsibility **zérèn** 责任 267

rest (v.) **xiē** 歇 236, **xiūxi** 休息 240

(the) rest **qíyú** 其余 170

restaurant **cāntīng** 餐厅 22, **fàndiàn** 饭店 61, **fànguǎn** 饭馆 82, **jiǔdiàn** 酒店 121

restaurant (colloquial) **guǎnzi** 馆子 82

restore **huīfù** 恢复 96

restrict **xiànzhì** 限制 231

restroom **xǐshǒujiān** 洗手间 227

result **jiéguǒ** 结果 115, **xiàoguǒ** 效果 235

result (of examination) **chéngjì** 成绩, **kǎoshì chéngjì** 考试成绩 28

result in **zàochéng** 造成 267

retain **bǎoliú** 保留 7

retell **fùshù** 复述 68

reticent **chénmò** 沉默 27

retreat **tuì** 退 218

return (v., something) **huán** 还 95

return (v., to place) **huí** 回 96

reveal **gōngkāi** 公开 76, **lù** 露 145

reverse (adj.) **fǎn** 反 60

review (lesson) **fùxí** 复习 68

revise **xiūgǎi** 修改 240

revolution **gémìng** 革命 73

reward (n.) **shōuhuò** 收获 198

rice **dàmǐ** 大米 39, **mǐ** 米 151, **shuǐdào** 水稻 203

rice (cooked) **fàn** 饭 61, **mǐfàn** 米饭 151

rice bowl **fànwǎn** 饭碗 61

rich **fēngfù** 丰富 66, **fù** 富 68, **yǒuqián** 有钱 259

ride (v.) **qí** 骑 171

ride a bicycle **qí chē** 骑车 26

(the) right hand **yòushǒu** 右手 199

school (n.) **xuéxiào** 学校 242
school (of thought) **pài** 派 164
school assignment **zuòyè** 作业 288
schoolbag **shūbāo** 书包 6, 200
schoolmate **tóngxué** 同学 215
schoolwork **gōngkè** 功课 77
science **kēxué** 科学 127
scientific research **kēxué yánjiū, kēyán** 科学研究, 科研 127
scientist **kēxuéjiā** 科学家 106, 127
scold **pīpíng** 批评 166
scope **fànwéi** 范围 61
scrape, scratch (v.) **huá** 划 94
script **wénzì** 文字 224
sea **hǎi** 海, **hǎiyáng** 海洋 86
seaport **hǎigǎng** 海港 72
search for **tànsuǒ** 探索 209, **zhǎo** 找 269
season (n.) **jìjié** 季节 104
seat (n.) **zuòwèi** 座位 288
second (n.) **miǎo** 秒 153
secondary school **zhōngxué** 中学 278
secondhand **jiù** 旧 121
secondly **qícì** 其次 170
secret **mìmì** 秘密 151, 152
secret police **mìmì jǐngchá** 秘密警察 152
secretary **mìshu** 秘书 152
section (of something long) **duàn** 段 54
secure, security **ānquán** 安全 2
security guard **bǎo'ān** 保安 7
see **jiàn** 见 108, **kànjiàn** 看见 126
see a doctor **kànbìng** 看病 126
seed **zhǒngzi** 种子 279
seek **tànsuǒ** 探索 209, **xúnzhǎo** 寻找 242
seem to be **hǎoxiàng** 好像 89, **xiǎnde** 显得 230
(it) seems **sìhū** 似乎 205
seize **qiǎng** 抢 174, **zhuā** 抓 282
seldom **bù cháng** 不常 25, **shǎo** 少 189
select (v.) **jiǎn** 拣 108, **tiāo** 挑, **tiāoxuǎn** 挑选 212, **xuǎn** 选 241, **xuǎnzé** 选择 241
self **zìjǐ** 自己 285
self-contradictory **zìxiāng máodùn** 自相矛盾 149
self-study **zìxué** 自学 285
self-supporting **zìfèi** 自费 285
sell **mài** 卖 148
sell out **màidiao** 卖掉 49
semester **xuéqī** 学期 241
send a fax **fā chuánzhēn** 发传真 58
send off **huānsòng** 欢送 95
send out **fā** 发, **fāchū** 发出 58

senior high school **gāoji zhōngxué (gāozhōng)** 高级小学 (高中) 72
sentence (n.) **jùzi** 句子 122
sentence-making **zàojù** 造句 267
separate (adj.) **dān** 单 41
separate (v.) **gé** 隔 73
(be) separated from **fēnbié** 分别 64
serene **ānjìng** 安静 2
serial number **hàomǎ** 号码 89
serious **rènzhēn** 认真 182, **yánsù** 严肃, **yánzhòng** 严重 243, **yàojǐn** 要紧 246
serve **fúwù** 服务 67
serve (in armed forces) **dāng bīng** 当兵 15
service industry **fúwù yè** 服务业 67
set free **jiěfàng** 解放 116
set off (on journey) **chūfā** 出发 31, **dòngshēn** 动身 52
set out from … **cóng...chūfā** 从...出发 35
set up (v.) **chénglì** 成立 28, **jiàn** 建, **jiànlì** 建立 109
settle (an issue) **jiějué** 解决 116
seven **qī** 七 170
sever **tuōlí** 脱离 218
several **jǐ** 几 103
severe **lìhai** 厉害 139
sew **féng** 缝 66
shake (v.) **yáo** 摇 246
shake hands **wòshǒu** 握手 225
shall **jiāng** 将, **jiāngyào** 将要 110
shallow **qiǎn** 浅 173
Shanghai **Shànghǎi** 上海 188
shape (n.) **xíngshì** 形式 238, **xíngzhuàng** 形状 239
share (joy, benefits, etc.) **fēnxiǎng** 分享 64
share (n.) **gǔpiào** 股票 79
shared (adj.) **gòngtóng** 共同 78
sharp **jiān** 尖 107
shave (beard/whiskers) **guā húzi** 刮胡子 92
she **tā** 她 207
shear **jiǎn** 剪 108
sheep **yáng** 羊 245
sheepskin **yángpí** 羊皮 245
shift (v.) **yí** 移, **yídòng** 移动 250
shift (work) **bān** 班 4
shine (v.) **zhào** 照 270
ship (n.) **chuán** 船 33, **lúnchuán** 轮船 146
shirt **chènshān** 衬衫, **chènyī** 衬衣 27
(be) shocked **chījīng** 吃惊 29
shoe (n.) **xié** 鞋 236
shop (n.) **diàn** 店 49, **shāngdiàn** 商店 187

shop assistant **shòuhuòyuán** 售货员 200,
  yíngyèyuán 营业员 255

shopping center **shāngchǎng** 商场 186

shore (n.) **àn** 岸 3

short **ǎi** 矮 1

short (length, time) **duǎn** 短 54

(be) short of **shǎo** 少 189

short story **duǎnpiān xiǎoshuō** 短篇小说 235

short-term **duǎnqī** 短期 54

shortcoming **quēdiǎn** 缺点 179

shorthanded **quē rénshǒu** 缺人手 179

should **gāi** 该 68, **yào** 要 246, **yīnggāi** 应该 254

shoulder (n.) **jiān** 肩 107

shout (v.) **hǎn** 喊 87, **rǎng** 嚷 180

shout at **zhāohu** 招呼 269

show (n.) **biǎoyǎn** 表演 14, **zhǎnlǎn** 展览 268, **zhǎnlǎnhuì** 展览会 268

show (v.) **biǎoshì** 表示, **biǎoxiàn** 表现 14, **lù** 露 145, **shuōmíng** 说明 204, **yǎn** 演 244

shower **xǐzǎo** 洗澡 227, **zhènyǔ** 阵雨 272

shower room **xǐzǎojiān** 洗澡间 227

shrink (v.) **suō** 缩 206

shuffle cards **xǐpái** 洗牌 164

shut up **bì** 闭 12

shuttlecock **yǔmáoqiú** 羽毛球 260

sick leave **bìng jià** 病假 16

sick room **bìngfáng** 病房 62

side (n.) **biān** 边 12, **fāngmiàn** 方面 62, **páng** 旁 164, **pángbiān** 旁边 164

sightseeing **yóulǎn** 游览 257

(go) sightseeing **yóu-shān-wán-shuǐ** 游山玩水 186

sign (v.) **qiāndìng** 签订 172

sign up for **bàomíng** 报名 8

signboard **páizi** 牌子 164

significance **yìyì** 意义 253

silent **chénmò** 沉默 27, **jìng** 静 120

silk **sīchóu** 丝绸 204

silver **yín** 银 254

similar to **xiāngsì** 相似 231

simple **chéngshí** 诚实 29, **jiǎndān** 简单 108

simple and plain **pǔsù** 朴素 169

simply (adv.) **gāncuì** 干脆 70

simultaneously **tóngshí** 同时 214

since **jì** 既 104, **jìrán** 既然 105, **yǐlái** 以来 250, **zìcóng** 自从 284

since then **cóngcǐ** 从此 35

sincere **chéngkěn** 诚恳 29

sincerity **zhēnxīn** 真心 271

sing **chàng** 唱, **chànggē** 唱歌 25

sing a song **chànggē** 唱歌 73

Singapore **Xīnjiāpō** 新加坡 237

singer (professional) **gēshǒu** 歌手 73

single **dān** 单 41

single bed **dānrén chuáng** 单人床 33

sink (v.) **chén** 沉 27

sir **xiānsheng** 先生 229

sister (elder) **jiějie** 姐姐 115

sister (younger) **mèimei** 妹妹 151

sister-in-law (brother's wife) **dìmèi** 弟妹, **sǎozi** 嫂子 185

sit **zuò** 坐 288

situation **qíngkuàng** 情况, **qíngxíng** 情形 176, **xíngshì** 形势 239, **zhuàngkuàng** 状况 283

six **liù** 六 144

size **chǐcùn** 尺寸 29, **chǐmǎ** 尺码 30, **dàxiǎo** 大小 39, **hàomǎ** 号码 89

size up **gūjì** 估计 79

ski, skiing **huáxuě** 滑雪 94

skilful **shúliàn** 熟练 201

skill **běnlǐng** 本领 10, **jìshù** 技术 104

skilled **qiǎo** 巧 174, **shúliàn** 熟练 201

skilled worker **jìshù gōngrén** 技术工人 104

skin (human) **pífū** 皮肤 166

skin (n.) **pí** 皮 166

skirt (n.) **qúnzi** 裙子 179

sky **tiān** 天 211

slacken **sōng** 松 205

slanting **xié** 斜 236

sleep **shuì** 睡, **shuìjiào** 睡觉 203

slender **xì** 细 228

slice (v.) **qiè** 切 175

slightly **shāowēi** 稍微 188, **yǒu(yì)diǎnr** 有(一)点儿 258

slippers **tuō xié** 拖鞋 236

slippery **huá** 滑 94

slogan **kǒuhào** 口号 131

slope **pō** 坡 169

sloppy **mǎhu** 马虎 147

slow **màn** 慢 148

small **bó** 薄 16, **xiǎo** 小 234

small amount **shǎo** 少 189

small arms **qiāng** 枪 173

small change **língqián** 零钱 142

small of the back **yāo** 腰 246

small talk **xiánhuà** 闲话 230

smear **tú** 涂 217

smelly **chòu** 臭 31

smile **wēixiào** 微笑 221, **xiào** 笑 235

smoke (v.) **xīyān** 吸烟 226

smoking (n.) **xīyān** 吸烟 226

smooth (adj.) **píng** 平 168, **shùnlì** 顺利 204

snack **diǎnxīn** 点心 48

snake (n.) **shé** 蛇 189

snap (v.) **duàn** 断 54

snapshot **zhàopiàn** 照片 270

snort (v.) **hēng** 哼 91

snow (n.) **xuě** 雪 242

snow (v.) **xià xuě** 下雪 242

so **yīncǐ** 因此, **yīn'ér** 因而 253, **zhème** 这么, **zhèyàng** 这样 271, **suǒyǐ** 所以 206

so as to **yǐ** 以 250

so far **zhìjīn** 至今 277

so long as **zhǐyào** 只要 276

so-called **suǒwèi** 所谓 206

soap (n.) **xiāngzào** 香皂 232

sob (v.) **kū** 哭 131

soccer **zúqiú** 足球 177, 286

social appointment **yuēhuì** 约会 263

social butterfly **jiāojìhuā** 交际花 111

social class **jiējí** 阶级 113

social contact **jiāojì** 交际 111

social custom **fēngsú** 风俗 66

socialism **shèhuì zhǔyì** 社会主义 189

society **shèhuì** 社会 189

sociology **shèhuìxué** 社会学 189

sock (n.) **wàzi** 袜子 218

soda, soda water **qìshuǐ** 汽水 172

sofa **shāfā** 沙发 185

soft **ruǎn** 软 184

soft (of voice) **qīng** 轻 176

soft drink **qìshuǐ** 汽水 172

software **ruǎnjiàn** 软件 184

soil (n.) **tǔ** 土 217

soirée **wényì wǎnhuì** 文艺晚会 224

soldier (n.) **bīng** 兵 15, **jūnrén** 军人 124, **zhànshi** 战士 268

sole (adj.) **guāng** 光 83, **wéiyī** 唯一 221

solemn **yánsù** 严肃 243

solicit **zhēngqiú** 征求 272

solid **gǒnggù** 巩固 78

solid and hard **jiānyìng** 坚硬 107

solitary **dú** 独 53

solve **jiějué** 解决 116

some **jǐ** 几 103, **xiē** 些 235, **yǒude** 有的 258, **yǒuxiē** 有些 259

some time ago **yǐqián** 以前 250

sometimes **yǒushí** 有时, **yǒushíhou** 有时候 259

somewhat **yǒu(yì)diǎnr** 有(一)点儿 258

son **érzi** 儿子 57

song **gē** 歌 73

song lyric **gēcí** 歌词 73

soon **bùjiǔ** 不久 19

sorry (adj.) **bàoqiàn** 抱歉 8

sort (category) **zhǒng** 种 279

sound (n.) **shēng** 声, **shēngyīn** 声音 192

sound recorder **lùyīnjī** 录音机 144

soup **tāng** 汤 209

sour **suān** 酸 205

south side **nánbiān** 南边, **nánmiàn** 南面 158

south, southern **nán** 南 158

southeast **dōngnán** 东南 51

southern part **nánfāng** 南方 158

southerner **náifāngrén** 南方人 158

southwest **xīnán** 西南 226

soy sauce **jiàngyóu** 酱油 111

space **kōngjiān** 空间 130

spare time (adj.) **yèyú** 业余 247

speak **shuō** 说 204

speak (at a meeting) **fāyán** 发言 59

special **tèbié** 特别 209, **tèshū** 特殊 210

special features **tèdiǎn** 特点 210

specialist (adj.) **zhuānmén** 专门 282

specialist (n.) **zhuānjiā** 专家 282

specialized (adj.) **zhuānmén** 专门 282

specialty (study) **zhuānyè** 专业 282

specific **jùtǐ** 具体 122

specified (adj.) **yídìng** 一定 248

spectacles **yǎnjìng** 眼镜 244

spectator **guānzhòng** 观众 82

speech **fāyán** 发言 59, **huà** 话 95, **jiǎnghuà** 讲话 110, **kǒuyǔ** 口语 131

speed (n.) **sùdù** 速度 205

speedy **xùnsù** 迅速 242

spend **fèi** 费 64, **huā** 花 93

spend (a period of time) **dùguò** 度过 54

spend (time) **guò** 过 85

spin and weave **fǎngzhī** 纺织 63

spit (v.) **tǔ** 吐 217

splendid **guānghuī** 光辉 83

spoken language **kǒuyǔ** 口语 131

sponsor (n., for membership) **jièsháo rén** 介绍人 116

spoon (n.) **sháozi** 勺子 188

sport shoes **yùndòngxié** 运动鞋 264

sports **tǐyù** 体育 211

sports ground **cāochǎng** 操场 22, 25

sports meeting **yùndònghuì** 运动会 264

sports shoes **yùndòng xié** 运动鞋 236

sportsman, sportswoman **yùndòngyuán** 运动员 264

spouse (colloquial) **àirén** 爱人 2

spray (v.) **pèn** 喷 165, **sǎ** 洒 185

structure **gòuzào** 构造 78, **jiégòu** 结构 115

struggle **dòuzhēng** 斗争 53, **fèndòu** 奋斗 65

student **xuésheng** 学生 242

study (in school) **dúshú** 读书 53, **niàn** 念 161

study **xuéxí** 学习 242, **yánjiū** 研究 244

study abroad **liúxué** 留学 143

study intensively **zuānyán** 钻研 287

stuffed dumpling **jiǎozi** 饺子 112

stupid **bèn** 笨 10, **dāi** 呆 40, **shǎ** 傻 186

sturdy **jiēshi** 结实 113

subject (n.) **tímù** 题目 211

subjective **zhǔguān** 主观 281

sublime **chónggāo** 崇高 30

submit to **fúcóng** 服从 66

substance **nèiróng** 内容 159

substandard **chà** 差 24

substitute (v.) **tì** 替 211

substitute for (v.) **dàitì** 代替 40

subtract **jiǎn** 减 108

subtrahend **jiǎnshù** 减数 108

suburbs **jiāoqū** 郊区 111

subway **dìxià tiělù (dìtiě)** 地下铁路 (地铁) 47

succeed **chénggōng** 成功 27

successful **chénggōng** 成功 28, **shùnlì** 顺利 204

successively **xiānhòu** 先后 229

such **zhèyàng** 这样 271

such as **lìrú** 例如 139

suck (v.) **xī** 吸 226

suck up **xīshōu** 吸收 226

sudden **tūrán** 突然 216

suddenly **hūrán** 忽然 92, **tūrán** 突然 216

sue **gào** 告 73

suffer **zāodào** 遭到, **zāoshòu** 遭受 266

suffer hardship **chīkǔ** 吃苦 131

sufficient **chōngzú** 充足 30, **gòu** 够 78

sugar **táng** 糖 209

suggest **jiànyì** 建议 109, **tí jiànyì** 提建议 210

suit (v.) **shìhé** 适合 198

suitable **héshì** 合适 90, **shìdàng** 适当, **shìyòng** 适用 198, **xiāngdāng** 相当 231

suitcase **xiāngzi** 箱子 232

sum of money **kuǎn** 款 132

sum up **zǒngjié** 总结 286

summarize **gàikuò** 概括 70

summary **zǒngjié** 总结 286

summer **xiàtiān** 夏天 229

summer holiday **shǔjià** 暑假 201

summit **dǐng** 顶 50

sun (n.) **tàiyang** 太阳 208

sunbathe **shài tàiyang** 晒太阳 186

Sunday **Lǐbàitiān** 礼拜天 137, **Xīngqīrì** 星期日 238, **Xīngqītiān** 星期天 238

sundry **zá** 杂 264

sunglasses **tàiyang yǎnjìng** 太阳眼镜 244

sunlight **yángguāng** 阳光 83, 245

sunshine **tàiyang** 太阳 208, **yángguāng** 阳光 245

super **chāojí** 超级 26

superannuation **tuìxiū jīn** 退休 117

superior (n.) **shàngjí** 上级 188

supermarket **chāojí shìchǎng** 超级市场 26

superpower **chāojí dàguó** 超级大国 26

supervise **zhǐdǎo** 指导 277

supper **wǎnfàn** 晚饭 220

supple **ruǎn** 软 184

supplement **bǔchōng** 补充 18

supply (v.) **gōng** 供, **gōngjǐ** 供给 77, **tígòng** 提供 210

support (n.) **zhīyuán** 支援 274

support (v.) **yǎng** 养 245, **zànchéng** 赞成 266, **zhīchí** 支持, **zhīyuán** 支援 274

(be) sure to **kě** 可 128, **qiānwàn** 千万 172

surely **ma** 嘛 147

surf the Internet **shàngwǎng** 上网 188

surface (n.) **biǎomiàn** 表面 14

surgery room **shǒushùjiān** 手术间 199

surname **xìng** 姓 239

surround **wéi** 围 221

surrounding area **zhōuwéi** 周围 280

swallow (v.) **yàn** 咽 245

swan **tiān'é** 天鹅 57

swap (v.) **diào** 调 50

swear **mà** 骂 147

sweat (n.) **hàn** 汗 87

sweat (v.) **chūhàn** 出汗 87

sweater (woolen) **máoyī** 毛衣 149

sweep (v.) **sǎo** 扫 185

sweet-smelling **xiāng** 香 232

sweets **tángguǒ** 糖果 209

swift (adj.) **xùnsù** 迅速 242

swim **yóuyǒng** 游泳 258

swimming pool **yóuyǒngchí** 游泳池 258

swindler **piànzi** 骗子 167

switch (n.) **kāiguān** 开关 124

switch on **kāi** 开 124

sympathize, sympathy **tóngqíng** 同情 214

system **xìtǒng** 系统 228, **zhìdù** 制度 277

T

table (n.) **tái** 台 207, **zhuōzi** 桌子 284

table tennis **pīngpāngqiú** 乒乓球 168

tail (n.) **wěiba** 尾巴 222

Taiwan **Táiwān** 台湾 207

take (by force) **duó** 夺 57

take (time) **huā** 花 94

take (v.) **dài** 带 41, **lǐng** 领 143, **sòng** 送 205

take apart **chāi** 拆 24

take away **ná zǒu** 拿走 156

take back **shōuhuí** 收回 198

take care of **guānzhào** 关照 81, **guǎn** 管 82

take effect **shíxíng** 实行 195

take measurements **liáng** 量 141

take medicine **chī yào** 吃药 246

take notes (in class) **jì bǐjì** 记笔记 11, 103

take notice of **zhùyì** 注意 282

take off (clothes etc.) **tuō** 脱 218

take off a hat/cap **tuō màozi** 脱帽子 149

take photo(s) **pāizhào** 拍照 163, **zhào** 照 270, **zhàoxiàng** 照相 270

take shape **xíngchéng** 形成 238

take the place of **dài** 代 40

tale **gùshi** 故事 80

talented person **réncái** 人才 181

talk (n.) **jiǎnghuà** 讲话 110

talk (v.) **huìhuà** 会话 98, **jiǎng** 讲 110, **tán** 谈 208, **yìlùn** 议论 253

talk (v., formal) **huìtán** 会谈 98

tall **gāo** 高 72

tangerine **júzi** 橘子 122

tap water **zìláishuǐ** 自来水 203

target (n.) **mùbiāo** 目标 156

tariff **guānshuì** 关税 203

taste (n.) **wèidao** 味道 223

taste (v.) **cháng** 尝 25

tasteless (food) **dàn** 淡 42

taut **jǐn** 紧 117

tax (n.) **shuì** 税 203

tax bureau **shuìwùjú** 税务局 203

taxi **chūzū qìchē** 出租汽车 32

taxi stand **chūzū qìchē zhàn** 出租汽车站 26, 268

tea **chá** 茶 23

tea (black) **hóngchá** 红茶 91

teach **jiāo** 教 111, **jiàoyù** 教育 113

teacher **jiàoshī** 教师 112, **lǎoshī** 老师 134

teaching (n.) **jiàoxué** 教学 113

teaching material **jiàocái** 教材 112

teaching staff **jiàoyuán** 教员 113

teacup **chábēi** 茶杯 9, 23

team **duì** 队, **tuán** 团 56, 217

team leader **duìzhǎng** 队长 56

teapot **chá hú** 茶壶 23

tear (n.) **yǎnlèi** 眼泪 244

tease **dòu** 逗 53

technician **jìshùyuán** 技术员 104

technique, technology **jìshù** 技术 104

teeth **yá** 牙 243

telegram **diànbào** 电报 48

telephone (n.) **diànhuà** 电话 48

telephone call **diànhuà** 电话 48

telephone pole **diànxiàn gān** 电线杆 70

television **diànshì** 电视 49

tell **gào** 告, **gàosu** 告诉 73, **shuō** 说 204, **dǎzhāohu** 打招呼 269

tell (what to do) **fēnfù** 吩咐 65

tell a story **jiǎng gùshi** 讲故事 80

temper (n.) **píqi** 脾气 166

temperament **xìnggé** 性格 239

temperature **qìwēn** 气温 172, **wēndù** 温度 223

temple **miào** 庙 153

temporary **zànshí** 暂时 265

ten **shí** 十 194

ten thousand **wàn** 万 220

tender **nèn** 嫩 159

tennis **wǎngqiú** 网球 220

tense **jǐnzhāng** 紧张 117

tentative **chūbù** 初步 32, **línshí** 临时 142

term **xuéqī** 学期 241

terminate **jiéshù** 结束 115

terrible **zāogāo** 糟糕 266

terrific **liǎobuqǐ** 了不起 142

terrifying **kǒngbù** 恐怖 130

terrorism **kǒngbù zhǔyì** 恐怖主义 130

terrorist **kǒngbù fènzi** 恐怖分子 130

test **cèyàn** 测验 23, **kǎoshì** 考试 127, **shíyàn** 实验 195

testify **zhèngmíng** 证明 273

text **kèwén** 课文 129

text message (by cell phone) **duǎnxìn** 短信 54

textbook **jiàocái** 教材 112, **kèběn** 课本 129

textile goods **fǎngzhīpǐn** 纺织品 63

textile industry **fǎngzhī gōngyè** 纺织工业 63

than **bǐ** 比 11

thank **gǎnxiè** 感谢 71, **xièxie** 谢谢 236

that **nà** 那 156

that one **nàge** 那个 157

thatched cottage **cǎofáng** 草房 62

theatre **jùchǎng** 剧场 123

theatrical performance **yǎnchū** 演出 245

themselves **tāmen zìjǐ** 他们自己 285

then **dāngnián** 当年 42, **dāngshí** 当时 43, **jiēzhe** 接着 114, **nà** 那 157, **zé** 则 267

theory **lǐlùn** 理论 138

there **nàli** 那里 157
there (colloquial) **nàr** 那儿 157
there is/are no **méiyǒu** 没有 149
thereby **cóng'ér** 从而 35
therefore **suǒyǐ** 所以 206, **yīncǐ** 因此, **yīn'ér** 因而 253
thermos flask **rèshuǐpíng** 热水瓶 181
these **zhèxiē** 这些 271
thesis **lùnwén** 论文 146
they (female, human) **tāmen** 她们 207
they (human) **tāmen** 他们 207
they (not human) **tāmen** 它们 207
they say **jùshuō** 据说 123
thick **cū** 粗 36, **hòu** 厚 92
thick (gas/liquid) **nong** 浓 162
thief **xiǎotōu** 小偷 235
thin (adj.) **báo** 薄 7, **shòu** 瘦 200, **xì** 细 228
thing **dōngxi** 东西 51
think **dàng** 当 43, **juéde** 觉得 124, **rènwéi** 认为 182, **xiǎng** 想 232
think (incorrectly) **yǐwéi** 以为 251
think up a plan **xiǎng bànfǎ** 想办法 5
thinker **sīxiǎngjiā** 思想家 204
thinking (n.) **sīxiǎng** 思想 204
thirsty **kě, kǒukě** 渴, 口渴 128
this **cǐ** 此 34, **zhè** 这, **zhège** 这个 271
thorax **xiōng** 胸 240
thorough **chèdǐ** 彻底 26, **tòu** 透 216, **zhōudào** 周到 280
those **nàxiē** 那些 157
though **suīrán** 虽然 206
thought (n.) **sīxiǎng** 思想 204
thoughtful **zhōudào** 周到 280
thousand **qiān** 千 172
thread (n.) **xiàn** 线 231
three **sān** 三 185
throat **sǎngzi** 嗓子 185
through **jīngguò** 经过 119, **tōngguò** 通过 214
throughout **shǐzhōng** 始终 196
throw **rēng** 扔 183
throw a tantrum **nào píqi** 闹脾气 159, **fā píqi** 发脾气 167
throw away **rēngdiao** 扔掉 49, **diū** 丢 51
thumb **shǒuzhǐ** 手指 200
thunder **léi** 雷, **dǎ léi** 打雷 136
thunderstorm **léi yǔ** 雷雨 136
Thursday **Xīngqīsì** 星期四 238
thus **cóng'ér** 从而 35
ticket **piào** 票 167
tidy **zhěngqí** 整齐 273
tidy up **shōushi** 收拾 199, **zhěnglǐ** 整理 273

tiger **lǎohǔ** 老虎 134
tight **jǐn** 紧 117
till (prep.) **zhídào** 直到 275
till now **zhìjīn** 至今 277
timber **mù** 木, **mùtou** 木头 155
time (n.) **gōngfu** 工夫 75, **gōngfu** 功夫 77
time-honored **gǔlǎo** 古老 79, **yōuxiù** 优秀 257
timely **jíshí** 及时 102
timetable (for schedule) **rìchéngbǎo** 日程表 183
timetable (railway, coach) **shíkèbiǎo** 时刻表 195
tin **guàntou** 罐头 83
tinned food **guàntou shípǐn** 罐头食品 83
tip (n.) **xiǎofèi** 小费 234
tired **lèi** 累 136, **píláo** 疲劳 166
title (n.) **tímù** 题目 211
title of book **shūmíng** 书名 200
to **cháo** 朝 26, **duì** 对 55, **duìyú** 对于 56, **gěi** 给 74, **tì** 替 211, **zhì** 至 277
to some degree **bǐjiào** 比较 11
toast (v., with drink) **gānbēi** 干杯 70
today **jīntiān** 今天 117
tofu **dòufu** 豆腐 53
together **yídào** 一道 248, **yíkuàir** 一块儿 249, **yìqǐ** 一起 251, **yìtóng** 一同 252
together with ... **gēn ... yìqǐ** 跟 ... 一起 75, **hé ... yìqǐ** 和 ... 一起 90
toilet **cèsuǒ** 厕所 23, **xǐshǒujiān** 洗手间 227
toilet soap **xiāngzào** 香皂 232
tolerate **rěn** 忍 182
tomato **xīhóngshì** 西红柿 226
tomorrow **míngtiān** 明天 154
ton **dūn** 吨 56
tone (n.) **yǔqì** 语气 261
tone (of Chinese word) **shēngdiào** 声调 192
tongue (n.) **shétou** 舌头 189
too **tài** 太 207, **yě** 也 247
tool (n.) **gōngjù** 工具 75
tooth **yá** 牙 243
toothbrush **yáshuā** 牙刷 243
toothpaste **yágāo** 牙膏 243
topple **dǎo** 倒 43
torn **pò** 破 169
torturous **tòngkǔ** 痛苦 215
toss **rēng** 扔 183
(in) total **gòng** 共 78, **yígòng** 一共 249
totally **shífēn** 十分 194
touch **diǎn** 点 48, **mō** 摸 155
touch emotionally **gǎndòng** 感动 71
touching (adj.) **dòngrén** 动人 52
tough **jiānkǔ** 艰苦 107, **yìng** 硬 255

uncle (father's brother) **bófù** 伯父 16, **shūshu** 叔叔 200

uncomfortable **nánshòu** 难受 158

uncompromising (adj.) **jiānruì** 尖锐 107

uncooked **shēng** 生 191

under **dǐxia** 底下 46, **xià** 下, **xiàbian** 下边 228, **xiàmiàn** 下面 229, **zhī xià** 之下 274

undergo **āi** 挨 1, **jīnglì** 经历 119

underground (n.) **dìxià** 地下 47

underneath **dǐxia** 底下 46, **xià** 下 228

undersell **yājià** 压价 243

understand **dǒng** 懂 52, **lǐjiě** 理解 138, **liǎojiě** 了解 142

understand **míngbai** 明白 154, **rènde** 认得, **rènshi** 认识 182

undertaking **shìyè** 事业 197

(be) underway **shīgōng** 施工 194

undo **jiě** 解 115

(be) unemployed **xiàgǎng** 下岗 229

(become) unemployed **shīyè** 失业 193

uneventful **píngjìng** 平静 168

unexpected **yìwài** 意外 253

unexpectedly **què** 却 179

unfold **pū** 铺 169

unforeseen **yìwài** 意外 253

unfortunate **búxìng** 不幸 17

unified (adj.) **tǒngyī** 统一 215

unify **tǒngyī** 统一 215

unilateral **piànmiàn** 片面 167

unite **liánhé** 联合 140, **tuánjié** 团结 217

(the) United Nations (UN) **Liánhé Guó** 联合国 140

(the) United States of America **Měiguó** 美国 150

university **dàxué** 大学 39

university department **xì** 系 228

university entrance examination **gāoděng xuéxiào rùxué kǎoshì** 高等学校入学考试, **gāokǎo** 高考 127

university president **dàxué xiàozhǎng** 大学校长 235

university professor **jiàoshòu** 教授 112

unnecessarily **búbì** 不必 16

unoccupied **xián** 闲 230

unprecedented **kōngqián** 空前 130

unpromising **búmiào** 不妙 153

unreliable **kàobuzhù** 靠不住 127

unrestrained **zìyóu** 自由 285

unripe **shēng** 生 191

untie **jiě** 解 115

until **zhídào** 直到 275, **zhì** 至 277

until now **zhìjīn** 至今 277

untrue **jiǎ** 假 106

untrustworthy **kàobuzhù** 靠不住 127

unusual **qíguài** 奇怪 170

unusual **tèshū** 特殊 210, **yìcháng** 异常 252

unusually **fēicháng** 非常 64

(be) unwell **shūfu** 舒服 201

up to **dào** 到 43

uphold **jiānchí** 坚持 107

upright **zhèng** 正 273

upstairs **lóu shang** 楼上 144

urban area **chéngshì** 城市 29

urge (v.) **cuī** 催 36

urgent **jí** 急 102, **pòqiè** 迫切 169, **yàojǐn** 要紧 246

urine, urinate **xiǎobiàn** 小便 234

us **wǒmen** 我们 225, **zánmen** 咱们 265

US dollar **Měiyuán** 美元 150

(the) USA **Měiguó** 美国 150

use (v.) **cǎiyòng** 采用 21, **shǐyòng** 使用 196, **yòng** 用, **yòngchu** 用处 256, **yùnyòng** 运用 264

use up **yòngdiao** 用掉 49, **yòngwán** 用完 219

(be) used to **xíguàn** 习惯 227

useful **shíyòng** 实用 195, **yǒuyòng** 有用 259

useless **méiyòng** 没用 149, **yòngbuzháo** 用不着 256, **méiyǒu yòng** 没有用 259

usually **píngcháng** 平常 168

utility (water and electricity) bill **shuǐdiàn fèi** 水电费 64

utility pole **diànxiàn gān** 电线杆 70

V

vacuum **zhēnkōng** 真空 271

valid **yǒuxiào** 有效 259

valuable **bǎoguì** 宝贵 7

value (n.) **jiàzhí** 价值 106

value (v.) **zhòngshì** 重视 279

vanish **xiāoshī** 消失 234

vapor **qì** 汽 172

variety **pǐnzhǒng** 品种 168

vase **huā píng** 花瓶 93

vast **guǎngdà** 广大 83, **guǎngkuò** 广阔 84

vegetable **cài** 菜 21, **shūcài** 蔬菜 201

vegetable market **cài shìchǎng** 菜市场 196

vehicle **chē** 车 26

velocity **sùdù** 速度 205

venue **dìdiǎn** 地点 46, **huìchǎng** 会场 97

verdict **jiélùn** 结论 115, **pànduàn** 判断 164

very **fēicháng** 非常 64, **hǎo** 好 88, **hěn** 很 91, **jíle** 极了 102, **tǐng** 挺 213

very few (exceptional) **gèbié** 个别 74
Very Important Person (VIP) **dà rénwù** 大人物 38
very much **hǎo** 好 88
very sharp **jiānruì** 尖锐 107
vexing (adj.) **tǎoyàn** 讨厌 209
vice chancellor (of university) **xiàozhǎng** 校长 235
(be) victorious **shèng** 胜 193
victory **shènglì** 胜利 193
video recorder **lùxiàngjī** 录像机 144
view (n.) **guāndiǎn** 观点 82, **kànfǎ** 看法 126, **yìjiàn** 意见 252
viewpoint **guāndiǎn** 观点 82
vigor **jīnglì** 精力, **jīngshén** 精神 120
village **cūnzi** 村子 36
vinegar **cù** 醋 36
vineyard **pútaoyuán** 葡萄园 169
violate the law **wéifǎn fǎlǜ** 违反法律 59, **fàn fǎ** 犯法 61
violent **qiángliè** 强烈 174
VIP (Very Important Person) **dà rénwù** 大人物 38
visit (a place) **cānguān** 参观 22
visit (v.) **fǎngwèn** 访问 63, **zuòkè** 做客 289
visit a relative **zǒu qīnqi** 走亲戚 175
visitor **kèren** 客人 129
vitality **jīngshén** 精神 120
vivacious **huópo** 活泼 99
vivid **shēngdòng** 生动 191
vocation **zhíyè** 职业 275
vocational work **yèwù** 业务 247
voice (n.) **sǎngzi** 嗓子 185, **shēng** 声, **shēngyīn** 声音 192
volleyball **páiqiú** 排球 163, 177
volume (book) **cè** 册 23
volume (mathematics) **tǐjī** 体积 211
voluntary **zìjué** 自觉 285
voluntary work **yìwù gōngzuò** 义务工作, **yìgōng** 义工 252
vomit (v.) **tù** 吐 217
vote **xuǎnjǔ** 选举 241

W

wages **gōngzī** 工资 76
waist **yāo** 腰 246
wait **děng** 等, **děngdài** 等待 46
wait for **děng** 等 46
waiter/waitress **fúwùyuán** 服务员 67
wake **xǐng** 醒 239
walk (v.) **zǒu** 走 286

wall **qiáng** 墙 174
wallet **qiánbāo** 钱包 6, 173
want (v.) **yào** 要 246, **yuànyì** 愿意 263
war (n.) **zhànzhēng** 战争 268
ward (n.) **bìngfáng** 病房 16, 62
warm (adj.) **nuǎn** 暖 162, **nuǎnhuo** 暖和 163, **rèliè** 热烈 180
warmhearted **rèqíng** 热情 180, **rèxīn** 热心 181
wash (v.) **xǐ** 洗 227
washbasin **xǐliǎnpén** 洗脸盆 165
washing machine **xǐyījī** 洗衣机 227
washroom **xǐshǒujiān** 洗手间 227
waste (v.) **làngfèi** 浪费 134
watch (n.) **biǎo** 表 14, **shǒubiǎo** 手表 199
watch (v.) **guānchá** 观察 82, **kàn** 看 126
watch a game/sports event **kàn bǐsài** 看比赛 11
watch TV **kàn diànshì** 看电视 49
water (n.) **shuǐ** 水 203
water buffalo **shuǐniú** 水牛 161
water stain **shuǐdiǎn** 水点 48
watercolor (painting) **shuǐcǎi huà** 水彩画 94
watermelon **xīguā** 西瓜 226
wave (n.) **làng** 浪 134
wave (v.) **yáo** 摇 246
wavering (adj.) **yóuyù** 犹豫 257
way **fāngshì** 方式 62
we **wǒmen** 我们 225, **zánmen** 咱们 265
weak **ruò** 弱 184, **sōng** 松 205
weak (flavor) **dàn** 淡 42
wealthy **fù** 富 68, **yǒuqián** 有钱 259
wean (a child) **duàn nǎi** 断奶 54
weapon **wǔqì** 武器 225
wear (v.) **chuān** 穿, **dài** ，戴 33, 41
wear a hat/cap **dài màozi** 戴帽子 149
wear a watch **dài biǎo** 戴表 14
weather (n.) **qìxiàng** 气象 172, **tiān** 天, **tiānqì** 天气 211
weather forecast **qìxiàng yùbào** 气象预报 172
Web site **wǎngzhàn** 网站 220
wedding banquet **jiéhūn yànhuì** 结婚宴会 245
wedding present **jiéhūn lǐwù** 结婚礼物 137
wedge between(v.) **jiā** 夹 105
Wednesday **Xīngqīsān** 星期三 238
weed (n.) **cǎo** 草 22
weed (v.) **chú cǎo** 除草 32
week **xīngqī** 星期 238, **zhōu** 周 280
weekend **zhōumò** 周末 280
weep **kū** 哭 131
weigh **chēng** 称 27
weight **fènliàng** 分量 65, **zhòngliàng** 重量 279
welcome **huānyíng** 欢迎 95

welcome banquet **huānyíng yànhuì** 欢迎宴会 245

well-developed **fādá** 发达 58

well-known **yǒumíng** 有名 259, **zhùmíng** 著名 282

well-lit **míngliàng** 明亮 154

west **xī** 西 226

(the) West **xīfāng** 西方 226

west side **xībian** 西边 226

western medicine **xīyào** 西药 246

wet (adj.) **shī** 湿 194

wharf **mǎtóu** 码头 147

what **hé** 何 90, **shénme** 什么 190

what's more **bìngqiě** 并且 15, **érqiě** 而且 57

whatever **nǎ** 哪 156, **rènhé** 任何 182

whatever (plural) **nǎxiē** 哪些 156

wheat **xiǎomài** 小麦 234

when **dāng, chèn** 当, 趁 42, 27

when … **dāng … de shíhou** 当 … 的时候 42

(the time) when **shíhou** 时候 194

whenever **suíshí** 随时 206

where **nǎli** 哪里 156

where (colloquial) **nǎr** 哪儿 156

which **hé, nǎ** 何, 哪 90, 156

which (plural) **nǎxiē** 哪些 156

whichever **nǎ** 哪 156

whichever (plural) **nǎxiē** 哪些 156

while **chèn** 趁 27

while … **yìbiān … yìbiān …** 一边 … 一边 … 251

whiskers **húzi** 胡子 92

white **bái** 白 4

who, whom, whoever **shuí** 谁 202

whole (adj.) **quán** 全 178, **zhěng** 整 272, **zhěngge** 整个 273

whooping cough **bǎirìké** 百日咳 4

why **wèishénme** 为什么 222, **zěnme** 怎么 267

wide **guǎngkuò** 广阔 84, **kuān** 宽 132

wide-ranging **guǎngfàn** 广泛 83

widespread **guǎngfàn** 广泛 83, **pǔbiàn** 普遍 169

wife **fūrén** 夫人 66, **qīzi** 妻子 170, **tàitai** 太太 208

will (adv.) **jiāng** 将, **jiāngyào** 将要 110

will (modal v.) **huì** 会 97

will (n.) **yìzhì** 意志 253

willing (adj.) **gāoxìng** 高兴 72

(be) willing **kěn** 肯 129, **yuànyì** 愿意 263

win (v.) **duó** 夺 57, **huòdé** 获得 100, **yíng** 赢 255

win victory **shènglì** 胜利 193

wind (n.) **fēng** 风 66

wind force **fēnglì** 风力 66

window **bōli chuāng** 玻璃窗, **chuāng** 窗, **chuānghu** 窗户 16, 33, 33

(go) window-shopping **guàng dàjiē** 逛大街 39, **guàng jiē** 逛街 84

wine (from grapes) **pútaojiǔ** 葡萄酒 169

wine bar **jiǔbā** 酒吧 121

wine shop **jiǔdiàn** 酒店 121

wineglass **jiǔbēi** 酒杯 9

wing (of bird) **chìbǎng** 翅膀 30

winter **dōngtiān** 冬天 51

winter vacation **hánjià** 寒假 87

wipe out **xiāomiè** 消灭 233

wire (n.) **xiàn** 线 231

wish **xīwàng** 希望 227, **yuànwàng** 愿望 262, **zhù** 祝 282

with **gēn** 跟 75, **hé** 和 90, **jí** 及 101, **tóng** 同 214, **yǐ** 以 250, **yóu** 由 257

withdraw money **qǔkuǎn** 取款 178

within **nèi** 内 159, **yǐnèi** 以内 250

wok **guō** 锅 85

wolf (n.) **láng** 狼 133

woman **fùnǚ** 妇女 68, **nǚrén** 女人 162

woman (young, unmarried) **gūniang** 姑娘 79

wonderful **liǎobuqǐ** 了不起 142, **miào** 妙 153

wood **mù** 木, **mùtou** 木头 155, **shùlín** 树林 202

woods **shùlín** 树林 202

wool **yángmáo** 羊毛 245

woolen sweater **máoyī** 毛衣 149

word (n.) **cí** 词 34, **dāncí** 单词 41

word processing **wénzì chǔlǐ** 文字处理 224

words **huà** 话 95

words (of song) **gēcí** 歌词 73

work (literary) **zhùzuò** 著作 282

work (n.) **gōngzuò** 工作 76, **huór** 活儿 99

work (v.) **bàngōng** 办公 5, **gàn** 干 71, **gōngzuò** 工作 76, **zuògōng** 做工 289

work as **dāng** 当 42

work for **fúwù** 服务 67

work of art/literature **chuàngzuò** 创作 34

work overtime **jiābān** 加班 5

work unit **dānwèi** 单位 41

worker **gōngrén** 工人 76

worker (skilled) **jìshù gōngrén** 技术工人 104

working conditions **gōngzuò tiáojiàn** 工作条件 212

working hours **bàngōng shíjiān** 办公时间 5

workman **gōngrén** 工人 75

workshop (in factory) **chējiān** 车间 26

(the) world **shìjiè** 世界 196
(the) World Wide Web **hùliánwǎng** 互联网 93
worm (n.) **chóngzi** 虫子 30
(be) worried **zháojí** 着急 269
worry (v.) **chóu** 愁 30, **dānxīn** 担心 41
(be) worth **zhíde** 值得 275
wound (n., v.) **shāng** 伤 186
(be) wounded **shòushāng** 受伤 186
wrap up **bāo** 包 6
wristwatch **shǒubiǎo** 手表 199
write **xiě** 写 236
writer **zuòjiā** 作家 288
(great) writer **wénxué jiā** 文学家 224
writings **zhùzuò** 著作 282
wrong **cuò, cuòwù** 错, 错误 36

Y

(the) Yangtze River **Cháng Jiāng** 长江 25
year **nián** 年 160
year (of age) **suì** 岁 206
yell (v.) **rǎng** 嚷 180
yellow **huáng** 黄 96
yen **Rìyuán** 日元 183, 261
yes **shì** 是 197
yesterday **zuótiān** 昨天 287
yet **dànshì** 但是 42, **ér** 而 57, **què** 却 179,
　　rán'ér 然而 179

yield (n.) **chǎnliàng** 产量 24
you (honorific) **nín** 您 161
you (plural) **nǐmen** 你们 160
you (singular) **nǐ** 你 160
young (adj.) **niánqīng** 年轻 161, **xiǎo** 小 234
young and tender **nèn** 嫩 159
young lady **xiǎojiě** 小姐 234
young man **nán qīngnián** 男青年 158,
　　shàonián 少年 189, **xiǎohuǒzi** 小伙子 234
young person **niánqīngrén** 年轻人 161,
　　qīngnián 青年 175, **qīngshàonián** 青少年
　　189
young woman **nǚ qīngnián** 女青年 162,
　　shàonǚ 少女 189
younger brother **dìdi** 弟弟 47
younger sister **mèimei** 妹妹 151
your family name **guìxìng** 贵姓 239
yourself **nǐ zìjǐ** 你自己 285
yourselves **nǐmen zìjǐ** 你们自己 285
youth **qīngnián** 青年 175

Z

zeal **jījíxìng** 积极性 101
zero **líng** 零 142
zoo **dòngwùyuán** 动物园 52
zoology **dòngwùxué** 动物学 52

Meaningful Character Components

Most of Chinese characters are made up of two or more component parts. "Signific graphs" (义符 **yìfú**) are components that suggest the meaning of characters. Hence, learning the meaning of these component parts will deepen your understanding of characters you know, and help you guess the meaning of unfamiliar characters. The following is a list of such meaningful character components.

冫 = freezing, ice (e.g. 冰 **bīng**, 冷 **lěng**, 寒 **hán**)

讠, 言 = word (e.g. 语 **yǔ**, 词 **cí**)

八 = dividing (e.g. 分 **fēn**, 半 **bàn**)

亻, 人 = man, person (e.g. 他 **tā**, 信 **xìn**)

刂, 刀 = knife (e.g. 利 **lì**, 剩 **shèng**)

力 = muscle, strength (e.g. 男 **nán**, 办 **bàn**)

阝 (on the left) = mound, steps (e.g. 院 **yuàn**, 附 **fù**)

阝 (on the right) = city, region (e.g. 部 **bù**, 邮 **yóu**)

氵, 水 = water (e.g. 河 **hé**, 海 **hǎi**)

忄, 心 = the heart, emotions (e.g. 情 **qíng**, 怕 **pà**)

宀 = roof, house (e.g. 家 **jiā**, 室 **shì**)

广 = roof, hut (e.g. 庭 **tíng**, 店 **diàn**)

门 = door, gate (e.g. 闻 **wén**, 间 **jiān**)

土 = earth (e.g. 场 **chǎng**, 城 **chéng**)

女 = woman (e.g. 妇 **fù**, 妈 **mā**)

饣, 食 = food (e.g. 饭 **fàn**, 饱 **bǎo**)

口 = the mouth, speech, eating (e.g. 问 **wèn**, 吃 **chī**)

囗 = boundary (e.g. 围 **wéi**, 园 **yuán**)

子, 孑 = child (e.g. 孩 **hái**, 学 **xué**)

艹 = plant, vegetation (e.g. 草 **cǎo**, 菜 **cài**)

纟 = silk, texture (e.g. 组 **zǔ**, 纸 **zhǐ**)

辶 = walking (e.g. 道 **dào**, 过 **guò**)

彳 = path, walking (e.g. 行 **xíng**, 往 **wǎng**)

巾 = cloth (e.g. 布 **bù**, 带 **dài**)

马 = horse (e.g. 骑 **qí**)

扌, 手, 攵 = the hand, action (e.g. 拿 **ná**, 擦 **cā**)

灬, 火 = fire, heat (e.g. 烧 **shāo**, 热 **rè**)

礻, 示 = spirit (e.g. 神 **shén**, 祖 **zǔ**)

户 = door, window (e.g. 房 **fáng**)

父 = father (e.g. 爸 **bà**)

日 = the sun (e.g. 晴 **qíng**, 暖 **nuǎn**)

月 = the moon (e.g. 阴 **yīn**, 明 **míng**)

月, 肉 = flesh, human organ (e.g. 脸 **liǎn**, 脚 **jiǎo**)

贝 = shell, treasure (e.g. 贵 **guì**)

止 = toe (e.g. 步 **bù**)

木 = tree, timber (e.g. 树 **shù**, 板 **bǎn**)

王, 玉 = jade (e.g. 理 **lǐ**, 球 **qiú**)

见 = seeing (e.g. 视 **shì**, 现 **xiàn**)

气 = vapor (e.g. 汽 **qì**)

车 = vehicle (e.g. 辆 **liàng**)

疒 = disease, ailment (e.g. 病 **bìng**, 疼 **téng**)

立 = standing (e.g. 站 **zhàn**, 位 **wèi**)

穴 = cave, hole (e.g. 空 **kōng**, 窗 **chuāng**)

衤, 衣 = clothing (e.g. 裤 **kù**, 袜 **wà**)

钅, 金 = metal (e.g. 银 **yín**, 钱 **qián**)

石 = stone, rock (e.g. 碗 **wǎn**, 磁 **cí**)

目 = the eye (e.g. 眼 **yǎn**, 睡 **shuì**)

田 = farm, field (e.g. 界 **jiè**, 里 **lǐ**)

禾 = seedling, crop (e.g. 种 **zhǒng**, 秋 **qiū**)

鸟 = bird (e.g. 鸡 **jī**)

米 = rice (e.g. 糖 **táng**, 精 **jīng**)

竹 = bamboo (e.g. 筷 **kuài**, 笔 **bǐ**)

舌 = the tongue (e.g. 话 **huà**, 活 **huó**)

舟 = boat (e.g. 船 **chuán**)

酉 = fermentation (e.g. 酒 **jiǔ**)

走 = walking (e.g. 起 **qǐ**)

足 = the foot (e.g. 跳 **tiào**, 踢 **tī**)

Measure Words

Measure words are a special feature of Chinese. A particular measure word, or set of measure words, occurs with each noun whenever one is speaking of numbers. The measure word may function like a collective noun (like a *pride* [of lions] or a *school* [of fish]) or may be related to the shape of the object. Nouns phrases using measure words often have the structure "number + measure word + noun," e.g.

- 一把刀 **yì bǎ dāo** = *a knife*
- 两道难题 **liǎng dào nántí** = *two difficult questions*

Some measure words occur with verbs, and may be related to the frequency or duration of the action. For verbs, the expression may have the structure "verb + number + measure word," e.g.

- 看了三遍 **kànle sān biàn** = *read three times*
- 去过两次 **qùguo liǎng cì** = *have been ... twice.*

bǎ 把 for objects with handles; a handful

bān 班 class (in school)

bèi 倍 fold, time

běn 本 for books

bǐ 笔 for a sum of money

biàn 遍 times, indicating the frequency of an action done in its complete duration from the beginning to the end

cè 册 volume (books)

céng 层 story, floor

chǎng 场 for movies, sport events

chǐ 尺 a traditional Chinese unit of length (equal to ⅓ meter)

cùn 寸 a traditional Chinese unit of length (equal to ¹⁄₃₀ meter)

cì 次 time, expressing frequency of an act

dào 道 for questions in a school exercise, examination, etc.; for things in the shape of a line

dī 滴 drop (of liquid)

diǎn 点 o'clock

dù 度 degree (of temperature, longitude, latitude, etc.)

duàn 段 section of something long

dùn 顿 for meals

duǒ 朵 for flowers

fēn 分 Chinese currency (1 分 **fēn** = 0.1 角 **jiǎo** = 0.01 元 **yuán**), cent

fèn 份 for a set of things or newspapers, documents, etc.

fēng 封 for letters

fú 幅 for pictures, poster, maps, etc.

gè 个 the most commonly used measure word for nouns that do not take special measure words, or in default of any other measure word

gēn 根 for long, thin things

gōngchǐ 公尺 meter (formal)

gōngjīn 公斤 kilogram

gōnglǐ 公里 kilometer

háng 行 used with nouns that are formed in lines; line, row, queue

hù 户 used with nouns denoting households and families

huí 回 number of times

jiā 家 for families or businesses

jiān 间 for rooms

jiàn 件 for things, affairs, clothes or furniture

jiǎo 角 Chinese currency (0.1 *yuan* or 10 *fen*), ten cents, a dime

jiē 节 a period of time

jīn 斤 *jin*, unit of weight equivalent to half a kilogram

jù 句 for sentences

kē 棵 for trees

kè 克 gram

kè 刻 quarter of an hour

kǒu 口 for members of a family

kuài 块 for things that can be broken into lumps or chunks; for money; *yuan*, dollar

lǐ 里 a Chinese unit of length, equivalent to 0.5 kilometers

lì 粒 for rice, pearls

liǎng 两 a traditional Chinese unit of weight, equivalent to 50 grams; ounce

liàng 辆 for vehicles

liè 列 for trains

máo 毛 a Chinese money unit, colloquialism for 角 **jiǎo** (= 0.1 元 **yuán** or 10 分 **fēn**)

mēn 门 for school subjects, languages, etc.

mǐ 米 meter (colloquial)

miàn 面 for flat objects

míng 名 for people, especially for those with a specific position or occupation

miǎo 秒 second (of time)

mǔ 亩 a traditional Chinese unit of area, especially in farming (equal to ¹⁄₁₅ hectare or 667 square meters)

pái 排 for things arranged in a row

pī 批 for a batch of goods, and for things/people arriving at the same time

pǐ 匹 for horses

piān 篇 for a piece of writing

piàn 片 for a thin and flat piece, slice

píng 瓶 a bottle of

qún 群 a crowd/group of

shēn 身 for clothes

shǒu 首 for songs and poems

shuāng 双 a pair of (shoes, chopsticks, etc.)

suì 岁 year (of age)

suǒ 所 for houses, or institutions housed in a building

tái 台 for machines, big instruments, etc.

tàng 趟 for trips

tào 套 a set of

tiáo 条 for things with a long, narrow shape

tóu 头 for cattle or sheep

wèi 位 a polite measure word for people

xià 下 used with certain verbs to indicate the number of times the action is done

xiàng 项 item, component

xiē 些 some, a few, a little

yè 页 for pages (of a book)

yīngchǐ 英尺 foot (as a measurement of length)

yīngcùn 英寸 inch

yuán 元 the basic unit of Chinese currency (1 元 **yuán** = 10 角 **jiǎo** / 毛 **máo** = 100 分 **fēn**), dollar

zhāng 张 for paper, beds, tables, desks

zhèn 阵 for an action or event that lasts for some time

zhī 支 for stick-like things

zhī 只 for animals, utensils, or objects

zhǒng 种 kind, sort

zuò 座 for large and solid objects, such as a large building

The 100 Most Common Chinese Family Names

(Arranged in order of frequency)

1.	李	Lǐ	35.	许	Xǔ	68.	熊	Xióng
2.	王	Wáng	36.	傅	Fù	69.	金	Jīn
3.	张	Zhāng	37.	沈	Shěn	70.	陆	Lù
4.	刘	Liú	38.	曾	Zèng	71.	郝	Hào
5.	陈	Chén	39.	彭	Péng	72.	孔	Kǒng
6.	杨	Yáng	40.	吕	Lǚ	73.	白	Bái
7.	赵	Zhào	41.	苏	Sū	74.	崔	Cuī
8.	黄	Huáng	42.	卢	Lú	75.	毛	Máo
9.	周	Zhōu	43.	蒋	Jiǎng	76.	邱	Qiū
10.	吴	Wú	44.	蔡	Cài	77.	秦	Qín
11.	徐	Xú	45.	贾	Jiǎ	78.	江	Jiāng
12.	孙	Sūn	46.	丁	Dīng	79.	史	Shǐ
13.	胡	Hú	47.	魏	Wèi	80.	顾	Kù
14.	朱	Zhū	48.	薛	Xuē	81.	侯	Hóu
15.	高	Gāo	49.	叶	Yè	82.	邰	Tái
16.	林	Lín	50.	阎	Yán	83.	孟	Mèng
17.	何	Hé	51.	余	Yú	84.	龙	Lóng
18.	郭	Guō	52.	潘	Pān	85.	万	Wàn
19.	马	Mǎ	53.	杜	Dù	86.	段	Duàn
20.	罗	Luó	54.	戴	Dài	87.	雷	Léi
21.	梁	Liáng	55.	夏	Xià	88.	钱	Qián
22.	宋	Sòng	56.	钟	Zhōng	89.	汤	Tāng
23.	郑	Zhèng	57.	汪	Wāng	90.	尹	Yǐn
24.	谢	Xiè	58.	田	Tián	91.	黎	Lí
25.	韩	Hán	59.	任	Rèn	92.	易	Yì
26.	唐	Táng	60.	姜	Jiāng	93.	常	Cháng
27.	冯	Féng	61.	范	Fán	94.	武	Wǔ
28.	于	Yú	62.	方	Fāng	95.	乔	Qiáo
29.	董	Dǒng	63.	石	Shí	96.	贺	Hè
30.	肖	Xiāo	64.	姚	Yáo	97.	赖	Làn
31.	程	Chéng	65.	谭	Tán	98.	龚	Gōng
32.	曹	Cáo	66.	廖	Liào	99.	文	Wén
33.	袁	Yuán	67.	邹	Zōu	100.	施	Shī
34.	邓	Dèng						

Chinese Transcriptions for 100 Common English Names

The Chinese translation of common foreign names follows an established convention. Here are examples.

Aaron 艾伦 **Àilún**

Adam(s) 亚当(斯) **Yàdāng(sī)**

Amanda 阿曼达 **Āmàndá**

Amy 艾米 **Àimǐ**

Anderson 安德森 **Āndésēn**

Andrew 安德鲁 **Āndéluó**

Angela 安姬拉 **Ānjīlā**

Anthony 安东尼 **Āndōngní**

Austin, Austen 奥斯丁 **Àosīdīng**

Baker 贝克 **Bèikè**

Benson 本森 **Běnsēn**

Brian 布兰恩 **Bùlán'ēn**

Brown 布朗 **Bùlǎng**

Campbell 坎贝尔 **Kǎnbèi'ěr**

Carson 卡森 **Kǎsēn**

Charles 查尔斯 **Chá'érsī**

Christopher 克里斯托弗 **Kèlǐsītuōfú**

Claire 克莱尔 **Kèlái'ěr**

Collins 柯林斯 **Kēlínsī**

Daniel 丹尼尔 **Dānní'ěr**

David 戴维(or 大卫) **Dàiwéi (or Dàwèi)**

Diana 黛安娜 **Dài'ānnà**

Edison 爱迪生 **Àidíshēng**

Elizabeth 伊丽莎白 **Yīlìshābái**

Emily 爱米丽 **Àimǐlì**

Emma 艾玛 **Àimǎ**

Eric, Erik 埃里克 **Āilǐkè**

Ford 福特 **Fútè**

Forster 弗雷斯特 **Fúléisītè**

Fox 福克斯 **Fúkèsī**

Garrison 加里森 **Jiālǐsēn**

George 乔治 **Qiáozhì**

Hall 霍尔 **Huò'ěr**

Harrison 哈里森 **Hālǐsēn**

Heather 海德 **Hǎidé**

Helen 海伦 **Hǎilún**

Jackson 杰克逊 **Jiékèxùn**

James 詹姆斯 **Zhānmǔsī**

Jason 贾森 **Jiāsēn**

Jeffrey 杰夫利 **Jiéfūlì**

Jenkin(s) 詹金(斯) **Zhānjīn(sī)**

Jennifer 詹妮弗 **Zhānnífú**

Jessica 杰西卡 **Jiéxīkǎ**

Joanne 乔安娜 **Qiáo'ānnà**

John 约翰 **Yuēhàn**

Jonathan 乔纳森 **Qiáonàsēn**

Joseph 约瑟夫 **Yuēsèfū**

Joshua 乔舒亚 **Qiáoshūyà**

Julie 朱莉 **Zhūlì**

Justin 贾斯廷 **Jiǎsītíng**

Katherine 凯瑟琳 **Kǎisèlín**

Kelly 凯利 **Kǎilì**

Kennedy 肯尼迪 **Kěnnídí**

Kenneth 肯尼思 **Kěnnísī**

Kerry 克里 **Kèlǐ**

Kimberly 金本莉 **Jīnběnlì**

Knox 诺克斯 **Nuòkèsī**

Larry 拉里 **Lālǐ**

Laura 劳拉 **Láolā**

Lauren 劳恩 **Láo'ēn**

Lindsay 林赛 **Línsài**

MacDonald 麦克唐纳 **Màikètángnà**

Marcus 马库斯 **Mǎkùsī**

Mark 马克 **Mǎkè**

Martin 马丁 **Mǎdīng**

Mary 玛丽 **Mǎlì**

Matthew 马修 **Mǎxiū**

Michael 麦克尔 **Màikè'ěr**

Michelle 米歇尔 **Míxiē'ěr**

Monica 蒙妮卡 **Méngníkǎ**

Newman 纽曼 **Niǔmàn**

Nicola(s) 尼克拉(斯) **Níkèlā(sī)**

Nicholson 尼科尔森 **Níkè'ěrsēn**

Osbo(u)rn(e) 奥斯本 **Àosīběn**

Paul 保罗 **Bǎoluó**

Peter 彼得 **Bǐdé**

Philip(s) 菲利浦(斯) **Fēilìpǔ(sī)**

Pitt 皮特 **Pítè**

Rachel 雷切尔 **Léiqiè'ěr**

Rebecca 丽贝卡 **Lìbèrkǎ**

Richard 理查德 **Lǐchádé**

Robert 罗伯特 **Luóbótè**

Robin(s) 罗宾(斯) **Luóbīn(sī)**

Ryan 莱恩 **Lái'ēn**

Scott 斯科特 **Sīkētè**

Sarah 萨拉 **Sālā**

Sean 肖恩 **Xiāo'ēn**

Simpson 辛普森 **Xīnpǔsēn**

Smith 史密斯 **Shǐmìsī**

Spencer 斯潘塞 **Sīpānsài**

Stephanie 斯蒂芬妮 **Sīdìfēnní**

Stephen 斯蒂芬 **Sīdìfēn**

Steven 斯蒂文 **Sīdìwén**

Taylor 泰勒 **Tàilè**

Thomas 托马斯 **Tuōmǎsī**

Tiffany 提芬尼 **Tífēnní**

Timothy 提摩太 **Tímótài**

Wallace 华莱士 **Huáláishì**

White 怀特 **Huáitè**

William(s) 威廉(士) **Wēilián(shì)**

Provinces and Other Administrative Regions

China is administratively divided into provinces, autonomous regions, municipalities under direct jurisdiction of the central government and special administrative regions. Under each province and autonomous region major cities are listed, with the first city listed being the capital of the province or autonomous region.

Provinces (省 shěng)

Anhui 安徽 **Ānhuī**
  Hefei 合肥 **Héféi**
  Bangbu 蚌埠 **Bàngbù**
  Huainan 淮南 **Huáinán**

Fujian/Fukien 福建 **Fújiàn**
  Fuzhou/Foochow 福州 **Fúzhōu**
  Xiamen/Amoy 厦门 **Xiàmén**
  Zhangzhou 漳州 **Zhāngzhōu**

Gansu 甘肃 **Gānsù**
  Lanzhou 兰州 **Lánzhōu**
  Tianshui 天水 **Tiānshuǐ**
  Dunhuang 敦煌 **Dūnhuáng**

Guangdong 广东 **Guǎngdōng**
  Guangzhou 广州 **Guǎngzhōu**
  Zhuhai 珠海 **Zhūhǎi**
  Zhanjiang 湛江 **Zhànjiāng**

Guizhou 贵州 **Guìzhōu**
  Guiyang 贵阳 **Guìyáng**
  Liupanshui 六盘水 **Liùpánshuǐ**
  Zunyi 遵义 **Zūnyì**

Hainan 海南 **Hǎinán**
  Haikou 海口 **Hǎikǒu**
  Sanya 三亚 **Sānyà**

Hebei 河北 **Héběi**
  Shijiazhuang 石家庄 **Shíjiāzhuāng**
  Baoding 保定 **Bǎodìng**
  Tangshan 唐山 **Tángshān**

Heilongjiang 黑龙江 **Hēilóngjiāng**
  Harbin 哈尔滨 **Hāěrbīn**
  Qiqihar/Ch'i-ch'i-ha-erh 齐齐哈尔 **Qíqíhāěr**
  Daqing 大庆 **Dàqìng**

Henan 河南 **Hénán**
  Zhengzhou 郑州 **Zhèngzhōu**
  Kaifeng 开封 **Kāifēng**
  Luoyang 洛阳 **Luòyáng**

Hubei 湖北 **Húběi**
  Wuhan 武汉 **Wǔhàn**
  Xiangfan 襄樊 **Xiāngfán**
  Yichang 宜昌 **Yíchāng**

Hunan 湖南 **Húnán**
  Changsha 长沙 **Chángshā**
  Zhuzhou 株洲 **Zhūzhōu**
  Hengyang 衡阳 **Héngyáng**

Jiangsu 江苏 **Jiāngsū**
  Nanjing 南京 **Nánjīng**
  Wuxi 无锡 **Wúxī**
  Suzhou 苏州 **Sūzhōu**

Jiangxi 江西 **Jiāngxī**
  Nanchang 南昌 **Nánchāng**
  Jiujiang 九江 **Jiǔjiāng**
  Jingdezhen 景德镇 **Jǐngdézhèn**

Jilin 吉林 **Jílín**
  Changchun 长春 **Chángchūn**
  Jilin 吉林 **Jílín**
  Siping 四平 **Sìpíng**

Liaoning 辽宁 **Liáoníng**
  Shenyang 沈阳 **Shěnyáng**
  Dalian 大连 **Dàlián**
  Jinzhou 锦州 **Jǐnzhōu**

Qinghai/Tsinghai 青海 **Qīnghǎi**
  Xining 西宁 **Xīníng**

Shaanxi 陕西 **Shǎnxī**
  Xi'an 西安 **Xī'ān**
  Xianyang 咸阳 **Xiányáng**
  Baoji 宝鸡 **Bǎojī**

Shandong 山东 **Shāndōng**
  Jinan 济南 **Jǐnán**
  Qingdao/Tsingtao 青岛 **Qīngdǎo**
  Yantai 烟台 **Yāntái**

Shanxi 山西 **Shānxī**
  Taiyuan 太原 **Tàiyuán**
  Changzhi 长治 **Chángzhì**
  Datong 大同 **Dàtóng**

Sichuan/Szechuan 四川 **Sìchuān**
Chengdu 成都 **Chéngdū**
Mianyang 绵阳 **Miányáng**
Leshan 乐山 **Lèshān**

Yunnan 云南 **Yúnnán**
Kunming 昆明 **Kūnmíng**

Dali 大理 **Dàlǐ**
Jinghong 景洪 **Jǐnghóng**

Zhejiang 浙江 **Zhèjiāng**
Hangzhou 杭州 **Hángzhōu**
Ningbo 宁波 **Níngbō**
Wenzhou 温州 **Wēnzhōu**

(Taiwan 台湾 **Táiwān**
Taipei 台北 **Táiběi**
Kaoshiung 高雄 **Gāoxióng**
Taichung 台中 **Táizhōng**)

Autonomous regions (自治区 zìzhìqū)

Guangxi Zhuang Autono-
mous Region 广西壮族
自治区 **Guǎngxī
Zhuàngzú zìzhìqū**
Nanning 南宁 **Nánníng**
Guilin 桂林 **Guìlín**
Liuzhou 柳州 **Liǔzhōu**

Inner Mongolia Autono-
mous Region 内蒙古自
治区 **Nèiménggǔ
zìzhìqū**

Hohhot 呼和浩特
Hūhéhàotè
Baotou 包头 **Bāotóu**
Chifeng 赤峰 **Chìfēng**

Ningxia Hui Autonomous
Region 宁夏回族自治
区 **Níngxià Huízú
Zìzhìqū**
Yinchuan 银川 **Yínchuān**

Tibet Autonomous Region
西藏自治区 **Xīzàng
Zìzhìqū**
Lhasa 拉萨 **Lāsà**
Xigaze/Shigatse 日喀则
Rìkāzé

Xinjiang Uygur Autono-
mous Region 新疆维吾
尔自治区 **Xīnjiāng
Wéiwúěr Zìzhìqū**
Ürümqi/Urumchi 乌鲁木
齐 **Wūlǔmùqí**

Municipalities under direct jurisdiction of the central government (直辖市 zhíxiáshì)

Beijing municipality 北京市 **Běijīng shì** (the capital of the People's Republic of China)
Chongqing/Chungking municipality 重庆市 **Chóngqìng shì**
Shanghai municipality 上海市 **Shànghǎi shì**
Tianjin/Tientsin municipality 天津市 **Tiānjīn shì**

Special administrative regions (特别行政区 tèbié xíngzhèngqū)

Hong Kong 香港 **Xiānggǎng**
Macao/Macau 澳门 **Àomén**

Useful Words

Numbers

0	零	líng
1	一	yī
2	二	èr
3	三	sān
4	四	sì
5	五	wǔ
6	六	liù
7	七	qī
8	八	bā
9	九	jiǔ
10	十	shí
11	十一	shíyī
12	十二	shí'èr
13	十三	shísān
14	十四	shísì
20	二十	èrshí
21	二十一	èrshíyī
22	二十二	èrshí'èr
23	二十三	èrshísān
30	三十	sānshí
40	四十	sìshí
50	五十	wǔshí
100	一百	yìbǎi
200	两百	liǎngbǎi
300	三百	sānbǎi
1,000	一千	yìqiān
1,234	一千两百三十四	yìqiān liángbǎi sānshísì
2,000	两千	liángqiān
3,000	三千	sānqiān
4,000	四千	sìqiān
10,000	一万	yíwàn
12,345	一万两千三百四十五	yíwàn liǎngqiān sānbǎi sìshíwǔ

23,456	两万三千四百五十六	liǎngwàn sānqiān sìbǎi wǔshíliù
100,000	十万	shíwàn
1 million	一百万	yìbǎiwàn
10 million	一千万	yìqiānwàn
100 million	一亿	yíyì
1 billion	十亿	shíyì
6 billion	六十亿	liùshíyì

Days of the Week

Monday	星期一	Xīngqīyī
Tuesday	星期二	Xīngqī'èr
Wednesday	星期三	Xīngqīsān
Thursday	星期四	Xīngqīsì
Friday	星期五	Xīngqīwǔ
Saturday	星期六	Xīngqīliù
Sunday	星期日	Xīngqīrì
Sunday	星期天	Xīngqītiān
Sunday	礼拜天	Lǐbàitiān

Months

January	一月	Yīyuè
February	二月	Èryuè
March	三月	Sānyuè
April	四月	Sìyuè
May	五月	Wǔyuè
June	六月	Liùyuè
July	七月	Qīyuè
August	八月	Bāyuè
September	九月	Jiǔyuè
October	十月	Shíyuè
November	十一月	Shíyīyuè
December	十二月	Shí'èryuè

October 24, 1942 一九四二年十月二十四日
yījiǔsì'èr nián Shíyuè èrshísì rì

August 2, 2006 二零零六年八月二日
èrlínglíngliù nián Bāyuè èr rì

Seasons

spring 春 **chūn**
summer 夏 **xià**
fall, autumn 秋 **qiū**
winter 冬 **dōng**

Time

five minutes 五分钟 **wǔfēnzhōng**
a quarter of an hour (= 15 minutes) 一刻
　　(钟) **yí kè (zhōng)**
half an hour 半小时 **bàn xiǎoshí**
three quarters of an hour 三刻 **sān kè**
three hours 三小时 **sān xiǎoshí**
early morning (approximately 6–9 a.m.) 早
　　晨 / 早上 **zǎochén/zǎoshang**
morning (approximately 8 a.m.–noon) 上午
　　shàngwǔ
noon 中午 **zhōngwǔ**
afternoon 下午 **xiàwǔ**
evening 晚上 **wǎnshang**
at night 夜里 **yèli**
one o'clock 一点 **yīdiǎn**
two o'clock 两点 **liángdiǎn**
7:30 a.m. 早上七点半 **zǎoshang qī diǎn bàn**
10:45 a.m. 上午十点三刻 **shàngwǔ shí diǎn**
　　sān kè
2:20 p.m. 下午两点二十分 **xiàwǔ liáng diǎn**
　　èrshí fēn
9:15 p.m. 晚上九点一刻 **wǎnshang jiú diǎn**
　　yī kè
12:50 a.m. 十二点五十分 **yèli shí'èr diǎn**
　　wǔshí fēn

the day before yesterday 前天 **qiántiān**
yesterday 昨天 **zuótiān**
today 今天 **jīntiān**
tomorrow 明天 **míngtiān**
the day after tomorrow 后天 **hòutiān**

the year before last 前年 **qiánnián**
last year 去年 **qùnián**
this year 今年 **jīnnián**
next year 明年 **míngnián**
the year after next 后年 **hòunián**

Money

In China, the currency is called Renminbi
(literally "The People's Currency"). The
basic unit is the *yuan* (元 **yuán**). Each *yuan*
is divided into 10 *jiao/mao* (角 / 毛 **jiǎo/**
máo) or 100 *fen* (分 **fēn**)

50 cents 五毛 **wǔ máo**
¥8.65 八块六毛五分 **bā kuài liù máo wǔ**
　　fēn
¥398.99 三百九十八元九角九 **sānbǎi**
　　jiǔshíbā yuán jiǔ jiǎo jiǔ
US dollar 美元 **Měiyuán**
Japanese yen 日元 **Rìyuán**
Euro 欧元 **Ōuyuán**

Distance

meter 公尺 **gōngchǐ**, 米 **mǐ**
li, a Chinese unit of length, equivalent to 0.5
　　kilometers 里 **lǐ**
kilometer 公里 **gōnglǐ**

Weights

gram 克 **kè**
jin, unit of weight, equivalent to 0.5 kilome-
　　ters 斤 **jīn**
kilogram 公斤 **gōngjīn**
ton 吨 **dùn**

Directions

east 东 **dōng**
south 南 **nán**
west 西 **xī**
north 北 **běi**
center, middle 中 **zhōng**
northeast 东北 **dōngběi**
southeast 东南 **dōngnán**
northwest 西北 **xīběi**
southwest 西南 **xī'nán**

Animals

cow, bull 牛 **niú**
water buffalo 水牛 **shuǐniú**
ox 黄牛 **huángniú**

horse 马 **mǎ**
pig 猪 **zhū**
sheep, goat 羊 **yáng**
chicken 鸡 **jī**
dog 狗 **gǒu**
cat 猫 **māo**
fish 鱼 **yú**
bird 鸟 **niǎo**
goose 鹅 **é**
swan 天鹅 **tiān'é**
wolf 狼 **láng**
elephant 象 **xiàng**
tiger 老虎 **lǎohǔ**
lion 狮子 **shīzi**
monkey 猴子 **hóuzi**
panda 熊猫 **xióngmāo**
frog 青蛙 **qīngwā**
dragon 龙 **lóng**

Colors
red 红 **hóng**
yellow 黄 **huáng**
blue 蓝 **lán**
white 白 **bái**
black 黑 **hēi**
green 绿 **lǜ**, 青 **qīng**
purple 紫 **zǐ**

Sports
baseball 棒球 **bàngqiú**
basketball 篮球 **lán qiú**
dancing 跳舞 **tiàowǔ**
diving 跳水 **tiào shuǐ**
high jump 跳高 **tiào gāo**

jogging 跑步 **pǎobù**
long distance running 长跑 **chángpǎo**
long jump 跳远 **tiào yuǎn**
mountain climbing, mountaineering 爬山 **páshān**
rope-skipping 跳绳 **tiào shéng**
soccer 足球 **zúqiú**
swimming 游泳 **yóuyǒng**
volleyball 排球 **páiqiú**
swimming pool 游泳池 **yóuyǒngchí**
indoor swimming pool 室内游泳池 **shìnèi yóuyǒngchí**
running track 跑道 **pǎodào**
sports ground 操场 **cāochǎng**
stadium 体育场 **tǐyùchǎng**
gymnasium 体育馆 **tǐyùguǎn**

Clothes
overcoat 大衣 **dàyī**
shirt 衬衫 **chènshān**, 衬衣 **chènyī**
swimming trunks 游泳裤 **yóuyǒng kù**
swimsuit 游泳衣 **yóuyǒng yī**
skirt 裙子 **qúnzi**
trousers 裤子 **kùzi**

glove 手套 **shǒutào**
hat, cap 帽子 **màozi**
stocking, sock 袜子 **wàzi**
shoes 鞋 **xié**
sports shoes 运动鞋 **yùndòngxié**
sandals 凉鞋 **liángxié**
leather shoes 皮鞋 **pí xié**
slippers 拖鞋 **tuō xié**
rubber boots 雨鞋 **yǔxié**

Kinship Terms

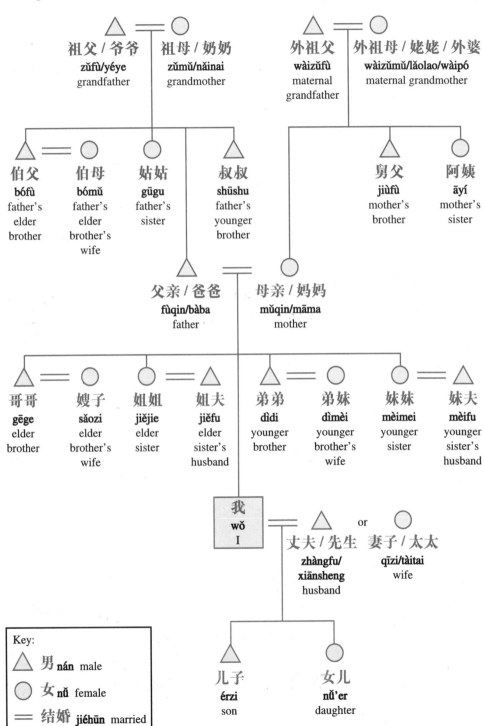